THE
COLLEGE
PRESS
NIV
COMMENTARY

1 & 2 CHRONICLES

THE COLLEGE PRESS NIV COMMENTARY

1 & 2 CHRONICLES

JOHN MARK HICKS, PH.D.

Old Testament Series Co-Editors:

Terry Briley, Ph.D.
Lipscomb University

Paul Kissling, Ph.D.
Great Lakes Christian College

COLLEGE PRESS
PUBLISHING COMPANY
Joplin, Missouri

Library of Congress Cataloging-in-Publication Data

Hicks, John Mark.
  1 & 2 Chronicles/John Mark Hicks.
    p.   cm. — (The College Press NIV commentary. Old
  Testament series)
  Includes bibliographical references.
  ISBN 0-89900-883-6
  1. Bible. O.T. Chronicles—Commentaries. I. Title:
First & Second Chronicles. II. Title: First and
Second Chronicles. III. Title. IV. Series.
BS1345.3.H53 2001
222'.6077—dc21

                                        2001017169

A WORD
FROM THE PUBLISHER

Years ago a movement was begun with the dream of uniting all Christians on the basis of a common purpose (world evangelism) under a common authority (the Word of God). The College Press NIV Commentary Series is a serious effort to join the scholarship of two branches of this unity movement so as to speak with one voice concerning the Word of God. Our desire is to provide a resource for your study of the Old Testament that will benefit you whether you are preparing a Bible School lesson, a sermon, a college course, or your own personal devotions. Today as we survey the wreckage of a broken world, we must turn again to the Lord and his Word, unite under his banner and communicate the life-giving message to those who are in desperate need. This is our purpose.

ABBREVIATIONS

ABD . . . . *Anchor Bible Dictionary*
ABR . . . . *Australian Biblical Review*
ANEP . . . . . *Ancient Near Eastern Pictures Relating to the Old Testament*
ANET . . . . . *Ancient Near Eastern Texts Relating to the Old Testament*
AUSS . . . . . . *Andrews University Seminary Studies*
BA . . . . *Biblical Archaeologist*
BASOR . . . . *Bulletin of the American Society of Oriental Research*
BBR . . . . *Bulletin for Biblical Research*
BETL . . . . . . *Bibliotheca Ephemeridum Theologicarum Lovaniensium*
BETS . . . . . . *Bulletin of the Evangelical Theological Society*
BI . . . . *Biblical Interpretation*
Bib . . . . *Biblica*
BibSac . . . . . *Bibliotheca Sacra*
BJRL . . . . . . *Bulletin of the John Rylands Library*
BN . . . . *Biblische Notizen*
BR . . . . *Biblical Research*
BRv . . . . *Bible Review*
BT . . . . *Bible Today*
BTB . . . . *Biblical Theology Bulletin*
CBQ . . . . *Catholic Biblical Quarterly*
CR . . . . *Currents in Research: Biblical Studies*
CTM . . . . . . *Concordia Theological Monthly*
Dtr . . . . *Deuteronomist, Deuteronomistic or Deuteronomic (1 Sam–*
  2 Kgs – see footnote on p. 17)
ET . . . . *Expository Times*
EQ . . . . *Evangelical Quarterly*
GNB . . . . . . *Good News Bible*
HS . . . . *Hebrew Studies*
HSM . . . . . . *Harvard Semitic Monographs*
HTR . . . . . . *Harvard Theological Review*
IBD . . . . *Interpreter's Bible Dictionary*
IEJ . . . . *Israel Exploration Journal*

Int . . . . *Interpretation*
JAAR . . . . . . *Journal of the American Academy of Religion*
JAOS . . . . . . *Journal of the American Oriental Society*
JANES . . . . . *Journal of the Ancient Near Eastern Society*
JANESCU . . . *Journal of the Ancient Near Eastern Society of Columbia University*
JASCG . . . . . *Journal of the American Society for Church Growth*
JBL . . . . *Journal of Biblical Literature*
JBQ . . . . *Jewish Bible Quarterly*
JETS . . . . . . *Journal of the Evangelical Theological Society*
JNES . . . . . . *Journal of Near Eastern Studies*
JNSL . . . . . . *Journal of the Northwest Semitic Languages*
JP . . . . *Journal for Preachers*
JS. . . . . *Journal for Semitics*
JSOT . . . . . . *Journal for the Study of the Old Testament*
JSS. . . . . *Journal of Semitic Studies*
JTS . . . . *Journal of Theological Studies*
JQR . . . . *Jewish Quarterly Review*
KJV . . . . *King James Version*
LTQ. . . . . . . *Lexington Theological Quarterly*
LTSB. . . . . . *Lutheran Theological Seminary Bulletin*
LXX. . . . . . . *The Septuagint (Greek Translation of the Hebrew Bible)*
MT . . . . *Masoretic Text (Hebrew Bible)*
NEB. . . . . . . *New English Bible*
NT. . . . . *New Testament*
OT. . . . . *Old Testament*
PEQ. . . . . . . *Palestine Exploration Quarterly*
RB. . . . . *Revue Biblique*
RQ. . . . . *Restoration Quarterly*
SBLDS . . . . . *Society of Biblical Literature Dissertation Series*
SBT . . . . *Studia Biblica et Theologica*
SJOT . . . . . . *Scandanavian Journal of the Old Testament*
ST . . . . *Studia Theologica*
TB. . . . . *Tyndale Bulletin*
TJ . . . . *Trinity Journal*
TR. . . . . *Theological Review*
VE. . . . . *Vox Evangelica*
VT. . . . . *Vetus Testamentum*
WTJ. . . . . . . *Westminster Theological Journal*
ZAW . . . . . . *Zeitschrift für Altestamentliche Wissenschaft*

Simplified Guide to Hebrew Writing

Heb. letter	Translit.	Pronunciation guide
א	’	Has no sound of its own; like smooth breathing mark in Greek
ב	b	Pronounced like English B *or* V
ג	g	Pronounced like English G
ד	d	Pronounced like English D
ה	h	Pronounced like English H
ו	w	As a consonant, pronounced like English V or German W
וּ	û	Represents a vowel sound, pronounced like English long OO
וֹ	ô	Represents a vowel sound, pronounced like English long O
ז	z	Pronounced like English Z
ח	ḥ	Pronounced like German and Scottish CH and Greek χ (chi)
ט	ṭ	Pronounced like English T
י	y	Pronounced like English Y
כ/ך	k	Pronounced like English K
ל	l	Pronounced like English L
מ/ם	m	Pronounced like English M
נ/ן	n	Pronounced like English N
ס	s	Pronounced like English S
ע	‘	Stop in breath deep in throat before pronouncing the vowel
פ/ף	p/ph	Pronounced like English P *or* F
צ/ץ	ṣ	Pronounced like English TS/TZ
ק	q	Pronounced very much like כ (k)
ר	r	Pronounced like English R
שׂ	ś	Pronounced like English S, much the same as ס
שׁ	š	Pronounced like English SH
ת	t/th	Pronounced like English T *or* TH

Note that different forms of some letters appear at the end of the word (written right to left), as in כָּפַף (*kāphaph*, "bend") and מֶלֶךְ (*melek*, "king").

Vowels in Hebrew (except where the ו is used to represent a vowel sound), are represented by "vowel points" added to the consonant. For example: הַ (*ha*, "the"). The letter *yod* (י, y) also becomes a *part of* certain vowel sounds, as in the conjunction כִּי (*kî*, "that"). Originally, Hebrew was written as "unpointed" text, with just the consonants. For convenience, the different vowel points are shown below on the letter Aleph (א).

אָ	ā	Pronounced not like long A in English, but like the broad A or AH sound
אַ	a	The Hebrew short A sound, but more closely resembles the broad A (pronounced for a shorter period of time) than the English short A
אֶ	e	Pronounced like English short E
אֵ	ē	Pronounced like English long A, or Greek η (eta)

א	i	Pronounced like English short I
א	î	The same vowel point is sometimes pronounced like אִ (see below)
אָ	o	This vowel point sometimes represents the short O sound
אֹ	ō	Pronounced like English long O
א	u	The vowel point ֻ sometimes represents a shorter U sound and
א	ū	is sometimes pronounced like the וּ (û, see above)
אֵ	ê	Pronounced much the same as א
אֵ	ê	Pronounced much the same as א
אִ	î	Pronounced like long I in many languages, or English long E
אְ	ə	An unstressed vowel sound, like the first E in the word "severe"
אֳ, אֲ, אֱ	ŏ, ă, ĕ	Shortened, unstressed forms of the vowels אָ, א, and א, pronounced very similarly to א

PREFACE AND ACKNOWLEDGMENTS

"Chronicles?" my friend asked, "Write a commentary on Chronicles? That is the last book I would spend years studying." An understandable reaction since Chronicles is probably the most ignored text in Scripture. Chronicles has been called the "Cinderella" of the Bible (Kleinig, "Research," 43). It begins with nine chapters of genealogies, covers the same historical ground as 2 Samuel, 1 Kings, and 2 Kings, and is filled with details about ancient rituals surrounding a temple that no longer exists.

However, Chronicles is filled with excitement — God's promise to David, his gracious presence in the temple, and the faith-response of his people. David and Solomon are the new Moses and Joshua. The Temple follows the Exodus/Conquest just as David/Solomon followed Moses/Joshua. God establishes a people, cares for them, tests them and, if necessary, punishes them. Chronicles describes the worship of God's people and the hope that worship engenders. It assures Israel of God's presence and the "messianic" hope of the Davidic kingdom. The Chronicler's themes are significant: worship, grace, providence, hope, divine testing, faith, prayer, divine retribution.

"Why are you writing a commentary on Chronicles?" another friend questioned. "You are trained in historical and systematic theology. What gives you a passion for Chronicles?"

I studied under Raymond Dillard at Westminster Theological Seminary. He instilled in me an appreciation of Chronicles as biblical theology. The Chronicler bridged the gap between his generation and the canon of the OT available to him. He had the Pentateuch, Samuel–Kings, some of the prophets, and some of the Psalms in front of him (as well as noncanonical resources). He attempted to make sense of God's past work in Israel in his post-exilic situation. As an interpreter of Scripture, he applied the meaning of God's promises to his own context. As a narrative theologian, he retold the history of Israel through the eyes of God's dynastic promise to David and his redemptive promise to Solomon (temple). He restored hope to his discouraged postexilic community. The Chronicler models narrative theology.

While paying attention to the historical and literary dimensions of the Chronicler's text, I will often concentrate on theological exegesis. I am a theologian reading a theologian. I intend to probe the story of God in Chronicles in order to more fully appreciate the meaning of God's story in our contemporary setting.

I recognize that I am not a specialist in Old Testament studies. I will defer many questions to the specialists (e.g., what is "late biblical Hebrew" and questions of textual transmission). The reader should not use my commentary in isolation from the more substantial works that engage the minutiae of exegetical detail (e.g., Williamson, Braun, Dillard, and Japhet).

Many have helped in the process of writing this commentary, including the staff and editors of College Press and the OT commentary series. But first and foremost is my graduate assistant Keith Stanglin. He has done the grunt work of bibliographical research, read the manuscript with me, and provided helpful suggestions.

Other students worked through Chronicles with me as we discussed the manuscript: David Black, Tommy Drinnen, Steve Dye, Paul Glover, Jeremy Hopkins, Daniel Joliff, Robert Lee, Shawn Moore, Justin Tedesco, Chris Thompson, Bobby Valentine, and Ivan Voser. I profited from their comments and suggestions.

A special thanks is due the Wednesday afternoon Bible class at the Ross Road Church of Christ in Memphis, TN, which included my mother. They cheerfully endured thirty weeks of study. Other congregations provided similar opportunities, including seven weeks at the White Station Church of Christ in Memphis, TN.

The librarians and staff at Harding University Graduate School of Religion were extremely helpful as I adopted their holdings. I piled interlibrary loan and purchase requests on their already full plates. I am continuously amazed at how rarely I must look elsewhere as HUGSR's library provides access to a wealth of material.

Mostly, however, I am grateful for my family. They have endured long hours away from me as I have completed this task. Barbara,

Ashley, Joshua, and Rachel are my emotional support and I find my greatest fulfillment in knowing that they love me.

May reading the Chronicler's story enable you to make the story of God your own story so that you may live in hope, faithfulness and assurance.

John Mark Hicks
http://johnmarkhicks.faithsite.com

Dedicated to the students, staff, administration, and faculty of Harding University Graduate School of Religion from whom I have learned much and through whom I have experienced the Chronicler's message of divine faithfulness.

INTRODUCTION

First and Second Chronicles were originally one book. It is the longest and last book in the Hebrew Bible. Its Greek translation (LXX) divided Chronicles into two books and placed them after Kings. The LXX titled Chronicles παραλειπομενων (*paraleipomenōn*) which means "the things omitted" (the things that remained). The title implies that Chronicles was written to supplement the material found in 2 Samuel and 1 & 2 Kings. The name "Chronicles," however, comes from Jerome (d. 420) who translated the Latin Vulgate. He described 1 & 2 Chronicles as a "a chronicle of the whole of sacred history" (*Chronicon totius divinae historiae*). Thus, English Bibles use the title "1 and 2 Chronicles."

HISTORY OF INTERPRETATION

The interpretation of Chronicles is a history of neglect (Japhet, "Chronicles," 1:179-187; Peltonen). Chronicles's Aramaic targum did not receive its final form till the ninth century A.D., no early midrash was ever written, and only a few medieval Jewish commentaries are known (Kalimi, "History," 5-41). With the exception of Jerome and Theodoret of Cyrrhus, Chronicles was neglected by early Christians. Chronicles was the stepchild of OT studies till the early nineteenth century.

Chronicles became the center of attention in the early nineteenth century only to move back to the periphery by the century's end (Graham, "Utilization"). While prior to the nineteenth century the Chronicles history was accepted as reliable (with a few exceptions like Spinoza), the application of the historical-critical method attacked its credibility. In 1806 DeWette published the first critical analysis of the relationship between Samuel–Kings and Chronicles. He concluded that Chronicles was unreliable for reconstructing preexilic Israelite history. Because Chronicles assumes Levitical priestly developments, it was important for DeWette to discredit Chronicles in the light of a late dating of the Pentateuch.

Chronicles, therefore, became the center of a controversy concerning the authorship and dating of the Pentateuch. Consequently, the nineteenth century was consumed with the deconstruction or defense of the Chronicles history. The credibility of Chronicles, according to some, was further eroded by the Graf-Wellhausen theory. In particular, when it was decided that the Priestly Code (e.g., Leviticus) was a late tradition, the Chronicler's history suffered because he used some of this priestly material in his history of Israel. Consequently, it was concluded, the Chronicler's history is late, unreliable, and biased toward the Levitical class.

However, by the early twentieth century, archaeological evidence, according to some (e.g., Albright), actually supported the Chronicler's history of Israel. As a result, scholars have moderated their complete dismissal though the discussion continues (Japhet, "Historical," 83-107).

While the interest in Chronicles was primarily historical in the first 150 years of critical study, the last 40 years (especially, 1980–90s) have witnessed a renewal in Chronicles research (Kleinig, "Research," 43-76; McKenzie, *Chronicler's,* 17-32). Instead of historical reliability, the primary concern has become the Chronicler's theological interests (e.g., Ackroyd, "History and Theology," "Theology," et al.).

The study of Chronicles has moved into a new era. While the debate over historical reliability continues, the emphasis has shifted. Scholars now seek to reconstruct the setting of the Chronicler's postexilic community and understand his applied theological perspective. The Chronicler is not just a historian. He is also an exegete and a theologian. Standing last in the Hebrew canon, he is unique in biblical literature because he has a large portion of the OT canon before him and writes his text as historian, exegete, and theologian.

GENERAL CONTENT AND SIGNIFICANCE

Chronicles covers the same historical period as Samuel–Kings. Consequently, we have two histories of Israel, much as we have four histories of Jesus (Matthew, Mark, Luke, and John).

While the two histories cover the same period, they write in different settings, with different purposes, and for different audiences. First–Second Kings was compiled during the Babylonian exile. Exilic questions in that time were: "Why were we exiled?" or "Did the Babylonian gods overrule Yahweh?" or "Where is God and his promises?" Dtr[1] focuses on the sins of Israel and Judah. David and Solomon do not escape judgment, and the whole nation is judged for its sins. Judah is in exile because it sinned. The Babylonian gods did not win, but rather God removed Judah from their homeland. Dtr explains God's judgment.

Chronicles was written during the postexilic period, that is, after the return of the exiles from Babylon in 536 B.C. The Chronicler's audience lived in Judah. Postexilic questions differed from exilic ones. The postexilic community asked: "Will God still dwell among his people in this new temple?" "Will God take us back as his people?" or "Will God keep his promise to David?" While the Chronicler explains the exile as a divine judgment, he stresses God's yearning to restore his people. God will keep his promises and God will dwell among his people as in the days of Solomon. If the postexilic community will seek God, then he will dwell among them.

COMPARISON OF HISTORIES

	1 Sam–2 Kgs	1–2 Chr
Authorship	Exilic Scribes/Prophets	Postexilic Levites
Date of Composition	ca. 550 B.C.	515–200 B.C.
Audience	Exilic Community	Restored Community
Content	Northern and Southern Kingdoms	Only the Southern Kingdom
History	From Samuel through David to the Exile	From Adam through David to Restoration
Question	"Why are we here in exile?	"Will God remember his covenant with David?"
Theme	Sin and Judgment	King and Temple
Point	Punishment for Sin	Grace for Seekers

Chronicles begins with a genealogy from Adam to Zerubbabel (1 Chr 1–9). God has preserved a people throughout history. The genealogies emphasize the royal (Judah) and priestly (Levi) lines to

---

[1]"Dtr" refers to the unified theological perspective of Deuteronomy through Second Kings. While 1–2 Kings likely were compiled during the exile, other books in Dtr were written earlier.

ensure the continuity of the Davidic royal house and the Aaronite priesthood. The postexilic community shares in the dynastic promises to David (kingdom) and Solomon (temple).

First Chronicles 10 through 2 Chronicles 9 is the history of David and Solomon. The Chronicler does not tell us about the sins of David (except the moving of the ark and the census) and Solomon because he is not interested in their frailties. He is concerned with their role as founders of the kingdom and temple worship. He provides the postexilic community with hope based upon the Davidic promises fulfilled in the Solomonic temple.

Second Chronicles 10–36 is the history of the kings of Judah after David and Solomon. The Chronicler does not merely repeat material found in Kings (60% of Chronicles is unique). Rather, he demonstrates how God blessed kings when they sought him and how he punished them when they did not. He details their relation to the temple, their faithfulness to God, and God's faithfulness to his promises. When the kings sought God, he was found. But when they did not seek him, God forsook them. Faithfulness meant the enjoyment of God's presence at the temple, but unfaithfulness ultimately meant Godforsakenness.

The primary significance for the Chronicler's first readers was the assurance that the Davidic covenant is still operative and that God dwells among his people in his temple just as he did in the days of Solomon. God yearns for his people, and he will keep his promises. God returns the exiles to the land in order to dwell among them. Indeed, the climax of Chronicles is the decree to rebuild the temple. Chronicles, therefore, offers the postexilic community a gracious hope. The Chronicler tells the story of Judah with a concern for his contemporary community (Fishbane, 385-403).

What is significant for modern Christians? The story of God's graciousness culminates in Jesus Christ. The presence of God in the temple is the presence of the Holy Spirit in Christians. God seeks a people who seek him. God seeks worshipers (John 4:23-24) and yearns to share his communion with people who trust him with all their hearts. Just as the Exodus is our story, so the building of the temple is our story. When Christians study Chronicles, they study the significance of God's temple-building for their own faith and life. They learn something about God's faithfulness and grace; about worship, holiness, faith, and perseverance; and about the God of David and Solomon who is also the God of Jesus Christ.

AUTHOR AND RELATIONSHIP TO EZRA–NEHEMIAH

The Babylonian Talmud (*Baba Bathra* 15a) credits Ezra with penning Chronicles. This traditional position held sway for centuries and has been defended by some (Albright, "Date," 104-114; MYERS, lxxxvi-lxxxvii; Young, 389-392; Archer, 405-407; PAYNE, 304-307).

However, the book is anonymous. The identification with Ezra hinges on whether or not one thinks Chronicles–Ezra–Nehemiah is a single work written by a single author. Because this was once the common belief, Ezra was assumed the author of the whole corpus.

Contemporary scholarship, however, has either (1) rejected the idea that a single author lies behind the three books in favor of a "Chronicler" tradition that shaped the books into their present form over a process of years or (2) separated Chronicles from Ezra–Nehemiah as an independent work. Few scholars would argue that Ezra was the author of the whole corpus though a number argue that Chronicles–Ezra–Nehemiah is a single work (Clines, 9-12; Blenkinsopp, *Ezra,* 47-54).

The emerging consensus is that Chronicles is an independent work. However, this is not unanimous (Ackroyd, "Chronicles–Ezra–Nehemiah," 189-201; Talshir, "Reinvestigation," 165-193). Four arguments tend to unite Chronicles and Ezra–Nehemiah (Dillard, *Introduction,* 171). First, Chronicles (2 Chr 36:23) ends and Ezra (Ezra 1:1-4) begins with the decree of Cyrus to rebuild the temple which may indicate that the two histories were originally one. Second, the apocryphal book 1 Esdras (ca. 150 B.C.) contains 2 Chronicles 35–36, Ezra, and Nehemiah as if Chronicles and Ezra–Nehemiah were one book. Third, Chronicles and Ezra–Nehemiah share lexical and syntactical similarities. Fourth, they share a common theological emphasis and setting as well as similar literary forms (e.g., lists).

Despite these arguments, I regard Chronicles as a separate work (Japhet, "Supposed," 5-11; JAPHET, 3-5; WILLIAMSON, 5-11; Braun, "Chronicles," 42-64). The reasons for uniting the books are not absolute. There are alternative explanations for the above arguments

(Williamson, *Israel*, 5-82). The overlapping section at the end of Chronicles and the beginning of Ezra may have been intended to unite what was originally separate. First Esdras may combine two separate traditions or perhaps 1 Esdras is a secondary development of Chronicles–Ezra–Nehemiah (McKenzie, *Chronicler's*, 17-25). There is also evidence of wide lexical and syntactical differences between Chronicles and Ezra–Nehemiah.

The strongest reason for regarding Chronicles as an independent work is its different purpose and theological interests. The chart below represents some of these different emphases.

Chronicles	Ezra-Nehemiah
Inclusivist Attitude toward the North	North as Unclean and Hostile
Little Discussion of the Sabbath	Sabbath a Major Topic
Davidic Succession Important	No Role for Davidic Interests
Little Reflection on the Exodus	Exodus as Primary
No Mention of Solomon's Sins	Solomon as Bad Example
Little Comment on Mixed Marriages	Mixed Marriages as Primary Sin
Emphasis on the Prophets	Little Emphasis on Prophets
Theology of Retribution	No Application of Retribution
Strong Role for Levites	Weak Role for Levites

These differences indicate that Chronicles and Ezra–Nehemiah did not come from the same author. Chronicles seeks to unite "all Israel" on the basis of the Davidic promises and the temple cult in accordance with prophetic utterances. Ezra–Nehemiah seeks to re-vision the postexilic community as a "new exodus" under the scribal leadership of Ezra and Nehemiah who focus on Torah cultic purity. Both of these interests might exist simultaneously within the same postexilic community, but the different interests separate the books instead of uniting them. What they share in common is a postexilic setting, but they differ in terms of how each addresses the needs of that community. This commentary assumes Chronicles is an independent work by an anonymous Levite.

DATE AND SETTING

The earliest possible date for Chronicles is 538 B.C., the date of Cyrus's decree (2 Chr 36:23). Also, it is generally conceded that the book could not have been written before 515 B.C. because

1 Chronicles 29:7 refers to a coin that was minted during the reign of Darius (Williamson, "Eschatology," 123-126). The latest possible date is ca. 150 B.C. when Eupolemos (Jewish historian) of Alexandria quoted Chronicles. In addition, Ben Sira (ca. 180 B.C.) alludes to 1 Chronicles 15-16 as he comments on David's role in organizing the temple singers (Sirach 47:8-10). This means that the date of Chronicles is no later than 200 B.C. Within these limits, there are three primary positions (Dyck, 16-29).

First, some place Chronicles in the early Persian period ca. 515 B.C. (Newsome, 201-217; Freedman, 436-442; Cross, "Reconstruction," 4-18; McKenzie, *Chronicler's*, 25-26; Welch, *Chronicler;* Throntveit, *Kings*, 97-107; BRAUN, xxv-xxix; Holdridge). The major reason for dating Chronicles this early is the combination of several themes which find their most natural application during the time of Zerubbabel. The Chronicler emphasizes the Davidic dynasty in conjunction with the temple's priestly cast. The Chronicler employs the prophets as supporters of the temple cultus and the Davidic dynasty. This fits the milieu of the prophets Haggai and Zechariah. The Chronicler is a Levitical historian/theologian who encourages the postexilic community by recalling their Davidic and Levitical heritage as they begin again under Davidic leadership in a rebuilt temple.

The problem with this scenario is that 515 B.C. is not the date of the final form of Chronicles. The genealogy of Jehoiachin (1 Chr 3:17-24) contains at least two generations and possibly six generations beyond that date into the fifth century, possibly as late as 450-420 B.C. Further, Chronicles's genealogical list in 1 Chronicles 9:2-34 is about a generation later than the list contained in Nehemiah 11:3-19. Some propose two forms of Chronicles. An early form (1 Chr 10-2 Chr 36) dated around 515 B.C. and a final form with the addition (or updating) of 1 Chronicles 1-9 by a final editor around 450-400 B.C. This is possible, but 1 Chronicles 1-9 appears integral to the rest of Chronicles since it articulates the same themes and reflects the same style (Johnson, *Purpose*, 44-76). Consequently, a 520-500 B.C. date is unlikely (Williamson, "Eschatology," 120-130).

Second, some place Chronicles in the early Hellenistic period ca. 300-200 B.C. (Torrey, *Ezra*, 209; Noth, 69-75). They believe Chronicles is a polemic against the rise of Samaritanism. However, one of the key theological themes of Chronicles is that "all Israel" is invited to Jerusalem. Chronicles has a positive outlook on the potential of the north to share in the temple cultus (Braun, "Reconsideration," 59-62). Further, there is no indication of any Greek influence in Chronicles (Ackroyd, *Age,* 7-8).

Third, some place Chronicles in the middle or late Persian period ca. 450–350 B.C. Those who unite Chronicles with Ezra–Nehemiah date it around 450 B.C. (MYERS, lxxxvi-lxxxix; Albright, "Date," 104-114; cf. SELMAN, 1:69-71) while others generally favor a late Persian date around 400–350 B.C. (JAPHET, 23-28; WILLIAMSON, 15-17; DE VRIES, 16-17). The later date has gained the widest acceptance among OT scholars. The consensus is that Chronicles is "late biblical Hebrew" with affinities to Ezra–Nehemiah, Esther, Dead Sea Scrolls, and the Samaritan Pentateuch (Japhet, "Supposed," 5-11; cf. Polzin).

Since neither the early (515 B.C.) nor the late dates (200 B.C.) are feasible, and since the Chronicler probably had Ezra–Nehemiah in front of him, it is best to date the book in the late Persian period (ca. 350 B.C.). If this is the case, then Chronicles is the last OT book written (given conservative datings of other texts). It is fitting that the Chronicler occupies the last place in the Hebrew Bible since he is a theologian of the whole Hebrew canon.

THE CHRONICLER'S SOURCES

Biblical authors often used sources and researched material. Luke did this for his Gospel (Luke 1:1-4). He talked to eyewitnesses and read the works of others. Nevertheless, as he composed his Gospel, he did so under the influence of the Spirit. God superintended the writing of Scripture in such a way that human authors wrote in their own style, vocabulary, and in the light of their own research. The final product is inspired but the exact dynamics of inspiration are unknown.

The Chronicler (like Luke) used sources. He cites them and points his readers to them for more details (e.g., the reigns of the kings). However, the nature, use, and reliability of these sources are hotly debated.

His sources include both canonical (biblical) and noncanonical literature. The biblical literature includes the Torah (five books of

Moses), Joshua–Kings, many of the prophets, Ezra–Nehemiah, and some psalms. The apparent extrabiblical literature (no longer extant) includes the "books of the kings" and the "books of the prophets" as well as additional Levitical, military, and genealogical lists.

The Chronicler used the text of 1–2 Samuel and 1–2 Kings. Some of this material is copied verbatim. Indeed, the Chronicler's history of the kings of Judah in 2 Chronicles is a redaction and elaboration of 2 Kings. In addition, the Chronicler had access to a wide range of biblical texts. While 1–2 Samuel and 1–2 Kings provided the basic historical frame, the Chronicler's interests reflect themes and continuities with the whole OT. The chart below is only representative (cf. ENDRES).

Chronicles' Use of Biblical Sources	
Biblical Materials	**Appearance in Chronicles**
Genealogical Lists in Genesis	1 Chronicles 1:1–2:2
Joshua 19:2-8	1 Chronicles 4:28-33
Joshua 21:10-39	1 Chronicles 6:54-81
Joshua 17:11-12	1 Chronicles 7:29
Joshua 7:1	1 Chronicles 2:7
Ezra 1:1-4	2 Chronicles 36:22-23
Nehemiah 11:3-19	1 Chronicles 9:2-17
Numbers 26:5-11	1 Chronicles 5:2-10
Exodus 6:16-26	1 Chronicles 6:2-4
Numbers 3:2-4	1 Chronicles 6:50-53
Psalm 105:1-15	1 Chronicles 16:8-22
Psalm 96:2-13	1 Chronicles 16:23-33
Psalm 106:1,47-48	1 Chronicles 16:34-36
Psalm 132:8-10	2 Chronicles 6:41-42

Chronicles refers to the "books of the Kings" quite often (cf. the top chart on p. 24). The different titles are probably variations on the basic title "book of the Kings." Many have concluded that they refer to the canonical books of 1–2 Samuel and 1–2 Kings or at least to a single comprehensive history of Israel.

Chronicles also refers to the "books of the prophets" (second chart overleaf). These references are more elusive. If we compare them with Dtr, we discover similar source notes (cf. 1 Chr 29:29 with 1 Kgs 14:29). Further, some of the prophetic references are said to be contained in the "books of the Kings of Judah and Israel" (2 Chr 32:32) or the "book of the Kings of Israel" (2 Chr 20:34). Second

Chronicles 33:18 says that the words of the seers are recorded in the "Annals of the Kings of Israel." What Chronicles calls "the books of the prophets" may be the reports of the prophets contained in the "books of the Kings." In other words, these are not independent sources from the "books of the Kings," but they are prophetic speeches or records contained in those books. However, some prefer to see the independent references to the prophets as additional sources beyond the "books of the Kings."

Books of the Kings	
Title	Texts
Books of the Kings of Israel and Judah	2 Chr 27:7; 35:27; 36:8
Books of the Kings of Judah and Israel	2 Chr 16:11; 25:26; 28:26; 32:32
Books of the Kings of Israel	1 Chr 9:1; 2 Chr 20:34
Annals of the Kings of Israel	(2 Chr 33:18) 2 Chr 33:18
Interpretation of the Book of Kings	2 Chr 24:27
Annals of King David	2 Chr 27:24
Directions of David and Solomon	2 Chr 35:4

Books of the Prophets	
Prophet	Text
Samuel, Nathan, and Gad	1 Chr 29:29
Nathan, Ahijah, and Iddo	2 Chr 9:29
Shemaiah and Iddo	2 Chr 12:15
Iddo	2 Chr 13:22
Jehu	2 Chr 20:34
Isaiah	2 Chr 26:22; 32:32
Chronicle of the Seers	2 Chr 33:19

More than likely, Dtr and the Chronicler had access to the same source, that is, the "books of the kings" which included the words and deeds of various prophets. If this is correct, the Chronicler not only had access to Joshua–Kings, but also to some of the same sources as underlie those books.

In addition, the Chronicler apparently had access to other kinds of sources, including genealogical and military lists (e.g., the further generations of Jehoiachin, 1 Chr 3:17-24). He also probably had access to some census records (1 Chr 5:17; 7:1-11,30-40; 24:6).

The Chronicler may have had other kinds of sources available to him. For example, he refers to what is "written in the Laments"

(2 Chr 35:25) which should not be confused with the canonical
Lamentations. The various literary genres that appear in Chronicles
indicate that he had a wide range of resources upon which to draw
(DE VRIES). He includes many prophetic or Levitical speeches/ser-
mons (e.g., 1 Chr 12:18; 17:4-14; 21:9-12; 2 Chr 7:12-22; 12:5,7-8;
15:1-8; 16:7-10; 18:7-27; 19:1-3; 20:14-19,27; 21:12-15; 24:20; 25:7-
9,15-16; 28:9-11; 34:23-28). He includes many prayers (e.g., 1 Chr
14:10,13; 16:8-36; 17:16-27; 19:13; 21:8,17; 29:10-20; 2 Chr 1:8-10;
6:1-2,14-42; 14:11; 20:3-13; 30:18-20,27; 32:20,24; 33:12-13). These
sermons and prayers may have come from collections of similar
material.

In contrast to late nineteenth and early twentieth-century scholarship (Torrey, "Chronicler," 157-173, 188-217), the Chronicler did
not invent sources. The current debate is the nature and use of these
sources.

Second Samuel and 1-2 Kings are the Chronicler's major source
since he consistently appropriates them. Yet, he probably had access
to another history as well which he generally cites as "books of the
Kings and prophets." Whatever we may say, the Chronicler uses
materials that predate him, and he cites his sources as a mark of
authenticity.

The Chronicler is selective. He does not reproduce 1-2 Samuel
and 1-2 Kings. He omits some things (David's relationship with
Bathsheba), rewords others (Nathan's oracle to David), and adds
additional details (Manasseh's repentance). He retells the story of
Judah in order to apply its significance to his own time. He verifies
his story with sources, but he tells the story in a way that has meaning for his contemporary readers.

PURPOSE: HISTORIAN, EXEGETE, AND THEOLOGIAN

Israelite historiography has been hotly discussed in the last few
decades (e.g., Handy, *Age of Solomon;* Long, *Art*). On one extreme
are those who believe that OT histories (e.g., Solomon) are theological fiction without any real historical basis ("the minimalists"). On
the other extreme are those who believe that the Old Testament histories are strict chronicles analogous to modern scientific history.

The question focuses on the Chronicler's intent. Does he intend to write a "history," and what is meant by "history"?

The Chronicler does not intend to offer a comprehensive history. He does not record every detail (e.g., he omits the sins of Solomon). But neither does the Chronicler intend fiction. He notes his sources, and he assumes a knowledge of Dtr. However, despite his name, he is not a chronicler. He is an interpreter.

The Chronicler writes history as an exegete of the Hebrew canon. He utilizes the whole canon in order to shape a history that speaks to his own context. In other words, he writes a theological history. The Chronicler is concerned about what really happened, but he is also concerned with how those events are interpreted. He is a historian for theological purposes.

Consequently, to say the Chronicler is a "historian" might be a misnomer if we mean by "historian" one who simply chronicles events. While he is a historian in that he makes factual claims about the past, he is a theologian who uses history to proclaim a message. He is a narrative theologian. He writes history in a "representational" manner so that he reliably interprets its meaning (Long, "History," 232-254).

THE BASIC THEOLOGY OF CHRONICLES

The fundamental theological hermeneutic of Chronicles is "God seeks seekers." The faithful and gracious God seeks hearts that seek him. The God of Chronicles is a relational God who seeks authentic reciprocal relationship. Those who seek him will find him, but he will forsake those who forsake him (1 Chr 28:9; 2 Chr 15:2).

Two of the most significant terms in Chronicles are "seek" (דרש, בקש, dāraš, bāqaš) and "heart" (לב, לבב, lēb, lēbāb). They are thematic for Chronicles (Begg, "Seeking," 128-141; Schaefer). These terms are linked 11 times (1 Chr 16:10; 22:19; 28:9; 2 Chr 11:16; 12:14; 15:12,15; 19:3; 22:9; 30:19; 31:21), that is, hearts that seek God. "Seek" appears 54 times (the most in biblical literature) and "heart" 64 times (only Jeremiah and Psalms use it more often). God seeks hearts and yearns for hearts that seek him.

The flip side of God's relational nature is that he will forsake those who forsake him (1 Chr 28:9; 15:2). The history of Israel is filled with example after example of this Godforsakenness. Ultimately, because Israel forsakes God, God exiles Israel.

Consequently, God enters history to create, discipline, probe, test, and redeem in order to find hearts that seek him as he seeks them. Chronicles is the story of Yahweh who moves among his people to know their hearts and find those who seek him (2 Chr 16:9). In Chronicles, Yahweh creates the world and preserves a people throughout history (1 Chr 1–9). Yahweh establishes a covenant with David as he inaugurates a kingdom (1 Chr 17). Yahweh graciously dwells among his people in the temple (2 Chr 6–7). Yahweh disciplines, blesses, and tests his people in order to know their hearts (1 Chr 29:17-19; 2 Chr 32:31). The story of Chronicles is the dynamic engagement between God and his people as God seeks to establish a gracious relationship with those who seek him.

The two theological pillars of God's relationship with his people are (1) the promise to David (1 Chr 17) and (2) the presence of God in the Solomonic temple (2 Chr 6–7). Both ground the hope of the postexilic community. The kingdom is incomplete without Davidic king and Solomonic temple (divine presence).

The Davidic promise involves God's commitment to rule the nations through Israel. The move from Sinaitic theocracy to Davidic kingdom was not incidental. The postexilic restoration was incomplete without a Davidic king even though the temple was fully operational. The Davidic promise grounds the hope of the restored community in a future Davidic king (Raison, 292-308; cf. Kelly, 135-185). The postexilic community depends on the God's faithfulness to David.

However, the Davidic kingdom finds its pinnacle in God's presence in his temple. God comes to "rest" among his people (2 Chr 6:40-42) as they rest in the land God has given them through Davidic victories. The temple is God's redemptive, gracious, and reconciling presence. It is the place of communion between God and his people. The postexilic community trusts the gracious presence of God in the temple.

Thus, standing on the promise of God to David and the gracious presence of God in his temple, the postexilic community is called to hope, holiness, and perseverance. If they will seek God in his temple, trusting in his promises, then God will find them.

Christians understand this dual theme of Davidic promise and gracious presence. God has demonstrated his faithfulness in Jesus Christ who sits on David's throne, and God has given his presence to the church through the indwelling of the Holy Spirit. The theological themes that ground the hope of the postexilic community are fulfilled in Jesus Christ who grounds the hope of the Christian community.

God still seeks seekers. Those who seek him will be found, but he will forsake those who forsake him. In this sense the story of Chronicles is our story. The same God seeks the same kind of hearts. The same God is still at work in history to find those hearts and give them his rest.

There are several helpful theological summaries of Chronicles. At the popular level, Braun (*Understanding*) is an excellent treatment. At the scholarly level, Japhet's *Ideology* is a must read (cf. Petter). Most major commentaries summarize the key themes of Chronicles, but especially helpful are WILLIAMSON (24-33), BRAUN (xxix-xli), and SELMAN (1:45-65). The best single survey of theological themes in Chronicles is PRATT (14-55) who interprets them in both a postexilic and Christological context.

SPECIAL PROBLEM:
LARGE NUMBERS IN CHRONICLES

One of the most puzzling questions in Chronicles is its large numbers. Though numbers are typically taken at face value, some are problematic. For example, Judah and Israel send 1.2 million men into battle and 500,000 are killed (2 Chr 13:3,17) which is larger than American casualties in WWII. Also, on a few occasions, the numbers in Chronicles differ from those in Samuel–Kings.

Some are explained by textual corruption. Through years of transmission, numerals were especially susceptible to copyist errors (Wenham, "Large," 21-24). These accidental changes might involve a letter change (cf. 2 Sam 10:18, "700 chariots" with 1 Chr 19:18, "7,000 chariots") or confusion of nouns. (2 Sam 10:18, "40,000 horsemen" and 1 Chr 19:18, "40,000 footmen").

Obvious textual issues aside, other difficulties remain. Two options are available. One interprets large numbers objectively as precise numerical values. This assumes that the numbers have been interpreted incorrectly. Several attempts have been made to determine the meaning of these large figures (Davies, 452-465). The most convincing solutions interpret the use of אֶלֶף (*'lp*). When pointed אֶלֶף (*'eleph*), it is translated "thousand," but sometimes it bears a general collective meaning, e.g., "cattle" (Isa 30:24) or "clan/family" (Judg 6:15). When it is pointed אַלּוּף (*'allûph* [defectively as אַלֻּף, *'allūph*]), it carries an individual meaning of "chief" (e.g., Gen 36:15-43). In an unpointed text there is no difference in the spelling of the words. Hence, some apply these alternative meanings to numbers over a thousand. Wenham ("Large," 27, 45) takes the 3,700 of the house of Aaron to mean three "captains of thousands" and seven "captains of hundreds" (1 Chr 13:1).

The difficulty is knowing when to translate something other than "thousand." Inanimate objects cannot be grouped into military units or clans (e.g., 1 Chr 22:14; cf. Klein, "Thousand," 275-277). In 1 Chronicles 5:21 the 44,760 transjordanian Israelite soldiers defeated the Hagrites and took "50,000 camels, 250,000 sheep, 2,000 donkeys . . . also . . . 100,000 people." Should we apply "units" to donkeys and sheep as well as military personnel?

Others interpret the numbers hyperbolically (Fouts, "Hyperbolic," 377-387; "Large Numbers," 205-211). Ancient Near Eastern historiography often employed extraordinary numbers, especially in military contexts and royal inscriptions. Though many are intended to be precise (Millard, "Large," 215), some are exaggeration. The texts concerning David and Solomon may resemble the genre of classic royal inscriptions (Fouts, "Hyperbolic," 387). The function of hyperbole is theologically grounded. It exalts Yahweh, the house of David, and the fulfillment of God's promises.

Interpreting 1 Chronicles 12 as hyperbole resolves the problem of the "unit interpretation." The nearest tribes to Hebron were the least represented (e.g., Judah, 6,800). The most remote tribes had larger representations (e.g., Zebulun, 50,000). Klein ("Large," 279-280) interprets the numbers as symbolic of the popular enthusiasm for David's kingship among the "fringe" tribes. Even with a "unit interpretation" it is difficult to comprehend why Judah had only six troops/chiefs and Zebulun had 50.

Fouts ("Another," 209) cites a text from Ugarit which describes a strong army numbering "three hundred ten thousands." In the next line this same army is described as "without number" and "beyond counting." The Chronicler makes the same point when he describes the sheep and oxen as too many to count (2 Chr 5:6).

The unit interpretation of '*lp* may be appropriate in some contexts and the hyperbolic appropriate in others. Sometimes the numbers are precise and sometimes they are figurative (even typological). When the literal statement makes little or no sense in its context, it is probably figurative.

However the large numbers are interpreted, one should recognize two things in Chronicles. First, the Chronicler was not simply inventing historical fiction. Of the 213 numbers in Chronicles which are paralleled elsewhere in Scripture, 194 agree. Only 19 differ and some are smaller (Payne, "Validity," 23-24). Second, his primary purpose is theological interpretation. This affects the book's genre and interpretation in comparison with other records.

RECOMMENDED READING

Exegetical Detail. The most comprehensive commentaries on the Hebrew text in English are those by JAPHET (1993), WILLIAMSON (1982), BRAUN (1986), and DILLARD (1987). WILLIAMSON is the least detailed, while BRAUN and DILLARD provide extensive bibliographical resources. JAPHET, however, is the single most comprehensive commentary. DILLARD is more theological and conservative, but JAPHET touches on almost every question the text might raise. Her conclusions are usually moderate.

Theological Reflection. The three most significant theological commentaries are SELMAN (1994), MCCONVILLE (1984), and JOHNSTONE (1997). They think theologically and canonically (especially SELMAN's Christological applications). While they do not neglect exegetical questions (MCCONVILLE is the least helpful), their quest is theological understanding. Of the three, SELMAN is the better theologian though JOHNSTONE and MCCONVILLE are often quite insightful. A book which combines exegetical substance with theological interests is Japhet's *Ideology* (1997).

For the Serious Student in the Pew. PRATT (1998) is the best single commentary for the person in the pew. It is filled with rich theology and covers problem areas in a conservative vein. THOMPSON

(1994) is conservative on critical issues and often applies the text Christologically, but lacks PRATT's detail and theological insight.

Homiletical Help. WILCOX (1987) is an excellent teaching tool with many applications. ALLEN's (1987) work is designed for preachers. Both are quite theological and oriented toward practical application.

Overall, the most balanced, helpful and instructive commentary for a broad audience is SELMAN.

OUTLINE

PART ONE:
THE GENEALOGY OF ALL ISRAEL —
1 CHR 1:1–9:44

I. FROM ADAM TO ISRAEL — 1:1–2:2
A. The Descendants of Adam — 1:1-27
1. The Lineal Descent of Adam — 1:1-4
2. The Segmented Descent of Noah — 1:5-23
3. The Lineal Descent of Shem — 1:24-27

B. The Descendants of Abraham — 1:28–2:2
1. Descendants of Ishmael and Keturah — 1:28-34a
   a. Descendants of Ishmael — 1:28-31
   b. Descendants of Keturah — 1:32-34a
2. Descendants of Esau, Son of Isaac, the Edomites — 1:34b-54
   a. Descendants of Esau — 1:34b-37
   b. Descendants of Seir — 1:38-42
   c. The Kings of Edom — 1:43-51a
   d. The Chiefs of Edom — 1:51b-54
3. Descendants of Israel, Son of Isaac — 2:1-2

II. THE GENEALOGY OF ISRAEL — 2:3–9:1a
A. Judah — 2:3–4:23
1. Judah's Five Sons — 2:3-4
2. The Descendants of Judah's Sons, Perez and Zerah — 2:5-8
3. The Descendants of Perez's Son Hezron — 2:9–3:24
   a. Sons of Ram to David — 2:9-17
   b. Sons of Caleb to Bezalel — 2:18-24
   c. Sons of Jerahmeel — 2:25-33
   d. Further Descendants of Jerahmeel — 2:34-41
   e. Further Descendants of Caleb — 2:42-55
   f. Further Descendants of Ram from David — 3:1-24

PART TWO:
THE UNITED MONARCHY —
1 CHR 10:1–2 CHR 9:31

I. THE REIGN OF DAVID — 10:1-22:1
A. David Becomes King — 10:1-12:40
  1. The Death of Saul — 10:1-14
    a. The Battle of Gilboa — 10:1-7
    b. The Body of Saul — 10:8-12
    c. A Theological Obituary — 10:13-14
  2. The Enthronement of David in Hebron — 11:1-12:40
    a. David's Coronation at Hebron — 11:1-9
    b. Support for David at Hebron — 11:10-47
    c. Support for David at Ziklag — 12:1-7
    d. Support for David at the Stronghold — 12:8-15
    e. Support for David at the Stronghold — 12:16-18
    f. Support for David at Ziklag — 12:19-22
    g. Support for David at Hebron — 12:23-37
    h. David's Coronation at Hebron —12:38-40
B. David and the Ark of the Covenant — 13:1-17:27
  1. Object Defined: Bring the Ark to Jerusalem —13:1-4
  2. Process of Actualization — 13:5-15:29
    a. The First Attempt Aborted — 13:5-14
    b. The Solidification of David's Reign — 14:1-17
    c. The Second Attempt Successful — 15:1-29
  3. Object Reached: Celebration of the Ark's Arrival — 16:1-43
    a. God's Blessing for Every Israelite — 16:1-3
    b. Levites Appointed for Worship — 16:4-7
    c. Psalm of Praise — 16:8-36
    d. Levites and Priests Appointed for Worship — 16:37-42
    e. God's Blessing for David's House — 16:43
  4. A House for the Ark — 17:1-27
    a. Introductory Dialogue between David and Nathan — 17:1-2
    b. Nathan's Prophecy — 17:3-15
    c. David's Prayer — 17:16-27
C. David Wins Wars — 18:1-22:1
  1. Davidic Victories — 18:1-20:8
    a. Victory over the Nations — 18:1-17
    b. Victory over the Ammonites — 19:1-20:3
    c. Victory over the Philistines — 20:4-8

4. The Rejection of Rehoboam — 10:16-19
5. Conclusion to the Schism — 11:1-4
B. Rehoboam Consolidates His Base — 11:5-23
  1. City-Building — 11:5-12
  2. Faithful Israelites — 11:13-17
  3. Rehoboam's Family — 11:18-23
C. Rehoboam's Punishment — 12:1-12
  1. The Invasion of Shishak — 12:1-4
  2. The Prophetic Word — 12:5-8
  3. Jerusalem Subdued but Saved — 12:9-12
D. Evaluation of Rehoboam — 12:13-16

II. THE SOUTHERN KINGDOM — 13:1–28:27
  A. The Reign of Abijah — 13:1–14:1a
    1. The Formulaic Introduction — 13:1-2
    2. The Battle with Jeroboam —13:3-21
      a. Abijah's Speech — 13:3-12
      b. The Battle Report —13:13-19
      c. The Results — 13:20-21
    3. The Formulaic Conclusion — 13:22–14:1a
  B. The Reign of Asa — 14:1b–16:14
    1. Formulaic Introduction — 14:1b-8
      a. Religious Reform — 14:1b-5
      b. National Reform — 14:6-8
    2. War with Zerah the Cushite — 14:9–15:19
      a. The War Described — 14:9-15
      b. Covenant Renewal — 15:1-18
      c. Conclusion — 15:19
    3. War with Baasha, King of Israel — 16:1-10
      a. The War Described — 16:1-6
      b. Prophetic Opposition — 16:7-10
    4. Formulaic Conclusion — 16:11-14
      a. Source Notation — 16:11
      b. The Faithlessness of Asa — 16:12
      c. Death and Burial of Asa — 16:13-14
  C. The Reign of Jehoshaphat — 17:1–21:1
    1. Expanded Formulaic Introduction — 17:1-19
      a. Fortifications and Army — 17:1-2
      b. Commendation — 17:3-4
      c. Tribute and Respect — 17:5
      d. Reform — 17:6

BIBLIOGRAPHY

COMMENTARIES ON CHRONICLES
(Cited by name in SMALL CAPS; for recommendations see the last section of the Introduction)

ACKROYD, Peter R. *I & II Chronicles, Ezra, Nehemiah*. TBC. London: SCM Press, 1973.

ALLEN, Leslie C. *1, 2 Chronicles*. CC. Waco, TX: Word, 1987.

BRAUN, Roddy L. *1 Chronicles*. WBC. Waco, TX: Word, 1986.

COGGINS, R.J. *The First and Second Book of the Chronicles*. CBC. Cambridge: Cambridge University Press, 1976.

DEVRIES, Simon John. *1 and 2 Chronicles*. FOTL. Grand Rapids: Eerdmans, 1989.

DILLARD, Raymond B. *2 Chronicles*. WBC. Waco, TX: Word, 1987.

ENDRES, John C., William R. Millar, & John Barclay Burns, eds. *Chronicles and Its Synoptic Parallels in Samuel, Kings and Related Biblical Texts*. Collegeville, MN: Liturgical Press, 1998.

JAPHET, Sara. *I & II Chronicles: A Commentary*. OTL. Louisville, KY: Westminster/John Knox, 1993.

JOHNSTONE, William. *1 and 2 Chronicles*. 2 volumes. JSOTSup 253. Sheffield: Sheffield Academic Press, 1997.

KEIL, C.F. "The Books of the Chronicles." In *Biblical Commentary on the Old Testament*. Vol. III. Ed. C.F. Keil and F. Delitzsch (Grand Rapids: Eerdmans, 1982).

MANGAN, Celine. *1-2 Chronicles, Ezra, Nehemiah*. OTM. Wilmington, DE: Michael Glazier, 1982.

MCCONVILLE, J.G. *I & II Chronicles*. DSB. Philadelphia: Westminster Press, 1984.

MYERS, Jacob M. *I Chronicles* and *II Chronicles*. AB. Garden City, NY: Doubleday, 1965.

PAYNE, J. Barton. "1, 2 Chronicles," 4:301-562. In *The Expositor's Bible Commentary*. Ed. Frank E. Gaebelein. Grand Rapids: Zondervan, 1988.

PRATT, Richard L. *1 and 2 Chronicles: A Mentor Commentary*. Fearn, Ross-Shire: Mentor, 1998.

SAILHAMER, John. *First & Second Chronicles*. EBC. Chicago: Moody Press, 1983.

SELMAN, Martin J. *1 Chronicles: An Introduction and Commentary* and *2 Chronicles: A Commentary*. Tyndale. Downers Grove, IL: Inter-Varsity, 1994.

THOMPSON, J.A. *1, 2 Chronicles*. NAC. Nashville: Broadman & Holman, 1994.

WILCOX, Michael. *The Message of Chronicles*. BST. Downers Grove, IL: InterVarsity, 1987.

WILLIAMSON, H.G.M. *1 and 2 Chronicles*. NCB. Grand Rapids: Eerdmans, 1982.

MONOGRAPHS, ARTICLES, AND THESES

Ackerman, Susan. "The Queen Mother and the Cult in Ancient Israel." *JBL* 112 (1993): 389-395.

Ackroyd, Peter R. *The Chronicler and His Age*. JSOTSup 101. Sheffield: JSOT Press,

_____."Chronicler as Exegete." *JSOT* 2 (1977): 3-32.

_____. "Chronicles-Ezra-Nehemiah: The Concept of Unity," *Beihefte zur ZAW* 100 (1988): 189-201.

_____. "History and Theology in the Writings of the Chronicler." *CTM* 38 (1967): 501-515.

_____. "The Temple Vessels — A Continuity Theme." In *Studies in the Religion of Ancient Israel*. VTSup 23. Ed. P. de Boer. Leiden: Brill, 1972.

_____. "The Theology of the Chronicles." *LTQ* 8 (1973): 101-116.

Albright, William F. *Archaeology and the Religion of Israel*. 5th ed. Baltimore: Johns Hopkins, 1968.

_____. "The Date and Personality of the Chronicler." *JBL* 40 (1921): 104-114.

_____. "The Judicial Reform of Jehoshaphat." In *Alexander Marx Jubilee Volume*. New York: Jewish Theological Seminary of America, 1950.

Andreasen, N. "Role of the Queen Mother in Israelite Society." *CBQ* 45 (1983): 179-194.

Applegate, John. "Jeremiah and the Seventy Years in the Hebrew Bible: Inner-Biblical Reflections on the Prophet and His Prophecy." In *The Book of Jeremiah & His Reception*. BETL 128. Ed. A.H.W. Curtis and T. Romer. Leuven: Leuven University Press, 1997.

Archer, Jr., Gleason L. *A Survey of Old Testament Introduction*. Rev. ed. Chicago: Moody Press, 1974.

Aufrecht, William E. "Genealogy and History in Ancient Israel." In *Ascribe to the Lord: Biblical and Other Studies in Memory of Peter C. Craigie*. JSOTSup 67. Ed. Lyle Eslinger and Glen Taylor. Sheffield: Sheffield Academic Press, 1998.

Avigad, N. "Excavations in the Jewish Quarter of the Old City Jerusalem 1969/1970, Preliminary Report II." *IEJ* 20 (1970): 129-134.

Bailey, Noel. "David's Innocence: A Response to J. Wright." *JSOT* 64 (1994): 83-90.

Ball, E. "The Co-Regency of David and Solomon (1 Kings I)." *VT* 27 (1977): 268-279.

Bar, Shaul. "A Better Image for Solomon." *BT* 36 (1998): 221-226.

Beentjes, Pancratius. "Jerusalem in the Book of Chronicles." In *The Centrality of Jerusalem: Historical Perspectives*. Ed. M. Poorthuis and C. Safrai. Kampen, Netherlands: Kok Pharos, 1996.

_____. "Tradition and Transformation: Aspects of Innerbiblical Interpretation in 2 Chronicles 20." *Bib* 74 (1993): 258-268.

Begg, Christopher T. "Babylon and Judah in Chronicles." *Ephemerides Theologicae Lovanienses* 65 (1988): 142-152.

_____. "Constructing a Monster: The Chronicler's *Sondergut* in 2 Chronicles 21." *ABR* 37 (1989): 35-51.

_____. "The Death of Josiah in Chronicles: Another View." *VT* 37 (1987): 1-8.

_____. "'Seeking Yahweh' and the Purpose of Chronicles." *Louvain Studes* 9 (Fall 1982): 128-141.

Bellinger, Jr., W.H. "Psalms of the Falsely Accused: A Reassessment." In *SBL 1986 Seminar Papers Series.* Atlanta: Scholars Press, 1986.

Black, Matthew. "The Doxology of the *Pater Noster* with a Note on Matthew 6.13B." In *A Tribute to Geza Vermes: Essays on Jewish and Christian Literature and History.* JSOTSup 100. Ed. Philip R. Davies and Richard T. White. Sheffield: JSOT Press, 1990.

Blenkinsopp, J. *Ezra–Nehemiah: A Commentary.* OTL. Louisville: Westminster/John Knox Press, 1988.

_____. *Gibeon and Israel.* SOTSMS 2. Cambridge: Cambridge University Press, 1972.

Bowman, Craig D. "An Analysis of the Chronicler's Use of Sources: Methodological Concerns and Criteria." Ph.D. dissertation, Princeton Theological Seminary, 1997.

Braun, Roddy L. "Chronicles, Ezra and Nehemiah: Theology and Literary History." *VT* 30 (1979): 42-64.

_____. "The Message of Chronicles: Rally 'Round the Temple.'" *CTM* 42 (1971): 502-514.

_____. "A Reconsideration of Chr's Attitude toward the North." *JBL* 96 (1977): 59-62.

_____. "Solomon, the Chosen Temple Builder: The Significance of 1 Chronicles 22, 28, and 29 for the Theology of Chronicles." *JBL* 95 (1976): 581-590.

_____. "Solomonic Apologetic in Chronicles." *JBL* 92 (1973): 503-516.

_____. *Understanding the Basic Themes of 1, 2 Chronicles.* Dallas: Word, 1991.

Brettler, Marc Zvi. *The Creation of History in Ancient Israel.* New York: Routledge, 1995.

Broshi, M. "The Expansion of Jerusalem in the Reigns of Hezekiah and Manasseh." *IEJ* 24 (1974): 21-26.

Bulbach, Stanley W. "Judah in the Reign of Manasseh as Evidenced in Texts during the Neo-Assyrian Period and in the Archaeology of the Iron Age." Ph.D. dissertation, New York University, 1981.

Butler, Trent C. "A Forgotten Passage: From a Forgotten Era (1 Chr. XVI 8-36)." *VT* 28 (1978): 142-150.

Byl, John. "On the Capacity of Solomon's Molten Sea." *VT* 48 (1998): 309-314.

Cahill, Jane. "A Rejoinder to 'Was the Siloam Tunnel Built by Hezekiah?'" *BA* 60 (1997): 184-185.

Chisholm, Jr., Robert B. "Does God Deceive?" *BibSac* 155 (1998): 11-28.

Clines, D.J.A. *Ezra, Nehemiah, Esther,* New Century Bible. Grand Rapids: Eerdmans, 1984.

Cogan, Mordechai. "The Chronicler's Use of Chronology as Illuminated by Neo-Assyria." In *Empirical Modes for Biblical Criticism.* Ed. J. Tigay. Philadelphia: University of Pennsylvania Press, 1985.

Cohen, Ralph. "The Fortresses King Solomon Built to Protect His Southern Border." *BAR* 11.3 (1985): 56-70.

Crocker, P.T. "Cush and the Bible." *Bible History* 22 (1986): 27-38.

Cross, Jr., Frank Moore. *Canaanite Myth and Hebrew Epic: Essays in the History of the Religion of Israel.* Cambridge, MA: Harvard University Press, 1973.

_____. "A Reconstruction of the Judean Restoration," *JBL* 94 (1975): 4-18.

Cross, Frank Moore, and David Freedman. "Josiah's Revolt against Assyria." *JNES* 12 (1953): 56-58.

daSilva, A.A. "A Comparison between the Avenging Angel of 1 Ch 21 and Analogous 'Angel-like' Figures in the Ugaritic Ba'al Cycle." *JS* 6 (1994): 154-169.

Davies, Eryl W. "A Mathematical Conundrum: The Problem of the Large Numbers in Numbers I and XXVI." *VT* 45 (1995): 452-465.

Dawes, Stephen B. "'Bless the Lord': An Invitation to Affirm the Living God." *ET* 106 (1995): 293-296.

Day, John. "Asherah in the Hebrew Bible and Northwest Semitic Literature." *JBL* 105 (1986): 385-408.

Day, Peggy. *An Adversary in Heaven.* HSM 43. Atlanta: Scholars Press, 1988.

Deboys, David G. "History and Theology in Chr's Portrayal of Abijah." *Bib* 71 (1990): 48-62.

Demsky, A. "The Genealogy of Gibeon [I Chronicles 9:35-44]: Biblical and Epigraphic Considerations." *BASOR* 202 (1971): 20-23.

Derby, Josiah. "David's Conquest of Jerusalem." *JBQ* 25 (1997): 241-245.

DeVries, Simon J. "Festival Ideology in Chronicles." In *Problems in Biblical Theology: Essays in Honor of Rolf Knierim*. Ed. Hendry T.C. Sun et al. Grand Rapids: Eerdmans, 1997.

_____. "The Land's Sabbath in 2 Chr 36:21." *Proceedings, Eastern Great Lakes & Midwest Biblical Societies* 6 (1986): 96-103.

_____. "Moses and David as Cult Founders in Chronicles." *JBL* 107 (1988): 619-639.

_____. "The Scheme of Dynastic Endangerment in Chronicles." *Proceedings, Eastern Great Lakes and Midwest Bible Society* 7 (1987): 59-77.

Dillard, Raymond. "1 Chronicles." *NIV Study Bible*. Grand Rapids: Zondervan, 1985.

_____. "The Chronicler's Jehoshaphat," *TJ* 7 (1986): 17-22.

_____. "The Chronicler's Solomon," *WTJ* 43 (1980): 289-300.

_____. "David's Census: Perspectives on II Samuel 24 and I Chronicles 21." In *Through Christ's Word*. Ed. W. Robert Godfrey and Jesse L. Boyd III. Phillipsburg, NJ: Presbyterian and Reformed, 1985.

_____. "The Literary Structure of the Chronicler's Solomon Narrative," *JSOT* 30 (1984): 85-93.

_____. "The Reign of Asa (2 Chr 14–16): An Example of Chr's Theological Method." *JETS* 23 (1980): 207-218.

_____. "Reward and Punishment in Chronicles: The Theology of Immediate Retribution." *WTJ* 46 (1984): 164-172.

Dillard, Raymond, and Tremper Longman. *An Introduction to the Old Testament*. Grand Rapids: Zondervan, 1994.

Dion, P.E. "The Angel with the Drawn Sword (I Chr. 21,16)." *ZAW* 97 (1985): 114-117.

Dirksen, Piet B. "1 Chronicles 9,26-33: Its Position in Chapter 9." *Bib* 79 (1998): 91-96.

_____. "I Chronicles 16:38: Its Background and Growth." *JNSL* 22 (1996): 85-90.

_____. "1 Chronicles XXVIII 11-18: Its Textual Development." *VT* 46 (1996): 429-438.

_____. "Why Was David Disqualified as Temple Builder? The Meaning of 1 Chronicles 22:8." *JSOT* 70 (1996): 51-56.

Dorsey, David A. "Another Peculiar Term in the Book of Chronicles: מסלה, 'Highway'?" *JQR* 35 (1985): 385-391.

Dyck, Jonathan. "Dating Chronicles and the Purpose of Chronicles." *Didaskalia* 8 (Spring 1997): 16-29.

Eaton, M.R. "Some Instances of Flyting in the Hebrew Bible." *JSOT* 61 (1994): 3-14.

Edelman, Diana V. "The Asherite Genealogy in 1 Chronicles 7:14-40." *BR* 33 (1988): 13-23.

_____ . "The Manassite Genealogy in 1 Chronicles 7:14-19: Form and Source." *CBQ* 53 (1991): 179-201.

_____ . "Saul Ben Kish in History and Tradition." In *The Origins of the Ancient Israelite States*. JSOTSup 228. Ed. Volkmar Fritz and Philip R. Davies. Sheffield: Sheffield Academic Press, 1996.

Elayi, Josette. "The Name of Deuteronomy's Author Found on Seal Ring." *BAR* 13.5 (1987): 54-56.

Eskenazi, Tamara C. "A Literary Approach to Chronicles' Ark Narrative in 1 Chronicles 13–16." In *Fortunate the Eyes that See*. Ed. Astrid B. Beck et al. Grand Rapids: Eerdmans, 1995.

Estes, Daniel J. "Metaphorical Sojourning in 1 Chronicles 29:15." *CBQ* 53 (1991): 45-49.

Eves, Terry L. "The Role of the Passover in the Book of Chronicles: A Study of 2 Chronicles 30 and 35." Ph.D. dissertation, Annenberg Research Institute, 1992.

Fewell, Dana N. "Sennacherib's Defeat: Words at War in 2 Kings 18:13–19:37." *JSOT* 34 (1986): 79-90.

Fishbane, Michael. *Biblical Interpretation in Ancient Israel*. Oxford: Clarendon Press, 1985.

Fouts, David M. "Another Look at Large Numbers in Assyrian Royal Inscriptions." *JNES* 53 (1994): 205-211.

_____ . "A Defense of the Hyperbolic Interpretation of Large Numbers in the Old Testament." *JETS* 40 (1997): 377-387.

Freedman, D.N. "The Chronicler's Purpose." *CBQ* 23 (1961): 436-442.

Friedman, R.E. "The Tabernacle in the Temple." *BR* 43 (1980): 241-248.

Fritz, Volkmar. "The 'List of Rehoboam's Fortresses' in 2 Chr. 11:5-12 — A Document from the Time of Josiah." *Eretz-Israel* 15 (1981): 46-53.

Frost, Stanley Brice. "The Death of Josiah: A Conspiracy of Silence." *JBL* 87 (1968): 369-382.

Galil, Gershon. "Chr's Genealogies of Ephraim." *BN* 56 (1991): 11-14.

_____ . "The Sons of Judah and the Sons of Aaron in Biblical Historiography." *VT* 35 (1985): 488-495.

Gane, Roy. "The Role of Assyria in the Ancient Near East during the Reign of Manasseh." *AUSS* 35 (1997): 21-32.

Garfinkel, Yosef. "2 Chr 11:5-10 Fortified Cities List and the *lmlk* Stamps—Reply to Nadav Na'aman." *BASOR* 271 (1988): 69-73.

Glatt-Gilead, David A. "The Role of Huldah's Prophecy in the Chronicler's Portrayal of Josiah's Reform." *Bib* 77 (1996): 16-31.

Goldberg, Jeremy. "Two Assyrian Campaigns against Hezekiah and Later Eighth Century Biblical Chronology." *Bib* 80 (1999): 360-390.

Goldingay, J. "The Chronicler as Theologian." *BTB* 5 (1975): 99-126.

Good, Robert M. "The Just War in Ancient Israel." *JBL* 104 (1985): 385-400.

Graham, J.N. "Vinedressers and Plowmen." *BA* 47 (1984): 55-58.

Graham, M. Patrick. "Aspects of the Structure and Rhetoric of 2 Chronicles 25." In *History and Interpretation: Essays in Honour of John H. Hayes.* JSOTSup 173. Ed. M. Patrick Graham et al. Sheffield: JSOT Press, 1993.

_____ . "Setting the Heart to Seek God: Worship in 2 Chronicles 30.1–31.1." In *Worship and the Hebrew Bible: Essays in Honour of John T. Willis.* JSOTSup 284. Ed. M. Patrick Graham, Rick R. Marrs, and Steven L. McKenzie. Sheffield: Sheffield Academic Press, 1999. Pp. 124-141.

_____ . *The Utilization of 1 and 2 Chronicles in the Reconstruction of Israelite History in the Nineteenth Century.* SBLDS 116. Atlanta: Scholars Press, 1990.

Green, Alberto R. "David's Relations with Hiram: Biblical and Josephan Evidence for Tyrian Chronology." In *The Word of the Lord Shall Go Forth.* ASORSV 1 Ed. Carol L. Myers and M. O'Conner. Winona Lake, IN: Eisenbrauns, 1983.

_____ . "The Fate of Jehoiakim." *AUSS* 20 (1982): 103-109.

Handy, Lowell K. "Hezekiah's Unlikely Reform." *ZAW* 100 (1988): 111-115.

_____ . "On the Dating and Dates of Solomon's Reign." In *The Age of Solomon: Scholarship at the Turn of the Millennium*. Ed. Lowell K. Handy. Leiden: Brill, 1997. Pp. 96-106.

Handy, Lowell K., ed. *The Age of Solomon: Scholarship at the Turn of the Millennium*. Leiden: Brill, 1997.

Hanson, Paul D. "1 Chronicles 15-16 and Chronicler's Views of the Levites." In *Sha'arei Talmon*. Ed. Michael Fishbane et al. Winona Lake, IN: Eisenbrauns, 1992.

_____ . *The Dawn of Apocalyptic*. Philadelphia: Fortress Press, 1975.

Haran, Menahem. "Explaining the Identical Lines at the End of Chronicles and the Beginning of Ezra." *BRv* 2.3 (1986): 18-20.

Hart, Stephen. "'Sela': The Rock of Edom?" *PEQ* 118 (1986): 91-95.

Hauer, C. "David and the Levites." *JSOT* 23 (1982): 33-54.

Hendel, Id S. "The Date of the Siloam Inscription: A Rejoinder to Rogerson and Davies." *BA* 59 (1996): 233-237.

Herrmann, Siegfried. "The So-Called 'Fortresses of Rehoboam,' 2 Chron 11:5-12: Theoretical Considerations." *Eretz-Israel* 20 (1989): 72-78.

Hicks, John Mark. "The Lord's Table: A Covenant Meal." *Leaven* 3.3 (1995): 4-7.

_____ . "Numerical Growth in the Theology of Acts: The Role of Rhetoric, Reason and Pragmatism." *Journal of the American Society for Church Growth* 8 (1997): 17-34.

_____ . "Preaching Imprecatory Psalms." In *A Heart to Study and Teach: Essays Honoring Clyde M. Woods*. Ed. Dale Manor. Henderson, TN: Freed-Hardeman University, 2000. Pp. 28-51.

_____ . "The Sabbath Controversy in Matthew: An Exegesis of Matthew 12:1-12." *RQ* 27.2 (1984): 79-92.

_____ . "What Did God Do to Sin and Death through Jesus Christ?" In *Theology Matters: Answers for the Church Today, In Honor of Harold Hazelip*. Ed. Gary Holloway, Randall J. Harris, and Mark C. Black. Joplin, MO: College Press, 1998. Pp. 53-63.

_____ . *Yet Will I Trust Him*. Joplin, MO: College Press, 1999.

Hill, Andrew. "Patchwork Poetry or Reasoned Verse? Connective Structure in 1 Chronicles XVI." *VT* 33 (1983): 97-101.

Ho, Craig Y.S. "Conjectures and Refutations: Is 1S XXXI 1-13 Really the Source of 1 Chronicles X 1-12?" *VT* 45 (1995): 82-106.

Hobbs, T.R. "The 'Fortresses of Rehoboam': Another Look." In *Uncovering Ancient Stones: Essays in Memory of H. Neil Richardson.* Ed. Lewis M. Hopfe. Winona Lake, IN: Eisenbrauns, 1994.

Hognesius, Kiell. "A Note on 1 Chr 23." *SJOT* 1 (1987): 123-127.

Holdridge, Donald Wesley. "An Argument for a Late Sixth Century Date for the Book of Chronicles." Th.D. dissertation, Dallas Theological Seminary, 1992.

Horn, Siegfried H. "The Chronology of King Hezekiah's Reign." *AUSS* 2 (1964): 40-52.

Huffmon, H.B. "The Treaty Background of Hebrew *Yada'*." BASOR 181 (1966): 31-37.

Hulse, E.V. "The Nature of Biblical 'Leprosy' and the Use of Alternative Medical Terms in Modern Translations of the Bible." *PEQ* 107 (1975): 87-105.

Hurowitz, Victor A. "The Form and Fate of the Tabernacle: Reflections on a Recent Proposal." *JQR* 86 (1995): 127-151.

_____. *I Have Built You an Exalted House: Temple Building in the Bible in Light of Mesopotamian and Northwest Semitic Writings.* JSOTSup 115. Sheffield: Sheffield Academic Press, 1992.

Hurvitz, Avi. "Terms and Epithets Relating to the Jerusalem Temple Compound in the Book of Chronicles: The Linguistic Aspect." In *Pomegranates and Golden Bells.* Ed. David P. Wright et al. Winona Lake, IN: Eisenbrauns, 1995.

_____. "The Usage of שש and בוץ in the Bible." *HTR* 60 (1967): 117-121.

Japhet, Sara. "Chronicles, Books of." In *Dictionary of Biblical Interpretation*, Volume 1. Ed. John H. Hayes. Nashville: Abingdon, 1999.

_____. "Conquest and Settlement in Chronicles." *JBL* 98 (1979): 205-218.

_____. "From the King's Sanctuary to the Chosen City." *Judaism* 46 (1997): 132-139.

_____. "The Historical Reliability of Chronicles: The History of the Problem and Its Place in Biblical Research," *JSOT* 33 (1985): 83-107.

_____. *The Ideology of the Book of Chronicles and Its Place in Biblical Thought.* Rev. ed. Trans. Anna Barber. New York: Peter Lang, 1997.

_____ . "Interchanges of Verbal Roots in Parallel Texts in Chronicles." *HS* 8 (1987): 22-23.

_____ . "Israelite Legal and Social Reality as Reflected in Chronicles: A Case Study." In *"Sha'arei Talmon": Studies in the Bible, Qumran, and the Ancient Near East Presented to Shemaryahu Talmon.* Ed. Michael Fishbane and Emmanuel Tov. Winona Lake, IN: Eisenbrauns, 1992.

_____ . "The Prohibition of the Habitation of Women: The Temple Scroll's Attitude toward Sexual Impurity and Its Biblical Precedents." *JANES* 22 (1993): 69-87.

_____ . "The Supposed Common Authorship of Chronicles and Ezra–Nehemiah Investigated Anew." *VT* 18 (1968): 5-11.

Johnson, A.R. *The Cultic Prophet and Israel's Psalmody.* Cardiff: University of Wales, 1979.

Johnson, M.D. *The Purpose of Biblical Genealogies.* New York: Cambridge University Press, 1969.

Johnstone, William. *Chronicles and Exodus: An Analogy and Its Application.* JSOTSup 275. Sheffield: Sheffield Academic Press, 1998.

_____ . "Guilt and Atonement: The Theme of 1 and 2 Chronicles." In *A Word in Season: Essays in Honor of William McKane.* JSOTSup 42. Ed. J.D. Martin and P.R. Davids. Sheffield: JSOT Press, 1986).

Jones, Gwilym H. "From Abijam to Abijah." *ZAW* 106 (1994): 420-434.

Kalimi, Isaac. "The Contribution of the Literary Study of Chronicles to the Solution of Its Textual Problem." *BI* 3 (1995): 190-212.

_____ . "History of Interpretation: The Book of Chronicles in Jewish Tradition from Daniel to Spinoza." *RB* 105 (1998): 5-41.

_____ . "The Land of Moriah, Mount Moriah, and the Site of Solomon's Temple in Biblical Historiography." *HTR* 83 (1990): 345-362.

_____ . "Paronomasia in the Book of Chronicles." *JSOT* 67 (1995): 27-41.

Kaufman, A. "Determining the Length of the Medium Cubit." *PEQ* 116 (1984): 120-132.

Kelly, Brian E. *Retribution and Eschatology in Chronicles.* JSOTSup 211. Sheffield: Sheffield Academic Press, 1996.

Kitchen, K.A. "Sheba and Arabia." In *The Age of Solomon: Scholarship at the Turn of the Millennium*. Ed. Lowell K. Handy. Leiden: Brill, 1997.

_____ . "Shishak's Military Campaign in Israel Confirmed." *BAR* 15.3 (1989): 32-33.

_____ . *The Third Intermediate Period in Egypt (1100–650 B.C.)*. 2nd Rev. Ed. Warminster: Aris & Phillips, 1986.

_____ . "Where Did Solomon's Gold Go?" *BAR* 15.3 (1989): 30.

Klein, Ralph W. "Abijah's Campaign against the North (II Chr 13)— What Were Chr's Sources." *ZAW* 95 (1983): 210-217.

_____ . "How Many in a Thousand?" In *Chronicler as Historian*. JSOTSup 238. Ed. M. Patrick Graham et al. Sheffield: Sheffield Academic Press, 1997.

_____ . "Reflections on Historiography in the Account of Jehoshaphat." In *Pomegranates & Golden Bulls*. Ed. David P. Wright et al. Winona Lake, IN: Eisenbrauns, 1995.

Kleinig, John W. "The Divine Institution of the Lord's Song in Chronicles." *JSOT* 55 (1992): 75-83.

_____ . *The Lord's Song: The Basis, Function and Significance of Choral Music in Chronicles*. JSOTSup 156. Sheffield: Sheffield Academic Press, 1993.

_____ . "Recent Research in Chronicles." *CR* 2 (1994): 43-76.

Kleven, Terence. "Up the Waterspout: How David's General Joab Got inside Jerusalem." *BAR* 20 (July-August 1994): 34-35.

Kline, Meredith. *The Structure of Biblical Authority*. 2nd ed. Grand Rapids: Eerdmans, 1972.

Knoppers, Gary N. "Jehoshaphat's Judiciary and 'The Scroll of YHWH's Torah.'" *JBL* 113 (1994): 59-80.

_____ . "Jerusalem at War in Chronicles." In *Zion: City of Our God*. Ed. Richard S. Hess and Gordon J. Wenham. Grand Rapids: Eerdmans, 1999.

_____ . "Reform and Regression: The Chronicler's Presentation of Jehoshaphat." *Biblica* 72 (1991): 500-524.

_____ . "Rehoboam in Chronicles: Villain or Victim?" *JBL* 109 (1990): 423-440.

_____ . "'There Was None Like Him': Incomparability in the Books of the Kings." *CBQ* 54 (1992): 411-431.

_____ . "'Yahweh Is Not with Israel': Alliances as a *Topos* in Chronicles." *CBQ* 58 (1996): 601-626.

Konkel, A. "Hezekiah in Biblical Tradition." Ph.D. dissertation, Westminster Theological Seminary, 1987.

Laato, Antti. "The Levitical Genealogies in 1 Chronicles 5–6 and the Formation of Levitical Ideology in Postexilic Judah." *JSOT* 62 (1994): 77-99.

Lipinski, Edward. "The Syro-Palestinian Iconography of Woman and Goddess (Review Article)." *IEJ* 36 (1986): 87-96

Loader, J.A. "Redaction and Function of the Chronicler's 'Psalm of David.'" *OTWSA* 19 (1976): 69-75.

Long, Thomas G. "The Fall of the House of Uzzah and Other Difficult Preaching Texts." *JP* (1983): 13-19.

Long, V. Philips. *The Art of Biblical History*. Grand Rapids: Zondervan, 1994.

_____ . "History and Fiction: What Is History?" In *Israel's Past in Present Research: Essays on Ancient Israelite Historiography*. Ed. V. Philips Long. Winona Lake, IN: Eisenbrauns, 1999.

Luria, B.Z. "Obed—A Prophet of God," *Dor le Dor* 15 (1987): 256-259.

Machinist, Peter. "The Transfer of Kingship: A Divine Turning." In *Fortunate the Eyes that See: Essays in Honor of David Noel Freedman in Celebration of His Seventieth Birthday*. Ed. Astrid B. Beck et al. Grand Rapids: Eerdmans, 1995.

MacKenzie, J.A. Ross. "Valiant against All: From Text to Sermon on I Chronicles 11:22,23." *Int* 22 (1968): 18-35.

Malamat, Abraham. "The Historical Background of the Assassination of Amon, King of Judah." *EIJ* 3 (1953): 26-29.

_____ . "Josiah's Bid for Armageddon: The Background of the Judean-Egyptian Encounter in 609 B.C." *JANESCU* 5 (1973): 267-278.

_____ . "King Lists of the Old Babylonian Period and Biblical Genealogies." *JAOS* 88 (1968): 163-173.

_____ . "Kingship and Council in Israel and Sumer: A Parallel." *JNES* 22 (1963): 247-253.

_____ . "The Last Kings of Judah and the Fall of Jerusalem." *IEJ* 18 (1968): 135-156.

_____ . "The Twilight of Judah: In the Egyptian-Babylonian Maelstrom." In *Congress Volume*. VTSup 28. Leiden: Brill, 1975.

Mason, R. *Preaching the Tradition: Homily and Hermeneutics after the Exile*. Cambridge: Cambridge University Press, 1990.

Mayhue, Richard L. "False Prophets and the Deceiving Spirit." *The Master's Seminary Journal* 4 (1993): 135-163.

Mazar, Benjamin. "The Aramean Empire and Its Relations with Israel." *BA* 25 (1962): 98-120.

_____. "The Campaign of Pharaoh Shishak to Palestine." *VT*Sup 4 (1957): 57-66.

Mazar, Eliat. "King David's Palace: It's There." *BAR* 23 (1997): 50-57, 74

McCarter, Jr., P. Kyle. "The Historical David." *Int* 40 (1986): 117-129.

McCarthy, Dennis J. "An Installation Genre?" *JBL* 90 (1971): 31-41.

McConville, J.G., "1 Chronicles 28:9: Yahweh 'Seeks Out' Solomon." *JTS* ns37 (1986): 105-108.

_____. *Law and Theology in Deuteronomy*. JSOT 33. Sheffield: JSOT, 1984.

McKenzie, Steve. *The Chronicler's Use of the Deuteronomistic History*. HSM 33. Atlanta: Scholars Press, 1985.

_____. "The Source of Jeroboam's Role at Shechem." *JBL* 106 (1987): 297-304.

McKinnon, James W. "The Exclusion of Musical Instruments from the Ancient Synagogue." *Proceedings of the Royal Music Association* 106 (1979–80): 77-87.

_____. *Music in Early Christian Literature*. Cambridge: Cambridge University Press, 1987.

McMillion, Phillip. "Manasseh and the Chronicler." Unpublished paper, presented at the Annual Meeting of the Society of Biblical Literature, Kansas City, 1991.

Mendenhall, G.E. "The Census Lists of Numbers 1 and 26." *JBL* 77 (1958): 52-66.

Mercer, M.K. "Daniel 1:1 and Jehoiakim's Three Years of Servitude." *AUSS* 27 (1989): 179-192.

Meulen, Harry E. Faber van der. "One or Two Veils in Front of the Holy of Holies?" *Theologia Evangelica* 18 (1985): 22-27.

Milgrom, Jacob. "Hezekiah's Sacrifices at the Dedication Services of the Purified Temple (2 Chr 29:21-24)." In *Biblical and Related Studies Presented to Samuel Iwry*. Ed. Ann Krot and Scott Morshauser. Winona Lake: Eisenbrauns, 1985.

Millard, Alan R. "Does the Bible Exaggerate King Solomon's Golden Wealth?" *BAR* 15.3 (1989): 20-31, 34.

_____. "King Solomon in His Ancient Context." In *The Age of Solomon: Scholarship at the Turn of the Millennium.* Ed. Lowell K. Handy. Leiden: Brill, 1997.

_____. "Large Numbers in the Assyrian Royal Inscriptions." In *Ah, Assyria . . . Studies in Assyrian History and Ancient Near Eastern Historiography.* Ed. Mordechai Cogan and Israel Eph'al. SH 33. Jerusalem: Magnes Press, Hebrew University, 1991.

_____. "Sennacherib's Attack on Hezekiah." *TB* 36 (1985): 61-77.

_____. "Solomon in All His Glory." *VE* 12 (1981): 14-16.

Miller, J. Maxwell. "Rehoboam's Cities of Defense and the Levitical City List." In *Archaeology & Biblical Interpretation.* Ed. Leo G. Perdue et al. Atlanta: John Knox Press, 1987.

Monson, John. "The New 'Ain Dara Temple: Closest Solomonic Parallel." *BAR* 26 (May/June 2000): 20-35, 67.

Moriarty, Frederick L. "The Chronicler's Account of Hezekiah's Reform." *CBQ* 27 (1965): 399-406.

Mowinckel, S. *The Psalms in Israel's Worship.* Trans. D.R. Ap-Thomas. Oxford: Basil Blackwell, 1967.

Music, David. *Instruments in the Church: A Collection of Source Documents.* Landham, MD: Scarecrow Press, 1998.

Na'aman, Nadav. "The Date of 2 Chr 11:5-10 — A Reply to Y. Garfinkel." *BASOR* 271 (1988): 74-77.

_____. "Hezekiah's Fortified Cities and the *LMLK* Stamps." *BASOR* 261 (1986): 5-21.

_____. "The List of David's Officers (*SALISIM*)." *VT* 38 (1988): 71-79.

_____. "Prophetic Stories as Sources for the Histories of Jehoshaphat and the Omrides." *Bib* 78 (1997): 153-173.

_____. "Sennacherib's Campaign to Judah and the Date of the *LMLK* Stamps." *VT* 29 (1979): 61-86.

_____. "Sources and Redaction in Chr's Genealogies of Asher and Ephraim." *JSOT* 49 (1991): 99-111.

Newsome, J.D. "Toward a New Understanding of the Chronicler and His Purposes." *JBL* 94 (1975): 210-217.

Nielsen, E. "Political Conditions and Cultural Developments in Israel and Judah during the Reign of Manasseh." In *Proceedings of the Fourth World Congress of Jewish Studies, Jerusalem, 1965.* Jerusalem: World Union of Jewish Studies, 1967.

Norin, Stig. "The Age of the Siloam Inscription and Hezekiah's Tunnel." *VT* 48 (1998): 37-48.

North, Robert. "Does Archaeology Prove the Chronicler's Sources?" In *A Light unto My Path: Old Testament Studies in Honor of Jacob Meyers.* Ed. Howard M. Bream et al. Philadelphia: Temple University Press, 1974.

Noth, Martin. *The Chronicler's History.* Trans. H.G.M. Williamson. JSOTSup 50. Sheffield: Sheffield Academic Press, 1987.

Ogden, Graham S. "The Northern Extent of Josiah's Reforms." *ABR* 26 (1978): 26-34.

Oswalt, J. "The Golden Calves and the Egyptian Concept of Deity." *EQ* 45 (1973): 13-20.

Payne, J. Barton. "The Relationship of the Reign of Ahaz to the Succession of Hezekiah." *BS* 126 (1969): 40-52.

_____. "Validity of Numbers in Chronicles." *Near East Archaeological Society Bulletin* 11 (1978): 5-58.

Peltonen, Kai. *History Debated: The Historical Reliability of Chronicles in Pre-Critical and Critical Research.* 2 vols. Finnish Exegetical Society 64. Helsinki: Finnish Exegetical Society, 1996.

Petersen, David. *Late Israelite Prophecy: Studies in Deutero-Prophetic Literature and in Chronicles.* SBLMS 23. Missoula, MT: Scholars Press, 1977.

Peterson, Eugene. "Why Did Uzzah Die? Why Did David Dance? 2S 6–7," *Crux* 31.3 (September 1995): 3-5, 7-8.

Petter, G.J. "A Study of the Theology of the Books of Chronicles." Ph.D. dissertation, Vanderbilt University, 1985.

Plum, Karin Friis. "Genealogy as Theology." *SJOT* 1 (1989): 66-92.

Polk, Timothy. "The Levites in the Davidic-Solomonic Empire." *SBT* 9 (1979): 12-14.

Polzin, R. *Late Biblical Hebrew.* Missoula, MT: Scholars Press, 1976.

Porter, J. Roy. "The Succession of Joshua." In *Proclamation and Presence: OT Essays in Honour of Gwynne Henton Davies.* Ed. John I. Durham and J.R. Porter. London: SCM Press, 1970.

Priest, John. "Huldah's Oracle." *VT* 30 (1980): 366-368.

Pritchard, James B., ed. *Ancient Near Eastern Texts*. Princeton: Princeton University Press, 1971.

Rainey, Anson F. "Hezekiah's Reform and the Altars of Beer-sheba and Arad." In *Scripture & Other Artifacts: Essays on the Bible and Archaeology in Honor of Philip J. King*. Ed. Michael D. Coogan, J. Cheryl Exum, and Lawrence E. Stager. Louisville: Westminster/John Knox, 1994.

_____. "Wine from the Royal Vineyards." *BASOR* 245 (1982): 57-62.

Raison, Stephen John. "From Theocracy to Kingdom: Royalist Hope in Chronicles." Ph.D. dissertation, Westminster Theological Seminary, 1992.

Rasmussen, Carl G. "The Economic Importance of Caravan Trade for the Solomonic Empire." In *A Tribute to Gleason Archer*. Ed. W. Kaiser, Jr. and R. Youngblood. Chicago: Moody Press, 1986. Pp. 153-166.

Redford, Donald B. "Studies in Relations between Palestine and Egypt during the First Millennium B.C. II. The Twenty-Second Dynasty." *JAOS* 93 (1973): 3-17.

Rendsburg, Gary A. "The Internal Consistency and Historical Reliability of the Biblical Genealogies." *VT* 40 (1990): 185-206.

Riley, William. *King and Cultus in Chronicles: Worship and the Reinterpretation of History*. JSOTSup 160. Sheffield: Sheffield Academic Press, 1993.

Roberts, J.J.M. "Does God Lie? Divine Deceit as a Theological Problem in Israelite Prophetic Literature." In *Congress Volume: Jerusalem, 1986*. VTSupp 40. Ed. J.A. Emerton. Leiden: Brill, 1988.

Rogerson, John, and Philip R. Davies, "Was the Siloam Tunnel Built by Hezekiah?" *BA* 59 (1996): 138-149.

Rosenbaum, Jonathan. "Hezekiah's Reform and the Deuteronomistic Tradition." *HTR* 72 (1979): 23-43.

Rowley, H.H. "Hezekiah's Reform and Rebellion." *BJRL* 44 (1961-62): 395-431.

_____. *The Relevance of the Bible*. New York: Macmillan, 1944.

Rowton, M.B. "Jeremiah and the Death of Josiah." *JNES* 10 (1951): 128-130.

Runnalls, Donna. "The *PARWAR*: A Place of Ritual Separation," *VT* 41 (1991): 324-331.

Sailhamer, John H. "1 Chronicles 21:1 — A Study in Inter-Biblical Interpretation." *TJ* 10ns (1989): 33-48.

Schaefer, G.E. "The Significance of Seeking God in the Purpose of the Chronicler." Th.D. dissertation, Southern Baptist Theological Seminary, 1972.

Schley, Donald G. "I Kings 10:26-29: A Reconsideration." *JBL* 106 (1987): 595-601.

_____. "The *SALISIM*: Officers or Special Three-Man Squads." *VT* 40 (1990): 321-326.

Schniedewind, William M. "The Source Citations of Manasseh: King Manasseh in History and Homily." *VT* 41 (1991): 450-461.

Schwertley, Brian. *Musical Instruments in the Public Worship of the Church*. Southfield, MI: Reformed Witness, 1999.

Selman, Martin J. "The Kingdom of God in the Old Testament." *TB* 40 (1989): 163-171.

Shanks, H. "Jerusalem's Underground Water Systems." *BAR* 20 (July-August 1994): 20-38, 64.

_____. "Nelson Glueck and King Solomon — A Romance That Ended." *BAR* 1 (March 1975): 10-16.

Shea, William H. "Sennacherib's Second Palestinian Campaign." *JBL* 104 (1985): 401-418.

Shipp, R. Mark. "'Remember His Covenant Forever': A Study of Chronicler's Use of the Psalms," *RQ* 35 (1993): 33-37.

Smelik, Klaas A.D. "The Representation of King Ahaz in 2 Kings 16 and 2 Chronicles 28." In *Intertextuality in Ugarit and Israel*. Ed. Johannes C. deMoor. Boston: Brill, 1998.

Snyman, Gerrie. "Who Is Responsible for Uzzah's Death? Rhetoric in 1 Chronicles 13." In *Rhetoric, Scripture and Theology: Essays from the 1994 Pretoria Conference*. JSNTS 13. Ed. Stanley E. Porter and Thomas H. Olbricht. Sheffield: Sheffield Academic Press, 1996.

Solomon, Ann M. Vater. "Jehoash's Fable of the Thistle and the Cedar." In *Saga, Legend, Tale, Novella Fable: Narrative Forms in OT Literature*. JSOTSup 35. Ed. George W. Coats. Sheffield: JSOT Press, 1985.

Spanier, Ktziah. "The Northern Israelite Queen Mother in the Judaean Court: Athalia and Abi." In *Boundaries of the Ancient*

Near Eastern World: A Tribute to Cyrus H. Gordon. JSOTSup 273. Ed. Meir Lubetski et al. Sheffield: Sheffield Academic Press, 1998.

Sparks, Kent. "The Prophetic Speeches in Chronicles: Speculation, Revelation, and Ancient Historiography." *BBR* 9 (1999): 233-245.

Spencer, F. Scott. "2 Chronicles 28:5-15 and the Parable of the Good Samaritan." *WTJ* 46 (1984): 317-349.

Stapert, Calvin. "Historical and Theological Perspectives on Musical Instruments in Worship." In *The Complete Library of Christian Worship*. Vol. 4. Ed. Robert E. Webber. Nashville: Star Song, 1994.

Steiner, Vernon J. "The Asa Narrative and Chronicler's Exegetical Method: Intertextuality and the Question of Relevance in the Proclamation of Old Testament Narrative Texts." Ph.D. dissertation, Trinity Evangelical Divinity School, 1992.

Stern, E. "Israel at the Close of the Period of the Monarchy: An Archaeological Survey." *BA* 38 (1975): 26-54.

Stigers, H. "The Interphased Chronology of Jotham, Ahaz, Hezekiah, and Hoshea." *BETS* 9 (1966): 81-90.

Sugimoto, Tomotoshi. "Chronicles as Independent Literature." *JSOT* 55 (1992): 64-70.

Tadmor, Hayim. "Chronology of the Last Kings of Judah." *JNES* 15 (1956): 226-230.

Talshir, D. "A Reinvestigation of the Linguistic Relationship between Chronicles and Ezra-Nehemiah." *VT* 38 (1988): 165-193.

Talshir, Zipora. "The Three Deaths of Josiah and the Strata of Biblical Historiography (2 Kings XXIII 29-30; 2 Chronicles XXXV 20-5; 1 Esdras I 23-31)." *VT* 44 (1996): 213-236.

Tatum, Lynn W. "From Text to Tell: King Manasseh in the Biblical and Archaeological Record." Ph.D. dissertation, Duke University, 1988.

Thiele, Edwin R. *The Mysterious Numbers of the Hebrew Kings.* 3rd ed. Grand Rapids: Zondervan, 1983.

Throntveit, Mark A. "Hezekiah in the Books of Chronicles." In *SBL 1988 Seminar Papers*. Ed. David J. Lull. Atlanta: Scholars Press, 1988. Pp. 302-311.

_____. "The Idealization of Solomon as the Glorification of God in the Chronicler's Royal Speeches and Royal Prayers." In *The Age of Solomon: Scholarship at the Turn of the Millennium*. Ed. Lowell K. Handy. Leiden: Brill, 1997.

_____. *When Kings Speak: Royal Speech and Royal Prayer in Chronicles*. SBLDS 93. Atlanta: Scholars Press, 1987.

Tidwell, N.L. "The Philistine Incursion into the Valley of Rephaim (2 Sam. v. 17ff.)." In *Studies in the Historical Books of the Old Testament*. VTSup 30. Ed. J.A. Emerton. Leiden: Brill, 1979.

Todd, E.W. "The Reforms of Hezekiah and Josiah." *SJT* 9 (1956): 288-293.

Torrey, Charles C. "The Chronicler as Editor and as Independent Narrator." *American Journal of Semitic Literature* 25 (1908/1909): 157-173, 188-217.

_____. *Ezra Studies*. Chicago: Chicago University Press, 1910.

Ulrich, E.C. *The Qumran Text of Samuel and Josephus*. HSM 19. Missoula, MT: Scholars Press, 1978.

Ussishkin, D. *The Conquest of Lachish by Sennacherib*. Tel Aviv: University Institute of Archaeology, 1982.

Van Keulen, Percy S.F. *Manasseh through the Eyes of the Deuteronomists: The Manasseh Account (2 Kings 21:1-18) and the Final Chapters of the Deuteronomic History*. OS 38. Leiden: Brill, 1996.

Vaughn, Andrew G. "The Chronicler's Account of Hezekiah: The Relationship of Historical Data to a Theological Interpretation of 2 Chronicles 29–32." Ph.D. dissertation, Princeton Theological Seminary, 1996.

von Rad, Gerhard. "There Remains Still a Rest for the People of God: An Investigation of a Biblical Conception." In *The Problem of the Hexateuch and Other Essays*. Trans. E.W. Trueman Dicken. New York: McGraw-Hill, 1966.

Walters, Stanley D. "Saul of Gibeon." *JSOT* 52 (1991): 61-76.

Washburn, David L. "Perspective and Purpose: Understanding the Josiah Story." *TJ* 12ns (1991): 59-78.

Webb, Robert L. *John the Baptizer and Prophet: A Socio-Historical Study*. JSNTSup 62. Sheffield: Sheffield Academic Press, 1991.

Welch, Adam C. "The Death of Josiah." *ZAW* 42 (1925): 255-260.

_____. *The Work of the Chronicler: Its Purpose and Date*. London: Oxford University Press, 1939.

Wenham, G. J. "Were David's Sons Priests?" *ZAW* 87 (1975): 79-82.

Wenham, John W. "Large Numbers in the Old Testament." *TB* 18 (1967): 44-53.

Whitelam, Keith W. *The Just King: Monarchical Judicial Authority in Ancient Israel* JSOTSup 12. Sheffield: JSOT Press, 1979.

Whitley, C.F. "The Term Seventy Years Captivity." VT 4 (1954): 60-72.

Williamson, H.G.M. "The Accession of Solomon in the Books of Chronicles." *VT* 26 (1976): 351-361.

_____ . "The Death of Josiah and the Continuing Development of the Deuteronomistic History." *VT* 32 (1982): 242-248.

_____ . "The Dynastic Oracle in the Books of Chronicles." In *Isac Leo Seeligmann Volume: Essays on the Bible and the Ancient World*. Ed. Alexander Rofe and Vair Zakovitch. Jerusalem: E. Rubinstein's Publishing House, 1983.

_____ . "Eschatology in Chronicles," *TB* 28 (1977): 115-154.

_____ . *Israel in the Book of Chronicles*. Cambridge: Cambridge University Press, 1977.

_____ . "A Note on I Chronicles 12." *VT* 23 (1973): 375-379.

_____ . "The Origins of the Twenty-Four Priestly Courses: A Study of 1 Chronicles xxiii-xxvii." In *Studies in the Historical Books of the Old Testament*. Ed. J.A. Emerton. Leiden: Brill, 1979.

_____ . "Reliving the Death of Josiah: A Reply to C.T. Begg." *VT* 37 (1987): 9-15.

_____ . "Source and Redaction in Chr's Genealogy of Judah." *JBL* 98 (1979): 351-359.

_____ . "'The Sure Mercies of David': Subjective or Objective Genitive," *JSS* 23 (1978): 31-49.

_____ . "The Temple in the Books of Chronicles." In *Templum Amicitia: Essays on the 2nd Temple Presented to Ernst Bammel*. JSNTSup 48. Ed. David E. Orton. Sheffield: JSOT Press, 1991.

_____ . "'We Are Yours, O David': The Setting and Purpose of 1 Chronicles 12:1-23." In *Remembering All the Way*. OS 21. Ed. Bertil Albrektson. Leiden: Brill, 1981.

Wilson, R.H. *Prophecy and Society in Ancient Israel*. Philadelphia: Fortress, 1980.

Wilson, Robert R. "Between 'Azel' and 'Azel': Interpreting the Biblical Genealogies." *BA* 42.1 (1979): 11-22.

_____ . *Genealogy and History in the Biblical World*. New Haven: Yale University Press, 1977.

_____ . "Israel's Judicial System in the Preexilic Period." *JQR* 74 (1983): 229-248.

Winkle, Ross E. "Jeremiah's Seventy Years for Babylon: A Re-Assessment. Part I: The Scriptural Data." *AUSS* 25 (1987): 201-214.

_____ . "Jeremiah's Seventy Years for Babylon: A Re-Assessment. Part II: The Historical Data." *AUSS* 25 (1987): 289-299.

Wiseman, D.J. "'Is it Peace?' — Covenant and Diplomacy." *VT* 32 (1982): 311-326.

Wolfers, David. "Who Killed Goliath? A Response to Steven Moss." *JBQ* 18 (1989): 14-16.

Wright, G. Ernest. "The Boundary and Province Lists of the Kingdom of Judah." *JBL* 75 (1956): 202-226.

Wright, John W. "The Founding Father: The Structure of Chronicler's David Narrative." *JBL* 117 (1998): 45-59.

_____ . "From Center to Periphery: 1 Chronicles 23–27 and the Interpretation of Chronicles in the Nineteenth Century." In *Priests, Prophets and Scribes: Essays on the Formation and Heritage of 2nd Temple Judaism in Honour of Joseph Blenkinsopp.* JSOTSup 149. Ed. Eugene Virich et al. Sheffield: JSOT Press, 1992.

_____ . "Guarding the Gates: 1 Chronicles 26.1-19 and the Roles of Gatekeepers in Chronicles." *JSOT* 48 (1990): 69-81.

_____ . "The Innocence of David in 1 Chronicles 21." *JSOT* 60 (1993): 87-105.

_____ . "The Legacy of David in Chronicles: The Narrative Function of 1 Chronicles 23–27." *JBL* 110 (1991): 229-242.

Yadin, Yigael. "Goliath's Javelin and ארגים מנור." *PEQ* 87 (1955): 58-69.

Young, Edward J. *An Introduction to the Old Testament.* Rev. Ed. Grand Rapids: Eerdmans, 1964.

Zalewiski, Saul. "The Purpose of the Story of the Death of Saul in 1 Chronicles X." *VT* 39 (1989): 449-467.

Zvi, Ehud Ben. "A Gateway to the Chronicler's Teaching: The Account of the Reign of Ahaz in 2 Chr 28,1-27." *SJOT* 7 (1993): 216-249.

1 CHR 1:1–9:44 – PART ONE

THE GENEALOGY OF ALL ISRAEL

The genealogy of 1 Chronicles 1–9 is the "tree of the Lord's planting." First Chronicles 1–3 are the "roots," 1 Chronicles 4–7 the "branches," and 1 Chronicles 8–9 the "fruit." (WILCOX, 7). Chronicles geneaologically portrays the historic progression of God's purposes through time. God is growing his tree — he cares for it, waters it, and has a purpose for it.

The postexilic community needs to appreciate their roots. They live in the backwater of a huge Empire. Jerusalem is no longer the center of the universe, and Judah is a meaningless province. The genealogy reminds Israel of God's active planting and watering. God has always had Israel in mind — from the beginning with Adam — and he will not forget his people.

The genealogies demonstrate God's faithfulness. They evidence God's love for Israel. God is faithful even while Israel is unfaithful (1 Chr 9:1; Hos 1–3). The genealogies connect Israel with their divine election, past history, and legitimate lines of royal and priestly service. They give the postexilic community their identity. The genealogies highlight God's election of Israel. They trace the line of promise. Cain is not in the genealogical history. The elect line is important, and the line of promise is Adam — Seth — Noah — Shem — Abraham — Israel (Jacob).

The genealogies highlight the history of Israel. MYERS (1:6) compares the genealogical list to "sermon notes." JOHNSTONE (1:25) considers them a "cryptic code, allusively bringing to mind in the most condensed form possible the stories of the primeval and of the patriarchal periods." When Chronicles invokes a name, it reminds Israel of their stories, which evokes memories of God's faithfulness throughout history. While the names are sometimes obscure to us, they were probably "commonplace to [the Chronicler] and to his audience and merely part of their awareness of the world in which they lived" (JOHNSTONE, 1:29). Each name contributes to the plot that culminates in the reigns of David and Solomon. The genealogies prepare us for the coming narrative.

The genealogies also legitimate the royal and priestly lines of descent (Johnson, *Purpose*, 77-82). This assures the postexilic community that their leadership and religious cult is secure. The temple and its servants are legitimate.

Chronicles's genealogy is laid out in three major sections: (1) Adam to Israel (1 Chr 1:1–2:2); (2) The Sons of Israel (1 Chr 2:3–9:2); and (3) Postexilic Israel (9:3-44). The structure is concentric.

    I. From Adam to Israel (1 Chr 1:1–2:2)
        II. All Israel (1 Chr 2:3–9:1a)
            A. Judah (1 Chr 2:3–4:23)
                B. Northern Tribes near Judah (1 Chr 4:24–5:26)
                    C. Levites (1 Chr 6:1–81)
                B′. Northern Tribes Distant from Judah (1 Chr 7:1-40)
            A′. Benjamin (1 Chr 8:1-9:1a)
    I′. Postexilic Israel (1 Chr 9:1b-44)

SELMAN (1:86) suggests three reasons why this structure is important. First, the genealogy of the nations in 1 Chronicles 1:1–2:2 "shows that all nations were God's creation and therefore part of his special purposes for Israel." Second, 1 Chronicles 2:3–9:1 confirms that "the present small Jewish community was still descended from Jacob's twelve sons and from 'all Israel' who had inherited the Promised Land." The postexilic community includes the northern tribes, "all Israel" (1 Chr 9:1). Third, 1 Chronicles 9:2-44 shows that "the exile had not cut the umbilical cord of the postexilic community's life, for those who now lived and worshiped in Jerusalem remained heirs of the promises of God." The fact that the Chronicler brings the genealogical lists down into the postexilic community, and into his own time (1 Chr 3:17-24), indicates that this genealogy is no mere historical curiosity. It demonstrates God's faithfulness to Israel as an elect people.

Given this theological context, 1 Chronicles 1–9 is bound up with the themes and theological emphases of 1 Chronicles 10–2 Chronicles 36. While some argue that parts of 1 Chronicles 1–9 might be the hand of a later editor, there is little to defend separating 1 Chronicles 1–9 from the rest of the book (JAPHET; WILLIAMSON).

BRAUN (1-12) summarizes the issues related to genealogical forms, sources, and purposes (cf. Johnson, *Purpose*, and Wilson, *Genealogy*). The form of a genealogy is either linear or segmented. The linear provides the depth of relationship within a family (e.g., grandparent-parent-child): Abraham, Isaac, Jacob. Its purpose is to legitimate the last person named. The segmented provides the breadth of relationship within a family (e.g., siblings): Jacob and Esau. Its purpose is to establish relationships among various branches of a family. Chronicles uses both kinds. In addition, these lists are not comprehensive, that is, not every descendent is listed.

Chronicles shares the characteristics of the genealogical genre found in ancient and contemporary oral cultures. The accuracy of a genealogy is not modern precisionism and comprehensiveness. Rather, it is theological function (Plum, 66-92). Consequently, ancient genealogies (and modern oral ones) have a certain "fluidity" that serves the purpose of the community and establishes relationships between peoples and cultures, including "adoptions" from other genealogical lines (Wilson, "Between," 11-22; Malamat, "King," 163-173). The Chronicler used appropriate sources and methods which would legitimate postexilic Israel in the eyes of his community. This means that none of the genealogical data was simply pure invention. On the contrary, he gathered canonical data, military and census lists, and used other sources available to him to accomplish his purpose in a way that it would be received and valued by his community. We should not impose on Chronicles the expectations of modern, scientific genealogists, but neither should we think that the Chronicler is a propagandist who invents genealogical records. The Chronicler works with sources, both canonical and noncanonical, to report a sanctioned and legitimate genealogical record according to the conventions of the ancient genre (Rendsburg, 185-206; Aufrecht, 205-235).

These genealogies may seem as interesting as a dictionary, but their total impact is theologically significant. The African-American community was reinvigorated in the 1970s by the appearance of Alex Haley's *Roots*. In contrast to our mobile, urban culture, *Roots* reminded us that we are connected in important ways with our past. These genealogies serve the same function. This is the story of God among his people. It is the story of Israel. It is the Christian story.

Adam, Abraham, and David are our forefathers. God has preserved his family. The story continues in the genealogies of Jesus Christ, and in Christ we are Abraham's children. These genealogies are our genealogies not just because we are now part of Israel's story, but because Israel's God is our God. His grace and faithfulness, demonstrated in this genealogical history, belong to us. The function of these genealogies is not to date the history but to root Israel's present in the past. Continuity, not exhaustiveness, is critical.

Teaching these genealogies is a difficult but fruitful task. One method is to let the names evoke their stories. From Adam to Israel is the story of God's relationship with people. As each name evokes a story, it reminds God's people of their forefathers. But the names are put together so that each individual story serves the broader continuity of God's purposes (e.g., the royal line in 1 Chr 3:1-24). Another method is to stress genealogical themes (e.g., inclusiveness [racial and gender], continuity, divine faithfulness) and illustrate them with various lines. Further, the genealogies contain some narrative examples (1 Chr 2:3-4; 4:9-10; 5:1-3,18-22; 6:31-32,48-49). A teacher can use these narratives to illustrate the broader values of the genealogical record. Still further, one may teach these genealogies in light of the broader themes: (1) world history, (2) Israel's history, and (3) the needs of the postexilic community. Chronicles stresses Israel's link with the "nations," the importance of Judah (royal), Levi (temple servants), and Benjamin (Jerusalem). He offers hope in the present through the postexilic community's link to the past.

I. FROM ADAM TO ISRAEL (1:1–2:2)

Since the word "Israel" does not appear until 1 Chronicles 2:1, this section has sometimes been called the "preamble" or "preface." (BRAUN, 13; JOHNSTONE, 1:24). It is the Chronicler's Genesis from which all the genealogical material is derived. "Preamble" is an appropriate term because "Adam to Israel" provides the setting of Israel as a nation. Israel is "the Way" for the nations (ALLEN, 31). God has elected Israel from the beginning, even in Adam (Japhet, *Ideology*, 116-124). "Israel has the task of realizing in its life the ideal once intended by God for all" (JOHNSTONE, 1:30). All nations will be blessed through Abraham and Israel.

Seventeen of the place names found in this section are repeated by the Chronicler in his discussion of David and Solomon (ALLEN, 34-35). These two kings represent God's regency over the world, and the whole earth seeks them and submits to them. This genealogy anticipates their rule in Chronicles's history.

The genealogical history presented in this section (1 Chr 1:1–2:2) is summarized in the following chart (SELMAN, 1:90).

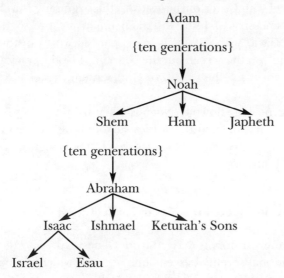

A. THE DESCENDANTS OF ADAM (1:1-27)

BRAUN (16) notes the symmetry of this section. From Adam to Noah are ten generations (1 Chr 1:1-4) and from Shem to Abraham are ten generations (1 Chr 1:24-27). These generations are succinct, one-name lineal lists which form an inclusio (JAPHET, 53-54). The author moves quickly without stopping to note the details, but he moves through history rather than skipping it. This section introduces the main event, that is, the sons of Abraham and then on to the sons of Israel, but also intentionally links Adam and Abraham through Noah. God has ordered this history and progressively brought his purposes into play with Adam, Noah, and Abraham. God's purpose does not exclude other nations, but includes them.

1. The Lineal Descent of Adam (1:1-4)

The first word in Chronicles is the beginning of history: **Adam**. The history of Israel is linked to the history of the world. Israel did not drop out of the sky. The history of Israel begins with Adam. This "is a bold theological statement to trace Israel's ancestry back not just to Abraham, but to creation itself."

This links Israel with God's purposes from the beginning. Just as Luke traces the ancestry of Jesus to Adam in Luke 3:38, so the Chronicler links David with Adam. Israel is part of world history. Israel is not a "blip" on the screen but the conduit of God's gracious purposes in the world for the world. In God's intent, Israel serves the nations.

The Adamic genealogy down to **Noah** is taken from Genesis 5:1-32. The Chronicler has deleted the stories surrounding each name and given us the lineal descent to Noah where his line is segmented: **Shem, Ham and Japheth**.

2. The Segmented Descent of Noah (1:5-23)

The Noahic family history is derived from Genesis 10:1-32 where we find the traditional seventy descendants of Noah which symbolize the seventy peoples of the world (the "table of nations"; cf. PAYNE, 4:327-329). He reverses the order in Genesis so that **Shem** receives the emphasis: **Japheth, Ham**, and then Shem (in Gen 11:10ff). The Chronicler also deletes the territorial comments (Gen 10:5,9-12,19-21,30-32). For example, he does not tell us about Nimrod's kingdom (Gen 10:9-12), though he retains the characterization of Nimrod as a **mighty warrior** (cp. 1 Chr 1:10 with Gen 10:8). He streamlines the account in terms of descendants in a way that parallels Genesis. He includes all the names Genesis provides.

Some have argued that the descendants of Japheth and Ham were not original. The focus of this section is 1 Chronicles 1:1-4 and 24-27. However, the lineage of Japheth and Ham marks off those sections as significant and provides a sense of the world history to which Israel is linked. Israel does not appear in a vacuum but alongside the history of other peoples.

3. The Lineal Descent of Shem (1:24-27)

Shem's family history is derived from Genesis 11:10-32. The Chronicler deletes all the material except the bare descent from **Shem** to **Abraham**. He identifies **Abram** (Gen 11:26) as **Abraham** (Gen 17:5). While the identification should have been obvious to the reader, the Chronicler emphasizes his status as the father of many nations as he begins his genealogy of Abraham with Ishmael. The genealogy demonstrates the promise to Abraham was fulfilled.

First Chronicles 1:1-27 teaches, in genealogical form, that Israel is part of a world community. It participates in the "brotherhood" of humanity. The nations are bound together by God's creation and providence. Israel, however, is the elect nation for the sake of the nations. Through Abraham God will bless all nations.

B. THE DESCENDANTS OF ABRAHAM (1:28-2:2)

Chronicles begins the genealogy of Abraham with the eldest, Ishmael, and then moves to the younger, Isaac. The line of promise comes last. Since the Chronicler focuses on the descendants of Israel, he segments the line between Ishmael and Isaac, and then segments the line from Isaac between Esau and Israel (Jacob).

The Chronicler titles his next section. He begins with both sons of Abraham ("Isaac and Ishmael") where Genesis simply begins the genealogy of Ishmael. The Chronicler provides structure to the genealogical account.

Theologically, while David and Solomon are the focus of the Chronicler's history, he recognizes the significance of Abraham by calling attention to the fullness of his family (Ishmael, Keturah, and the Edomites). This is a genealogical restatement of the fulfillment of God's promise to Abraham. Just as God kept his promise to Abraham, so he will keep his promise to David and Solomon. The genealogical record testifies to the faithfulness of God, which is most fully demonstrated in the genealogy of Jesus Christ (Matt 1:1-17; Luke 3:23-38).

1. Descendants of Ishmael and Keturah (1:28-34a)

JAPHET (54) notes how 1 Chronicles 1:28 introduces and 1:34a concludes this section. These are the children of Abraham other than Isaac.

Descendants of Ishmael (1:28-31)

Ishmael's family history is derived from Genesis 25:12-16. While Keturah's genealogy is provided before Ishmael's in Genesis 25:1-4, the Chronicler inverts the order because Ishmael is the firstborn. The Chronicler omits details except that **Nebaioth** is Ishmael's **firstborn**.

Descendants of Keturah (1:32-34a)

Keturah's family history is derived from Genesis 25:1-4. The Chronicler omits the sons of Dedan but changes the description of Keturah. While Genesis 25:1 refers to **Keturah** as Abraham's "wife," the Chronicler calls her his **concubine**. This is consistent with Genesis' distinction between Isaac and Abraham's other children. In fact, Genesis 25:5-6 may be interpreted as including Keturah among Abraham's concubines. The explicit change reflects the Chronicler's intention to make the distinction between Isaac and Abraham's other children clear. Only Isaac is the child of promise.

The inclusion of Keturah is rather surprising since she is not mentioned in 1 Chronicles 1:28. Further, the Chronicler intentionally inverts the order of **Ishmael** and Keturah. Thus, the inclusion of Keturah is not simply a matter of slavishly following Genesis. The Chronicler places Israel in the wider world in which she lived, but the Chronicler does not include all the Genesis genealogies (cf. Gen 4:17-22; 19:30-38; 22:20-24).

2. Descendants of Esau, Son of Isaac, the Edomites (1:34b-54)

First Chronicles 1:34b functions as a "title" much like 1 Chronicles 1:28, as the Chronicler has changed his source in order to structure his account (cf. Gen 36:1). Indicative of the Chronicler's interests, he does not use "Jacob" but "Israel." Only in 1 Chronicles 16:13,17 does the author use "Jacob." Everywhere else it is "Israel," even when the patriarchal formula of "Abraham, Isaac and . . ." appears he uses "Israel" instead of "Jacob" (cf. 1 Chr 29:18; 2 Chr 30:6). This underscores Israel's divine election, the nation's identity, and the inclusive character of the Chronicler's purpose ("all Israel").

Esau's family history is derived from Genesis 36:1-43. The Chronicler omits the incidental stories surrounding some of the names and provides a bare-bones genealogy extracted from Genesis. Significantly, he omits Genesis 36:2-9 where Esau's Hittite and Ishmaelite wives are noted as well as his move to Seir (later Edom). The Chronicler omits all references which link Esau with Edom though he provides the genealogy of Edomite Kings and clans in this section (1 Chr 1:43,51).

Descendants of Esau (1:34b-37)

This section depends on Genesis 36:1-19, but the Chronicler has streamlined the names without comment. One difference from Genesis is that while **Timna** is a concubine of **Eliphaz** (one of Esau's sons) in Genesis 36:12 (omitted in 1 Chronicles), the Chronicler lists Timna as one of the sons of Esau (1 Chr 1:36). The Chronicler later recognizes that Timna was the daughter of Seir (1 Chr 1:39). The reference to Timna in 1 Chronicles 1:36 is probably the additional wife that bore **Amalek** (which is contained in Gen 36:12). In other words, the Chronicler has conflated Genesis 36:11-12 into a single lineal descendent where Timna is understood as the wife of Eliphaz who gave birth to Amalek. The Chronicler could not miss this in his source, and he recognizes the gender of her name in his own document. Consequently, while the Hebrew is a simple list of names, the NIV (also LXX) correctly interprets this relationship – by **Timna, Amalek**. WILLIAMSON (44) attributes this to "compression" and a dependence upon the reader's knowledge of Genesis. Dillard (*Study*, 584) believes this as an example of "genealogical fluidity" where descendants are sometimes "promoted" into the primary list because of their later importance.

Descendants of Seir (1:38-42)

This section is dependent upon Genesis 36:20-27. Seir's name is not found in any of the previous genealogies. **Seir** is not descended from any previous name. The Chronicler does not tell us he is a descendent of Esau (neither does Genesis). This reflects a common genealogical practice of associating the inhabitants of a general area together in genealogical lists, a kind of "adoption." Esau had moved to the region of Seir (Gen 36:9), so the inclusion of the descendants of Seir is given along with Esau. BRAUN (23) suggests that Seir should be understood as a geographical region rather than a person.

The Kings of Edom (1:43-51a)

This list is derived from Genesis 36:31-39. It only adds that **Hadad died** (1 Chr 1:51a). Apparently, **kings reigned in Edom** before Israel, but after the rise of David, Edom served Israel (1 Chr 18:13) when they were then led by "chiefs" (JAPHET, 64).

The Chiefs of Edom (1:51b-54)

Derived from Genesis 36:40-43, this list contains the same names and sequence, but it omits the references to territories or lands. It also omits the reference to Esau as the father of Edom.

Edom reminds Israel that physical descent from Abraham is not sufficient. It also reminds them of familial relationships with their surrounding neighbors. It is another element of the "world history" vision. Perhaps the Chronicler envisions a time coming when Israel will again take center stage among the nations (ACKROYD, 32). Indeed, the last king of Edom is generationally coordinate with the reign of David (the fourteenth generation from Abraham). "At that moment," JOHNSTONE (1:35) comments, "the rule of the Edomites passes from kings to tribal chieftains and monarchy itself passes from Edom to Israel." The reign of God finds reality in the reign of Israel over the nations, and Edom serves their younger brother (cf. Gen 25:23).

3. Descendants of Israel, Son of Isaac (2:1-2)

The **sons of Israel** (Jacob) are listed, but the listing does not follow any order in Genesis or Exodus (though the closest is Gen 35:22-26 where only Dan is placed differently; cf. BRAUN, 9). Neither does it follow any other list in Chronicles (even the genealogical order in 1 Chr 2–8). There does not seem to be any obvious rationale for the way in which the sons are listed except that the sons of Leah are together. They are not listed by order of birth or importance in the history of Israel (e.g., **Judah** is not listed first).

Whatever the origin or reason for this order, it transitions the reader from the "world history" of chapter one to the "Israelite" history of chapters two through nine. This is the hinge that swings the door between the two worlds.

II. THE GENEALOGY OF ISRAEL (2:3–9:1a)

The Chronicler now focuses on Israel against the backdrop of world history. He provides a genealogical account of every tribe except Dan and Zebulun. There is no apparent reason for the absence of these two tribes even though both are in the list of Israel's sons in 1 Chronicles 2:1-2. Perhaps neither tribe was significantly represented in the postexilic community. There may be a theological reason since Dan was associated with idolatry (cf. Judg 18; Rev 7:5-8 excludes Dan).

Finding an intentional structure is difficult. Nevertheless, the broad picture seems clear. The largest blocks of material are Judah (1 Chr 2:3-4:23), Levi (1 Chr 6:1-81) and Benjamin (1 Chr 8:1-9:1). This indicates the Chronicler's primary interests. The other tribes are scattered among these three. Chronicles utilizes a concentric structure (WILLIAMSON, 46-47).

    A. Judah (2:3-4:23)
       B. "Northern" Tribes near Judah (4:24-5:26)
          C. Levi (6:1-81)
       B′. "Northern" Tribes Distant from Judah (7:1-40)
    A′. Benjamin (8:1-9:1a)

Judah and Benjamin receive emphasis because of their relation to David. He descended from Judah and reigned in Jerusalem (located in the territory of Benjamin). Judah comes first because of the preeminence of David. Benjamin is last because it provides an entrée into the genealogy of Saul. Levi is the centerpiece of the chiasm which emphasizes the importance of the temple and its servants.

The "northern" tribes are not forgotten, but they are surrounded by David, Jerusalem, and the temple. The inclusion of "all Israel" in the genealogy (cf. 1 Chr 9:1) serves the Chronicler's inclusivist interest. He intends for the postexilic community to include the "northern" tribes as well as the southern ones. God seeks reconciliation with "all Israel," and "all Israel" is invited to the temple to commune with their God.

The Chronicler's inclusivistic interests are evidenced by the way he draws attention to non-Israelite ancestors (e.g., 1 Chr 2:3). The Chronicler could have easily excised these references to Canaanite ancestry, but he intentionally included them. He encouraged an inclusivism within Israel without undermining the continuity of the Jewish people.

A. JUDAH (2:3-4:23)

WILLIAMSON (48-50; "Source," 351-359) sees a chiastic structure in the Chronicler's organization of Judah's genealogy, which gives order to an apparently chaotic genealogical list. According to his theory, this section is composed of two chiastic arrangements: one (a,b,c,c',b',a') inside the other (1,2,3,2',1').

1. Judah's Five Sons (2:3-4)
2. The Descendants of Perez [and Zerah] (2:5-8)
3. The Descendants of Perez's Son Hezron (2:9-3:24)
   a. Sons of Ram to David (2:9-17)
      b. Sons of Caleb to Bezalel (2:18-24)
         c. Sons of Jerahmeel (2:25-33)
         c.' Further Descendants of Jerahmeel (2:34-41)
      b.' Further Descendants of Caleb (2:42-55)
   a.' Further Descendants of Ram from David (3:1-24)
2'. The Descendants of Perez (4:1-20)
1'. The Descendants of Judah's Son, Shelah (4:21-23)

Within the inner chiastic structure the family of David forms the inclusio while at the same time forming the inner structure of the larger chiasm where the family of Hezron is the central theme. This structure places the emphasis on the Davidic family. The chief descendant of Judah is David (cf. 1 Chr 28:4), who is the central person in the genealogy of Judah.

1. Judah's Five Sons (2:3-4)

The Chronicler developed this list from Genesis 38 and 46:12. He repeats Genesis 46:12a: "The sons of Judah: Er, Onan, Shelah, Perez and Zerah." He also repeats Genesis 46:12c in 1 Chronicles 2:5: "The sons of Perez: Hezron and Hamul." The reference to Judah's Canaanite wife is based on Genesis 38:5. The comment on Er's death is copied from Genesis 38:7 with only one word difference.

As JAPHET (70) comments, the Chronicler was not satisfied with the brief genealogy of Genesis 46:12. He elaborates on the immediate family of **Judah** by calling attention to the wickedness of **Er** and Judah's wives. Chronicles invokes the name of "Yahweh" (**LORD**) for the first time in a case of divine retribution. It also illustrates God's sovereign election through the demotion of the firstborn.

Judah's relations with women involved covenant transgressions. He married a Canaanite woman and bore children through his **daughter-in-law** (cf. Lev 18:15; 20:12). But, for the Chronicler, this is God's gracious continuation of the line of Judah even though he sinned. His sons were born either to non-Israelite women or through sexual immorality. Women, especially non-Israelite women, are included in the genealogies of Chronicles as indications of God's grace. This reflects the Chronicler's inclusivist tendencies which parallels Matthew's specific inclusion of fallen and Gentile women in Jesus' genealogy (Matt 1:3,5-6).

The Chronicler's brief comment on Judah's sons, then, provides an opportunity to note God's retribution in one verse, but his grace in another. The dialectic between grace and wrath, between God's elect purposes and God's holiness, is a constant theme in Chronicles.

Since only three **sons of Judah** survived, the genealogy of Judah only continues through Zerah (1 Chr 2:6-8), Perez (1 Chr 2:5,9; 4:20) and Shelah (1 Chr 4:21-23). The emphasis falls to Perez, the line of David.

2. The Descendants of Judah's Sons, Perez and Zerah (2:5-8)

While 1 Chronicles 2:5 is dependent upon Genesis 46:12c, the construction of 1 Chronicles 2:6-8 is consciously parallel with 1 Chronicles 2:3-4. The five sons of Judah are paralleled by the five

sons of Zerah which presupposes Joshua 7:1 (where **Zimri** is "Zabdi" due to textual corruption) and 1 Kings 4:31 (where **Ethan** is called an Ezrahite; cf. Ps 89). "Ezrahite" (הָאֶזְרָחִי, *hā'ezraḥî*) and Zerah (זֶרַח, *zeraḥ*) are easily exchangeable terms in textual transmission. In 1 Chronicles 2:7 **Carmi** is a son of Zimri though this is not noted in the text. Zimri was probably lost in textual corruption (BRAUN, 29; cf. Josh 7:1,18).

The Zerah genealogy may be an example of genealogical fluidity where Judah and Levi shared interests in these men as given in 1 Kings 4:31. Indeed, **Heman** and Ethan are listed among the Levites in 1 Chronicles 6:33-42 and 15:19. Perhaps, as WILLIAMSON (50-51) suggests, these individuals are "adopted" into the tribe of Judah, and Chronicles identifies them strongly with Judah through Zerah. Chronicles, then, connects Levites (temple) and Judahites (David). Albright (*Archaeology*, 123; also BRAUN, 30-31; THOMPSON, 59) suggests these names represent musical guilds and were adopted into the genealogy of Judah. The men of 1 Kings 4:31 may not be the same as those in 1 Chronicles 2:6. Others believe that Chronicles has simply skipped ahead several generations ("as later descendants, not immediate 'sons'") because they were prominent in the temple (PAYNE, 4:334).

The Chronicler makes only one explicit comment. He identifies **Achar** ("Achan" in Josh 7:1) as the "troubler" (NRSV; cf. Josh 7:25-26) of Israel who violated the ban on booty at Jericho. The difference is probably due to a word play (paronomasia) between עָכָר (*'ākār*, Achar) and עָכָן (*'ākān*, Achan) which the original readers would have recognized as an artistic but theologically meaningful adaptation (cf. Kalimi, "Paronomasia," 39.) It not only reminds the reader of Achan, but also the great "troubler" of northern Israel, Ahab (same word in 1 Kings 18:17-18). Chronicles specifies that Achar was guilty of מָעַל (*mā'al*, "violating"; "evil, unfaithfulness"). This is a significant term in Chronicles (37 times as noun or verb; cf. 1 Chr 9:1; 10:13). The Chronicler is laying the groundwork for his theology of retribution. "The Achar incident thus already marks the beginning of the end." But, at the same time, the graciousness of God is demonstrated by the use of the sons of Zerah as temple musicians (JOHNSTONE, 1:43).

3. The Descendants of Perez's Son Hezron (2:9–3:24)

This is the Chronicler's main point. The Davidic line interests him most. Consequently he concentrates on the genealogy of Hezron, the grandson of Judah (JOHNSTONE, 1:45).

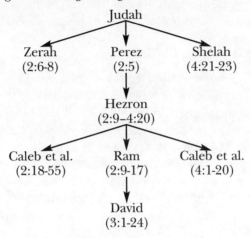

Sons of Ram to David (2:9-17)

First Chronicles 2:10-12 is derived from Ruth 4:19-22, 1 Chronicles 2:13-15 from 1 Samuel 16:6-13, 1 Chronicles 2:16 from 2 Samuel 12:18 and 1 Chronicles 2:17 from 2 Samuel 17:25.

David descends from **Ram**, the secondborn. David's line does not come from the firstborn of **Hezron**. This is another indication of God's election of the "younger," and it explains why Chronicles added the other sons of Hezron to the text of Ruth.

Problematically, David is identified as the **seventh** son of his father Jesse, but in 1 Samuel 16 he is the eighth. The Chronicler knows this from his source (1 Chr 27:18 names the brother [Elihu] that is missing here). Chronicles may call him seventh for the theological significance of the word (cf. 1 Chr 3:24), which indicates prominence. Others (rabbis; THOMPSON, 61) suggest, however, that one of the brothers is not listed because he died childless. The two solutions are not mutually exclusive.

Two other references are interesting. The Chronicler calls **Nahshon, the leader of the people of Judah** or a "prince" (NRSV) among his people (cf. Num 2:3). There is no apparent reason why the Chronicler comments on this individual other than he had a reputation as a leader foreshadowing David's own prowess. Also, the Chronicler calls **Jether**, the father of **Amasa**, an **Ishmaelite**. This is yet another indication of his inclusivist interests and links Israel with Ishmael. However, he is called an "Israelite" in 2 Samuel 17:25 (where יִתְרָא [Jethra] stands for יֶתֶר [Jether], a slight alteration in Hebrew), though this is probably due to textual variation.

Sons of Caleb to Bezalel (2:18-24)

There is no canonical source for Caleb's genealogy. Whatever sources the Chronicler had available no longer exist.

The text returns to 1 Chronicles 2:9 and another son, **Caleb**, is added to the list of the sons of **Hezron** or perhaps Caleb should be identified with "Chelubai" (MT; 1 Chr 2:9) as the NIV does. This Caleb is not the Caleb of "Joshua and Caleb" fame (Num 13; cf. 1 Chr 4:15) since he was "a contemporary of **Bezalel**, Caleb's great-grandson" (1 Chr 2:20; WILLIAMSON, 52; BRAUN, 37; JAPHET, 81-82). Bezalel is the important figure because he supervised the building of the tabernacle (Exod 31:1-5; cf. 2 Chr 1:5).

After Bezalel, Chronicles continues with Hezron's additional wife whom he married at the age of sixty. The section concludes with his death (1 Chr 2:21-24). The significance is difficult to determine. Perhaps it simply fills out the family of Hezron, but the emphasis on Gilead (1 Chr 2:21-22) points toward a strong association between Judah and Manasseh. Machir (**Makir**) was a son of Manasseh who settled on the eastern side of the Jordan (Num 32:39-41). Chronicles is interested in the settlement of the land of promise, including the transjordan area.

A difficulty does emerge in 1 Chronicles 2:24. While the NIV reads **after Hezron died in Caleb Ephrathah**, it is probably best to read with WILLIAMSON (53; LXX; Vulgate), "After the death of Hezron, Caleb went in to Ephrath, and she bore him Ashhur, the father of Tekoa." The textual difficulties permit such a reading, and Chronicles has already identified Ephrath as Caleb's wife (1 Chr 2:19,50; 4:4). It is unlikely that Caleb married his stepmother.

Sons of Jerahmeel (2:25-33)

There are no canonical parallels for this genealogy and the Chronicler's sources are unknown. Its beginning and ending mark it off as a self-contained entity that may have been drawn from a single source. The descendants of **Jerahmeel**, the **firstborn of Hezron**, are given with only the addition of some names for a couple of wives (**Atarah** and **Abihail** in 1 Chr 2:26,29) and the fact that **Seled** and **Jether** died childless (1 Chr 2:30,32). It is difficult to judge whether the Chronicler intended any theological judgment based on childlessness. The notation, however, underlines the grace of God. Lineage is not "automatic" and the "harsh realities of life" meant that some families were not continued. Consequently, the "genealogical survival of the appointed, such as the royal and high priestly houses, were a tribute to the sustaining grace of God's hand across the ages" (THOMPSON, 63).

Further Descendants of Jerahmeel (2:34-41)

This section is a self-contained unit about the family of **Sheshan**. It has no canonical parallels. This linear genealogy ends with **Elishama** (1 Chr 2:41). While we do not know who Elishama is (sometimes identified with the person in 2 Kgs 25:25), this genealogy is provided to legitimize his family status and social role.

First Chronicles 2:34 may hint at why Elishama needed legitimization. His racial purity had been compromised by male **Egyptian** blood. Because Sheshan had no sons, he married his daughter to his Egyptian slave **Jarha**. Since Jarha was a non-Israelite slave, his children belonged to his master. Thus, the son of Jarha, **Attai**, was the son of Sheshan (Japhet, "Israelite," 79-91).

Further Descendants of Caleb (2:42-55)

This section resumes the topic of 1 Chronicles 2:18-24 and more fully elaborates Caleb's family relationships. Whatever the source, its presentation is in two parts: (a) **The sons of Caleb the brother of Jerahmeel** (1 Chr 2:42-50a) and (b) **The sons of Hur the firstborn of Ephrathah** (1 Chr 2:50b-55). Some, however, think that 1 Chronicles 2:53-55 is a third list derived from a separate source or previously attached to the Chronicler's source because of the overlap with **Kiriath Jearim**. Both lists are rather straightforward and offer little extraneous comment. Kiriath Jearim, however, is important for its later associations with the ark of the covenant in the Chronicler's history (JOHNSTONE, 1:54; cf. 1 Chr 13:5-6; 2 Chr 1:4).

The first section is structured around Caleb's different wives: (a) sons by an unnamed wife (1 Chr 2:42-45); (b) sons by **Ephah** (1 Chr 2:46-47); and (c) sons by a second **concubine** (1 Chr 2:48-50a; BRAUN, 41). Many of these Judean cities are known from Joshua 15.

The genealogy reflects some fluidity when it associates the **Kenites** with Judah (1 Chr 2:55). Thus, there was an "ongoing amalgamation of previously unrelated tribal elements into the mainstream of Judah" (BRAUN, 43). Nomadic tribes and perhaps others living in the settlement areas (particularly the southern regions) were "adopted" into particular clans and formed part of the people of Israel. This is another piece of the Chronicler's inclusivistic patchwork.

Further Descendants of Ram from David (3:1-24)

With 1 Chronicles 3:1 we return to the lineage of David (1 Chr 2:17). The genealogical lists of 1 Chronicles 2 brought us down to the time of the monarchy. Now the Chronicler resumes David's line with the royal lineage of Judah, the theological center of Hezron's genealogy. This section takes us from David through the Judean Kings to the postexilic community. Here is the heartbeat of Judah's genealogy.

The Davidic line receives more attention than any other among the Judahites. It is the royal line. All the royal lines of the Northern Kingdom were extinguished. The royal line of Judah continues. The royal list points towards the Chronicler's messianic interests. He expects a renewal of Davidic glory because God is faithful to his promises (ALLEN, 43).

This section divides into three parts: (1) David's sons (1 Chr 3:1-9), (2) the kings of Judah (1 Chr 3:10-16), and (3) the exilic and postexilic line (1 Chr 3:17-24). Some of this material (1 Chr 3:1-8) is derived from 2 Samuel 3:2-5; 5:5,14-16. The list of David's sons born in Jerusalem also appears in 1 Chronicles 14:4-7. The origin of the royal list – the Kings of Judah – in 1 Chronicles 3:10-16 is unknown, but it may have been composed by the Chronicler from the records before him, especially the canonical source of 1–2 Kings. The origin of the third section is unknown but probably based on postexilic records that were available to the Chronicler.

The List of David's Sons (3:1-9)

The list of David's **sons** is given in three sections: (a) those born in

Hebron (1 Chr 3:1-4a from 2 Sam 3:2-5), (b) those born in **Jerusalem** (1 Chr 3:4b-8 from 2 Sam 5:14-16), and (c) a summary statement that includes **Tamar**, David's daughter (1 Chr 3:9 from 1 Sam 13). In addition, (a) and (b) are joined by the note that David ruled in Hebron **seven years** and in Jerusalem for **thirty-three years** (1 Chr 3:4 is derived from 2 Sam 5:5). While he records the place and years of 2 Samuel 5:5, he omits the reference to the different subjects over which he reigned. He excises the difference between ruling "over Judah" in Hebron and ruling "over all Israel and Judah" in Jerusalem, which does not suit his inclusivist and Davidic purposes.

The Chronicler reproduces 2 Samuel almost without change in 1 Chronicles 3:1-4a (though "Chileab" becomes **Daniel**, probably due to textual corruption). Significantly, he does not omit references to the non-Israelite background of some of David's wives (e.g., **Maacah daughter of Talmai king of Geshur**, 1 Chr 3:2).

The list of the sons born in Jerusalem has a few problems. After noting the four sons of **Bathsheba** (Solomon is listed last due to his elect status), nine more sons are listed without their mothers. Three problems result. First, **Eliphelet** is repeated twice. Since it is doubtful that David named two sons by the same name, this is probably a textual corruption that has been lost to us (BRAUN, 50). Second, the list contains two names that do not appear in 2 Samuel, Eliphelet and **Nogah**. The inclusion of these names is not accidental since the Chronicler counts "nine" as the additional number of sons beyond Bathsheba's. The names also appear in 1 Chronicles 14:5-6. Samuel's text was probably corrupted through textual transmission. Third, **Eliada** was originally named "Beeliada" (1 Chr 14:7), but the name was probably changed (as in 1 Sam 5:16) in order to avoid associations with Baal imagery (PAYNE, 4:338).

The Kings of Judah (3:10-16)

The second major section of 1 Chronicles 3:1-24 is the list of Judah's kings (1 Chr 3:10-16). This is given in a linear manner down to Josiah where the genealogical pattern shifts to a mixed approach (segmentation followed by linear). The only difficulty, other than varied spellings, is a listing of four sons (**Johanan, Jehoiakim, Zedekiah** [Mattaniah in 2 Kgs 24:17], and **Shallum**) for **Josiah** when 2 Kings only mentions three and one of them is not one of the

Chronicler's four (Jehoahaz, Jehoiakim, and Zedekiah; 2 Kgs 23:31, 34,36; 24:17-18). Many identify Jehoahaz with Shallum (cf. Jer 22:10-12), and it may be surmised that Johanan was a son who either did not survive long enough to reach the throne or was unfit for the throne (JAPHET, 97). The NIV reads **successors** where the Hebrew reads "sons" or "descendants" (NRSV) and this means that Zedekiah in 1 Chronicles 3:16 is the same as the Zedekiah in 1 Chronicles 3:15. But Zedekiah in 1 Chronicles 3:16 is probably a descendant of Jehoiakim even though 2 Kings does not mention him. After surveying the seemingly confused state of the evidence, BRAUN (51-52) concludes that there were two Zedekiahs and that Chronicles offers a complete genealogy.

The fiftieth generation from Adam goes into exile (JOHNSTONE, 1:57). This is symbolic for the Chronicler. His goal is "the fiftieth generation in which eschatological release is proclaimed to the exiles, as in the Jubilee of Leviticus 25" (cf. 2 Chr 36:20-21). Of course, the fiftieth generation in the Chronicler's history is not literal since that would only take us back 1250 years to ca. 1855 B.C. Chronicles is using generations symbolically just as Matthew arranges his genealogy in groups of fourteen (Matt 1:17). The symbolism of the organization is significant. There is no intention to be precise in the count of generations.

Beyond the Exile (3:17-24)

The third major section of 1 Chronicles 3:1-24 is the exilic and postexilic royal genealogy. The genealogical line takes us from **Jehoiachin** (or, Jeconiah in Hebrew, the exiled king of Judah) to the time of the Chronicler. The generational list offers some means of dating Chronicles, unless it was added to the book at a later time (e.g., those who would date the Chronicles ca. 515 B.C.). If the list is regarded as original, then Chronicles could not have been written prior to the last person in the genealogical list (which would be Anani, the son of Elioenai, 1 Chr 3:24).

The final list (1 Chr 3:17-24) follows a set form (JAPHET, 93-94). The father (e.g., Josiah) has sons (e.g., Johanan, Jehoiakim, Zedekiah, Shallum), and then one of the sons (Jehoiakim) becomes a father to other sons (Jehoiachin and Zedekiah), etc. The NIV follows this organizational pattern. Given this pattern (except the problematic counting in 1 Chr 3:21), from **Zerubbabel** to **Elioenai** there are at least "seven to fourteen" generations of approximately twenty years each, which would push the list back to between "460 to 320 B.C." as the *terminus ad quem* of the Chronicler's writing (JAPHET, 94; BRAUN, 52). Based on a generational span of twenty-five years, MYERS (1:21) places the generation of the last son (**Anani**) ca. 405 B.C.

One problem, other than varied spellings, is the lineage of Zerubbabel. While Ezra 3:2 and Haggai 1:1 name his father as **Shealtiel**, Chronicles names **Pedaiah**. The LXX corrects this and replaces Pedaiah with Shealtiel. KEIL's (81-82) explanation is generally accepted. Shealtiel may have died childless and, through a levirate marriage, Pedaiah became the father of Zerubbabel (WILLIAMSON, 57; SELMAN, 1:100).

Shelomith in 1 Chronicles 3:19 has recently drawn attention. Her name has been discovered on a seal found near Jerusalem that dates from the postexilic era (THOMPSON, 70). The woman on the seal was married to the governor and that may be the reason she is mentioned in the Zerubbabel genealogy.

The fact that David's line remains intact through the exile testifies to the faithfulness of God. He has not forgotten David. While it is probably true, as COGGINS (26) suggests, that there is no political hope in the mere listing of these names, the centrality of this list in the genealogical scheme, the importance of David in the coming narrative, and the messianic expectations of the royal line give more weight to future hopeful expectations from the Davidic line than a mere list. While the list may not be sufficient for that hope, without the list there is no hope.

ALLEN (43) reflects on the historic situation of Anani, the seventh son of Elioenai (1 Chr 3:24). Could Anani have entertained the possibility that he could reign as king of Israel? Living in a small Persian province, removed from the trade routes of his century, and the seventh son of his father, it would have been a sheer act of faith to believe that he could have become king. Yet, David was in a similar situation. The "seven" of 1 Chronicles 3:24 reminds us of the "seven" of 1 Chronicles 2:15. If God could make David king, surely he could also make Anani king too. Hope lives because God is both gracious and faithful.

4. The Descendants of Perez (4:1-20)

There does not appear to be any structure to this grouping of genealogies relating to the sons of **Perez**. First Chronicles 4:1 (Perez, etc.) resumes the line of 1 Chronicles 2:52 (part of the larger block that began with Perez in 1 Chr 2:5). Consequently, the continuation of the sons of Perez marks off the lineage of David that comes between them. The resumption of the line from Judah through Perez begins with a linear list in 1 Chronicles 4:1. However, where 1 Chronicles 4:1 reads **Carmi** we expect "Caleb" (cf. 1 Chr 2:9). JAPHET (106) believes this reflects a further textual variation of Caleb's name ("Chelubai" in 2:9; as well as "Caleb" in 2:18,42 and perhaps "Chelub" in 4:11). After Caleb, there are simply alternate groupings of various clans and families: **Shobal** (1 Chr 4:2), **Etam** (1 Chr 4:3-4a), **Hur** (1 Chr 4:4b-8), **Jabez** (1 Chr 4:9-10), **Kelub** (1 Chr 4:11-12), **Kenaz** (1 Chr 4:13-14), **Caleb** (1 Chr 4:15), **Jehallelel** (1 Chr 4:16), **Ezrah** (1 Chr 4:17-18), **Hodiah** (1 Chr 4:19), **Shimon** (1 Chr 4:20a), and **Ishi** (1 Chr 4:20b).

These genealogies have no canonical parallels. The Chronicler probably includes such an assorted list for the sake of comprehensiveness, completing the chiasm begun in 1 Chronicles 2:3 and legitimizing the descendants of Judah that live in his community.

This section contains the Chronicler's first narrative. Jabez, the subject of the narrative, is not mentioned in the genealogical lists though the city Jabez (1 Chr 2:55) in the hill country of **Hur** associates it with Judah. The Chronicler draws no connection between the story and the city. Jabez was probably related to the surrounding Judahites who preserved his story.

The embedded theology of this story is significant. The Hebrew words for **Jabez** (יַעְבֵּץ, ya'ªbbēṣ) and **pain** (עֹצֶב, 'ōṣeb) are similar. Out of the pain of childbirth a mother names her son. Jabez prays to be free from pain. In this he was more honorable than his Judahite kinsmen. The Jewish mind could not miss the irony of a man associated with pain as the most honorable among his brothers.

The prayer requests blessing (cf. 1 Chr 17:27). It contains three requests that are dependent on the opening wish (**bless me**): (1) **enlarge my territory**; (2) keep God's hand near; and (3) **keep from harm** (disaster). The first verb describes God's promise to David to enlarge his armies (1 Chr 27:23). In 1 Chronicles 29:12,14,16 the **hand** of God is a prominent theme. Second Chronicles 18:22 uses the term "disaster" to refer to God's judgments against his people. These themes are scattered throughout the Chronicler's narrative.

This story, set in the genealogical list of Judah, reflects God's gracious promise to hear the prayers of his people, avert disaster, enlarge their territory, and bless his people when they cry out to him (1 Chr 20:9). Jabez epitomizes the situation of the postexilic community. They were born out of pain, and they cry out to God for peace and rest. The assurance of this story is that God will hear the prayer of faith and graciously respond. The hope of the postexilic community is God's gracious disposition. God will give his people rest (cf. 1 Chr 23:25; 2 Chr 14:1-6; 15:15; 20:30; 32:22).

5. The Descendants of Judah's Son, Shelah (4:21-23)

Shelah returns to 1 Chronicles 2:3. He is the son of a Canaanite woman (another indication of inclusiveness). Shelah completes the Judean chiasm. The genealogy of **Judah** closes with his ancestry. There are no canonical parallels with this genealogy, but the Chronicler cites a source in 1 Chronicles 4:22.

B. THE "NORTHERN" TRIBES: SOUTH AND EAST OF JUDAH (4:24-5:26)

This section and 1 Chronicles 7:1-40 are the only places where Chronicles offers any kind of history of the Northern Kingdom. In the span of these short genealogies, Chronicles offers a brief history from their settlement after the conquest to their exile under the Assyrians.

The Chronicler sandwiches his genealogies of the "other" tribes between Judah and Levi and then between Levi and Benjamin. Judah, Levi, and Benjamin take up the major space, but the Chronicler does not omit "all Israel." This is another sign of his inclusiveness. He emphasizes David, the temple, and Jerusalem (located in Benjamin), that is, Judah, Levi, and Benjamin, but he also includes the other tribes of Israel.

In this first section of the "Northern" tribes the Chronicler provides a genealogical account of the tribes located south (Simeon) and
east of Judah in the transjordan region (Reuben, Gad, and half of
Manasseh). The rest of the tribes, which lived due north of Judah, are
described in 1 Chronicles 7:1-40. Thus, the Chronicler geographically
structures his groupings so that "all Israel" is included while the focus
is still on Judah, Jerusalem (Benjamin), and the temple (Levi).

1. South of Judah: Simeon (4:24-43)

Despite the fact that **Simeon** was a rather minor tribe, even
excluded from the blessing in Deuteronomy 33, it is given more
space than any tribe other than Judah, Levi, and Benjamin. This may
reflect Simeon's close association with Judah, which continued
despite the fact that Simeonites apparently sided with the northern
tribes during the reign of Rehoboam (2 Chr 15:9; 34:6). Its geographical location, however, made their opposition insignificant.

Simeon was given land on the southern border of Judah. Joshua
19:1,9 describes Simeon's territory as "within the inheritance" of
Judah. Many of the cities listed in 1 Chronicles 4:28-31 are Judahite
cities in Joshua 15:28-42. Chronicles underscores their geographical
relationship by noting that the Judahites outnumbered the
Simeonites (1 Chr 4:27). This indicates that early in the history of
Israel Simeon was absorbed into Judah even though Simeonites
retained some genealogical distinction into Hezekiah's reign (1 Chr
4:41; cf. Wright, "Boundary," 202-226). Some may have still lived in
the land at the time of the Chronicler.

JAPHET (119) discerns a threefold structure which evidences compositional unity. The first section is strictly genealogical (1 Chr 4:24-
27), the second is a series of place names where Simeonites settled
(1 Chr 4:28-33), and the last contains their history distinguished by
western (1 Chr 4:34-41) and eastern expansions (1 Chr 4:42-43).
Such expansions indicate that the conquest was never absolute but
was an ongoing task (cf. Judg 1-2).

In addition to the parallel material in canonical sources (Gen 46:10;
Exod 6:15; Num 26:12-14; and Josh 19:1-9), other materials probably
came from such sources as a census, a tribal genealogical list (cf. 1 Chr
4:33), and military lists (SELMAN, 1:102, cites Johnson, *Purpose*, 62-68).

While 1 Chronicles 4:24-26 could be a linear eight-generation list, the NIV and NRSV both see a different pattern of linear plus segmented genealogies. In either event, **Shimei** is the object of the genealogical list. Its purpose is to comment on his fruitfulness in contrast with his brothers. As a result, the Judahites began to outnumber the Simeonites with the ultimate result that Simeon is absorbed into Judah's clan.

The list of cities in 1 Chronicles 4:28-33 is based on Joshua 19:1-9 (though the language has changed from "inheritance" to "settlement"; cf. JAPHET, 122) but is also paralleled by Joshua 15:21-41 and Nehemiah 11:25-30. The identifiable cities are located in the southern regions of Israel within a 20-mile radius of Beersheba. Chronicles adds that these were Simeonite cities **until the reign of David** (1 Chr 4:31). This indicates their inclusion into the administrative district of Judah though cities belonging to Simeon were still extant in the time of Josiah (2 Chr 34:6). Nevertheless, Chronicles recognizes that there was a time when "Simeon once had a tribal identity before it was absorbed into Judah" (THOMPSON, 76). Their inclusion may indicate that a small number of Simeonites were still identifiable during the Chronicler's time. The reference to Ziklag (1 Chr 4:30) reminds readers that the Simeonites could not effectively control this area until the King of Gath gave it to David (1 Sam 27:6).

First Chronicles 4:34, the beginning of a new genealogical list, is not specifically linked to the previous one. JAPHET (124) thinks it is possible that **Shemaiah** (1 Chr 4:37) is a formalized spelling of Shimei (1 Chr 4:27) so that this is a further genealogy of Shimei from which the leaders of the clan arose. This clan moved in a western direction where they found pastureland in the region formerly belonging to Ham (1 Chr 4:39-40), probably somewhere between Gaza and Beersheba (**Gedor**, or perhaps due to corruption it should read Gerar as in the LXX; THOMPSON, 76). Apparently, they defeated the Philistines to settle this land, and it may have been part of a larger military campaign that took place under Hezekiah (cf. 2 Kgs 18:8). They are apparently known by the Chronicler through a registry compiled at the time of Hezekiah (1 Chr 4:41).

JOHNSTONE (1:69) calls attention to the importance of "registry" for the Chronicler as a consistent theme in Chronicles (1 Chr 5:1,7,17; 7:5,7,9,10; 9:1,22; 2 Chr 12:15; 31:16-19). "The registering of people is thus a sacral undertaking" that legitimates lineage and territory.

The last note on the Simeonites (1 Chr 4:42-43) brings their line to the time of Chronicles ("to this day") and reflects an eastern expansion into the regions of Edom (Mt. **Seir**). This involved military action against the **Amalekites**. While this may be Saul's action against the Amalekites in 1 Samuel 15 (or, possibly David's in 1 Sam 30), it is probably best to plead ignorance.

2. East of Judah (5:1-26)

The Chronicler turns his attention to the tribes that lived east of the Jordan river. This section divides into three separate genealogical accounts: Reuben (1 Chr 5:1-10), Gad (1 Chr 5:11-22), and half of Manasseh (1 Chr 5:23-26). The themes of settlement (1 Chr 5:9,16,23) and exile (1 Chr 5:6,22,26) are apparent in each section. The unity of the chapter is the unity of these three groups (cf. their concert action and punishment in 1 Chr 5:18,26 which parallels settlement and exile). Their geographical unity is underscored by Gad's description of dwelling "next" to Reuben (1 Chr 5:11) and Manasseh's description of dwelling "in the land" (1 Chr 5:23; BRAUN, 72). Consequently, this is the Chronicler's intentional "Transjordan" section of the genealogy. The Chronicler still maintains the birthright of the sons of Joseph — he is interested in the fortunes of "all Israel."

First Chronicles 5:1-3,25-26 are taken generally from canonical sources, but only 1 Chronicles 5:3 is cited verbatim (Exod 6:14; cf. Gen 46:9). Chronicles acknowledges a genealogical record as an unknown source for the Gadites (1 Chr 5:17). Chronicles's use reflects "authentic sources" rather than "fictitious composition" (JAPHET, 130).

Reuben (5:1-10)

The genealogy of **Reuben** begins with an explanation of why he does not have preeminence among the sons of Israel even though he was firstborn (1 Chr 5:1-2). The question of **firstborn** ("firstborn" and **birthright** used 6 times) is the primary topic. Why is preeminence

given to **Judah** when **Joseph** received the rights of firstborn that originally belonged to Reuben? Chronicles "suggests three levels of priority among the sons of Jacob: the biological firstborn, the legally nomi-
nated elder, and the one who wielded actual authority" (JAPHET, 133).

The loss of the birthright was a punishment for sin. Reuben slept
with his father's concubine (cf. Gen 35:22). This is another expression of the Chronicler's retribution theology as only he among the
canonical authors draws this theological connection.

But where did the Chronicler get the idea that the birthright had
passed to Joseph? This is his interpretation of Genesis 48:5 where
Jacob says that Ephraim and Manasseh will become to him as
Reuben and Simeon are. Joseph, then, stands in for Reuben (JAPHET,
135). In other words, the birthright belongs to Ephraim and
Manasseh, the largest and most significant of the northern tribes.
Thus, the Chronicler "wished to affirm that the Joseph tribes, representing now the Northern Kingdom, had been given the birthright
and apparently still enjoyed it" thereby legitimating their inclusion
in "all Israel" (BRAUN, 73). As a result, the "core of the old northern
kingdom" — the sons of Joseph — is safeguarded as part of Israel
(WILLIAMSON, 63). They had not lost their privileges.

Yet, Judah still has the preeminence (1 Chr 2:3-4) as the messianic tribe from which a ruler will emerge. David emerges as king of "all
Israel" and the promise to David grounds the hope of the postexilic
community. The Chronicler's interpretation of Genesis legitimizes
Israel's historical development where Ephraim and Manasseh receive
the double portion of the firstborn (territory and population) but the
ruler (cf. 1 Chr 11:2; 17:7; 28:4) comes out of Judah.

This is yet another example of the Chronicler's interest in the
demotion of the firstborn (1 Chr 2:3; 26:10). God grants status by
privilege rather than right; by grace rather than merit (SELMAN,
1:105). The older serves the younger.

The rest of the Reubenite material follows something similar to
Simeon's. The genealogical record is followed by a linear descent to
Beerah who, as a chief among the Reubenites, was taken into exile
by **Tiglath-pileser** (1 Chr 5:4-6; cf. 2 Chr 28:20) with a few relatives
(1 Chr 5:7-8a). The Reubenites settled the east side of the Jordan
and were exiled when it was conquered by Tiglath-pileser (745–727
B.C.) in 733 B.C. (1 Chr 5:8b-10). Theologically, God graciously gave

them the land and by retribution took it away through the Assyrian king.

Interestingly, war with the **Hagrites** during the "days of Saul" is without canonical parallel (1 Chr 5:10). A fuller comment on this war appears below (1 Chr 5:19-20). This ethnic group is unknown (though one of David's officers was a Hagrite, 1 Chr 27:30), but Psalm 83:6 associates them with Moab, Edom, and the Ishmaelites who are Israel's "traditional enemies" in the transjordan region (BRAUN, 76).

Gad (5:11-22)

The Moabite Stone (ca. 830 B.C.) refers to the "men of Gad" (*ANET*, 320). A Moabite king, living south of Israel's transjordan territory, recognized the presence of **Gadites** in the region.

The immediate children of Gad, known from Genesis 46:16 and Numbers 26:15-17, are not listed, and "none of the descendants of Gad listed here is otherwise known" in the OT (BRAUN, 74). Nevertheless, the citation of a source from the reigns of Jeroboam (Israel) and Jotham (Judah) bespeaks their authenticity (1 Chr 5:17). Some contend that Jotham and Jeroboam II did not reign at the same time (1 Kgs 15:32). However, Jotham probably reigned as a coregent with his father while he was stricken with leprosy (cf. 2 Kgs 15:5). Consequently their reigns did overlap, and a joint census ca. 750 B.C. is possible given the peace between the north and south during the late reign of Jeroboam II and the rise of the Assyrian empire (BRAUN, 76). The military material in 1 Chronicles 5:18-22 may indicate that Chronicles's source was some kind of military record and may suggest that "such genealogies originally served a military function" (BRAUN, 74).

The military excursion provides the Chronicler an opportunity to press some of his theological themes (cf. 1 Chr 4:9-10). This is the Chronicler's first battle report (cf. 2 Chr 13:13-19; 14:9-15; 18:31; 20:1-27; 26:7; 32:7-8,20-22) and it is his longest narrative in the genealogical accounts. While based upon an earlier source, this is the Chronicler's composition because it is couched in his language and theology (though **trained for battle** [1 Chr 5:18] is unique in Chronicles). In particular, 1 Chronicles 5:20 is clearly an editorial comment (cf. 2 Chr 18:31 as an addition to the account in 1 Kgs

22:32). SELMAN (1:106) underscores the three key ideas found in 1 Chronicles 5:20: divine "*help* (cf. 2 Ch 20:15; 25:8; 32:8), answered *prayer* in battle (cf. 2 Ch 14:11-15; 20:5-30; 32:20-21) and *trust* in God (cf. 2 Ch 32:10)." Theologically, the war belongs to God (1 Chr 5:22), and victory is assured if the people of God will cry out to him and trust him.

The seeming inconsistency between a well-prepared army and trusting in God raises an interesting question. Why does the Chronicler emphasize the preparedness and skill of the army when trusting God truly wins the battle? The Chronicler's theology is "sacramental," that is, "since the seen and the unseen are but the two sides of the one indivisible reality, in order to be the fitting agent of this cosmic power, Israel must be totally prepared and equipped with the best of all the temporal forces available" (JOHNSTONE, 1:75). Yet, they must rely on God. God equips and prepares his people as his agents in the world and intends that they use the best available means to accomplish divine goals. But their victories are by his strength and power. This has a wide application to preaching, apologetics, and evangelism as well as to the perennial problem of human responsibility and divine sovereignty (cf. Hicks, "Numerical," 17-34).

JAPHET (139-140) thinks it is unlikely that all of Transjordan would be united in a military expedition without monarchical leadership. She thinks a genuinely historic local initiative underwent "literary elaboration." However, there is no reason why a regional interest would not unite these tribes to prosecute a war in which the monarchy could not involve itself (e.g., a weak central government). The patterns of military organization in early Israel do not exclude such a possibility (JOHNSTONE, 1:74-75), especially if this war is identified with the one in 1 Chronicles 5:10. In that case the central government is acknowledged even if it is not involved.

For the first time, however, we encounter some of the "large numbers" that appear in the Chronicler's account (see Introduction; cf. comparative charts in JOHNSTONE, 1:76). The numbers are not as large as those found in Numbers 1 and 26. However we might interpret some of the details, it is unlikely that the Chronicler would falsify numbers because he had access to census and military records. While exaggeration and hyperbole are legitimate literary tools, it is possible these numbers "represent groups rather than arithmetic realities" (THOMPSON, 81) or we think in terms of "total mobilization of the males of arm-bearing age" (JOHNSTONE, 1:76).

The exile mentioned in 1 Chronicles 5:22 is not Babylonian, but Assyrian. The exile of 1 Chronicles 5:22 is the exile of 1 Chronicles 5:26. The Chronicler's readers had experienced their own exile (Babylon) and so "all Israel" reads their history with postexilic eyes. God exiled both north and south, and he will renew fellowship with both north and south if they will trust him as they did in the days of this battle.

East Manasseh (5:23-26)

This geneaological list is only for the half of **Manasseh** which lived next to Reuben and Gad in the Transjordan (the other half in 1 Chr 7:14-19). The genealogy is brief (1 Chr 5:23-24). As with Gad, Manasseh's sons are not named (Num 26:29; Josh 17:2). The Chronicler emphasizes settlement (1 Chr 5:23, including **Mount Hermon** near Damascus) and the **heads** of the clans (1 Chr 5:24).

The record of the transjordanian tribes, however, reaches its climax in the summary of their exile (1 Chr 5:25-26) which is derived from 2 Kings 17:7-23 (SELMAN, 1:107). Just like Achan (1 Chr 2:7), the transjordanian tribes acted unfaithfully (מָעַל, *ma'al*) and God punished them (cf. 1 Chr 9:1). The theology of retribution is assumed. The Chronicler describes their idolatry as prostitution. They "played the harlot" (cf. 2 Chr 21:11,13) with the idolatry of the Canaanites (**peoples of the land**) that God had rooted out of the land he had given to Israel. This is the ultimate theological insult — to worship the very gods that God had destroyed the previous inhabitants of the land for worshiping.

First Chronicles 5:26 describes the punishment. The **king of Assyria** carried them away into exile. Instead of the land of their fathers, they inhabited the land of **Halah, Habor, Hara and the river of Gozan** (cf. 2 Kgs 17:6) which is located in upper Mesopotamia. Chronicles emphasizes their continued exile (**to this day**). Theologically, he does not exclude them from the renewal of the Davidic promise. He stresses the seriousness of their unfaithfulness and that unfaithfulness does have a price. His message is that renewal comes through repentance and not on the mere expectation that God will redeem his people no matter what their unfaithfulness.

The Chronicler used two names for the Assyrian king. One is an appositional description of the other (cf. NIV). The **king of Assyria** who exiled the transjordanian region was **Pul** (Pulu in Neo-Babylonian sources). He was also called **Tiglath-pileser**. Instead of conflating two different kings (cf. 2 Kgs 15:19,29), the Chronicler provides both names. That the Chronicler intends one king is clear from the fact that he uses singular verbs (he came, he took, etc.).

The divine role is underscored by the significant phrase, **the God of Israel stirred up the spirit of Pul king of Assyria** (1 Chr 5:26). This language indicates divine initiative (cf. 2 Chr 21:16; Ezra 1:1). The God of Israel punished Israel through Assyria. However God may accomplish such a movement among human beings, God takes credit for the exile.

The same God, however, will move the heart of a Persian king (2 Chr 36:22). That king will return "all Israel" to their land to rebuild their temple. The sovereign God is a gracious God, and if his people will return to him, he will return to them.

C. LEVI (6:1-81)

The Levites not only receive the most lengthy attention (except for Judah), but they are the centerpiece of Chronicles's genealogical structure. This is not simply a structural center, but a theological one (ALLEN, 55, 60). The genealogical structure of the sons of Israel puts "God at the center" and the presence of the Levites bears "witness to the temple." Chronicles's structure may have been influenced by Numbers 1–2 where the Levites camped in the center with the tabernacle while they were surrounded by the other tribes.

The importance of Levi is underscored in two ways. First, they are temple servants. Chronicles supplies a list of the high priests and musicians. This establishes continuity between the Davidic origins of the temple cult and the postexilic community. While Chronicles's Levitical genealogy has often been regarded as contrived, recent scholarship recognizes the layers of traditions present. Chronicles's genealogy utilizes preexilic sources (cf. Laato, 77-99). Also, JAPHET

(148) notes that fifty percent of these materials are derived from canonical sources.

Second, the Levites are the religious backbone of Israel. Even their settlements reflect their role as "holy presence" in the land. They are scattered throughout Israel — from north to south, from east to west — in Levitical cities. The Levites, as religious leaders, provide continuity and cohesiveness within Israel. "Levi thus provides a religious leadership which acts as a binding force through the length of Israel's history and the breadth of its territory" (WILCOX, 38).

JOHNSTONE (1:82) discerns a threefold structure to 1 Chronicles 6: (1) the genealogy of the Levites (1 Chr 6:1-30), (2) the chief duties of the Levites (1 Chr 6:31-49), and (3) the Levitical cities (1 Chr 6:50-81). Thus, Chronicles moves from people to duties to settlements.

1. The Levitical Genealogy (6:1-30)

First Chronicles 6:1 and 6:16 have the same beginning line. Consequently, this section falls into two natural divisions. Chronicles first provides the High Priestly line through Levi's son Kohath (1 Chr 6:1-15), and then provides a fuller Levitical line through Levi's other sons (Gershon [MT reads Gershom] and Merari) as well as the nonpriestly line from Kohath (1 Chr 6:16-30).

The importance of the High Priestly line cannot be overestimated. It is the religious link between preexilic and postexilic Israel. It legitimates the temple. Consequently, Chronicles provides a linear genealogy of the High Priests from Aaron to Jehozadak (the High Priest who went into exile and father of the postexilic High Priest Joshua, cf. Hag 1:1; Ezra 3:2).

While the High Priestly line is a linear genealogy (with some segmentation), Chronicles provides a segmented genealogy for the rest of the Levites. Laato (81) suggests that Chronicles "presents us with seven main genealogical lists: two for Gershom and Merari (each containing genealogical links with the Levitical clans and singers) and three for Kohath (one each for Levites, high priests and singers)." Laato furnishes this schematization:

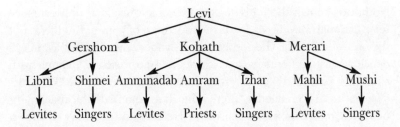

The High Priestly Line (6:1-15)

The sons of **Levi** are given in the normal canonical order (Gen 46:11; Exod 6:16), but the focus is on the middle son, **Kohath**. His is the high priestly line. Consequently, the Chronicler does not follow the pattern of Exodus 6, but deals only with the line of Kohath. He provides a segmented genealogy for Kohath, **Amram**, and **Aaron** (1 Chr 6:2-3), but begins a linear genealogy with **Eleazar** (1 Chr 6:4-15). JAPHET (146) notes that the segmented section serves as an introduction to the linear tree and that 1 Chr 6:16-30 follows the same pattern.

The segmented genealogy is beautifully structured to narrow down to the high priestly line (BRAUN, 83-84). The linear list from **Eleazar** contains twenty-two names which involves a "reasonable period between the settlement and the destruction of the Temple" (JAPHET, 150). WILLIAMSON (70-71) suggests that when the editorial comment of 6:10 is moved to 6:9, there are twelve generations from Aaron to the temple and twelve from the temple to Joshua. If we give forty years for each generation, then the Chronology matches 1 Kings 6:1 as well as the timeline from the building of the temple to the exile. Thus, we move from settlement (Aaron) to temple (**Azariah**) to resettlement (Joshua) through the genealogical list (similar to Matt 1).

One of the main problems with this list is the repetition of **Amariah**, **Ahitub**, and **Zadok** (1 Chr 6:7b-8a,11b-12a). Zadok is an important name in the history of Israel. He was the high priest at the time of David along with Abiathar (1 Chr 18:16), but after the rise of Solomon Zadok alone was high priest (1 Chr 29:22). Abiathar was expelled due to his rebellion (1 Kgs 2:26-27). The Chronicler does not mention this intrigue since he is unconcerned with the political problems surrounding Solomon's accession (e.g., 1 Kgs 1). The high priestly line continued through Zadok.

Zadok's descent from the Aaronic line has often been doubted.

Nothing is known about his descent except this text. The only evidence for a fictional, Davidic Zadok is the repetition of names. But this is not the only alternative. The "repetition of names (e.g., vv. 8,12) is no evidence against authenticity, and is not at all surprising in a family with a strong sense of history and tradition" (SELMAN, 1:109). Cross (*Canaanite*, 214) concludes "there is much to commend the attachment of Zadok to the house of Aaron in Hebron and to the well-known shrine there where both David and Absalom were anointed king."

Another problem is the list's omissions. Several high priests are missing. For example, among those missing are: Jehoiada (2 Kgs 12:2), Zechariah (2 Chr 24:20), Uriah (2 Kgs 16:10-16), a third and fourth Azariah (2 Chr 26:17,20; 31:10-13), Eli (1 Sam 1:9; 14:3), Meraioth (1 Chr 9:11), and Abiathar (2 Sam 8:17). Why does the Chronicler omit these names when he includes others he knows from the same canonical sources (e.g., **Azariah** [1 Kgs 4:2], **Hilkiah** [2 Kgs 22:4ff], and **Seraiah** [2 Kgs 25:18])? Perhaps this list is not strictly genealogical, but rather an official linear list sufficient to preserve the line and cover the time from the settlement to the exile.

One other problem is that 1 Chr 6:10 places the dedication of the temple during the time of Azariah, the son of **Johanan**, but 1 Kings 4:2 identifies the high priest as Azariah, the son of Zadok. The editorial note was probably misplaced in the textual tradition and belongs in 1 Chronicles 6:9 rather than 6:10 (WILLIAMSON, 70).

The Nonpriestly Line (6:16-30)

Chronicles begins with segmented genealogies in order to introduce the fuller Levitical clan (1 Chr 6:16-19a), but then moves quickly to linear genealogical trees (1 Chr 6:19b-30). The first section offers a segmented genealogy of the three **sons of Levi: Gershon** (2 sons), **Kohath** (4 sons) and **Merari** (2 sons). With the editorial comment in 1 Chronicles 6:19b, the Chronicler gives a linear genealogy for **Gershon, Kohath and Merari**. He follows Gershon through **Libni** (1 Chr 6:20) for seven generations and he follows Merari through **Mahli** for seven generations (1 Chr 6:29). The center of this linear list, however, is the lineal descent from Kohath through **Amminadab** (1 Chr 6:21-28).

The Chronicler's interests lie with Kohath. The lengthy recitation of the Kohathites through Amminadab includes **Samuel**, the prophet, among the **Levites** (1 Chr 6:27-28). This is problematic because Samuel is an Ephraimite (1 Sam 1:1) even though he did minister in the tabernacle (1 Sam 3:1). Some believe that Samuel's family was Levitical but only lived in a Levitical city in Ephraim (PAYNE, 4:351; SELMAN 1:111). WILLIAMSON (72) suggests he was "adopted" into the Levitical ministry through his dedication. In either event, the inclusion of Samuel prepares the way for the Levitical function of his grandson, Heman (1 Chr 6:33-38), whom the Levitical record legitimates.

Several problems emerge in Kohath's linear list. Amminadab is not listed elsewhere as a descendant of Kohath (1 Chr 6:22). Izhar appears in other lists where Chronicles has Amminadab (cf. 1 Chr 6:2,37-38; Exod 6:18,21). It seems Izhar is intended rather than Amminadab and so some emend the text accordingly (BRAUN, 87). Some think it might be an alternative spelling/name for the same individual. However, Galil ("Sons," 488-495; cf. Dillard, *Study*, 593) suggests that this is an example of genealogical fluidity where Aaron's marriage to the daughter of Amminadab of Judah (Elisheba, Exod 6:23) is used as a genealogical reference point. If so, this means that all the priests of Israel were descendants of Aaron the Levite and Elisheba the Judahite (Galil, "Sons," 493). I prefer Laato's solution which sees Izhar and Amminadab as brothers, both sons of Kohath.

2. The Chief Duties of the Levites (6:31-49)

This section begins (16:31-32) and concludes (16:48-49) with a narrative. Sandwiched between are linear genealogies of Levitical servants whose two main duties are musical/liturgical (16:31-32) and sacrificial/expiatory (16:48-49).

The introduction anticipates the later narrative where David institutes the musical liturgy (1 Chr 15-16). The conclusion recalls the institution of Levitical and priestly orders during the time of Aaron. Thus, the genealogies link Moses and Aaron with David. The Davidic service of the temple, then, is an extension of the Mosaic Levitical institutions. The Chronicler has not forgotten Moses and Aaron.

The Levitical descriptions assign three roles to the descendants of Levi. First, the priestly class, descended from Aaron (1 Chr 6:49), performed the expiatory rituals. They served the altar and the Holy Place. Second, there are singers or musicians (1 Chr 6:31-32; cf. Kleinig, *Song*, 30-39). Third, the rest of the Levites perform other duties. The first and third were instituted by Moses, but the second by David. Thus, David completes what Moses began.

The language of the introduction and conclusion is typical of Chronicles. The "**house** (temple) of Yahweh" is used 95 times in Chronicles. The singers **ministered** (19 times) with music, and they performed their service (10 times). The other Levites performed their **duties** (or, ministries, 37 times in reference to the temple). The Aaronic descendants officiated at the sacrificial rituals, including the altars of sacrifice and incense (50 times). The Chronicler lays the groundwork for his further elucidation of the temple cultus in the coming narrative.

The genealogical details are covered adequately by others (BRAUN, 91-94; WILLIAMSON, 73-74), but the three major families of musicians are significant. Hauer (33-54) defends a Davidic dating. JAPHET (156-157) notes that the singers flow through the second sons of Gershon, Kohath, and Merari, and that the lineage is intended to legitimate the musical ministries of **Asaph** (from Gershon), **Heman** (from Kohath), and **Ethan** (from Merari) during the time of David and Solomon. This is the basic structure of the text to which several other items are added, and it is written in the interests of legitimizing their role in temple service. This is particularly true of Heman who is not listed among the singers of Ezra (ch. 2) and Nehemiah (ch. 7).

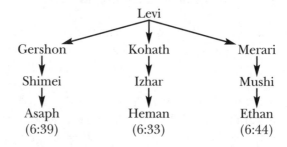

3. The Levitical Cities (6:50-81)

The Levitical settlements are prefaced by reproducing the high priestly line previously stated in 6:3b-8. Why is it reproduced? It is

probably a thematic reintroduction. God's priests do not simply officiate at the temple, but they are scattered among the people
throughout the land. They "constitute," according to JOHNSTONE
(1:94), "an indwelling presence of local teaching and example."
Their dwellings among the people represent the God who not only
dwells in his temple but also has a holy presence throughout the
land. In the same way, Christians are a sacral presence in the world
as we bear witness to God's light and salt the earth with holiness.

The list of **settlements** (lit., "dwelling-places"), based on Joshua
21, is divided into five sections: (1) Aaronite settlements (1 Chr 6:54-
60; cf. Josh 21:9-19) and (2) the remaining allotments (1 Chr 6:61-
65). The Levites receive a total of forty-eight cities, which BRAUN
(100) believes is an equal distribution throughout the country (four
cities in each tribal territory).

The remaining allotments are divided between the three
Levitical families: (3) **Kohathite** settlements (1 Chr 6:66-70; cf. Josh
21:20-26); (4) Gershomite settlements (1 Chr 6:71-76; cf. Josh 21:27-
33); and (5) Merarite settlements (1 Chr 6:77-81; cf. Josh 21:34-40).
Each tribe contributes land and cities to one of the Levitical families.
Chronicles's list reflects a Davidic situation, and modern scholarship
is increasingly accepting its historical value (JAPHET, 163-165).

Dan is absent though present in his source (Josh 21:23). This
reflects the consistent theological exclusion of Dan from "all Israel"
due to its idolatrous associations. The two halves of Manasseh make up
for the loss of Dan so that there are twelve tribes, that is, "all Israel."

The list includes the Levites in "all Israel" (cities) and distributes
the sacral presence of the Levites throughout the land. Israel is settled in its land, and God is present among his people. The presence
of the Levites demonstrates God's acceptance of his people as God
receives their sacral ministry in his name.

D. "NORTHERN" TRIBES: NORTH OF JUDAH (7:1-40)

This section completes the genealogical record of "all Israel." It
compliments the previous "northern" section (1 Chr 4:24–5:26).
These tribes settled north of Judah (including Benjamin).

There is no apparent reason for the order of the remaining
northern tribes: (1) Issachar (1 Chr 7:1-6), (2) Benjamin (1 Chr 7:7-

12), (3) Naphtali (1 Chr 7:13), (4) the sons of Joseph (1 Chr 7:14-29), and (5) Asher (1 Chr 7:30-39). There is a difference between the type of record for the sons of Joseph than for the other tribes listed here. Issachar, Benjamin, and Asher, for example, have military overtones, whereas Ephraim and Manasseh are more settlement records. The Chronicler may have used a military census as his scheme, listing them from the largest (Issachar) to the smallest (Asher). For completeness, he inserted a settlement record of the sons of Joseph ("all Israel"; JAPHET, 168-169). Naphtali (1 Chr 7:13) was derived from Genesis 46:24 and apparently the Chronicler had no other independent source.

There is no mention of Dan (unless 1 Chr 7:12 is so interpreted), no mention of Zebulun, and scant mention of Naphtali (1 Chr 7:13). While there may be theological reasons for the Chronicler's attitude toward Dan, the short rendition of Naphtali and the absence of Zebulun may reflect something else in which Dan might be included. JAPHET (169) theorizes that the most northern tribes, which suffered the earliest and most from Assyrian incursions, may have left few records.

Chronicles maintains the number twelve. If Dan is included at 1 Chronicles 7:12 (see below), then the exclusion of Zebulun makes the number twelve since Levi effectively takes his place. However, if Dan is absent, Chronicles counts Manasseh twice (two settlements), so the number is still twelve. Either way Chronicles keeps the important and symbolic number twelve (WILCOX, 40).

1. Issachar (7:1-5)

The source for the **Issachar** record is a genealogical enrollment (1 Chr 7:5) and/or a Davidic military census (1 Chr 7:2). The sons of Issachar are also listed in Genesis 46:13 and Numbers 26:23-24.

The structure is fairly simple. The sons of Issachar (1 Chr 7:1) are followed by the sons of **Tola**, Issachar's firstborn (1 Chr 7:2), who are followed by the sons of **Uzzi**, Tola's firstborn (1 Chr 7:3). Other comments in the section relate to the numbers of the **fighting men** derived from each clan and from the total of the entire clan (87,000 in 1 Chr 7:5).

2. Benjamin (7:6-12)

There is considerable difference between the four canonical lists of Benjamin's **sons** (Gen 46:21; Num 26:38; 1 Chr 7:6; 1 Chr 8:1). Their differences, especially within Chronicles itself, probably reflect the sources from which these names were gleaned. The Chronicler knows the canonical sources, and he himself includes two different lists. It is best to think that he is following his source closely and that the sources had different purposes. SELMAN (1:114-115) theorizes that 1 Chronicles 7:6-12 reflects Davidic loyalties and military interests while 1 Chronicles 8:1 reflects geographical concerns and a loyalty to Saul.

Why does the Chronicler include a genealogical list for Benjamin in this section when he will devote a large amount of space (40 verses) to the Benjamites in 1 Chronicles 8? Each list has a different purpose. While 1 Chronicles 7:6-12 serves a military purpose, 1 Chronicles 8 serves a settlement purpose and enables the Chronicler to prepare us for the reign of Saul in 1 Chronicles 10.

The basic structure of this section is a segmented genealogy that encompasses three generations from **Benjamin** through **Bela** and **Beker**, and four generations from Benjamin through **Jediael**. The primary data is genealogy and military strength.

The major problem in this section is 1 Chronicles 7:12b which reads ". . . the sons of Ir, Hushim, the son of Aher" (NRSV). Genesis 46:23 pegs Hushim as the son of Dan. Consequently, some have favored emending the text to read: "The sons of Dan: Hushim, the sons of Aher" (BRAUN, 106) or "the sons of Dan: Hushim, his one son" (JAPHET, 174). This involves a change of **Ir** to "Dan," and possibly reading "Aher" as "one" or even "another" instead of reading it as a name. However, WILLIAMSON (78; "Note," 375-379) has argued that it is a continuation of Benjamite names (cf. "Hushim" in 1 Chr 8:8,11). The plural sons does not mean that the Chronicler intended to list more than one (cf. 1 Chr 7:3). Chronicles excludes the idolatrous clan of Dan for theological reasons. WILLIAMSON's more natural and unemended reading seems best.

3. Naphtali (7:13)

The genealogical record of **Naphtali** is the briefest in Chronicles, limited to one generation, and reproduced from Genesis 26:24. It points to the Chronicler's inclusiveness. Apparently, he had no genealogical record or military census for Naphtali, so he included the only thing he did have — the canonical record. This does not answer the question as to why the Chronicler would include Naphtali from a canonical source and not include Zebulun (cf. Gen 46:14; Zebulun appears in 1 Chr 12:33,40; 27:19; 30:10,11,18). Perhaps he did not need Zebulun to retain the symbolic number of twelve.

4. Sons of Joseph (7:14-29)

Manasseh and Ephraim are given in their birth order. They are grouped as the sons of Joseph (1 Chr 2:1-2), inhabit contiguous territories, and 1 Chronicles 7:29 ties the two sons together with the conclusion: **the descendants of Joseph son of Israel lived in these towns**.

West Manasseh (7:14-19)

While this genealogical record is based on Numbers 26:29-34 and Joshua 17:1-3, it is, according to Edelman ("Manassite," 179-201), informed by an "administrative" list which probably dates from the time of David and Solomon. This accounts for its rather "disjointed" appearance (JOHNSTONE, 1:105). It lacks the detail of the canonical sources (e.g., other sons of Manasseh in Josh 17; the daughters of Zelophehad) but includes otherwise unknown items (e.g., the sons of Makir's wife, **Maacah**). Some textual problems make this text more difficult than usual (e.g., the meaning of **Huppites and Shuppites** and whether **Makir** is the wife or sister of Maacah in 1 Chr 7:1510; cf. JAPHET, 174-177; Edelman, "Manassite," 184).

Whatever the difficulties, the Chronicler calls attention to the **Aramean concubine** of **Manasseh**. This signals the Chronicler's inclusivism. He provides the descent of Gilead through this Aramean and includes **Gilead** to solidify the unity of East and West

Manasseh. The Manasseh clan is still connected even though they settled on different sides of the Jordan.

Seven of the thirteen clans of Manasseh are known independently of canonical sources through inscriptions on the Samaria ostraca (65 inscribed potsherds) which date from the eighth century B.C. (Dillard, *Study*, 596). These include **Shemida** and **Abiezer** (MYERS, 1:54).

Ephraim (7:20-29)

This genealogical record contains four sections: (1) a linear genealogy from **Ephraim** to **Shuthelah** (1 Chr 7:20-21a) partly based on Numbers 26:35-37; (2) the birth narrative of **Beriah** (1 Chr 7:21b-24); (3) a linear genealogy from **Rephah** to **Joshua**, the son of **Nun** (1 Chr 7:25-26); and (4) the settlement record of Ephraim (1 Chr 7:27-28).

The major historical difficulty is 1 Chronicles 7:21b-24. JAPHET (178, 183-184; cf. "Conquest," 205-218) argues that Chronicles projects both Manasseh ("Aramean" concubine) and Ephraim (sons **killed** by **men of Gath**) back into pre-Conquest Canaan. But the accounts in Genesis assume they never lived in Canaan. Consequently, according to JAPHET (184), Chronicles (here "more than any other passage") provides an alternative historiography that neglected the Exodus-Conquest. However, an "Aramean" could have lived in Egypt at the time of Manasseh, and the Ephraim of 1 Chronicles 7:22 may not be the immediate son of Joseph. He may be someone named after his illustrious ancestor (e.g., this Ephraim had "brothers," [1 Chr 7:22 where the NIV reads "relatives"] but the patriarch only had one brother, Manasseh; cf. Galil, "Chr's," 11-14). SELMAN (1:116-117; cf. BRAUN, 115) argues that the incident described in 1 Chronicles 7:21-24 took place either during the conquest or in the process of settlement. Another possibility is that the raid against Gath was carried out from Egypt during the lifetime of Joseph's son because the name Ephraim in 1 Chronicles 7:22 seems to assume the Ephraim of 1 Chronicles 7:20. In that case, Joshua may be ten generations from Ephraim which fits the timeframe of the Exodus (Dillard, *Study*, 596; cf. JOHNSTONE, 1:106; PAYNE, 4:358). Either way, the Chronicler is not offering a revisionist Conquest.

The Chronicler provides a linear genealogy for Joshua (1 Chr 7:26). This leads naturally to a discussion of the **settlements** of the sons of Joseph (which is based on Josh 16–17). In the name "Joshua" the Conquest comes into focus and the settlements are given a historical context.

This narrative recounts the story surrounding the naming of Beriah (בְּרִיעָה sounds like "in" + "misfortune, evil" [רָעָה, *rā'āh*], or to be born "in tragedy" [ALLEN, 71]). This is a local story that the Chronicler includes because it is probably in his Ephraimite source (Na'aman, "Sources," 108). Why the naming of Beriah is significant is unclear except that there is a traditional association of the cities of Beth Horon (where the descendants of Beriah settled) with Joshua. Perhaps the connection between Joshua and **Beth Horon** motivated the inclusion of this Ephraimite incident.

5. Asher (7:30-40)

This genealogical material is unknown except for its beginnings in Genesis 46:17 (cf. Num 26:44-47). The rest is probably derived from a census or military list (1 Chr 7:40) from the Davidic era (cf. Edelman, "Asherite," 17). Given the geographical associations of **Heber** (1 Chr 7:32), the present genealogy is most likely linked to an Asherite community in the region of Ephraim and Benajmin (Edelman, "Asherite," 13-23; JAPHET, 185). As a result, the biblical materials contain almost nothing of the actual development of the Asherite settlement in northwest Palestine. **Asher** concludes the "northern tribes" (1 Chr 7). While the genealogies are scanty, they enable the Chronicler to include "all Israel."

E. BENJAMIN (8:1-9:1a)

Chronicles provided a genealogical record for Benjamin in 1 Chronicles 7:6-12. While it is unclear why Chronicles duplicates Benjamin, this extended genealogy gives closure to the whole genealogical record of "all Israel" (1 Chr 9:1). The structure, therefore, emphasizes Judah-Levi-Benjamin with the "northern" tribes interspersed between Judah-Levi and Levi-Benjamin. Only Judah and Levi have more extensive genealogical lists than Benjamin. Consequently, Chronicles focuses on the southern kingdom (Benjamin and Judah – often mentioned together, cf. 2 Chr 11:1,3,10,12;

15:2,8,9; 25:5; 31:1; 34:9) and temple (Levites) while at the same time including "all Israel." Further, Benjamin is the clan of Israel's first king, Saul. Since the Chronicler begins his narrative with the death of Saul (1 Chr 10), the family of Saul the Benjamite is considered last (1 Chr 8:29-40). Saul's genealogy leads us into the narrative of his death and David's rise to power.

JAPHET (189) divides the chapter into two sections: (1) the growth of the Benjamites (1 Chr 8:1-32) and (2) the genealogy of Saul (1 Chr 8:33-40). The recurring idea of family "heads" (along with the interest in geography, especially Jerusalem in 1 Chronicles 8:28 and 8:32) binds the section together. The introduction of Saul in 1 Chronicles 8:33 begins a new section.

1. The Growth of the Benjamites (8:1-32)

JAPHET (189-190) subdivides the first section in this pattern: (a) introduction (1 Chr 8:1-2), (b) Sons of Bela (1 Chr 8:3-7), (c) Sons of Shaharaim (1 Chr 8:8-14), (d) Benjamites in Jerusalem (1 Chr 8:15-28), and (e) Benjamites of Gibeon (1 Chr 8:29-32).

Introduction: Sons of Benjamin (8:1-2)

The list of Benjamin's sons parallels lists in Genesis 46:21, Numbers 26:38-39 and 1 Chronicles 7:6. None of these lists are exactly the same. Some differences may be due to "transcriptional variations" (BRAUN, 123), such as Ahrach (אחרח), Ahoah (אחוה), and Ahiram (אחירם) or **Nohah** (נוחה) and Naaman (נעמן). The differences in the genealogical lists probably reflect different purposes and sources for the list, e.g., while the Chronicler knows Beker and Jediael as sons of Benjamin (1 Chr 7:6), he does not mention them here (1 Chr 8:1-2).

Sons of Bela (8:3-7)

Chronicles lists the sons of **Bela** for a second time (1 Chr 7:7). None match. This may reflect different sources and purposes as well as transcriptional problems (e.g., **Gera** is listed twice as a son of Bela in 1 Chr 8:3,5). Further, the appearance of **Ehud** in 1 Chronicles 8:6 is rather abrupt in the NIV text. However, it is better to translate "Abihud" (1 Chr 8:3) as "father of Ehud" (cf. NIV fn.; WILLIAMSON, 83).

These problems are probably best understood when 1 Chronicles 8:4-5 are taken as the sons of Ehud, and after the narrative note in 1 Chronicles 8:6 some of the sons are repeated in 1 Chronicles 8:7 (SELMAN, 1:119-120; JAPHET, 190-191). The resultant linear line would be: Benjamin–Bela–Gera–Ehud–Gera et al. Thus, the text concentrates on Ehud, a descendent of Benjamin, probably the leader of Israel in Judges 3:15 (the genealogy assumes some telescoping).

The descendants of Ehud lived in **Geba**, a Levitical city located in Benjamin (1 Chr 6:60) just north of Judah. However, some **were deported to Manahath**. The nature, timing, and location of this deportation is obscure. This may refer to a migration south of Judah or perhaps in Edom, or it may refer to military action or "internal tribal struggles" in the region (JAPHET, 192; BRAUN, 125).

Sons of Shaharaim (8:8-14)

The genealogical records of this section and the next (1 Chr 8:15-28) are unique to Chronicles. First Chronicles 8:8 resumes the descendants of Bela through **Shaharaim** (1 Chr 8:5). The text reflects two migrations of Benjamites — one to **Moab**, and another to **Aijalon** (originally assigned to Dan, Josh 19:42). The Chronicler emphasizes settlement patterns. The inhabitation of the land is significant. The reference to **Ono** and **Lod**, which were cities known in Egypt prior to the Exodus, must mean "rebuilt" (THOMPSON, 100).

Benjamites in Jerusalem (8:15-28)

First Chronicles 8:28 identifies these families with Jerusalem. This editorial note does not include 1 Chronicles 8:1-14 as Chronicles has separated groups according to the **heads** of families (1 Chr 8:6,10,13). In contrast with the previous families which lived in Geba, Moab, and Aijalon, these heads (families) lived in **Jerusalem** which was a Benjamite city bordering Judah.

Benjamites of Gibeon (8:29-32)

The Chronicler introduces the Gibeonite Benjamites to set up his genealogy of Saul (1 Sam 14:49; 31:2; 2 Sam 9:12; cf. MYERS, 1:62). The reference to **Gibeon** is significant. Saul's genealogy is twice linked to **Jeiel** (LXX, contra MT), the father of Gibeon (1 Chr 8:29; 9:35). While the Benjamites who descended from Bela lived in **Jerusalem**, another group from which Saul descended lived in Gibeon (1 Chr 8:29; 9:34-35). Demsky (20-23) notes that **Ner** (1 Chr 8:33) and **Gedor** (1 Chr 8:31) are family names discovered on jar handles from preexilic Gibeon. They lived near but not in Jerusalem. The contrast between Gibeon and Jerusalem is strong. It may reflect a royal rivalry. Gibeon was an early capital during the reign of Saul (Edelman, "Saul," 154-156). While some (Demsky, 16-23, and Blenkinsopp, *Gibeon*) argue that Saul was a Gibeonite rather than a Benjamite (Saul's line is not traced back to Benjamin, so Gibeon may be another case of adoption in genealogical record), it is sufficient to call attention to the geographical contrast in order to emphasize the difference between Saul of Gibeon and David of Jerusalem (Walters, 69-72). SAILHAMER (27-28) also contrasts the divine choice of Jerusalem for his resting place (2 Chr 6:6) with the Israelite decision to place the tabernacle in Gibeon (1 Chr 16:39; 21:29). The contrast between David and Saul is also the contrast between divine election and human manipulation.

2. The Genealogy of Saul (8:33–9:1a)

This is the first of two Saulide genealogies in Chronicles (cf. 1 Chr 9:39-44). The second one introduces 1 Chronicles 10 where Saul's death is narrated. This one concludes the Benjamite genealogies before Chronicles moves to a different topic in 1 Chronicles 9.

The genealogy is a combination of linear and segmented relationships. With the exception of the segmentation of Saul's four sons (**Jonathan, Malki-Shua, Abinadab and Esh-Baal** [Ish-Bosheth in 2 Sam 2:8]) in 1 Chronicles 8:33b, the text provides a linear genealogy: **Ner** (not in MT, but supplied from LXX and 1 Chr 9:36)–**Kish–Saul** (segmented with his four sons)–**Jonathan–Merib-Baal** (Mephibosheth in 2 Sam 4:4)–**Micah** (with segmentation for his four sons in 1 Chr 8:35)–**Ahaz–Jehoaddah** (with segmentation for his three sons)–**Zimri–Moza–Binea–Raphah–Eleasah–Azel** (with segmentation for his six sons). The genealogy of a second son of Eleasah (brother of Azel) is also provided through segmentation. The conclusion in 1 Chronicles 8:40 is that the sons of **Ulam** were

brave warriors and fertile. This is the most comprehensive genealogy of Saul, spanning 15 generations into the postexilic period. This is fairly unique in Chronicles, more like the genealogies of the high priests, David, and the Levites (BRAUN, 127).

Theologically, even though "all his house" (1 Chr 10:6) was destroyed at Gilboa, God graciously continued Saul's line. Even though Saul was rejected as king, the faithfulness of God to "all Israel" was demonstrated in his continuation of Saul's genealogy into postexilic times.

Benjamin is the first and last Hebrew term in this chapter (8:1,40). This functions as an inclusio. The Chronicler's interest in Benjamin is both genealogical and geographical. The Benjamites were spread over southern Palestine and grew in significance through Saul and their subsequent association with David. Despite Benjamin's past failures (e.g., Saul), they are, along with Judah and Levi, the most significant postexilic clan.

Since Benjamin is used as an inclusio in 1 Chronicles 8:1,40, 1 Chronicles 9:1a is the conclusion for the section which began in 2:3. **All Israel** was recorded in the genealogies. The land was settled. The Chronicler yearns for Israel to once again fully occupy the land under the reign of another Davidic king. The genealogies point to the inheritance of Israel and the inclusiveness of the coming reign.

III. POSTEXILIC ISRAEL IN JERUSALEM (9:1b-44)

Chronicles began with world history (Adam to Israel), moved the reader through the history of Israel (Judah–Levites–Benjamin), and concludes with the return of Israel to Jerusalem after the exile. Several of the genealogies included postexilic times (David, Aaron, and Saul). Now the Chronicler narrows his postexilic concern to the settlement of Jerusalem. This emphasizes Judah (David), Levi (temple), and Benjamin (Jerusalem). "Genealogies that once seemed dead are now alive again (cf. Ezek 37:1-14), and [the Chronicler] and his community are living witnesses to a hope rooted in the very creation of humanity" (SELMAN, 1:125).

First Chronicles 9 summarizes the postexilic situation and brings the history of Israel down to his own time (between a half generation to three generations after the repopulation of Nehemiah's

Jerusalem, e.g., 420–350 B.C.; cf. SELMAN, 1:124). First Chronicles 1–9 tells the whole story, but it is only the skeleton. The skeleton emphasizes continuity, God's faithfulness, and God's gracious redemption of Israel from exile. The narrative of 1 Chronicles 10–2 Chronicles 36 puts flesh on the bones. It not only explains the exile, but, more importantly, it explains the mercy of God in the light of the Davidic promise. It offers the postexilic community the hope of renewed communion through the experience of God in the temple and the hope of a Davidic heir.

JAPHET (202) structures 1 Chronicles 9 into three major divisions: (1) Introduction (1 Chr 9:1b-2), (2) Inhabitants of Jerusalem (1 Chr 9:3-34), and (3) The Genealogy of Saul (1 Chr 9:35-44).

A. INTRODUCTION (9:1b-2)

Judah was exiled into Babylonia because of **their unfaithfulness** (1 Chr 9:1b; cf. 2:7; 5:25), but now some resettled their land. This brief introduction anticipates the conclusion of Chronicles (2 Chr 36:20-23). God punished the unfaithfulness of Judah in exile but also graciously resettled them in their land. The twin themes of retribution and grace are present. The postexilic community lives in the era of grace: they are a redeemed, restored community.

The introduction outlines the next section. The first to resettle were **Israelites, priests, Levites and temple servants** (1 Chr 9:2; cf. Neh 11:3 though Chronicles drops "the descendants of Solomon's servants"). First Chronicles 9:3-34 describes the resettlement of Jerusalem according to this structure except that temple servants are not mentioned again.

B. INHABITANTS OF JERUSALEM (9:3-34)

This section is divides into three major parts: (1) Israelites (1 Chr 9:3-9), (2) Priests (1 Chr 9:10-13), and Levites (1 Chr 9:14-34). The Levites receive the most attention since Chronicles has an extended section concerning their temple functions (1 Chr 9:19-33). The list of inhabitants follows Nehemiah 11:4-19 (1 Chr 9:3-18; cf. BRAUN, 132-138, and JAPHET, 202-206, for detailed discussions of differences, and see SELMAN, 1:123-124 on why it is more likely that Chronicles depended on Nehemiah than vice versa). The additional material is unparalleled in canonical literature (1 Chr 9:19-33).

1. Israelites (9:3-9)

While Nehemiah 11:4 only includes Judahites and Benjamites, Chronicles adds **Ephraim** and **Manasseh** to the inhabitants of **Jerusalem** (1 Chr 9:3). The largest clans of the northern kingdom are represented among the redeemed community in Jerusalem. However, his genealogical lists only include **Judah** and **Benjamin**.

Chronicles includes some genealogical data for three sons of Judah: **Perez** (1 Chr 9:4), Shelah (1 Chr 9:5; variant of "Shilon"), and Zerah (1 Chr 9:6). Nehemiah only includes Perez, and Chronicles omits the reference to the "warriors" (Neh 11:6). The Benjamites are grouped under four family heads (1 Chr 9:7-8): **Sallu, Ibneiah, Elah,** and **Meshullam**.

After these genealogies Chronicles counts the total of their descendants living in Jerusalem (1 Chr 9:6,9). This provides continuity with the past and solidifies their presence in the restored community. The Judahites numbered 690 and the Benjamites numbered 956. Jerusalem has been repopulated with its ancestral people. God is faithful.

2. Priests (9:10-13)

Not only has Israel resettled Jerusalem, but the priests are present too. Their number (1,790) overshadows Judah and Benjamin.

The genealogical list of priests has been telescoped so that the general line is documented. The text has six priestly families: **Jedaiah, Jehoiarib** (presumably Nehemiah's Joiarib), **Jakin, Azariah, Adaiah,** and **Maasai** (a variant of Nehemiah's Amashsai; cf. BRAUN, 134-135, 140).

While Chronicles drops Nehemiah's reference to "warriors" (Neh 11:14), they both refer to **Ahitub** as an **official** (נָגִיד, $n^e g\hat{\imath}d$) in the "house of God" (1 Chr 9:11; Neh 11:11). This term occurs in

Chronicles 21 times but only once in Nehemiah. This may refer to the high priest, but not necessarily (cf. 2 Chr 35:8).

Chronicles also adds that the priests are **responsible for ministering in the house of God** (1 Chr 9:13). "Responsible" might be better translated "qualified" as this probably reflects some kind of registration system (cf. 1 Chr 6:32,48).

3. Levites (9:14-34)

JAPHET (202) divides this section into three parts: (1) Registration (1 Chr 9:14-18), (2) Functions (1 Chr 9:19-33), and (3) Conclusion (1 Chr 9:34). While 1 Chronicles 9:14-17 parallels Nehemiah 11:15-19, 1 Chronicles 9:18-33 is unique material.

Registration of Levites (9:14-18)

BRAUN (141) believes the emphasis of this section is the correlation of the families of **Shemaiah**, **Mattaniah**, and **Obadiah** with their ancestors **Merari** (1 Chr 9:14), **Asaph** (1 Chr 9:15), and **Jeduthun** (1 Chr 9:16).

While it may seem that 1 Chronicles 9:17-18 belongs more with 1 Chronicles 9:19-33 than with 1 Chronicles 9:14-16, the concluding statement of 1 Chronicles 9:18 binds it with what comes before it. Chronicles solidifies the Levitical character of the gatekeepers. Thus, **Levites** serves as an inclusio for this section (1 Chr 9:14,18). Perhaps this is intended to legitimize the gatekeepers (cf. 1 Chr 9:26). The next section attends to their functions.

Four gatekeepers are mentioned by name with **Shallum** as the chief (**head**). Stationed at the **King's Gate**, where royalty would enter the temple, Shallum bears the major responsibility for the purity and honor of the temple. **Gatekeepers** were temple guardians which included opening the temple doors in the morning, guarding it at night, and responsibility for the temple's rooms and treasuries (1 Chr 9:26-27; 26:1-19).

Levitical Functions (9:19-33)

This section highlights the gatekeepers, but it also describes different roles in the temple.

The Gatekeepers (9:19-29)

JAPHET (214) calls this the Magna Carta of the **gatekeepers** as it grounds their role in biblical history. The gatekeepers are **Korahites** (1 Chr 9:19). Their role is derived from the historic example of the high priest **Phinehas** in Numbers 25:7-13. The Chronicler assumes his readers know the story (1 Chr 9:20). Phinehas defended the honor of God against idolatry. The gatekeeper emulates Phinehas. This highlights the seriousness of their task. Just as **the LORD was with** Phinehas (1 Chr 9:20), so he is with the gatekeepers in the Chronicler's day. They guard the entrance into the presence of the Lord so that nothing impure or ritually defiled may enter (cf. 2 Chr 23:19).

Not only did the gatekeepers have their historic beginnings in the zeal of Phinehas, but they were also confirmed in their task by **David** and **Samuel** (1 Chr 9:22). The authority of the gatekeepers, then, is priestly (Phinehas), royal (David), and prophetic (Samuel). This kind of legitimization may indicate that the role of the gatekeepers at the time of the Chronicler was suspect (Dirksen, "1 Chronicles 9," 95). Since Samuel died before David's reign, how could Samuel be involved in this Davidic action? The reference is not to Samuel's concert action with David, but Samuel's own gatekeeping function at the tabernacle (SELMAN, 1:129; cf. 1 Sam 3:15). Perhaps Samuel had already begun to organize the gatekeepers and David completed the task (PAYNE, 4:367).

They **numbered 212** and rotated service in the temple for seven-day periods. Levites were stationed at the four doors into the temple and these **principal** (or, mighty) gatekeepers had the **key** (lit., "over the opening") to the doors of the temple (1 Chr 9:27). **Their brothers** lived in surrounding villages so as to have easy access to Jerusalem and its temple (like the singers, Neh 12:29).

While some see 1 Chronicles 9:28-29 as relating the functions of other Levites (BRAUN, 132; WILLIAMSON, 91), these verses are a further elaboration of the role of the gatekeepers (JAPHET, 217). In addition to "guarding" the doors, they also cared for temple articles, furniture, and materials for offerings of bread and wine as well as incense (JOHNSTONE, 1:126-127).

JOHNSTONE (1:125) calls attention to the various ways in which the sanctuary is described: **Tent** (1 Chr 9:19), **Tent of Meeting** (1 Chr 9:21), **dwelling of the LORD** (1 Chr 9:19), **house of the LORD**

(1 Chr 9:23), the **house called the Tent**, (1 Chr 9:23), and **the house of God** (1 Chr 9:26-27). These descriptions are "panchronic," that is, they come from various moments in Israel's history — Phinehas, David, Samuel, postexilic community. This testifies to the "enduring significance" of the Lord's presence in his house as the "mechanism for securing the holiness of the people." The Holy God dwells among a holy people through the atonement offered by his priestly servants (1 Chr 6:48-49).

Other Levitical Functions (9:30-33)

The introduction of the word **priest** in 1 Chronicles 9:30 separates this task from the gatekeepers. The preparation of the incense (1 Chr 9:30) is a priestly task. Levites may serve in the other roles. Some mixed the **spices**, others baked the **bread**, and others prepared for the **sabbath**. Some of these functions are even attributed to gatekeepers (**Mattithiah** bakes the bread). These functions are probably listed here because they are closely associated with the gatekeepers. Even the **musicians** are mentioned (1 Chr 9:33), not to detail their duties, but to indicate their relationship to the gatekeepers. In other words, while the musicians stayed in the rooms of the temple, they were not responsible for its daily maintenance. That was the task of the gatekeepers (Dirksen, "1 Chronicles 9," 96).

Conclusion (9:34)

The formula **heads of the Levite families** closes the discussion of the Levites, and the final phrase, **they lived in Jerusalem**, recalls 1 Chronicles 9:2. This concludes Chronicles's discussion of the Israelites, priests, and Levites who lived in postexilic Jerusalem.

This inclusio about postexilic Jerusalem concludes the genealogies of all Israel beginning with Adam. It underscores the continuity of God's people throughout history and God's accompanying faithfulness. WILCOX (48-50) calls attention to the continuity between the 10th and 5th centuries in Chronicles. David, the temple, the Levites, Jerusalem, and "all Israel" ground the hope of God's people. Christians find God's faithfulness in Jesus Christ through whom we trace our heritage of faith back through David and Abraham (Matt 1:1) to Adam (Luke 3:38). Consequently, we are one people of God united by one faith in the one God.

C. THE GENEALOGY OF SAUL (9:35-44)

This genealogical list is practically the same as 1 Chronicles 8:29-38 (with some differences, e.g., **Jeiel** appears in the MT here, while it is absent in 1 Chronicles 8:29; and **Ahaz** is omitted in 1 Chronicles 8:35 but retained here). The previous list emphasized settlement, but this is Saul's royal line. It anticipates 1 Chronicles 10. The historical narrative begins with the death of **Saul** and the fall of his dynasty. Consequently, the repetition of the genealogy serves as a transition from the genealogical genre to the narrative genre of 1 Chronicles 10.

First Chronicles 10:13-14 contains a negative assessment of Saul's fall. Just as Judah was unfaithful and went into exile (1 Chr 9:1b), Saul was unfaithful and lost his dynasty (1 Chr 10:13). But Judah returns to possess Jerusalem, and Saul's descendants live in the city (1 Chr 9:38). This testifies to the grace of God. Saul's descendants live in Jerusalem alongside Davidic and Levitical families. Postexilic Jerusalem is filled with "all Israel," and it bears witness to God's mercy and faithfulness.

1 CHR 10:1–2 CHR 9:31 – PART TWO

THE UNITED MONARCHY

The United Monarchy in Chronicles is the reign of David and Solomon. During their reigns Israel achieved territorial integrity, united their worship and located their religio-political center in Jerusalem. Before these kings, Israel never had territorial integrity, and after these kings Israel was divided in its religious and political life. David and Solomon are the kings of the "Golden Age" of Israel.

First and Second Samuel and 1–2 Kings (Dtr) paint a different picture. Even though Dtr lauds the territorial, religious, and political achievements of David and Solomon, it also shows that David's reign is marred by sin, rebellion, and disunity and that Solomon's reign is tainted by foreign influence and idolatry. These stains are missing in Chronicles. The Chronicler intentionally omits all the scars (except two). Why does he omit what everyone knows? The Chronicler is focused on a specific theme. Even when he tells the history of David and Solomon, it is not comprehensive. He selects materials from Dtr and other sources that serve his purpose. He is interested in the Davidic promise, the temple, and Jerusalem. He applies these themes to his postexilic community. To rehearse the sins of David would not serve his purpose as he engenders faith in the Davidic promises and the meaning of God's presence in the temple. He does not ignore David's sins when they are part of the temple's story, that is, moving the ark (1 Chr 13) and the census (1 Chr 21).

The story of the United Monarchy, then, is the story of the temple in the context of Israel's achievement of territorial integrity where God gives his people rest in the land of promise. The "Golden Age" of Israel underscores God's promises, presence, and faithfulness.

This section falls into three parts (BRAUN, xli): (1) The Reign of David (1 Chr 10:1–22:1), (2) The Transition from David to Solomon (1 Chr 22:2–29:30), and (3) The Reign of Solomon (2 Chr 1:1–9:31).

The reign of David is focused on the ark, temple, and military victories that gave Israel rest. The transition period describes the preparations for the temple and the institution of the temple cultus. The reign of Solomon describes the building and dedication of the temple.

Chronicles tells the story of the temple during the United Monarchy. But "temple" is not simply a building. It is the presence of God among his people. The holy God sanctifies a people for himself and enjoys rest in communion with his people. The temple is God's sabbatical presence among his people, that is, the "rest of God" where his people enjoy communion with him (1 Chr 23:25; 28:2; Ps 95:11; Heb 4:1-11). While God is omnipresent, he is present in the temple in a special redemptive sense.

Christians read Chronicles with an eye on God's grace, presence, and faithfulness. It is our story too. God gives his presence to his people, sanctifies them, and demonstrates his faithfulness. This is the story of God in Jesus Christ. God gives his presence to his people by dwelling in them through the Holy Spirit (Eph 2:21-22). God sanctifies his people through that indwelling presence (1 Pet 1:2). God is faithful to his promises as that presence seals our future redemption (2 Cor 1:21-22).

I. THE REIGN OF DAVID (10:1–22:1)

This section covers the reign of David from his enthronement to the wars which secured Israel's territorial integrity. The nation moves from chaos to order, from war to peace, and from neglect of the ark to the centralization of worship. The reign of David is the establishment of God's rest among his people in the land he promised. In this sense, David is the "founding father" of Israel (Wright, "Founding," 45-59).

The structure of the text is threefold: (1) David Becomes King (1 Chr 10:1–12:40), (2) David Establishes the Religious Cult (1 Chr 13:1–17:27), and (3) David Wins Wars (1 Chr 18:1–22:1). David basically does two things after he becomes King. First, he renews the worship of God around the ark. Second, he brings peace to Israel. In both cases, he corrects the failings of his predecessor, King Saul, who did not inquire of the ark (1 Chr 13:3) and who could not bring peace and territorial integrity (1 Chr 10:7). David does both. As a result the nation is ready to build a temple for Yahweh.

A. DAVID BECOMES KING (10:1–12:40)

This section begins with the death of Saul (1 Chr 10:14) and ends with a royal banquet in David's honor (1 Chr 12:38-40). The account is not as extensive as 2 Samuel, but it provides the material necessary to accomplish the Chronicler's dual purpose: military success (including Jerusalem) and divine appointment as king over "all Israel."

David's accession is focused on his time in Hebron. While the death of Saul is the occasion of his accession (1 Chr 10), David's rise is grounded in the support he received while in the wilderness, Ziklag, and Hebron (1 Chr 11–12).

1. The Death of Saul (10:1-14)

The Chronicler has little interest in the reign of Saul. He knows Saul (1 Chr 10:13-14), but Saul does not figure into his temple theme.

However, there are several reasons for including the death of Saul though there is no discussion of his reign. The chapter is more than just "secondary" (MYERS, 1:78). One purpose is to lead the reader into the reign of David. The death of Saul serves as a transition to a major topic of Chronicles — David. The death of the villain Saul leads to the heroic David. An ignoble death gives way to a noble life. The transitory reign of Saul leads to the permanent rule of the Davidic dynasty (Zalewiski, 449-450).

Another purpose contrasts the faithlessness of Saul with the faithfulness of David. Saul shares in the unfaithfulness of Israel. In fact, "unfaithful" in 1 Chronicles 10:13 recalls the term "unfaithful" in 1 Chronicles 9:1. Saul is removed as king just as Judah was removed from the land. The death of Saul is paradigmatic for the other kings of Judah (ACKROYD, "Chronicler," 3-32; *Chronicler*, 311-343). Will the subsequent kings of Judah follow the example of Saul or David? More importantly, will the readers of Chronicles recognize that the "exile" of Saul is followed by the "restoration" of David? Since a David can follow a Saul, Chronicles teaches that restoration can follow exile (WILLIAMSON, 93).

This narrative also clarifies David's accession to the throne. Some have suspected that there was an oral tradition that accused David of overthrowing Saul. Chronicles makes it clear that the Lord removed Saul and installed David as king. "Thus," Zalewiski (466) concludes, "it enables the reader to see David's rise to kingship as legitimate and ideal." It is divine election.

This section divides into three parts: (1) The Battle of Gilboa (1 Chr 10:1-7), (2) The Body of Saul (1 Chr 10:8-12), and (3) A Theological Judgment (1 Chr 10:13-14). The Chronicler follows the order of the account in 1 Samuel 31:1-13 and depends on it, though he may have some independent sources that shape his account differently (cf. Ho, 82-106, for the possibility of a common source behind 1 Sam and 1 Chr). Ackroyd (*Chronicler*, 313-323) believes the Chronicler is "exegeting" 1 Samuel 31.

The Battle of Gilboa (10:1-7)

The battle is described in 1 Chronicles 10:1-5 and its aftermath in 1 Chronicles 10:6-7. In the first part the Chronicler makes few changes to the Samuel account (linguistic preferences, stylistic changes, and a few omissions). Essentially, 1 Chronicles 10:1-5 reproduces 1 Samuel 31:1-5.

The Chronicler begins with this Philistine battle because he is interested in the transfer of the kingdom from Saul to David. The Chronicler emphasizes the death of Saul and his dynasty (**died** occurs at the beginning and end of 1 Chr 10:6).

Ancient military tactics intended to capture or kill the king. So, after killing his three sons (named in 1 Chr 10:2), they pursue the king (cf. 1 Kings 22:31). Saul is wounded but he fears torture. His request for death at the hands of his **armor-bearer** is a request for mercy. The armor-bearer refuses. Dtr sanctions the armor-bearer's response when David confronts the liar who claims to have killed Saul with the question, "Why were you not afraid to lift your hand to destroy the Lord's anointed?" (2 Sam 1:14). The suicide of Saul is, as a narrative, the bad ending of a bad life (though many suicides are cries for help rather than defiant acts of unfaithfulness). The narrative rings with disapproval since it is Saul's climactic act of rebellion. Not even the anointed one has the right to take his own life. Saul dies because he is **unfaithful**.

In describing the aftermath of the battle, the Chronicler makes important changes to 1 Samuel. Two are particularly significant. While 1 Samuel 31:6 says that "all his men died" on that day, the Chronicler substitutes **all his house died** (1 Chr 10:6). Both note that Saul's **three sons died**. The Chronicler knows there was a fourth son, Esh-Baal (or, Ish-Bosheth) since he included him in the earlier genealogies (1 Chr 8:33; 9:39) and Saul's line extended into postexilic times. Does he intend to say that Ish-Bosheth died in this battle which would conflict with 1 Samuel? His readers knew better. Ish-Bosheth's reign is assumed in 1 Chronicles 3:4 and 29:27. This language reflects the end of the Saulide dynasty. THOMPSON (111; cf. WILLIAMSON, 93) points out that the Chronicler also omitted "that same day" so that the point may effectively mean the end of the dynasty rather than the death of all of Saul's sons. Since the genealogies continue the house of Saul, the Chronicler's point is that "so far as maintaining kingly power and a royal line was concerned, his house was hereafter in reality defunct" (JOHNSTONE, 1:133; SELMAN, 1:134). The royal dynasty (**house**) of Saul is finished. The Chronicler has telescoped history. As Zalewiski (462) comments, "what interests [the Chronicler] is not making an exact description of the historical event. Rather, he concentrated on the subject that served his purpose. The death of Saul and his sons on **Mount Gilboa** reflects the work of the providential hand which put an end to the line of Saul."

The Body of Saul (10:8-12)

This section divides into two parts: (1) the desecration of Saul's body (1 Chr 10:8-10) and (2) its burial (1 Chr 10:11-12).

The Desecration of Saul's Body (10:8-10)

The Chronicler's changes to Samuel's account have been the "object of over-interpretation" (BRAUN, 150). Chronicles omits the beheading (1 Sam 31:9), substitutes **gods** for "Ashtoreths" (1 Sam 31:10), and hangs the **head** of Saul **in the temple of Dagon** instead of fastening "his body to the wall of Beth Shan" (1 Sam 31:10). These changes have been taken to not only have tendentious meaning (though some may be textual; cf. McKenzie, Chronicler's, 59) but also, by some, to involve historical fiction.

Chronicles assumes the beheading when Saul's head is hung in the temple of Dagon. It may be that the head of Saul was hung in one temple while his body was hung on the wall of another. Samuel does not say what was done with the head, only what the Philistines did with the body. Archaeological evidence confirms the existence of several temples in Beth Shan during the Iron Age. Chronicles is interested in the head of Saul, not the body.

The explicit mention of Saul's head in the temple of Dagon may have theological significance. Perhaps the Chronicler contrasts the fall of Dagon before the ark (1 Sam 5:1-4) and the loss of Goliath's head (1 Sam 17:54) with the defeat of Saul by the **Philistines** (Ackroyd, *Chronicler*, 316-318). The Philistines win only because the power of the Lord permits them. While the Philistines celebrate as if their gods had accomplished some great victory, Chronicles clarifies that this was the Lord's hand. Yahweh defeated Saul.

The Burial of Saul's Body (10:11-12)

First Chronicles 10:12 differs from 1 Samuel 31:12-13 in a few particulars as he omits: (1) the reference to Beth Shan and (2) the burning of the bodies. Beth Shan is probably omitted because he has not mentioned it previously. SELMAN (1:136) suggests that the burning of the bodies is omitted to "avoid associating" Saul "with criminal activity (cf. Lv. 20:14; 21:9; Jos. 7:25)." McKenzie (*Chronicler's*, 59-60), on the other hand, thinks it is more likely that Chronicles was using a different text-type of Samuel that did not include the burning. The main point, however, is that the people of **Jabesh Gilead** honored **Saul and his sons** by providing a burial and fast for them. The people of Jabesh Gilead were particularly indebted to Saul's military exploits (cf. 1 Sam 11).

A Theological Obituary (10:13-14)

This theological judgment is unique to Chronicles. Dtr would regard the judgment as sound since his narrative is the fulfillment of a prophecy by Samuel that Saul and his dynasty would be dethroned. Chronicles makes this explicit. Saul is not a tragic figure, but a dethroned sinner.

Yahweh executed Saul (1 Chr 10:14; **the LORD put him to death**). He offers three reasons why this was a just judgment. First, Saul was **unfaithful**, a word used to describe Judah's exile (1 Chr 9:1). This word is only used in Chronicles where there is no other biblical parallel to his text (16 times in this sense; 1 Chr 2:7; 5:25; 9:1; 2 Chr 12:2; 26:16,18,19,22; 29:6,19; 30:7; 33:19; 36:14). This theological judgment is doubly emphasized: "Saul died in his unfaithfulness with which he was unfaithful to the Lord." Second, Saul **did not keep the word of the LORD and even consulted a medium for guidance**. This is an example of paronomasia (Kalimi, "Paronomasia," 37). Saul (שָׁאוּל) consulted (שְׁאוֹל, *šᵊʾōl*) a medium for advice. "Saul" and "consult" are the same Hebrew consonants. Third, Saul **did not inquire of the LORD** (Saul seeks the Lord in 1 Sam 28:6 inappropriately). "Seek" (דָּרַשׁ, *dāraš*) is important in Chronicles (occurs 33 times in this sense; cf. 1 Chr 28:9; 2 Chr 7:14). Saul did not seek the Lord like David (1 Chr 14:10). Instead, he sought a medium for guidance (לִדְרוֹשׁ, *lidrôš*). The unfaithful one forsakes the Lord, but the faithful one seeks the Lord.

Whether the Chronicler has three specific events in mind drawn from the Dtr account is uncertain, though the "medium" is surely a reference to Saul's visit to the witch of Endor (1 Sam 28:8-25). That visit was a death sentence for Saul (cf. Deut 18:9-13). SELMAN (1:137) comments, "Saul's syncretism is a microcosm of Israel's unfaithfulness in the Old Testament." The Chronicler may also be thinking about Saul's other disobedient acts (1 Sam 13:8-9; 15:2-3). But the Chronicler is not just talking about Saul. They are general descriptions of Israel's sin. They are the reasons Israel went into exile, and they are the reasons **Saul died**.

Chronicles legitimizes the reign of David by attributing his installation to God himself. The Lord **turned the kingdom** (אֶת־הַמְּלוּכָה יַסֵּב, *yassēb eth-hammᵊlûkah*) over to David (1 Chr 10:14). Chronicles uses this expression in 1 Chronicles 12:23 where, according to the word of the Lord, armed men came to **turn Saul's kingdom** over to David (לְהָסֵב מַלְכוּת שָׁאוּל, *lᵊhāsēb malkûth šāûl*). This is a divine transfer. The noun form of the verb "to turn" also describes the transfer of rule to the northern kingdom from Rehoboam (2 Chr 10:15; נְסִבָּה, *nᵊsibbāh*, "turn of events"). God turned events so that the north sought their own king (Machinist, 105-120).

God has transferred the kingship from Saul to David. This is the main point of 1 Chronicles 10–12 as is clear from the use of the verb "to turn" at the beginning (1 Chr 10:14) and end (1 Chr 12:23) of this section.

2. The Enthronement of David in Hebron (11:1–12:40)

Williamson ("We Are Yours," 169) suggests a chiastic organization which emphasizes the growing strength and resultant enthronement of David.

(a) David's Coronation at Hebron (11:1-9)
  (b) Support for David at Hebron (11:10-47)
    (c) Support for David at Ziklag (12:1-7)
      (d) Support for David at the Stronghold (12:8-15)
      (d′) Support for David at the Stronghold (12:16-18)
    (c′) Support for David at Ziklag (12:19-22)
  (b′) Support for David at Hebron (12:23-37)
(a′) David's Coronation at Hebron (12:38-40)

These chapters contain the only material about David in Chronicles that predates his reign. This is the only indication in Chronicles that David was a wandering warrior and his rise to the throne was a long process. While the Chronicler does not reproduce the Saul-David intrigue of 1 Samuel, he was not ignorant of it. He did not include it because it did not suit his purpose. His intent is to demonstrate that David's enthronement was supported by "all Israel," including various representatives of the clans that joined him at the stronghold, Ziklag, and Hebron before he captured Jerusalem.

This material also demonstrates that David was a great military leader as he gathered an army around him. It highlights the warrior dimension of David's life as Chronicles anticipates his successes on the battlefield (McCarter, 117-129).

Chronicles highlights David's coronation. It is a thematic rather than chronological account. It begins with "all Israel" coming to Hebron to crown David king, and it ends with a coronation banquet in Hebron. Between those two bookends is a "flashback" to David's growing support before he was crowned. Instead of the Chronicler manipulating material and putting it in the wrong chronological order, he has carefully crafted a history that moves into the past and back to the future in order to emphasize David's national strength.

All Israel came to David. Divine providence brought David the support he needed. The phrase "coming to David" pervades the narrative (cf. 1 Chr 11:1,3,10; 12:1,8,16,19-20,22,23,31,38).

David's Coronation at Hebron (11:1-9)

The Chronicler moves directly to the coronation of David and skips over Dtr's history of the reign of Ish-Bosheth. He has no interest in that story because it does not serve his purpose and he has dealt summarily with the end of Saul's dynasty in 1 Chronicles 10. The Chronicler wants to move into the heart of his concerns: David, Jerusalem, the ark, and the temple. The "incidental" history of Ish-Bosheth would divert his attention and lengthen his story (THOMPSON, 115). The Chronicler does not reject Dtr's version (the gathering of support in Hebron, Ziklag, and the stronghold indicates the Chronicler knew there was opposition). Rather, he quickly gets to the end game — David's reign. The Chronicler is interested in the "final result rather than the process" (JOHNSTONE, 1:142). He is "selecting and simplifying" rather than contradicting (McCONVILLE, 22).

David Anointed King (11:1-3)

This text parallels 1 Samuel 5:1-3 (1 Sam 5:4-5 is present in 1 Chr 3:4). There are several differences between them. Chronicles changes Samuel's "all the tribes of Israel" (1 Sam 5:1) to **all Israel** (1 Chr 11:1). While in Samuel "Israel" refers to the northern tribes, in Chronicles "Israel" refers to the whole nation. The emphatic "all Israel" underscores not only the Chronicler's inclusiveness, but also the united character of David's support throughout the nation. Further, the Chronicler says they **came together** (or, "gathered"; 1 Chr 11:1) rather than merely "came" (1 Sam 5:1). There is a stress on the twin ideas of "gathering" and "acknowledgement" in Chronicles and this first appears here at the coronation of David (cf. 2 Chr 15:9-10; 20:4; 23:2; 24:5; 25:5; 32:4,6; cf. JOHNSTONE, 1:142).

Chronicles also adds a prophetic fulfillment motif in 1 Chronicles 11:3: **as the LORD had promised through Samuel.** The prophecy is quoted in 1 Chronicles 11:2. Chronicles assumes the story of

Samuel's anointing of David as the elect one (1 Sam 15:28; 16:1-3; cf. WILLIAMSON, 97; ACKROYD, 52).

When all Israel comes, they acknowledge his leadership during the reign of Saul (1 Chr 11:2 is the only time Saul is called **king** in Chronicles). This assumes the stories in Samuel when David led Saul's army to victories. Literally, the Hebrew text reads that David "led out" and "led back" Israel so that his **military** prowess and the sanction of Yahweh was demonstrated. David's military leadership endeared him to the people.

Yahweh appointed David the leader of Israel, and all Israel acknowledges it. **Shepherd** is a common description of a king and fits Israel's nomadic past. **Ruler** or leader is a common word for a guardian (to be in charge of a special task) and may refer to his military role as protector (cf. 1 Chr 11:10ff). God chose David as a leader among his people (Chronicles adds **my people** in 1 Chr 11:2).

David's installation was by covenant (**compact**) with **all the elders of Israel**. Representative leaders act on behalf of various tribes in Israel. The relationship between David and Israel, just as between God and Israel, is a covenantal one. Even though David is from the house of Judah, by covenant David reigns over all Israel. In light of the covenant, David is **anointed** and proclaimed **king**. The anointing by the elders acknowledges David's status as king: it is a "sacramental" recognition of a divine anointing (SELMAN, 1:138). The transition from Saul to David is complete.

David is king by virtue of prophetic affirmation, military victory, and acknowledgement by the **elders** of the people. These coalesce to legitimize the reign of David as king over all Israel (Ps 78:70-71).

David Conquers Jerusalem (11:4-9)

The conjunction of Jerusalem and Hebron as royal cities is not as incongruous as might first appear, especially since David will ultimately reign from Jerusalem. Chronicles has already noted the divided reign of David: seven years in Hebron and thirty-three in Jerusalem (1 Chr 3:4). Consequently, the conjunction of the two is not surprising. The Chronicler accounts for the move from Hebron to Jerusalem as he anticipates his focus on Jerusalem. The conquest of Jerusalem is the culmination of his coronation in Hebron where it is his "first and foremost" act as king even though the Chronicler knows David ruled in Hebron for seven years (JAPHET, 234). This is a thematic, not a chronological, structure. It anticipates the next major topic: the move of the ark to Jerusalem in 1 Chronicles 13–16.

As the relocated capital of Israel, **Jerusalem** is the nation's central city. Yahweh is the "God of Jerusalem" (2 Chr 32:19), and Jerusalem is the place of his residence (1 Chr 23:25). The city is named 151 times in Chronicles which is 22% of the 669 times it appears in the Hebrew Bible (Beentjes, "Jerusalem," 17). The Chronicler has a special interest in the city. He introduces us to the city at the beginning of David's reign even though he knows that David reigned in Hebron for seven years (1 Chr 3:4; 29:27). The Chronicler does not follow Samuel but intentionally introduces Jerusalem at the beginning of David's reign. WILLIAMSON (97-98) notes that the Chronicler sometimes rearranges Samuel's material. Consequently, when he preserves it in Samuel's order, it is intentional.

While there is no evidence that Jerusalem was ever known by a different name (the Amarna letters refer to the city as "Jerusalem" before the entrance of Israel into the land), those who inhabited the city and lived around it were **Jebusites**, and thus the city was called **Jebus** by Israel as a way of referring to the city before it became the **City of David** (19 times in Chronicles), that is, **Jerusalem** (WILLIAMSON, 98-99). It is David's city because his royal throne was located there.

The Chronicler's account differs in several particulars from 1 Samuel 5:6-10 (cf. McKenzie, *Chronicler's*, 41-45). He omits the Jebusite taunt (or curse; Derby, 241-245) that even the lame and blind could defend the city against David (1 Sam 5:6,8). The Chronicler also stresses the role of **Joab** who is not mentioned in 1 Samuel (cf. WILLIAMSON, 99). He probably supplied this information from another source (McKenzie, *Chronicler's*, 44). Joab is the leader of the attack on **Jebus** (Josh 15:18; 18:16,28) and is also involved in its repair (1 Chr 11:8; cf. the same word in Neh 4:2). The city must have suffered some damage during the capture or perhaps the terraces had fallen into disrepair. The city was built on a hill with terraces flowing down the hillside. They needed constant repair. Another difference is the absence of the "water shaft" as the means of entrance into the city (1 Sam 5:8; cf. Kleven, 34-35). He may have omitted it because it was no longer obvious in postexilic Jerusalem. Overall these changes reflect the Chronicler's interest in the simple event rather than the drama, though he uses it to introduce Joab. In contrast to Dtr, Joab always appears in a good light in Chronicles. But the Chronicler's purpose is not the political intrigue of the royal house, but the establishment of the Davidic kingdom in which Joab plays a role.

Chronicles emphasizes the support of **all the Israelites** (lit., "all Israel") and the presence of the Lord. Whereas 1 Samuel 5:6 reads "the king and his men," 1 Chronicles 11:4 reads **David and** all Israel **marched to Jerusalem**. The change is emphatic. The capture of Jerusalem was an act of "all Israel" under David's leadership. Further, the Chronicler concludes his story with the words of 1 Samuel 5:10: **the LORD Almighty** (יְהוָה צְבָאֹות, *YHWH ṣᵉbā'ôth*) **was with him** (cf. 1 Chr 17:24). His appointment as king and his capture of Jerusalem were expressions of divine activity within Israel. God has chosen David and Jerusalem (JAPHET, "King's Sanctuary," 132-139). Unlike Saul, who was defeated by the Philistines, David defeated the inhabitants of Jebus.

Support for David at Hebron (11:10-47)

While 1 Chronicles 11:11-41a is derived from 1 Samuel 23:8-39, 1 Chronicles 11:10 is the Chronicler's "heading." This section includes two different units: (1) a heroic deed list (1 Chr 11:11-25), and (2) a list of names (1 Chr 11:27-47). The last part of the second section (1 Chr 11:41b-47) is not found in 1 Samuel.

Though this section might read like a telephone book at times, it is theologically significant. These are Israel's heroes. Just as the United States has its Daniel Boones and Davy Crocketts, so Israel had its Benaiah and Jashobeam. These names are not familiar to us, but they reminded Israel of their heroic past. Every community needs their heroes of faith. Congregations have local heroes. These are God's "mighty people" whom he has made great through faith (cf. Heb 11). More significantly this is God's army (1 Chr 12:22). God helps David by rallying a warrior community around him. The Lord of Hosts will lead this army of heroes. David does not accomplish his divine mission alone. God surrounds him with a community.

God's leaders are not lone rangers nor do they lead without the help of others.

The Heading (11:10)

The heading (1 Chr 11:10) sets the tone for the whole section. It displays David's support from **all Israel** according to the Lord's promise (**the whole land** is "Israel" in Hebrew). Even the list of **mighty men** is inclusive and legitimates David's reign. Chronicles follows the order of Samuel by first recounting the heroic deeds of David's men and then filling out the mighty men by a simple list of names.

The Commanders or "the Three" (11:11-25)

One problem in this chapter is the designations **officers** (1 Chr 11:11), **three** (1 Chr 11:12,18,19,20,21,24,25), and **thirty** (1 Chr 11:15,25). The problem is that the plural **the officers** (הַשָּׁלוֹשִׁים, haššālôšîm) is very similar to the term **the thirty** (הַשְּׁלִישִׁים, haššālîšîm) and **the three** (הַשְּׁלוֹשָׁה/הַשְּׁלֹשָׁה, haššəlō[ô]šāh). The parallel to 1 Chronicles 11:11 in 2 Samuel 23:8 reads "the three" instead of "officers." The relationship between these three groups is rather confusing. BRAUN correctly suggests that whatever these designations mean the numerical forms have lost their original function (that is, "three" no longer means only three but refers to a class of officers). The general term "officers" is equally adequate though Braun (157, 160) unenthusiastically prefers "three" in 1 Chronicles 11:11. More specifically, Na'aman ("List," 71-79) argues that **Jashobeam** (1 Chr 11:11) is the chief of "the Three," who are **Eleazar** (1 Chr 11:12), Shammah (drawn from 2 Sam 23:11, perhaps lost in textual transmission in Chronicles; cf. MYERS, 1:142; WILLIAMSON, 102), and **Abishai** (1 Chr 11:20) followed by **Benaiah** (1 Chr 11:22) in charge of the king's **bodyguard** and then the rest of the officers ("the thirty"). On the other hand, Schley ("SALISIM," 321-326) argues that the "three" refer to special three-man squads who carried out specific and daring feats for the king, two of whom are singled out in this text because of their heroism, that is, Abishai and Benaiah. Whichever is correct (perhaps neither), the list of mighty men ("the thirty") is led by this group called "the three."

First Chronicles 11:11 begins the recounting of heroic deeds by some of David's more prominent mighty men, including the three.

Chronicles supplies some heroic snippets: Jashobeam, the **chief of the officers** (1 Chr 11:11), Eleazar, **one of the three** (1 Chr 11:12-14), three unnamed officers from the thirty but perhaps identified as the three (1 Chr 11:15-19), Abishai, the **chief of the Three** (1 Chr 11:20-21), and Benaiah, the royal bodyguard, who was not included among the thirty (1 Chr 12:22-25).

The described exploits did not necessarily happen prior to the time they came to Hebron. Rather, they are descriptive of their heroism whether before or after David becomes king. Their heroic deeds explain why they are commanders in the army.

Jashobeam successfully killed **three hundred men** (1 Chr 11:11; 1 Sam 23:8 read "eight hundred" due to textual corruption; cf. WILLIAMSON, 102). Eleazar fought with David at **Pas Dammim** despite the fact that the troops had fled the field. There the LORD gave them a **great victory** over the **Philistines** (1 Chr 11:12-14). **Three** anonymous men of the thirty secured a cup of **water** from the Philistine-held city of **Bethlehem**, and due to their valor David gave it as a drink-offering to **the LORD** (1 Chr 11:15-19). The NIV says **before the LORD**, but it should read "to the LORD" (NRSV). This was an act of worship which honored the loyalty and dedication of his men. Abishai, whose exact relationship with the "three" (some read "thirty") is difficult (cf. JAPHET, 246), killed **three hundred men and became as famous as the Three** (1 Chr 11:20-21). Benaiah receives the most extensive notice (MacKenzie, "Valiant," 18-35): he killed **two of Moab's best**, a **lion** and a tall **Egyptian** with his enemy's **spear** (1 Chr 11:22-25). He was not one of the Three, but he was put in charge of protecting David's life.

The "Mighty Men" or "the Thirty" (11:26-47)

This section comes from two sources. First Chronicles 11:26-41a is based on 2 Samuel 23:23-39 with several variant spellings and textual corruptions (JAPHET, 248-251). The source of 1 Chronicles 11:41b-47 is unknown. It does not appear in 2 Samuel 23.

The first section (1 Chr 11:26-41a) contains a list of thirty-one names, almost without comment. The presence of **Asahel** (1 Chr 11:26), who was killed during the war between David and Ish-Bosheth (2 Sam 2:23), indicates that this list originates prior to David's reign over Israel. Most of these names are from areas inhabited by Judah, Benjamin, and Simeon as well as the first Dan settlement. There are others from outside this southern region, but David's major support is drawn from the south. Nevertheless, some non-Israelites support David's rise (cf. 1 Chr 11:38-41a; **Zelek the Ammonite** in 1 Chr 11:39a and **Uriah the Hittite** in 1 Chr 11:41a [cf. 2 Sam 11–12]). The list is inclusive — David receives support from different quarters.

The second list (1 Chr 11:41b-47) is even more inclusive than the first, primarily individuals from the Transjordan. It includes **Reubenites** (1 Chr 11:42) and a **Moabite** (1 Chr 11:46). David's coalition is inclusive. It includes "all Israel" and more.

Just as David gathers a kingdom, so the postexilic community gathers one. David was inclusive in his gathering, so also must the postexilic community be. As JOHNSTONE (1:159) comments, "The presence of such foreigners recognizing David's role as leader of Israel among the world of nations is integral to the C[hronicler]'s overall theme."

Support for David at Ziklag (12:1-7)

This material has no canonical parallel. Nevertheless, JAPHET (257-258; cf. Williamson, "We Are Yours," 165-176) argues that the Chronicler's text is based upon earlier sources that lend it historical credibility (1 Chr 12:1-22).

The reference to **Ziklag** assumes the events of 1 Samuel 27 when the area was given to David by the Philistine king of Gath (1 Sam 27:6). This happened between David's wilderness period and his reign in Hebron. The Chronicler moves back in time to when David gathered support in Ziklag. The Chronicler is skillfully revisiting the past as it leads to the present. First Chronicles 12:1-7 chronologically precedes 1 Chronicles 11:1-9.

Besides the list of names (1 Chr 12:3-7), the first two verses offer an interesting aside concerning these mighty **warriors** ("mighty men," as in 1 Chr 11:26). They were with David when he was fleeing from **Saul**, but they were also Saul's own kinsmen, Benjamites. Twenty-three from **Benjamin** joined David against Saul and these were well-trained militia. They were gifted in archery and slings so that they could use either hand. Why these Benjamites joined David is unknown, but Chronicles emphasizes them because it legitimizes

David's rule over Israel. Indeed, for Chronicles, Saul is no longer king, but David is the anointed one. So the Benjamites are not traitors, but part of the army of God (1 Chr 12:22).

A group of **Korahites** is mentioned in 1 Chronicles 12:6. While some (JOHNSTONE, 1:161; PAYNE, 4:377) may identify these with Levites living in the territory of Benjamin, it is likely that this is just another group of Benjamites. "Korah" was a "very common name" (JAPHET, 261; cf. 1 Chr 2:43 for one from the tribe of Judah).

Support for David at the Stronghold (12:8-15)

This material has no canonical parallel. The reference to the **stronghold** differentiates both the time and place when these warriors joined David's ranks. The stronghold refers to David's hiding place in the wilderness (**desert**) near the Dead Sea. Many believe the stronghold is Engedi on the Dead Sea (1 Sam 24:1) or Adullam (1 Sam 22:1), but it may refer to various hiding places in wilderness caves.

Significantly, **Gadites** joined David at the stronghold. Gad is a northern tribe. David draws support from various parts of Israel while Saul still reigns. "All Israel" is coming to David.

The military character of this support (they are ranked and called **commanders**, 1 Chr 12:14) and their renowned abilities are highlighted by metaphorical language common to the ancient Near East. Their military skill is compared to **lions** (strength and courage) and **gazelles** (speed). The "main purpose" for lauding their abilities is to enhance David's status; that is, "the best and most capable men became his followers because they recognized in him the chosen vessel of Yahweh" (MYERS, 1:97).

Their expertise in military matters is stressed by their worth: one is worth a **hundred**, but their best is worth a **thousand**. This hyperbole emphasizes their value. Their memory is preserved by the heroic deed of clearing out opposition in the valley when the **Jordan** was torrentially flowing into the Dead Sea. The **first month** was springtime when the melting snows of Mt. Hermon flooded the valley and created a hazardous river crossing (THOMPSON, 124; cf. Josh 3:15f).

Support for David at the Stronghold (12:16-18)

When David fled from Saul into the wilderness, **Benjamites** and Judahites joined him which was the major part of his support (1 Chr

11:26-41). While the wilderness was David's lowest point, the Chronicler's "portrayal of the period presents David's star so clearly in ascendant that members of Saul's tribe, the Benjamites, cross over to him" (MANGAN, 34).

David's hesitation is natural. He is uncertain whether they have come to **help** or to **betray** (he was betrayed by Doeg, the Keilahites, and the Ziphites in 1 Sam 21-23, 26). If they have come to betray him, then David curses them (imprecation) according to God's judgment (cf. 1 Sam 24:12). If they have come to help, David offers them **peace** and unity (NRSV, "my heart will be knit to you"). Embedded in his oath is an assertion of innocence — he has done no violence (cf. possible quotation of Job 16:7; cf. JAPHET, 265). David invites others to join him with an oath.

Amasai, the **chief of the Thirty,** prophesies. He speaks as one clothed (lit., "the Spirit clothed Amasai"; cf. 2 Chr 24:20; Judg 6:34) with the Spirit of God. This fits a "soldier-prophet" model (THOMPSON, 125). "God himself," JOHNSTONE (1:162) writes, is "controlling the response and vindicating David." Amasai's reply, then, is no mere acclamation of loyalty, but a divine assessment of David's growing strength. Benjamin and Judah (and all Israel) belong to David by God's own appointment (cf. the opposite in 2 Chr 10:16). Amasai repeats the key term **success** (שָׁלוֹם, *šālôm,* "peace, wholeness") three times so as to "bring emotional encouragement to David. He is surrounded by '*helpers*' on every side, and not least aided by God as patron of his cause" (ALLEN, 94). It is not only a blessing for success but the assurance of success because **God** has helped David (better to translate, "God has helped you," instead of **God will help you**). The course of David's life is given prophetic assurance through a blessing.

The two stronghold sections (1 Chr 12:8-18) constitute the beginning of David's support. It comes from Gad, Benjamin, and Judah. Solidarity is emphasized by the prophetic word of Amasai. This word comes at the heart of Chronicles's structure (the middle of the chiasm). Consequently, it colors the whole narrative. The people of Israel — Gadites, Reubenites, Benjamites, Danites, Simeonites, Judahites — recognized God's hand in David's dispute with Saul. They came to help David in battle (1 Chr 12:1) because God was David's help (1 Chr 12:18). David's rise to the throne was by divine appointment (election).

The word "help" (עֵזֶר, *'ēzer*) is significant (1 Chr 12:22,33). It is the "theme" of this chapter and an important term throughout Chronicles (MCCONVILLE, 27). The noun and verb occur 30 times. It is a theological word for the Chronicler that evidences divine assistance (cf. 2 Chr 14:11; 18:31; 25:8; 26:7; 32:8). The Lord is present to help Israel when it cries out to him.

God helped David through the men he sent him. ALLEN believes Chronicles stresses this help motif through the names of the individuals who joined David. For example, Ahiezer (1 Chr 12:3), Joezer (1 Chr 12:6), Ezer (1 Chr 12:9), Eleazar (1 Chr 11:12) and Abiezer (1 Chr 11:28) all include the word "help" (*'ēzer*) in their names (ALLEN, 94-95). God helps David through the mighty men he sends to secure the kingdom he will turn over to him (1 Chr 12:23).

The thematic quality of help reminds us that Amasai's prophetic oracle is not a "mere military annal," but "a meditation on the nature of *help*." The term is "tantamount to salvation" (MCCONVILLE, 29). God saves David and appoints him king. This was God's intent even while Saul reigned. David's growing support in the wilderness and at Ziklag testifies to David's divine election.

Nevertheless, this support came slowly and over many years. The Chronicler has telescoped this history. David's election was not always so clear to him (cf. Ps 142). The years in the wilderness, just as our own wildernesses, are times of trial, patience, and waiting. God will make his election clear, but in his own time. God will help, but according to his timing.

Support for David at Ziklag (12:19-22)

Some of **Manasseh defected to David** from Saul (1 Chr 12:19-20) — the verb is used three times. Consequently, there is a shift in allegiance by a significant number from a key northern tribe (JAPHET, 266). The **men of Manasseh** apparently intended to fight **against Saul** with David, but the **Philistines** would not trust their help (cf. 1 Sam 29). Nevertheless, **they helped David against raiding bands**.

The term **thousand** in 1 Chronicles 12:20 may refer to a military unit or clan in the Davidic army and not to an actual number (Mendenhall, 52-66; JAPHET, 267). Whatever may be the case, these Manassahites were leaders in David's army.

First Chronicles 12:22 summarizes the effect of David's pilgrimage into the wilderness and his relocation at Ziklag. David gains support daily. He builds an army. Chronicles emphasizes that this is a divine act in history (1 Chr 12:18). This army is like an **army of God** (similar to "Lord of Hosts"). David's army was like the Lord of Host's own army; "there is a fleeting picture also of the host of heaven itself gathering to David's cause (cf. 2 Kings 6:17)" (McCONVILLE, 29).

Support for David at Hebron (12:23-37)

First Chronicles 12:23 functions as a heading for the list of men who joined David at Hebron. The text recalls 1 Chronicles 10:14 where God turned **Saul's kingdom** over to David. Consequently, this heading binds the whole of 1 Chronicles 10–12 together as a unit: God turns the kingdom over to David. God has chosen his king, and the people joyfully and peaceably submit to God's choice.

First Chronicles 12:23-40 has no canonical parallels. While JAPHET (267) does not believe it is the Chronicler's "free composition," she does think he has "elaborated" his source (a military list; cf. WILLIAMSON, 110) in order to shape a picture of David's victory at Hebron. Indeed, the small number of Judahites in comparison with other tribes (more from Simeon than Judah) and the "typological" character of **40,000** for the last four tribes (where the first four tribes only had a total of 25,200) have created doubts about the historicity of this story (JAPHET, 258-259).

However, instead of doubting the story, perhaps it is better to understand the function of the list. One could argue that the difference in numbers between, say, Judah (**6,800**) and Asher (40,000) reflect the Chronicler's integrity with his sources for surely he would have inflated Judah's numbers if he were merely interested in contriving a narrative that exalts David (McCONVILLE, 32-33). Interestingly, while thirteen tribes are listed, they are grouped in a way that maintains the symbolic number of twelve (Levi has a military contingent) and includes "all Israel" (every tribe is mentioned by name — even Dan). The transjordanian tribes (Reuben, Gad, and half of Manasseh) are grouped as one so that the count is twelve (Dillard, *Study*, 602). The Chronicler is interested in symbolism. All Israel (cf. 1 Chr 12:38-39) supports David's coronation at **Hebron**.

The larger numbers (40,000) may be hyperbolic in order to exalt David's status according to ancient Near Eastern royal conventions (much like, "I've seen that movie a hundred times"; see Introduction). He emphasizes the divine appointment of David through these helpers whom God sent to David. David's army is like the host of heaven (Dillard, *Study*, 602-603; cf. 1 Chr 12:22). Further, it is possible that in reference to Judah and other tribes that the number **thousand** may refer to military units rather than specific individuals. So, MYERS (1:98) believes 1 Chronicles 12:24 might be translated, "the sons of Judah who bore shield and spear numbered six units with eight hundred armed men with military training" (cf. PAYNE, 4:378). Further, Wenham ("Large Numbers," 27, 45) understands the 3,700 from the house of Aaron as three "captains of thousands" and seven "captains of hundreds." Consequently, the numbers are lower than might first appear. Whether hyperbole or literal, their function is clear: all Israel – in massive support – comes to Hebron to anoint David king (BRAUN, 170).

Saul still lies in the background of the narrative (1 Chr 12:29), but now even those who had remained loyal to Saul among the Benjamites give their allegiance to David. The comment underscores the complete victory of David so that even Saul's relatives come to crown David.

Interestingly, **Issachar** and **Zebulun** receive the fullest comment in the list of tribes (1 Chr 12:32-33). Wisdom is attributed to the men of Issachar – they **understood the times** and knew what Israel should do. The nature of the wisdom is vague, but the point is clear: the northern tribes recognized the divine election of David as king. God brings Israel to David in overwhelming numbers. The huge number of **50,000** for Zebulun, the largest in the list, underlines that recognition and support. The huge number from Zebulun contrasts with the small number from Judah which is, according to Klein ("How Many," 279-280), the Chronicler's way of emphasizing David's support from distant tribes (the numbers are larger as the distance from Judah increases).

David's Coronation at Hebron (12:38-40)

This is the climax of 1 Chronicles 10–12. Whereas the Chronicler begins with the death of Saul, it ends with a royal banquet in David's honor. Several elements are significant. First, **all Israel** is emphasized. **All the rest of the Israelites**, not just the warriors, participated. Even the most distant tribes from the Galilean hills (**Issachar, Zebulun,** and **Naphtali**) came to celebrate David's royal appointment. Second, Israel is united in its purpose (lit., "one heart"; 1 Chr 12:38) to crown David king. They came to Hebron wholly dedicated (1 Chr 12:38; **fully determined,** בְּלֵבָב שָׁלֵם, *bᵉlēbab šālēm*). The Chronicler's "heart" language involves determination and unity. "The 'whole-heartedness' is directed towards the realization of Yahweh's full blessing for Israel" (MCCONVILLE, 33). Third, Israel gathered to celebrate David's victory with a **three**-day royal banquet. Thus, Israel was characterized by plenty and **joy** (1 Chr 12:40). This contrasts with how this narrative began (gloom, defeat, fasting, death, and mourning, 1 Chr 10).

The banquet is not only a royal celebration, but a covenant meal. All Israel came to make a covenant with David (1 Chr 11:3). The enactment of this covenant was liturgical and included both the sacrifice and the sacrificial meal (cf. Gen 26:26-30; 31:54; Exod 24:11; Josh 9:11-15). When Israel and David sat down to eat together, they ate in the presence of God and bound themselves in covenant. Their meal celebrated the covenant so that there was **joy in Israel** (1 Chr 12:40).

Theologically, this royal covenant meal anticipates the messianic banquet. The Chronicler's postexilic community yearned for such a banquet. The Christian community enjoys the foretaste of that banquet through the Lord's Supper (Hicks, "The Lord's Table," 4-7). The triumphal picture of 1 Chronicles 12:38-40 is a reflection of the triumphal picture of the eschatological messianic banquet where death is destroyed and tears are no more (Isa 25:6-9). The reign of David, then, and the banquet which began it, point us to the eschatological joy of God's fellowship with a united people. Christians share the joy of that fellowship whenever they meet at the Lord's table.

B. DAVID AND THE ARK OF THE COVENANT (13:1-17:27)

Chronicles moves from enthronement to holy procession. Now that David is established as king over all Israel in Jerusalem, his first concern is to bring the ark to the city.

The structure of 1 Chronicles 10:1-22:1 is disputed. Wright ("Founding Father," 45-59) argues that the ark motif is in the background and that the reign of David as a model king dominates. He believes the enthronement motif runs from 1 Chronicles 10:1–14:2. First Chronicles 14:2 functions as a concluding summary for the enthronement section. He then understands 1 Chronicles 14:3–22:1 as the "Acts of David." However, Eskenazi (258-274) demonstrates that the ark motif dominates 1 Chronicles 13–16. The repetition of key terms ties this narrative together (e.g., "ark" occurs 28 times in 1 Chr 13–16 while only 18 times in the rest of Chronicles), and it moves to a crescendo as the ark is brought into Jerusalem.

First Chronicles 10–12 is an enthronement motif. First Chronicles 13–17 is the ark narrative. There are several problems, however, with this structure. First, why is the ark narrative interrupted with an account of Philistine wars in 1 Chronicles 14? Second, should 1 Chronicles 17, which contains the Davidic promise, belong to 1 Chronicles 13–16 or 1 Chronicles 18–21? If 1 Chronicles 17 is wedded to the structure of 1 Chronicles 13–16, how does the Davidic promise serve the ark motif? These problems are discussed below.

Given 1 Chronicles 13–17 as a literary unit (BRAUN, 172; JAPHET, 272), the ark narrative may be divided into four sections (Eskenazi, 264): (1) Object Defined: Bring the Ark to Jerusalem (13:1-4), (2) Process of Actualization (13:5–15:29), (3) Objective Reached: Celebration of the Ark's Arrival (16:1-43), and (4) A House for the Ark (17:1-27).

1. Object Defined: Bring the Ark to Jerusalem (13:1-4)

This section does not appear in 2 Samuel. The Chronicler frames the ark narrative. The context may be the coronation celebration in Hebron, but not necessarily. The shift to an ark motif may indicate a chronological shift (David is living in Jerusalem). Whichever is the case, Chronicles begins the ark narrative with a self-conscious deliberation on the part of "all Israel."

While in Samuel the ark narrative (2 Sam 6:1-11) follows the Philistine wars (2 Sam 5:11-25), in Chronicles the ark narrative (1 Chr 13) begins before the Philistine wars (1 Chr 14). This is a thematic reordering of Samuel's account in order to stress the ark and to give the Philistine wars a supporting role in the drama. The Chronicler is not concerned about chronology but thematic arrangement. His restructuring, according to Cogan (206), "does not occasion surprise: it is an editorial procedure not unfamiliar in history writing, one which has been documented in Assyrian historical texts." The Chronicler emphasizes David's piety rather than his wars so he recontextualizes the wars in order to serve his larger purpose. Accordingly, repositioning the military victories after David's decision to seek the Lord (1 Chr 13:3) is "part of a wider pattern employed by [the Chronicler] in the account of kings such as Abijah (2 Chr 13), Jehoshaphat (2 Chr 17–20), and Hezekiah (2 Chr 29–32). According to this pattern, a king's military victories and his sovereignty over other peoples are understood as consequences that result from seeking the Lord" (SELMAN, 1:149).

The Chronicler begins the drama of the ark narrative by providing his own introduction (1 Chr 13:1-4). While the reference to David's consultation with all (כָּל, *kol*, **each**) his military commanders links 1 Chronicles 13 with the events of 1 Chronicles 11–12, the emphasis lies on the **whole assembly** (כֹל קָהֵל, *kl qhl*) of Israel (1 Chr 13:2,4). David consulted the leadership, but he spoke to the whole assembly and **the whole assembly agreed** because **all the people** (כָּל־הָעָם, *kol-hā'ām*) thought it was a good idea (1 Chr 13:4). He suggests that Israel go **to the rest of our brothers throughout** (lit., "in all," בְּכֹל, *bᵉkōl*) **the territories of Israel**, including the **priests and Levites**. SELMAN (1:151) notes that "in Chronicles, the kings who consult their people are also those who seek Yahweh" (2 Chr 1:5; 2 Chr 20:3-4; 30:18; 31:21).

Chronicles uses the term "all" (כֹל, *kol/kōl*) five times in 1 Chronicles 13:1-4. This emphasis is no mere repetition of Chronicles's inclusivist theme. Rather, all Israel desired to renew their relationship with God. The contrast with **Saul** is explicit (1 Chr 13:3). Whereas Saul did not inquire of the ark, David makes it the centerpiece of his religious life. Just as the Lord turned the kingdom over to David (1 Chr 10:14), so David now seeks the Lord in a way that Saul did not (1 Chr 13:3). The term "assembly" has religious overtones. This is a communal event in the life of Israel. Bringing the ark to Jerusalem is a national moment of rededication to the LORD. The transition from **Saul** to **David** is not only political but religious. Renewal, as well as the unity of North and South in all Israel, is an important theme for the Chronicler's postexilic community.

However, something is wrong with this picture. Yes, David seeks the Lord through the ark. Yes, he seeks covenant renewal in concert with the people. But he seeks God in an inappropriate way. **Let us bring the ark of our God back to us** reflects a manipulative stance. David places God's ball in his court. He will reposition the ark in order to achieve his own ends. The people agreed **because it seemed right to** them. This is an expression of moral evil in Dtr — what seems right in the eyes of the people (cf. Deut 12:8; Judg 17:6; 21:25; 2 Sam 17:4). Chronicles contrasts doing what is "right in the eyes of Yahweh" (2 Chr 14:2; 20:32; 24:2; 25:2; 26:4; 27:2; 29:2; 34:2) and what is right in human eyes (1 Chr 13:4; but 2 Chr 30:4, due to its context, has a positive meaning). He acted by what was right in his own eyes instead of fully seeking the Lord.

The Chronicler makes this clear in 1 Chronicles 15. David takes responsibility for the debacle in 1 Chronicles 13. "*We* did not inquire of him about how to do it in the prescribed way" and consequently "the Lord our God broke out in anger against *us*" (1 Chr 15:13). David sought the Lord, but he did not seek the Lord. He sought the ark for his own reasons. David, not just Uzzah, failed to keep the command of God in this situation.

The ark is of paramount significance as Chronicles gives more attention to it than does Dtr. Its descriptors verify this. In 1 Chronicles 13–17 it is variously identified as the **ark of our God** (1 Chr 13:3), "ark of God" (1 Chr 13:5-7,12,14; 15:1,2,15,24; 16:1), "the ark that is called by the Name" (1 Chr 13:6), "ark of the LORD" (1 Chr 15:3,12,14; 16:4), "the ark of the covenant of the LORD" (1 Chr 15:25,26,28,29; 16:37; 17:1), and "the ark of the covenant of God" (1 Chr 16:6). The ark is the presence of God among his people. First Chronicles 13:8 underscores this perspective when the people dance and sing "before God" as they move the ark. The Lord sits enthroned above the cherubim of the ark (1 Chr 13:6). To **inquire** of the ark is to inquire of the Lord (1 Chr 13:3). Thus, Chronicles "emphasizes the sacramental character of the ark: to be in the presence of the ark is to be in the very presence of God himself" (JOHNSTONE, 1:167). SAILHAMER (38) comments, "the Ark was no mere symbol of God's presence. It was the place where God had chosen to center His presence among His people (Ex. 25:22)."

Why is the Chronicler so interested in the ark when the ark no longer exists? The Chronicler is interested in the close identification of the ark with the temple and more specifically with God, that is, the presence of God. Consequently, even though the postexilic community does not possess the ark, they do have a temple. God's presence is assured by the symbolic significance of the temple even though there is no ark since God's presence is not dependent upon the ark (and neither is it dependent upon the temple). Rather, the ark and temple symbolize the same point: God is present. David's attitude toward the ark is the kind of attitude the postexilic community must have for the temple. Just as David sought God through the ark, so postexilic Israel must seek God through the temple. The heart of the ark narrative, then, is the theological point that "God is with us and that God is holy" (THOMPSON, 135). The postexilic community yearned for the presence of God (cf. Zech 2:10-11). In the same way Christians seek God through the provision of his own mercy-seat in Jesus Christ and know the presence of God through his indwelling Spirit.

2. Process of Actualization (13:5–15:29)

Eskenazi (265-268) argues that this whole section is a carefully pictured religious drama which climaxes in the entrance of the ark into Jerusalem. David announces his intention to move the ark (1 Chr 13:2) and the narrative concludes with the ark in Jerusalem (1 Chr 15:29). The first attempt to move the ark is aborted (1 Chr 13:5-14), but the second succeeds (1 Chr 15:1-29). Sandwiched between the attempts are three subnarratives which serve the Chronicler's larger interests: (a) David's Palace (1 Chr 14:1-2), (b) The Sons of David (1 Chr 14:3-7), and (c) The Philistine Wars (1 Chr 14:8-17).

The First Attempt Aborted (13:5-14)

The Chronicler does not indicate how much time transpired between Hebron (1 Chr 12:38-40) and the first attempt to move the ark (1 Chr 13:5). He assumes that David has already conquered Jerusalem (1 Chr 13:13). Consequently, the Chronicler indicates that some time has passed between the events in Hebron and the movement of the ark, though David's initial interest may have begun at Hebron.

First Chronicles 13:5-14 follows the wording of 2 Samuel 6:1-11 with a few significant differences (cf. Ulrich, 193-221; JAPHET, 278-282). One underscores the Chronicler's theme — **all the Israelites** (three times in 1 Chr 13:5,6,8). While 2 Samuel 6:1 refers to 30,000 men of Israel, the Chronicler speaks of all the Israelites along with an inclusive south-north geographical range (Shihor River in Egypt to Lebo Hamath in Josh 13:2-5; cf. JAPHET, 277-278). "All Israel" was scattered throughout the land that God had given them.

The Chronicler emphasizes the religious meaning of this narrative. Whereas 2 Samuel 6:1 states that "David again gathered" (דָּוִד וַיֹּסֶף עוֹד, *wayyōseph 'ôd dāwid*), the Chronicler writes **David assembled** (דָּוִד וַיַּקְהֵל, *wayyaqhēl dāwid*). The verb "assembled" is from the same root as the noun "assembly" (1 Chr 13:2,4). This is an assembly of Israel which dances and rejoices before the Lord (1 Chr 13:8). As MYERS (1:102) notes, the Chronicler thinks of this as a "religious matter" rather than "a semimilitary ceremony." The addition of the priests and Levites in 1 Chronicles 13:2 stresses the holy nature of the assembly. Chronicles places the ark in its own house rather than in the house of Obed-Edom though it is in the care of Obed-Edom (BRAUN, 173; "its house" rather than "his house").

The participation of "all Israel" and the religious significance of the event provide an air of expectation and exhilaration. But, as SELMAN (1:150) notes, the "enthusiasm" of 1 Chronicles 13:3 with all the attendant dancing and singing "gives way swiftly to David's despair" (1 Chr 13:12). The move from joy and anticipation to anger and fear is dramatic. The first attempt to move the ark is a bust. Something went wrong, and interpreters have been perplexed by the nature of this misstep. But the misstep has something to do with the ark as a symbol of divine presence in Israel.

The Ark Is Moved (13:5-8)

All Israel convenes to move the ark from Kiriath Jearim with a festive and processional celebration **before God**. **Kiriath Jearim** was located on the Philistine-Judean border about seventeen miles from Jerusalem. The ark is placed on a **new cart** (perhaps built for this occasion). The Philistines moved the ark on a cart (1 Sam 6:7), and David continues their practice. SELMAN (1:153) notes that "Israel got into difficulties because they failed to recognize that worship of the true God meant they could no longer simply follow contemporary pagan practices."

JOHNSTONE suggests that David's consultation with all Israel in 1 Chronicles 13:2 implied a hasty action that did not take full account of the seriousness of this move. David suggested that Israel "break out" ("send word far and wide," 1 Chr 13:2; פָּרַץ, *pāraṣ*) and gather the people from all the territories to relocate the ark. Given the use of this term in 1 Chronicles 13:11, 14:11, and 15:13, JOHNSTONE (1:169) believes that the Chronicler has "deliberately chosen" this word "to express the hot-headed and unconsidered way in which David sets about an action that is perfectly laudable in itself." In other words, it was a good idea, but a hasty way of doing it (WILLIAMSON, 114). Perhaps David's pride led to this decision to move the ark without adequate preparation. Because David chose an unacceptable delivery method, God "broke out" on Uzzah when he reached out to touch the ark. The whole narrative, then, constitutes a warning against taking "sacred actions and holy objects lightly" (SAILHAMER, 39).

As is clear from the Chronicler's own commentary (1 Chr 15:2, 13-15), the way in which the ark is moved is a violation of divine prescriptions (cf. Exod 25:12-15). Even though David intended to inquire of the Lord (1 Chr 13:3, דְרַשְׁנֻהוּ, *dᵉrašnuhû*), he did not inquire how to move the ark (1 Chr 15:13). He did not seek God's guidance. While he intended to seek the Lord (perhaps for his own purposes), his method was faulty. This movement, then, is a blemish on David's record. The Levites alone were not responsible for this movement, but David is ultimately accountable. Indeed, he takes responsibility in 1 Chronicles 15:13 when he says "*we* did not give it proper care." Chronicles does not whitewash David's sin, but highlights it more than 2 Samuel. David did not inquire of the Lord as he should have. This point, along with the religious nature of the event, must contextualize what happens in the narrative.

The Procession Is Stopped (13:9-12)

The **ark of God** is the presence of God. It embodies his holiness and majesty. The ark cannot be treated carelessly or irreverently. The brief story about Uzzah underscores these themes, and modern interpreters should not mischaracterize God (e.g., a vindictive tyrant) or underestimate the seriousness of Uzzah's actions (e.g., he was just trying to keep the ark from falling). The text forcefully states: the

Lord **struck him down** (contra Rowley, *Relevance*, 28). What is the significance of this divine act?

First, God's holiness, often associated with cultic practices and articles, "possessed genuine power and could have striking physical and spiritual effects" (SELMAN, 1:153; cf. Lev 10:1ff; Isa 6:1ff). Indeed, the ark itself was the focus of some powerful effects when it was among the Philistines (1 Sam 5) and at Beth Shemesh (1 Sam 6:19-20). Those experiences should have warned Israel "that to be in the possession of the ark was no unqualified guarantee of divine blessing" (SELMAN, 1:153). The ark's holiness punished those who abused the divine presence it symbolized. This "mode of God's revelation and presence in the OT — a presence much sought and graciously granted (Exod. 33:3,12-23; 34:9ff.) — brought with it the need to deal carefully with it" (McCONVILLE, 38). The Holy Mount of Sinai was not to be touched. The unholy cannot touch the face of God. Uzzah did not respect the divine presence. So, Uzzah died **before God** (1 Chr 13:10). The Chronicler changed 1 Samuel's wording ("beside the ark of God") to "before God" which has liturgical meaning.

Modern Westerners are rather irreverent when it comes to holy objects. We do not understand holy objects and are rather flippant with those kinds of traditions. However, in the ancient world, holy objects were revered. The ancient community understood the distance they must keep. They know the rules for handling or not handling such objects. Israel, if they did not have, should have had a sense of the holy. Israel's irreverence testifies to their lack of appreciation for the significance of the ark as a bearer of divine presence.

Second, many have read this story as Uzzah's well-intentioned attempt to save the ark from harm (ALLEN, 99-101). But given that its movement on a cart was the continuation of a pagan practice, Uzzah's act reflected a disregard for its holiness. Uzzah's attempt to steady the ark was part of a larger profaning. Snyman (203-217) sees the function of 1 Chronicles 13 as a legitimization of the Levites. They should have been carrying the ark rather than Uzzah steadying it. The holiness of the ark was disturbed, and Uzzah paid the price. JOHNSTONE (1:172) notes that the musical praise is restricted to the Levites in 1 Chronicles 15 which suggests that in 1 Chronicles 13 "Israel's rejoicing is at best a disorganized, over-exuberant tumult, a cacophony of raucous chant and blaring fanfare." Israel's procession was disorderly rather than holy. Israel trifled with the presence of God.

Third, read as a narrative, there is an "implicit invitation to us to fill in the blanks" as we participate in the narrator's world (Peterson, 5). Peterson (5-7) sees Uzzah as one who takes "charge of God" and manages God's presence by his own care. Indeed, "Uzzah is the patron saint of those who uncritically embrace technology without regard to the nature of The Holy." The story of Uzzah posts a danger sign "Beware the God." Long ("Fall," 18) also sees this theme. Human beings believe they can manipulate or control the divine presence. By his spontaneous act, "Uzzah confessed his real faith: a God so impotent that if the box falls God falls; a God so weak that his God needs the help of the likes of Uzzah to dotter across the street; an empty shell of a God trapped inside fragile religious symbols."

Fourth, read in the context of Chronicles as a whole, this story illustrates the Chronicler's retribution motif which will become more prominent in 2 Chronicles 10–36 (Snyman, 203-217). Uzzah dies as a punishment from the Lord. This motif functions alongside "seeking" in Chronicles. God punishes those who do not seek him, and he rewards those who do. When people are punished in Chronicles, it is not just a technical violation; it reflects their hearts. When others technically violate the law but their hearts are seeking God, they are accepted (cf. 2 Chr 30:17-20). Within the theology of Chronicles, Uzzah is not punished based on a technicality, but because his heart did not seek God. David and the priests technically violated the law, but they were not struck like Uzzah. "Uzzah's death was not sudden; it was years in the making, the 'dead' works accumulating like dead men's bones within him, suffocating the spirit of praise and faith and worship" (Peterson, 7).

When Yahweh is pictured as the "God of technicalities" who jumps to zap his people, the nature of God's holiness is seriously misunderstood. God is not searching for technical law-breakers; he is searching for hearts that seek him. He punishes those who rebelliously violate his commands but forgives those who seek him. Uzzah arrogantly violated the law (cf. Num 4:15) — he did something the law explicitly condemned.

God's reaction to Uzzah is contextualized by the disorderly procession and the pagan delivery method. Uzzah's act was the most profane of all — to touch the holiness of God. Israel profaned God's presence. Uzzah sought to manage and control God rather then serve him. Uzzah's act was a "presumptuous intrusion into the sphere of the Divine" (JOHNSTONE, 1:172). David did not seek out the Lord, but sought to get the Lord into his camp (Jerusalem). "The point is that Uzzah is the victim of a carelessness on the part of his leaders, ultimately David himself" (McCONVILLE, 38). The first attempt to move the ark was a debacle, and it signaled that Israel was not yet ready to serve God in his majesty. The holiness of God broke out against sin in Israel.

Consequently, it is inappropriate to think Uzzah's problem was a mere "technical" violation of the law. David himself violated the law as he superintended the movement of the ark on a cart. David was in technical violation himself, but he was not struck down that day. Uzzah's was part of a much larger context where the holy was profaned. God is not some vindictive judge who anxiously watches for any technical violation. Rather, God is the holy one whom Israel must honor if they are to serve him. This episode, in the context of Chronicles, points to the heart rather than to technicality as the culprit. Uzzah was struck because he arrogantly presumed to touch God, but David was not struck because his heart was oriented toward God even though he mistakenly moved the ark in a way that violated God's law. Both David and Uzzah violated the law, but only Uzzah was struck. More was involved than technical law-breaking. In the larger context of Chronicles's theology, David sought God with his heart, but Uzzah did not.

David's response to Uzzah's death is both anger (1 Chr 13:11; same word as in 1 Chr 13:10) and fear (1 Chr 13:12). Both are directed at God. This mixture is understandable. Anger is his response to the reversal he has just experienced. One minute all Israel is celebrating, and the next minute the **LORD's anger** breaks out against **Uzzah**. The sudden shift angered David, shocked by the divine response. David did not understand the problem nor did he see the disrespect. But his anger soon turned to despair as stated in the question, **How can I ever bring the ark of God to me?** David recognized that something went wrong (though he sought to blame God more than himself at this point: McCONVILLE [38-39] writes, "In any case his exclamation in v. 12 is less pure enquiry than petulant self-justification. His naming of the place Perez-Uzzah belongs to his attempt to deflect the blame from the incident upon God."). Consequently, David decided to wait for another occasion. He took the death of Uzzah as "God's active objection to the removal of the ark, which put the whole project in jeopardy" (JAPHET, 281).

David's anger is memorialized by the name he gave to the place: **Perez Uzzah**. "Perez" means to "break out" (פָּרַץ, *pāraṣ*). David names the place as the point where the Lord broke out against Uzzah. The memory of that event is seared into the conscience of Israel as the place name remained even into the Chronicler's time.

The theology of Israel did not take lightly the holiness of God. When his holiness was violated, God's anger responded. His holiness consumes those who treat him with irreverence. The exile itself was an exclusion of an unholy nation from a holy God. The post-exilic community must revere God's holiness. They must not dishonor the temple of God, but acknowledge his presence and worship his majesty. In the same way, Christians must respect the divine presence within them and honor him with their bodies (1 Cor 6:20).

Neither may we treat what is holy as something for manipulation. Contemporary worship discussions need to wrestle with the sense of the holy that must pervade our assemblies as we gather before God. As much as we seek God to "break out" for us in blessing, church growth, and conflict resolutions, we too often fail to recognize that God sometimes breaks out in judgment and against sin. The call to holiness is perpetual and unbending. God says, "Be holy, for I am holy" (Lev 11:14,45; 1 Pet 1:16).

The Ark Is Placed (13:13-14)

David waits for another day to move the ark. In the meantime, he places the ark in the care of **Obed-Edom the Gittite**. The identification of Obed-Edom is problematic though it is clear that he lives in the Philistine city of Gath. Some believe he is a Levite (Polk, 6-7; JOHNSTONE, 1:173; cf. 1 Chr 15:18,21,24; 16:5,38; 26:4). Others believe he is a Philistine (JAPHET, 281).

SELMAN (1:154) suggests that "the non-Israelite form of the name and the epithet *Gittite* (= inhabitant of Gath) make it more likely that he was a Philistine." If so, then this is a further comment on divine sovereignty. David may have thought the ark was too much trouble for Israel, so he left it in the hands of a Philistine. Consequently, David protected Israel from the ark. But, instead of cursing Obed-Edom, the ark blessed him. God will not be pegged and limited by human beings. He will show mercy on whom he wishes (Exod 33:19; cf. Rom 9:15). God blessed the Philistine Obed-Edom even though he punished the Israelite Uzzah. If Obed-Edom is a Levite, then the point of reversal still remains. While Uzzah was punished for his unfaithful handling of the ark, Obed-Edom is blessed. God's blessing comes to those who honor his holiness, but he curses those who disregard it (cf. Ps 50).

The Solidification of David's Reign (14:1-17)

Chronicles's narrative legitimizes David's reign by recognizing divine blessings (SAILHAMER, 40-41): a palace (1 Chr 14:1-2), children (1 Chr 14:3-7), and the defeat of the Philistines (1 Chr 14:8-17). Buildings, family, and military victories are characteristic blessings in Chronicles. Despite David's misstep, he was still God's king.

Though the Chronicler rearranged 2 Samuel 5-6 to emphasize the ark (placing it first in his narrative), he uses these blessings to enhance David's status and enables the continuation of the ark narrative (BRAUN, 177-178). He thematically reorganized 1 Samuel. The Chronicler's arrangement serves the themes articulated in 1 Chronicles 13 (SELMAN, 1:155): (1) seeking God (1 Chr 14:10,14), (2) "all Israel" (1 Chr 14:8), (3) divinely blessed Jerusalem (1 Chr 14:3), and (4) divine "out-breaking" (1 Chr 14:11).

The key is 1 Chronicles 14:17. This summary addition, along with 1 Chronicles 14:1-2, establishes David as an international player whom the Lord has blessed. Brettler (44) believes that the Chronicler has patterned the order of his material after Deuteronomy 11-12. Once David is at peace, then he may concern himself with temple building just as Deuteronomy moves from peace (Deut 11:25) to the sanctuary (Deut 12:14). Consequently, 1 Chronicles 14 is best perceived as the solidification of David's reign in preparation for his renewed attempt to move the ark to Jerusalem (1 Chr 15-16).

The Building of David's Palace (14:1-2)

The building of his **palace** was a concrete expression of divine blessing, and the assistance of **Hiram king of Tyre** indicates David's international presence. Hiram recognizes David as king by which David recognizes that the Lord has **established** him as king. David's palace (lit., "house") is a divine testimony.

The NIV misses a significant point through its adaptation (1 Chr 14:2) of 2 Samuel 5:12 which reads "David knew that the LORD had established him as king over Israel *and* had exalted his kingdom for the sake of his people Israel" (italics supplied). The "and" (ו) is not present in 1 Chronicles 14:2. A better translation is: **David knew that the LORD had established him as king over Israel** *because* . . . . David understood his divine election as king because God had exalted his kingdom (Japhet, "Interchanges," 22-23; JAPHET, 286). "It is God's purpose that David's kingship should be recognized not merely for its own sake, but for the fulfilling of God's purpose through Israel" (JOHNSTONE 1:177).

The reference to Hiram is problematic. Since David reigned ca. 1010-970 B.C. and Solomon followed David with another forty years, and Hiram was involved with both Kings, some believe that the chronology here is impossible. Did Hiram reign long enough for David to build his palace early in his reign and then help Solomon build the temple as well (MYERS, 1:106)? First, chronology is not the Chronicler's interest here. While the palace was probably built early in David's reign, this may mean ca. 990 or later because David reigned in Hebron the first seven years. Also, David may not have built a palace nor have been internationally recognized until he had secured the significant borders of his kingdom. Second, Hiram probably ruled over a fifty year span, beginning in the 980s, that overlapped both David and Solomon (Green, "David's," 373-397).

The Sons of David (14:3-7)

God increased David's family — a clear indication of God's intent to bless the Davidic house. Chronicles assumes that the reader knows 2 Samuel 3:2-5 so the emphasis is on the **more** that David received in Jerusalem. The children born in Hebron are omitted. This solidifies his position in Jerusalem as king over Israel. Moreover, the house of David stands in contrast to the dethroned "house" of Saul (1 Chr 10:6; WILLIAMSON, 117). The list of children is repeated from 1 Chronicles 3:5-8. The Chronicler does not believe that all these children were born in the three months of 1 Chronicles 13:14. The Chronicler is not thinking in chronological categories.

The Philistine Wars (14:8-16)

As long as David reigned in Hebron and over Judah alone, the **Philistines** probably considered him a vassal, even an ally. But as soon as David is proclaimed king over **all Israel** (1 Chr 14:8), he is a threat. Consequently, the Philistines seek to control David. The exact chronology and geographical location of the two conflicts are disputed (Tidwell, 190-212), but the theological point is clear. David defeats the enemy that defeated Saul. God has elected David king over all Israel.

The Philistine wars are tied to the previous context by the use of the verb "break out" (*pāraṣ*) in 1 Chronicles 13:2,11 and 14:11 (also 15:13). Thus, Chronicles links the Philistine wars with the ark narrative (Eskenazi, 265). Even though God "broke out" against David's procession through striking Uzzah, God also "broke out" against the Philistines to bless David. The holiness of God breaks against sin but the grace of God breaks out for the sake of his people against their enemies. By this device the Chronicler contextualizes the Philistine wars so that David's victory over the Philistines is a divine blessing in preparation for the movement of the ark to Jerusalem. "Had Chr not wished to bring this into close association with the theme of seeking the ark," WILLIAMSON (117) writes, "he would probably have grouped this paragraph with his collection of David's military successes in chs 18–20."

The First War with the Philistines (14:8-12). It is uncertain whether this first battle is before or after the capture of Jerusalem. Second Samuel 5:17 states that the Philistines "went up" to search for David and that David "went down to the stronghold." First Chronicles 14:8 states that David **went out to meet them**. Chronicles has streamlined the events and avoided a reference to the stronghold in the Judean wilderness (Mazar, "Palace," 54-55, believes the stronghold refers to a citadel in Jerusalem). Yet, it appears that this battle took place prior to David's capture of Jerusalem — why else would the Philistines need to search for David if he was located in Jerusalem (JAPHET, 287)? Once again, the Chronicler is not interested in chronology as much as he is in thematic association.

The Philistine purpose is clarified in Chronicles. While 2 Samuel 5:18 only refers to the presence ("spread out") of Philistines in the Valley of Rephaim, 1 Chronicles 14:9 tells us they **raided** the valley.

The Philistine hostile intention is clear. The **Valley of Rephaim** is located southwest of Jerusalem near Bethlehem.

The theological heart of this narrative is found in the act of seeking God. This term contrasts David with Saul. Whereas Saul did not inquire of the Lord (1 Chr 10:13), David does (1 Chr 14:10,14). Saul was defeated (1 Chr 10:2; "killed") by the Philistines, but David defeated (1 Chr 14:11,16) the Philistines. The difference between the kings is their desire to seek God. The Sovereign God controls the battle and gives it to Israel by the hand of David (1 Chr 14:11).

Interestingly, the God who "struck" (1 Chr 13:10) Uzzah is the same God who struck (1 Chr 14:11,16; **defeated**) the Philistines. The connections between the Philistine and ark narratives are strengthened by the use of "break out" (1 Chr 13:11; 14:11) to describe God's active involvement. God broke out against the Philistines so the place is named **Baal Perazim**, meaning "the Lord who breaks out" (or, "Lord, or owner, of irruptive powers"; JOHNSTONE, 1:179). "Perazim," then, becomes a name which celebrates a victory (1 Chr 14:11) but also provides a warning (1 Chr 13:11): God will not be mocked, but he will bless those who seek him.

In 1 Chronicles 14:12 the idols are burned instead of carried off (2 Sam 5:21). This illustrates the Chronicler's tendency to interpret his source (JAPHET, 289). The Chronicler tells us, in keeping with Deuteronomy 7:5 and 12:3, that Israel carried off the idols to burn them. BRAUN (179) agrees: "David and his men do not 'pick them up,' i.e., as booty; rather at David's command his men destroy them by burning."

The Second War with the Philistines (14:13-16). The Philistines returned to the valley, but the battle is enlarged. This time the battle envelopes the territory from **Gibeon to Gezer** (1 Chr 14:16; 2 Sam 5:17 reads "Geba" [גֶּבַע] rather than "Gibeon" [גִּבְעוֹן] which is probably due to textual transmission or associative because it is the same geographical region; cf. Kalimi, "Contribution," 208). Gibeon is located northwest of Jerusalem. This was probably an attack on Jerusalem. Whatever the case, David secures the region of Benjamin and Judah by these two battles, and the last battle was rather wide-ranging (even including Rephaim again, 2 Sam 5:22) as it pursued the Philistines into their territory (Gezer is a Philistine city). He defeats the Philistines so that they are no longer a threat to his newly established reign.

The second battle narrative highlights God's acts. David receives an answer to his inquiry that includes a battle plan. God will signal when to attack by his presence in the **tops of the . . . trees.** The Lord of Hosts will march ahead of David **to strike the Philistine army.** BRAUN (179) compares this to a "Holy War" where God leads the battle himself. As the verb indicates (נָכָה, *nākāh*), God strikes the Philistines (1 Chr 14:11,15), just as he struck Uzzah (1 Chr 13:10). The holiness of God means he defeats those who profane his name and blesses those who seek him.

Theological Comment (14:17)

This is unique to the Chronicler — perhaps patterned after Deuteronomy 11:25 (Brettler, 44). Just as he commented on Saul's defeat (1 Chr 10:13-14), so here he comments on David's victories. David now has an international presence and **all the nations** respect his new position. David is feared by the nations (cf. Ps 2), and this **fear** has messianic overtones for the hope of a restored postexilic community. Dillard (*Study*, 605) comments: "Here and elsewhere [the Chronicler] uses an expression that refers to an incapacitating terror brought on by the sense that the awful power of God is present in behalf of his people. . . . Thus David is seen by the nations as the very representative of God (similarly Asa, 2Ch 14:14; Jehoshaphat, 2Ch 17:10; 20:29)." David, then, is established by God as king over all Israel.

The Second Attempt Successful (15:1-29)

The second attempt to move the ark comes in two stages: (1) Preparations (1 Chr 15:1-24) and (2) Transfer (1 Chr15:25-29). The second section is paralleled by 2 Samuel 6:12b-16, but the first section has no canonical parallels. Second Samuel assumes some preparation since David had set up a tent for the ark (2 Sam 6:17), the people were assembled (2 Sam 6:15), the ark was carried instead of put on a cart (2 Sam 6:13), animals were sacrificed (2 Sam 6:13), and musicians were prepared (2 Sam 6:15). Chronicles makes explicit what is implicit in 2 Samuel. Chronicles adds some details 2 Samuel does not mention. For example, **the elders of Israel and the commanders** went up to bring the ark (1 Chr 15:25), the Levites carry the ark (1 Chr 15:26), and the musical procession is led by the

Levites (1 Chr 15:27). Second Samuel and 1 Chronicles complement each other (JAPHET, 292-294).

The two sections are bound together by a single theme (SELMAN, 1:159) which is seen in the repeated phrases to "bring up the ark" (עֲלֹה אֶת־אָרוֹן [*'lh 'eth-ʾărôn*]; 1 Chr 15:3,12,14,25,28) or to "carry the ark" (נָשָׂא אֶת־אָרוֹן [*ns' 'eth-ʾărôn*]; 1 Chr 15:2,15,26,27). The dominating interest of 1 Chronicles 15 is the transfer of the ark. Chronicles introduces preparations in the first section that are implemented in the next. Since Chronicles gives so much narrative space to the ark (1 Chr 13, 15–16) — in contrast with the space given the Philistine wars (1 Chr 14:8-16) — this "forces the reader to recognize what [the Chronicler] values most" (Eskenazi, 267).

Since the ark is at the center of this narrative, Chronicles's Levitical interest is also prominent. They carry the ark, lead the procession, and perform the musical worship. The Levitical lists (1 Chr 15:4-10,17-24) emphasize their place in the reconstituted worship of Israel. The Levitical interest arises from at least three considerations. First, David parallels Moses in his arranging of Levitical functions in accordance with Moses' instructions from the LORD (1 Chr 15:15). David functions as a new Moses. Second, the Chronicler rehabilitates the influence of the Levites in his own day. Their tasks were neglected (Neh 13:10). The beginnings of Davidic Levitical functions call for renewed appreciation of the Levites in Israel's worship (SELMAN, 1:161). Third, the conjunction of David, Zadokian priests, and the Levites serves as a model for reconciliation in the postexilic community where priests, Levites, and potential Davidic heirs may have been engaged in a struggle for preeminence (Hanson, "Levites," 75-76).

While some have suggested that 1 Chronicles 15 is a patchwork piece of redaction from variant sources (Noth, 35; MYERS, 1:110-113; BRAUN, 187-188), this chapter is a literary masterpiece that unites several thematic interests: David, ark, Levites, Jerusalem, divine blessing, and worship. JAPHET (296; cf. SELMAN, 1:159-161) concludes that "this material was not added in a secondary stage, but compiled and composed by [the Chronicler] himself, in the service of his literary and historical interests."

Preparations for Transferring the Ark (15:1-24)

This section, unique to Chronicles, divides into four parts (SELMAN, 1:162-165): (1) preparing a place for the ark (1 Chr 15:1-3), (b) preparing the people to carry the ark (1 Chr 15:4-10), (c) preparing the leaders (1 Chr 15:11-15), and (d) preparing the musicians (1 Chr 15:16-24). The lists not only identify, but also heighten, the literary drama as it moves slowly toward its goal. The lists are more than functional; they are part of the rhetoric that underscores this important moment in the history of Israel (Eskenazi, 265-269).

A Place for the Ark (15:1-3). The key phrase is: **he prepared a place for the ark** (1 Chr 15:1,3). David had not given up on his intent expressed in 1 Chronicles 13:3. Even though David had spent some time in building dwellings (lit., "houses") for himself (including his palace, 1 Chr 14:1-2), his main interest was to provide. He provided a sanctuary in which the ark might dwell different from the one at Gibeon (1 Chr 16:39; 21:29).

The preparation for the ark's placement in Jerusalem also involved calling the Levites into service. They were chosen **to carry the ark of the LORD and to minister before him forever** (1 Chr 15:2). Chronicles assumes the role of the Levites in Deuteronomy 10:8; 18:5. They lead the worship of God's people, including the procession that brings the ark to Jerusalem. The first attempt to move the ark failed due to improper leadership: David did not call upon the Levites, and the Levites did not assume their proper responsibility. This is corrected as David reinstitutes Mosaic procedures. Kleinig (*Song*, 30-39; "Divine Institution," 75-83) notes that Chronicles finds divine sanction for the musical ministry of the Levites in the Torah itself. The ministry of music is a divine institution. Chronicles patterns events according to the Torah (Brettler, 28). Indeed, canonical authority already functions for the Chronicler as he looks to an authoritative body of writings to legitimize his procedure (ALLEN, 111-112).

The final preparation for removal of the ark to Jerusalem is the assembling of the people. Just as in 1 Chronicles 13:5, **David assembled all Israel** (1 Chr 15:3). The religious overtones of this language are unmistakable. David assembles a holy procession to bring the ark to Jerusalem. But this time the assembly will have proper leadership.

Divine grace is evident in this "second chance" for David and Israel. As McCONVILLE (44) comments, "second opportunities, in the grace of God, do come."

Levites to Carry the Ark (15:4-10). David gathers the **descendants of Aaron** (i.e., the priests) **and the Levites**. The designation "Levites" is used in two ways throughout the chapter. Sometimes it refers to sons of Levi excluding the priests (1 Chr 15:4,11,14,17), and sometimes to the sons of Levi including the priests (1 Chr 15:12). This creates some ambiguity (e.g., 1 Chr 15:15-16). Yet, the correlation of priests and Levites tends to exalt the position of the Levitical order while at the same time maintaining respect for the priestly class.

The Levitical order is divided into six groups. The division is schematized below where the leader is given beneath the family name. This is the only place where we find this sixfold division among the Levites though the relationships among them are present in Exodus 6:18-22. Kohathites were charged with responsibilities for the ark (Num 4:4-6,15; 7:9). Consequently, as JOHNSTONE (1:182) notes, emphasis is given to the Kohathite groups (four of the six are Kohathite).

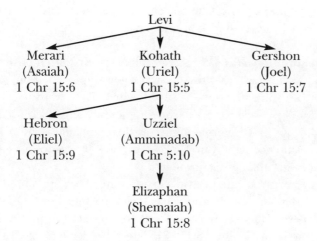

Levi

Merari	Kohath	Gershon
(Asaiah)	(Uriel)	(Joel)
1 Chr 15:6	1 Chr 15:5	1 Chr 15:7

Hebron	Uzziel
(Eliel)	(Amminadab)
1 Chr 15:9	1 Chr 5:10

Elizaphan
(Shemaiah)
1 Chr 15:8

Leaders Are Briefed (15:11-15). David summoned the **priests** and the leaders of the **Levites** (listed in 1 Chr 15:5-10). **Zadok** and **Abiathar** appear together as the chief priests without any hint of the rivalry that existed between the two (cf. 1 Kgs 1–2). These leaders must prepare their respective groups for the holy procession.

The structure of this section consists of two parts: (1) Davidic instruction (1 Chr 15:12-13) and (2) Levitic implementation (1 Chr 15:14-15). In each part, the first half focuses on consecration (sanctify or make yourselves holy; 1 Chr 15:12,14), and the second half focuses on obedience to divine instructions (1 Chr 15:13,15). Consequently, this is the heart of David's response to the debacle of 1 Chronicles 13: holiness and obedience.

The holy leaders of God's people must **consecrate** themselves to this holy service in accordance with the Mosaic prescriptions. This probably involved some rituals of purification, including bathing and separation from uncleanness (cf. Exod 19:14-15). The priests and Levites must take seriously the holy character of the procession. The atmosphere and method of moving the ark in this procession is different.

The mood has changed. Holiness is at the forefront. David knows the first attempt to move the ark failed because the Levites did not carry it (Exod 25:10-15; 37:1-5; Num 4:10-12; 7:9). David failed to inquire of God about how to move the ark. David does not blame Uzzah. He takes responsibility for the failure: **We did not inquire of him** . . . (1 Chr 15:13). The problem was not Uzzah's alone. Israel's leadership is accountable for the life and worship of Israel.

Levitical Musicians (15:16-24). Unlike the first attempt to move the ark, David prescribes the musical leadership of the holy procession by assigning this task to the **Levites**. They were to provide **singers** and musicians in order to **sing joyful songs** (lit., "to lift up sounds of joy"). The term "joy" is in the emphatic position in the Hebrew sentence (cf. 1 Chr 15:25). This holy procession was a celebration rather than a solemn march.

The Levites executed David's instructions. They appointed three leaders (**Heman, Asaph,** and **Ethan**), eleven other Levites, and two **gatekeepers** (**Obed-Edom** and **Jeiel**) to conduct the music of the holy procession (1 Chr 15:17-18). The three leaders are assigned **cymbals** (1 Chr 15:19), and the other eleven are divided into those who play **lyres** (eight; 1 Chr 15:20) and those who play **harps** (six, adding **Azaziah** who is not in the previous list; 1 Chr 15:21). These are the three instruments listed in 1 Chronicles 15:16 (cf. the addition of priestly trumpets and horns in 1 Chr 15:28).

In addition, **Kenaniah** was given responsibility for vocal music (1 Chr 15:22). Interestingly, Chronicles notes the giftedness (skill) of Kenaniah as the reason for his appointment (lit., "he understood it"). Leaders recognize the giftedness of their people and assign them appropriate tasks. God gifts his people to serve, and leaders must empower that service.

Sandwiched between the assignment of the four **doorkeepers** (**Berekiah** and **Elkanah** in 1 Chr 15:23) and the harp musicians **Obed-Edom** and **Jehiah** (probably a variant of Jeiel in 1 Chr 15:18) in 1 Chronicles 15:24b (apparently the latter served a dual role) is the appointment of seven priests **to blow the trumpets before the ark** (1 Chr 15:24a). Trumpeting is a priestly function (cf. Num 10:2,7-10; 29:1; Josh 6:6).

Transferring the Ark (15:25-29)

Chronicles depends upon 2 Samuel 6:12b-16. As Eskenazi (267) points out, "a grammatical shift in 15:25-29 underscores the unique importance of this final act of transfer." Chronicles changes the perfect tense of the verbs in 2 Samuel to participles which emphasize "continuous action." David and the elders are walking (1 Chr 15:25), God is helping (1 Chr 15:26), David has been dressed (1 Chr 15:27), all Israel is bringing up (1 Chr 15:28), and the ark of the covenant was coming (1 Chr 15:29). "Such grammatical turns," Eskenazi (267-268) writes, "make the final movement of the ark the climactic event, the one on which the narrator lingers." This moment is unlike any other moment in the history of Israel. The ark is coming to Jerusalem, the city of God. God is coming to dwell in his city.

Just as God helped David become King (1 Chr 12:18), so God helps the Levites bring the ark to Jerusalem (1 Chr 15:26). Whereas before, God "broke out" against Uzzah and the previous dishonorable procession (1 Chr 13:10-11), now God blesses this holy procession.

While 2 Samuel 6:12b only says "David went down," the Chronicler includes the **elders** and **commanders** (much like 1 Chr 13:1). Further, the Chronicler collapses 2 Samuel 6:15 ("all the house of Israel") into his characteristic phrase **all Israel** (1 Chr 15:28). This is a national event rather than the work of a few leaders. This is a "corporate act" by all Israel "rather than an expression of David's personal faith" (SELMAN, 1:165).

The Chronicler also emphasizes its religious significance. The procession involved sacrificial rituals (1 Chr 15:26). Also, not only does Chronicles specifically mention the Levites as those who carry the ark (2 Sam 6:13 does not; cf. 1 Chr 15:26) as well as the fact that Levites are dressed in **fine linen** (sacral uniform worn by the holy procession; JAPHET, 307) along with David (2 Sam 6:14 does not; cf. 1 Chr 15:27), he also consistently refers to the **ark of the covenant of the LORD** (1 Chr 15:25,26,28,29) while 2 Samuel only calls it the "ark of the LORD" or the "ark of God" (2 Sam 6:12,13,15,16). The introduction of the term "covenant" is significant in the light of the covenant God will establish in 1 Chronicles 17. The ark is a symbol of the covenant between God and Israel.

The role of David in this liturgical procession is significant. Not only does he wear the fine linen but also the **ephod** (1 Chr 15:27). This may mean that David assumed priestly functions since an ephod (a cape) was a priestly indicator (cf. 1 Sam 22:18; Exod 28:4-14; cf. Hurvitz, "Usage," 117-121). THOMPSON (138; contra PAYNE, 4:388-389) comments that "probably we should see some priestly function for David here, but not as a pretext for Israelite kings to assume Levitical prerogatives. This was, in the history of Israel, an exceptional and significant event. David functioned as the type of the Messiah as a king who is also a priest." In 2 Samuel 6:13 it is David who sacrifices the animals. The Chronicler assumes this as well ("ephod"), but broadens the reference to include the Levites who are carrying the ark (1 Chr 15:26; lit., "they sacrificed"). David is a new Moses as the founder of the temple cult just as Moses was the founder of the tabernacle rituals (cf. 1 Chr 16:1-3).

The religious significance is underscored by the musical presence of the Levites. While 2 Samuel 6:14 only mentions David's dancing before the Lord, Chronicles stresses the choral leadership of **Kenaniah**. Further, Chronicles stresses the musical instruments (1 Chr 15:28) and 2 Samuel 6:15 does not (except for the priestly trumpets). This highlights the holy character of this celebratory event.

Saul's daughter, Michal, despises David as he dances and celebrates before the Lord. While 2 Samuel 6:20-23 explains this as her jealousy as well as David's loincloth appearance, Chronicles leaves it in the context of her attitude toward the holy event itself. The daughter of Saul, like Saul, did not appreciate the holy things of God and could not understand this celebratory joy. "Michal's attitude in this matter," JAPHET (308) writes, "reflects the traditional position of the house of Saul: a negative stand toward the ark of the Lord" (1 Chr 13:3). Saul and Michal, then, become "typical of unfaith" (ACKROYD, 63). David is now king instead of Saul. The moment the ark is brought into Jerusalem "David's kingship is finally fully actualized" by the unity of king, ark, city, and people (Eskenazi, 268).

3. Object Reached: Celebration of the Ark's Arrival (16:1-43)

The narrative lingers to savor the entrance of the ark into Jerusalem. While only a few verses are dedicated to the conquest of Jerusalem (1 Chr 11:4-9), this whole chapter celebrates the arrival of the ark. In addition to the space provided in the narrative, Eskenazi (269) notes three other points. First, "[Chronicles] replicates the song and makes the reader a participant in the celebration." Second, "the reiteration of the lists once again forces the narrative to linger." Third, "there is a persistent reminder of permanence and continuity."

SELMAN (1:166) sees a chiastic structure with the psalm at its center. The two outer sections are derived from 2 Samuel 6:17-20, but the Levitical lists have no parallel in canonical sources. The psalm itself is a conflation of three canonical Psalms (1 Chr 16:8-22 from Ps 105:1-15; 1 Chr 16:23-33 from Ps 96:1-13; and 1 Chr 16:34-36 from Ps 106:1,47-48).

   a. God's Blessing for Every Israelite (16:1-3)
      b. Levites Appointed for Worship (16:4-7)
         c. Psalm of Praise (16:8-36)
      b.́ Levites and Priests Appointed for Worship (16:37-42)
   a.́ God's Blessing for David's House (16:43)

The psalm, as the centerpiece of the chapter, celebrates what is theologically important about the ark's arrival.

God's Blessing for Every Israelite (16:1-3)

The ark's arrival is narratively emphasized by repeating themes found at the beginning of 1 Chronicles 15. The ark is brought to its **tent** (prepared in 1 Chr 15:1), the Levites carry out their cultic functions (1 Chr 15:2), and David assembles the people (1 Chr 15:3).

First Chronicles 16:1-3 is the narrative fulfillment of in 1 Chronicles 15:1-3.

All Israel is assembled for this event and they receive the Davidic blessing. All Israel brings the ark to the tent David has prepared for it. The sacrificial offerings in Jerusalem were unusual, but the event is unique so this accounts for sacrifices before the Lord that are not also at the tabernacle.

Two sacrificial offerings are mentioned: (1) **burnt offerings** and (2) **fellowship offerings** (הַשְּׁלָמִים, *haš°lomîm*; from *šalôm*, peace or right relations). Burnt offerings are sacrifices of dedication (Lev 1). The whole animal is given to God as an act of commitment and consecration. Fellowship offerings are sacrifices where the fat is burned to God, the priests eat the breasts and right thigh, and the worshipers eat the rest of the animal (Lev 3; 7:11-21). The meal celebrates the peace between God and his people. The meal involved bread and drink. Thus, David's gift to the people in 1 Chronicles 16:3 is a function of the fellowship offering itself. The people gather to eat the sacrificial meat (NRSV reads "portion of meat;" cf. MYERS, 114) and celebrate the arrival of the ark. It begins with table fellowship: the king (along with the priests), the people, and God share a meal together. The psalm of thanksgiving (1 Chr 16:8-36), then, is contextualized by fellowship offerings (ACKROYD, 63). Likewise Christians sit at a table hosted by a son of David to celebrate his victory over death.

Chronicles does not necessarily portray David as the one who offered the sacrifices personally, but only that he authorized them or led the procession (JAPHET, 314). But it is possible, given the fact that he wears the linen ephod (1 Chr 15:27), that David performed priestly functions (SELMAN, 1:166-167). JOHNSTONE (1:190) notes the parallel between David and Moses. Just as Moses was an officiant at the altar when the Aaronic priesthood was instituted (Lev 8; cf. Exod 24:7-8), so David is an officiant at the altar during the Levitical celebration of the ark's arrival and the institution of Levitical duties in Jerusalem.

Levites Appointed for Worship (16:4-7)

This section is framed by Davidic appointments. David assigns ("gives," נָתַן, *nāthan*; **appointed** in 1 Chr 16:4 and **committed** in 1 Chr 16:7) tasks to the **Levites** and to **Asaph**. He assigns the Levites

to minister before the ark of the LORD (1 Chr 16:4). He assigns **Asaph and his associates** a **psalm** to sing before the Lord.

The ministry of the Levites (cf. 1 Chr 16:37) is described by three verbs: **make petition**, **give thanks**, and **praise**. Their appointed task is to "minister before him forever" (1 Chr 15:2; cf. Deut 10:8; 18:5). The three verbs anticipate 1 Chronicles 16:8-36. They describe the function of liturgical ministry.

The meaning of the first verb, "make petition" (זכר, *zākar*, "to remember"), is disputed. Kleinig (*Song*, 36) suggests it refers to the function of the trumpets in Numbers 10:9-10 which serve as "memorial for you" (לְזִכָּרוֹן לִפְנֵי], *l*ᵉ*zikkārôn liphnê*). "The singing of the Lord's song to instrumental accompaniment," according to Kleinig, "was therefore regarded as an extension of the priestly mandate to sound the trumpets over the public sacrifices." Consequently, Chronicles roots the musical ministry of the Levites in the Torah.

Therefore, in addition to "thanking" and "praising" God, another function of the Levitical song was to "proclaim" ("invoke," NRSV; or "cause to remember") the name of God. Their musical ministry, then, was to remind Israel of their God, to thank God, and to praise God. Chronicles provides a theological function for the Levitical choir which, in turn, provides a theological ground for the priestly function of singing in the contemporary church. The church sings to proclaim the grace of God, thank him, and praise him (Col 3:16; Eph 5:19).

The Levitical musicians named in 1 Chronicles 16:5 are present in 1 Chronicles 15:17-24 except for Jahaziel. Asaph, who played the **cymbals**, was the leader of the group that included those who play **lyres** and **harps** as well as two priests (Eliezer in 1 Chr 15:24 but **Jahaziel** in 1 Chr 16:6; probably a textual corruption, JAPHET, 315) who blew the **trumpets**. Trumpeting was a priestly function (cf. Num 10:8-10). Chronicles emphasizes both the sacrificial rituals (1 Chr 16:1-3) and the importance of the musical ministry of the Levites. They facilitate the praise of God's people as they lead them in proclamation, thanksgiving, and praise.

Kleinig (*Song*, 82, 84, 89) describes the ritual role of these instruments. The trumpets proclaim "the gracious presence of the LORD with his people" in worship. The cymbals announce "the LORD's acceptance of [the burnt offerings] and assisted in proclaiming his gracious presence with his people." The harps and lyres accompanied the "ritual performance of praise." In summary, the instruments served "to announce the LORD to his people, to proclaim his presence, and to praise him for his goodness." The following chart (Kleinig, *Song*, 99) represents their ritual function and significance:

	Trumpets	Cymbals	Lyres and Harps
Normal Number	Two	One	Two Harps, Nine Lyres
Institution	Moses	Nathan, Gad, David	Nathan, Gad, David
Players	Priests	Leader of Levitical Choir	Levitical Musicians
Class	Sounding Instruments	Sounding Instruments	Instruments of Song
Status	Holy Instruments	Instruments of Service	Instruments of Service
Role	Proclamation (Remembrance)	Announcement (Hearing)	Thanksgiving and Praise
Ritual Function	Announcement of burnt offering and of congregational prostration	Announcement of sacred song and call for congregational attention	Accompaniment of sacred song
Ritual Significance	Proclamation of divine presence	Proclamation of divine acceptance of sacrifices	Proclamation of divine goodness and generosity

Since the function of singing is proclamation through thanksgiving and praise, those who listened to this singing received the ministry of music. Music ministered to them in much the same way that choruses and special singing groups minister today. Music may minister to people in worship much like sermons do. The ministry of song edifies and proclaims.

Psalm of Praise (16:8-36)

This hymn uses parts of two Psalms (Ps 105:1-15 with 1 Chr 16:8-22; 106:1,47-48 with 1 Chr 16:34-36) along with the full incorporation of another (Ps 96 with 1 Chr 16:23-33). While this psalm may have circulated previous to its inclusion into Chronicles's narrative (JAPHET, 313), the Chronicler probably constructed it for this specific occasion. While some think it was composed by David and given to Asaph (PAYNE, 4:390), 1 Chronicles 16:7 "does not claim that

David gave this psalm to the Asaphites but that he appointed them to give thanksgiving to the Lord" (Kleinig, *Song*, 133).

Some significant differences exist between the canonical Psalms and 1 Chronicles 16 (noted below). They are old prayers in a new context (Loader, 69-75). None of the Psalms utilized are ascribed to David. The Chronicler involves his readers in the celebration that accompanied the ark's arrival. The psalm, then, speaks to his readers. As SELMAN (1:168) comments, it is "almost certain that earlier Scripture has been reinterpreted and applied to the circumstances of [the Chronicler's] time."

The psalm is framed by the use of the Hebrew term תָּמִיד (*tāmîd*, "continually, regularly"; only used 8 times in Chronicles, 4 times in 1 Chr 16). The word appears in 1 Chronicles 16:6,37,40 as well as in the Psalm (1 Chr 16:11). The "day" of 1 Chronicles 16:7 becomes a continual activity. The ministry of proclaiming, thanking, and praising is a daily ministry. It is the continual seeking of God's presence: to **seek his face always**. This is an appropriate response to the **everlasting covenant** (1 Chr 16:17; cf. 1 Chr 16:15) whereby God blesses Israel. The love of the Lord **endures forever** (1 Chr 16:34,41; cf. 16:36) and so does the praise of God's people. The ministry of the Levites is an unceasing ("forever" in 1 Chr 15:2) ministry of worship.

As the only sacred song that appears in Chronicles (other than refrains taken from it), it is paradigmatic for what sacred song is. Sacred songs remember, thank, and praise God.

This psalm epitomizes the Levitical ministry of song. The threefold function (1 Chr 16:4) of the musical ministry is present in the song. The psalm remembers (זכר, *zkr*) the Lord in 1 Chronicles 16:12,15, praises him (הלל, *hll*) in 1 Chronicles 16:10,25,36 and thanks (ידה, *ydh*) him in 1 Chronicles 16:7,8,34,35. Yahweh (**LORD**) is used 16 times in the psalm (1 Chr 16:8,10,11,14,23,25,26,28[2], 29[2],31,33,34,36[2]). In addition, the psalm reflects the joyous celebration (1 Chr 16:10,31) of God through song (1 Chr 16:9,23). The psalm is not a piece of patchwork but a carefully elaborated celebration of Levitical functions (Hill, 99-100). Thus, the song is a psalm of thanks to the LORD. Consequently, far from interrupting the narrative, the psalm illustrates the Levitical ministry and proclaims the theology of the Chronicler (Butler, 142-150; MCCONVILLE, 51-52; Kleinig, *Song*, 135-136).

Shipp (33-37) argues that the psalm structurally highlights the Levitical functions of remembering, praising, and thanking the Lord. First Chronicles 16:8-14 constitutes an introductory preamble which contains the three Levitical functions of remembering (1 Chr 16:12), praising (1 Chr 16:10), and thanking (1 Chr 16:7-8). The rest of the psalm concentrates on each of these functions. First Chronicles 16:15-22 remembers the Lord, 1 Chronicles 16:23-33 praises him, and 1 Chronicles 16:34-36 thanks him. Each section begins with an imperative (1 Chr 16:8,10,12,15,23[where **sing** is equivalent to "praise"], 34).

(1) Thank the Lord (1 Chr 16:8-9)
   (2) Praise the Lord (1 Chr 16:10-11)
      (3) Remember the Lord (1 Chr 16:12-14)
      (3′)Remember the Lord (1 Chr 16:15-22)
   (2′)Praise the Lord (1 Chr 16:23-33)
(1′)Thank the Lord (1 Chr 34-36)

This means that the whole of 1 Chronicles 16 is structured chiastically. Placing 1 Chronicles 16:8-36 in the context of the whole chapter the schematization looks like this:

a. God's Blessing for Every Israelite (16:1-3)
   b. Levites Appointed for Worship (16:4-7)
      c. Psalm of Praise (16:8-36)

      (1) Thank the Lord (1 Chr 16:8-9)
         (2) Praise the Lord (1 Chr 16:10-11)
            (3) Remember the Lord (1 Chr 16:12-14)
            (3′)Remember the Lord (1 Chr 16:15-22)
         (2′)Praise the Lord (1 Chr 16:23-33)
      (1′)Thank the Lord (1 Chr 34-36)

   b.′ Levites and Priests Appointed for Worship (16:37-42)
a.′ God's Blessing for David's House (16:43)

The Chronicler beautifully portrays an elaborate celebration of the ark's arrival with a literary masterpiece. He framed the chapter with 2 Samuel 6 (1 Chr 16:1-3,43), but added the Levitical appointments (1 Chr 16:4-7,37-42) and a hymnic celebration of this significant moment in the history of Israel (1 Chr 16:8-36).

The heart of this celebration is the call to remember the Lord which evokes praise and thanksgiving. The theological center of the ark narrative is the covenant faithfulness of God. His covenant is an everlasting covenant (1 Chr 16:15,17). His covenant love endures forever (1 Chr 16:34). The ministry of the Levites celebrates that covenant love (1 Chr 16:41). Shipp (31) calls attention to the significance of the liturgical refrain **for he is good; his love endures forever** (1 Chr 16:34,41; 2 Chr 5:13; 7:3,6; 20:21 which are additions to Dtr). It calls "upon the community and the Lord to remember the everlasting nature of the covenant commitment of the Lord to Israel, to remind God of his promise to deliver Israel in light of the present distress, and to remind them that they could rely on God for covenant faithfulness because he is good."

The significance for postexilic readers cannot be overestimated (Butler, 147-150). Their temple worship reminded them of God's covenant love. "*The covenant of God,*" WILCOX (71) writes, "*means the grace of God.*" In response to this memory, they praise and thank God as they seek his redeeming presence. Thus, worship generates hope in the postexilic community, just as it does when Christians remember God's unfailing love in Jesus Christ (Rom 8:31-39).

Thank the Lord (16:8-9)

This thanksgiving is based on Psalm 105:1-2 with only stylistic changes. The poetry is perfectly balanced: each verse contains three imperatival sentences (**give thanks, call, make known** and **sing, sing praise, tell**). The last line in each recalls the mighty acts of God. In the light of God's mighty deeds, the people of God give thanks and honor him with music.

Praise the Lord (16:10-11)

This praise is based on Psalm 105:3-4 with no changes. The poetry is balanced: each verse contains two imperatival sentences (**glory, rejoice** and **look, seek**). The call to praise (*hll*) is translated "glory" by the NIV and paralleled with "rejoice." The object of praise and joy is the Lord, but it only belongs to those who seek the Lord. The verb "seek" (בקשׁ, *bqš*) is used twice and its synonym ("seek"; דרשׁ, *drš*) is translated "look" (cf. 1 Chr 28:9; 2 Chr 7:14). Those who seek the Lord will find joy in the praise of his holy name.

Remember the Lord (16:12-14)

This proclamation is based on Psalm 105:5-7 but with one significant change. Where Psalm 105 reads "seed of Abraham" (Ps. 105:5), Chronicles reads **descendants** (seed) **of Israel** (1 Chr 16:13), which probably particularizes the application to postexilic Judah (WILLIAMSON, 129).

The first two sections emphasized God's mighty deeds ("strength" in 1 Chr 16:11). This section has only one imperative: **remember** (1 Chr 16:12). The emphasis is what (**wonders, miracles, judgments**) to remember and who (**Israel, Jacob**) should remember. Israel, as the elect servant nation, should remember what God has done for them. With such a memory they can confess that he is **the LORD our God**. The God of the universe (**in all the earth**) is the God of Israel.

Remember the Lord (16:15-22)

This proclamation is based on Psalm 105:8-15 with some significant changes. The Chronicler changes the first word from "he remembered" (3rd person sing) to you **remember** (2nd person pl); from a declarative to an imperative which the NIV does not preserve. Further, the Chronicler changes the Hebrew suffixes from third ("they were" in Ps 105:12) to second person ("you were" in 1 Chr 16:19) which the NIV obscures. The change contemporizes the statement for the Chronicler's audience. "In this way," Kleinig (*Song*, 137) comments, the Chronicler "identified his contemporaries with the patriarchs, whose experience was of vulnerability as a landless minority. Like their ancestors they were aliens in their own land which was ruled by the Persians. Yet like them they were also protected by the LORD as a people with royal status and a prophetic mission."

The rest of Psalm 105 recounts the remaining history of Israel, particularly the Exodus. However, the Chronicler is not concerned with the Exodus but with the Davidic-Solomonic kingdom. He does not deny the Exodus, but it is not his theological focus. Psalm 105:1-15 addresses the point he wants to make.

First Chronicles 16:15-22 consists of four parts. (1) Verses 15-16 call upon Israel to remember the **covenant** God made with them. (2) Verses 17-18 remind Israel how God had promised **the land of Canaan**. (3) Verses 19-20 remind Israel how they were once **few** and

wandered from nation to nation. (4) Verses 21-22 remind Israel how God protected them in their wanderings. Thus, the first part is the call to remember, and the three succeeding parts specify the content of that memory. In other words, remember what God has done (cf. 1 Chr 15:8-9).

The application to the postexilic community is apparent. Their situation is similar to the patriarchs. They are few in number, living within another nation, and strangers in the land of promise. Postexilic Israel must remember the covenant God made with Abraham, Isaac, and Jacob. Though they are strangers in the land, the land is theirs. Though they are in distress, God will deliver. As BRAUN (192) notes, "by concluding with v 15 of the psalm [105], the writer has permitted vv 12-15 (=1 Chr 16:19-22) to stand more in the nature of a timeless principle applicable therefore in his own day: *It is the people Israel, reduced in number and without a homeland, which is protected by God*." The promise and protection afforded to the patriarchs (God's "anointed" and "prophets") is also applicable to postexilic Israel.

When Christians feel the "fewness and vulnerability" of the postexilic community, the Chronicler points us to the "great things God has done" (MCCONVILLE, 53). His mighty deeds testify to his faithfulness. That faithfulness engenders hope in distress and inspires confidence in God's ultimate deliverance. Consequently, no matter what the distress, believers petition God with expectant hopefulness: "Save us, O God our Savior" (1 Chr 16:35).

Praise the Lord (16:23-33)

This section is the full incorporation of Psalm 96 with a few changes. The Chronicler uses Psalm 96:1b,2b and omits Psalm 96:1a,2a so that 1 Chronicles 16:23 is a truncated version of Psalm 96:1-2. More significantly, the Chronicler omits the refrain "he will judge the earth . . ." (Ps 96:10b,13b). Apparently, the idea of universal judgment, already present in 1 Chronicles 16:14, is redundant. Kleinig (*Song*, 138) suggests that the omission is due to the Chronicler's intent to project international praise for God in 1 Chronicles 16:23-30 and cosmic praise for God in 1 Chronicles 16:31-33. Judgment, then, is inappropriate to the context.

Psalm 96 was originally a Psalm designed for the temple, but the

Chronicler has adapted it to the new setting in which it appears. For example, "sanctuary" (Ps 96:6) is changed to **strength** (1 Chr 16:28) and "courts" (Ps 96:8) is changed to **before him** (1 Chr 16:29).

Praise language dominates this section as Israel is called to **sing** (1 Chr 16:23; same word in 1 Chr 16:9), **rejoice** (1 Chr 16:31) and **sing for joy** (1 Chr 16:33). Israel's praise confesses that the Lord is king over all the earth. God is **above all gods** (1 Chr 16:25). All other gods are **idols**, but the Lord is the creator of the heavens (1 Chr 16:26). All the nations should hear about his works (1 Chr 16:24), glorify him (1 Chr 16:28), and **bring an offering** (1 Chr 16:29). All the earth should **tremble** before him (1 Chr 16:30). The whole cosmos (**heaven and earth**) should **rejoice** because the Lord God **reigns** (1 Chr 16:31). All nature should rejoice (1 Chr 16:32-33). So, praise is not just the praise of Israel, but the nations and the cosmos as well. The international and cosmic character of this section reminds the reader how Chronicles's history began (1 Chr 1:1). "All Adam's children are now summoned to acknowledge God's purpose portrayed in Israel's history, his sole deity and transcendent power" (JOHNSTONE, 1:194).

The Lord's reign is cosmic. SELMAN (1:168) titles the whole Psalm: "The Lord Is King." The theme resounds with the proclamation, **The LORD reigns** (1 Chr 16:31). The postexilic community might have questioned the reign of God. How can God reign when the situation of Judah is a backwater province of the Persian empire? Nevertheless, faith confesses that God reigns even when it looks like he does not. Postexilic Israel should seek God's presence in the temple, remember his covenant, and praise the one who reigns over the whole earth. The psalm, then, constitutes an appeal for hope in the midst of distress (ALLEN, 116-119).

Thank the Lord (16:34-36)

This section is based on Psalm 106:1,47-48 with some significant changes. The Chronicler changes the first verb from "praise" (*hll*) in Psalm 106:1 to **give thanks** (*ydh*) in 1 Chronicles 16:34. This maintains the symmetry of his chiastic structure. Also, 1 Chronicles 16:35 has **our Savior** where Psalm 106:47 does not. Another change is the addition of the words **cry out** (lit., "and say") in 1 Chronicles 16:35. The Chronicler also adds **deliver us** to the text of Psalm 106:47.

Gather us was not sufficient since Israel in the postexilic situation had already been gathered, but they had not yet been delivered from their oppressors — the Persians. The Chronicler also changes "let all the people say" (Ps 106:48) to **all the people said** (1 Chr 16:36).

While this section is headed by a call to thanksgiving, it also contains a petition. As SELMAN (1:171) notes, the additions to Psalm 106:35 indicate that it has been augmented with a "plea for deliverance or salvation." This does not fit the original Davidic situation (though all his enemies are not necessarily conquered at this point; cf. PAYNE, 4:392). The Chronicler applies this psalm to his audience. It appeals to God to renew his mighty deeds for his postexilic community which must (1) confess the covenant faithfulness of God (1 Chr 16:34) and (2) depend on that faithfulness through petition (1 Chr 16:35). Yet, in their cry for relief they also are able to "bless" (**praise**, 1 Chr 16:36) the everlasting Lord.

SELMAN (1:172) argues that the "whole psalm is, therefore, much more than an illustration of the postexilic liturgical cultus . . . or an establishing of the identity of the Jerusalem cultus. It is an impassioned plea for God to restore his own and his people's identity in [the Chronicler's] own generation by performing fresh acts of salvation."

The Chronicler models for believers how to apply an old Psalm to a new situation. Whatever the original contexts of Psalms 105, 96 and 106, the Chronicler understands that the eternal covenant and the eternal God mean that those same theological principles are always applicable. The people of God confess God's faithfulness and cry out for redemption. Thus, through the canonical Psalms, the Chronicler speaks to his own audience. They must seek the presence of God in worship, trust his eternal covenant, and petition the one who reigns over the cosmos. God is faithful. He will hear the prayers of his people.

Just as the Chronicler appropriated ancient Psalms for his new context, so we read the Psalms in our new situation as well. Those songs express our hearts, emotions, and feelings. They are our laments and petitions too. Just as the Chronicler, we cry out for fresh acts of redemption and deliverance from the God who has demonstrated his faithfulness throughout history.

Levites and Priests Appointed for Worship (16:37-42)

At the conclusion of the Psalm, **David left Asaph** and **Obed-Edom**, along with their **associates, to minister** daily **before the ark** in Jerusalem. He also appointed **Zadok** and **his fellow priests** to minister before the Lord **at the high place in Gibeon.** Israel, then, had two sanctuaries during the reign of David: Jerusalem (ark) and Gibeon (tabernacle). These were united in Solomon's temple (BRAUN, 193-194).

The cultic center at Gibeon is problematic (Dirksen, "1 Chr 16:38," 85-90). No other OT source refers to this except 1 Kings 3:5 (cf. 2 Chr 1:3). Scholars have suggested that the Chronicler invented this story in order to legitimate Solomon's worship at Gibeon (Blenkinsopp, *Gibeon*, 102; Noth, 94-95). Chronicles probably preserves an ancient tradition about a worship center at Gibeon during the time of David (WILLIAMSON, 130-132; JAPHET, 321-323), and Gibeon is only a few miles from Nob where 1 Samuel recognizes a worship center (1 Sam 21:1-9; 22:19; SELMAN 1:173). This explains why Israel has two high priests, Abiathar and Zadok. The former serves before the ark in Jerusalem, and the latter serves at the tabernacle in Gibeon (Kleinig, *Song*, 53).

David maintains the requirements of the law concerning the tabernacle. In addition to the Mosaic legislation, however, David adds the musical praise of God focused on the liturgical refrain: **his love endures forever**. The sacrificial rituals continue at the tabernacle while at the same time the musical liturgy is established in Jerusalem.

The Davidic institution of choral music is distinguished from the priestly sacrificial ritual. While sacrifices continued at the tabernacle, the choral ministry served before the ark in Jerusalem. "The Lord's presence and power, symbolized by the ark, was to be solicited and announced in praise" (Kleinig, *Song*, 144). Levitical song proclaimed the presence of God in Jerusalem.

But proclamation is not simply a cognitive exercise. This is God's sacramental presence among his people. "The proclamation of the LORD's name was a performative enactment. It did not merely impart information about the LORD but actually effected his presence, for wherever his name was proclaimed, he was present with his people, as he had promised in Exodus 20:24" (Kleinig, *Song*, 124).

The ministry of music stands alongside the ministry of the Word because it is a proclamation of the Word in song and the exaltation of God in praise.

God's Blessing for David's House (16:43)

The story of 2 Samuel 6 is resumed exactly where the Chronicler left off in 1 Chronicles 16:1-3 as 2 Samuel 6:19b-20a is incorporated with only stylistic changes. With the ark in place, blessings flow upon Israel and David (just as they did upon Obed-Edom in 1 Chr 13:14). While the NIV reads that David blessed his **family**, the Hebrew term is "house" (בֵּית, *bêth*). This is significant because God will bless the "house" of David in the next chapter (1 Chr 17 where *bêth/bāyith* occurs 14 times). The Chronicler omits Michal's reaction to David in 2 Samuel 6:20b-23 (already noted in 1 Chr 15:29) because he wants to strengthen the link between the arrival of the ark in Jerusalem and the blessing of David's house in 1 Chronicles 16:43–17:1 (where *bêth/bāyith* is used in both verses, translated "family" and "palace" in the NIV).

David's attention to the worship provides a model for the contemporary church. The current attention devoted to the nature of worship in the Christian assembly is quite healthy. The worship of God is holy, celebratory, and God-centered. It deserves the church's focused attention, significant planning, and reverent execution.

4. A House for the Ark (17:1-27)

The movement of the ark of the covenant to Jerusalem leads thematically to God's establishment of a covenant with David. Just as David built a house (1 Chr 17:1) for himself and intended to build a house for God, so now God builds a house for David. A house for the ark becomes a house (a dynasty) for David. House (*bêth/bāyith*) is the key term, occurring 14 times in 1 Chronicles 17 with a range of meaning from "palace," "temple," and "dynasty."

The temple is variously described in Chronicles. Hurvitz ("Terms," 165-183) identifies seven descriptors: "house of sanctuary" (2 Chr 36:17), "house of the holy" (1 Chr 29:3), "house of the most holy" (2 Chr 3:8), "house of the mercy seat" (1 Chr 28:11), "house of rest" (1 Chr 28:2), "house of sacrifices" (2 Chr 7:12), and "house of tent" (1 Chr 9:23). These descriptors bear witness to the holy, atoning, and gracious presence of God in his temple.

First Chronicles 17 is based on 2 Samuel 7 with some significant differences. The chapter contains a prophecy (1 Chr 17:3-15) and a prayer (1 Chr 17:16-27). The structure of the text is: (1) Introductory Dialogue between David and Nathan (1 Chr 17:1-2), (2) Nathan's Prophecy (1 Chr 17:3-15), and (3) David's Prayer (1 Chr 17:16-27).

Some (Hanson, *Dawn*, 301) have thought that since the Chronicler is following 2 Samuel that the Davidic dynasty is not particularly significant. It only serves the ends of the temple. However, the Chronicler does not slavishly follow his sources (he omits some things, rearranges the order, lengthens and shortens, according to his purposes). The fact that he has retained 2 Samuel 7 intact and gives it so much space indicates its importance. Interpreters of the Chronicler must give full weight to its significance in his narrative without assuming its weight is less because it also appeared in his source. Therefore, it is inappropriate to downplay the Davidic covenant and the dynastic overtones because it first appeared in 2 Samuel 7. The Chronicler emphasizes the importance of the Davidic dynasty for his readers (Kelly, 158-167). Indeed, SELMAN (1:174) argues that 2 Chronicles 7:11-22 and 1 Chronicles 17:3-15 "are the two 'words of God' around which [the Chronicler's] entire work is constructed."

Scholars have debated whether the Davidic dynasty is theocratic, messianic, or royalist (Kelly, 135-155). They are divided along two major lines. On the one hand, many believe that the Chronicler is theocratic, that is, he finds the fulfillment of Israel's hope in the temple. When the temple cultus is restored, then Israel is restored and the hope of redemption has been fulfilled. Thus, postexilic Israel is a redeemed theocracy where God reigns through the temple cultus (Mason, 32). On the other hand, others argue that the Chronicler looks forward to a renewed Davidic king. Chronicles is oriented toward the future where a restored Davidic king will reign over Israel. The nature of this future is disputed. Some believe it is premillennial — a period at the end of history where one of David's sons will reign in Jerusalem (cf. PAYNE, 4:396). Others believe it is messianic (e.g., another David) where the Chronicler's expectations are undefined but fulfilled in Jesus Christ who reigns on David's throne (Dillard, *Study*, 608). Still others believe it is royalist — the Chronicler expects another Judean king in the line of David to rule in the post-exilic period (Newsome, 201-217).

The text evidences a profound belief in the eternal character of the dynastic promise to David. This dynasty is both theocratic (temple) and messianic (sons of David). As the story unfolds, David and Solomon function messianically. This dynastic promise, in turn, is linked to the reality of God's presence among his people in the temple cultus. Consequently, the royal (messianic) and priestly (theocracy) interests unite in David and Solomon. The exile dashed the hopes of Israel, but the postexilic community grounds their hope for a renewed Israel in the eternal promise of God to David. The Chronicler's expectation finds fulfillment in the reign of Jesus Christ on the throne of David (cf. Luke 1:31-33). The eternal character of the Davidic kingdom is fulfilled in Jesus Christ who, as a son of David, reigns forever in his eternal kingdom.

Introductory Dialogue between David and Nathan (17:1-2)

First Chronicles 17 has a significant theological twist (THOMPSON, 144-145). The human initiative to build God a temple is not a central divine concern. God does not need a temple — he has dwelt in a tent for years. Instead, divine initiative takes precedence. God elects David and gives his house a permanent quality ("forever," 1 Chr 17:27). Unlike the tent or the temple that Solomon will build, divine election ensures the permanence of David's house. The twist, then, is that though David wanted to do God a favor, God graced David.

Nevertheless, David's desire was not unusual in the ancient Near East. If the king has a house (palace), then the God who gave it also deserves a house (temple). When a king builds a temple, it is an expression of his gratitude (Hurowitz, *Exalted*, 32-90). While it is not unusual for a god to deny a king's request, what is unusual (unparalleled in the ancient Near East; cf. Hurowitz, *Exalted*, 165-167) is the divine explanation for rejecting the proposal. David wants to build God a house, but instead God builds David a house. Instead of demanding and receiving, God continues his gracious giving to David by entering into an eternal covenant with him.

David consults with the prophet Nathan, but Nathan's approval is his own personal discernment. There is no "word of the LORD" (as in 1 Chr 17:3). Nathan apparently offered his own personal counsel which seemed appropriate to everyone concerned — except the Lord.

While there are some minor differences between 1 Chronicles 17 and 2 Samuel 7 (e.g., Chronicles reads **David** in 1 Chr 17:1 where Samuel reads "king" in 2 Sam 7:1), one major difference is the deletion of the reference to David's rest from his enemies in 2 Samuel 7:1. While the reference to "rest" is problematic due to the ensuing discussion of "wars" in 1 Chronicles 18–20, this is not the reason the Chronicler deleted it (2 Sam 7 does not find it problematic). More likely, the Chronicler deletes the reference to "rest" (נוח, *nwḥ*) in 2 Samuel 7:1 because this idea belongs to the reign of Solomon in Chronicles (cf. 1 Chr 22:9,18; 23:25; cf. (BRAUN, 198-199; SELMAN, 1:177; JAPHET, 328). David is the warrior king, and Solomon is the peace king. David did not, at this moment, have the kind of rest that awaited Solomon, and Chronicles reserves that term for the Solomonic era.

Nathan's Prophecy (17:3-15)

Nathan's prophecy falls into four sections. The first (1 Chr 17:3) is the introductory formula. The next two are marked off by the phrase "say to my servant David" (1 Chr 17:4,7). The second section is the divine response to David's intention (1 Chr 17:4-6). The third, and longest section, is the divine promise to build David a house (1 Chr 17:7-14). The last is a conclusion formula (1 Chr 17:15).

The Introductory Formula (17:3)

The **word of God** comes to Nathan that night, and David recognizes what Nathan says to him as something God has spoken (1 Chr 17:17,26). It is what "the LORD says" (1 Chr 17:4,7). Nathan's words reveal God's desires through a divine vision (v. 15, חזון, *ḥāzôn*, "revelation"; the Chronicler's only other use is 2 Chr 32:32). While Nathan gave his best advice in 1 Chronicles 17:2, the divine word countermands Nathan's previous approval.

The Divine "No" (17:4-6)

The rhetorical crescendo builds in this brief answer. The divine answer comes in three stages: (1) You will not build me a house

(1 Chr 17:4), (2) I have never lived in a house (1 Chr 17:5), and (3) I never asked to have a house built (1 Chr 17:6).

Chronicles changes the question in 2 Samuel 7:5 ("Are you the one to build me a house to dwell in?") to a declarative statement (**You are not the one to build me a house to dwell in**). The divine answer, however, is softened by the introductory **my servant** (1 Chr 17:4) and the concluding **my people** (1 Chr 17:6). God does not reject David nor speak harshly. Rather, he affirms his relationship with David and Israel.

The divine answer recognizes two truths in redemptive history. First, God does not need a house. From the day he **brought Israel up out of Egypt to this day** God has dwelt in a tent. The tent moved from place to place, and God dwelled among his people. A temple, then, is not necessary to God's presence in Israel. Second, God never asked for a house. Throughout God's journey **with all the Israelites** (1 Chr 17:6), he never revealed a desire for a house to be built. He never asked any of the judges (שֹׁפְטֵי, *šōphṭê*, **leaders** in NIV). A house is not a divine priority. The divine answer emphasizes God's mobility — "since the people have not yet settled down permanently, God accompanies them in their wanderings" (JAPHET, 300). God will live with his people wherever they are (the Exodus, the wilderness, the worship centers at Shiloh, Nob, Gibeon), even when they do not have a temple (cf. Acts 7:44-50). The postexilic community needed to hear that word.

But why may not David build a temple when, in fact, God will sanction a temple through Solomon? The answer is not given here (1 Chr 22:28). It is enough that David hear the word of the Lord and submit. Just as Moses did not enter the promised land, so David will not experience the redemptive presence of God in the temple though he will prepare Israel for it.

The Divine "Yes" (17:7-14)

This section rehearses God's relationship with David and promises him a future — both immediate and eternal (**forever**). It declares God's faithfulness to David. This section divides into two parts: what God has done (1 Chr 17:7-8a) and what he will do (1 Chr 17:8b-14).

What God Has Done (17:7-8b). God describes his past faithfulness to David. First, he elected David a ruler over his people (1 Chr 17:7).

He was neither a descendant of Saul nor the firstborn of his own family. God made the shepherd of sheep to be the shepherd of Israel. Second, wherever David has gone (wilderness, Ziklag, Hebron, Jerusalem), God has been with him (1 Chr 17:8a). God did not need a temple to be with David in the wilderness ("stronghold" in 1 Chr 12:8,16). Third, God defeated David's enemies throughout his journey to the throne and since he has been enthroned (1 Chr 17:8b; the Philistines in 1 Chr 14). Just as God was faithful to Israel and dwelled among them throughout their journey to the land, so God has been faithful to David in his journey to the throne.

What God Will Do (17:8c-14). The tense of the verbs changes (**I will**). God commits himself to David by promising what he will do. The future promises involve: the kingdom of Israel (1 Chr 17:8c-10a) and the house of David (1 Chr 17:10b-14).

God Will Make a Kingdom for Israel (17:8c-10a). As SELMAN (1:179) notes, "the Davidic covenant represents a new stage in the fulfillment of the Abrahamic and Mosaic covenants." The promise is communal. It applies to Israel as a people (**my people**, 1 Chr 17:9) or kingdom. In fact, just as David had brought the ark up to the place (מָקוֹם, *māqôm*) he had prepared (1 Chr 15:3), so God will plant Israel in this land as a place (*māqôm*) they can call their own (1 Chr 17:9).

In particular, two points recall the patriarchal promises (Japhet, *Ideology*, 386-393; Williamson, *Israel*, 65-66): the promise of a great name (1 Chr 17:8c; Gen 12:2) and the promise of a land without disturbance and oppression (1 Chr 17:9-10a; Gen 13:14-17; 15:18-21). God commits to fulfill the Abrahamic promises through David.

The promise is best viewed in the context of the "kingdom of God" in Chronicles (Selman, "Kingdom," 163-171). The term "kingdom" (מַלְכוּת, *malkûth*) occurs 28 times (including 1 Chr 17:11,14). It is the kingdom of David (1 Chr 14:2), Solomon (1 Chr 22:10), and Yahweh (1 Chr 28:5). God's promise to David is a promise to manifest his own reign over the world through David and his heirs.

God Will Make a House for David (17:10b-14). This section repeats key terms that bind it together as a whole and emphasize the "core of the prophetic message" (JAPHET, 335): **throne** (1 Chr 17:12,14); **kingdom** (1 Chr 17:11,14), **house** (1 Chr 17:12,14), **forever** (1 Chr 17:12,14[2]), **father** (1 Chr 17:11,13), **establish** (1 Chr 17:11,12,14), to **be** (היה, *hāyāh*; 11,13[2],14), and take **away** (סור, *sûr*; 13[2]). God will establish David's throne (kingdom) as an eternal dynastic house (father-son) which God will never take away.

While David intended to build God a house which would not last, God intended to build David a house that would last forever. Chronicles emphasizes this contrast. While 2 Samuel 17:11b reads "make" (עשׂה, *'āśāh*, "establish"), 1 Chronicles 17:10b reads "build" (בנה, *bānāh*) as it does in 2 Samuel 7:13a and 1 Chronicles 17:12a. This balances 1 Chronicles 17:10b and 1 Chronicles 17:12b in a way that subtly heightens the point (Kelly, 157). The building of the two houses is linked to the Davidic covenant. Just as Solomon will build a house for God, so God will build a house for David. The priestly and royal dimensions are linked – both houses are part of the Davidic covenant (ALLEN, 124-125). Kelly (158) argues that this integrative approach to the Chronicler's broadly futuristic concerns (i.e., a future king) best suits the Chronicler's use of the promise.

The permanence of the kingdom is promised through the reign of David's family dynasty. At this point (1 Chr 17:11) Chronicles's account differs from 2 Samuel 7:12. While 2 Samuel reads "I will raise up your offspring to succeed you, who will come from your own body," Chronicles reads **I will raise up your offspring to succeed you, one of your own sons**. Why change from "who will come from your own body" to "one of your own sons"? JAPHET (333) thinks it is purely stylistic in order to emphasize the link with sonship in 1 Chronicles 17:13 (**he will be my son**). BRAUN (199) thinks it evidences the Chronicler's intent to link this promise specifically to Solomon. Whatever the case, Chronicles focuses on the one son of David who will build the temple (1 Chr 17:12-14 – **he**, **his throne**, **his father**, **my son**, **from him**, **set him**). Solomon is the object of this promise, as the rest of Chronicles demonstrates. It is probably too much to read a kind of messianism into the specific promise (Williamson, "Dynastic Oracle," 306-311), but the eternal nature of the promise entails a messianic hope.

The covenant involves a divine adoption of David's family. God and the Davidic king will be father and son, and this relationship is grounded in God's **love**. This "bond transcends even that of covenant: it goes beyond the voluntary, contractual status of a mere agreement between two parties and has become the necessary and inescapable tie as between members of the same family" (JOHNSTONE, 1:206).

God will never take away his love (חֶסֶד, *ḥesed*) from the son of David, as he did from Saul (cf. 2 Sam 7:15). The steadfast love of God for Israel (1 Chr 16:34, 41) is linked to his steadfast love for the Davidic dynasty. God has elected David and his offspring on the ground of his love. It is an eternal election.

Chronicles omits 2 Samuel 7:14b ("when he does wrong, I will punish him with the rod of men, with floggings inflicted by men"). At the very least, this is excluded because it removes the potential hint of Solomonic sins which Chronicles will not detail. Thus, the concession of wrongdoing by Dtr, necessary due to his account of Solomon, is unnecessary for the Chronicler. Others think that the omission of 2 Samuel 7:14b means that the Chronicler believes that the Davidic promise is conditional rather than unconditional (Japhet, *Ideology*, 460-467; JAPHET, 334). But this is unnecessary. If the promise is conditional, this omission may confirm it but it does not establish it.

Is the promise conditional? The conditions are not present in the text. But JAPHET (334) argues that they are present throughout the Chronicler's narrative (e.g., 1 Chr 22:12; 28:7,9). WILLIAMSON (133-134) argues that the promise is conditioned upon Solomonic obedience as the temple-builder, and since he obediently completed his task, the promise is now an eternal one. However, the promise of love to David involves God's commitment to never take that love away from his posterity (or, Solomon). It is an eternal ("forever") commitment. But if it is unconditional, how is this played out in the rest of Chronicles? While individual kings rise and fall, the promise to David remains secure. Indeed, the Davidic covenant is the ground of hope (cf. 2 Chr 7:12-22; 13:5; 21:7; 23:3). God's promise to David is the faith of postexilic Israel, and it grounds the expectation that God will again raise up a Davidic king to restore his people (WILLIAMSON, 134; "Dynastic Oracle," 316-318).

The Davidic dynasty is not independent but participates in the kingdom of God. Chronicles changes the pronouns in 2 Samuel 7:16 to emphasize this point. While 2 Samuel reads "Your house and your kingdom will endure," 1 Chronicles 17:14 reads **I will set him over my house and my kingdom forever**. Thus, the kingdom of Israel is identified with the kingdom of God. The throne of David is God's throne (1 Chr 28:5). As SELMAN (1:180) notes, "it is only

[Chronicles] . . . which sees the kingdom of God expressed directly in the Davidic kingdom." Just as the kingdom of God is forever, so is the Davidic kingdom. That identification is significant for a messianic reading of Chronicles because the kingdom of God is ultimately the kingdom of Jesus Christ.

Theologically, God brings his presence to the world through Israel, the Davidic king, and the temple cultus. "Here," JOHNSTONE (1:206) writes, "the sacramental role of Israel as earthly counterpart to the cosmic forces of the LORD of hosts finds its sharpest focus in the sacramental role of the Davidic king whose rule and status are the living expression of God's own reign." That sacramental role, of course, is climaxed in the incarnational ministry of Jesus, Immanuel (Matt 1:21; John 1:14). It is present by the indwelling of the Holy Spirit by whom we become the temple of God (1 Cor 6:18-20). Ultimately, it anticipates the new heaven and new earth when God will dwell among his people in the new Jerusalem (Rev 21:1-4). The promise of God is secure and eternal.

The Concluding Formula (17:15)

This enables the narrative to transition from Nathan's oracle to David's prayer. Nathan delivers a divine word through a vision, and David responds to the divine word with prayer.

David's Prayer (17:16-27)

The introductory formula is significant (1 Chr 17:16a). Having heard Nathan's oracle, David goes into God's presence to pray: **King David went in and sat before the LORD**. Apparently, David entered the tent where the ark of the covenant had been placed and offered his prayer (cf. 1 Chr 16:1).

JAPHET (338-339) discerns three movements in this prayer. First, David humbles himself before the Lord as he submits to God's word (1 Chr 17:16-19). Second, David bears witness to the exalted place of God who has graciously chosen Israel as his people (1 Chr 17:20-22). Third, David petitions God to fulfill his promise by blessing his house forever (1 Chr 17:23-27). The prayer moves from submission to awe to petition. Along the way, the prayer is filled with ten invocations: **O LORD God** (1 Chr 17:16-17), **O God** (1 Chr 17:17); **O LORD** (1 Chr 17:19-20,26), **you, O LORD** (1 Chr 17:22,27), **now, LORD**

(1 Chr 17:23), and **you, my God** (1 Chr 17:25). This reflects the "great excitement in which the prayer is uttered" (JAPHET, 336) as well as the overwhelming sense of relationship with God.

The prayer is David's resignation to the divine "no." David must have been disappointed. The prayer has no overflowing joy in it. There is no call for rejoicing or praise. Rather, there is the respectful submission of one who is amazed by the divine promise to preserve his house, but who nevertheless is disappointed that God has said "no."

David's Humility (17:16-19)

In the light of God's promise to David, one would expect an extended thanksgiving (along the lines of 1 Chr 16:8-9). However, David's prayer lacks the usual features of a thanksgiving. There is no exuberance of praise (as in 1 Chr 16) though there is excitement. David must have been disappointed by the "no" he received, but he is also awed by the divine promise.

The prayer reflects, as SELMAN (1:182) comments, "a marked change in David's perspective. He has a new perception of his dependence" on God. Consequently, David's first question is about himself: **Who am I** and **what is my family** (lit., "house")? These rhetorical questions reflect David's awe and humility as he acknowledges that he is the Lord's **servant**. David knows that it is nothing that he has done, but that God has acted **for the sake of** his **servant** and **according to** his **will**. David recognizes his humble origins. **What more can David say** to his elector?

David's Confession of Yahweh (17:20-22)

David's confession is twofold: (a) **there is no one like** Yahweh (1 Chr 17:20), and (b) there is no one like **your people Israel** whom Yahweh has chosen (1 Chr 17:21-22). The first exalts the God of Israel as the only true God.

The second part acknowledges the divine election of Israel as a people. The Exodus and Conquest come into full view. God chose Israel and redeemed them from Egyptian bondage. The faithfulness of God entailed the conquest of the promised land when God drove **out nations before** his people. Further, this election is no temporary act. God made Israel his **very own forever**. Just as the election of

David's house is forever, so also is the election of Israel. David confesses Yahweh's gracious, electing redemption.

Theologically, this text underscores a significant dimension of redemptive history. God seeks a **people for himself**. He yearns for a people who will call him **their God**. This is a pervasive theme in Scripture. When God entered into covenant with Abraham, he promised that Abraham's descendants would be God's people and he would be their God (Gen 17:7-8). When God came to Israel in Egypt through Moses, he promised redemption and assured them that "I will take you as my own people, and I will be your God" (Exod 6:7). When Israel set up the tabernacle in the wilderness, God's glory descended on it with the promise that there God would dwell among his people and be their God (Exod 29:45; 40:34-35; Lev 26:11-12). The glory was repeated with the completion of the temple under Solomon (1 Kgs 8:11; 2 Chr 5:14; 7:1-3). The prophets constantly reminded Israel of God's promise to be present among them (Ezek 34:30). Israel would be God's people and he would be their God (Jer 7:23; 11:4; 24:7; Ezek 11:20; 14:11; 36:28; 37:27; Zech 2:11; 8:8; 13:9).

Further, this promise was at the heart of the "new covenant." Through Jeremiah, God declared his intent to forgive Israel's sin so that he could fulfill his promise, that is, "I will be their God and they will be my people" (Jer 31:33). Paul, in the context of thinking about the ministry of this new covenant (2 Cor 3:6), reminds us that this promise has found expression in God's church where "we are the temple of the living God" (2 Cor 6:16). Leviticus 26:11-12 is fulfilled in the church, as God has said: "I will live with them and walk among them, and I will be their God, and they will be my people" (2 Cor 6:16 quoting Lev 26:12). The ultimate goal is the eschatological dwelling of God with his people which he will establish. When the new Jerusalem descends out of heaven, then a loud voice will announce: "Now the dwelling of God is with men, and he will live with them. They will be his people, and God himself will be with them and be their God" (Rev 21:3).

This redemptive-historical motif, that God seeks a people for himself, demonstrates that God's intent in redemption/re-creation is to dwell with his people in a communion of love. God seeks fellowship with his people (Hicks, *Trust*, 52-59).

David's Petitions (17:23-27)

David petitions the Lord to do as he promised. This section divides into two parts: (a) the petition itself (1 Chr 17:23-24) and (b) the acknowledgement of divine blessing (1 Chr 17:25-27).

First Chronicles 17:23 contains the single imperative in the prayer: **do as you promised**. But it is flanked on either side with wish-prayers (**let the promise . . . . it will be established**). The wish-prayers petition that the Lord should establish David's dynasty **forever** so that everyone will acknowledge that **the LORD Almighty** (or, Yahweh of Hosts) is the God of Israel. The **name** of God will be **established forever** just as David's dynasty is **forever**. When God blesses David, he thereby glorifies his name. God is glorified in the redemption of his people.

The second part does not contain any petitions. Unlike 2 Samuel 7:25 where David uses two imperatives ("be pleased" and "bless"), the Chronicler changes the mood of the verb "please," **you have been pleased to bless**. The Chronicler recognizes the divine oracle as a present blessing which is also a past act — a sovereign election (it pleased God).

Because God is trustworthy, David acknowledges the blessing that is yet to come. The extension of his house is yet future, but David is confident based on the trustworthiness of the divine word. The Hebrew roots for "speak" (4 times), "bless" (3 times), "house" (4 times), "forever" (4 times), and "servant" (6 times) bespeak the emphasis of 1 Chronicles 17:23-27. God promised to bless the house of his servant David forever.

David's goal to build a house for the Lord is denied, but the Lord declares that he will build a house for David. While David could not build anything truly permanent ("forever") — temples are eventually destroyed, the Lord will build something eternal for David — a house that will never be destroyed. "What better way was there for [the Chronicler] to reaffirm Israel's hope and trust in the coming Deliverer than to recount for his readers the trust and confidence with which David responded to the promise of His coming?" (SAILHAMER, 50-51).

David's response is a humble acknowledgement of electing grace. Sometimes God says "No" to seemingly "good" things; he is not a "vending machine" but the Sovereign Lord. Yet, even when

God answers "No," he still extends his grace. God said "No" to David's temple plans, but he said "Yes" to something for which David did not ask. Even though he received a divine "no," he submits, trusts in God's goodness, and leans on the divine promise. Perhaps this models how we should respond to "No" answers. More importantly, this redemptive-historical moment points to its ultimate fulfillment in Jesus Christ (cf. Luke 1:31-33).

C. DAVID WINS WARS (18:1-22:1)

These four chapters report David's wars. While most tend to separate 1 Chronicles 21:1-22:1 from 1 Chronicles 18-20, the Davidic census (1 Chr 21) is best contextualized by the Davidic wars.

The Chronicler follows 2 Samuel closely, but omits large chunks of material and does not add any of his own (SELMAN, 1:184; BRAUN, 201).

Content	1 Chronicles	2 Samuel
David's Victories over the Nations	18	8
David's Kindness to Mephibosheth		9
The Ammonite War	19	10
Beginning of the Siege of Rabbah	20:1a	11:1
David, Bethsheba, and Uriah		11:2-27
David's Sin and Consequences		12:1-25
Joab's Call for Support		12:26-28
The End of the Ammonite War	20:1b-3	12:29-31
Amnon and Absalom		13–14
Rebellion in David's Family		15–20
Death of Saul's Descendants		21:1-14
A Philistine Battle		21:15-17
Philistine Wars	20:4-8	21:18-22
David's Song of Praise		22:1-51
David's Last Words		23:1-7
David's Mighty Men	(11:10-41)	23:8-39
Davidic Census	21:1–22:1	24:1-25

Is there a pattern to this inclusion and exclusion of 2 Samuel material? In the past, most believed the Chronicler was fashioning an ideal (even fictional) David. For example, he omits David's dysfunctional family. Thus, the principle by which the Chronicler selects his material is driven by a messianic or "golden age" view of David. He omits stories that hinder this idealization. However, the Chronicler does not wince at pointing out David's failings when they are related to his themes, that is, the ark (1 Chr 13) and the census (1 Chr 21). In both Chronicles accentuates David's responsibility more than does Dtr. Since the ark and the location of the temple are central concerns, he does not overlook David's sins. Further, Chronicles omits David's kindness to Mephibosheth which surely would have enhanced David's idealization. Thus, the Chronicler is not primarily interested in an idealized David (Sugimoto, 64-70).

The stories in 1 Chronicles 18–20 are Davidic victories over enemies. Chronicles has collected war stories from 2 Samuel into one literary unit. What, then, motivates their selection and collection? Sugimoto (69; cf. McCONVILLE, 63) suggests that these "victory reports are placed immediately after the Davidic promise (1 Chr 17) to show the beginning of its fulfillment and God's establishment of David's kingdom." God promised David, "I will also subdue all your enemies" (1 Chr 17:10). First Chronicles 18–20 confirms the divine promise.

Consequently, the Chronicler does not tell family stories because, as SELMAN (1:185) notes, he is focused on the fulfillment of the divine promise to make a name for David (1 Chr 18:8a), to secure his territory (1 Chr 18:9), and to subdue his enemies (1 Chr 18:10). This is exactly what 1 Chronicles 18–20 does. What he excludes from 2 Samuel would have detracted from that purpose. Further, that divine purpose includes Solomon. The inclusion of the revolts of Absalom (2 Sam 13–19) and Sheba (2 Sam 20) would have weakened the strong relationship that Chronicles builds between David and Solomon. The exclusion of Solomon's rivals reinforces the divine establishment of Solomon's kingdom.

But why is 1 Chronicles 21 included? The Davidic victories provide the backdrop for the census. God had blessed David's military campaigns in 1 Chronicles 18–20, but his anger is aroused in 1 Chronicles 21 over a military census. Whereas in 2 Samuel David's military success is scattered throughout the narrative, the Chronicler connects them. He concentrates the military adventures not only to signal the fulfillment of divine promises, but also to contextualize the census.

WILLIAMSON (137-138) and BRAUN (202) suggest subthemes. The wars explain why David could not build the temple (1 Chr 22:8; 28:3) since he is pictured as a "great warrior" (JAPHET, 344; cf. ACKROYD, 68-70). The booty provides some of the wealth that enables Solomon to build the temple (2 Chr 5:1 with 1 Chr 18:8,11). But while the temple looms ahead, the focus of 1 Chronicles 18–20 is military victory in fulfillment of the divine promise, and 1 Chronicles 21 is contextualized by these military victories.

Though 1 Chronicles 18–20 should be united with 1 Chronicles 21, their concerns are different. First Chronicles 18–20 reports David's victory and 1 Chronicles 21 reports his sin. Further, 1 Chronicles 18–20 are united by a literary structure (18:1; 19:1; 20:4) that begins with the words **in the course of time**.

1. Davidic Victories (18:1–20:8)

This section falls into three sections (1 Chr 18:1; 19:1; 20:4). The first is a general overview of David's victories (1 Chr 18:1-17), and the second and third focus on two of David's most prominent enemies, the Ammonites (19:1–20:3) and the Philistines (20:4-8). As ALLEN (132-133) notes, the two subjugations of the Philistines (1 Chr 18:1; 20:4) function as structural markers to bind the whole. The narrative, then, is a rehearsal of God's mighty acts through David.

Victory over the Nations (18:1-17)

Theologically, the most significant phrase is repeated twice (1 Chr 18:6,13): **The Lord gave David victory everywhere he went**. The one who promised the subjugation of his enemies is carrying out his promise. This phrase also divides the text into three parts: (1) Military Victories (1 Chr 18:1-6), (2) Vassal Tribute (1 Chr 18:7-13), (3) David's Personnel (1 Chr 18:14-17).

Military Victories (18:1-6)

Chronicles reproduces 2 Samuel with a few minor variations and one major omission. Chronicles omits 2 Samuel 8:2b which describes David's execution of two-thirds of the Moabites. While MYERS (1:137; cf. BRAUN, 204) sees this as another example of "whitewashing" David, JAPHET (346) speculates that it was omitted either "from textual corruption or literary preferences." The Chronicler is not averse to executing God's enemies (cf. 2 Chr 25:12) so it would not have been a negative point.

The flow of the narrative is annalistic as it reports David's victories over Philistia (1 Chr 18:1), Moab (1 Chr 18:2), Zobah (1 Chr 18:3-4), and Aram (1 Chr 18:5-6). It is a quick-hitting recital of significant victories that enlarge David's kingdom.

Philistia was located southwest of Jerusalem along the Mediterranean coast. David took control of **Gath** (2 Sam 8:1 reads Metheg Ammah [as does 4QSamᵃ] which is unknown but Chronicles associated it with Gath). His subjugation of Philistia does not necessarily entail the removal of their king (cf. 1 Kings 2:39). Rather, they became his vassals. Just like the **Moabites** (1 Chr 18:2), the **Philistines** paid tribute. Moab is located east of Jerusalem across the Dead Sea. Thus, David secures his southern borders to the east and west of Jerusalem.

Zobah was one of the Aramaean states to the immediate north of Israel in the Becca valley (southeastern Lebanon; cf. Mazar, "Aramean," 98-120). Apparently, **Hadadezer** proclaimed his sovereignty over this northern region (**he went to establish his control** [lit., "hand"]) and threatened the emerging state of Israel. David decimated Hadadezer's army. The Hebrew of 2 Samuel 8:4, smoothed over by the NIV through textual emendation, reads: "a thousand and seven hundred horsemen." Chronicles's reading of **a thousand of his chariots** is supported by 4QSamᵃ and the LXX. It is the superior textual reading. The difference between "seven hundred" and **seven thousand** is another example of textual corruption (LXX reads 7,000) rather than an exaggeration by the Chronicler since he does not exaggerate the **twenty thousand foot soldiers** (same number as in 2 Sam 8:4). JAPHET (347) suggests that the loss of "chariots" in 2 Samuel 8:4 led to the reduction of the number from 7,000 to 700 in textual transmission. On the whole the better textual reading is the present text of Chronicles (NIV).

When other Aramean states (particularly **Damascus**) came to the aid of Hadadezer, David defeated them as well. His victory was sufficient to place **garrisons** in the region of Damascus which lies northeast of Dan. JOHNSTONE (1:211) perceives an implied contrast between Hadadezer and David. The royal name Hadadezer means "Hadad is help" where "Hadad" is an alternate name for Baal. Thus, while Hadazer depended on Baal, **the LORD gave David victory**. The Lord reigns over the nations.

Interestingly, the expansion of the Davidic kingdom from the southwest to the east across the Jordan and into the northeast represents a significant land gain. It recalls the patriarchal land promises (SELMAN, 1:186-187).

Vassal Tribute (18:7-13)

The booty from Hadadezer is brought to Jerusalem. This included the decorative **gold shields** of Hadadezer's officers. David also took spoils from the conquered cities of **Tebah** and **Cun** (Betah and Berothai in 2 Sam 8:8). "Tebah" is probably the original reading and Samuel is textually corrupted, but Berothai is known from Ezekiel 47:16 and "Cun" is attested in extrabiblical sources. JAPHET (348) is probably right when she proposes that the name change is based on "an inclination to 'modernize' the historical testimony." Perhaps **Cun** is another name for Berothai.

Chronicles adds a piece of information in 1 Chronicles 18:8 not present in 2 Samuel 8:8. Solomon used the bronze taken from Hadadezer **to make the bronze Sea, the pillars and various bronze articles**. This links the Davidic wars with preparations for the temple. Chronicles strengthens the connections within the whole context: God builds David's house through military victories, and David prepares for God's house with the spoils of military victories. Dedicating the booty to the temple is David's grateful response.

When other northeast states heard of David's victory, they submitted to his sovereignty by paying tribute. **Tou** (Toi in 2 Sam 8:9 is a variant spelling; cf. JAPHET, 349) **of Hamath**, who rejoiced in David's victory because he had been at war with Hadadezer as well, sent his son as an emissary **to greet him** (lit., "ask for peace") and **congratulate him on his victory in battle**. This diplomacy and tribute indicated the initiation of a vassal relationship (Wiseman, 311-326). The son's name has suffered textual corruption between 2 Samuel 8:10 (Joram) and 1 Chronicles 18:10 (**Hadoram**), or it may be a variant spelling. The divine promise gave David sovereignty over the region of Hamath near the Euphrates river.

The final words in this section are summary in character (1 Chr 18:11-13). It includes **Edom** (2 Sam 8:12 reads "from Aram" [מֵאֲרָם, *mē'ărām*] rather than "from Edom" [מֵאֱדוֹם, *mē'ĕdōm*]; Aram is a textual corruption), Ammon and **Amalek** which were not previously mentioned. This indicates that there were fuller lists of David's conquests that Chronicles does not supply here. The Chronicler comments on the Edom campaign in 1 Chronicles 18:12-13, which expanded David's kingdom southeast of the Dead Sea. However, there is a question as to who gets the credit for leading this expedition. While 2 Samuel 8:13 gives it to David, 1 Chronicles 18:12 attributes it to **Abishai son of Zeruiah** who is the brother of Joab, the commander of David's army. While this may be easily harmonized to think that David acted through his military commanders (just as **David had defeated the entire army of Hadadezer** in 1 Chr 18:9) and Joab himself is associated with the defeat of Edom (cf. Ps 60:2; 1 Kgs 11:15-16), why does Chronicles introduce Abishai? We may attribute it to the historical memory that Abishai (already known from 1 Chr 2:16 and 11:20) led the campaign under the direction of David and Joab. Chronicles's specification, however, does not obscure the honor due David.

David's Personnel (18:14-17)

This section summarizes David's primary administrative, cultic and military personnel. SELMAN (1:189-190) calls it his "cabinet." David reigns over **all Israel** and executes justice. Foreign oppression is gone as God promised. Peace and justice pervade the land.

David's cabinet included six groups: (1) commander of the army; (2) the **recorder**; (3) the **priests**; (4) the **secretary**; (5) the commander of the **Kerethites and Pelethites**; and (6) **chief officials** (identified as **David's sons**). This organization is loosely patterned after Egyptian administrations (MYERS, 1:138). The role of the recorder (מַזְכִּיר, *mazkîr*) is parallel with the chief of protocol in Egypt (who regulated admissions to royal audiences; cf. THOMPSON, 153), and the secretary (סוֹפֵר, *sôphēr*) is "responsible for official correspondence" (SELMAN, 1:190). JOHNSTONE (1:213) believes these offices were held by Levites because the recorder is a temple official in 2 Chronicles 34:8 and the secretary in 1 Chronicles 24:6 is a

COLLEGE PRESS NIV COMMENTARY

Levite. The Kerethites (Crete) and Pelethites (Philistines) probably
refer to David's bodyguards.

Zadok and **Ahimelech** are the priests, but one would expect it to
read Zadok and **Abiathar** since those are David's two high priests
(cf. 1 Chr 15:11). It may be that Ahimelech served alongside of his
father Abiathar just as Aaron and his sons served together (SELMAN,
1:191).

A further problem is the difference between 2 Samuel 8:18 and
1 Chronicles 18:17. While the Hebrew of 2 Samuel 8:18 reads
"priests" (כֹּהֲנִים, *kōhănîm*; NIV reads "royal advisers"), 1 Chronicles
18:17 reads **chief officials** (הָרִאשֹׁנִים, *hāri'šōnîm*). Some believe that
the Chronicler could not have possibly envisioned David's sons as
priests, so he changed the reading in his source to reflect his own
theological standpoint (MYERS, 1:139; MANGAN, 51). However,
Chronicles has already pictured David in priestly functions (cf. 1 Chr
15–16), but this would be dubiously extended to his sons who did
not act *ex officio*. The best solution, proposed by Wenham ("David's
Sons," 79-82; cf. WILLIAMSON, 140, and JAPHET, 352), regards
2 Samuel 8:18 as a textual corruption where "chief official" (סֹכֵן,
sōkēn) was corrupted into "priest" (כֹּהֵן, *kōhēn*). This is supported by
the reading "chief officials" (or something similar) in the LXX,
Syriac, the Targum, and other ancient versions. Thus, the NIV
emendation of 2 Samuel 8:18 is probably correct. The sons of David
were not priests but officials in the government.

Victory over the Ammonites (19:1-20:3)

This section is based on 2 Samuel 10:1-19 (1 Chr 19:1-19),
2 Samuel 11:1 with 12:26 (1 Chr 20:1), and 2 Samuel 12:30-31 (1 Chr
20:2-3). Aside from the "customary differences due to textual errors
and style" and "the desire to update the text," the "writer has shown
relatively little interest in the narrative" (BRAUN, 207). The
Chronicler has adopted 2 Samuel into his narrative for the sake of
his larger purpose, that is, to confirm the divine promise of Davidic
victories over his enemies (SELMAN, 1:191-192). The Bathsheba story
is incidental to that purpose, and consequently is excluded from his
narrative though "he assumes knowledge of the fuller account"
(WILLIAMSON, 140).

JAPHET (354) divides the text into five parts. The following chart represents the flow of the narrative.

2 Sam	1 Chr	Topic	The Nations
10:1-5	19:1-5	(a) David's Delegation to Hanun	Ammon
10:6-7	19:6-8	(b) The Mustering of Troops	Ammon & Aram
10:8-14	19:9-15	(c) The First Battle	Ammon & Aram
10:15-19	19:16-19	(d) War with the Aramaeans	Aram
11:1; 12:26, 30-31	20:1-3	(e) The Final Battle with Ammon	Ammon

First Chronicles 18 reports David's defeat of the Aramaeans (1 Chr 18:3-8) and the Ammonites (1 Chr 18:11). First Chronicles 19 is a further report. The exact chronological sequence between 1 Chronicles 18 and 1 Chronicles 19 is unclear. Since 1 Chronicles 18 is annalistic, it may reflect summary accounts that are now detailed in narrative form. It may be that the defeat of the Ammonites precedes the defeat of the Arameans in 1 Chronicles 18:3-8 and that the description of the war with the Arameans in 1 Chronicles 19:16-19 is the same as the war in 1 Chronicles 18:3-8. Or, because the war in 1 Chronicles 18:3-8 seems final, it may be that 1 Chronicles 19:16-19 is the first war with the Arameans and that 1 Chronicles 18:3-8 is the final battle between them. Thus, SELMAN (1:191-192) suggests this order for the battles: (1) first Ammonite battle (1 Chr 19:1-15), (2) first Aramean battle (1 Chr 19:16-19), (3) final Ammonite battle (1 Chr 20:1-3), and (4) final Aramean battle (1 Chr 18:3-8).

David's Delegation to Hanun (19:1-5)

Nahash king of the Ammonites dies and his son **Hanun** reigns in his place. David sends **a delegation to express sympathy**. This served a political as well as benevolent function. David intended peaceful relations between the two nations. JOHNSTONE (1:215) believes Chronicles implies a suzerain relationship where Ammon pays tribute to Israel. The **Ammonite nobles** believed there was a sinister purpose for this delegation. Israel had come to **explore and spy out the country and overthrow it** (the Hebrew order is explore, overthrow, and spy out).

Hanun listens to his advisors. As a sign of rejection and "intentional provocation," he humiliates the delegation (JAPHET, 356-357).

The Ammonites prepare for war in 1 Chronicles 19:6-7. David prepared for battle when it was clear that this was what the Ammonites intended.

The act of humiliation involved two personal affronts. First, Hanun **shaved them**. While 2 Samuel 10:4 specifies that only half their beard was shaved, Chronicles generalizes without necessarily implying more than what 2 Samuel intends. Chronicles abbreviates the account. Second, Hanun **cut off their garments in the middle at the buttocks**. This exposed them in a humiliating manner (cf. Isa 47:2-3).

The Mustering of Troops (19:6-8)

The textual differences between 2 Samuel 10 and 1 Chronicles 19 are greatest in this section. JAPHET (357-358) and Ulrich (152-156) examine them in detail though they arrive at somewhat different conclusions. The most significant example is the difference between 2 Samuel 10:6 and 1 Chronicles 19:6 (in agreement with 4QSam[a]). Second Samuel includes 20,000 foot soldiers from Aram (Euphrates region), 1,000 from the king of Maacah (Mt. Hermon region) and 12,000 from Tob. This totals 33,000. Chronicles reads **32,000**, but the 1,000 from the **king of Maacah** is not included in the Chronicler's number. JAPHET (357) regards this as an "intentional abbreviation," e.g., the deletion of the names of the kings and only the inclusion of place names in 1 Chronicles 19:6. The substitution of the term "foot soldiers" with **chariots and charioteers** is more problematic, but Chronicles's text is also found in 4QSam[a]. There were, no doubt, both chariots and foot soldiers in the Ammonite army. Samuel emphasizes one and Chronicles the other. Because the difference is a matter of textual tradition, it is inappropriate to attribute it to fictional exaggeration. In addition, the price of **a thousand talents of silver**, while absent from 2 Samuel, is present in 4QSam[a].

Whatever the complications of the textual tradition, the **Ammonites** called upon their northern neighbors (**Aram**) to assist them. No doubt David was a rising threat to the rulers of Ammon and Aram (east and northeast of Palestine). The army camped at the Moabite town of **Medeba** northeast of the Dead Sea. While some (WILLIAMSON, 141; JAPHET, 359) have seen this as problematic (a

Moabite town becomes the scene of a battle between David and Ammon), Joab may have just conquered Moab and this threatened Ammon's southern border. Further, Mazar ("Arameans," 102) believes that this whole incident is part of the larger battle between Aram and David over the important trade route called the "King's Highway." Medeba sits on that trade route. Thus, the Ammonite move into Moab threatens Israel, and David responds.

The First Battle (19:9-15)

The **Ammonites** had formed lines in front of the city and the **Arameans** were in the open country behind **Joab**. Given the situation, Joab divided his army. He led some of his **best troops** against the Arameans, but **Abishai his brother** led the rest of the army against the Ammonites. The general cautioned his brother that they might be squeezed in the middle. When Joab routed the Arameans, the Ammonites retreated into the walled city. The Ammonites probably prepared for a siege, but Joab returned to Jerusalem. JAPHET (360) thinks Joab disengaged because his force was too small and he knew he was about to war on two fronts (Aram and Ammon). It seems likely that Joab disengaged, formed an army for the war with Aram, and, after their subjugation, returned to Ammon to complete the conquest. The battle, therefore, shifted from Medeba to Rabbah (cf. 1 Chr 19:9,15; 20:1).

The theological heart of the narrative is Joab's exhortation to his brother (1 Chr 19:13): **Be strong and let us fight bravely for our people and the cities of our God. The LORD will do what is good in his sight**. While the NIV makes the final sentence a declarative one, it is probably a prayer (NRSV): "May the LORD do what seems good to him." The Lord decides the outcome of battle. Victory is the Lord's gift (1 Chr 18:6,13) and defeat is the Lord's punishment. Either way the outcome of the battle is based on the sovereign will of God.

This exhortation recalls Moses' instructions to Joshua to "be strong and courageous" in the conquest of the promised land (Deut 31:6-7; Josh 1:6,7,9). Joshua acted on God's land promise, and Joab does the same. When Israel is threatened, God will protect his cities (**cities of our God**, 1 Chr 19:13).

War with the Arameans (19:16-19)

While the participation of the Arameans at Medeba was mercenary in nature, the situation has changed. **David** now threatens their
own interests. Consequently, they mustered troops from beyond the
Euphrates in Mesopotamia. **Hadadezer** intended to mobilize all
Arameans against David. David also prepared for a war. As JAPHET
(360) comments, "David has three objectives in this war: to diminish
the threat of Aramaean might; to challenge the supremacy of
Hadadezer by throwing Aramaean unity into disarray; and to prevent a pact between Aram and Ammon" (cf. 1 Chr 19:18-19).

The significance of this battle is found in the words that David
gathered all Israel and crossed the Jordan. David's hegemony over
the transjordan region was at stake. The ancestral lands of Reuben,
Gad, and half of Manasseh were in the balance. It appears that David
himself led this battle (though "David" may not mean his personal
presence but the presence of his representatives; e.g., **David killed
seven thousand** in 1 Chr 19:18). The result of the battle is that **the
vassals of Hadadezer** secured a **peace with David**. Now David functioned as the suzerain where once Hadadezer had. The peace
between the Arameans and David, then, isolated the Ammonites.
Since the Ammonites no longer had allies and there was no one to
rescue them from the north, David turned his attention to the
Ammonite capital city — Rabbah (1 Chr 20:1). Once the Ammonites
were totally defeated, the Arameans again rose up against David and
were finally defeated (cf. 1 Chr 18:3-8); this time the Arameans paid
the tribute which is absent from 1 Chronicles 19:16-19.

There is a difference in the numbers of charioteers between
2 Samuel 10:18 and 1 Chronicles 19:18 (cf. 1 Chr 18:4). While
2 Samuel reads "seven hundred" charioteers (MT reads "forty thousand horsemen" where the NIV says "foot soldiers"), Chronicles
reads **seven thousand charioteers** and **forty thousand foot soldiers**
(LXX agrees with Chronicles). The problem is again best solved in
the light of textual transmission with Chronicles's reading as the
original one (WILLIAMSON, 141).

The Final Battle with Ammon (1 Chr 20:1-3)

Chronicles condenses the account of the Ammonite war in
2 Samuel 11–12 into three verses. It is an abbreviated rendition

which creates some difficulties. While it appears that **David** is the one who captured **Rabbah** in 2 Samuel 12:29, in 1 Chronicles 20:1 **Joab** captures Rabbah. Further, while Chronicles leaves David **in Jerusalem** at the beginning of the siege (1 Chr 20:1) and never says he came to Rabbah, nevertheless David accepts its surrender in 1 Chronicles 20:2 (and returns to Jerusalem in 1 Chr 20:3). By omitting the sequences of events in 2 Samuel 11–12, Chronicles has created a narrative that is seemingly at variance with 2 Samuel.

Chronicles retains the statement **David remained in Jerusalem** to remind the readers of 2 Samuel 11–12. Thus, the Chronicler reminds his readers of the broader context. The transition from 1 Chronicles 20:1 to 20:2 is awkward because the David who was in Jerusalem is now in Rabbah. We are not told he came to Rabbah (as we are in 2 Sam 12:29). The Chronicler assumes his readers are able to connect the dots. Instead, he presses what is important, that is, Ammon capitulated to David. This surrender involved the plunder of Ammon's wealth and the enslavement of its people (or, "he sawed them with saws," but enslavement is more likely, cf. JAPHET, 364 and BRAUN, 209). David's victory was complete and God's faithfulness was confirmed.

Victory over the Philistines (20:4-8)

This section contains three stories about David's mighty men who encountered descendants of **Rapha** (1 Chr 20:8) in skirmishes with Philistines. The **Rephaites** ("giants") were prominent warriors among the Canaanites (cf. Gen 15:20). The stories are derived from 2 Samuel 21:18-22. They form another account of Davidic victory whose exact chronology is uncertain, though these three "cameos" are perhaps "associated with David's assault on Gath" in 1 Chronicles 18:1 (SELMAN, 1:198). Their presence at the end of the Davidic victory stories is literary rather than chronological. Rhetorically, this unity (1 Chr 18–20) begins and ends with Philistine victories (1 Chr 18:1; 20:4-8). The triumph of David over the **Philistines** is a sign of God's election just as Saul's defeat by the Philistines was an indication of divine rejection (cf. 1 Chr 10:13-14).

The first "cameo" is a contest between **Sibbecai the Hushathite** and **Sippai** the Rephaite during a Philistine war at **Gezer**. While 2 Samuel 21:18-19 reads "Gob," the Chronicler is probably updating a location for his readers. "Gob" is unknown elsewhere in the OT, but perhaps associated with Gezer in the postexilic period.

The second "cameo" contains a difficult reading. While 2 Samuel 21:19 reads "Elhanan son of Jaare-Oregim the Bethlehemite killed Goliath the Gittite," 1 Chronicles 20:5 reads **Elhanan son of Jair killed Lahmi the brother of Goliath the Gittite**. Second Samuel 21:19 raises a tension within Samuel itself since David is the one who killed Goliath. Most believe that the text in 2 Samuel 21:19 is corrupt and that 1 Chronicles 20:5 is the original sense (Wolfers, 115; SELMAN, 1:199; JAPHET, 368-369). The Chronicler rehearses the exploits of David's men to remind his readers of David's own heroic exploit in killing Goliath the Gittite, **who had a spear with a shaft like a weaver's rod** (Yadin, 58-69; cf. 1 Chr 11:23).

The third "cameo" takes place at **Gath**. One of David's mighty men, **Jonathan**, David's nephew, **killed** a Raphaite who was known for **his six fingers on each hand and six toes on each foot**. Such a mutation is not problematic, but the real connection for Chronicles is the taunting motif. Just as this Rephaite **taunted Israel**, so had Goliath (1 Sam 17:10,25,26,36,45). "The duel," according to SELMAN (1:199), "was a recognized form of combat in Canaan." Just as David killed Goliath, so a relative of David killed the Rephaite who taunted Israel. Thus, divine faithfulness to David and Israel is confirmed.

Since these encounters took place in the context of the Philistine wars, they bind the literary unit of 1 Chronicles 18–20 together. "The Philistines function," ALLEN (134) writes, "as the A and Z of opposition to God's people." Perhaps more importantly, the three "cameos" recount encounters with the Rephaites. **These were descendants of Rapha in Gath, and they fell at the hands of David and his men**. The Chronicler brings the past into the present in order to bear witness to the faithfulness of God. At the same time he calls his postexilic community to hope on the basis of God's faithfulness to David.

From the details of David's victories we gain a picture of the extent of his kingdom. David reigned over all the territories of Israel — the land of the twelve tribes. He conquered his southeastern flank (Edom), his eastern flank (Moab and Ammon), and his northeast flank (Arameans of Damascus). In addition, he secured a vassal relationship with the Philistines to the southwest and the Hamath

Arameans to the northeast. Due north, along the coast, David was allied with Hiram of Tyre. David's conquests garnered him the promised land. God had, just as he promised, given Israel the land through David (Japhet, *Ideology*, 352-362). His faithfulness engenders hope in the postexilic community.

In the larger picture, David has established the divine kingdom among the nations. The nations recognize the kingdom of God in the world. Theologically, God's universal intent is present — God intends to reign over all nations. "The oneness between God and the human race, already lost in Adam," JOHNSTONE (1:223) comments, "is in process of restoration." David is God's "sacral" agent through whom he will establish "holiness which lies at the heart of Israel's vocation among the nations." In the same way, the church is God's sacral instrument in the world to bear witness to the holiness of God in a fallen world.

2. David's Sin (21:1–22:1)

Though dependent upon 2 Samuel 24, Chronicles gives the story a new context as well as a new ending. The new context is the narrator's transition from Davidic victories as a divine gift (1 Chr 17–20) to preparations for building the temple (1 Chr 22–29). The census is a military count (cf. 1 Chr 21:5) which links it to the previous exploits of David, but the ending relates to the building of the temple (1 Chr 21:28–22:1).

While the Chronicler has consistently excluded material about David's dark side (e.g., Bathsheba), this Davidic sin exacts a tremendous price from Israel. Scholars have almost unanimously noted that the Chronicler attributes this sin to David (contra Wright, "Innocence," 87-105; rebutted by Bailey, 83-90), and that this account is included because it is integrally related to the foundation of the temple in Jerusalem (MYERS, 1:146). The account describes the purchase of the land upon which the temple is built. The additional material (1 Chr 21:28–22:1) confirms this interest. Thus, the temple theme outweighs the narrator's interest in presenting David in a positive light (WILLIAMSON, 142-143). The Chronicler's emphasis on the temple drives his narrative rather than an idealization of David (cf. 1 Chr 13).

However, there is another interest at work. The census is not simply a pretext for introducing the temple site. The census is not only the occasion for purchasing the temple site but also stresses important theological concerns which are best explored through the lens of guilt and atonement. The census generates guilt, and the sacrifice on Mt. Moriah (the temple site) provides forgiveness and reconciliation. Thus, the theological themes of restored peace, forgiven sin, and atoning sacrifice are significant (Johnstone, "Guilt and Atonement," 123-124).

First Chronicles 21:1–22:1 falls into three sections (JAPHET, 373): (1) The Census (1 Chr 21:1-6), (2) The Punishment (1 Chr 21:7-14), and (3) Averting the Plague (1 Chr 21:15–22:1). In comparison with 2 Samuel 24, Chronicles shortens the first section (omitting 2 Sam 24:5-8), but lengthens the last (adding 1 Chr 21:28–22:1).

However, not every difference between 2 Samuel 24 and 1 Chronicles 21 is attributable to the Chronicler's theological interests. The recent discovery of 4QSam[a] provides a needed caution (Ulrich, 91-92, 156-160). For example, it was once thought that the addition of the angel in 1 Chronicles 21:16 reflected the Chronicler's postexilic angelology. The angel story appears in 4QSam[a] and should not be attributed to the Chronicler (Dion, 114-117). Other differences between 1 Chronicles 21 and 2 Samuel 24 are probably textual rather than theological, but the evidence of 4QSam[a] only includes 2 Samuel 24:16-20 (BRAUN, 213-218; Dillard, "Census," 97-98).

The Census (21:1-6)

David decides **to take a census of Israel**. This census is military because (1) the command is directed toward Joab, the commander of the army, and (2) the count is **the number of fighting men** who are able to **handle a sword** (1 Chr 21:5). But the census raises several questions. Why did David decide to take a census? Further, why does Joab object?

While 2 Samuel 24:1 credits the "anger of the LORD" as the occasion of the census and states that God incited David, Chronicles attributes the census to the prompting of **Satan** (שָׂטָן, śāṭān, "accuser or adversary"). Whatever the reason for the census, the Chronicler believes David was **incited** by Satan. Some (THOMPSON,

161; SELMAN, 1:202-203; MCCONVILLE, 69-77) believe this refers to the traditional evil angel (the Devil). Others (JOHNSTONE, 1:225; cf. Day, *Adversary*, 142-144) believe Satan is a celestial being who functions as "counsel for the prosecution" rather than a malicious spirit. The Chronicler may be drawing on the same theology that is evidenced in Job. There Satan incites God against Job (Job 2:3), but functions under God's sovereignty. As WILLIAMSON (144) observes, Chronicles's use of Satan is not "intended to contradict, but rather to elucidate." In other words, God used Satan to prompt the census (as in the case of Job) so that 2 Samuel 24:1 and 1 Chronicles 21:1 are consistent (SELMAN 1:203-204; MCCONVILLE, 70).

Others believe *śāṭān* is a human adversary (Japhet, *Ideology*, 145-149; Wright, "Innocence," 92-93; Sailhamer, 33-48). Here *śāṭān* appears without the article and may not refer to a specific celestial being. There is no evidence that the noun is a proper name. Sailhamer (42, n. 42) believes the lack of article before *śāṭān* actually distinguishes its use from the angelic being ("the" Satan) in Job (1:6,7,9,12; 2:1-4,6-7) and Zechariah (3:1-2). Further, SAILHAMER (53) argues that the Chronicler is exegeting 2 Samuel 24:1 in the context of Deuteronomy. In 1 Kings 5:4 God provides rest for Solomon so there is no adversary (*śāṭān*), but in punishment of Solomon's sins God raises up an adversary (*śāṭān*) in 1 Kings 11:14,23-25 (cf. the motif of burning anger in Judg 2:14,20; 3:8; 10:7; 2 Kgs 13:3; 23:26 where God raises up a human adversary to punish Israel; cf. 1 Sam 29:4; 2 Sam 19:23). The anger of the Lord "against Israel commonly resulted in oppression from her enemies" (SAILHAMER, 53). God gave them over to their enemies so that they could no longer stand against them (Judg 2:14). Consequently, Sailhamer (42) concludes that, "using the context of the whole of his sources as his 'lexicon,' [the Chronicler] could have read 2 Samuel 24:1a as an abbreviated statement that God had again (וַיֹּסֶף, *wayyōseph*) raised up the enemy against them." Thus, Chronicles interprets the anger of the Lord in 2 Samuel 24:1 as the presence of a threatening enemy. The enemy incites David to order a military census. God used a human adversary to test David.

But why is the census sinful? Wright ("Innocence," 90-92) points out that every other census in Chronicles is positive (cf. 2 Chr 14:8; 17:12-19; 25:5-6) and that many of Chronicles's lists are based on censuses. Further, the Torah prescribes various kinds of censuses (Num 3:40-51; Exod 30:12). There is nothing inherently wrong with a census. It does not necessarily imply a lack of trust in God's protection.

Some believe the census was sinful because David did not follow prescribed ritual forms (THOMPSON, 160-161; JOHNSTONE, 1:227-229). For example, Exodus 30:12 requires that each counted Israelite "pay the LORD a ransom for his life . . . . Then no plague will come on them when you number them." However, Chronicles usually points out ritual violations (as in 1 Chr 13, 15).

Chronicles presents the census itself as a sin. Joab protests the census (1 Chr 21:3) and David admits guilt (1 Chr 21:8). Nothing in the text attributes the sinfulness of the census to David's attitude or his failure to follow prescribed rituals. The census itself is sinful, and David did not heed Joab's warning (JAPHET, 377). Apparently, Joab did not complete the census because he did not agree with David's intent (1 Chr 21:6).

But why is the census sinful? The Chronicler is not specific. His interest is more about guilt and atonement. Dillard ("Census," 104-107) offers an illuminating explanation. Joab rejects the census proposal because, counted or uncounted, they are all David's subjects (1 Chr 21:3). Since David's house cannot be broken, Joab counsels that David should rest in the Lord's blessing for "the number of people is a matter of the blessing of the LORD; as the blessings of the LORD are unnumbered, so the people blessed by him, potentially a hundred-fold, are innumerable" (JOHNSTONE, 1:226). In addition, on another occasion (unlike this one) David did not take a census "because the LORD had promised to make Israel as numerous as the stars in the sky" (1 Chr 27:23). According to Dillard ("Census," 105; cf. SELMAN, 1:205), "the arena of David's transgression appears to be that taking a census impugns the faithfulness of God in the keeping of His promises."

God had promised David rest from his enemies and a land in which Israel would dwell without oppression (1 Chr 17:9-10). God demonstrated his faithfulness through military victories (1 Chr 18-20). David ruled over the promised land (cf. 1 Chr 27:23-24; 2 Chr 1:9 with Gen 12:1-6; 15:12-20; 22:15-18; 26:2-4). Dillard ("Census," 106) proposes that David's sin was his intent to expand his territory beyond the promised land. By so doing David "not only impugns the realization of divine promise but also reflects preparation for military conquest presumably directed to territories beyond the divine land grant to Israel, a transgression of the fixed boundaries allotted to Israel by her suzerain." The sin of the census was the preparation for further military activity that was beyond David's legitimate right as the Shepherd of Israel. In other words, the census was a sign of territorial greed.

Given the sustained military conquests of 1 Chronicles 18–20, God tested David's faithfulness (cf. 2 Chr 32:31). Japhet (*Ideology*, 193-198) argues that when God raises up an enemy to attack Israel in Chronicles, it is a test of faithfulness (cf. JOHNSTONE, 1:225; MANGAN, 53; ALLEN, 139). If Satan (*śāṭān*) is understood as a military adversary, then 1 Chronicles 21 fits this model. In the light of God's faithfulness and grace, would David be content with his military conquests? To answer the question, God raised up an enemy (*śāṭān*) that threatened Israel and incited David's military census. He tested David to reveal David's greed. David failed the test, and Israel was punished.

The total sum of the census is problematic when 1 Chronicles 21:5 is compared with 2 Samuel 24:9. Second Samuel reports the number as 800,000 from Israel and 500,000 from Judah. First Chronicles reports 1,100,000 from **all Israel**, but included in that number are 470,000 from Judah. We may suppose that 500,000 and 470,000 are nontechnical counts representing round numbers. Nevertheless, the total count differs: 1,300,000 in 2 Samuel, but 1,100,000 in 1 Chronicles. There seems to be no theological or redactional purposes for a change. It is probably best explained as a problem in textual transmission, though some have suggested that the missing 200,000 in 1 Chronicles is the total number of Levi and Benjamin which Joab did not count (WILLIAMSON, 145).

The Punishment (21:7-14)

This command (lit., "this thing") was evil in God's sight and as a result **he punished** (lit., "struck") **Israel**. The "thing" is the census. It was an **evil** act which God punished. David admits his sin (lit., "I did this thing"; 1 Chronicles 21:8) and begs for forgiveness. Interestingly, 1 Chronicles 21:7-8 are additions to 2 Samuel 24 and for the

first time in Chronicles the word "sin" (חָטָא, *ḥāṭā'*) is used (also
1 Chr 21:17). Where 2 Samuel 24:10 reads "David was conscience
stricken" ("David smote [נָכָה, *nākāh*] his own heart"), 1 Chronicles
21:7 reads that God smote (*nākāh*) Israel because of David's evil act.
The Chronicler supplies David's motivation for repentance and this
leaves the nature of this (first) punishment unspecified (JAPHET,
379). Perhaps the adversary (*śāṭān*), a human enemy, defeated David
in a battle. **Struck** (*nākāh*) has described previous military victories
(1 Chr 11:14; 14:11,16; 18:1-3,5,9,10,12; 20:1,4,5,7). As a result of
that defeat, David realizes his sin.

SELMAN (1:201) calls attention to the parallels between this
account and the revelation of David's sin with Bathsheba in
2 Samuel 11–12.

Topic	2 Sam	1 Chr
David confesses, "I have sinned."	12:13; 24:10	21:8
Sin results in death among Israel.	11:17-26; 12:15-19; 24:15	21:14
Prophetic disapproval is voiced.	12:1-4; 24:11-14	21:9-13
God punishes with the sword.	12:10	21:12,16,27
David is forgiven by word of promise.	12:10; 24:16	21:15
God grants forgiveness by covenants of promise connected to houses.	12:10,24-25	21:28–22:1

The chapter is filled with the language of sin, guilt, and forgiveness just as is 2 Samuel 12. JOHNSTONE (1:229) observes that **guilt**
(אַשְׁמָה, *'ašmāh*) has now become "one of the key terms" of the
Chronicler's theology (e.g., 2 Chr 24:18; 28:10,13; 33:23). In this
connection, sacrifice, atonement, and forgiveness also become central. Chronicles's account is narrative atonement theology.

Theologically, David encounters God's gracious forgiveness. Just
as in the Bathesheba story God remained faithful to David despite
David's sin, so God remains faithful here. Consequently, as Johnstone (*Chronicles*, 103) writes, "as David's adultery with Bathsheba is
the hinge of the presentation of the reign of David in [2 Sam 11–12],
so David's census of the people in [1 Chr 21], the presumptuous act
of numbering the people of God, is the pivot of the presentation of
the reign of David in [1 Chr]." While 2 Samuel follows out the consequences of David's sin in his reign, the Chronicler pursues the
consequences of David's repentance which involves the establish-

ment of the temple cultus where Israel finds forgiveness and reconciliation. The Chronicler portrays the gracious presence of God
through the temple. Thus, Dtr carries out his purpose of demon-
strating the nasty exilic consequences of sin, but Chronicles bears
witness to the grace of God through the temple.

The story moves through various phases in order to reach its climax. God tests David. David sins. God punishes David. David
repents. God atones. In the aftermath of reconciliation, God dwells
among his people in the temple. Through atonement, he comes to
dwell among them.

Just as the faithfulness of God brings hope to the postexilic community, so the faithfulness of Jesus Christ brings hope to the church.
God demonstrated his righteousness in Jesus Christ, and through
the "faith of Christ" (KJV) we are declared righteous in the sight of
God (Rom 3:21-26).

David's repentance moves God to relieve the punishment of his
people. Consequently, the Lord spoke to **Gad, David's seer**. Like
Nathan in 1 Chronicles 17, Gad comes to David with a word from
God. David must choose the consequences of his sin. He is given
three choices: (1) **three years** (2 Sam 24:13 reads "seven" but
Chronicles preserves the best reading; JAPHET, 380) **of famine**, (2)
three months of military defeats (the **swords** of David's enemies do
not necessarily entail David's own death), or (3) **three days** of plague
(through a divine messenger) throughout **every part of Israel**.

The three choices (in descending order of three years, months,
and days) represent three kinds of punishment: economic (famine),
military, and health. The choice itself is merciful since God did not
impose all three. Each would affect all Israel because the census was
"throughout Israel" (1 Chr 21:4). The people will share the consequences of David's act. This exemplifies corporate solidarity. The
actions of the king affect the lives of his people. Israel is not a collection of isolated individuals but one corporate people before God.
Thus, Israel bears the consequences of David's sin just as humanity
bears the consequence of Adam's sin. So, as in Adam all die (1 Cor
15:22), so through David Israel suffers.

The Chronicler clarifies David's choice by his contrast between
the swords of his enemies (or, to **fall into the hands of men**) and the
sword of the LORD (or, **the hands of the LORD**). David wants to **fall
into the hands of the LORD**. He chooses God's direct act over the

mediating work of his enemies (note the contrast in 1 Chr 21:13) because **his mercy is very great**. David appeals to the compassion or mercy of God. This is not a selfish choice on David's part since the people would have suffered with any of the three choices. David has the Lord's mercy in view. He knows he can appeal to the Lord's mercy whereas his enemies might not heed such pleas. The mercy of the Lord is, as SELMAN (1:206) calls it, a "permanent hope." The people of God call upon their Lord to "in wrath remember mercy" (Hab 3:2). In their lamentations, even during times of punishment, Israel remembers that mercy of the Lord (Ps 79:8; Lam 3:22). The post-exilic community hopes in that mercy (cf. 2 Chr 30:9).

The text is clear and straightforward: **So the LORD sent a plague on Israel, and seventy thousand men of Israel fell dead**. It is an act of God and 70,000 die. Due to corporate solidarity, the sin of one causes the whole nation to suffer. The irony of the census is that the men David sought to number are the ones who die in the plague. The strength David sought in a military census is decimated in a divine plague.

Averting the Plague (21:15–22:1)

This section describes the end of the plague and the purchase of the temple site. Thus, it connects the Davidic promise (1 Chr 17) with the temple (1 Chr 21). The climax is 1 Chronicles 21:28–22:1 (unique to Chronicles). David's conclusion, **The house of the LORD God is to be here, and also the altar of burnt offering for Israel** (1 Chr 22:1), states the significant point. Divine presence ("house") and mercy ("altar") are gifts. The census provided the occasion for the acquisition of the site where the house and altar will be built.

This section divides into three parts (JAPHET, 373): (1) David's Petition (1 Chr 21:15-21), (2) Negotiations with Ornan (1 Chr 21:22-25), and (3) Building the Altar (1 Chr 21:26–22:1).

David at the Threshing Floor (21:15-21)

The plague had already ravaged all Israel, and it was coming to Jerusalem. God sends an angel (מַלְאָךְ, *mal'āk*, "messenger") to destroy Jerusalem. The plague had not yet touched the city.

The text contains some tension (JAPHET, 383). It appears from 1 Chronicles 21:15 that God determines to stop the plague, but

1 Chronicles 21:22 indicates that David wants to build an altar to avert the plague. When did the plague stop? Before David built the altar or after he built it? First Chronicles 21:15 is a general summary that is explained by the subsequent narrative. The story is: David sees the angel over Jerusalem (1 Chr 21:16), David repents (1 Chr 21:17), Gad delivers a word from God (1 Chr 21:18), David does what God instructed (1 Chr 21:19-26), and God ends the plague (1 Chr 21:27). God, then, relents in response to David's repentance. First Chronicles 21:15 serves as a plot summary, and 1 Chronicles 21:16-27 tells the story (WILLIAMSON, 146, 151).

Divine Sovereignty (21:15). First Chronicles 21:15 assumes some important theological perspectives. God is sovereign. He decides when to send the plague and when to end it. But God changed his mind about the timing, that is, he **was grieved** (יִּנָּחֶם, *yinnaḥem*) and commanded the **angel** to stop. The Hebrew verb (נחם, *nḥm*) means to change one's mind or relent; it does not carry any notion of remorse for sin. Similar to Genesis 6:5-7, when God saw the **calamity** ("disaster or evil," הָרָעָה, *hārā'āh*), he changed his mind. Whatever we might say about God's immutable character, God does sometimes change his plans in relationship with human beings. God relents in response to repentance (e.g., Jonah 3:9-10; 4:2) or petitions (e.g., Exod 32:12-14; Amos 7:3-6). Thus, though **God sent an angel to destroy Jerusalem**, he relented.

Another perspective is the role of angels. Chronicles alludes to the Exodus slaying of the firstborn of Egypt. Both were plagues and both involved God's destroying (שָׁחַת, *šāḥath*) presence (Exod 12:23). Chronicles identifies the destroyer as one of God's providential agents ("angel"). Chronicles's text, based upon a different text of Samuel than the MT, has a more elaborate description of the angel (Dion, 117). In particular, the "drawn sword" (1 Chr 21:16; cf. vv. 12,27,30) identifies the angel as the agent of divine judgment (cf. Gen 3:24; Num 22:22-35; Josh 5:13-15), but, as SELMAN (1:208) notes, for the first time this angelic sword is drawn against Israel. Avenging angel motifs were not postexilic inventions, but were also part of earlier ancient cultures, e.g., Ugarit (daSilva, 154-169). Consequently, nothing necessarily identifies this as postexilic embellishment.

David's Petition (21:16-17). David takes responsibility for the census, but **the elders** prostrate themselves as well. This is a communal seeking of God, but David confesses sin as the offending party. David pleads for Jerusalem on the ground that he alone is responsible. Why does Israel suffer for David's sin? The Hebrew Bible assumes a corporate personality or a communal accountability. Thus, when Achan sinned, Israel suffered (Josh 7). So, when David sins, Israel suffers. David invokes this corporate idea when he asks God to punish his house (**family**) rather than Israel. In other words, David hopes that corporate accountability would only extend to his family rather than to the whole city of Jerusalem.

David's petition engages God. It confesses sin and offers an alternate scenario. Prayer seeks God and confesses sins, makes petitions, and provides God with alternatives. Petition seeks to change God's mind. This model empowers prayer. "God in his mercy," McCONVILLE (74) writes, "responds to the cry of the human heart, here in the form of intercession, and provides a means whereby sin can be atoned for."

God's Response (21:18-21). God's prophet tells David to go up to the **threshing floor**. God chooses the place of his altar and the site of his house in Jerusalem (Deut 12:5,11,14). Also, the role of the prophet is significant as the interpreter of God's mighty acts of judgment and blessing. The prophet is the agent of communication just as the **angel** is the agent of divine action.

The threshing floor belongs to Ornan (אָרְנָן, *'ornān*). The NIV reads **Araunah** (אֲרַוְנָה, *'ărawnāh*) as in 2 Samuel 24. The difference is probably due to textual corruption or variation in spelling. The addition of 1 Chronicles 21:20 to 2 Samuel is not tendentious since the incomplete fragment from Qumran contains part of the verse as well (Ulrich, 157-159, 179-180). Araunah is identified as a **Jebusite**. Apparently, Jebusites still lived on, owned, and worked land in the Jerusalem environs.

Negotiations with Ornan (21:22-25)

SELMAN (1:209) observes that this section has several echoes of previous events in Israel's history. First, the purchase of the whole **site** for the **full price** reminds canonical readers of Abraham's purchase of the cave at Machpelah (Gen 23:9), the first Caananite land owned by God's people. Just as Abraham bought land from a Caananite, so does David. Second, Gideon was commanded to build an altar at his threshing floor, and God sent a heavenly fire to consume that sacrifice just as he does in this narrative (Judg 6:11-24). We should not ignore the canonical connections. The divine presence (redemptive grace), land, and altar are intimately connected. Williamson ("Temple," 21) regards these associations as an example of the Chronicler's typological exegesis of earlier canonical traditions.

David will not accept the land as a gift from **Araunah**. He will not give to the Lord what **costs** him **nothing**. David's repentance means self-humiliation and sacrifice. Divine forgiveness, however, is not exacted by merit, but by grace through atonement. David expresses the significance of discipleship just as God offers his mercy by relenting. At the cross of Jesus, the cost of discipleship (the obedience of Jesus Christ) and the mercy of God (the forgiveness by atonement) are both exhibited.

The purchase price for the temple site is problematic. While 1 Chronicles 21:25 says that David purchased **the site** for **six hundred shekels of gold**, 2 Samuel 24:24 says that he purchased "the threshing floor and the oxen for fifty shekels of silver." Some have explained the difference as the Chronicler's attempt to glorify the temple **site** by inflating its price or that the difference is simply a matter of economic inflation. JAPHET (387) suggests that 600 is the multiplication of 50 by 12 (tribes) so that the number is "typological" and the value of the land is increased by the change from silver to gold. However, the difference in price reflects the difference between what is purchased. While 2 Samuel refers to only "the threshing floor and the oxen," 1 Chronicles includes the whole temple **site** (the whole top of the mount; cf. THOMPSON, 163, n. 57; WILLIAMSON, 150).

Building the Altar (21:26–22:1)

David built the **altar** on the threshing floor which was usually a flat rock surface on a high point so the wind could separate the wheat from the chaff. Thus, David erects an altar on a high place, but this high place is the site chosen by God as his holy place.

While the NIV says that David **sacrificed** there, the literal translation is that he offered up ("presented," NRSV) **burnt offerings and fellowship offerings**. Whether David acted as a priest or not, it is possible that others were involved and David officiated as king.

Nevertheless, David does assume personal guilt and the sacrifice may reflect David's personal act.

The offerings and the divine response are significant. Burnt offerings involved the burning of the whole offering, but fellowship (peace) offerings involved eating the sacrifice in the presence of God as a symbol of restored fellowship. God responds to the burnt offerings and the fat of the peace offerings by consuming them with fire. The divine response is gracious. The peace offerings testify to reconciliation. The **fire from heaven** reminds the canonical reader of the first Levitical sacrifice where God sent fire from heaven in Leviticus 9:24 (also Gideon [Judg 6:21] and Elijah [1 Kgs 18:38]). The sacrifice was atoning, the mercy of God accepted it, and peace was restored. In the wake of reconciliation, the plague ends. The sovereign decision of God, based on his mercy, told the **angel** to **put his sword back into its sheath**.

Given the fire from heaven David now regards this place as an appropriate sacrificial altar in addition to the **altar of burnt offering** that was at the **tabernacle** in **Gibeon**. Israel has two high places for burnt offerings: Gibeon and Jerusalem. The story of the census, then, legitimizes sacrificial rituals on Mt. Moriah in Jerusalem. Thus, Chronicles explains the origins of two high places and begins the story of the shift from Gibeon to Jerusalem — the shift from tabernacle to temple. As ALLEN (145) notes, "the atmosphere of the whole passage is electric with the sense of a new dispensation dawning. We trace our spiritual heritage back to this point in time, [the Chronicler] is saying, for the temple is dedicated to bringing repentant sinners back to God." The Lord's altar still functions in the Chronicler's postexilic situation, and the cross of Christ is the fulfillment of that altar (Heb 13:10).

David's inability to go to Gibeon is due to the presence of **the sword of the angel of the LORD**. The threshing floor of Mt. Moriah was located between Jerusalem and Gibeon to the north of Jerusalem. Consequently, David could not **inquire of God** at Gibeon because he was **afraid** to pass by the angel's sword. The message of Gad, then, gave David another option: build an altar in Jerusalem. The Jerusalem altar becomes the place for the house of God.

First Chronicles 22:1 is David's theological conclusion. This is where the **house of the LORD God** will be built along with the **altar**

of burnt offering. The shift from Gibeon to Jerusalem has begun. In Jerusalem God will dwell among his people, and the holy God will dwell through the atonement.

"Forgiveness has its proper channels," writes ALLEN (143). Given the themes of mercy, altar, and peace in this narrative, BRAUN (218) offers an appropriate application: "That same grace of God which triumphed over David's sins and led to the establishment of God's house remains God's principal attribute available to human beings. Available through repentance and reaching out to draw and sustain the weak. God himself always takes the lead in lifting up the fallen."

The temple, then, is the place of sacrifice. God's gracious presence redeems. This previews God's atoning work in Jesus Christ. The mercy and wrath of God meet in Jerusalem at the cross of Jesus. There God makes atonement for sin and in his mercy calls a people to himself.

II. THE TRANSITION FROM DAVID TO SOLOMON
(22:2–29:30)

First Chronicles 22:2–29:10 has no canonical parallel. This alerts us to its importance for the Chronicler. The move from David to Solomon is significant. First, it highlights David's involvement in the preparations for the temple. David prepares the temple materials, builders, personnel, and treasury. He charges his son to complete the task. In this way Chronicles portrays David as the temple's patron even though he is not its builder. Second, it anoints Solomon as the temple builder (Braun, "Solomon," 581-590). Solomon's significance for Chronicles is on par with David. They both have a role in the inauguration of the temple and the glory of the kingdom of God in Israel (Braun, "Solomonic," 503-516). Third, it attributes the cultic orders in the temple to David's appointment. Thus, David is the founding authority of the temple cult just as Moses was the founding authority for the tabernacle (De Vries, "Founders," 619-639). Fourth, it unites the reigns of David and Solomon around the theme of the temple. The United Monarchy is the Golden Age of Israel.

The most significant theme is the transition from David to Solomon. The Chronicler parallels the transition from Moses to Joshua and from David to Solomon. Several have noted this (McCarthy, 33-34;

Williamson, "Accession," 351-361; Braun, "Solomon," 586-588). First Chronicles 22 and 28 are dependent upon Joshua 1 (BRAUN, 222-223; SELMAN, 1:211-212; Porter, 102-132). By framing the transition from David to Solomon in this way Chronicles identifies another peak moment in redemptive history. The move from David to Solomon is comparable to the move from Moses to Joshua. The unity of Moses and Joshua resides in the redemptive inheritance of the promised land. The unity of David and Solomon resides in the secured "rest" in the promised land and the erection of God's permanent dwelling place in his chosen city.

Temple-building is theologically significant for Chronicles. It is the single most important event in the history of Israel in the promised land. But why is the temple so important? Earlier scholars believed it was important as a polemic against the Samaritan temple in Shechem (Torrey, *Ezra*, 208-251; Noth, 97-106). However, current scholarship has discredited this theory because the Chronicler's attitude toward the north is inclusive rather than exclusive (Williamson, *Israel*, 87-140; Braun, "Reconsideration," 59-62; Japhet, *Ideology*, 308-333). The importance of the temple, according to Williamson ("Temple," 29), is unity. The temple stands "as a focus for the reunification of the divided and scattered people of Israel." For the Chronicler, the temple is a symbol of both God's redemptive presence and the unity of Israel (north and south). The Chronicler calls his audience to the gracious presence of God in the temple and the reunification enabled by that presence.

Similarly, the redemptive presence of God in Jesus Christ through the Spirit enables a reunion of God's people through God's own gracious presence. Worship, whether in the temple or in the gathering of God's people as church, engages the personal presence of the redemptive God, and the people of God are united in their devotion to God.

The structure of 1 Chronicles 22–29 is determined by the installation/commission texts of 1 Chronicles 22 and 28–29. The material between those chapters focuses on David's arrangements for the temple cultus (1 Chr 23–27). First Chronicles 22:2–29:30 falls into three major parts (BRAUN, xli): (1) Initial Preparations for the Temple (1 Chr 22:2-19), (2) The Order of the Temple Cultus (1 Chr 23:1–27:34), and (3) Final Preparations for the Temple (1 Chr 28:1–29:30).

A. INITIAL PREPARATIONS FOR THE TEMPLE (22:2-19)

This section consists of three major parts: (1) David Prepares Workers (1 Chr 22:2-5), (2) David Prepares Solomon (1 Chr 22:6-16), and (3) David Prepares the Leaders of Israel (1 Chr 22:17-19). David's speeches, however, are the focus. The first is a self-reflection (1 Chr 22:5), the second charges Solomon (1 Chr 22:7-16), and the third addresses the leaders (1 Chr 22:18-19). The narrative supports the speeches.

1. David Prepares Workers (22:2-5)

This section falls into two parts. First, David provides workers and materiel for the temple (1 Chr 22:2-4). Second, he determines to **make preparations** for the building of God's house (1 Chr 22:5).

David Gathers Workers and Materiel (22:2-4)

He gathers the **aliens** in the land and **appointed** them **stonecutters** to prepare the **stone** for the temple. Aliens, as foreign residents in Israel, were used as the primary labor force in state projects, though Israelites were sometimes conscripted (cf. 2 Chr 2:17-18).

There is some question whether stonecutters are taken from among the aliens (NIV) or whether the stonecutters are a separate group from the aliens (NRSV). The NRSV is probably correct since stonecutters are skilled laborers.

The materiel, in addition to limestone, included **iron**, **bronze**, and **cedar**. These are common to elaborate buildings in the ancient world; **iron** was an expensive commodity. The quantity (**more . . . than could be weighed** and **more . . . than could be counted**) is emphasized through hyperbole.

David Resolves to Prepare for Temple-Building (22:5)

Instead of a speech to the workers, Chronicles provides a window into David's mind. David, for all practical purposes, intends to prefabricate the temple because his son is too young to begin the arduous task of temple-building (THOMPSON, 164).

David recognizes the youth and inexperience of Solomon. **Inexperienced** (רָךְ, *rāk*) "implies someone who needs further training and instruction" (SELMAN, 1:214). Its primary meaning is "tender" or "gentle" (cf. Prov 4:3; 15:1; Isa 47:1). David uses the term to describe Solomon in 1 Chronicles 29:1 and the Chronicler uses it to describe Rehoboam in 2 Chronicles 13:7. While Solomon sought the wisdom of God (2 Chr 1), Rehoboam sought the wisdom of his peers (2 Chr 13).

Just as David was disqualified from building, so Solomon was unable to plan due to his inexperience and youth (MCCONVILLE, 78). The unity of David and Solomon is underscored by their complementary roles. This cooperative spirit is a model for God's people who are assigned a common task but must take up different roles in order to accomplish it.

David expects the temple to excel in **magnificence, fame,** and **splendor.** The **nations** will marvel at it. The temple must testify to the glory of God. "An essential part of their *raison d'être* as God's people is to demonstrate before all the world that God alone is worthy of worship" (MCCONVILLE, 80).

2. David Prepares Solomon (22:6-16)

While David later charges Solomon publicly (1 Chr 28–29), here the charge is private.

Narrative Setting (22:6-7a)

David charges (צָוָה, *ṣāwāh*) Solomon to build the temple (1 Chr 22:6), just as he will charge (*ṣāwāh*) "all the leaders of Israel to help his son Solomon" (1 Chr 22:17).

David Addresses Solomon (22:7b-16)

JAPHET (396) divides this speech into three parts that follow a similar form — introductory invocation, content, and concluding exhortation (except the first section does not have a conclusion). The first begins with **my son** (1 Chr 22:7b-10), the second with **Now, my son** (1 Chr 22:11-13), and the third with "behold" (omitted in the NIV; 1 Chr 22:14-16).

The Word of the Lord to David (22:7b-10)

David intended **to build a house for the Name of the Lord,** but

the word of the LORD denied him that privilege. Chronicles reveals why David was not permitted to build the temple (1 Chr 28:3).

It seems rather strange that David was not permitted to build the temple. Was he not the "cult founder" of temple rituals? So, why did Solomon build the temple instead of David? The Chronicler supplies one. Though it is already present in his source (1 Kgs 5:3), the Chronicler places the explanation in the divine oracle itself (though not present in 1 Chr 17). Indeed, this version of the divine oracle explicitly identifies Solomon as the son who will build the temple (1 Chr 22:9). God has elected (1 Chr 28:5-6,10; 29:1; בָּחַר, *bāḥar*) Solomon (cf. Deut 17:11).

David cannot build the temple because he **shed much blood** and **fought many wars**. But the immediate rationale for this judgment is not apparent (Dirksen, "Disqualified," 51-56). David is God's devout servant who regained Israel's territory according to the promise of God, gathered materiel for the temple and founded the temple cult. If his wars and bloodshed did not prevent this, why should it prevent his erection of the temple? JAPHET (397-398) argues that shedding blood in war is an unholy thing (e.g., according to some, "shedding of blood" is always sinful in the OT) and that this was sufficient to disqualify David. But wars in Chronicles are not unholy. They are the means by which God kept his promise to David. Others (WILLIAMSON, 154; ACKROYD, 79) argue that David had become ritually impure through his military involvement. But Chronicles does not adduce this rationale though there is ample opportunity to specify it. Dirksen ("Disqualified," 54) believes David is "disqualified because of sinful behaviour." God rejected David as temple builder in the light of his sinful census. Just as Saul was rejected for his unfaithfulness (1 Chr 10:13-14), so David was rejected as temple builder for his sinful census. David prosecuted some wars with goals that were not consistent with God's purposes. But the census apparently occurs after the promise in 1 Chronicles 17. Wars and bloodshed may simply contrast with Solomon's situation and nothing more is implied (SELMAN, 1:215). Perhaps the Chronicler's only interest is to articulate the vision that temple-building "is a project which belongs not to a period of turmoil but to one of tranquility" (WILCOX, 99).

Whatever the exact backdrop of David's disqualification, Solomon was elected by God to build the temple because he **will be**

a man of peace and rest. The contrast between David and Solomon is strong. David was a "man of wars" (1 Chr 28:3) while Solomon was a "man of rest" (1 Chr 22:9). Solomon (שְׁלֹמֹה, *š^elōmōh*) is named for the peace (שָׁלוֹם, *šālôm*) that will characterize his reign. Temple-building, according to Chronicles, is a task for a man of peace in a time of rest (Deut 12:10-11). David prepared the temple, but Solomon is the builder (1 Chr 22:5).

Solomon is included in the Davidic promise. According to 1 Chronicles 22:10, it is Solomon's **throne** and Solomon's **kingdom** that will be established **forever**. This indicates that Solomon is not simply David's son, but God elected him to carry out a significant task. Just as David regained the land of Israel, so Solomon will build God's redemptive dwelling place. David and Solomon act as a unit. Their roles are complementary. Through them God reconquered Canaan and placed his Name in Jerusalem.

This is the divine gift of "rest" (מְנוּחָה, *m^enûḥāh*). The noun is used in 1 Chronicles 22:9 and 28:2. The verb ("to give rest," נוּחַ, *nûaḥ*) is used 12 times in Chronicles (1 Chr 16:21; 22:9,18; 23:25; 2 Chr 1:14; 4:8; 6:41; 9:25; 14:6,7; 15:15; 20:30). Usually it refers to the divine act of securing rest for the people of God, but it also refers to the fact that God himself comes to "rest" among his people. The ultimate "rest" is God's own redemptive presence. Chronicles finds this rest in the temple. It offers hope to the postexilic community (von Rad, 94-102; BRAUN, 224-225). In turn, through Christ Christians hope to rest with God in an eschatological sabbath (Heb 4:1-11).

The Charge to Keep the Law (22:11-13)

The introductory evocative (**now, my son**) is followed by a charge to keep the law and a blessing. As SELMAN (1:215) notes, this links the temple with the covenant "by stressing the need to obey God's word." Just as God is faithful to his covenant to David, so Solomon must be faithful to the Mosaic covenant.

Temple-building will be completed through divine assistance and Solomonic obedience (JAPHET, 399). God enables Solomon's obedience through his gift of **discretion and understanding** (cf. 2 Chr 2:12). Solomon cannot complete his task without divine grace and gifts. But he must also persevere in the task and **observe the decrees and laws that the LORD gave Moses for Israel**.

First Chronicles 22:11 contains an installation genre which consists of three parts (McCarthy, 31; BRAUN, 222): (a) assurance of divine blessing (**the LORD be with you**); (b) encouragement (**may you have success**); and (c) charge for the task (**build the house of the LORD your God**). David's installation of Solomon is based on Moses' installation of Joshua in Deuteronomy 31:23.

A further indication of the parallel between Joshua and Solomon is found in David's exhortation in verse 13. The phrase **be strong and courageous** (חֲזַק וֶאֱמָץ, *ḥăzaq we'ĕmāṣ*) is also found in Deuteronomy 31:6-7,23; Joshua 1:6-7,9,18; 10:25 (cf. 1 Chr 28:20; 2 Chr 32:7). The phrase **do not be afraid or discouraged** (אַל־תִּירָא וְאַל־תֵּחָת, *'al-tîrā' wə'al-tēḥāth*) occurs in Deuteronomy 1:21; Joshua 8:1; 10:25 (as well as in 1 Chr 28:20; 2 Chr 20:15,17; 32:7). Chronicles sees the transition from David to Solomon, and the task of Solomon (parallel to Joshua) as a key redemptive-historical moment. The postexilic community, having returned to the land, looks to the promise of David and the election of Solomon with hope. Their temple, just like Solomon's, is a symbol of God's redemptive presence among them.

The Exhortation to Begin the Work (22:14-16)

The NIV omits the introductory invocation ("behold"), but it is an attention-grabber for Solomon. David's accumulation of wealth for the future temple includes **gold**, **silver**, **bronze**, **iron**, **wood** (cedar), and **stone**. Again, not only quality, but quantity is emphasized. David expects Solomon to add to this amount, especially since he took such **great pains** to accumulate this for him. With such a large stockpile of wealth the temple is already a glorious testimony to the majesty of God.

The quantity of **100,000 talents of gold** and **1,000,000 talents of silver** is quite excessive (cf. 1 Kgs 10:14 where Solomon's annual revenues were only 666 talents of gold). WILLIAMSON (156) thinks that the numbers are exaggerated while SELMAN (1:217) suggests a textual corruption in transmission. THOMPSON (165-166) argues that these figures are hyperbolic in order to stress the magnificence of the temple (e.g., **craftsmen beyond number** in 1 Chr 22:16) and to draw "attention to David's vast preparations for the temple" (ALLEN, 151). On the other hand, PAYNE (4:412) invokes "God's special providence" and accepts the numbers literally.

Not only has David prepared materiel, but he has also prepared workers: **stonecutters**, **masons**, **carpenters**, and other **skilled** people. It is not just quality, but quantity. Even the workers, in good hyperbole, are beyond number.

The final exhortation is to complete the work with the assurance that God will be with him. Literally the text reads, "Arise and do!" (קוּם וַעֲשֵׂה, *qûm wa'ăśēh*). Solomon is called to begin his work immediately.

If Solomon is understood as already reigning with David, this may explain why the intrigues of Absalom and Adonijah are omitted (Ball, 268-279; 1 Kgs 1-2). They were inconsequential to the Chronicler's purpose. The commissioning of Solomon as temple-builder did not occur till after Solomon became David's co-regent. Thus, the history of 1 Kings 1 is skipped, not because it detracts from Solomon's status, but because it is incidental to the Chronicler's purpose.

3. David Prepares the Leaders of Israel (22:17-19)

Just as David charged Solomon, so he charges **all the leaders of Israel**. They are **ordered** to assist Solomon. David reminds the leaders of God's presence and gifts. Grace motivates service. God has given his people **rest** and they now inhabit the **land** in peace. Just as other theologians of Israel appeal to the Exodus as a redemptive moment that calls for a grateful faith, so David appeals to God's recent work as the basis for Israel's grateful response. This homiletical move (appealing to God's grace as the basis for faithful response) is theological motivation. We proclaim what God has done and then call people to seek God with all their heart.

Since God gave Israel rest, therefore (**now**) they should **devote their hearts and souls to seeking the LORD your God**. "Seek" (דָּרַשׁ, *dāraš*) is one of the most significant words in Chronicles (1 Chr 28:9; 2 Chr 7:14). It reflects an orientation toward God, a committed entrance into his presence, and a yearning to know his will.

David, as with Solomon, says "arise and build" (וְקוּמוּ וּבְנוּ, *w^eqûmû ûb^enû*). The goal of the work is explicitly stated. It is to **bring the ark of the covenant of the LORD and the sacred articles belonging to God into the temple that will be built for the Name of the LORD**. In other words, the goal is to give the ark a permanent resting place among God's people (in contrast to its present tent). Since God has given his people rest, so they must now prepare a place where God can rest among his people (cf. 2 Chr 6:41).

God has returned the postexilic Judah to their land, and he has come to rest again in the temple. The people of God seek God there and trust his gracious presence. In the same way, the Christian community rests assured in the gracious work of God in Jesus Christ.

B. THE ORDER OF THE TEMPLE CULTUS (23:1–27:34)

While 1 Chronicles 22, 28–29 are "installation" genres, 1 Chronicles 23–27 is a collection of lists which detail administrative personnel for the temple and state (Wright, "Center," 20-42). Some (Noth, 31-33; BRAUN, 231; MANGAN, 57) believe this section disrupts the flow of the narrative and consequently regard it as a secondary addition. WILLIAMSON (157-159; "Origins," 251-268) argues that much of the material belongs to the original Chronicler but that some elements come from a later hand. Others argue that it is original (JAPHET, 406-409; Wright, "Legacy," 229-242). While there may yet remain problems in the organization of the lists (they appear to come from a variety of sources), this "shows merely that [the Chronicler] did not harmonize the lists into a single chronological scheme" (SELMAN, 1:121).

While the details are complex, Wright ("Legacy," 229, 233) argues that the function of 1 Chronicles 23–27 confirms its originality. First Chronicles 23–27 provides the "chief legacy of David within [the Chronicler's] history." His legacy is rooted in temple and official preparations that enable a "smooth transference of power" so that Solomon may rule his kingdom "in peace and build the temple." This is consistent with De Vries' point that David legitimizes the Levitical order as "cult founder" alongside of Moses (De Vries, "Founders," 619-639). First Chronicles 23–27 does not interrupt the installation genre as much as it gives content to its significance. It pictures David as one who shared the task with Solomon. David prepared the temple and its cultus. Solomon built it and inaugurated its rituals. The two were a united royal house acting on the promise of God to inhabit the house that Solomon would build in confirmation of God's redemptive intentions for Israel.

The Levitical material of 1 Chronicles 23–26 "legitimates the proper temple personnel system within the temple." This legitimizes the reforms which Chronicles will describe during the reigns of Jehoiada (2 Chr 23:18-19), Hezekiah (2 Chr 29:25), and Josiah (2 Chr 35:4,15). Consequently, 1 Chronicles 23–26 is an "indispensable part of Chronicles" because "the unit functions to authorize and legitimate national beginnings and reform efforts whenever they arise" (Wright, "Legacy," 237).

1. David Makes Solomon King and Gathers his Leaders (23:1-2)

First Chronicles 22–29 should not be pressed into a strict chronology. It is a bird's-eye view of the final circumstances of David's reign. First Chronicles 23–29 are the details of that preparation and the installation of Solomon as king and temple builder. First Chronicles 23–29 is an elaboration of 1 Chronicles 22.

First Chronicles 23:1 heads this section, perhaps the whole of 1 Chronicles 23–29 (JAPHET, 407, 409, 411), as a topic sentence. It contextualizes David's actions in 1 Chronicles 23–27. David shares his throne with Solomon as co-regent. Theologically, as SELMAN (1:223) notes, this ties the temple cultus with the Davidic promise.

Many regard 1 Chronicles 23:2 and 1 Chronicles 28:1 as a doublet, the residue of a later redactor. However, Wright ("Legacy," 231) demonstrates that the two events are quite different. First Chronicles 28:1 is a holy assembly or convocation (קָהָל, *qāhāl*) called "to perform a national duty and celebrate a national festival." However, 1 Chronicles 23:2 uses a different term (אָסַף, *'āsaph*) that portrays "the gathering of officials to receive specific assignments." David gathers his leaders (royal and Levitical) in 1 Chronicles 23–27, but in 1 Chronicles 28–29 he gathers the whole nation. While the assembly in 1 Chronicles 28–29 is a national event, the assembly in 1 Chronicles 23:2 is "strictly business."

2. David Appoints Levitical/Priestly Personnel (23:3–26:32)

The bulk of the appointments in 1 Chronicles 23–27 are Levitical. While Moses installed the tabernacle cult, David installed the temple cult. There is a literary device by which Chronicles makes this distinction which De Vries ("Founders," 620-633) has called the "authorization formula" (Moses/Torah) and the "regulation formula" (David). The former (1 Chr 6:49; 15:15; 16:40; 2 Chr 8:13; 23:18; 30:5,18; 31:3; 35:6,12) refers to cultic obligations based on the Torah/Moses. The latter (1 Chr 15:13; 23:31; 24:19; 28:19; 2 Chr 4:7,20; 8:14; 23:18; 29:15,25; 30:6,12,16; 35:4,10,13,15,16) refers to David's prescriptions regarding the temple. Thus, Moses and David are parallel "cult founders" in Chronicles. David's innovative actions (such as the appointment of singers, selection of the temple site, etc.) are grounded in his legitimate role as "cult founder." Solomon, and other kings, regulated the temple according to the prescriptions given by David. Just as the tabernacle called for new institutions and procedures, so does the temple. Moses founded the cult on divine authority and David adjusted the cult to the new situation on divine authority. What David prescribes was "commanded by the LORD through his prophets" (2 Chr 29:25).

David sees value in an organized service with assigned tasks and people equipped to fill those roles. Proper organization, planning, and leadership are important. As ALLEN's (153) chapter title ("Varieties of Ministry") suggests, David sees value in a variety of roles. He trains, equips, and appoints people to different tasks for the common goal — in this case, the worship of God.

David Appoints Levitical Personnel (23:3-32)

First Chronicles 23:3-32 is separated from 1 Chronicles 24:1 where the list of Aaron's sons begins even though Aaron appears in 1 Chronicles 23:13. The Chronicler's purpose in 1 Chronicles 23 is broader than 1 Chronicles 24:1-19 where he specifies the priests.

The Levitical Census (23:3-5)

The total number of Levites 30 years or above was **38,000**. This is larger than other numbers of Levites in Chronicles (1 Chr 12:27). JAPHET (412) suggests the numbers are typological (based on multiples of four and six: 24,000, 6,000, 4,000 and 4,000) so as to enhance David's project (cf. WILLIAMSON, 159). However, SELMAN (1:223), given the counts of 288 musicians and 93 gatekeepers in 1 Chronicles 25:7-31 and 1 Chronicles 26:8-11, believes, "the figure of *thirty-eight* *thousand* is best understood as thirty-eight groups or clans." Others believe that the wealth and population of David's reign supports this large number (THOMPSON, 169; PAYNE, 4:419). JOHNSTONE (1:245-246) believes 38,000 is "easily accommodated within the statistical discrepancy noted in 1 Chron. 21:5-6; the clergy thus amount to about one in thirty of the adult male population" though the "round figures suggest the ideological nature of the writing."

Another problem with the census is the age difference between the census in 1 Chronicles 23:3 (age 30) and 1 Chronicles 23:24,27 (age 20). Age qualifications may have varied based on the availability of personnel or the nature of the tasks assigned (2 Chr 31:17; cp. Num 4:34-38 with 8:24; cf. JAPHET, 412; THOMPSON, 169). The inclusion of Levites 20 or above may have been an adjustment David made in the latter years of his reign or due to special circumstances (SELMAN, 1:226). The Chronicler, who is careful with style and language, left the "problem" in the text because he did not find it disconcerting.

David grouped the Levites into four task forces: (1) 24,000 **to supervise the work of the temple**, (2) 6,000 as **officials and judges**, (3) 4,000 as **gatekeepers**, and (4) 4,000 **to praise the LORD with the musical instruments**. The largest number refers to leaders in the temple who supervised not only the construction of the temple, but also its liturgical functions and mundane tasks (cf. 2 Chr 34:12-13). Though three of the groups are detailed in 1 Chronicles 23–26, only the officials and judges are not discussed further (1 Chr 26:29). Some Levites exercised judicial functions within Israel (cf. 2 Chr 19:4-11; 34:13). The term "officials" may refer to secretaries or scribes (ACKROYD, 82).

The Organization of the Levites (23:6-23)

David organized the Levites into three groups following the pattern of Levi's three sons: **Gershon, Kohath and Merari**. Verses 7-11 list the descendants of Gershon, verses 12-20 the descendants of Kohath, and verses 21-23 the descendants of Merari. Chronicles specifies **David** as the organizer.

Levi's descendants also appear in 1 Chronicles 6:1-30 (cf. BRAUN, 231-234). However, several problems appear in this list. Some are minor, such as the spelling variation of **Ladan** (1 Chr 23:7) where it is Libni in 1 Chronicles 6:17. However, the **sons of Shimei** appear twice (1 Chr 23:9 and 1 Chr 23:10). Perhaps it is a different Shimei since 1 Chronicles 23:9 contains the **heads of the families of Ladan** (WILLIAMSON, 161; PAYNE, 4:419), or perhaps it is a textual corruption (JAPHET, 414). Some emend Shimei to Jehiel which restores symmetry to the text (MYERS, 1:158; Hognesius, 123-127).

The expanded comment in 1 Chronicles 23:13-14 is significant. The Chronicler includes Moses' sons among the Levites, but he can only do this by introducing Moses' father **Amram**. But when Amram appears in genealogical lists, it is normal to list both sons: **Aaron and Moses**. Yet, the Chronicler also wants to distinguish the Aaronites (the priestly office) from the Levites: **Aaron was set apart, he and his descendants forever**.

The theological significance of 1 Chronicles 23:13 is important. It contains, according to SELMAN (1:225), "the most detailed list of priestly duties in Chronicles" (cf. 1 Chr 6:49). The Aaronites were separated out to serve as priests. Their task involved four functions: (1) **to consecrate** (קָדַשׁ, *qdš*) **the most holy things**, (2) **to offer** (קָטַר, *qṭr*) **sacrifices before the Lord**, (3) **to minister** (שָׁרַת, *šrt*) **before him**, and (4) **to pronounce blessings** (בָּרַךְ, *brk*) **in his name forever**. The priests "made holy" the "holiest of holy things." As the separated servants, they protected and dedicated the holy things of God. They offered sacrifices as atoning gifts to God and mediated God's blessings to his people. The mediatorial role of the priesthood is assumed. Just as the promise to David was forever, so the role of the priests before God is forever. The eternal character of the priesthood, just as the eternal character of the dynasty, is ultimately found in Jesus Christ who is the mediator between God and humanity. As priests, Christians also assume the priestly tasks of worship, spiritual sacrifices, intercession, and holiness.

The Tasks of the Levites (23:24-32)

JAPHET (417-418) believes that 1 Chronicles 23:24 serves as the conclusion to the previous section and the introduction to the following. She also believes the language of the verse is heavily dependent upon "census phraseology" found in Numbers 1. Chronicles numbers the Levites just as Numbers numbers all Israel. Chronicles numbers the people of God for the service of God.

The Transition from Tabernacle to Temple (23:24-27). The reason for these new tasks and regulations is the anticipated shift from tabernacle to temple. David is the one who authoritatively regulates the new situation.

The tabernacle involved certain duties for the Levites that would no longer be needed in the context of a temple (e.g., carrying the tent and the utensils). David reassigns and expands their duties.

The theological rationale for the move from tabernacle to temple is located in God's dwelling presence in Jerusalem. Israel is no longer a wandering nation nor is she oppressed within her own borders. At the end of David's life, God **has granted rest to his people and has come to dwell in Jerusalem forever**. Now God will have a permanent dwelling place rather than a portable tent. Israel will find security in that permanence since God has determined to give his presence to his people in a temple.

This encourages the Chronicler's postexilic audience. They, too, can find God's rest in his temple presence. This is the assurance of God's grace.

The Service of the Levites in the Temple (23:28-32). This section is bounded by the phrase **the service of the temple of the LORD** (1 Chr 23:28,32). This identifies the function of the Levites in the temple cultus and distinguishes them from priests. The Levites had a supporting role administering three major areas: (1) maintaining the purity of the grounds and utensils of the temple (1 Chr 23:28), (2) maintaining the required **bread** and **flour** for **baking and mixing** in appropriate quantities (1 Chr 23:29), and (3) leading the communal **praise** at the daily sacrifices and **appointed feasts** (1 Chr 23:30-31). As assistants to the priests, they maintained the cleanliness of the temple, prepared the bread and cereal offerings required for the daily burnt offerings (Exod 29:38-41; Num 28:3-8), and engaged in the constant worship of God.

JAPHET (419) suggests that these three functions correspond to the three major groups in 1 Chronicles 23–26: (1) gatekeepers, (2) Levites, and (3) musicians. SELMAN (1:226), however, believes that these are general tasks of the Levites, and that the other groups (gatekeepers, officials and judges, musicians, and treasurers) detailed by the Chronicler are separate and more specialized servants. In the latter case, praise and thanksgiving is something that all the Levites did, but there were specially trained musicians who led them.

SELMAN's approach seems best. The Chronicler begins broadly — the general tasks of all Levites. Then he focuses on special duties: priests (1 Chr 24:1-19), musicians (1 Chr 25:1-31), gatekeepers (1 Chr 26:1-19), and treasurers (1 Chr 26:20-32). Consequently, Levites, if they were not appointed to one of these specific offices, were given the broader tasks recorded in 1 Chronicles 23:28-32.

David Appoints Levitical Priests (24:1-19)

One of the major concerns of the postexilic community was the legitimization of its priests. Consequently, postexilic works contain several lists of the priestly line (1 Chr 6:3-15; 9:10-13; Ezra 2:36-39; Neh 10:1-8; 11:10-12; 12:1-21). This text is not a high priestly list (as in 1 Chr 6), but moves from Aaron to his sons to the heads of the families in the time of David. The purpose, however, is not to legitimate the lines of descent, but to legitimate the 24 divisions of the priestly organization. Thus, the section begins: **These were the divisions of the sons of Aaron.**

The Aaronite Origin of the Priesthood (24:1-5)

First Chronicles 24:1 resumes the genealogical list begun at 1 Chronicles 23:13 from Amram to Aaron. The sons of Aaron are priests and therefore distinct from the rest of the Levites. Interestingly, however, as JAPHET (425) points out, the priests receive the "least attention" of all the groups in 1 Chronicles 23–27. There is no detailed description of their function as with the other groups. The Chronicler, for the purposes of his own audience and setting, emphasizes the role of the Levites in general rather than the priests.

The priests are the **officials of the sanctuary and officials of God**. This designation underscores the centrality and importance of the priestly class without devaluing the significance of other Levitical functions in the temple. The priests are the **officials** of what is holy, and they represent God (intercessors and mediators through the sacrificial ritual).

Chronicles, then, has carefully balanced the importance of priests and the "rest of the descendants of Levi" (1 Chr 24:20; cf. 1 Chr 23:32). Levites and priests together serve before God. They are holy servants dedicated to the service of the holy God in his holy place.

The present list is not genealogical. It organizes the 24 divisions according to the descendants of only two of Aaron's sons. The incident of **Nadab** and **Abihu** (Lev 10) was sufficiently well known to permit the Chronicler to simply note that they did not have any sons. The Chronicler is not concealing a piece of information but assumes his readers know the story.

All the priests descend from Eleazar and Ithamar. The two most prominent priests represent these lines: **Zadok a descendant of Eleazar and Ahimelech a descendant of Ithamar**. Zadok and Ahimelech (the son of the high priest Abiathar, cf. 1 Chr 18:16) were David's two high priests. Zadok served at the tabernacle (1 Chr 16:39) and Abiathar at the ark. The two will serve together in the temple, and representative lines of Eleazar and Ithamar will divide the responsibilities.

The 24 divisions were assigned by **lots**, but the largest group was the descendants of Eleazar. This was done under the leadership of both David and his priests, Zadok and Ahimelech. The Chronicler legitimizes the 24 divisions by royal (**David separated** in 1 Chr 24:3) and priestly authority (**they divided** in 1 Chr 24:5). While most believe the divisions reflect postexilic conditions, there is little reason to doubt that the roots do not reach back to the beginnings of the temple cultus itself (SELMAN, 1:230). The number of divisions may have varied at times (Neh 10:3-9 has 21) and Chronicles's text may reflect a final stage of development (MYERS, 1:166; cf. charts of priestly divisions in PAYNE, 4:422). The number 24 is typological of the twelve tribes. The 24 divisions may refer to a two-year cycle of one division per month (as in Egypt; MYERS, 1:167-168) or a one-year cycle of one division per two weeks (as in Luke 1:5; cf. SELMAN, 1:232, n. 1).

The Twenty-Four Divisions (24:6-18)

Eleazar's descendants are the largest with sixteen divisions and the remaining eight are derived from Ithamar. On details pertaining to the names and problems associated with them, see more substantial commentaries (JAPHET, 429-432).

Conclusion (24:19)

The legitimization reaches back to Aaron rather than to just David, Zadok, and Ahimelech (cf. Ezra 7:1-5). This is an example of

Torah authorization (Moses and Aaron) rather than simply Davidic regulation.

David Appoints Levitical Ritual Assistants (24:20-30)

Most believe this section has been added by a later editor. It repeats the names found in 1 Chronicles 23:16-23 with the addition of another generation (updating the material; WILLIAMSON, 165). Further, this material omitting the Gershonites may indicate that some of the text has been lost in transmission since it is unlikely such a list would ignore the largest Levitical group (JAPHET, 432).

However, while these points are possible, there is another way to account for the text. SELMAN (1:232) suggests that this group of Levites "may have been restricted to priestly assistants, who shared the responsibility for temple administration (cf. 23:4) alongside those mentioned in 23:28-31." The exclusion of the Gershonites from this task may parallel the exclusion of the Merarites from treasury duty (1 Chr 26:20,32) and the Gershonites from the gatekeepers (1 Chr 26:19). Consequently, this list is a specific task group much like the following lists of musicians, gatekeepers, and treasurers. They are ritual assistants (JOHNSTONE, 1:255).

As ritual assistants, this Levitical group, just like the priests, are divided into groups by **lots**. God assigns servants by his own election (16:33). However, this is not the only similarity between the priests and their ritual assistants. JOHNSTONE (1:254) suggests that "24 Levites of the fourth and subsequent generations are here listed, a number which would indeed correspond with the 24 divisions of the priesthood."

David Appoints Levitical Musicians (25:1-31)

Musicians are an important part of the ritual event. Music was integral to ritual sacrifices in the temple. It was no mere addendum. "The choral service," Kleinig (*Song*, 131) writes, "did not exist by itself as a separate entity within the worship at the temple, but was closely coordinated with the public burnt offering. It had no independent ritual function but was part and parcel of the sacrificial ritual." It forms a necessary part of the temple ritual as instituted by David upon divine authority. Kleinig ("Divine Institution," 75-83; *Song*, 28-63) points out that the function of the Levitical choir is, in part, rooted in their responsibility to pronounce blessings in the name of God (cf. Deut 10:8 and 18:5). Thus, Levitical musicians are consistent with the prescriptions of the law itself. As SELMAN (1:234) notes, the Chronicler's "aim was presumably to stimulate regular musical praise as an important ministry in itself and as a vital accompaniment to the offerings of the priests."

The Three Families (25:1-6)

The section begins and ends by enumerating the three major families: Asaph, Heman, and Jeduthun. At the center of this section (1 Chr 25:2-5) is a list pertaining to each. Heman had more sons than the rest as a sign of God's blessing (1 Chr 25:5; cf. Job 42:13).

David, together with the commanders of the army, set apart the musicians. Literally, the Hebrew reads "the officers [or chiefs] of the host." Contrary to the NIV, this does not refer to military personnel, but, as JAPHET (439) believes, to the Levitical host (Num 4:3,23,30,35; 8:24,25) or Levitical officials (cf. 1 Chr 15:16). The text emphasizes the royal supervision of the musicians (1 Chr 25:6). Levitical worship was an **army** (host) that engaged in spiritual service (JOHNSTONE, 1:256).

First Chronicles 25:1, as an introduction to the whole chapter, refers to the **ministry of prophesying, accompanied by harps, lyres and cymbals**. This is their **service** (1 Chr 25:1) or **ministry** (1 Chr 25:6). **Asaph, Heman**, and **Jeduthun** are prophets or seers (1 Chr 25:2,3,5). Chronicles emphasizes the prophetic function of the Levitical singers (Kleinig, *Song*, 153-154). The ministry of music is a prophetic one (on cultic prophecy, see Petersen, 55-96; Wilson, *Prophecy*, 292-297; Johnson, *Cultic Prophet*).

Nowhere else is musical service identified with "prophesying" (except when the prophetess Miriam sang to Israel in Exod 15:20-21). While there is a tendency to tone down the use of this term, Chronicles emphasizes something significant rather than simply saying they "sang." The singers "prophesied." Further, it is more than simply how they prophesied (some argue that these singers looked like prophets in ecstasy). But the text states what they did, not how they did it. Interestingly, Chronicles changes "priests and prophets" in 2 Kings 23:2 to "priests and Levites" in 2 Chronicles 34:30. Chronicles associates the Levitical liturgy with prophetic ministry.

Kleinig (*Song*, 155-156) identifies three major approaches to this identification. First, some believe the singers are cultic prophets (Mowinckel). Consequently, singers prophesied in liturgical forms and proclaimed the word of God. Second, others believe these were inspired songs that were given power through their performance with musical instruments (THOMPSON, 177). Thus, Chronicles already regards the Psalms as inspired literature (JAPHET, 440). Third, as Kleinig (*Song*, 155) argues, the "singing of the psalms by the temple choir was a form of prophetic proclamation." They may or may not have received hymns directly from God by inspiration (perhaps some did; 2 Chr 20:14-17), but they performed the prophetic function of proclamation. They proclaimed the deeds of God to the people through song. Thus, singing was a form of prophesying (Johnson, *Cultic Prophet*, 69-72; PAYNE, 4:424).

The singers may be understood as prophetic in four ways (Kleinig, *Song*, 155-156). First, they mediated between God and his people, often speaking to the people for God through songs. Second, they addressed the people in a prophetic manner, that is, through poetry and song. Third, their function was connected to the daily burnt offering where the Lord's acceptance of his people was proclaimed. Fourth, their proclamation was by the power of the Lord who acted through the singers. "Their praise was effectual because in it they proclaimed the LORD's name and announced his goodness to his people. Thus, the proclamation of the singers was prophetic in status, manner, function and power."

This is liturgical proclamation. ALLEN (163) distinguishes between the "temple prophet" and the "classical prophet." The New Testament prophet, he believes, is the "descendant" of the former rather than the latter. Thus, New Testament prophesying is more like exhortation and worship than inspired (apostolic) preaching. It is teaching through song. Singing is a form of teaching (Eph 5:19 and Col 3:16), and the singers are analogous to soloists (or choruses) who exhort through song (1 Cor 14:26). These musical servants were constantly **thanking and praising the LORD** (1 Chr 25:3).

The ritual, then, involved the priest (offering the sacrifices), the ritual assistants (managing the details of the ritual), and the musicians (proclaiming the message of redemption through song). This entailed a combination of table (eating the sacrifices) and word (levitical sermons and the proclamation through song). The combination of song (praise), word (preaching), and table (Lord's Supper) is also at the heart of Christian worship.

Music was an integral part of this ritual. It was neither an addendum nor a mood-setter. It proclaimed salvation and praised God. Christianity is witnessing a revival of music. Yet, this importance should be rooted in its function as proclamation, thanksgiving, and praise rather than in its energy and mood. In contrast to the pagan use of music in temples, the music of Israel (and the church) is logocentric (proclamation; Stapert, 387-393). The message, not the medium, is important.

The Twenty-Four Groups (25:7-31)

The 24 groups follow the analogy of the priests and their ritual assistants (the number 288 is 24×12). Consequently, Chronicles posits one set of priests, assistants, and musicians that rotate on a periodic basis according to 24 divisions.

Chronicles unveils the highly organized character of temple worship. The priests, their assistants, and the musicians work closely together in regular shifts to complete their task. Every day and throughout the years, servants of God are present in his holy place to praise him.

David Appoints Levitical Gatekeepers (26:1-19)

"Gatekeeper" sounds antiquated. There is nothing analogous in modern culture. Consequently, many underestimate their significance as if they were dispensable personnel or received the "lower order" assignments (MYERS, 1:176). The common perspective that this was a menial task is probably accentuated by the supposed contrast in Psalm 84:10 between a lowly doorkeeper in the temple and a popular presence at the parties of the wicked. But this misunderstands the contrast, which is not between lowly and mighty but between holy and wicked. **Gatekeepers**, according to 1 Chronicles 26:12, **had duties for ministering in the temple of the LORD**. What was this ministry?

Wright ("Gatekeepers," 69-81) provides a helpful synopsis. Gatekeepers served four functions: (1) a paramilitary inner city security force, (2) political governance of the state, (3) the administration of temple revenue, and (4) the maintenance of the temple and its paraphernalia. Gatekeepers are guards (Levitical warriors, cf. 1 Chr 12:26). They protect the temple from theft and from "illegal entry into sacred areas." They are invested with the responsibility of maintaining the temple's holiness, warning those who seek to enter, and maintaining order. Thus, this military connotation has sacramental functions — it admits, restricts, and protects the holy place (Wright, "Gatekeepers," 70-74). GNB calls them "temple guards."

Other roles are political, custodial, and economic. Gatekeepers were "high-ranking government officials, involved in the political administration of the state" (Wright, "Gatekeepers," 74-75). In Persian contexts the "gate of the king" (cf. Dan 2:49) was a high political office. Further, one gatekeeper, **Zechariah**, is called a **wise counselor** who is stationed at the **North Gate** (1 Chr 26:14). This term describes royal advisers in Chronicles (cf. 1 Chr 27:32,33; 2 Chr 22:3,4; 25:16). Gatekeepers were active administrators and advisors in the government (Wright, "Gatekeepers," 76).

Apparently, they not only administered funds but they were also tax-collectors (1 Chr 9:26; 2 Chr 31:14-16; 34:8-13). "[The Chronicler] thus portrays gatekeepers as involved in all aspects of temple revenue — its collection, its storage, and its distribution" (Wright, "Gatekeepers," 77).

In addition to the general ministry of temple upkeep and ritual assistance (cf. 1 Chr 9:27-32), the gatekeepers were significant players in maintaining, administering, and governing the temple to ensure its security, holiness, and continued operation.

Psalms 15 and 23 indicate that the gates were "spiritual checkpoints" (ALLEN, 167). The gatekeepers excluded the unclean (2 Chr 23:19). They protected the temple's holiness and worship. Theologically, this unites ethics (holiness) and worship (Jer 7; Isa 1:13-17; Micah 6:1-8). Those who seek God's presence must reflect his holiness.

The List of the Gatekeepers (26:1-12)

The gatekeepers are taken from the **Korahites** (thus, from Asaph; 1 Chr 26:1), from **Obed-Edom** (1 Chr 26:4), and from the Merarites (1 Chr 26:10). The sons of Heman are lacking among the gatekeepers (1 Chr 26:19).

JAPHET (451) points out that this section follows the general pattern of "'genealogy' first and 'statistics' second." She outlines it in the following manner:

I. (a) Genealogy of Meshelemiah, the Korahite (1 Chr 26:1b-3)
   (b) Genealogy of Obed-Edom (1 Chr 26:4-7)
   (c) Number of Gatekeepers of Obed-Edom (1 Chr 26:8)
   (d) Number of Gatekeepers of Meshelemiah (1 Chr 26:9)
II. (a) Genealogy of the Merarites (1 Chr 26:10-11a)
   (b) Number of the Merarites (1 Chr 26:11b)

The Organization of the Gatekeepers by Lot (26:13-19)

East Gate	North Gate	South Gate and Storehouses	West Gate and Shalleketh Gate
Shelemiah with six guards	Zechariah with four guards	Obed-Edom with four guards and two at the storehouses	Shuppim and Hosah with four guards at the road and two at the court itself

Just as with the priests and musicians, the divisions and tasks are assigned by casting **lots**. Divine selection is at work in these lots (cf. Prov 16:33).

There are several problematic words. One is twice translated **court** (פַּרְבָּר, *parbar*) in 1 Chronicles 26:18. A second problematic term is translated **road** (מְסִלָּה, *məsillāh*) in 1 Chronicles 26:16,18. Dorsey (385) argues that this latter term does not refer to a road but to an "architectural structure" which Solomon "constructed in his palace/temple complex on the Temple Mount." The word describes a "particular type of gate . . . associated with the palace or the Temple, where gate-keepers would be stationed," perhaps even with an "outer stairway." If this is the correct understanding, 1 Chronicles 26:16 identifies the chambers (instead of reading a proper name **Shalleketh**; Dorsey, 387) of this special gate, and 1 Chronicles 26:18 refers to four who were stationed at this gate and two who were stationed at the **court**. Runnalls (329) argues that the term translated **court** by the NIV refers to a ritual separation site. Consistent with the Qumran *Temple Scroll*, this was a "columned structure in which the purgation offerings of the priests could be kept separate from those of the people."

David Appoints Other Levitical Officials (26:20-32)

The narrative separates these lists from the previous one. But the heading of 1 Chronicles 26:20 (**their fellow Levites**) links them. The heading marks off the next set of personnel as distinct from the gatekeepers, but the link also closely associates them with the gate-keepers.

First Chronicles 26:20-32 appoints personnel to two functions: (1) treasurers (1 Chr 26:20-28) and (2) officials and judges (1 Chr 26:29-32). First, the treasurers are closely associated with the gate-keepers (some were treasurers, 1 Chr 9:26) because the **treasuries** and storehouses were located near the gates (SELMAN, 1:241; cf. Neh 12:25). Second, if the gatekeepers are involved in state government, then it is natural to link them with officials and judges. Conse-quently, this section is not a simple addendum to the lists. It fills out the remaining economic and judicial functions of gatekeepers or those closely associated with them.

Treasurers (26:20-28)

While the gatekeepers were derived from the Kohathite and Merarite lines, the treasurers are appointed from the **Gershonites** though shared with the Kohathites descended from Amram's line. In general, the Gershonites were the treasurers, but the other two major lines were gatekeepers. The **Izharites** and **Hebronites** (1 Chr 26:23; also Kohathites, cf. 1 Chr 6:2,28; 1 Chr 23:12) are the officials and judges described in 1 Chronicles 26:29-32.

The treasuries are divided into two major parts. First, the **treasuries of the temple of the LORD** (1 Chr 26:22) are supervised by the **Gershonites**. Second, the **treasuries for the things dedicated by King David** are supervised by **Shelomith**, a Kohathite (1 Chr 26:26). The former probably refers to the regular financial transactions of the temple, but the latter are the spoils of war collected in David's military victories (cf. 1 Chr 18:11).

First Chronicles 26:28 also includes what was dedicated by **Samuel the seer**, **Saul**, **Abner**, and **Joab**. This apparently refers to a time prior to the reign of David (or, in the case of Joab partly concurrent with David's reign). The order of Abner and Joab probably assumes the time of the divided kingdom before David reigned over all Israel (2 Sam 2–4). Thus, the Chronicler's addendum tacitly recognizes the existence of an interval kingdom. Their spoils (from Samuel to Joab) were collected and administered for temple-building.

First Chronicles 26:27 says that these dedicated items were for the **repair of the temple of the Lord**. The problem is that the articles are dedicated to the repair of something that does not yet exist. However, the NRSV (BRAUN, 250) reads "maintenance" rather than "repair." The Hebrew term (לְחַזֵּק, *l*ᵉ*ḥazzēq*) means "to strengthen." "Maintenance" is the preferable rendering and refers to a fund for the upkeep of the temple (though it refers to temple repairs in 2 Chr 24:5,12; 34:8,10).

Interestingly, JAPHET (462) points out that the "genealogical pedigree" of Shelomith is given in full (unlike others in 1 Chr 23–26). His line conforms to a ten-generation pattern. Like Zadok (1 Chr 6:1-8), Joshua (1 Chr 7:20-27), and David (1 Chr 2:1-15), Shelomith is the tenth generation from the son of Jacob. This has typological significance, that is, the time is right to build the permanent house of the Lord.

Officials and Judges (26:29-32)

The phrase **officials and judges** (וְשֹׁטְרִים שֹׁפְטִים, *w*ᵉ*šōṭ*ᵉ*rîm w*ᵉ*šōph*ᵉ*ṭîm*) occurs 6 times in the Hebrew Bible (Deut 16:18; Josh 8:33; 23:2; 24:1; 1 Chr 23:4; 26:29). They are judicial figures who administer legal judgments in the cities. WILLIAMSON (173) believes that officials were subordinate executives who enforced the rulings of judges. In David's time, they are governmental officials who administer the king's justice. These Levites served God and king outside of Jerusalem (**away from the temple**, 1 Chr 26:29).

While WILLIAMSON (173) separates the role of the **Izharites** (1 Chr 26:29) from the task of the **Hebronites** (1 Chr 26:30-32), JAPHET (463-464) argues that the described tasks in verse 30 (**the work of the LORD and for the king's service**) and verse 32 (**for every matter pertaining to God and for the affairs of the king**) are the tasks of officials and judges. Her evidence is 2 Chronicles 19:5,11 where judges are appointed to serve in the things pertaining to the Lord and king. In other words, judges represent the Lord and king. The Levites are God's chosen representatives among the people, and they serve the king's interests because the king is God's deputy in a theocracy. However, since the Hebronites cover both **west**

(**Hashabiah and his relatives**; 1 Chr 26:30) and east of the Jordan (**Jeriah** and his relatives over **Reubenites, the Gadites and the half-tribe of Manasseh**, 1 Chr 26:31-32), some kind of judicial hierarchy was in place.

First Chronicles 23:4 numbers the officials and judges at six thousand. First Chronicles 26:29-32 identifies their Levitical lineage. The two texts together form an inclusio where 1 Chronicles 23–26 details the Levitical appointments and separates this section from the next one (1 Chr 27) which involves all Israel rather than just the Levites. That this occurred in the **fortieth year of David's reign** (his last) indicates that the whole program in 1 Chronicles 23–26 was done in his last years. The whole land is filled with God's appointed royal judges. As JOHNSTONE (1:264) notes, the unfaithfulness of East and West in 1 Chronicles 2–5 is reversed in the kingdom of David. Chronicles shows how "through David's actions, the sorry tale of *ma'al* [evil] can be arrested, and the primal idea of the sanctification of the people can be attained through the system of monarchy and Temple."

Theologically, the Levites are involved in the whole of the kingdom. They perform not only priestly functions, but royal and prophetic ones as well. The priestly functions are obvious, but for Chronicles they also serve a prophetic role in the musical liturgy. Further, they are involved in royal functions as treasury administrators and judges throughout Israel. The Levites, then, typify the role of prophet, priest, and king. The Levites, more than any other tribe, are God's royal and priestly nation. Though God intended all Israel to be a royal and priestly nation by selecting the firstborn of all Israel as priests, the Levites were separated out after the Golden Calf incident (cf. Exod 19:6; 32:29). The Levites point forward to the priesthood of all believers. As a royal priesthood, they offer spiritual sacrifices to God through the prophetic Spirit (1 Pet 2:5-9). The Levitical function in the temple is the contemporary function of Christians in the service of God (1 Chr 23–26).

Consequently, this section is more significant than a mere rehearsal of minutiae. It exalts David as the founder of the temple cult. He builds on Moses and adapts the Mosaic prescriptions to a new situation. For Chronicles's first readers, it legitimizes the role of the Levites. The restoration of Davidic regulations reflects God's return to his people. This portrait of the Levitical institutions is a mirror which reflects the Christian's status before God. We are Levites and our privilege is priestly, royal, and prophetic (Rom 12:1-2; Heb 13:15-16).

3. David Appoints Royal Officials (27:1-34)

The connection between 1 Chronicles 23–26 and 1 Chronicles 27 is not obvious, but life in a theocracy intimately connects the two. Chapter 27 in relation to 23–26 connects "the administration of the Temple to that of the nation as a whole." Consequently, the text emphasizes "that the character of the nation's life is fundamentally religious, even mundane matters being ultimately controlled by the worship of God" (MCCONVILLE, 90-91). The Levites are scattered throughout the land as officials and judges. The transition from the "semisecular" activities of the official and judges to the "secular" activities of the military and royal personnel is an easy one (THOMPSON, 183-184). First Chronicles 27, then, fills in the missing elements of Israel's administrative picture.

While 1 Chronicles 23:3–26:32 addressed the priests and Levites, 1 Chronicles 27 addresses all the leaders of Israel. Thus, the details of chapter 27 are within the intended scope of the Chronicler as he provides a comprehensive picture of David's administration. In fact, SAILHAMER (56) believes 1 Chronicles 23:2 outlines 1 Chronicles 23–27 in reverse: "David gathered together all the leaders of Israel, as well as the priests and Levites." Further, 28:1 assumes a knowledge of the details of chapter 27. This chapter serves the Chronicler's purpose and is carefully situated in his narrative.

National Organization (27:1-24)

This first section organizes national institutions, the army (1 Chr 27:1-15), and officials from the various tribes (1 Chr 27:16-22). The national quality of this section derives from its attention to a standing **army** for Israel and the organization of the officials around the tribes of Israel.

The Organization of the Army (27:1-15)

The twelve divisional commanders are also named in 1 Chronicles 11:10-31. David's standing army is led by his most loyal servants (David's mighty men). The symmetry is striking. There are twelve commanders of twelve divisions consisting of 24,000 men each. These serve one month out of the year on a rotating basis.

The total number is large. Some (WILLIAMSON, 175; PAYNE, 4:430) believe that we should read "units" instead of "thousand." The total number, then, would be 288 fighting units with an unspecified number of fighting men in each. Or, the numbers are typological multiples of 12.

The Officers of the Tribes (27:16-22)

The "order of the tribes in vv. 16-24 does not correspond exactly with any other listing" in the OT (BRAUN, 260). In particular, Gad and Asher are missing, but Aaron is his own tribe alongside Levi. Further, Manasseh is divided into east and west to reach the total of twelve. The Chronicler has a typological interest in "all Israel." Consequently, he numbers the **tribes** according to the list he has (the source is in front of him) to achieve the total of twelve. He does not slavishly borrow from previous lists but is faithful to the one in front of him (THOMPSON, 186).

The role of these **officers** is unclear. SELMAN (1:246) suggests they are either Joab's assistants in the census or David's royal appointees. He favors the latter, and this is a move away from tribal government toward a more centralized authority. Thus, the officials are royal representatives scattered through all Israel. The phrase **officers over the tribes of Israel** (1 Chr 27:16,22) forms an inclusio marking this section off from the previous one.

Comment on the Census (27:23-24)

The theological heart of 1 Chronicles 27 is verses 23-24. The administrative order and the population of Israel is the Lord's doing. God is faithful to his promises. Unlike 1 Chronicles 21, David trusted God's promise to Abraham. Contrary to BRAUN (261), the text does not blame Joab instead of David, but rather it contrasts David's actions in 1 Chronicles 27 with his order in 1 Chronicles 21 (which Joab halfheartedly fulfilled). More importantly, David acts on God's faithfulness, and God blesses his kingdom in preparation for the building of the temple. As SELMAN (1:243) notes, "the temple preparations bear a sharper testimony to the reliability and effectiveness of the kingdom of God (cf. 17:14; 29:11,23) than to the kingdom of David."

These verses are not an interpolation that interrupts the context, as is commonly argued (JAPHET, 473). Chronicles accounts for the difference between divine curse in 1 Chronicles 21 and divine blessing in 1 Chronicles 27 since, presumably, David took a census for the organization of his kingdom. The difference is that David trusts the promise of God in 1 Chronicles 27 whereas he did not in 1 Chronicles 21.

David's Administrative Personnel (27:25-34)

This section focuses on David's administration of his royal property (1 Chr 27:25-31) and advisers (1 Chr 27:32-33). These are narrower concerns than the administration of a national organization.

David's Stewards (27:25-31)

The function of these officials is stated in 1 Chronicles 27:31. They are **in charge of King David's property** (stewards of his possessions). The list betrays the wide agricultural (**field workers, vineyards, olive and sycamore-fig trees, herds, camels, donkeys,** and **flocks**) and economic (**storehouses**) interests of the king.

David's Advisers (27:32-34)

This is David's inner circle — his most intimate counselors. Some are not otherwise known, e.g., **Jonathan** and **Jehiel**. Nevertheless, the description of Jonathan is the most elaborate: **counselor, a man of insight** [understanding] **and a scribe**. Whatever the job of a scribe might have entailed (presumably an official secretary), Jonathan was more than a stenographer for David. He was family, and David apparently valued his wisdom.

The presence of Ahithophel is interesting since it raises the specter of Absalom's failed coup d'état. Ahithophel sided with Absalom, while **Hushai the Arkite** remained loyal. The Chronicler assumes a knowledge of political intrigues without commenting on them. His only hint is that **Ahithophel was succeeded by Jehoiada son of Benaiah and by Abiathar**. He does not say why Ahithophel was replaced, but he assumes his readers know the story. **Joab**, of course, is the **commander of the royal army** described in 1 Chronicles 27:1-15.

Interestingly, the total number of names is seven. Perhaps this is typological or it reflects the Persian practice of a council of seven around the Persian King (JAPHET, 480). However, it is not seven at one time. Indeed, it was five, and then after the death of **Ahithophel**, it was six. Nevertheless, the number seven may have a typological function that concludes the whole of 1 Chronicles 23–27.

C. FINAL PREPARATIONS FOR THE TEMPLE (28:1–29:25)

First Chronicles 28:1–29:25 constitute a single literary unit. While BRAUN (267) believes 1 Chronicles 23–27 interrupts 1 Chronicles 22, 28–29, 1 Chronicles 28–29 is probably a climactic development. In 1 Chronicles 22 David privately charged Solomon and in 1 Chronicles 23–27 he appointed personnel. In 1 Chronicles 28–29 David assembles all Israel for a public celebration. First Chronicles 23–27 is necessary for the climactic event in 1 Chronicles 28–29.

JAPHET (482) structures 1 Chronicles 28–29 into six parts. I see a concentric structure.

  1. Introduction (28:1)
      2. David Addresses the Leaders (28:2-10)
          3. David Plans for the Temple (28:11-21)
          3.́ The Leaders Contribute to the Temple (29:1-9)
      2.́ David Blesses the Lord (29:10-20)
  1.́ Conclusion (29:21-25)

The introduction and conclusion separate these chapters from 1 Chronicles 23–27. They identify the immediate occasion as Solomon's public enthronement. But that enthronement serves a larger purpose, that is, the building of the temple. David's addresses are temple-centered as Solomon is God's choice to build it.

This material is unique to Chronicles. Instead of following Dtr (1 Kgs 1–2), he offers a different scenario. While the Chronicler ignores the political intrigue that brought Solomon to the throne, his omission is not a denial. Rather, he continues his "temple" thrust and excludes material that does not serve his purpose. First Chronicles 28–29 is an expansion of 1 Kings 2:1-12 (SELMAN, 1:212).

Theologically, these chapters are filled with motifs that permeate Chronicles: divine election, temple-building, grace, testing, worship, etc. The themes in the speeches not only address David's situation, but the Chronicler's as well (Sparks, 233-245). The Chronicler does not write for history's sake, but for the sake of his people. These words, then, have a direct application to his own time. They are words of grace to a postexilic people. MANGAN (70-71) summarizes their function:

> The thrust of this speech has much in common with the type of writing contained in the Book of Deuteronomy and in some of the prophets. It is a type of preaching which is hortatory in character, insisting on the need to serve God with a 'whole heart' (cf. Deut 6:5; Jer 24:7) and to seek him in such a way that he may be found (cf. Deut 4:29; Jer 29:13). There are many such speeches in 2 Chronicles; they are often spoken of as 'levitical sermons' since they illustrate the kind of teaching engaged in by the Levites in the postexilic period (cf. 2 Chron 13:4-12; 16:7-9). . . . Sermons such as these were probably delivered by levitical teachers sent around the country to teach the people (cf. 2 Chron 30:6-10; Neh. 8). It is possible also that such sermons were written down and available to [the Chronicler] (cf. 2 Chron 21:12-15). Adapted to their contexts, they were a powerful means of forwarding [the Chronicler's] theology at given points of the text.

They are also words of grace to us. We are the temple of God in whom the Spirit dwells. We are the people of God among whom God is still at work just as he was in the days of David and the Chronicler.

1. Introduction (28:1)

The summons by David is different from the one in 1 Chronicles 23:2 (Wright, "Legacy," 231). While 1 Chronicles 23–27 gathered Israel for the purpose of assigning functions, the purpose in 1 Chronicles 28:1 is liturgical. **David** called (יַקְהֵל, *yaqhēl*) Israel together in a holy assembly just as he called Israel together to move the ark (1 Chr 13:5; 15:3). David calls this gathering an "assembly of the LORD" (קְהַל־יהוה, *q⁽ᵉ⁾hal-YHWH*; 1 Chr 28:8) and invites the whole assembly to "praise the LORD your God" (1 Chr 29:20; cf. 29:1,10; 2 Chr 1:3). Solomon will also assemble Israel for the dedication of the temple (2 Chr 5:2-3; cf. 6:3,12-13; 7:8).

However, the initial assembly, which is later expanded into "the whole assembly," only includes the **officials of Israel**. David had earlier gathered them (וַיֶּאֱסֹף, *wayye'ĕsōph*) to assign tasks (1 Chr 23:2). Now he assembles (*wayyaqhēl*) them for a religious convocation in order to enthrone Solomon. These officials are described in 1 Chronicles 27 except for the **mighty men and all the brave warriors** who were previously noted in 1 Chronicles 11–12. The priests and Levites, JOHNSTONE (1:275) concludes, are not included at this point "because they belong to the blueprint of the Temple and its personnel" (1 Chr 28:13,21).

2. David Addresses the Leaders (28:2-10)

David's speech divides into two parts. The first recounts the divine election of Solomon as king and temple-builder (1 Chr 28:2-7). The second is an exhortation marked off by the expression **so now** (1 Chr 28:8-10). The first part of this exhortation is to the assembly (pl verbs; 1 Chr 28:8). The second is addressed to Solomon (sg verbs and **my son**; 1 Chr 28:9-10).

Divine Purpose (28:2-7)

David recounts God's history with his people. The text contrasts what David intended and what God chose. Divine intention is contrasted with human purposes. God chose Judah as the royal clan (even though he was not firstborn; Gen 49:8-12). God chose David's house from among Judah (even though there was nothing special about it). God chose David (even though he was not firstborn). Now, God has chosen Solomon (even though he was not firstborn). God makes sovereign decisions that arise out of his love, faithfulness, and purposes. The enthronement of Solomon is a divine act. Theologically, election depends on divine grace. Judah did not deserve to be the royal house. David did not deserve to be king. Solomon did not rise to power by his own initiative and power. Consequently, the following exhortations are grounded in God's active grace rather than human achievement. Divine commands are rooted in God's gracious acts.

David intended to **build a house as a place of rest for the ark of the covenant of the LORD, for the footstool of our God**. This expanded characterization of the temple is theologically significant. The **ark** as a **footstool** is known elsewhere only in Psalm 132:7-8. The temple is God's resting place and the ark is God's footstool. The temple is the place where God himself rests just as he has given Israel rest. In the theology of Israel, this is God's sabbatical rest where he lives in covenant with his people. The ark, as a symbol of the covenant between God and Israel, is the place where Israel enters the rest of God. Indeed, the ark, as the mercy seat (Rom 3:25-26), anticipates the rest into which Jesus brings the people of God as we yet anticipate the full consummation of that rest in the presence of God (Heb 4).

Sometimes God does not permit the fulfillment of our intentions. He has other plans. God has chosen a "man of peace" (lit., "rest"; 1 Chr 22:9) to build his temple rather than a **warrior** who has **shed blood**. The temple, as the place where God and Israel find rest, must be built by a person of rest.

God's election sets the course of history. This language is more specific than 1 Chronicles 17 or 1 Chronicles 22. As the Chronicler recounts the Davidic promise for the third time, his narrative builds to a crescendo in the words of God: **Solomon your son is the one who will build my house and my courts, for I have chosen him to be my son, and I will be his father.** Solomon is designated as the heir of the Davidic promise given in 1 Chronicles 17, and Chronicles, unique in biblical literature, makes Solomon the object of election (Japhet, *Ideology*, 449-452). Solomon is God's elect one, the chosen temple builder (Braun, "Solomon," 581-590). Further, this is the language of adoption. The people of Israel are led by God's son since they are God's own family. This reflects the intimacy between God and his people. Israel is God's son, and the king of Israel is God's chosen leader among his sons. Thus, David addresses Israel as **my brothers and my people** (v. 2).

The promise to David is now the promise to Solomon. Solomon will **sit on the throne of the kingdom of the LORD** (1 Chr 28:5), and God will **establish his kingdom forever** (1 Chr 28:7). The kingdom of Solomon is the kingdom of the Lord. Israel embodies the kingdom of God on the earth; it bears witness to God's glory, grace, and righteousness. The church is also a signpost of the kingdom as it bears witness to the one who reigns from above.

Just as Solomon was commissioned to **build** (בנה, *bānāh*) a temple (1 Chr 28:6), so God will establish (*bānāh*) Solomon's kingdom (1 Chr 28:7). However, the commitment to establish Solomon's kingdom is conditioned on Solomon's faithfulness in building God's temple. If Solomon will carry out God's plans **as is being done at this time** (temple preparations), then God will demonstrate his faithfulness to Solomon. This does not undermine God's promise to David, but only that God's promise to Solomon is conditioned on Solomon's faithfulness.

Exhortation (28:8-10)

The phrase **so now** (וְעַתָּה, *wᵉ'attāh*) signals a shift from describing the divine election of Solomon to exhorting his hearers to trust in that promise. David shifts from the descriptive to the imperative (7 times in 1 Chr 28:8-10). Divine grace evokes committed obedience.

Exhortation to the People (28:8)

The plural verbs indicate that David speaks to the assembled leaders, and he does so (1) **in the sight of all Israel**, (2) in the sight **of the assembly of the LORD**, and (3) **in the hearing of our God**. This is a holy calling. The officials of Israel are called to serve God's intentions and plans. God, Israel, and the holy assembly are witnesses to this calling.

David commands his officials to watch (**be careful**) and seek (**follow**) God's commandments. The conditional quality of this obedience, as in the Solomonic promise, is explicit. Remaining in the **land** is conditioned upon Israel's obedient faithfulness. It is an **inheritance** they can pass on to their **descendants forever** if they will seek God.

In 1 Chronicles 28:8 the significant theological term "seek" (דרש, *dāraš*) appears (obscured by the NIV). Not only should the leaders seek ("follow") God's commandments, but the "LORD searches [*dāraš*] every heart" (1 Chr 28:9). Further, anyone who would "seek" (*dāraš*) God will be found by him (1 Chr 28:9).

Exhortation to Solomon (28:9-10)

David turns to Solomon as the singular verbs and invocation (**my son**) indicate. It contains five imperatives: **acknowledge**, **serve**, **consider**, **be strong**, and **do**. The first two imperatives address Solomon's general orientation, and the last three his specific task. David exhorts his son to orient his life toward the Lord, and then he charges him to fulfill the task God has given him.

The general orientation toward God is described as seeking the Lord. **If you seek him, he will be found by you; but if you forsake him, he will reject you forever** (cf. 2 Chr 15:2). The contrast between seeking and forsaking is strong. They are two modes of life. One yearns for God and is devoted to him with a whole heart and delighted soul (בְּלֵב שָׁלֵם וּבְנֶפֶשׁ חֲפֵצָה, *b*'*lēb šālēm ûb*'*nepheš ḥāphēṣāh*; cf. 2 Chr 6:38). This expresses the integrity of a person's life. A dedicated life finds peace and joy in serving God. The other, however, yearns for something or someone else. It forsakes God to serve other gods. Solomon is given this fundamental choice — the choice we all have — of seeking or forsaking God. It is the choice God gave humanity in Eden. As ALLEN (180) comments, "Each generation of God's people in turn is confronted by the challenge to live out their faith with ever-renewed commitment to God."

David, however, does not leave the "seeking" to Solomon alone. In addition, and indeed first of all, God "seeks" Solomon. God seeks ("searches") every heart. The NIV translates דּוֹרֵשׁ as searches (1 Chr 28:9). The translation is problematic. "Searches" is not consistent with the other usages in this context. The leaders and Solomon are to seek God (1 Chr 28:8,9). In the same way, God seeks Solomon, that is, he seeks every heart (cf. Isa 55:6). This is divine initiative and purpose. God seeks a people for himself where he can be their God and they his people. "Yahweh's 'seeking' would thus be understood as a kind of longing, rather than as the scrutiny suggested by" the NIV and NRSV (McConville, "1 Chronicles 28:9," 105).

The noun **every motive behind** describes potters in 1 Chronicles 4:23. It is what shapes or molds thoughts (cf. Gen 6:5). In addition, in this same context of 1 Chronicles 28–29, David prays that the Lord will keep this orientation (יֵצֶר, *yēṣer*; untranslated by NIV) of thought in their hearts forever (1 Chr 29:18). The verb **understands** (מֵבִין, *mēbîn*) is a causative which means "to give understanding" or "to cause to understand," or "to teach" (cf. Ps 119:34,73). God is active as he seeks a people. He gives them understanding or teaches every shape and form of their thoughts. God is engaged with his world to shape them into his own image. He seeks to reorient hearts.

God desires a reciprocal relationship (cf. "seek" in Ps 119:2,10,176). Yahweh is a relational God who yearns and longs for his people. God actively shapes a people for himself (e.g., gives understanding, cf. Ps 119:27,34,73,125,130,169). He keeps their heart and molds them as a potter does clay. This is how God approaches every heart. God is active in the world as he seeks those who are seeking him (cf. Acts 17:27; Heb 11:6; John 4:23). God's "'seeking out' of 'all hearts' is a search for response, not judgmental so much as longing" (McConville, "1 Chronicles 28:9," 108).

> This means that, by virtue of the creation-commitment, God's heart naturally goes out to man (seeking), and finds rest only when *he* finds rest. God's activity in v. 9 is therefore the seeking of a responsive heart. . . . The one who does not seek God is unworthy, in the strongest possible sense, of God's commitment to him, because he does not conform to God's own ancient and enduring decree concerning what constitutes true humanity. . . . It remains simply to notice that the idea of God's commitment to humanity in creation comes to its ultimate expression in the Incarnation. There is a sense in which the Incarnation is not a new intensity of commitment to humanity on God's part. The radical nature of that commitment was implied in the act of creation itself. It is because creation is *for relationship* that it brings in its train such possibilities, on the one hand, for *enjoying* God, and on the other — by the refusal to respond to him — for causing him offense (McCONVILLE, 99-100).

In this context, then, the term **acknowledge** is more intimate than simple cognitive recognition (e.g., "recognize the authority"; WILLIAMSON, 181; Huffmon, 31-37). The Hebrew term "know" (יָדַע, *yāda‘*) often involves intimacy, that is, to know in a relational way (cf. Jer 22:16; Hos 6:6). Thus, when David calls upon Solomon to know and **serve** God, it is a call to pursue an intimate relationship.

On the basis of this relationship Solomon takes up the task of temple-building. God has chosen him and seeks a relationship with him. If Solomon will reciprocate, he will be empowered to complete his task. David admonishes Solomon to be strong and do it (1 Chr 28:10 [cf. 1 Chr 28:7]; חֲזַק וַעֲשֵׂה, *ḥăzaq wa'ăśēh*). Election is gracious, but election also means responsibility.

3. David's Plans for the Temple (28:11-21)

First Chronicles 28:11-19 is syntactically one sentence in Hebrew. David entrusts the temple plan to Solomon. The long sentence is the content of the plan. This is followed by a further exhortation that parallels the imperatives in 1 Chronicles 28:10: **be strong and courageous, and do the work** (1 Chr 28:20). Thus, the section naturally divides into two parts: (1) The Temple Plan (1 Chr 28:11-19) and (2) The Exhortation (1 Chr 28:20-21).

The Temple Plan (28:11-19)

David gives Solomon the pattern that God gave David. Chronicles recalls the building of the tabernacle in Exodus 25. The Hebrew term (תַּבְנִית, *tabnîth*) rendered "pattern" in Exodus 25:9,40 is the same as the word for **plan** in 1 Chronicles 28:11-12,18-19 (4 times). Just as Moses was shown the pattern by God, so David was given **all the details of the plan** by inspiration when he wrote them down **from the hand of the LORD** (1 Chr 28:19). **The Spirit had put in** David's **mind** the layout and details of the temple and its courts (1 Chr 28:12; on the role of the Spirit, see Neh 9:30; Zech 7:12; cf. MYERS, 1:190). The parallel between Moses and David is obvious. It reinforces Chronicles's picture that just as Moses was the founder of the tabernacle, so David is the founder of the temple (but not its builder). Though both are founders, neither are innovators. They implement what God designed.

The lengthy sentence is a detailed list. It covers the architecture of the temple (**portico, buildings, rooms**), the various weights of the materials used (**gold, silver**), and various utensils (**articles, table, forks, bowls, pitchers, lamps, altar**). The plans included personnel (1 Chr 28:13; for technical details, see JAPHET, 493-500). Here the

priests and Levites are reintroduced into the narrative (absent from 1 Chr 28:1). The summary assumes a knowledge of 1 Chronicles 23–26 where their **divisions** and ministry are discussed. As JOHNSTONE (1:280-282) points out, the theological significance of this list is found in the rituals of sacrificial atonement. Everything in the temple serves the purpose of atonement so that the holy God might dwell among his people in a holy place.

The Exhortation (28:20-21)

The parallel with Joshua is highlighted when David, just as Moses did, charges Solomon to carry out his task (Deut 31:6,8; Josh 1:5). Chronicles models the transfer of leadership after Moses and Joshua. David and Solomon are the new Moses and Joshua (Williamson, "Accession," 351-353; Braun, "Solomon," 581-590).

Solomon's courage arises from God's presence. **The LORD God, my God, is with you**. This is a significant theme in Scripture (THOMPSON, 193, n. 100; Gen 21:22; 24:40; 26:3,24; Exod 3:12; 33:14; Num 14:43; Deut 2:7; 20:1,4; 31:6,8,23; Josh 1:5,9,17; 3:7; 7:12; 2 Sam 7:9; 1 Kgs 11:38; 1 Chr 22:11). This presence, however, is not simply a comforting one. It is the assurance that God will finish the task through Solomon. The enabling work of God empowers Solomon to fulfill his ministry.

Further, Solomon has the support of his community. The **priests and Levites** are prepared for their ministries in the temple. **Every willing man skilled in any craft will help you in all the work**. Everyone is supportive. **The officials and all the people** will follow Solomon's lead and his **every command**. The temple is a "unifying point for all Israel" (BRAUN, 276).

The task of ministry needs the resolve to seek God's face. Leaders must orient themselves toward God's purposes as they accept the lot God has given them. David accepted his role of preparation. But resolve is not enough. Leaders also need a supportive and equipped community who will follow them. Solomon cannot build the temple alone. But even community is not sufficient. The fundamental ingredient to successful ministry is the enabling presence of God who strengthens his people. Thus, personal commitment, community, and divine presence build temples. That combination also builds the church into a holy temple (1 Cor 3:1-18).

4. The Leaders' Contribution (29:1-9)

David has given his plan to Solomon. Now he turns his attention to solidifying support for his plan with the people. David speaks, not just to the leaders (1 Chr 28:2), but to the **whole assembly** (לְכָל־הַקָּהָל, *lᵉkol-haqqāhal*). David has gathered all Israel as a holy convocation.

The parallel with Moses is obvious (BRAUN, 279-280). Just as Moses sought free-will offerings for the support of the tabernacle (Exod 25, 35–36), so David seeks free-will offerings for the support of the temple.

David Addresses the Leaders (29:1-5)

Rather than commanding the people to set aside personal resources for the temple, David attempts to persuade them. JAPHET (503) summarizes the rhetorical quality of this appeal with five items: (a) the task is too enormous for any single person, (b) Solomon **is young and inexperienced**, (c) David models generosity, (d) David details some of the "necessary items," and (e) David's final question is "pregnant with expectation." This persuasive appeal is a model for leaders.

The beginning and end of the appeal are important. The beginning is communal. The task is great, and Solomon needs help. Though Solomon is God's **chosen** one, he is young and inexperienced. Even God's elect servants need community. The community must help build God's **palatial structure** (הַבִּירָה, *habbîrāh*), a term reflecting royal interests. This text and 1 Chronicles 29:19 are the only times the temple is so described. The Chronicler reminds his readers that though Solomon is king, "the kingdom ultimately belongs to God" (WILLIAMSON, 184). God lives in his palace.

The final appeal is inspirational: **Now, who is willing to consecrate himself today to the LORD?** The verb "consecrate" is literally "to fill the hand" which is technically "associated with the induction of a priest into his office" (BRAUN, 278; cf. Exod 28:41; 29:29; 32:29). The dedication of gifts to the Lord is a priestly act on the part of Israel. As JOHNSTONE (1:285) comments, "By their free-will offerings, the leadership and, by extension, the whole community, are dedicating themselves, as it were, by ordination as the priestly people of

God. Holiness, as sacramentally focused on the Temple, is the realized ideal for the community as a whole." The act of sacrificial giving is a priestly act (cf. Heb 13:16). Thus, "it is not simply the gift that is consecrated to God but the giver. As one bids the gift farewell, one takes on a new role before God, a role of consecration to the service of God" (ALLEN, 189).

Sandwiched between these two appeals are David's gifts to the temple. David collected resources from official sources (including booty from wars; cf. 1 Chr 29:2). The valuables are listed in their descending order of value: **gold**, **silver**, **bronze**, **iron**, and **wood** along with various precious stones. David also gave out of his **devotion**. He gave additional **gold and silver** out of his **personal treasures** beyond what he had already provided (1 Chr 29:3-4). Some was **gold** from **Ophir**. While this is more associated with Solomon (2 Chr 8:18), there is nothing to exclude the possibility that David also received treasure from that region. David provides effective leadership by modeling piety.

THOMPSON (195) notes that the Hebrew term behind "personal treasures" (סְגֻלָּה, *s⁽ᵉ⁾gullāh*) is only used elsewhere for Israel as God's own treasured possession (Exod 19:5; Deut 7:6; 14:2; 26:18; Ps 135:4; Mal 3:17). As David models for Israel, God has already modeled for David. David gives to God as God has given to Israel.

The Leaders Respond (29:6-9)

The leaders of **Israel** responded generously. The term נדב (*ndb*, **gave willingly**) is used 7 times in 1 Chronicles 29 (5,6,9[2],14,17[2]). It described Israel's response to Moses in Exod 25:21,29. Like David, they gave **gold**, **silver**, **bronze**, **iron**, and **precious stones**. The people saw the gifts of their leaders and **rejoiced** with David (lit., "rejoiced with great rejoicing"; 1 Chr 29:9). The joy was rooted in the spiritual significance and generosity of the gifts. They were an expression of the leaders' wholehearted (בְּלֵב שָׁלֵם, *b⁽ᵉ⁾lēb šālēm*; 1 Chr 28:9; 29:9) devotion **to the LORD**. This was an act of priestly dedication fitting for a holy nation that God intended to be a "kingdom of priests" (Exod 19:5).

McCONVILLE (103) comments that "people are closest to God-likeness in self-giving, and the nearer they approach God-likeness the more genuinely and rightly they become capable of rejoicing." Thus, this self-giving was a reflection of OT joy rather than grudging duty. The OT's "presentation of man's relationship with God is above all in terms of joy" and wholehearted devotion that rejects "the path of self-gratification." God loves a cheerful giver (2 Cor 9:7).

The use of the term **darics** is anachronistic. Darics were coins minted in honor of the Persian king Darius I (522–486 B.C.). Consequently, David could not have used this term. The Chronicler, however, is simply expressing "money value in terms of a later equivalent, a practice that is common enough in our day when Bible translators express ancient measures in terms of a modern equivalent" (THOMPSON, 195).

5. David Blesses the Lord (29:10-20)

This is one of the most paradigmatic prayers in the Bible. It is "probably the best known passage" in Chronicles (ALLEN, 191). The early church added part of it (1 Chr 29:11) to the Lord's Prayer (Matthew 6:13, NIV footnote; cf. Black, 327-328). The prayer is steeped in theological significance (SELMAN, 1:255-257). It acknowledges that the kingdom and the whole earth belong to the Lord. It thanks God for the grace he has demonstrated to Israel and his dynamic activity in the world for the sake of his people. It petitions God to move the hearts of Israel. The prayer assumes a dynamic, active God who yearns for his people and supplies their every need. This confidence evokes praise, but it also generates a confidence that enables generosity. Paul makes a similar appeal to the Corinthians in a didactic context (1 Cor 9:6-15). David appeals to his people through liturgical prayer (seven direct addresses to God).

Chronicles characterizes David's prayer as a blessing. While the NIV reads **David praised the LORD** (1 Chr 29:10), the Hebrew reads David "blessed" (יְבָרֶךְ, *y^ebārek*) the Lord (cf. 1 Chr 16:36; 29:20; 2 Chr 2:12; 6:4; 9:8; 20:26; 31:8; cf. Ps 145:21). The NIV tones down this "blessing" with the word "praise." To "bless" God is certainly to praise him, and perhaps they are rough equivalents. However, Dawes (295) argues that blessing God "is about acknowledging him, giving him due honor," an honor that belongs to no other. Yahweh is the only true God (cf. Ps 134:1-3; 135:19-21) and usually responds to some mighty act of divine revelation (cf. Exod 18:10; Deut 8:10).

JOHNSTONE (1:286) divides the prayer into three sections: (1) Blessing (1 Chr 29:10-12), (2) Thanksgiving (1 Chr 29:13-17), and (3) Petition (1 Chr 29:18-19). **Now** in 1 Chronicles 29:13 and the imperatives in 1 Chronicles 29:18 signal new sections.

BRAUN (283) sees this prayer as a blending "of three major psalm types, the hymn, the thanksgiving, and the petition, with marks of the lament as well." This prayer cannot be stereotyped easily. It models worship generally (WILLIAMSON, 185).

Blessing (29:10-12)

David's prayer begins with the verb בָּרוּךְ (*barûk*, blessed). Blessed is the LORD, **God of our father Israel, from everlasting to everlasting**. The blessing links the present experience of Israel to the past and secures the future. The eternal God is the LORD who was with Israel (Jacob), and is now with David, and will always be with Israel. David draws assurance from the eternal God as the God of his father Israel which is the same assurance available to the postexilic community. The LORD is the God of Israel yesterday, today, and forever (cf. Heb 13:8). The Lord's love is everlasting to everlasting (Ps 103:17).

Following this elaborate invocation (1 Chr 29:10), the blessing divides into two sections. The structure is indicated by the phrase **Yours, O LORD** (לְךָ יהוה, *l'kā YHWH*). The first stanza (1 Chr 29:11a) evidences Israel's praise language. BRAUN (284) points out the following parallels: (1) **greatness** (Ps 71:21; 145:3,6), (2) **power** (Ps 89:14; 90:10; 106:2,8; 145:11,12; 150:2), (3) **glory** (Ps 71:8; 78:61; 89:18; 96:6), **splendor** (Ps 8:1; 21:5; 45:3; 96:6; 104:1; 111:3; 145:5), and **in heaven and earth** (Ps 115:15; 121:2; 123:1; 124:8; 134:3; 135:6). This doxological language ascribes to God what rightly belongs to him as the sovereign Creator ("heaven and earth").

The second stanza (1 Chr 29:11b-12) locates the reign of God in Israel's situation. While the Lord reigns over all the earth and everything belongs to him, on this occasion God has demonstrated his reign in Israel. The references to **wealth and honor** refer to the dedicatory gifts to the temple. The God of Israel is the real king of Israel. The **kingdom** belongs to him. He is **head over all** and **the ruler** (Ps 22:29; 59:14; 66:7; 89:10) **of all things**. The term "ruler" is a "special term for leader, and appears to be the official title of the earliest kings, still distinguishing them from the kings of the surrounding countries." It is one of the terms the Chronicler prefers (22 times; only 44 times in the OT) and since it is "connected with anointing," it may reflect the theocratic interest of the Chronicler (MYERS, 1:196). **Strength and power** are associated with his reign and he decides whom he will **exalt**. God alone (**in your hands**) glorifies Israel, its king, and people. Thus, the reign of God over Israel is manifested in the election of Solomon and in Israel's wealth.

Thankful Dedication of Gifts (29:13-17)

First Chronicles 29:13 is the topic sentence of this section. It contains three common worship phrases that fill the Psalms of Israel: **our God** (אֱלֹהֵינוּ, *ĕlōhênû*; 48 times, Ps 18:32; 20:8; 42:4,11; 95:7; 99:5; 105:7; 115:2-3; 145:1; 147:1), give **thanks** (יָדָה, *ydh*; 67 times, Ps 7:17; 9:1; 18:49; 35:18; 75:1; 105:1; 106:1; 107:1; 118:1; 136:1-3), and **praise** (הָלַל, *hll*; 94 times, including Ps 22:22-23; 69:30,34; 105:45; 106:1; 107:1; 111:1; 112:1; 113:1; 135:1; 145:2-3; 146:1-2). God's gifts to Israel enable their gifts to him.

The contrast between verses 13 and 14 is important. The verbs "thanks" and "praise" are participles which suggest the ongoing nature of the action, that is, "Here we are thanking and praising [you] . . . *but* — and the word is strongly emphasized — what is our status before God?" (ACKROYD, 94). It is a contrast between divine greatness and human frailty.

First Chronicles 29:14-17 supports the thanksgiving of 1 Chronicles 29:13. The first part emphasizes human dependence (1 Chr 29:14-16) while the second stresses integrity (1 Chr 29:17). Thanksgiving comes from the recognition that **everything comes** from God's **hand** (1 Chr 29:14,16). The "hand" metaphor serves as a binding concept for 1 Chronicles 29:14-16 and links it with 1 Chronicles 29:12. With the realization that God has given this wealth for the building of the **temple** comes concomitant praise and thanksgiving. The generosity of the people is dependent upon God's generosity: **Who am I, and who are my people, that we should be able to give as generously as this?** Generosity does not flow from pride, but from humility. It flows from dependency, not self-sufficiency.

This humility and dependency are metaphorically expressed in

1 Chronicles 29:16. Just as "father Israel" in verse 10 recalled Israel's patriarchal heritage, so does the language of **aliens and strangers** (Gen 23:4; also 17:8; 21:23). This was the plight of Israel's **forefathers**, and Israel continues its pilgrimage. This seems a bit odd now that Israel has territorial integrity. How can Israel still be an alien and stranger? Israel sojourns among the nations as God's people. It is a spiritual pilgrimage **in your sight**, that is, "before your face." Israel has always had a sojourner status before God, and the allusion to the brevity of life confirms this (Estes, 45-49).

This recognizes "that Israel's privilege to worship Yahweh is not based on right, but on grace" (Estes, 47). Israel's presence in the land, the kingdom of David, the gifts to the temple, and everything that Israel has is a demonstration of God's graciousness. Israel has no claim other than the promise of God. They are "aliens and strangers." Further, the postexilic community, who felt like aliens and strangers in their own land, gained confidence from this graciousness. Their status before God does not depend on temple, king, or land, but upon God's grace. Christians are also "aliens and strangers" (1 Pet 2:11) in the world. As Estes (49) concludes, "Thus, the sojourning of the previous generation of Israel begins to be viewed also as a paradigm for the life of the believer on the earth."

While 1 Chronicles 29:14-16 stresses human dependency and divine graciousness, 1 Chronicles 29:17 stresses human **integrity**. Integrity is a proper response to divine testing. God pursues humanity through testing or probing their integrity. Job is such an occasion of divine testing (Job 1–2; 23:10), but also Abraham (Gen 22:1), Israel (Deut 8:2-5), righteous hearts (Jer 11:20; 20:12; cf. Prov 17:3), and Hezekiah (2 Chr 32:31). The Psalmists pray for it and recognize it in their lives (Ps 7:9; 11:5; 17:3; 26:2; 66:10; 139:23). God is active and "seeking" a people for himself through testing.

David recognizes this occasion as a test, and he rejoices in his people's integrity. The Hebrew term behind "integrity," used in two different forms in verse 17, means equity or justice (Ps 9:8; 58:1; 75:2; 96:10; 98:9; 99:4). "Integrity" is an appropriate translation in some contexts (Deut 9:5; 1 Kgs 9:4), but it mainly refers to doing what is right ("uprightness," NRSV). The proper response to God's testing is to do what is right. This integrity (וּמֵישָׁרִים, *ûmêšārîm*) manifested itself by a willing, joyful gift **with honest intent** (בְּיֹשֶׁר, *b⁰yōšer*). This is a model of obedient, grateful response to God's graciousness. As the narrative unfolds, Chronicles will note which kings did what was right and which did not. That theological evaluation utilizes the same word that appears in 2 Chronicles 29:17 (יֹשֶׁר, *yšr*). God is pleased with honest intent (or rightness), and thus he is pleased with kings who do what is "right" (cf. 2 Chr 14:2; 20:32; 24:2; 25:2; 26:4; 27:2; 28:1; 29:2,34; 31:20; 34:2).

The Chronicler teaches his community how to respond to God's grace. Second Corinthians 8 and 9 is another example. The theology is the same though the circumstances are different. Paul tests the integrity and sincerity of love by exhorting the Corinthians to give to the poor saints in Jerusalem (2 Cor 8:8). His appeal is based upon the grace that God had demonstrated in Jesus Christ (2 Cor 8:9). Paul uses the term "grace" more in 2 Corinthians 8 and 9 than in any other section of his writings (8:1,4,6,7,9,16,19; 9:8,14,15). The Corinthians ought to "grace" the poor because God has "graced" them so that "grace" (thanks) might return to God.

Petition (29:18-19)

David prays for the hearts of his people and son. Integrity and uprightness do not simply flow out of human self-resolve. Rather, God works good things in the hearts of his people. God moves in the hearts of people (1 Sam 10:9; 1 Kgs 18:37; Ezra 6:22; Prov 21:1) as they move their hearts toward him (Deut 30:17; 1 Kgs 11:9; Jer 5:23; 17:5). He seeks them as they seek him. He enables them as they yearn for him. David's prayer for his people and his son is a model for all believers as they pray for their churches and their children. The prayer assumes both human responsibility and divine activity. Both are complementary values in God's relationship with his people.

David's petition draws on the covenantal promise of God to **Abraham, Isaac and Israel**. The children of Jacob are the children of promise. David claims this relationship and asks God to **keep this desire in** their **hearts** and **keep** (וְהָכֵן, *w⁰hākēn*, "prepare") **their hearts loyal** to him. The heart is the crucial area of relationship. God seeks committed, loyal hearts which yearn for relationship with him. The desire refers to the willing, joyful generosity of 1 Chronicles

29:17. David prays that God will prepare their hearts just as he himself has prepared the temple (1 Chr 29:19, **provided**).

In a similar fashion, David prays for his son, just as all parents pray for their children. He prays that God will **give** peace or wholeness (שָׁלֵם, *šālēm*; a play on Solomon's own name, שְׁלֹמֹה, *šᵉlōmōh*) to his heart in order to **keep** God's Torah (cf. 2 Chr 34:31). In particular, he prayed that Solomon would complete what David intends, that is, to build God's **palatial structure**.

Israel's Response (29:20)

David invited the **whole assembly** to participate. He calls upon them to bless **the LORD your God**. The people responded by blessing **the LORD, the God of their fathers**. Their blessing emphasizes David's stress on their history with this God. The LORD has always been their God.

Their worship involved body language. **They bowed low and fell prostrate before the LORD and the king**. We worship God as whole persons, including bodily actions. Whether standing, sitting, bowing, or lifting holy hands, worship is not only a matter of the heart, but also manifested through our bodies. Israel humbles itself before God in recognition of their dependency upon him.

6. Conclusion (29:21-25)

The first day of the holy assembly involved prayer, thanksgiving, and gifts to the Lord. The second day focused on sacrifices and Solomon's anointing. Solomon's enthronement, as is fitting for a theocracy, took place in the context of a holy assembly.

Liturgical Sacrifices (29:21-22a)

While the term **sacrifices** is a general one, the day's activities included **burnt offerings** and, though unspecified, peace offerings. Burnt offerings are acts of consecration to God where the whole animal is consumed. Such sacrifices express Solomon's wholeheartedness. Since Israel **ate and drank with great joy in the presence of the LORD** in the context of other sacrifices, this included peace offerings (Deut 27:7). These sacrifices were eaten by the worshiper in conjunction with **drink offerings**.

Enthronement of Solomon (29:22b-24)

The Chronicler's purpose is not the celebration of Solomon's enthronement, but "the true goal is the building of the Temple as the place of rest" for the ark (JOHNSTONE, 1:289). Solomon's accession is a necessary means to that end. The Chronicler is not interested in the accession per se. Consequently, the Chronicler skips the political intrigue of 1 Kings 1 because it does not serve his purpose. The Chronicler does not deny the events of 1 Kings; he merely omits them (contra JAPHET, 512).

Chronicles assumes the 1 Kings account (SELMAN, 1:261-262; WILLIAMSON, 187). The MT reads that Solomon was anointed **a second time** (1 Chr 29:22). Since this phrase does not appear in the LXX and Vulgate, many believe that it was added by a later scribe in order to clarify the relationship between 1 Chronicles 23:1 and 1 Chronicles 29:22. This is possible. Nevertheless, there is nothing inconsistent with two anointings since both Saul (1 Sam 10:1,24; 11:14-15) and David (1 Sam 16:13; 2 Sam 2:4; 5:3) were anointed twice (Dillard, *Study*, 623). If 1 Chronicles 29:23 parallels 1 Kings 2:12, Chronicles is describing the public enthronement of Solomon in 1 Kings 2 rather than the private anointing in 1 Kings 1.

Another indication that Chronicles assumes the events of 1 Kings 1–2 is the anointing of **Zadok to be priest**. This is unusual since he is already a priest (1 Chr 16:39; 18:16), but, as SELMAN (1:262) comments, "he is either being promoted to high priest, or being reappointed under a new king." This is appropriate since Abiathar is removed by Solomon because of his involvement in Adonijah's attempted coup.

All Israel gathered in a holy assembly to acknowledge Solomon as king. He emphasizes all Israel by noting that David's **officers**, **mighty men**, and **sons** all **pledged their submission** (lit., "gave the hand under") to Solomon. Divine approval is signaled by the fact that **he prospered and all Israel obeyed him**.

Theologically, Solomon did not sit on David's throne (cf.1 Kgs 2:12). Chronicles places him on **the throne of the LORD**. The kingdom belongs to God, and the one who sits on the throne does so by grace rather than right. Solomon's kingdom is a manifestation of the kingdom of God on earth. The Chronicler's community yearns for a renewal of that kingdom, and the people of God still pray "Your kingdom come!" as we await the full consummation of God's reign.

Theological Summary (29:25)

Since Solomon reigns on the throne of the LORD, he receives honor due to God's chosen king. **The LORD highly exalted** him (lit., "made him great," וַיְגַדֵּל, *way°gaddēl*). Greatness was applied to the LORD in 1 Chronicles 29:11 and the power to exalt (lit., "to make great") is in God's hands. Further, God gave him **splendor** that also belongs to the LORD himself (1 Chr 29:11). God raised Solomon to a height, in view of the temple-building project, that **no king over Israel ever had before**. No king had ever been in a position of such wealth, honor, and territorial integrity as Solomon. Further, this approval is highlighted by the contrast between Solomon's surpassing greatness ("highly exalted") and Israel's unfaithfulness (1 Chr 9:1). The word play between מַעְלָה (*ma°lāh*, "highly") and מַעְלָם (*ma°ălām*, "unfaithfulness") is unmistakable (JOHNSTONE, 1:292). Solomon's greatness contrasts with Saul's unfaithfulness (1 Chr 10:13-14).

D. THE CONCLUSION OF DAVID'S REIGN (29:26-30)

The Chronicler's final words about David parallel 1 Kings 2:10-12, but he is dependent only on 1 Kings 2:11. Even in these last words, the Chronicler emphasizes his reign over all **Israel**.

The Chronicler adds to Dtr an attribution of honor to David. It is his theological judgment, just as he gave one about Saul (1 Chr 10:13-14). David was blessed with **long life, wealth and honor** (cf. 1 Chr 29:12; also 2 Chr 17:5; 18:1; 32:27). David died in the bosom of God's blessings. Honor attaches to the death of godly saints whose long lives testify to divine grace and faithfulness.

It is uncertain whether the reference to the prophetic **records of Samuel**, **Nathan**, and **Gad** should be identified with Dtr or whether it is an additional source. Most commentators seem to think the former, but the latter is possible (JAPHET, 517). The Chronicler appeals to these sources as historical verification of his narrative.

III. THE REIGN OF SOLOMON (2 CHR 1:1–9:31)

The presentation of the reign of Solomon is quite different from that found in Dtr (1 Kgs 1–11). The Chronicler only uses 167 of 434 verses and adds 34 of his own (JOHNSTONE,1:296). The Chronicler omits Solomon's sins. While his unfaithfulness was important to Dtr as part of the explanation for the exile, it was unimportant to the Chronicler who concentrates on Solomon as the chosen temple-builder. Some of Solomon's laudable activities are also missing from 2 Chronicles (e.g., wise rulings, administration, royal palace; cf. 1 Kgs 3:16-28; 4:1-34; 7:1-12). As DILLARD (2) notes, "even the endue-ment with wisdom is not wisdom in the abstract (1 Kgs 3:16–4:34) but is specifically wisdom to build the temple." The guiding princi-ple of inclusion/exclusion for the Chronicler is the temple.

ACKROYD (99) believes the Chronicler approaches Dtr homilecti-cally. He sees an "example of a homiletic technique, very familiar from the preaching of many ages and contexts, in which a biblical narrative . . . is paraphrased, the addition and omissions, the changes in wording, all being due to a desire on the part of the preacher to bring home the real significance of what is already familiar."

Typology is the Chronicler's hermeneutical method for homilet-ical applications. "Typological comparison is his way of describing the new era which was comparable with the old and succeeded it. What the tabernacle meant in the Torah and to Israel hitherto, henceforth the temple would mean. The old was a model for the new, and the new replaced it." This hermeneutical move is contin-ued in the New Testament (particularly Hebrews) where writers reuse "language relevant to the old even as it supersedes it." Re-demptive history, then, "is a series of decisive interventions, with each new intervention marked by features comparable with earlier revelations" (ALLEN, 207). Consequently, the postexilic community anticipates renewal and NT writers proclaim its arrival. Christians anticipate a fuller experience of the presence of God in the new Jerusalem (Rev 21). Typology recognizes recurring patterns in redemptive history.

The Chronicler portrays Solomon typologically as he fulfills pre-vious patterns in the history of redemption. DILLARD (2-5; "Solo-mon," 289-300) summarizes these models. First, Solomon is a second

David (Braun, "Solomonic," 503-516). Only David and Solomon are "chosen" (בחר, *bāḥar*) in Chronicles (1 Chr 28:4-5). Both David and Solomon are supported by "all Israel" (1 Chr 11:1; 12:38; 1 Chr 29:22-25). Both are engaged in building the temple and ordering its personnel. Chronicles links the two as paradigmatic for a time of blessing and faithfulness (2 Chr 7:10; 11:17).

Second, David and Solomon are analogous to Moses and Joshua (Williamson, "Accession," 351-356). Just as Moses transferred leadership to Joshua, so David transfers leadership to Solomon. Just as Dtr has a double announcement of Joshua's election (Deut 1:37-38; 31:2-8), so there is a double announcement of Solomon's (1 Chr 22:5-13; 28:2-8). Both Moses and David were disqualified from fulfilling their respective goals (Moses entering the land and David building the temple). Joshua and Solomon complete their respective missions. This unity connects leadership at two peak moments of redemptive history (conquest of Canaan and temple-building). As a result, both Joshua and Solomon are supported by all Israel (Josh 1:16-20; 1 Chr 29:23-24), and God exalts (גדל, *gādal*) both (Josh 3:7; 4:14; 1 Chr 29:25; 2 Chr 1:1). Both Joshua and Solomon bring the people of God into "rest" (DILLARD, 4; Josh 11:23; 21:44; 1 Chr 22:8-9).

Third, Solomon and Huram-Abi are the new Bezalel and Oholiab (DILLARD, 4-5). Bezalel was chosen to build the tabernacle, and Oholiab was his helper (Exod 31:1-6). Both were given wisdom and skills. In the same way, Solomon and Huram-Abi were gifted to build the temple. In addition, Bezalel was a Judahite. Huram-Abi had the same tribal ancestry as Oholiab (2 Chr 2:14). The only two references to Bezalel outside of Exodus are in Chronicles (1 Chr 2:20; 2 Chr 1:5).

Theologically, Chronicles parallels the redemptive significance of David and Solomon with the significance of the Exodus-Sinai-Conquest. For the Chronicler, temple-building is a peak moment in redemptive history. God places his name in a city and gives his presence to his people. It is a further fulfillment of Exodus 25:8, "make a sanctuary for me, and I will dwell among them." The building of the temple is the continuation of covenant relationship with God. This is the Chronicler's confidence: God dwells in the midst of his people through the temple. The Exodus-Conquest and Temple-

Building are redemptive moments that ground the Chronicler's confidence that the rebuilt temple in the restored postexilic community mediates God's presence.

God dwells among Christians by his Spirit (1 Cor 6:18-20). The work of God in Christ (incarnation, ministry, death, resurrection, and exaltation) is the climactic moment of redemption. God builds another temple and comes to dwell in it. We are the temple of the living God where God lives (2 Cor 6:16; Eph 2:20-22). Yet, the church anticipates a dwelling with God where the fullness of God lives among his people in a new heaven and new earth (Rev 21:1-4; 22).

DILLARD (5-7; "Literary," 85-93) suggests a chiastic structure for Chronicles's Solomonic account.

A. Solomon's Wealth and Wisdom (1:1-17)
> B. Recognition by Gentiles/Dealings with Hiram (2:1-16)
>> C. Temple Construction/Gentile Labor (2:17-5:1)
>>> D. Dedication of the Temple (5:2-7:10)
>>> D'. Divine Response (7:11-22)
>> C'. Other Construction/Gentile Labor (8:1-16)
> B'. Recognition by Gentiles/Dealings with Hiram (8:17-9:12)

A'. Solomon's Wealth and Wisdom (9:13-28)

This emphasizes the dedication of the temple and God's response. Solomon's wealth and wisdom are only important in the light of his temple-building. The recognition and assistance of Gentiles is only significant in light of what they are building. The temple has "sacramental" significance as God's dwelling place in Israel. Prayer, atonement, grace, wholeheartedness, glory, and divine speech are the significant moments in Chronicles's Solomonic account. Second Chronicles 1–9 are not a history of Solomon's reign. They are a liturgical witness to the glory of God. At the heart of Solomon's reign is worship which is also the heart of the postexilic community and the church. Worship generates hope as God draws near in grace and communion.

In addition, scattered throughout the narrative is the recurring theme that God and Solomon will build this temple together, just as God and Moses built the tabernacle (SELMAN, 2:291). DILLARD (10) summarizes the evidence and parallels it with the construction of the tabernacle.

1. A temple to be built	Exod 25:1-8	1 Chr 28:11-21
2. King visits a temple overnight	Exod 24:12-18	2 Chr 1:2-7
3. A god reveals plans and duties	Exod 25:8–30:38	1 Chr 28:2-3,11-19
4. King announces intent to build	Exod 35:4-10	2 Chr 2:1-10
5. Master builder and materials	Exod 31:1-6	2 Chr 2:7-14
6. Temple finished according to plan	Exod 39:42-43	2 Chr 5:1; 6:10
7. Offerings and dedications	Exod 40:9-11	2 Chr 6:12-42; 7:4-7
8. Assembly of people	Exod 39:32-33	2 Chr 5:2-13
9. God enters the temple	Exod 40:34-35	2 Chr 5:13-14; 7:1-3
10. King is blessed with dominion		2 Chr 7:12-18

The tabernacle and temple are parallel events in redemptive history. Moses and Solomon are parallel figures. Both ultimately anticipate the master builder Jesus Christ.

The reign of Solomon may be dated from 970–930 B.C. (Handy, "Dating," 96-106). Millard ("King Solomon," 30-53) defends the essential historicity of Solomon's role in Israel.

A. SOLOMON'S WEALTH AND WISDOM (1:1-17)

As the ends of the structural chiasm, this section and the last (2 Chr 9:13-28) emphasize Solomon's wisdom (2 Chr 1:10-12; 9:22-23) and wealth (2 Chr 1:14-16; 9:13-14,25,27). In particular, wisdom is given to Solomon as it had not been given to anyone else (2 Chr 1:12; 9:22), and his silver, gold, and cedar were plentiful (2 Chr 1:15; 9:27). These verbal parallels confirm Chronicles's "structural intent" to bear witness to Solomon's exalted (2 Chr 1:1) status (DILLARD, 6). Wealth and wisdom are divine gifts (cf. Jas 1:5; 2 Cor 8:11).

1. Introduction (1:1)

The Chronicler's introductory summary parallels 1 Kings 2:12b and 2:46b though he uses a different verb for **established** (חזק [ḥāzaq] instead of כון [kûn]). Nevertheless, the function is the same. The **kingdom** is firmly in the hands of Solomon. This is God's act. **The LORD his God was with him and made him exceedingly great**. God's presence is one of Chronicles's enduring themes. His presence is an aspect of his faithfulness and empowerment (1 Chr 4:10; 9:1; 11:9; 17:8; 22:11,16,18; 28:20). Just as Solomon will build Yahweh an exceedingly great house (לְהַגְדִּיל לְמַעְלָה, *lᵊhagdîl lᵊmaʿᵊlāh*; 1 Chr 22:5), so God has made Solomon exceedingly great (וַיְגַדְּלֵהוּ לְמָעְלָה, *wayᵊgaddᵊlēhû lᵊmāʿᵊlāh*; cf. 1 Chr 29:25).

2. Solomon's Wisdom (1:2-13)

While 1 Kings 3:1–4:1a is the source of this section, the Chronicler uses it for different purposes. Some have seen this as the Chronicler's purposeful recasting of the events described (JAPHET, 525-526; Bar, 221-226). For example, many regard 1 Kings 3 as a private affair, but 2 Chronicles 1 a public one. However, nothing in 1 Kings 3 is explicitly private. Rather, 1 Kings focuses on Solomon whereas Chronicles emphasizes "all Israel." It is unlikely that Solomon went to Gibeon alone, and it is likely that he was accompanied by representatives of "all Israel" when he went. Whatever the solution, Chronicles adds that all Israel went to Gibeon (2 Chr 1:2-3).

Journey to Gibeon (1:2-6)

The journey to Gibeon is a holy convocation (**assembly**, הַקָּהָל, *haqqāhāl*). Just as early in David's reign a holy convocation brought the ark to Jerusalem (1 Chr 13:4; cf. 15:3; 28:1), so Solomon leads a holy assembly to the tabernacle at Gibeon. Further, just as David inquired ("sought") of the LORD (1 Chr 13:3; 15:13), so does Solomon (2 Chr 1:5). **All Israel**, including leaders at all levels, **went to the high place at Gibeon.**

Chronicles omits the reference to Solomon's sacrifices in Jerusalem (1 Kgs 3:15b) and explains why Solomon could legitimately offer sacrifices at the high place in Gibeon. Second Chronicles 1:3b-5 is unique. Dtr is somewhat apologetic about Solomon's visit to the high place whereas Chronicles seeks to legitimize his sacrifices in Gibeon.

But why does Solomon go to Gibeon when he could have worshiped before the ark in **Jerusalem**? JOHNSTONE (1:299-300) suggests that Solomon unites the religious cult of Israel. Under David Israel worshiped at Gibeon (tabernacle) and at Jerusalem (**the ark of God**).

Solomon's presence at Gibeon prepares the reader for the union of the tabernacle and the ark. **Moses** established this unity but it was lost when the ark was lost (1 Sam 4). Solomon will reunite Israel's worship in the newly built temple.

Chronicles's description of the worship center at Gibeon is filled with allusions. It recalls David's movement of the ark from **Kiriath Jearim** to a **tent** in Jerusalem. But it notes that the **bronze altar** which **Bezalel** made (Exod 38:1-8) was in **Gibeon in front of the tabernacle of the LORD**. This is the Tent of Meeting which Moses constructed **in the desert**. The presence of the Mosaic tent and **altar** legitimate the worship center. Indeed, the phrase **God's Tent of Meeting** (2 Chr 1:3) may be rendered "the tent for meeting God" (NEB, TEV). Thus, Solomon goes to Gibeon to inquire of the Lord (2 Chr 1:5).

While there is no direct evidence in the Hebrew canon that the tabernacle was moved from Nob to Gibeon, Chronicles assumes this. Some regard this as fictionalized history, but others argue for its authenticity (WILLIAMSON, 130-131). There is no reason to doubt this account except the silence of other canonical sources. But the Chronicler's interests, not shared perhaps by other biblical writers, may explain why he is concerned to highlight this move from Gibeon to Jerusalem. The Chronicler's perspective, as JAPHET (528) notes, is that Gibeon was a "*temporary* cultic" site which gives way to "the *permanent* setting of the Jerusalem sanctuary."

Divine Revelation (1:7-12)

Chronicles abbreviates the longer account in 1 Kings 3:5-14. Their substance is essentially the same, but Chronicles rewords and shortens Dtr. The king encounters God and receives a revelation. Though some (COGGINS, 148) argue that the Chronicler's omission of "in a dream" in 1 Kings 3:5 (also 1 Kgs 3:15) reflects a postexilic negativity toward dreams, he is more likely abbreviating. The Chronicler's readers would not have "differentiated between a revelation 'to Solomon in a dream of the night' and simply 'at night'" (DILLARD, 12). The mode of encounter is not significant, but the substance of the revelation is.

God offers Solomon carte blanche: **Ask for whatever you want me to give you.** As WILCOX (124) observes, this is a promise to every believer: "Ask, and it will be given you" (Matt 7:7). "We must not imagine that God was making Solomon a private and unrepeatable offer." This is no one-time favor for Solomon, but God's general disposition toward his children. The uniqueness of Solomon's encounter is not rooted in the favor God gives but in the redemptive-historical task he has been given (temple-building).

Solomon's prayer is (1) thanksgiving (2 Chr 1:8) and (2) petition (2 Chr 1:9-10). Solomon acknowledges God's hand in the history of his family. Just as God had shown **kindness** (חֶסֶד, *ḥesed*) to his father, so God has **made** Solomon **king in his place**. *Ḥesed* ("love, covenant loyalty") was promised Solomon in 1 Chronicles 17:13, and God's *ḥesed* toward Israel is their continual praise (1 Chr 16:34,41; 2 Chr 5:13; 6:14,42; 7:6).

Solomon offers two petitions: (1) **let your promise to my father David be confirmed** and (2) **give me wisdom and knowledge**. The first request looks back to God's promise to David in 1 Chronicles 17 and particularly David's petition that God's promise be "established forever" (1 Chr 17:23-24). Solomon uses the same verb (אָמַן, *'āman*, "confirmed") from which we derive our English word "amen." Solomon requests God's "Amen" to his own promise. Solomon claims the promise (lit., "the word") God made to David. Moreover, Chronicles, by changing the wording of 1 Kings 3:8 ("a great people, too numerous to count"), recalls the patriarchal promise of Genesis 28:14 where the descendants of Jacob are as **the dust of the earth** (Williamson, *Israel*, 62-64). God has faithfully fulfilled his promise to Abraham, and he will also keep his promise to David.

The second petition requests **wisdom and knowledge**. Solomon's motive is not self-aggrandizement. Rather, he seeks to fulfill his ministry (**that I may lead this people**). Leadership (lit., "to go out before and come in") demands God's gifts of wisdom and knowledge. The language assumes Solomon's inexperience (1 Chr 22:5; 29:1). Chronicles's deletion of Solomon's confession of inexperience in 1 Kings 1:7 is abridgement rather than denial.

Solomon's request is granted because his heart is properly oriented toward God's goals. Solomon's interests are communal rather than individualistic. He seeks the welfare of his people rather than his own glory. The result is that God's blessings overflow beyond the bounds of mere wisdom and knowledge to include **wealth, riches**

and honor. Interestingly, while **long life** appears in 2 Chronicles 1:11, it is absent from 2 Chronicles 1:12. This is probably due to abbreviation though it alleviates the potential false impression that Solomon lived longer than any other king (DILLARD, 12). Because Solomon's heart is right, God will bless him as he has no other king — past or future. Leadership must seek God's interests rather than their own. This is modeled in the ministries of Paul (1 Thess 2:1-12) and Timothy (Phil 2:19-20).

Part of the Chronicler's aim in his "portrayal of Solomon is to show how God governed the events of history to impart to the kingdom of Israel, at least once, a splendour which was fit to symbolize his own" (MCCONVILLE, 110). Thus, the temple will reflect God's glory. Solomon provides a "guideline" in regard to material things. "The resolution to serve God whatever the implications for status or income is a biblical response." This permits discipleship "to allow God his freedom in the matter of our material well-being" (MCCONVILLE, 113). What counts is whether we approach God seeking him just as he seeks us. Whatever God's blessing, whether small or great, is inconsequential to the fundamental joy of that relationship.

As Solomon assumes the reigns of his kingdom, he does two things: (1) he worships God as he publicly consecrates himself to his calling and (2) he requests divine wisdom. This is paralleled in New Testament settings by prayer, fasting, and the public consecration with the laying on of hands (Acts 6:6; 13:1-4). When we seek to fulfill the ministry God has given us, we should seek his face in prayer and worship, dedicate ourselves to the task (e.g., fasting), and seek God's wisdom.

Solomon's prayer appeals to God's steadfast love (**kindness**) and faithfulness (**promise, dust of the earth**) in order to claim God's promise in humility. We approach God with a confidence grounded in his mercy and faithfulness as we boldly approach the throne of God (Heb 4:16).

Conclusion (1:13)

Confident in the promise of God, Solomon returned to **Jerusalem** where **he reigned over Israel**. The promise to David is confirmed. God is faithful, and Solomon is prepared for his task.

3. Solomon's Wealth (1:14-17)

In confirmation of God's promise to Solomon, the Chronicler summarizes Solomon's wealth. While the parallel account in 1 Kings 10:26-29 follows the building of the temple, the Chronicler places it here for the sake of his chiastic structure.

Horses, Treasures, and Cedar (1:14-15)

The description of the horses (2 Chr 1:14) is almost verbatim from 1 Kings 10:26 and is partly repeated in 2 Chronicles 9:25. JAPHET (533) accepts the authenticity of Solomon's wealth in horses. The numbers are not extravagant. Some buildings at Megiddo have been identified as stables though dated from the time of Ahab. Solomon may have stabled horses in major cities throughout the land.

The metaphorical expression of wealth in 1 Kings 10:27 is reproduced in 2 Chronicles 1:15 (adding **gold**) and 2 Chronicles 9:27. Precious metals, like **silver and gold**, and **cedar** were signs of wealth. The metaphor exaggerates their presence in Israel (there are many more **stones** in Israel than silver and gold), but it exalts Solomon and confirms God's promises.

The Value of the Horses (1:16-17)

Second Chronicles 1:16-17 reproduces 1 Kings 10:28-29 with minor variations. Second Chronicles 9:28 summarizes Solomon's trade in horses (also based on 1 Kings). Horse trading was one of the major sources of Solomon's wealth. However, while several believe this account is "legendary" (Schley, "Reconsideration," 600), JAPHET (534) defends its historicity because the "technical terminology" and the "precise geographical points" reflect an authentic tradition.

DILLARD (13-14) summarizes some other problems. Solomon probably functioned as a "middleman" between Egypt and Cilicia (e.g., **Hittites**). More than a century after Solomon, the Assyrians sought "Nubian horses" (Egyptian) and "foreign experts" for their chariots. Since Israel sat on the land bridge between Europe, Asia, and Africa, Solomon controlled the trade of horses from Egypt and other countries.

B. RECOGNITION BY GENTILES/
DEALINGS WITH HIRAM (2:1-16)

Second Chronicles 2:1–7:11 is the Chronicler's account of the building of the temple. Second Chronicles 2:1 states that Solomon **gave orders** to build, and 2 Chronicles 7:11 says that Solomon "finished" building. These verses, serve as bookends for the temple-building project.

This section divides into three parts: (1) Initial Preparations (2 Chr 2:1-2), (2) Solomon's Letter to Hiram (2 Chr 2:3-10), and (3) Hiram's Reply (2 Chr 2:11-16). Second Chronicles 2:17-18 belongs to the next section as part of the Chronicler's overall chiastic structure. The text parallels 1 Kings 5:1-18, but with considerable variation, including deletions and additions.

The thematic point, as JOHNSTONE (1:306) notes, is "an example of the ideal response of the world of the nations to the sovereignty of God expressed through the rule of the house of David in Jerusalem." This theme will return again in 2 Chronicles 8:17–9:12. When God reigns in Jerusalem, he reigns over the nations (Ps 47:8; 96:10; 99:1).

1. Initial Preparations (2:1-2)

Solomon intends **to build a temple for the Name of the LORD and a royal palace for himself** (lit., "a house for his kingdom"). While the Chronicler does not ignore Solomon's palace project (cf. 2 Chr 7:11; 8:1; 9:1), he omits its description (1 Kgs 7:1-12). The Chronicler is focused on the Lord's house.

On the conscription of workers, see the comments at 2 Chronicles 2:17-18.

2. Solomon's Letter to Hiram (2:3-10)

The letter has two parts: (a) Solomon Declares His Intent (2 Chr 2:3-6) and (b) Solomon Requests Hiram's Help (2 Chr 2:7-10). The first is descriptive and the second is petitionary. Just as Hiram sent cedars to David (2 Chr 2:3), so Solomon requests that Hiram send him cedars (2 Chr 2:8).

While in 1 Kings 5:1 it appears that Hiram initiated contact, Chronicles ignores this. This is another example of abbreviation. Chronicles omits 1 Kings 5:1 and begins with 1 Kings 5:2. In both cases Solomon initiates the request for help.

Solomon Declares His Intent (2:3-6)

The request of 2 Chronicles 2:3 is repeated in 2 Chronicles 2:7-8 (same verb, שָׁלַח, *šālaḥ*). This focuses the purpose of the letter and contextualizes the explanation of Solomon's intent to build a temple. Solomon needs **cedar** for the Lord's **temple** and his **palace** just as David needed cedar for his palace.

Between these requests, Solomon explains his purpose (1 Chr 2:4-6). Unique to the Chronicler, this material reflects his special interests. Just as God's promise to David is forever, so Solomon intends to inaugurate a **lasting** (לְעוֹלָם, *l'ôlām*) **ordinance**. Just as God's promise is forever, so Israel's worship is forever.

The nature of this ordinance is located in the continual presence of offerings before the Lord in a building dedicated ("consecrated," קָדַשׁ, *qādaš*) to the Lord. God will have a house in which Israel will daily (**every morning and evening**), weekly (**Sabbaths**) and monthly (**New Moons**) worship their God through various offerings (**incense**, **bread**, and **burnt offerings**). This is atonement language. It is the language of grace. Solomon wants a house where Israel will ever stand in God's presence.

Christians are present in the Holy of Holies through the blood of Christ (Heb 10:19-25). The Moons, Sabbaths, and offerings were shadows of the reality in Jesus (Col 2:16-17). The church, therefore, is called to continually offer their sacrifices to the Lord in the presence of God (Heb 13:15-16).

Solomon, of course, intends to build a **great** (גָּדוֹל, *gadôl*) temple, not only because God had made Solomon great (וַיְגַדְּלֵהוּ, *way'gadd'lēhû*; 2 Chr 1:1), but, more importantly, because God is **greater** (*gadôl*). Since this is the house in which God will dwell, it must reflect his majesty and glory. Solomon, therefore, uses gold, silver, and cedar. The temple must bear witness to the glory of God, not only for the sake of Israel, but for the nations. Nevertheless, Solomon recognizes that whatever he builds, it cannot encompass the one whom even **the highest heavens** cannot **contain**. This is a building for Israel, not for God. It is the place where Israel can meet God, seek his face, and experience reconciliation. It is a **place to burn sacrifices before him**. God is truly there, but he is not contained by it. The temple does not put God in a box, but God is graciously present through the temple. "This was the function of the liturgy carried on in the Temple," MANGAN (79) writes.

God's presence arises out of his gracious intent to commune with his people. This "localization is always voluntary on his part, undertaken on his initiative alone." It is God's self-giving. Thus, "God in his grace has seen fit, on various occasions, to manifest himself for purposes of revelation and redemption; the supreme demonstration of this fact lies in the incarnation of Jesus Christ" (PAYNE, 4:445).

Through Christ, God is still graciously present among his people. God dwells through his Spirit. We are the temple of God. This text does not encourage churches to build elaborate buildings. This misreads the typology, and it ignores the NT's application of this principle. Christians do not seek bodily adornment or material extravagance. Rather, since we are the temple of God, we seek a holiness that reflects God's glory. We honor God with our bodies and our lives. The Solomonic temple is not paradigmatic for building church buildings, but for building holy lives.

Solomon Requests Hiram's Help (2:7-10)

Solomon makes two requests. The first is unique to Chronicles (2 Chr 2:7), but the second is also found in 1 Kings 5:6 (2 Chr 2:8). First, he requests a person **skilled in gold and silver, bronze and iron**. Solomon needs a master builder who can construct the building David has detailed. This master builder will work with the **craftsmen** David has already arranged.

The second request is for lumber, **woodsmen**, and skilled craftsmen (2 Chr 2:8-10). Chronicles derives this material from 1 Kings 5:6,10-11. Solomon promises payment and assistance.

Twice in this context (2 Chr 2:5,9) Solomon emphasizes why this **temple** needs this kind of assistance. Since it is a temple consecrated to the Lord, it **must be large** (*gadôl*; "great" in 2 Chr 2:5) **and magnificent** (2 Chr 2:9). Large because God is great, and magnificent because God's works are wonderful (1 Chr 16:9,12,24). The temple, then, is a form of praise and testimony.

The temple was the sacramental presence of God in Israel. There God dwelt, atonement was enacted, and grace was experienced. Consequently, as a building, it demanded extravagance. The temple is a witness to God's glory, and this was true for the postexilic community as well.

First Kings 5:11 reads differently in the Hebrew from 2 Chronicles 2:10. Where 2 Chronicles has 115,000 gallons, 1 Kings reads 1,200 gallons (although the NIV main text follows the LXX in keeping the figures the same). But the oil in 1 Kings is perhaps a finer quality given only to Hiram (NRSV) whereas the oil in 2 Chronicles is given to the woodsmen. Or, 1 Kings may be an annual payment, but 2 Chronicles is a lump sum (PAYNE, 4:446).

3. Hiram's Reply (2:11-16)

This letter divides into two parts signaled by the term "and now" (left untranslated in the NIV) in 2 Chronicles 2:13: (a) Hiram Blesses God (2 Chr 2:11-12) and (b) Hiram Supplies Help (2 Chr 2:13-16). Hiram favorably responds to Solomon's request because he recognizes God's hand in Solomon's reign.

Hiram Blesses God (2:11-12)

While 2 Chronicles 2:12 is based on 1 Kings 5:7, 2 Chronicles 2:11 is the Chronicler's addition loosely based on 1 Kings 10:9 (cf. 2 Chr 9:8). His editorial activity serves the purpose of exalting both Solomon and Yahweh. It is a theological statement assessing the rationale for Solomon's royal appointment. Solomon is appointed king because God **loves his people** (the first use of "love" [אָהֵב, 'āhēb; cf. 2 Chr 9:8] in Chronicles). God graciously elects Solomon for the sake of his people.

The precise doxology that Hiram offers is unparalleled in the Hebrew canon: **Praise** (lit., "blessed") **be to the LORD, the God of Israel, who made heaven and earth!** It praises Yahweh as creator. These words are surprising on the lips of Hiram, but they may be nothing more than diplomatic politeness while at the same time the acknowledgment functions to declare Yahweh's standing in the world. Hiram, a Gentile king, blesses the God of Israel. Hiram is no convert, but he recognizes that Jerusalem belongs to Yahweh (much like the declaration of Gentile kings in Dan 4:34-35; 6:26-27; cf. SELMAN, 2:301).

God has gifted Solomon with **intelligence and discernment** (cf. 1 Chr 22:12). David's prayer has been answered. The Chronicler has adjusted Dtr's wording in order to emphasize that Solomon's wisdom is primarily for temple-building rather than governing the nation (2 Chr 2:12 with 1 Kgs 5:7).

Hiram Supplies Help (2:13-16)

This part of Hiram's letter (2 Chr 2:13-14) is based on 1 Kings 7:13-14. It describes the **skill** of **Huram-Abi**. Chronicles elaborates Dtr's account by articulating the fuller dimensions of his craftsmanship, adding his expertise in **fine linen** as well as with other materials (**gold and silver, bronze and iron, stone and wood**). Chronicles's expansion emphasizes the parallel between Huram-Abi and Oholiab, the craftsman who assisted Bezalel (DILLARD, 21; Exod 31:1-6; cf. Exod 35:31-35). Huram-Abi, as a person of wisdom (**a man of great skill**; אִישׁ־חָכָם, *îš-ḥākām*) will assist Solomon's wise men (**craftsmen**; חֲכָמֶיךָ, *ḥăkāmêkā*).

Huram-Abi was an Israelite. His Danite lineage provides another parallel with Oholiab (Exod 31:6). However, 1 Kings 7:14 states that his "mother was a widow from the tribe of Naphtali," but Chronicles says his **mother was from Dan** (his **father was from Tyre**). More than likely the Chronicler focuses on Dan in order to enhance his typology with Oholiab (DILLARD, 21). But has the Chronicler merely invented a parallel? SELMAN (2:302) suggests that "ancestry from more than one tribe cannot have been uncommon, either because of contrasting geographical and genealogical links or as a result of the lineage of earlier generations." It may be that Naphtali is a geographical reference while Dan is a genealogical one.

Even though Hiram addresses both Solomon and David as **my lord**, this does not necessarily imply a vassal relationship. Solomon pays and barters for Hiram's assistance. It probably reflects a mutual respect and the honor a supplier shows to a buyer (DILLARD, 21; THOMPSON, 212). The details of 2 Chronicles 2:15-16 are more suitable for a business arrangement than a suzerain-vassal relationship.

Theologically, Hiram's letter testifies to God's sovereignty. He uses Gentile rulers to accomplish his purposes. He drafts wise men from various parts of the world to equip Solomon for building the temple. The nations recognize that God has determined to bless Israel.

No doubt the postexilic community yearned for that recognition in contrast to their backwater situation. Will the Gentiles ever recognize Israel again? Indeed, many Gentiles today bless the name of Yahweh as they serve him through Jesus Christ.

C. TEMPLE CONSTRUCTION/GENTILE LABOR (2:17–5:1)

1. Gentile Labor (2:17-18)

The use of alien labor is another parallel between Solomon and Joshua. Joshua used Gibeonites at the place of worship (Josh 9:26-27). Solomon conscripts Gentile laborers (DILLARD, 4, 21). The number is probably based upon David's census and subsequent employment of aliens as stonecutters (1 Chr 22:2).

Chronicles concentrates on the employment of Gentile labor and does not mention the forced labor of Israelites (1 Kgs 5:13-18; cf. Dillard, "Solomon," 294-295). In addition to the more than 150,000 workers, 1 Kings 5:13 adds another 30,000 Israelites. Jeroboam served as an official in this labor force (1 Kgs 11:28), and Rehoboam's additional labor policies were the occasion of a northern rebellion (1 Kgs 12:3-4,18-19). Perhaps the Chronicler's intent, as SELMAN (2:303) suggests, is to emphasize "the submission of the non-Israelites in Canaan as a sign of Israel's full occupation of the land." This is consistent with the rare use of the phrase "the land of Israel" (**in Israel**, NIV) which is only used 10 times in Scripture (4 times in Chronicles; 1 Chr 22:2; 2 Chr 2:17; 30:25; 34:7 in connection with the four major kings: David, Solomon, Hezekiah, and Josiah).

2. Temple Construction (3:1–5:1)

This account parallels 1 Kings 6:1-7:51 but the eighty-nine verses of 1 Kings 6-7 are condensed to forty. As the chart below indicates (PRATT, 223), the Chronicler omits three major sections and adds five smaller ones. While it is not always clear why the Chronicler added or omitted material, the reasons probably relate to the function,

design, and condition of the temple in his postexilic situation. Some
details are significant for his readers, others are not.

Content	2 Chr	1 Kgs
Introduction (loosely parallel)	3:1-2	6:1
Overview of Temple (loosely parallel)	3:3-4	6:2-3
Details and Solomon's Conditional Promise		6:4-20
Main Hall (loosely parallel)	3:5-7	6:21-22
Most Holy Place: Details	3:8-9	
Most Holy Place: Cherubim (loosely parallel)	3:10-13	6:23-27
Most Holy Place: Huram-Abi	3:14	
Details and Solomon's Palace		6:28-7:14
Bronze Altar	4:1	
Metal Sea (closely parallel)	4:2-5	7:23-26
Details of Ten Movable Stands		7:27-37
Stands (roughly parallel)	4:6	7:28-39a
Furniture in the Main Hall	4:7-8	
Courts Distinguished	4:9	
Location of the Sea (loosely parallel)	4:10	7:39b
Additional Material on the Temple (loosely parallel)	4:11-22	7:40-50
Conclusion (closely parallel)	5:1	7:51

The Chronicler is not as interested in the details of temple-building as Dtr is. If the chiastic structure of 2 Chronicles 1–9 is correct,
the Chronicler's emphasis is liturgical rather than architectural. He
omits elaborate temple details and Solomon's palace. His interest is
sufficient to verify the magnificence of the temple, but he does not
detract from the central piece of his chiasm: divine presence and
human seeking. However, what he adds to Dtr was apparently significant for his interests.

Temples, of course, were quite pervasive in the ancient Near
East. Every major city had a temple. Most of these temples have
structural similarities though rarely identical. However, the closest
parallel to Solomon's temple (size, layout, and architecture) is the
recently discovered 'Ain Dara temple in northern Syria which predates Solomon's temple (ca. 1300 B.C.). Its excavation demonstrates
that temples like Solomon's were built in the ancient world
(Monson, 20-35, 67).

The structure of 2 Chronicles 3:1–5:1 is difficult. It has a clear introduction (2 Chr 3:1-2) and conclusion (2 Chr 5:1) but scholars differ as to how to organize what lies between. JOHNSTONE (1:313-314) divides the middle section into building (2 Chr 3:3-7) and furnishings (2 Chr 3:8–4:22).

Introduction (3:1-2)

Chronicles uniquely identifies the temple site with **Mount Moriah**. It is chosen because the **LORD had appeared to** king **David** there, but the reference to Moriah also recalls Abraham's sacrifice of Isaac (Gen 22:2). Mount Moriah is the "mountain of the LORD" (Gen 22:14). The Chronicler directly connects temple-building with Abraham's experience of divine presence when he uses נִרְאָה (*nir'āh*, **had appeared**; cf. Gen 22:14). The temple is built on this site because there God spoke to Abraham and David (Kalimi, "Moriah," 345-362).

The Chronicler omits a reference to the Exodus that appears in his source (1 Kgs 6:1) as well as Dtr's temporal indicator. The Chronicler does not record what year the temple was completed (unlike 1 Kgs 6:37-38; cf. 2 Chr 8:1). The Chronicler stresses the patriarchs more than the Exodus because the situation of the postexilic community is more analogous to the nomadic patriarchs than the Exodus-Conquest.

Theologically, the postexilic community seeks God's grace on Mount Moriah. There the reality of God's presence is experienced. The sacrifice of Isaac, the sacrifices of David (1 Chr 21), and the temple sacrifices typologically anticipate the sacrifice of Jesus Christ who died in the vicinity of that mount.

The Main Building (3:3-7)

The dimensions of the temple are: (a) The Holy of Holies is 20×20×20, (b) the Holy Place is 40×20×30, and (c) the Porch (a kind of vestibule) is 10×20×20. The MT (cf. NRSV) has the height of the Porch at 120 cubits, but most think this is a textual corruption (WILLIAMSON, 206). The temple structure (excluding the porch) is 60×20×20. The measurement is based on the **old standard** for cubits which is almost 18 inches. The new standard, found in Ezekiel 40:5; 43:13, is approximately 20 inches (Kaufman, 120-132). Following the short cubit, the floor space of the temple was approximately 7200 square feet.

Solomon luxuriously decorated the inside of the temple. **He overlaid** the walls with **pure gold** and **paneled the main hall** (Holy Place) **with pine** (or, cypress) **and covered it with fine gold**. The gold was from **Parvaim** which was apparently famous but now unknown (DILLARD, 29; WILLIAMSON, 207). He used elaborate designs as decorations (including **palm tree and chain designs**) and **he carved cherubim on the walls**. Further, **he adorned the temple with precious stones**. These decorations were symbols of God's greatness.

The temple was a reflection of the heavenly throne room. It was God's palace. Consequently, subsequent descriptions of God's throne room (Rev 4-5) take their clues from the temple itself.

The Furnishings (3:8-4:22)

JOHNSTONE (1:314-315) organizes the furnishings by the linguistic device וַיַּעַשׂ (wayya'aś, "and he made") found in 2 Chronicles 3:8,10, 14,15,16[2]; 4:1,2,6,7,8[2],9,11,18,19. Also, the verb עָשָׂה ('āśāh, "make") occurs an additional 5 times (4:11[2],14[2],16). The first series is what Solomon made (3:8-4:11a). The next series is what Huram made (4:11b-18). The final series is again what Solomon made (4:19-22). Theologically, WILLIAMSON (208) suggests that this device connects the building of the temple with the building of the tabernacle (Exod 36:8-39:32) where a similar series exists.

SELMAN (2:304) notes that most of these details would have been "unseen" to all Israelites except priests and Levites, and only the High Priest would see the Most Holy Place. "God had drawn near to them but the way to him was hedged with many restrictions." This testifies to the holiness of God and the awe which worshipers should feel in God's presence. Yet Israel experienced joy, and the presence of God at the temple. Christians follow Jesus through the veil into the throne room of God. We boldly approach the throne of grace (Heb 4:16), and we enter the Most Holy Place with confidence (Heb 10:19-22).

Solomon Made the Furnishings (3:8-4:11a)

This is a serial list of items Solomon "made" ('āśāh). JOHNSTONE groups it into five paragraphs: (1) Holy of Holies (3:8-14), (2) Pillars

of the Temple (3:15-16), (3) Inner Courtyard (4:1-6), (4) Furnishings
of the Holy Place (4:7-8), and (5) the Courts (4:9-11a).

Most Holy Place (3:8-14). This section is divided into three parts
by the linguistic device *wayya'aś* ("and he made") found in 3:8,10,14:
he made the **Most Holy Place** (3:8), the cherubim (3:10), and the
curtain (3:14).

The Most Holy Place is immersed in **gold**. The total weight of the
inside paneling is **six hundred talents** (ca. 20 tons). This was close
to Solomon's revenue in a single year (2 Chr 9:13). **Gold nails** probably refer to the "quantity of gold leaf used to cover the heads of
nails or tacks that held the sheets of gold in place on the walls" since
gold is too soft to function as nails (DILLARD, 29). The weight and
nails are additions to the account in Kings. These details lend
greater weight to the glory of the Most Holy Place. The reference to
upper parts may refer to an upper chamber. This may account for
some differences in height with 1 Kings 6:2 (10 extra cubits for the
upper room).

In the Most Holy Place Solomon placed two huge angelic statues
– **cherubim**. Chronicles lingers on their description. The cherubim
function as protectors of God's holiness (e.g., they guard the
entrance to his presence), and propel "the divine throne chariot
through the universe" (JOHNSTONE, 1:319; cf. 1 Chr 13:6; 28:18).
Their **wings** touched each other and the walls of the temple so that
they covered twenty cubits. **They stood on their feet, facing the
main hall**.

The **curtain** was **made** of **fine linen**. The veil is not mentioned
in 1 Kings 6 and only here in the Hebrew Bible. Herod's temple had
a veil (Matt 27:51). The Chronicler believed that Solomon's temple
had both a veil and doors (cf. 2 Chr 4:22). Some argue for two veils
that overlap so that the priest entered the veil from one side of the
building only to walk to the far side to pass through the veil again
and then to walk through the doors (Meulen, 22-27). They separate
the holy God from a sinful people though the grace of God permitted the High Priest to enter once a year to make atonement.

Theologically, the majesty of the temple is the point. The is the
holiest spot on earth – it is the place where God rests upon the ark.
The cherubim surround the throne of God (cf. Isa 6; Rev 4). They
represent the angelic host that worship and serve the Lord. The veil

symbolizes God's separateness (holiness) even though he dwells among his people.

Through Jesus Christ, we come to Mount Zion. We enter the Most Holy Place surrounded by angels who praise God continually. There is no more veil. The writer of Hebrews sees the fulfillment of God's Sinaitic and temple presence in the worship of the church (Heb 10:19-25; 12:24-28). The majesty of this temple is the holiness of its people as they are transformed into God's likeness.

Pillars of the Temple (3:15-16). Solomon **made** three items (**pillars**, **chains**, and **pomegranates**) and then **erected the** two **pillars in front of the temple**. They were placed on the north and south ends of the porch (DILLARD, 30). There is no certainty as to the meaning of the names for each pillar though **Jakin** and **Boaz** as a verbal sentence means "he establishes in strength" (DILLARD, 30; cf. JOHNSTONE, 1:322). Problematically, the height of the pillars differs from 1 Kings 7:15. Chronicles has **thirty-five cubits** but Dtr eighteen. SELMAN (2:309) suggests that Chronicles's number is a "combined figure for both pillars (the reverse seems to have happened with the *pomegranate decorations*, cf. v. 15 and 1 Ki. 7:20)."

Theologically, the pillars testify to God's strength. The chains of pomegranates, as a symbol of abundance (Num 20:5) and the promised land (Deut 8:8), testify to God's abundant provisions. Israel enters the temple confessing that Yahweh alone provides strength. Just as in the postexilic community, our lives also bear witness to that same truth and draw strength from the one who alone can establish strength.

Inner Courtyard (4:1-6). This section is divided into three parts by the linguistic device *wayya'aś* ("and he made") found in 4:1,2,6: he made **a bronze altar**, **the Sea**, and **ten basins**. These furnishings are placed in the inner courtyard in front of the porch.

The **bronze altar** has no parallel in 1 Kings 7 (though present in 1 Kgs 8:64). This is a huge altar (30×30×15 feet), probably with steps like Ezekiel 43:13-17 (DILLARD, 34). The base, then, would be 30×30 feet with the actual altar at its pinnacle.

The Sea was a large container of water in the corner of the temple courtyard (2 Chr 4:10). The tabernacle had a laver between the altar and the Tent, but this is much larger. It held approximately 17,500 gallons of water (PRATT, 226). Ezekiel's temple (Ezek 47:1-12) and the

eschatological Eden have a river (Rev 22:1-2). The Sea enabled priestly ablutions (immersions, cf. Webb, 95-108; Lev 15:5-15; 16:4,24; Heb
9:9). The weight of the water is supported by **twelve bulls**. "Twelve"
represents the tribes and bulls were sacrificial animals.

Second Chronicles 4:5 says the volume of the water is **three
thousand baths**, but 1 Kings 7:26 reads "two thousand." Explanations vary. Byl (313) suggests that the Chronicler is thinking about
the Sea filled to capacity while Dtr provides its normal volume. The
basins were smaller containers of water for cleaning animal parts (cf.
Lev 1:9).

Theologically, these furnishings symbolize what is necessary to
enter God's presence. The function of the altar is atonement and
water cleanses. Entrance into the presence of God is through the
blood of the animals and the cleansing of water. A sinful people
depend upon God's gracious atonement through the altar as they
approach him with cleansed bodies. Typologically, this anticipates our
own entrance into the presence of God through hearts sprinkled with
the blood of Christ and bodies washed in pure water (Heb 10:22).

Furnishings of the Holy Place (4:7-8). Solomon also **made**
(*wayya'aś*) **lampstands** (4:7), **tables** (4:8a), and **bowls** (4:8b). The temple has more furnishings than the tabernacle. While the tabernacle
only had one lampstand and one table, the temple has **ten gold
lampstands** and **ten tables** along with a **hundred gold sprinkling
bowls**.

Light and bread are symbols of God's sustaining presence. Indeed,
the bread of the table is sometimes called "the Bread of the Presence"
(2 Chr 4:19). Light and bread contrasts with darkness and hunger
(poverty). God graciously provides just as he is graciously present.

Theologically, Jesus himself is the light and bread of the world
(John 6:35; 8:12). He is God's gracious provision for life. Christians
celebrate this good news by sitting at the table of the Lord.

The Courts (4:9-11a). Solomon **made** (*wayya'aś*) **the courtyard of
the priests**, and **the large court** (4:9) and **pots and shovels and
sprinkling bowls** (4:11a; priestly utensils). The utensils were used to
remove fat and ashes as well as boil animal flesh (cf. Exod 27:3;
2 Chr 35:13). Two courtyards indicate the division between clergy
and laity. The priestly courtyard is where the altar and **Sea** are located. Only clergy were admitted in this space and **doors** separated the

two spheres. But the large court is where the people assembled. The separation between clergy and laity is no longer present in Christ. The priesthood of all believers enables every Christian to enter the Most Holy Place (Heb 10:19-25; 1 Pet 2:4-8).

Huram Made Bronze Objects (4:11b-18)

This section is marked off by the phrase **Huram finished the work** (לַעֲשׂוֹת, *la'ăśôth*). Chronicles recalls the work of Huram just as Exodus 36 accentuated the work of Oholiab. Bezalel made the tabernacle with the assistance of Oholiab, so Solomon built the temple with the help of Huram. This is the person Hiram supplied as a master bronze worker. The temple furnishings and architecture (none are in the Most Holy Place or the Holy Place) are rehearsed to emphasize the importance of Huram and the large amounts of **polished bronze** used. The quantity was so great that it was not even weighed (the Chronicler's hyperbole).

The geographical location of Solomon's mining and smelting works are obscure. The source of the copper is unknown though some have located it at Timnah north of Elath on the Gulf of Aqabah (but see Shanks, "Glueck," 10-16).

Solomon Made Golden Objects (4:19-22)

The resumption of **Solomon also made** (*wayya'aś*) is another paragraph marker. These are the golden objects which Solomon made as opposed to the bronze items which Huram made. This paragraph summarizes **all the furnishings** that Solomon had made and placed in **God's temple**. The **golden altar** of incense (cf. Heb 9:4) is mentioned for the first time.

Conclusion (5:1)

The conclusion is a play on Solomon's own name (McConville, 125). Just as the temple was **finished** (וַתִּשְׁלַם, *watišlam*), so **Solomon** himself was at peace in the accomplishment of his task (Johnstone, 1:331-333).

As Johnstone (1:329-330) notes, the text subtly marks off the **temple** and its furnishings as dedicated to God. Just as David **dedicated** ("sanctified"; קָדְשֵׁי, *qodšê*) **the silver and gold and all the furnishings**, so the completed temple is consecrated to God.

The temple is a copy of the heavenly sanctuary and thus the temple is filled with symbolism as it proclaims God's presence. The majesty, glory, and strength of the Lord are taught by the greatness and luxury of the building. In Christ we are a building of God, a holy temple in which God dwells by his Spirit (Eph 2:19-22). The majesty, glory, and strength of God are manifested through us as the Spirit transforms us into the image of God.

D. DEDICATION OF THE TEMPLE (5:2–7:10)

As the chiastic structure of 2 Chronicles 1–9 indicates, the dedication of the temple and the divine response are the theological heart of the narrative. God comes to rest in his temple through atoning sacrifices, the people celebrate and worship, and God responds graciously. The temple is not about a building but about the gracious and redemptive presence of God who sanctifies a people for himself in order to dwell among them.

Adapting DILLARD's (5) chiastic structure, the appearance of the glory cloud is this section's central feature. Its appearance is surrounded by assembling/dismissal, sacrifices, and musical praise. Framed by the glory cloud (5:13b and 7:1), Solomon exhorts his people and prays. The structure may be schematized in this way:

1. Summons (5:2-3)
   2. Sacrifice (5:4-10)
      3. Music (5:11-13a)
         4. Glory Cloud (5:13b–7:2)
      3'. Music (7:3)
   2'. Sacrifice (7:4-7)
1'. Dismissal (7:8-10)

The narrative portrays a liturgical assembly. The people are summoned. The priests prepare sacrifices which will atone for sin and sanctify the people. The people consecrate themselves to the Lord's service and praise him with songs of praise and thanksgiving. God comes among them and Solomon prays. This is followed by musical celebration and sacrificial meals. After several days of feasting in the presence of God, the people are dismissed to their homes. The liturgy of atonement, music, and meal frames the gift of God's presence.

1. Summons (5:2-3)

Solomon assembles (יַקְהֵל, *yaqhêl*) Israel in a holy convocation just as David did (1 Chr 13:2,4-5; 15:3; 28:1). All Israel is involved. This not only includes the leaders (**elders, heads of the tribes**, and **chiefs of the Israelite families**), but **all the men of Israel** (יִשְׂרָאֵל כָּל־אִישׁ, *kol-îš yiśrā'ēl*).

The purpose of this assembly is analogous to 1 Chronicles 15. While David brought the ark to Jerusalem, Solomon now brings the **ark of the LORD's covenant** into the temple. The movement of the ark is a holy moment and requires consecration. It coincides with the **festival** of the seventh month (the Feast of Tabernacles; Lev 23:33-43) which was a time of renewal.

According to 1 Kings 6:38, the temple was completed in the eighth month, but this celebration occurs in the seventh month. SELMAN (2:318) believes the nation prepared for this festive dedication for a year (contra DILLARD, 41, and PRATT, 229, who believe the dedication took place a month before the temple was completed).

2. Sacrifice (5:4-10)

The ark is placed in the temple's most holy place. The first phase is the movement of the ark to the temple area along with the furnishings of the tabernacle and appropriate sacrifices (2 Chr 5:4-6). The second moves the ark into the temple itself with a description of its interior (2 Chr 5:7-10).

The Movement of the Ark to the Temple (5:4-6)

Chronicles changes the wording of 1 Kings 8:3 so that the **Levites** (rather than "priests") carry the ark to the temple though they do not carry it into the temple (2 Chr 5:7). Chronicles protects the Levitical function of carrying the ark (cf. Num 4:15; 1 Chr 15:14-15) while **priests, who were Levites** (lit., "Levitical priests"), **carried** other articles belonging to the tabernacle. The **Tent of Meeting** itself is carried to the temple. Chronicles assumes that the tabernacle was moved to Jerusalem in preparation for the temple's dedication. But what was done with the tabernacle? Friedman (241-248) believes that the tabernacle was actually incorporated into the temple, possibly even occupying the space of the Most Holy Place (but see Hurowitz, "Form," 127-151).

The procession to the temple is a holy **assembly** of all (**entire**) Israel. This is the only time Chronicles uses this Hebrew term translated "assembly" (עֵדָה, *'dh*). It is a significant term in the history of Israel, normally translated "congregation." It is used here because a form of the noun is behind the term "meeting" (מוֹעֵד, *mô'ēd*) in "Tent of Meeting." It recalls Israel in the wilderness (cf. Num 1:2). The Israel of the wilderness has become the Israel of God's city (JOHNSTONE, 1:334).

Animals were sacrificed in celebration of the ark's movement to a permanent spot. The animals are not burned at this point – the fire from heaven has not yet been released (cf. 2 Chr 7:1-2). The animals are prepared, but the sacrifices are not burned until after Solomon's prayer. The number of animals anticipates the kind of feasting that will follow the dedication (cf. 2 Chr 7:7). The number of animals **could not be recorded or counted** (hyperbole).

The Movement of the Ark into the Temple (5:7-10)

The priests carry the ark to its resting place **in the inner sanctuary of the temple** since only priests could enter. The drama is heightened by the ark's description and its resting place: **the ark of the LORD's covenant** in **the Most Holy Place** beneath **the wings of the cherubim**. Holiness, covenant, and angelic hosts are envisioned in this simple majestic statement. The presence of God (the ark) is now in a permanent resting place.

At the time of the temple dedication, the ark only contained **the two tablets that Moses had placed in it at Horeb.** The ark is "the ark of the Lord's covenant" and the ten commandments are the symbol of this covenant because Sinai is where **the Lord made a covenant with** the children of Israel. The language of covenant begins and ends this section. The movement of the ark has covenantal meaning. God places his Name among his people in a permanent way. The covenant is God's gracious gift of himself. The two tablets are a reminder of that covenant, and the ark is a reminder of God's own presence.

3. Music (5:11-13a)

This material is unique to the Chronicler (except 5:11a) and reflects his special priestly and musical interests. **All the priests who were there had consecrated themselves** but not according to the regular **divisions**. The 120 **trumpeters** (2 Chr 5:12) – more than normal – were probably "an ad hoc group" since this event did not involve "their usual divisional rotations" (DILLARD, 42).

As the priests withdraw from **the Holy Place**, the Levitical musicians and the priestly trumpeters break out in praise. They **stood on the east side of the altar** and were **dressed in fine linen** (priestly garb for festive occasions) and were **playing cymbals, harps and lyres**. The whole assembly of musicians and singers offered **one voice** in praise and thanksgiving **to the LORD**. They celebrate the ark's arrival as the united people of God. The only other time this phrase occurs is Exodus 24:3 where Israel said "with one voice" that they would keep the covenant of God. With one voice Israel thanks God for the gracious presence of the ark of that covenant (cf. Rom 15:6).

The meaning of this celebration, however, is the Lord's mercy and grace. The refrain **raised in praise to the LORD** is: **He is good; his love endures forever.** This is the liturgical refrain of 1 Chronicles 16:34,41 when the ark was brought to Jerusalem. It is renewed as the ark is set in its resting place (cf. 2 Chr 7:3). It highlights the benevolence and mercy of God. It praises and thanks God for his eternal covenant loyalty (cf. 1 Chr 16:4).

4. Glory Cloud (5:13b–7:2)

This is the literary and theological center of Chronicles's Solomon narrative. There is no more significant moment in the whole of Chronicles. Its significance is located in the gracious presence of the holy God who dwells among his people. This presence is God's Sinaitic presence on the holy mountain, the cloud by day and the fire by night that led Israel through the wilderness, and the presence that enveloped the completed tabernacle. God now comes to dwell in a permanent house among his people as a testimony to his grace and faithfulness. This is a peak moment in redemptive history (like the Calling of Abraham or the Exodus-Conquest or the Restoration from Exile). It is *the* peak moment in the Chronicler's history — it is God's own self-disclosing revelation.

This section begins and ends with the appearance of the glory cloud (5:13b-14; 7:1-2). Sandwiched between are two Solomonic speeches — one to the people (6:3-11) and one to God (6:1-2,12-42); one a homily and the other a prayer.

The Glory Cloud Appears (5:13b-14)

The **cloud** is an important theological symbol. It recalls the Exodus where God led them through a cloud by day and fire by night (Exod 13:22). The cloud is the presence of God himself (cf. Exod 14:24; cf. Num 14:14; Deut 1:32-33). The glory of the Lord appears in the cloud (Exod 16:10), and God spoke from a cloud (Exod 19:9; 33:9-10; 34:5; Num 11:25; Ps 99:7). The glory of the Lord rested on Mt. Sinai in a cloud (Exod 24:15-16). When the tabernacle was finished, "the cloud covered the Tent of Meeting, and the glory of the Lord filled the tabernacle" (Exod 40:34). This became his dwelling-place as the cloud hovered over the mercy seat, the ark of the covenant (Lev 16:2). The cloud/fire led Israel through the wilderness (Num 9:15-22; Ps 78:14; 105:39). The cloud is the gracious presence of God.

This "overwhelming experience of God's self-disclosure is summed up in the word, 'glory'" (JOHNSTONE, 1:338). The phrase **glory of the LORD** only occurs in this section of Chronicles (2 Chr 5:14; 7:1-3; cf. at Mt. Sinai in Exod 24:16-17, at the tabernacle in Exod 40:34-35; Lev 9:23; Num 14:10; 16:19,42; 20:6; at the temple in Ezek 10:4,18; 11:23; 43:4-5; 44:4).

In redemptive history, the glory of the Lord would make another appearance. It shone around the shepherds on the night of Jesus birth (Luke 2:9), and the incarnate one himself revealed the glory of the Father (John 1:14). A voice from the cloud spoke at the transfiguration of Jesus and bore witness to the glory of Jesus Christ (Matt 17:1-7). It is the face of Jesus Christ that shines with the glory of God, and we reflect that glory just as Moses shone with that glory as he came out of the Tent of Meeting (2 Cor 3:18). One day, in the new Jerusalem, the city will shine with the "glory of God" (Rev 21:11,23). There God will dwell with his people forever (Rev 21:1-4).

Solomonic Speeches (6:1-42)

Solomon's speeches follow 1 Kings 8:12-53 though with significant differences. The structure emphasizes Solomon's long prayer
to God, but prefaces it with Solomon's direct response to God in the
wake of the glory cloud's appearance (2 Chr 6:1-2). This is followed
by a homily (2 Chr 6:3-11).

SELMAN (2:322) summarizes the meaning of this section for the
postexilic community. First, the temple is a witness to God's commitment to David and his house. Second, it is a witness to God's gracious presence that emboldens prayer and confidence. For the postexilic community, the temple is an appropriate place to seek God's
face and to pray, "Your kingdom come."

Solomon Speaks to God (6:1-2)

Solomon remembers the Sinaitic moment as he responds to the
cloud. He uses a word that evokes the memory of Mt. Sinai — "thick
darkness" (עֲרָפֶל, 'ărāphel; NIV, **dark cloud**). Moses approached God
at Sinai in thick darkness (Exod 20:21; cf. Deut 4:11; 5:22). God
dwells in thick darkness (Ps 97:2). It is a metaphor for God's gracious presence and healing (cf. 2 Sam 22:10; Ps 18:9). The **temple**
(lit., "a house of habitation") is for God. Solomon welcomes him to
his new home, **a place for you to dwell forever**. The glory cloud is
God's response to the building of the temple.

Solomon Speaks to the People (6:3-11)

Israel was gathered in a holy convocation (2 Chr 5:3; 6:3,12; 7:3).
They had watched the ark brought into the temple, seen the glory cloud
descend on the temple, and heard Solomon's initial response (2 Chr
6:1-2). Solomon interprets the meaning of this event with a homily.
Solomon becomes the interpreter of God's mighty act. Solomon takes
on prophetic functions with this short homily just as he assumed a
priestly function by blessing the people (2 Chr 6:3; cf. 1 Chr 16:2).

The homily divides into three parts: (1) the opening doxology
(2 Chr 6:4), (2) the Davidic promise (2 Chr 6:5-9), and (3) the fulfillment of the promise (2 Chr 6:10-11).

Doxology (6:3-4). Just as Solomon blessed the people, he now
blesses God (**praise**; בָּרַךְ, bārak, in 1 Chr 16:36; 29:10,20; 2 Chr

2:12). God is praised for his faithfulness since **with his hands** he **has fulfilled what he promised**. Solomon describes the nature of the promise in 2 Chronicles 6:5-9. The dedication of the temple is God-centered rather than Solomon-centered.

Davidic Promise (6:5-9). As DILLARD (47) notes, the citation of the Davidic promise in 2 Chronicles 6:5-6 is not identical with any of its other canonical forms (cf. 1 Chr 17; 28:2-10; 2 Chr 12:13; 33:7), but it is essentially the same thought. In comparison with 1 Kings 8:16, Chronicles emphasizes that God did not choose a city or a ruler after the Exodus, but in this moment God has confirmed the choice of a city and a ruler. When God came in his glory cloud to this temple, God confirmed the choice of Jerusalem and David. Chronicles's postexilic readers have returned to Jerusalem and they await a new David. They are in the right place leaning on an eternal promise.

While Japhet (*Ideology*, 382-388) believes Chronicles devalues the Exodus (cf. 2 Chr 6:11 with 1 Kgs 8:21), this text (cf. 1 Chr 17:21; 2 Chr 5:10; 7:22; 20:10) indicates that Chronicles does not obscure its importance (DILLARD, 47). On the contrary, the Exodus-Conquest anticipates this moment – the fulfillment of God's intention to dwell among his people. The Chronicler understands these two redemptive-historical moments as promise-fulfillment.

Second Chronicles 6:7-9 continues the narration of the events leading up to the present moment. It rehearses material from earlier in the narrative (1 Chr 17:4-14; 22:7-10; 28:2-7). Solomon did not build this temple on his own initiative or strength. God elected him as temple-builder and gifted him with sufficient strength and skill to complete the task. God receives the credit for the finished temple.

Fulfillment of the Promise (6:10-11). Solomon stresses the fulfillment motif. **The Lord has kept the promise he made**. He has kept both promises – Solomon **succeeded** his father, and **the temple for the Name of the LORD** has been completed. Literally, Yahweh has made his word stand. God is praised because he has inaugurated the Davidic covenant and confirmed his commitment to dwell among his people (2 Chr 6:4).

The completed temple houses the **ark, in which is the covenant of the LORD that he made with the people of Israel**. Solomon reminds the people that this is a covenantal moment and constitutes a covenant renewal festival.

Solomon Speaks to God (6:12-42)

Solomon's prayer follows 1 Kings 8:22-53 but with a different ending (cf. 2 Chr 6:41-42). After a narrative introduction (2 Chr 6:12-13), the prayer's structure is:

(1) Petition for Davidic Covenant (6:14-17)
   (2) Hear the Lament of Your People (6:18-21)
      (3) The Circumstances of Prayer (6:22-35)
   (2′) Hear the Lament of Your Exiled People (6:36-39)
(1′) Petition for God's Presence (6:40-42)

Solomon's plea is that God will hear the lament of his people when they turn their face toward the temple. God's temple is a place for sacrifice and grace, of atonement and reconciliation. This is the place toward which Israel may pray. Significantly, 19 of the 27 times Chronicles uses "pray" (פָלַל, *palal*) or "prayer" (תְּפִלָּה, *t*ᵉ*phillāh*) occur in 2 Chronicles 6–7.

The vocabulary and context identify these prayers as laments. The circumstance of each prayer in 2 Chronicles 6:22-35 and the vocabulary reflect the context of lament. The Hebrew-word group (חָנַן [*ḥānan*], תְּחִנָּה [*t*ᵉ*ḥinnāh*], and תַּחֲנוּנִים [*taḥănûnîm*]), variously translated **supplications** or **pleas**, evokes the lament world of the Psalter (used 43 times; e.g., Ps 4:1; 6:2,9; 9:13; 25:16; 27:7; 31:9; 41:4; 51:1; 55:1; 56:1; 86:3,6,16; 116:1; 119:170; 142:1; 143:1). This word group only occurs here in Chronicles (7 times; 2 Chr 6:19,21,24,29,35,37, 39) with the significant exception of Manasseh's lament for mercy in 2 Chronicles 33:13 that is patterned after Solomon's prayer. In addition, another lament word, **cry** (רִנָּה, *rinnāh*), appears in verse 19 (2 Chr 20:22; cf. Ps 17:1; 42:4; 88:2; 106:44; 146:6).

The structure of 2 Chronicles 6:14-42 enhances the lamentations. The beginning (2 Chr 6:14-17) and end (2 Chr 6:40-42) call upon God to keep his promise. The promises give the people courage to approach God in prayer (cf. 1 Chr 17:25). God's people do not presume they may barge into his throne room. The promises, however, are God's invitation to his people and the assurance of his gracious disposition toward them. The middle portion of the chiasm (2 Chr 6:22-35) details various circumstances.

The inner rings of the chiasm (2 Chr 6:18-21,36-39) provide the principle and the occasion of this prayer in the original setting of

Chronicles's readers. God will hear and forgive. The readers have returned from exile. This is a theological application of the prayer to the original readers. Whether exilic or postexilic, Solomon's prayer demonstrates that God will listen to the hearts of his people, forgive, and return them to their land. The hope of Israel is their gracious God.

The prayer seeks a gracious God who will **hear** and **forgive** (together 6 times; 2 Chr 6:21,25,27,30,39; 7:14). "Hear" occurs 14 times in 2 Chronicles 6–7. Solomon pleads for God to listen to the lament of his people, and his confidence is that God will hear and forgive.

Significantly, 2 Chronicles 6:16,41,42(3 times) are the only texts which employ an imperative in the prayer. Solomon calls upon God to (1) **keep** his **promises**, (2) to **arise** and come to his **resting place** and (3) to **remember** his **love** for **David**. Second Chronicles 6:14-17 and 6:40-42, then, serve a petitionary function. Solomon prays with the confidence of God's covenantal faithfulness and love. The postexilic community prayed on the same theological ground, and Christians pray with the same confidence (Heb 4:14-16; 10:19-24).

Introduction to the Prayer (6:12-13). While 2 Chronicles 6:12 essentially reproduces 1 Kings 8:22, verse 13 is unique. The addition portrays Solomon as elevated over the assembly so that he was visible to all. His prayer is **before the altar of the LORD** but at the same time **in the center of the outer court**. Probably, a temporary platform was erected in the outer court in sight of the altar (THOMPSON, 228).

He kneels with his hands lifted to God (cf. Ps 44:21). This is "a gesture of petition eloquent enough in itself to express unconditional dependence on the gracious response of God" (JOHNSTONE, 1:342). The king kneels to the true king, the God of Israel.

Petition for Davidic Covenant (6:14-17). Solomon appeals to God as a covenant-keeper (2 Chr 6:14-15) and petitions God to keep his covenant with David (2 Chr 6:16-17). Three times Solomon invokes the faithful one's name, **LORD, God of Israel** (2 Chr 6:14,16,17). The faithful, covenant love of God, then, is the ground of petition and praise.

The appeal to God's covenant-keeping character evokes a cosmic dimension (**in heaven or on earth**) but focuses on **David**. Whether universal or particular, God has a track record. He is the relational

God who keeps his **covenant of love** (lit., "covenant and steadfast love") with those who seek him **wholeheartedly** (lit., "walk before you with whole hearts"). Those who seek God are confident of his faithfulness. Solomon declares that **You have kept your promise to your servant David . . . and with your hand you have fulfilled it — as it is today**. The completion of the temple and the descent of the glory cloud bear witness to his faithfulness.

The petition cites God's promise to David (cf. 1 Chr 17:23; 2 Chr 1:9). Solomon asks God to continue to keep his promises (2 Chr 6:16). The word of the Lord remains trustworthy — let the word of the Lord be an Amen (אמן)!

Hear the Lament of Your People (6:18-21). God's temple presence grounds Solomon's intercessory appeal in 2 Chronicles 6:18-21. Even though **the highest heavens cannot contain** him, Solomon believes that God dwells in this temple. "The temple's function," as SELMAN (2:327) writes, "is to locate God, not to limit him, to bring human beings into direct contact with the one whose *dwelling-place* is in *heaven*" (cf. 2 Chr 6:21,30,33,39). The gracious God makes himself accessible. Solomon, for example, prays in the **presence** of God (2 Chr 6:19; lit., "before or to your face"). Second Chronicles 6:24 locates God's presence in the temple. The ark is his footstool though he fills the whole earth with his presence. His presence in the temple is a "gracious condescension" (JOHNSTONE, 1:344) which, indeed, is the incarnational character of God himself that culminates in the Incarnate One, Jesus Christ.

God's presence is redemptive — he hears and forgives. God hears from his heavenly **dwelling place**, but he is also present to forgive and commune in this particular place. God's earthly dwelling place is a place of prayer and sacrifice (cf. 2 Chr 2:5; Isa 56:7), of communion with the reconciling God. In the same way, God is in Christ reconciling the world to himself (2 Cor 5:16-17).

SELMAN (2:327-328) titles this section the "basic principles of intercession": the people plead, God opens his eyes and hears, prayers are offered in confidence toward the place where God has put his name, the people address Yahweh as their covenant God, and God forgives. The intersection of these ideas reflects the relational character of God and how he yearns for reconciliation. He will **hear** and **forgive**.

First Chronicles 6:19-21 contains the "gist of the long prayer" and its vocabulary. The middle section of the prayer (2 Chr 6:22-35) is repetitive as it applies these general principles to specific circumstances.

The Circumstances of Prayer (6:22-35). The center of the chiasm is a list of lamentable circumstances. It anticipates Israelite history, and, for the Chronicler, is a rehearsal of that history. That history tells one story: God will hear and forgive those who seek him. The grace of God is unimaginable. Consequently, the story must be told and retold. This prayer serves not only as petition and doxology, but also as a pedagogical tool. It teaches Israel that God is gracious.

The prayer envisions six scenarios. In each case there is a lamentable circumstance followed by a plea with the expectation that God will hear and act graciously.

1. When there has been injustice, hear and justify (6:22-23).
2. When Israel has been defeated in battle, hear and forgive (6:24-25).
3. When Israel suffers a drought, hear and forgive (6:26-27).
4. When Israel suffers any disaster, hear and forgive (6:28-31).
5. When a foreigner seeks God, hear and reveal yourself (6:32-33).
6. When Israel goes to war, hear and justify (6:34-35).

The first and last scenarios concern justice. The first scenario (2 Chr 6:22-23) asks God to **judge** (שָׁפַט, *šāphaṭ*) between the **guilty** and the **innocent** (righteous) who have been falsely accused and seek justice. In other words, Solomon seeks the right of imprecation, that is, to give justice over to God. He seeks redress for the innocent who have been falsely accused (Bellinger, 463-469; Hicks, "Preaching," 28-51; cf. Ps 7). The last scenario (2 Chr 6:34-35) asks God to **uphold their cause** (מִשְׁפָּט, *mišpāṭ*). It is a war against **enemies** (the enemies of God), and it is understood that God sends them into battle (cf. the use of the verb in 2 Chr 1:12). The first scenario is a legal judgment and the latter is a holy war (Knoppers, "Jerusalem," 57-76). God will act since he is the God of justice (cf. 1 Chr 16:14,33).

The second and fifth scenarios envision a negative and positive engagement with the nations. The second (2 Chr 6:24-25) assumes that Israel goes to battle against a nation without divine authority (i.e., God did not send them as in 2 Chr 6:34). Consequently, Israel is defeated. The defeat may entail exile since a divine response includes a return **to the land** (JAPHET, 595). However, the exile is explicit later (2 Chr 6:36-39). The point may be a return to their homeland after a battle. Perhaps this anticipates a time when Israel will go out to conquer new territory but fail (cf. 2 Chr 24–26). The fifth scenario views the nations in a positive way. The term **foreigner** (נָכְרִי, *nākrî*) only occurs here, but the theme of Gentile witness to the glory of God is present in the stories about Hiram (2 Chr 2:12-16) and the Queen of Sheba (2 Chr 9:1-12). The temple is a place where Gentiles may come to pray; it is a house of prayer for the nations (Isa 56:7; Mark 11:17). Gentiles are attracted to the temple because of God's **great name**, **mighty hand**, and **outstretched arm**. The revelation of God's mighty acts is so renown that even Gentiles confidently pray to Yahweh. Thus, any Gentile may pray **toward this temple**, and God will hear and **do whatever the foreigner asks**. In this way **all the peoples of the earth** will **know your name and fear you**. God never intended to leave the Gentiles on the outside. He has always offered grace to those who seek him.

The third and fourth scenarios (2 Chr 6:26-31) depict natural disasters, diseases, and hostile action by an enemy. They are just punishments. God **afflicted them** because of **their sin** (2 Chr 6:26). In the history of his people, Solomon expects — and Chronicles's history bears out — that God will use natural disasters (including drought, **locusts, famine**), diseases (including a **plague**), and war to turn the hearts of his people back to himself. God teaches (2 Chr 6:27) and turns (2 Chr 6:26; cf. 2 Chr 6:24,38) them. The Lord's discipline teaches righteousness (cf. Heb 12:4-12). When they learn and turn, then God hears, forgives, and heals. He renews peace and wholeness in the land of their inheritance (2 Chr 6:27,31). At the center of this turning is "heart" language. God knows their **hearts** and so he judges. God deals **with each man according to all he does**, but this "doing" is judged by the character of the person's heart. When God judges actions, he actually judges the heart that produced the action. If the heart seeks God — even if their actions are imperfect — God hears the heart, forgives, and heals (cf. 2 Chr 30:18-20).

Hear the Lament of Your Exiled People (6:36-39). The Chronicler applies the principles of 2 Chronicles 6:18-21 to the specific situation of his audience. It "brings together many themes in the prayer to describe the worst possible scenario" (SELMAN, 2:330). It also reflects the grandness of God's grace since he hears and forgives his people whether they are at the temple or in a distant land. God heard the prayers of his people in exile and returned them to their land. The postexilic community should see God's act as a testimony of grace. Instead of being discouraged by their current situation (no Davidic king), they should claim the promise and lean on the past demonstrations of God's steadfast love. Postexilic Israel asked Malachi, "How has God loved us?" (Mal 1:2). The answer is: you are in the land. Remember God's great love for you from your beginnings in Abraham through David and into the present. Hope is ever present because the faithful God will remember his covenant.

Since the exilic picture reflects the situations of both 1 Kings and Chronicles, this part of the prayer receives the most emphasis. It is a theological credo. It affirms the universal character of sin (**there is no one who does not sin**) and God's holy response to it (**you become angry with them**). Nevertheless, in the midst of punishment, if Israel will **have a change of heart** (lit., "return to their heart"), **repent, plead with you,** confess their sin (**we have sinned**), and **turn back** to God **with all their heart and soul**, then God will be gracious. God will **hear, uphold their cause** (same phrase as 2 Chr 6:35), and **forgive**. God is ever willing to forgive those who seek him with a whole heart. Israel is a national prodigal son (Luke 16:11-32). Just as the prodigal son "came to his senses" and confessed his sin, so Israel, when it "returned to its heart" and confessed its sin, was received graciously. When Israel returned to its heart, then God returned them to their land. That postexilic Judah now lives in Jerusalem with a rebuilt temple is a testimony to God's faithful and gracious love.

Petition for God's Presence (6:40-42). While 2 Chronicles 6:40 is based on 1 Kings 8:52, verses 41-42 utilize the thought-world of Psalm 132:8-10 which celebrates the Davidic covenant. Chronicles's addition of verses 41-42 is theologically significant.

Dtr's ending utilizes the language of the prayer — **may your eyes be open and your ears attentive to the prayers offered in this place**. However, Chronicles's ending is explicitly petitionary as it uses the imperative mood twice (**arise, remember**). It is a loose quotation of Psalm 132:8-10, **Remember the great love promised to David your servant** (Williamson, "Mercies," 31-49). By quoting this Psalm and adding a final word, the Chronicler has joined the Davidic covenant (cf. Isa 55:3) and God's presence in the temple. The hope of Israel is bound up with both.

The text identifies the **ark** as God's **resting place** (cf. 1 Chr 28:2). He is surrounded by his angels (cherubim), his **priests**, and his **saints**. However, the Chronicler has changed the plural "anointed ones" in Psalm 132:10 to the singular **anointed one** in 2 Chronicles 6:42. The Davidic promise is focused in Solomon (cf. 2 Chr 7:10).

Theologically, Solomon petitions God to come to his temple, that is, to arise from his heavenly dwelling place and come to his sabbatical rest in the temple as Israel's redeemer. By so doing, God acts upon his covenant love and faithfully fulfills his promise to David. Postexilic Judah also prays this prayer. They plead with God to remember his covenant faithfulness to David. They seek the presence of God in the temple.

Christians, filled with the Spirit, pray in the Spirit to the enthroned one. Through prayer we enter the throne room of God and our prayers come before him as a sweet-smelling incense. God hears the pleas of his people, forgives, and heals. The gracious God still continues to work among his people and hear their prayers. In communal worship, the congregation seeks the face of God and he lifts them up into his throne room presence to share the worship of millions.

The Glory Cloud Appears (7:1-2)

Some find it problematic that the text has two appearances of the cloud, one before (2 Chr 5:13b) and one after (2 Chr 7:1) Solomon's prayer. However, this is a literary device ("resumptive repetition") which intends "to express simultaneity of events" (JAPHET, 610). Consequently, the narrative picture is that the cloud descends and covers the temple area as Solomon prays. Second Chronicles 5:13–7:2 is one dramatic moment.

5. Music (7:3)

God revealed himself through cloud and fire. Just as in the Exodus, the **fire** and **glory** are the presence **of the LORD** among his people. The people respond in worship **with their faces to the ground**. While prior to God's revelation the worship was conducted by the priests and Levites (2 Chr 5:11-13), here all Israel confesses (**gave thanks**) the refrain, **He is good; his love endures forever**. The priests and Levites prepared the temple for God's arrival, and once he arrived, all Israel broke out in praise.

6. Sacrifice (7:4-7)

The fire from heaven lights the altar (cf. Lev 9:23-24). Divine fire burns the sacrifices of Israel. The number of animals sacrificed (22,000 cattle and 120,000 sheep and goats) seems extravagant until their purpose is understood. Israel is celebrating a two-week festival which included not only burnt offerings (where the whole animal is dedicated to God), but also fellowship offerings (where the fat is burned to God but the priests and worshipers eat the animal). Chronicles, in fact, adds "fellowship offerings" to the language of 1 Kings 8:62-63 (2 Chr 7:5 [NIV reads **sacrifices** instead of "fellowship offerings"] and 7:7). The festival is a holy banquet. Chronicles emphasizes the meal. They celebrate "the dedication of the altar" (2 Chr 7:9) by eating at the table. God himself joins the eating ritual since the fat of the animals is his food (cf. Lev 3:16). The number of animals is consistent with the presence of all Israel for the temple's dedication.

As sacrifices were slaughtered and eaten, the Levitical musicians continued their praise and thanksgiving, **saying, His love endures forever**. Thus, the combination of altar (sacrifice), table (eating), and musical proclamation is emphasized (2 Chr 7:6 does not appear in 1 Kings).

7. Dismissal (7:8-10)

The **vast assembly** (קָהָל, *qāhāl*) continued for two weeks, one week beyond what was planned. It was a festive celebration but at the same time a holy convocation. It represented the whole of Israel — **from Lebo Hamath to the Wadi of Egypt** — which inhabited the promised land (cf. 1 Chr 13:5).

Second Chronicles 7:10 articulates the basis of worship. It celebrates the **good things the LORD** has done. Israel celebrated what
God **had done for David and Solomon**. Christians also celebrate
God's work in Israel, but, in addition, they celebrate God's reconciling work in Jesus Christ. We worship because of what God has
done (Rev 4:11; 5:9). People from every nation have been grafted
into Israel so that in the church and before the throne of God (just
as Israel was before God's throne at the temple), we confess that the
Lamb has made us "a kingdom and priests to serve our God" (Rev
5:10; cf. Exod 19:5; 1 Pet 2:5-9).

E. DIVINE RESPONSE (7:11-22)

Second Chronicles 5:2–7:10 focuses on Israel's praise and
address to God. Solomon's prayer was bounded by sacrificial preparations on one side and followed by sacrificial offerings on the
other. It was preceded with a holy procession and followed by two
weeks of festive celebration.

Now God speaks. In these few verses God articulates his basic
disposition toward his people. He announces his willingness to hear
their prayers, forgive their sins, and heal their brokenness. God
answers Solomon's prayer with a resounding "Yes." This positive
response arises out of God's merciful and gracious disposition.

God's message divides into two parts. First, God speaks to
Solomon (2 Chr 7:11-18) in response to his prayer (**your** [sing.]
prayer). Second, God speaks to the people (2 Chr 7:19-22; pl. verbs).
The second part is particularly appropriate for a postexilic community which still sees the visible evidence of God's devastation in
Jerusalem, but the first part reminds that community of God's merciful disposition. Given the devastation (2 Chr 7:19-22), the people
should humble themselves and trust God's grace (2 Chr 7:13-14).

1. God Speaks to Solomon (7:11-18)

The festive celebration has run two weeks. Solomon has **finished
the temple of the LORD**, along with his **royal palace** (noted but not
emphasized). He has carried **out all he had in mind to do in the**

temple of the LORD. Solomon built a temple, prayed, sacrificed, and celebrated.

Chronicles provides a "programmatic" divine response (DILLARD, 58). Second Chronicles 7:12b-15 has no parallel in 1 Kings. It is the heart of Chronicles's theology and provides the principle that is worked out in the coming narrative (2 Chr 10–36; cf. ALLEN, 238; WILLIAMSON, 225-226).

God's Basic Disposition (7:11-16)

Second Chronicles 7:14 is probably the most well-known verse in Chronicles (SELMAN, 2:337-340). It has been the thematic text for revivals throughout history. Chronicles offers hope to fallen Israel. Whenever Israel finds itself in the midst of a drought, crop devastation, or **a plague**, their hope is God. Consequently, throughout the history of God's people, 2 Chronicles 7:14 has been recalled again and again to revive hope among broken people.

However, verse 14 should not be isolated from its larger temple context. The middle **when . . . if** (2 Chr 7:13-14) is bounded by explicit declarations of God's sovereign election. Second Chronicles 7:12 and 7:16 declare that God has **chosen** (בָּחַר, bāḥar) a **place** for his mercy and communion: **a temple for sacrifices**. Given the context of divine presence and the sacrifices of 2 Chronicles 7:1-10, JOHNSTONE (1:357) believes these sacrifices refer primarily to the fellowship offerings. "The temple," he writes, "will be the place where the restored harmony between God and his people will be celebrated." Consequently, God's **eyes** and **ears** are focused on this place since he has **consecrated** it for his **Name**. Prayer and sacrifice are "two sides of the same coin" in Chronicles (Japhet, *Ideology*, 80), and the temple is the locus of both.

This language is soaked in theological meaning. God knows his people need atonement, so he provides a place. God's intent is openness. His disposition is inviting — **my eyes will be open and my ears attentive**. The sacrifices and prayers of God's people are means of mercy, and the temple epitomizes God's graciousness. God provides forgiveness and healing. God dwells in the temple as a testimony of his intent. God declares, **My eyes and my heart will always be there**.

God seeks seekers (cf. 1 Chr 28:9). He takes the initiative, but yearns for a reciprocal relationship. Consequently, God acts in the world in such a way to turn the hearts of his people to himself. If necessary, he will **shut up the heavens so there is no rain, or command locusts to devour the land or send a plague among** his **people** (2 Chr 6:26-28). God will afflict his people in order to engender authentic relationship. As the Psalmist writes, "in faithfulness you have afflicted me" (Ps 119:75). God is faithful to his intent: he will find seekers, and he will use all available means (cf. 2 Chr 24:19) to turn his rebellious children into seekers.

The response God seeks is described in 2 Chronicles 7:14. If Israel will (1) **humble themselves**, (2) **pray**, (3) **seek my face**, and (4) **turn from their wicked ways**, then God will (1) **hear from heaven**, (2) **forgive their sin**, and (3) **heal their land**. Given the principle that God seeks seekers, 2 Chronicles 7:14 summarizes the theology of the Chronicler. This is his message to the postexilic community: God is willing to hear and forgive if his people will seek him.

God has located his gracious presence in Israel at this temple. It has been **consecrated** to mercy. God does not merely intend to forgive, but he also intends to restore (heal). This is the only time the phrase "heal their land" occurs in the Hebrew Bible. The Lord "comes to the rescue of harassed nations and restores the *shalom* on earth" (WILLIAMSON, 226, citing Moor).

However, God seeks authentic relationship. Consequently, God's forgiveness and healing is conditioned on the hearts of his people. To emphasize this, Chronicles describes their approach with four significant terms (cf. Kelly, 49-62). "Humble" (כנע, *kāna'*) appears 19 times (only 17 times in the rest of the Hebrew Bible), sometimes in reference to the subjugation of enemies (1 Chr 17:10; 18:1; 20:4; 2 Chr 13:18), but often in reference to the humility God demands (2 Chr 12:6-7,12; 30:11; 32:26; 33:12,19; 33:23; 34:27; 36:12) or God's act of humbling his people (2 Chr 28:19). "Pray" (פלל, *pālal*) occurs 15 times (including 1 Chr 17:25; 30:18; 32:20; 32:24; 33:13) but 10 times in 2 Chronicles 6–7 (6:19,20,21,24,26,32,38; 7:1,14). "Seek" (בקשׁ, *bāqaš*, but elsewhere דרשׁ, *dāraš*) has a theological sense 8 times (1 Chr 16:10,11; 2 Chr 7:14; 11:16; 15:6,15; 20:4). Its synonym (*dāraš*) is found, among other places, in 1 Chronicles 16:11; 28:9; 2 Chronicles 12:14; 15:2,12,13; 30:19; 34:3,21,26. "Turn" (שׁוב, *šûb*) is a synonym for repentance (2 Chr 6:24,37,38; 7:14; 15:4; 19:4; 30:6,9; 36:13). This heaping of terms (the only time these four verbs occur together) probably represents some kind of progression. If they will humble themselves, pray to him, seek his face, and turn from their sin, then God will hear, forgive, and heal.

Second Chronicles 7:13-14 evidences God's desire for relationality and 2 Chronicles 7:12,15-16 testify to God's gracious disposition. He will show mercy to those who humbly seek him. Chronicles's story repetitively demonstrates this principle — Rehoboam (2 Chr 12:12), Asa (2 Chr 15:1-15), the northern pilgrims (2 Chr 30:11,18-20), Hezekiah (2 Chr 32:24-26), Manasseh (2 Chr 33:12), and Josiah (2 Chr 34:27). Chronicles's story provides the confidence that God will show mercy. When his people seek him, he will be found (cf. 2 Chr 15:2).

God's Promise to Solomon (7:17-18)

While 2 Chronicles 7:13-16 concerned the prayers of God's people, 2 Chronicles 7:17-18 specifically addresses Solomon. God offers Solomon a conditional covenant. The unconditionality of the Davidic promise, realized messianically in Jesus Christ, is not the subject here. Rather, Solomon's **royal throne** (lit., "your kingdom throne") is.

The postexilic community lived without a Davidic king, but they hoped for one. God removed kings because they forsook him, but as long as they walked as David did, they reigned over Israel with God's blessing. While Chronicles does not detail the faults of Solomon, the inclusion of this conditional promise anticipates the division of the kingdom in 2 Chronicles 10 and the eventual exile of Judah in 2 Chronicles 36.

Nevertheless, the Davidic promise does not fail because Solomon and other kings were unfaithful. The Davidic line is fulfilled in Jesus Christ. The Chronicler hopes for another Davidic king as he expresses the confidence that even though no one sits on the throne (cf. 1 Kgs 9:5), Israel will always have a ruler (an echo of Micah 5:2). "The dynastic promise," DILLARD (59) comments, "has not lost its validity even with the loss of the throne." Chronicles changes the language of 1 Kings 9:5 from "as I spoke to David" to **as I covenanted with David**. The hope of postexilic Israel is the Davidic covenant. God will act faithfully regarding his promises. The promises of God are "Yes" in Jesus Christ (cf. 2 Cor 1:20). Whether the Chronicler had messianic hopes or not, a canonical reading of Chronicles points us in that direction.

2. God Speaks to the People (7:19-22)

The shift from the singular in 2 Chronicles 7:17-18 to the plural in 2 Chronicles 7:19-22 indicates that the divine oracle has broadened its intended audience. Solomon's descendants will reign as long as they do not **forsake** God's **decrees and commands**. When God's people seek him, he will be found, but when they forsake him, he will forsake them (cf. 1 Chr 28:9). JAPHET (616) notes that this section functions as a theodicy to explain the destruction of the temple and the loss of Davidic rule in postexilic Judah.

The term "forsake" is used theologically 17 times. Sometimes it is a divine promise that God will not forsake (1 Chr 28:20) or a testimony that Israel has not forsaken (2 Chr 13:10), but other times it is a divine warning that God will forsake (1 Chr 28:9; 2 Chr 7:22; 12:5; 15:2) if Israel does (1 Chr 28:9; 2 Chr 7:19; 12:1; 13:11; 15:2; 21:10; 24:18,24; 28:6; 29:6; 34:25). When Israel forsakes the way of God and turns toward other gods, God will forsake them (2 Chr 7:22).

The text describes this Godforsakenness. The Lord brings **disaster** (lit., "evil"; cf. 2 Chr 34:24-25) upon a rebellious people. In particular, the God who redeemed them from Egypt and gave them this land will also **uproot Israel from** that land. He will **reject this temple**. Given rebellion, God reverses the Exodus-Conquest, and he destroys the place of mercy (temple). The grace of God becomes the wrath of God. Even the nations, who were to be blessed by Israel, will deride Israel in the wake of God's judgment. "What had been intended to be the channel of universal restoration," JOHNSTONE (1:359) writes, "has through the failure of its commissioned agents become the object of universal derision" (2 Chr 7:21-22).

When the people ask, **Why has the LORD done such a thing to this land and this temple?** the answer is simple. They forsook the Lord. God forsakes those who forsake him. Despite God's gracious intentions, when God's people seek other gods, he rejects them.

God's relationship with his people is reciprocal. If they seek him, he will be found because he seeks them. But if they forsake him, he will forsake them. Just as with Saul, so with Solomon and other Judean kings, if they are unfaithful, God will forsake them. God seeks all hearts (1 Chr 28:9), but the question is whether any seek him. Nevertheless, God remains a seeker, and he will keep his promise to David by raising up an eternal king in the person of Jesus Christ.

Will the postexilic community seek God? Their current temple pales in comparison to Solomon's. They have no Davidic king. They see the insignificance of Jerusalem in the Persian empire. Yet, they remember God's great reversal in the Babylonian exile. But their question is, will God remember his great love for David? If they seek God, will he be found? The resounding answer of Chronicles is "Yes" (cf. 2 Chr 6:36-39). God seeks seekers.

F. OTHER CONSTRUCTION/GENTILE LABOR (8:1-16)

This section details further construction and Gentile labor. Its chiastic counterpart appears in 2 Chr 2:17–5:1. Both sections end with a summary statement (2 Chr 5:1; 8:16): **the temple of the LORD was finished** (Dillard, 61).

The expansion of Solomon's building projects include not only his palace, but projects in both northern and southern Israel. This is the rest that God has given Solomon. The use of Gentile conscript labor reflects God's intent that the nations serve Israel (as Esau served Jacob) though ultimately Israel will serve the nations as the conduit through which the blessings of God will flow. The theological function of this material, then, is to enhance the stature of Solomon which glorifies God.

This section parallels 1 Kings 9:10-28 though the Chronicler has omitted some material (1 Kgs 9:12-16) and added some details of his own (2 Chr 8:11b,13-16).

1. Other Construction (8:1-6)

Solomon's construction includes the (1) **temple of the LORD**, (2) **his own palace**, (3) **villages that Hiram had given him**, (4) rebuilding **Tadmor**, (5) **store cities . . . in Hamath**, (6) **fortified cities** in **Upper Beth Horon and Lower Beth Horon**, (7) **Baalath and all his**

store cities, and (8) **all the cities for his chariots and for his horses**. His construction activities extended from **Jerusalem** to **Lebanon and throughout all the territory he ruled**. The diverse locations and extensive construction are evidence of divine blessing.

The geographical diversity is impressive. He conquered new territories in **Hamath Zobah** in the north (a region David had under tribute) which is the only reference in Chronicles to any military activity by Solomon. He also **settled Israelites** in northern cities that Hiram had given him. He built cities in the south, particularly Baalath.

Solomon builds the store cities to house his immense wealth. They were probably located along his trade routes for storage of tribute and taxation. He also fortifies his borders. For example, occupying Hamath and the region of Gezer (southern Judah) means that he controls the major trade route through Palestine (i.e., the Way by the Sea). Further, rebuilding Upper Beth Horon and Lower Beth Horon fortifies the main road between Jerusalem and the trade route. In addition, Tadmor (later Palmyra, located northeast of Damascus) controls the only other Palestinian trade route. Solomon is protecting his commercial interests. Indeed, some of these cities Solomon built have been identified as fortresses in the Negev south of Beersheba (Cohen, 56-70).

The most problematic element in this account is the difference between 2 Chronicles 8:2a and 1 Kings 9:11b. The Chronicler believes Hiram gave Solomon some cities, but 1 Kings states that Solomon "gave twenty towns in Galilee to Hiram King of Tyre" as payment for his services. Since the Chronicler had 1 Kings in front of him, why does he make this obvious change? Some believe the Chronicler reverses the scenario in order to exalt Solomon (COGGINS, 174), but this underestimates the Chronicler's faithfulness to his sources and his assumption that his readers know 1 Kings (e.g., he assumes they know about Solomon's marriage to Pharaoh's daughter [2 Chr 8:11] though he omits the account in 1 Kgs 9:16). Others think that Hiram found these cities unacceptable (Solomon had to rebuild them) and returned them, or they were given to Hiram as collateral for a loan (THOMPSON, 238; WILLIAMSON, 228-229; DILLARD, 63; SELMAN, 2:345).

2. Gentile Labor (8:7-11)

Conscripted Labor and Israel (8:7-10)

The conscription of Gentile labor, especially **the descendants remaining in the land** who had not been **destroyed** in the Conquest, signals the full inhabitation of Canaan. Structurally, this section is the chiastic counterpart to 2 Chronicles 2:17-18.

Pharaoh's Daughter (8:11)

This is Chronicles's only reference to **Pharaoh's daughter** even though she is prominent in Dtr (1 Kgs 3:1; 7:8; 9:16,27; 11:1). Chronicles does not focus on her because she played a role in Solomon's sins, and Chronicles has a negative view of foreign alliances. In addition, she is mentioned here because it heightens Solomon's international reputation (Johnstone, 1:365).

Chronicles offers a reason for moving Pharaoh's daughter to her own **palace**. She could not **live in the palace of David king of Israel because the places the ark of the LORD has entered are holy**. Is the issue here gender or ethnicity? DILLARD (65) believes it is her gender because the language literally reads "no woman belonging to me" may live where the ark had been present. Thus, this anticipates the separation of the "court of the women" from the "court of the men" in the Second Temple period. JOHNSTONE (1:366; cf. Japhet, "Prohibition," 69-87) believes it relates to her married status since "sexual abstinence" is part of holiness preparations. However, SELMAN (2:348) argues that the context (Gentile relations) provides the explanation. As a foreigner, Pharaoh's daughter is not permitted in holy places. Consequently, foreign wives were given separate housing.

The Chronicler stresses the holiness of the ark. He has no interest in Solomon's relationship other than the preservation of temple holiness. Since Solomon's palace was adjacent to the temple, Solomon built his foreign wives separate homes to maintain a holy distance.

3. Temple Rituals Complete the Temple (8:12-16)

This is the Chronicler's literary device to close his parallel between 2:17–5:1 and 8:1-16. It expands 1 Kings 9:25. Other than a literary device, this section is out of place. Consequently, the Chronicler is more concerned about rhetoric (chiastic grouping) than he is strict chronology (Dillard, 66). Nevertheless, this section summarizes the full operations of the temple cultus according to Mosaic prescriptions (**commanded**) and Davidic regulations (**ordinance**).

Unique to Chronicles, it verifies Solomon's faithful pursuit of temple rituals. While the Chronicler never assigns the king any cultic roles (as he does Levites and priests), the king is always given a significant function as "founder, patron, and supervisor" (De Vries, "Founders," 619-639). The **king's commands** regulated the rituals (2 Chr 8:15). These rituals included (1) Mosaic prescriptions and (2) Davidic regulations. The former consisted of prescribed rituals: (a) **daily** morning and evening **burnt offerings**, (b) weekly **Sabbaths**, (c) monthly **New Moons**, and (d) **three annual** pilgrim **feasts**: **Unleavened Bread** (Passover), **Feast of Weeks** (Pentecost) and **the Feast of Tabernacles** (cf. 2 Chr 2:4; 31:3; cf. Deut 16:1-16).

The Davidic regulations included (1) **the divisions of the priests**, (2) the priestly assistants, and (3) musicians (**Levites to lead the praise**) in the daily sacrifices (cf. 1 Chr 15–16, 23–25). In addition, Solomon **appointed the gatekeepers by divisions for the various gates** (cf. 1 Chr 26). Solomon followed David's regulations because David was a **man of God**. This title gives him prophetic status (cf. 1 Chr 23:14; 2 Chr 11:2; 25:7,9; 2 Chr 30:16). "There could be no higher claim: the system conceived in Moses and realized in David, both accredited by God in the highest terms possible, has now been put into operation by Solomon" (Johnstone, 1:367). David is one of the prophets himself (cf. 2 Chr 29:25).

G. RECOGNITION BY GENTILES/DEALINGS WITH HIRAM (8:17–9:12)

This section is the chiastic counterpart of 2 Chronicles 2:1-16. Their common themes include Hiram's assistance and Solomon's international recognition. It demonstrates Solomon's international influence and reputation. Theologically, Solomon extends Yahweh's influence beyond the borders of Israel and blesses the nations surrounding him. Indeed, all wealth and wisdom flow to Jerusalem, and then it flows out again to bless the nations. The queen of Sheba serves a paradigmatic function.

1. The Expedition to Ophir via Elath (8:17-18)

Parallel with 1 Kings 9:26-28, **Solomon** imports large quantities of gold from Ophir with Hiram's help. JAPHET (629) sees this as quite feasible historically because **Hiram** had the naval ability and Solomon had control of the coastal regions of the Red Sea.

Israel had no natural resources close to home. The "gold of Ophir" (1 Chr 29:4) probably came from trade with western Arabia, the coastal regions of Africa, the Horn of Africa, or perhaps even India. As DILLARD (66) points out, the "three year durations of the voyages" (cf. 2 Chr 9:21 with 1 Kgs 10:22) "suggests a remote location." In addition, Solomon's control of the caravan trade through Palestine would enable the accumulation of great wealth (Rasmussen, "Economic," 153-166).

Is 450 **talents** (ca. 14.5 tons; 1 Kgs 9:28 reads 420 talents, due to textual variation) **of gold** too excessive? Alexander the Great captured 40,000 talents (1,178.5 tons) of gold at Persian Susa. Persia received 10.5 tons of gold from India on one occasion. Osorkon I of Egypt (924–889 B.C.) gave 17.8 tons of gold to his Egyptian temples in the first four years of his reign (Millard, "Glory," 14-16). Consequently, this amount is not excessive, especially if it indicates the total revenue from Solomon's trade with **Ophir** over his whole reign. Other parts of the trade with Ophir included imported wood that was used for the temple, palace, and musical instruments (2 Chr 9:10-11).

2. The Queen of Sheba Visits (9:1-12)

The queen sees Solomon in all his glory and splendor. Just as Hiram (2 Chr 2) recognized God's hand in raising up Solomon, so does the queen of Sheba. Hiram and the queen are internationally prominent royalty who recognize Solomon's status in the world.

Theologically, the nations come to Jerusalem bearing gifts. They acknowledge the throne of God in Jerusalem. The queen praises the God of Israel who has gifted Solomon with such abundance. The glory of Solomon, then, is the glory of God since Solomon sits on the throne of God (2 Chr 9:8; cf. Throntveit, "Idealization," 411-427).

This section follows 1 Kings 10:1-13 with some significant exceptions (noted below). The Chronicler's close attention to his source confirms historical credibility since later renditions of this story are quite expansive, including even a sexual relationship between the queen and Solomon.

The Queen Comes to Jerusalem (9:1-4)

Most believe the **queen of Sheba** (or Saba) is from the region of modern Yemen on the Arabian coast about 1400 miles from Jerusalem (Kitchen, "Sheba," 126-153). Sheba, SELMAN (2:353) writes, was "well-known in ancient times for its wealth, based on trade in frankincense and myrrh (cf. Ezk. 27:22-23)." Her identity, however, is unknown as there are no available texts from that region. Yet, there is no reason to doubt the story's historicity (DILLARD, 71-72).

The queen **came to Jerusalem to test** Solomon **with hard questions** because she had **heard** of his **fame**. While her intentions also involved trade (since she needed access to the Mediterranean), the narrative portrays this meeting as a "wisdom encounter" (DILLARD, 71). "Wisdom" is used four times (2 Chr 9:3,5,6,7). Solomon possesses divine wisdom (2 Chr 1:12), and so he is able to answer the queen's difficult questions. SELMAN (2:354) speculates that the questions may have been similar to what biblical wisdom literature engages (e.g., Ps 49, Proverbs, Job, etc.).

The queen was also impressed with Solomon's wealth. She herself brought evidence of her own wealth in a large **caravan** (including **spices**, **gold**, and **precious stones**). But **she was overwhelmed** (lit., "there was no longer any spirit in her") with Solomon's wealth (including his **palace**, **food**, his banquet arrangements, and the number of his **burnt offerings**). God's gifts to Solomon in wisdom and wealth were breathtaking. This awe translates into praise for the divine giver.

The Queen Testifies (9:5-8)

The queen's words belie her intention. She came to test and to see. What she had heard was unbelievable, but what she heard was not even the half of it. She is enthralled with Solomon's **achievements** and **wisdom**. As a Gentile she rejoices in the revelation of divine wisdom.

Second Chronicles 9:8 is the theological heart of Chronicles's pericope because the queen testifies to the glory of God. The most significant difference between 1 Kings 10:6-9 and 2 Chronicles 9:5-8 is this sentence: **placed you on his throne as king to rule for the LORD your God**. Chronicles refers to Solomon's throne as God's rather than the "throne of Israel" (1 Kgs 10:9). The Chronicler adds the idea that Solomon rules for Yahweh. The Chronicler's point, then, is that Solomon's kingdom is the kingdom of God, that his throne is God's throne, and that he rules as God's representative. Thus, the glory of Solomon is really the glory of God. As one who represents God, Solomon must rule God's people with **justice and righteousness**. Something obscured by the NIV, but stressed in the Hebrew text is that God "gave" (נתן, *nāthan*) Solomon his kingship.

Chronicles expands the statement in 1 Kings 10:9 from "because of the LORD's eternal love for Israel" to **because of the love of your God for Israel and his desire to uphold them forever**. The latter phrase stresses God's eternal purpose in Israel. This intent arises out of his great love for Israel. This parallels Hiram's statement in 2 Chronicles 2:11 (almost the same language): because God loves Israel, he gave Solomon a kingdom. The glory of Solomon not only evidences God's glory, but also his faithful love.

Christians recognize the evidence of God's glory and love. In Jesus Christ we see the glory (John 1:14-18) and love of God (John 3:16). God bears witness to himself through his mighty acts and most significantly in the mighty act of incarnation, atonement, and resurrection. All the nations, just like the queen and Hiram, recognize this as Gentiles pour into the church of God. If the nations came to visit Solomon to hear his wisdom, the nations come to the kingdom of God in Jesus Christ because one greater than Solomon is present (cf. Matt 12:42).

The Exchange of Gifts and Departure (9:9-12)

This section involves three topics: (1) the queen's gifts to Solomon (9:9), (2) the role of Hiram's men (9:10-11), and (3) Solomon's gifts to the queen (9:12). The first and third reflect the reciprocal relationship between Solomon and the queen, and point the reader to the dynamic that God's blessings flow to Jerusalem, but then they also flow out. Just as all the nations will come to Jerusalem, so there will also be a living stream that flows from Jerusalem to nourish all nations.

Their exchange includes the queen's gift of **120 talents of gold**, **spices**, and **precious stones**. The amount of gold (3.9 tons) is not excessive given analogous gifts in the ancient world. Tiglath-pileser III of Assyria received a tribute of 150 talents of gold from Tyre in 730 B.C. (Millard, "Bible," 31).

H. SOLOMON'S WEALTH AND WISDOM (9:13-31)

Chronicles details some of Solomon's vast wealth and wisdom (chi astically parallel with 2 Chr 1). Some have regarded this description as exaggerated. However, as Millard ("Solomon," 5-18; "Bible," 20-29, 31, 34) has demonstrated, the biblical narrative is quite consistent with what is known about the wealth of other ancient Near Eastern cultures. Utilizing JAPHET's (639) list of Solomon's wealth in 2 Chronicles 9, I have constructed the chart below from Millard's data.

Text	Solomon's Wealth	Ancient Near Eastern Parallels
9:1	Spices, gold, and precious stones	Sheba was famous for these items
9:9	120 talents (3.9 tons) of gold plus spices and precious stones	Tyre gave 150 talents of gold (4.4 tons) to Tiglath-pileser III of Assyria in 730 B.C.
9:10	gold from Ophir	"gold of Ophir" known on an 8th-century B.C. ostracon in Israel
9:10	algum wood and precious stones	see 9:1 and 9:11
9:11	steps, lyres, and harps, made of algum wood	precious wood known from Ugaritic lists of tribute and Akkadian texts
9:13	a yearly income of gold — 666 talents (21.6 tons)	The accumulated wealth of Persia that Alexander the Great confiscated was 8,020 tons of gold.
9:14	gold and silver from Arabia	mines have been discovered in western Arabia
9:15	two hundred large shields of gold and three hundred regular shields	Sargon II of Assyria boasts that he took gold shields as booty from Urartu
9:17	an ivory throne, with steps, 'footstool,' and lions	ivory throne found at Salamis in Cyprus; ivory furniture overlaid with gold at Assyrian Nimrud

9:20	golden drinking vessels	known from Egypt, Ur, and Ugarit
9:20	golden vessels for the House of the Forest of Lebanon	known from Egypt, Ur, and Ugarit
9:21	gold and silver from Tarshish	"going to the ends of the earth" (cf. Ps 72:10; Isa 2:16), that is, global wealth
9:21	apes and peacocks (baboons?)	exotic animals from Africa and other regions
9:24	articles of silver and gold	jewelry, chariots, furniture, even toiletry articles are known
9:24	yearly donations of garments, myrrh, spices, horses, mules	common articles of wealth and status
9:25	four thousand stalls for horses and chariots	Ugarit chariots used three horses per chariot (SELMAN, 2:357)
9:25	twelve thousand horses (NIV)	Ugarit chariots used three horses per chariot.
9:27	silver like stones and cedar like sycamore	hyperbole for pervasive presence of wealth
9:28	horses imported from all lands	imports from the known world

Solomon's wealth is consistent with what is known from the ancient Near East. His kingdom is adorned in splendor and glory but not unlike other empires. Further, his reign has imperial status as **he ruled over all the kings from the River to the land of the Philistines, as far as the border of Egypt**. The function of Solomon's wealth is to highlight his status among the kings of the earth.

Given this immense wealth, it is a legitimate question to wonder what happened to it. The best answer is Pharaoh Shishak's invasion (cf. 2 Chr 12:2).

Theologically, this wealth praises God, not Solomon. This is God's kingdom, not Solomon's. All that Solomon possesses is by grace. Since Solomon sits on God's throne, his reign must reflect God's glory. Solomon's wealth, then, is a testimony to God's splendor and majesty. Consequently, this is no mere accumulation of luxury, but rather the testimony of heaven on earth. The streets are paved with gold in the new Jerusalem because God lives there (not for our reward). In the same way, Jerusalem is filled with wealth because God has chosen to place his name in this city. The gold bears witness to God's presence.

WILCOX (152-163) reminds us that we should not take up Solomon's wealth as a goal for the Christian lifestyle. Solomon's wealth is not about a materialistic lifestyle but the glory of God. In the same way, our lifestyle manifests the glory of God in holiness not luxury (cf. Jas 5:1-6). Solomon's wealth is a function of God's presence in his chosen city. God, however, now resides in the human heart, and the evidence of his presence is the fruit of the Spirit in holiness.

1. His Wealth (9:13-21)

Parallel with 1 Kings 10:14-22, this section details his immense wealth. The section is chiastically structured in order to stress Solomon's throne.

a. Sources of Wealth (9:13-14)
  b. Gold Utensils (9:15-16)
    c. The Throne (9:17-19)
  b'. Gold Utensils (9:20)
a'. Sources of Wealth (9:21)

The outer rings of the chiasm provide a sampling of Solomon's sources of wealth. His annual income from tribute and taxation is **666 talents** of gold (21.6 tons). While this is a large amount, it is not inconceivable (Millard, "Solomon," 13-17).

The inner rings of the chiasm provide examples of Solomon's luxurious use of gold. Not only did he have golden cups and other **household articles**, he also had 300 **small shields of hammered gold**. Golden shields were useless for military purposes. They are decorative just as are golden helmets (one was discovered in Byblos dating from ca. 1800 B.C.; Millard, "Bible," 24, 26). Such a sign of wealth would be analogous to someone purchasing a number of Rembrandts to decorate their home.

At the center of the chiasm is Solomon's throne. It may seem strange to overlay ivory with gold, but this practice is known in the ancient world. Apparently, "ancient royalty showed their wealth by concealing the ivory beneath gold" as the throne found at Salamis in Cyprus demonstrates (Millard, "Bible," 22). The emphasis on the throne does not stress Solomon's wealth as much as it manifests the throne of God himself. Solomon's throne is God's throne (cf. 2 Chr 9:8). There was no other throne like Solomon's in the same sense that there was no mountain higher than Zion (cf. Isa 2:2), that is, this is God's throne on God's mountain (JOHNSTONE, 1:372).

2. His International Status (9:22-24)

Solomon's international status is due to his **riches and wisdom**. Indeed, the kings did not come simply to bring him tribute but to **hear the wisdom God had put in his heart** (lit., "God gave to his heart"). A similar expression appears in 2 Chronicles 30:12 where God gives unity to the hearts of the people. In Chronicles God is active in the hearts of people (cf. 1 Chr 29:18-19).

3. His Wealth (9:25-28)

DILLARD (71) notes that the Chronicler's repetition of material from 2 Chronicles 1:14-17 "should not be thought of as clumsy compositional technique or lapse of memory on the part of the author, but rather as deliberate signposts of the overall structure he has contrived." Chronicles is completing the chiasm of 2 Chronicles 1-9.

There are several textual difficulties between 1 Kings 4:21,26; 10:26b-27 and 2 Chronicles 9:25b-27 (JAPHET, 642-644). The 40,000 stalls of 1 Kings 4:26 are too large a number and are another example where Chronicles preserves the best variant reading. SELMAN's (2:357) solution is to see the 12,000 horses as a number needed for 1,400 chariots (cf. 2 Chr 1:14), including three horses per chariot with additional horses used for breeding and training. The number of horses is a sign of wealth and power.

Chronicles includes a note about the extent of Solomon's reign (cf. 1 Chr 13:5). Solomon, inhabits the promised land. God has kept his promise to Abraham (cf. Gen 15:18).

4. Conclusion to Solomon's Reign (9:29-31)

The Chronicler points his readers to additional sources (the prophets **Nathan**, **Ahijah**, and **Iddo**). JAPHET (645) argues that they refer to extrabiblical texts which are no longer extant. Kline (53-57) has argued that this reflects a canonical role for prophets as covenant historians as well as covenant messengers.

The main topic of 2 Chronicles 1-9 is not Solomon but the God of Israel. Chronicles omits the sins of Solomon because the "reign of Solomon" is not the topic. The subject of the narrative is God, not Solomon. Chronicles tells the story of Solomon to bear witness to the glory and grace of Yahweh, the King of Israel. Solomon is his representative.

Typologically, then, Solomon functions messianically, that is, he points to the true representative of God — one in whom the fullness of God dwelt (cf. Col 2:9). In Jesus Christ God became flesh, dwelt among us, and bore witness to the glory of God as the unique Son of the Father (John 1:14-18).

2 CHR 10:1–36:23 — PART THREE

THE DIVIDED MONARCHY

The "Golden Age" of Israel was the United Monarchy under David and Solomon. Just as the Exodus-Conquest was a unity of Moses and Joshua, so the Re-Conquest/Preparation (David) and Temple-Building (Solomon) was a unity of David and Solomon.

Upon the death of Solomon, the kingdom divides. Just as after the death of Joshua the period of the judges saw a time of schism (even civil war) and apostasy, so after the death of Solomon Israel degenerates — first into schism, and then into idolatry (both north and south). But the Chronicler is not so much interested in the reasons for the schism and idolatry as he is in the "principles by which restoration might take place" (SELMAN, 2:359).

The Chronicler narrates the history of Judah (the southern kingdom) alone. He does not tell the story of the northern kingdom except as it impinges on the history of Judah (e.g., Ahab's alliance with the south). His concern is the Davidic line and the Solomonic temple. Thus, his interests are the same as they were in 1 Chronicles 10–2 Chronicles 9 — the promise to David and God's temple presence.

Schism and idolatry are ever present dangers for the postexilic community. The Chronicler does not want a repeat of post-Solomonic Israel (e.g., schism and idolatry). Consequently, he tells the story of the Davidic dynasty in order to unite his community around the Davidic promise and temple cultus. He counsels adherence to the Torah through seeking the Lord. In order to resist schism and idolatry, postexilic Israel "needed to hear and rehear the story of the Davidic dynasty, ever the object of Yahweh's gracious fidelity and ever in danger of failing to receive the promise through infidelity" (De Vries, "Schema," 77). The Chronicler is interested in redemption, restoration, and healing.

Despite his focus on Judah, the Chronicler does not cut off the north from the Davidic heritage. Northern schismatics are invited to join the Davidic kingdom and Solomonic cultus. Chronicles's history promotes the inclusion of the north.

The danger of schism and idolatry is also ever present to the Christian community. Just as Paul counseled the Corinthians not to fall into the habits of wilderness Israel (1 Cor 10:1-13), so the Chronicler speaks both warning and hope. He warns that schism and idolatry destroy the people of God, and he teaches that hope is the Davidic promise.

The structure of 2 Chronicles 10–36 is uncertain. The final part of Chronicles is not a mere list of kings without any periodization or internal structural relationship. Throntveit (*Kings*, 113-121; cf. THOMPSON, 341) has suggested that 2 Chronicles 10–36 consists of two major sections: (1) the Divided Monarchy (2 Chr 10–28) and the Re-United Kingdom (2 Chr 29–36). The Re-United Kingdom is the renewal of the Davidic covenant (see 2 Chr 29).

The theological function of Throntveit's structure offers hope to the postexilic community. Just as God can reunite the kingdom after the devastation of Samaria in 722 B.C., so he can reunite Israel after the Babylonian exile. Hezekiah serves as a model for the postexilic community, and the remaining history of Judah warns that what has been restored can be lost again (e.g., Babylonian exile).

In light of this theological function, I have divided 2 Chronicles 10–36 into three parts: (1) The Schism (10:1–12:16), (2) The Southern Kingdom (13:1–28:27), and the (3) Re-United Monarchy (29:1–36:23).

Dating the kings of the divided kingdom is a difficult task. It is complicated by several factors (Thiele, 43-60). Some kings reigned as co-regents with their fathers though this is not always stated. Sometimes dates are counted according to an accession year system (where the year in which one becomes king is not counted in the total years of the reign) and sometimes according to a nonaccession year system (where the year in which one becomes king is counted in the total years of the reign). There are also complications regarding the month which began a regnal year (sometimes Tishri, sometimes Nisan). This commentary assumes Thiele's dating even though it is disputable.

While Chronicles is not interested in the history of the northern kingdom (Israel), the history of Judah often intersects with it. I have provided Thiele's (10) dates for both.

Judah, the Southern Kingdom		Israel, the Northern Kingdom	
Rehoboam	930–913	Jeroboam I	930–909
Abijah	913–910		
Asa	910–869	Nadab	909–908
		Baasha	908–886
		Elah	886–885
		Zimri	885
		Tibni	885–880
		Omri	885–874
Jehoshaphat (co-regent)	872–869	Ahab	874–853
Jehoshaphat (total reign)	872–848	Ahaziah	853–852
Jehoram (co-regent)	853–848	Joram	852–841
Jehoram (total reign)	853–841		
Ahaziah	841	Jehu	841–814
Athaliah	841–835		
Joash	835–796	Jehoahaz	814–798
Amaziah	796–767	Jehoash	798–782
		Jeroboam II (co-regent)	793–782
Uzziah (overlap)	792–767	Jeroboam II (total reign)	793–753
Uzziah (total reign)	792–740	Zechariah	753
		Shallum	752
		Menahem	752–742
Jotham (co-regent)	750–740	Pekah	752–732
Jotham (official reign)	750–735		
Jotham (total years)	750–732	Pekahiah	742–740
Ahaz (overlap)	735–732		
Ahaz (official years)	732–715	Hoshea	732–723
Hezekiah	715–686		
Manasseh (co-regent)	696–686		
Manasseh (total reign)	696–642		
Amon	642–640		
Josiah	640–609		
Jehoahaz	609		
Jehoiakim	609–598		
Jehoiachin	598–597		
Zedekiah	597–586		

JOHNSTONE (2:13) notes that each account of a Judahite king is framed by seven factors: (1) age of the new Davidic king at his succession, (2) the length of his reign in Jerusalem, (3) the name of his mother, (4) evaluation, (5) the record of the rest of his deeds, (6) his death and burial in the city of David, and (7) the succession of the next king. These seven elements appear at the beginning and/or end of the account of each king. This standard formula frames the story that is significant for Chronicles.

I. THE SCHISM (10:1–12:16)

The schism appears "out of the blue" — there is no hint in the previous narrative (1 Chr 10–2 Chr 9). The Chronicler does not prepare the reader even though his account traces it back to Solomon's oppressive labor policies (cf. 2 Chr 10:4,11).

Theologically, the schism is one of two great "turning" events in the history of Israel. Just as God turned (סבב, *sābab*) the kingdom over to David (1 Chr 10:14; 12:23), so God turned events (נְסִבָּה, *n'sibbāh*) so his kingdom was divided (2 Chr 10:15). The move from Saul to David and the move from united to divided kingdom are the two most significant events in the political history of Israel. God was active in both. He punished Saul and blessed David, and through the schism he judges both Jeroboam and Rehoboam.

WILLIAMSON (237-239, 251-252) argues that the northern tribes legitimately break with Judah but then become apostate when they turn to their own cultic practices (2 Chr 11:14-15) and reject Abijah's offer to reunite (2 Chr 13:4-12). On the other hand, Knoppers ("Rehoboam," 425) argues that Rehoboam is not so much a villain as "the victim of forces he is ill prepared to confront." Consequently, Chronicles regards the schism as a rebellion against the Davidic dynasty and the temple cultus.

Given the Davidic dynasty, Chronicles regards the schism itself as rebellious (2 Chr 10:19). Jeroboam is a villain even though he serves God's purpose. God often uses human rebellion to achieve his purposes (e.g., the use of evil empires to punish Israel and Judah). The northern kingdom's rejection of David is emphatic (2 Chr 10:16). Knoppers ("Rehoboam," 426; cf. Japhet, *Ideology*, 308-324) is correct to conclude that the "revolt of the northern tribes at Shechem in Chronicles is unwarranted and unprecedented."

However, Rehoboam is no mere victim. Chronicles does not provide the rationale for the northern disaffection (except the brief hints in 2 Chr 10:4,11). The northern schism is an "abrupt about-face from the allegiance they had continually displayed since early in David's reign" (Knoppers, "Rehoboam," 434). Rehoboam continues to oppress the north. The schism is God's judgment against Rehoboam and not merely the rebellion of Jeroboam.

Nevertheless, the emphasis is squarely on the northern rebellion. Inexperienced and unwise, Rehoboam "falls victim to Jeroboam's rebellion. The Chronicler does not exonerate Rehoboam; nevertheless, he does seem to place the brunt of the blame for the division upon Jeroboam" (Knoppers, "Rehoboam," 439).

The schism serves a significant structural purpose. Since the Chronicler is interested in the Davidic promise and the Solomonic temple, he does not follow the story of the northern kingdom. He excludes all material that is solely about the northern kingdom (e.g., 1 Kgs 15:25–21:29), which has rebelled against the Davidic covenant and, therefore, has no place in his history. Second Chronicles 10–12 – the reign of Rehoboam – is structurally an introduction to the narrative of the divided kingdom.

Contemporary theology must never forsake the central importance of divine covenant and presence as Jeroboam did. At the same time, partakers of the covenant must not abuse their privilege as Rehoboam did. The schism might have been avoided if Rehoboam's inexperience and self-righteousness did not abuse his northern brothers and if Jeroboam had remained committed to the Davidic covenant. Despite Rehoboam's faults, he is the bearer of the covenant and God's representative. Faithlessness, however, reverses Rehoboam's fortunes. The one who was named "may the people become enlarged" experiences, with great irony, a vast reduction of his people (JOHNSTONE, 2:21).

A. THE ABORTED CORONATION OF REHOBOAM
(10:1–11:4)

The section may reflect a chiastic structure as it follows 1 Kings 12:1-24 (though 1 Kgs 12:20 is omitted; cf. DILLARD, 84-85). The flow of the text moves from Israel to Rehoboam to more on Rehoboam then back to Israel. The dynamic of appeal, consultation, rejection of appeal, and rejection of Rehoboam is the framework of the schism. Rehoboam failed to take the advice of older, wiser counselors. Consequently, any hope of reconciliation between north and south was lost through Rehoboam's inexperience and foolishness. The structure may be schematized in this way.

1. Introduction to the Schism (10:1-2)
  2. The North Appeals to Rehoboam (10:3-4)
    3. Rehoboam Consults (10:5-11)
      a. Three-Day Break (10:5)
      b. Advice of the Elders (10:6-7)
      c. Advice of the Young Men (10:8-11)
    3′. Rehoboam Reports (10:12-15)
      a. Three-Day Break (10:12)
      b. Advice of the Elders (10:13)
      c. Advice of the Young Men (10:14-15)
  2′. The North Rejects Rehoboam (10:16-19)
1′. Conclusion to the Schism (11:1-4)

This illuminates the central feature of the text — Rehoboam's consultation with advisors and his report back to Israel. The twofold repetition of the advice also underscores its importance. The schism is due to inept leadership.

1. Introduction to the Schism (10:1-2)

Rehoboam goes to **Shechem** as "all Israel" **had gone there to make him king**. The immediate problem is why the king of Israel should go to Shechem for a coronation. Many suppose that the relationship between the north and south was based on a mutual contract. There may have been sufficient discontent in Israel that Rehoboam needed to consolidate his power. This is either a "sign of weakness" or "political ineptitude" or "probably both" (JAPHET, 652).

However, the occasion may have been covenant renewal. DILLARD (85) notes that Shechem has a long history in Israelite memory: Abraham (Gen 12:6-7) and Jacob (Gen 33:18-20) worshiped there, Joseph was buried there (Josh 24:26; Acts 7:16), Joshua led a covenant renewal ceremony there (Josh 24), and the abortive kingdom of Abimelech failed there (Judg 9). Shechem was drenched in covenantal meaning. The site probably reflects theological significance rather than mere pragmatism. Rehoboam probably goes to Shechem to celebrate the renewal of the Davidic covenant (cf. 2 Chr 23:3). To reject this renewal is to reject David, and consequently to reject God's own representative (his elect one). To reject the elect one is rebellion (2 Chr 10:19).

One difference between 2 Chronicles 10:2 and 1 Kings 12:2 is that Dtr states that **Jeroboam** "remained in Egypt" while Chronicles says he came to Shechem. McKenzie ("Source," 297-304) believes this is the result of textual transmission (haplography) and Chronicles preserves the best reading. Presumably when Jeroboam hears that Solomon is dead, he comes to Shechem as the leader of a potential schism.

2. The Appeal to Rehoboam (10:3-4)

Jeroboam, whom the Chronicler presumes his readers know, leads the delegation of **all Israel**. JAPHET (652) notes that the tone is not polite diplomacy but confrontational demand. There is no formulaic "if . . . then," but rather a positive demand. Further, the people are emphatic as they repeat the words **heavy yoke** and **your father** (the NIV leaves the second use untranslated). There is a play on words in the terms **harsh labor** (מֵעֲבֹדַת, *mē'ăbōdath*) and **we will serve you** (וְנַעַבְדֶךָ, *w'na'abdekka*). The clear implication is that if Rehoboam does not lighten the load, then Israel will not serve the Davidic dynasty.

The charge is a harsh one since it uses language that describes Israel's oppression in Egypt (Exod 5:9; 6:6-9; Lev 26:13). No more radical charge could be made against an Israelite king than that he was treating God's people like the hard-hearted Pharaoh of Egypt. The request seems innocuous, even reasonable. The implied threat is ominous. Israel will serve the Davidic king but it expects justice and fairness. The threat, however, to separate from God's elect is rebellious. Nevertheless, the schism could have been avoided with servant leadership.

3. Rehoboam's Consultation and Rejection of Appeal (10:5-15)

Wisely, Rehoboam seeks counsel. Unwisely, he accepts the wrong counsel. He consults with two groups: **elders who served his**

father Solomon and **the young men who had grown up with him and were serving him**. The precise identification of these groups is unnecessary, though the first group are the "elders of Israel" (probably longtime advisors to Solomon rather than city elders) and the latter are half-brothers or royal princes from Solomon's numerous wives (Malamat, "Kingship," 247-253). Ahab's seventy sons "constituted one such group" analogous to Rehoboam's young men (2 Kgs 10:1-6; DILLARD, 86).

The counsel of the older advisors is seasoned with kindness. Chronicles changes the wording of 1 Kings 12:7. Instead of saying "if today you will be a servant to these people and serve them," the Chronicler writes **if you will be kind** (lit., "good") **to these people and please them**. The Chronicler changes the wording to emphasize the covenantal dimensions of the relationship between Rehoboam and his people. To speak "good words" (**favorable answer**, טוֹבִים דְּבָרִים, d°bārîm ṭôbîm) is language that appears in ancient covenants with the meaning "to make an agreement" (DILLARD, 87). The counsel of the elders is to make peace.

The counsel of the younger advisors, however, is unmerciful and insensitive. If DILLARD (87) is correct, **my little finger** is a reference to the male sexual organ, a statement of sheer bravado and vulgarity. The young men intended to protect their own interests rather than the interests of the people. They are willing to **scourge** the people in order to achieve more than Solomon.

The contrast between the elders and young men reflects the contrast between service and selfishness. The former apply for mercy, but the latter increase the misery. The former invest in the dynamics of agreement and cooperation, but the latter consume the labors of others. The former model a humility that yields healing, but the latter model an arrogant egoism that fosters schism. When leaders look to their peers, they may be served by self-interestedness, but when they look to experience, they may be served by wisdom.

While the people requested relief from the harsh (הִקְשָׁה, hiqšāh) labor Solomon had imposed, Rehoboam responds to them **harshly** (קָשָׁה, qāšāh). God turned the **events** of that day as he fulfilled his prophecy to **Jeroboam through Ahijah** (cf. 1 Kgs 11:26-39). God stood behind the events of that day even though the people and Rehoboam were fully responsible for their own actions (JOHNSTONE,

2:23). God punished Israel for the sins of Solomon. The Chronicler does not mention the sins of Solomon — for reasons noted previously — but his readers would recognize the allusion to 1 Kings 11:29-33. The Chronicler presumes the readers' knowledge of the totality of the events assumed by the Chronicler's allusion. That the Chronicler regards this as God's work does not mean he understands the schism as neutral or even profitable. God can work through an agent without endorsing evil (cf. Gen 45:3-9; 50:10).

4. The Rejection of Rehoboam (10:16-19)

All Israel sees the king's refusal and so they **all** go home (lit., "they went to their tents"). The division of the kingdom is succinctly stated in a few narrative sentences, but the theological meaning is embedded in the poetic response of the people. The poem contrasts strongly with 1 Chronicles 12:18 (Williamson, "We Are Yours," 172-176).

1 Chr 12:18	2 Chr 10:16
We are yours, O David!	What share do we have in David,
We are with you, O son of Jesse!	what part in Jesse's son?
Success, success to you	To your tents, O Israel!
and success to those who help you	Look after your own house, O David!
for your God will help you.	

First Chronicles 12:18 stood at the center of David's growing army in the wilderness at Ziklag and Hebron, which included representatives from all Israel and culminated in David's coronation as king by all Israel. Those who once hitched their wagon to David now reject his dynasty.

This language alludes to the Conquest and subsequent inheritance (JOHNSTONE, 2:28). The north rejects the single corporate identity of Israel and atomizes it into parcels of inheritance. "So far as the northern tribes are concerned, this is the definitive break (cf. Gen. 31:14): they have freed themselves and their heirs from any allegiance to the house of David." In fact, JOHNSTONE (2:28) believes that "back to your tents" implies military preparation (cf. 2 Sam 20:1), and Rehoboam's planned military response may support this (2 Chr 11:1). The language is inflammatory and a call to "open revolt" (DILLARD, 87). While the Israel that lived in the **towns of Judah** remained loyal to David, **all the** other **Israelites went home**.

Rehoboam's response is rather dense. He attempts to impose his authority. He sends **Adoniram, who was in charge of forced labor,** to deal with the situation — the one who epitomizes Israel's harsh feelings toward their harsh labor — but he is stoned and Rehoboam escaped to Jerusalem. Ironically, David's grandson had to flee from fellow Israelites when it was Israel that came to David some eighty years earlier.

The final result is Israel's **rebellion**. SELMAN (2:364) believes this is a neutral term because it really only applies to apostate Israel under Jeroboam's idolatry. But there is no evidence that the term can be used neutrally (only other uses in Chronicles are 2 Chr 21:8,10[2]). Literally, the text reads that "Israel has transgressed against the house of David." Israel sinned against the house of David through schism, and this is a sin against Yahweh himself.

5. The Conclusion to the Schism (11:1-4)

In response to the schism and the implied threat of military conflict, Rehoboam returns to **Jerusalem** in order to muster an army from **the house of Judah and Benjamin**. He intended to **regain** his **kingdom**.

However, the **word of the LORD came to Shemaiah the** prophet. God stops Rehoboam from pursuing his military ends. He must not fight against his **brothers**, but every man is to "return to his home" (**go home**). In contrast with returning to "tents," the men of **Judah and Benjamin** return to their homes. Even when there is a schism, war is inappropriate. Rehoboam's gathered army **obeyed the words of the LORD** and did not march **against Jeroboam**. Whereas previously Rehoboam would not listen (שָׁמַע, *šāmaʻ*) to Jeroboam and Israel (2 Chr 10:15), he (along with the rest of Judah and Benjamin) did listen ("obeyed," וַיִּשְׁמְעוּ, *wayyišmᵊʻû*) to God (2 Chr 11:4).

The schism is an accepted reality. It is a divine judgment. The rebellion, as JAPHET (659) writes, was — in some sense — "the will of God." God's prophetic word explicitly says, "this thing is from me" (**this is my doing**). Through the agency of human beings (Jeroboam, Rehoboam, the people of Israel and Judah), God achieved his purpose.

B. REHOBOAM CONSOLIDATES HIS BASE (11:5-23)

Recognizing the de facto reality of the schism, Rehoboam moves to consolidate his remaining kingdom. He does this in three ways: (a) he strengthens some cities (2 Chr 11:5-12), (b) he encourages the Jerusalem temple cultus (2 Chr 11:13-17), and (3) his family administers Judah (2 Chr 11:18-23). Rehoboam will not lose the south. He attends to necessary administrative and religious functions that ensure his viability in the south.

This material is unique to Chronicles. Goldingay (102-104) suggests a contrast with Jeroboam (1 Kgs 12:25–14:20) who built cities, instituted an apostate cult, and was judged by God. Rehoboam is blessed, but Jeroboam is condemned. Most believe Rehoboam is blessed by God in his initial three years. The kingdom of Judah is first **strengthened** (2 Chr 11:17), and then Rehoboam "abandoned the law of the LORD" (2 Chr 12:1). Consequently, Rehoboam enjoyed peace and blessing because he obeyed God's prohibition against war with the north, but God punishes him when he forsakes the Lord (WILLIAMSON, 243; DILLARD, 92-99).

However, this material might serve to consolidate Rehoboam's position rather than signaling a time of communion with God. SELMAN (2:365-366) sees Rehoboam as a fundamentally evil king who enjoyed blessings in his early years due to the humility of the **priests and Levites** who joined the south. The Chronicler offers his general assessment of Rehoboam in 2 Chronicles 12:14: "He did evil because he did not set his heart on seeking the LORD." No other king who engaged in building projects and was blessed with large families is criticized. Only Rehoboam is judged negatively when at the same time he engages in city-building (cf. 2 Chr 14:5; 17:12; 26:6; 27:4; 32:29). Given his status as an evil king, "why [is] city building attributed to Rehoboam" at all? (Garfinkel, 72). Rehoboam's measures in 2 Chronicles 11:5-23 are political consolidation rather than spiritual devotion (JOHNSTONE, 2:31-39). The spiritual strength of the kingdom arises from the devotion of the northern Levites who sought the Lord. They strengthened the kingdom rather than Rehoboam (2 Chr 11:16-17). In any event, his success is short-lived since Pharaoh Shishak will remove his wealth and power in his fifth year (2 Chr 12:2). Just when Rehoboam is strong (2 Chr 12:1), God demonstrates how weak he really is.

1. City-Building (11:5-12)

Rehoboam's city-building has occasioned debate. The archaeological data does not support well-fortified cities at all these locations during the reign of Rehoboam, but it is generally agreed the list "represents historical information which [the Chronicler] derived from some ancient source" (Miller, 274). Some conclude that this list actually belongs to Hezekiah's preparation for an Assyrian invasion (Na'aman, "Hezekiah's," 5-21; "Date," 74-77) or Josiah's preparation for an Egyptian invasion (Fritz, 46-53). Others believe it was started during the reign of Rehoboam but only finished in later years (Herrmann, 72-78).

However, Hobbs (41-64) demonstrates that these studies are based on a false premise, that is, the cities were intended as defensive fortresses. Instead, they served an administrative function for taxation and internal security. They consolidate Rehoboam's political and economic control over Judah. The building program is not linked to Shishak's invasion, but to the succession narrative. These are Rehoboam's administrative measures to retain control. The conclusion of this section makes this very point: **So Judah and Benjamin were his**, literally, "Judah and Benjamin belonged to him" (cf. NEB, "Thus he retained possession of Judah and Benjamin.").

The defensive interpretation fails. The location of these cities leaves gaping holes in the defensive line, and there are no cities built for defense north of Jerusalem. Further, the archaeological evidence does not support walled, defensive cities, and the cities are located on major internal roadways rather than on defensive perimeters.

However, the key interpretive point is the meaning of the term **defense** (מְצֻרוֹת [m^eṣurôth] or מָצוֹר [māṣôr]; 2 Chr 11:5,10,11,23; cf. 2 Chr 8:5; 12:4; 14:6; 21:3; 32:10). The term primarily means "siege" with the idea of confining or restraining (Hobbs, 51-53). Thus, the cities were "built for *constraint*, and this is the method by which he retained Judah and Benjamin." Their function is "*internal security*." Supporting this thesis is the fact that Rehoboam disperses **some of his sons throughout the districts of Judah and Benjamin, and to all** these **cities** as administrative personnel (2 Chr 11:23). The list of cities resembles the administrative districts of Joshua 15 (Hobbs, 53-54, 62-63).

Rehoboam secures his kingdom by his own city-building project. He distributes loyal people throughout these cities, arms them, and lavishly supplies them. Rehoboam's goal is to maintain control of Judah and Benjamin. Theologically, Rehoboam has taken his future into his own hands. He secured his kingdom. Because Rehoboam worked against the purposes of God and rested in his own power, wealth, and status, God humbled him by an Egyptian invasion.

2. Faithful Israelites (11:13-17)

This material is unique to Chronicles. **The priests and Levites** who were scattered throughout the nation of Israel **sided with** the Davidic king. Thus, Chronicles unites the Davidic dynasty, Jerusalem, and the temple. The **Levites** left their **pasturelands and property** in order to come to **Judah and Jerusalem**. Levitical cities were situated throughout Israel (cf. 1 Chr 6:54; 13:2), but they were abandoned when the schism's religious ramifications became clear.

The northern king rejected the Levites as **priests of the LORD** and substituted his own priests at the altars he had erected. DILLARD (97-98) points out that Chronicles has enhanced Jeroboam's apostasy with a reference to **goat** idols (cf. Lev 17:7). Interestingly, the two instances of **calf** worship are on the heels of Egyptian experiences (Israel from Egypt at Sinai and Jeroboam from exile in Egypt). Otherwise, calf worship is unknown in Palestine (Oswalt, 13-20). Chronicles emphasizes the depth of Jeroboam's apostasy in contrast to Levitical faithfulness.

However, it was not just Levites who abandoned Jeroboam. Some from **every tribe of Israel** joined the exodus. It is significant that Chronicles not only emphasizes that **priests and Levites from all** (כֹּל, *kol*) regions, but that every (*kol*) tribe is represented in this migration (or pilgrimage). Just as "all Israel" came to David (1 Chr 11-12), so "all Israel" remains faithful to the Davidic dynasty. The unfaithfulness of Saul is paralleled by the unfaithfulness of Jeroboam. The faithful come to Judah and Jerusalem and separate themselves from the apostasy of the north.

Chronicles offers a theological interpretation. Those who come to Jerusalem **to offer sacrifices to the LORD, the God of their fathers**, are those who have **set their hearts on seeking the LORD,**

the God of Israel. The language is important ("seeking" cf. 1 Chr 28:8-9; 2 Chr 7:14). Yahweh is the God of their heritage (**Israel**). In other words, Yahweh is still Israel's God even though the northern kingdom is schismatic. Northern Israelites are invited to share in the worship of the common God of Judah (south) and Israel (north) — he is the "God of their fathers." But those who come must be authentic seekers. This constitutes the true kingdom.

Chronicles notes that *they* (pl.) **strengthened** and *they* walked (**walking** is a plural participle). The priests and Levites and the faithful from every tribe of Israel gave stability to the political and religious life of **the kingdom of Judah**. This stability remained for **three years** as they walked in the **ways of David and Solomon during this time**. Rehoboam does not receive credit for this peace.

The faithfulness of the people is defined by "walking in the ways of David and Solomon." The unity of the "Golden Age" of Israel is stressed by placing the two founding kings side by side — one founded the nation and the other the temple. This is the standard for Chronicles — whether one follows the values of David and Solomon as they sought the God of Israel.

By this example, the Chronicler invites all Israel to come to Jerusalem to offer sacrifices at the temple in postexilic Judah. God receives those who seek him, and if Israel will seek God through the Jerusalem temple, God will hear and forgive just as God has received Judah back from the Babylonian exile. God is gracious to those who seek him. Even in the midst of rebellion (or a dead church; Rev 3:4), God will be found by those who seek him (2 Chr 7:14).

3. Rehoboam's Family (11:18-23)

Most believe this section demonstrates how God blessed Rehoboam. Sometimes large families are a "sign of divine blessing" (cf. 1 Chr 14:2-7; 25:5; 26:4-5; 2 Chr 13:21; 21:1-3; DILLARD, 98). However it may have a different function in this context. If Rehoboam built cities as an internal security measure, the purpose of detailing the number of his children may complement the details of his city-building. Second Chronicles 11:23 links the two by noting that he put **his sons** in these **cities** (with luxury). The administrative focus is emphasized by the appointment of his son **Abijah** as the **chief prince** (cf. 1 Chr 11:2; 17:7; 29:22) **among his brothers**.

The family descriptions of other kings are not as extensive except for Jehoshaphat (which emphasizes the brutality of his son Jehoram; 2 Chr 21:1-7). This is the only king in the entire narrative of 1 Chronicles 10–2 Chronicles 36 whose concubines are noted (JOHNSTONE, 2:37). The number of wives is only counted for Rehoboam and his son Abijah (2 Chr 13:21). His many wives and concubines follow the example of Solomon. This family description is a backdoor condemnation of Rehoboam (cf. Deut 17:17) though he commends Rehoboam's wisdom in **dispersing** his sons **throughout the districts of Judah and Benjamin**.

C. REHOBOAM'S PUNISHMENT (12:1-12)

Just when Rehoboam was feeling secure, God sent an invader to remind him that the kingdom belongs to the Lord. Just as Saul was unfaithful (1 Chr 10:13-14; cf. 1 Chr 9:1), so was Rehoboam (2 Chr 12:2). God, therefore, punished him.

This section is bounded by the occasion of Shishak's invasion (2 Chr 12:1-4) and relief from it (2 Chr 12:9-12). The central focus of the pericope is the prophetic word and Judah's response (2 Chr 12:5-8). The centerpiece of the narrative illustrates "the effectiveness of Rehoboam's repentance" which is one of Chronicles's "constant reminders of God's offer of restoration" (SELMAN, 2:372). This is the Chronicler's (2 Chr 12:5-8,12) addition to 1 Kings 14:21-31. Rather than retribution, the main theme is grace to the humble.

1. The Invasion of Shishak (12:1-4)

Chronicles emphasizes that Rehoboam **established** (כוּן, *kûn*) himself as king (cf. 2 Chr 12:13 where חזק [*ḥzqh*] is translated "established" but **strong** in 2 Chr 12:1). Elsewhere the Lord establishes his kings (cf. 1 Chr 14:2; 17:24; 2 Chr 17:5), especially in the Davidic promises (1 Chr 17:11-12,14; 22:10; 28:7). Rehoboam sought strength in himself rather than in God (JOHNSTONE, 2:40). This sense of security was an abandonment of **the law of the LORD** rather than an effect (**after** is not necessarily a temporal indicator but may reflect simultaneity). To abandon the Torah is the epitome of unfaithfulness. To forsake the Torah is to forsake God himself (cf. 1 Chr 28:9; 2 Chr 7:14,19,22; 12:5; 15:2; 21:10; 24:18,20,24; 29:6; 34:25).

While Dtr briefly mentions the invasion of Shishak (1 Kgs 14:25), he does not explicitly connect it with Judah's unfaithfulness. Chronicles, however, leaves no doubt. Shishak invaded **because they had been unfaithful to the LORD** (2 Chr 12:2). "Unfaithful" (מעל, *ma'al*) is a key word that appears at the beginning and end of the genealogies (1 Chr 2:5; 9:1) and at the beginning and end of the monarchy (1 Chr 10:13; 2 Chr 36:14) as well as dispersed throughout the narrative of the divided monarchy (2 Chr 26:16,18; 28:19,22; 29:6,19; cf. SELMAN, 2:373). God punishes Judah's unfaithfulness through Shishak.

Shishak (Shoshenq I) was the first Pharaoh of the 22nd dynasty. He came to power ca. 945 B.C. when the previous Pharaoh (Psusennes II) left no male heir. He died in 924 B.C. (Kitchen, *Third*, 287-302). While Solomon reigned, Shishak made no attempt to reassert Egyptian power in the region. However, a divided Israel provided an opportunity. Shishak harbored the fugitive Jeroboam during the latter years of Solomon (1 Kgs 11:26-40).

Shishak used some border incidents (incursions into Egyptian territory by Semitic tribesmen) to launch his invasion of Palestine during the spring and summer of 925 B.C. (Kitchen, *Third*, 296-300; "Shishak's," 33; Mazar, "Campaign," 57-66). Details about the invasion come from a triumphal relief preserved in the Temple of Amon at Karnak. The main attack was launched against Gaza after which Shishak sent a task force into the southern regions of Judah and Simeon (including Beersheba, Hebron, and Arad). The main army proceeded through the borderlands of Philistia and Judah to Aijalon and Gibeon where Shishak camped a few miles outside of Jerusalem. Rehoboam paid the Egyptian Pharaoh a huge tribute. However, Shishak did not stop with Judah. He also invaded the northern kingdom and conquered the cities of Shechem, Tirzah, and Megiddo (among others). Instead of paying tribute, Jeroboam hid in Transjordan. Shishak did not pursue his onetime associate. The Egyptian Pharaoh left two impoverished kings in his wake along with several destroyed cities (as archaeological evidence confirms).

Shishak's goal was not to conquer and maintain territory. It may have been to open trade routes that Solomon had heavily taxed or simply to plunder the wealth of Solomon's kingdom (Redford, 11). Shishak probably returned to Egypt with Solomon's gold and the means to enrich his kingdom by a subdued Palestine. Because Shishak died the next year, his son Osorkon I (ca. 924–889 B.C.) controlled this wealth. "During the first 4 years of his reign," Kitchen (*Third*, 303) writes, "Osorkon I bestowed handsome gifts of gold and silver vessels and furnishings upon the temples of the major deities of Egypt." His total gift to the gods was "at least 383 tons of precious metal."

The 60,000 horsemen is probably a textual error that should read 6,000 (just as 2 Chr 9:25 preserves the better reading of 4,000 over against 1 Kings 4:26's 40,000). Otherwise, the numbers are reasonable. The 1200 chariots are comparable to the 924 chariots Tuthmosis III captured in Canaan and the 1,034 captured by Amenophis. Also, in 853 B.C., Ben-Hadad II of Syria (Aram) mustered 1200 chariots against Assyria (Kitchen, *Third*, 288-289; cf. *ANET*, 237, 246-247, 278). Chronicles's reference to **innumerable** is another example of hyperbole. The **Libyans** and **Sukkites** were conquered people from the west of Egypt and the **Cushites** were Nubians from the south of Egypt (Kitchen, *Third*, 290-292). Of the **fortified cities** listed in 11:5-12, only Aijalon appears on Shishak's list of cities, but the list is damaged and partial (Kitchen, *Third*, 300; Redford, 11, n. 74).

Theologically, God uses national events to serve his purposes. God desires that the nations of the earth come to Jerusalem to acknowledge his grace (as the Queen of Sheba), but when his people are unfaithful, God brings the nations to punish them (Assyria, Babylon). Shishak is the instrument of God's wrath against Judah. That Shishak invaded Palestine was obvious to all, but that he was the hand of God was a matter of prophetic insight. The Chronicler's postexilic community sees in God's exile of his people (2 Chr 9:1) the same divine work of judgment.

2. The Prophetic Word (12:5-8)

Unique to Chronicles, this material reflects his theological interests: prophetic confrontation, humble repentance, and God's gracious response. It offers the hope of restoration in postexilic Judah just as it continues to give hope to penitent believers.

Shishak did not capture Jerusalem, but he reached Gibeon. While **Rehoboam** and the **leaders of Judah** were assembled to discuss Shishak's presence, **the prophet Shemaiah** (cf. 2 Chr 11:2-4; 12:15) proclaimed the Lord's message: **You have abandoned me; therefore, I now abandon you to Shishak**. The prophet articulates the principle of 2 Chronicles 7:14: if God's people seek him, he will be found; but if they forsake him, he will forsake them. As JOHNSTONE (2:42) points out, this is not a function of retribution but a "corollary of sacramental thinking," that is, God is a relational God who seeks holy communion with his people. God will receive them as they receive him, and he will reject them as they reject him. God's holiness demands a sanctified oneness (thus, the people recognize the justice of God, cf. 2 Chr 12:6), but his love yearns for relationship.

Humility (כָּנַע, *kāna'*) is a key word (cf. 2 Chr 7:14) in this context (2 Chr 12:6,7[2],12). God responds to humility, and Israel's **leaders humbled themselves** with their confession that the **LORD is just** (NRSV, "in the right"). The people admit their guilt and accept their punishment. The text recalls Solomon's temple prayer and appeals to God's restoring grace.

In response, God offers grace, but with consequences. God spares Jerusalem but he removes its wealth. God grants Judah a "little escape" (כִּמְעַט לִפְלֵיטָה, *kim'aṭ liphlêṭāh*, **deliverance**). Nevertheless, divine righteousness and prudence teach Judah a lesson. They must **learn the difference between serving me and serving the kings of other lands**. God uses history pedagogically. He teaches his people through punishment and discipline in order to foster a genuine relationship. This is the function of God's narrative history both as he works in it and teaches through it.

3. Jerusalem Subdued but Saved (12:9-12)

Second Chronicles 12:9-11 essentially reproduces 1 Kings 14:26-28. The contextual adjustment, however, is that the loss of the **treasures of the temple of the LORD** is the consequence of Judah's unfaithfulness. Though God spared the city, he did not spare the gold. Jerusalem is impoverished, and so much so that

Rehoboam can only replace Solomon's decorative **gold shields** with **bronze** ones.

Chronicles highlights the gold shields because they were probably the most luxurious and decorative items in the temple. Judah enjoyed luxury and glory, but only for a short time. Stripping the temple's luxury reflects the diminished glory of God. The relationship between God and his people has suffered, and consequently the temple suffers. The bronze shields are a reminder of Judah's unfaithfulness.

Nevertheless, when confronted with the prophetic word, Rehoboam humbled himself. In response, **the LORD's anger turned from him, and he was not totally destroyed**. Chronicles adds, almost incidentally but also for the sake of explanation, that **there was some good in Judah**. We may presume that the "good things" include the devotion of the Levites detailed in 2 Chronicles 11:13-17 because 2 Chronicles 19:3 uses the same expression in reference to worship renewal.

Theologically, worship renewal, seeking God, and humbling ourselves before him are expressions of our continued yearning to know God. Despite failures and sins, God is gracious toward those who seek him. The critical point is whether the heart is dedicated to seek him, because God already seeks us (cf. 1 Chr 28:9). This is a message of grace for postexilic Israel as well as for contemporary Christians.

D. EVALUATION OF REHOBOAM (12:13-16)

The summary judgment about Rehoboam's reign is negative. He **established himself** (in contrast to God establishing him; cf. 2 Chr 12:1), and **he did evil because he had not set his heart on seeking the LORD**. The same language describes Saul (1 Chr 10:13-14). Rehoboam became a "new Saul" (JOHNSTONE, 2:47). His heart was not like the heart of his grandfather David. Rehoboam, based on how Chronicles evaluates future kings (cf. 2 Chr 21:6; 33:2; 36:5,9,12), is an evil king. This contrasts with the descriptions of good kings (2 Chr 14:4,7; 20:3-4; 26:4-5; 30:19; 31:21; 34:3). As WILLIAMSON (249) notes, Chronicles "probably intends us to view the account of that specific act of apostasy [described in 2 Chr 12] as illustrative of the general nature of Rehoboam's reign." What preserved Judah in their crisis was not Rehoboam, but the leaders of Judah and the "good things" among them.

The **continual warfare between Rehoboam and Jeroboam** is probably an indication of Rehoboam's (as well as Jeroboam's) continual evil. This detail probably comes from some noncanonical source, such as the prophetic records of **Shemaiah** and **Iddo**. The prophets were not only royal counselors (cf. 2 Chr 12:5-6), but recorders of royal history as witnesses to God's acts among them.

The schism is the topic of 2 Chronicles 10-12. Even the summary of Rehoboam's reign reminds the reader that **Jerusalem** is **the city the LORD had chosen out of all the tribes of Israel in which to put his Name**. God reigns from Jerusalem in his temple and the southern kingdom is the heir of the Davidic promise. Israel (northern kingdom) rebelled against the house of David (2 Chr 10:19), but the priests and Levites throughout Israel and some from every tribe remained loyal to God's choice of Jerusalem (2 Chr 11:13,16). Consequently, Judah is faithful Israel. Chronicles refers to the southern kingdom (Judah) as Israel (2 Chr 12:1,6). Everyone who sets their heart to seek the Lord is welcome at the Jerusalem temple (2 Chr 11:16). God seeks seekers, but the promises of God are through David and manifested at the temple. Postexilic Israel must cling to that promise and seek their God at the temple. God continues to seek seekers. God seeks worshipers (John 4:23-24) who worship him in Spirit (Holy Spirit) and Truth (Jesus Christ).

II. THE SOUTHERN KINGDOM (13:1-28:27)

The schism resulted in continual war between Jeroboam and Rehoboam (2 Chr 12:15). However, a new Davidic king brings hope for reunion. On the eve of a battle with Jeroboam, Abijah seeks reconciliation. While his attempt fails, his invitation sets the tone for Chronicles. The southern kingdom, as the Davidic kingdom, is true Israel. Nevertheless, the Davidic kingdom stands ready to reconcile with the north if they will acknowledge the Davidic king and the city where God has placed his Name. The Chronicler gives a prominent place to Abijah's speech (2 Chr 13:4b-12), which is unique to Chronicles.

The theme is the hope of reconciliation and the necessity of faithful obedience to Yahweh. As long as the northern kingdom exists, Judah does not give up that hope. But this hope is conditioned on the north's repentance. The story of the relationship between the north and south is the story of faith and apostasy. Sometimes the north influences the south to compromise its faith, and at other times the south is resolute in its intention to seek Yahweh. But the underlying theme, announced by Abijah, is the call for northern Israelites to return to Yahweh.

The Chronicler teaches his postexilic community to reconcile with northerners. The temple is the place of reconciliation between God and his people and among his people. Communal worship offered to Yahweh is the center of unity. In the Christian community, the Lord's Supper is that center. Christians yearn for reunion around the true worship of God in the place where he has provided reconciliation. Schisms are healed at tables — whether it is the table the north and south might share at a Jerusalem festival (cf. 2 Chr 7:3-10) or a table in the church of God.

The formulaic introduction and conclusion of each reign sets off one section from the next. Consequently, the structure below follows the successive reigns.

The thematic interests are signaled by Abijah's speech and the constant application of Chronicles's fundamental theological perspective. Articulated in 1 Chronicles 28:8-9 (cf. 2 Chr 12:5; 15:2; 20:20) and 2 Chronicles 7:13-22, God seeks seekers but he forsakes those who forsake him. The Chronicler applies this principle in the history of the kings. It is his theological method, that is, he applies the theological principle of "seeking and forsaking" to the particular history of kings and illustrates the blessings and punishments that follow seeking and forsaking.

The Chronicler is a theological interpreter of history. He elucidates the work of God in the history of Israel, and he understands the relational character of that history. God is at work seeking seekers, but when his people forsake him, he forsakes them. The Chronicler rehearses the reigns of the kings in order to encourage his postexilic community to see the pattern of God's relational interest in his people.

A. THE REIGN OF ABIJAH (13:1–14:1a)

The reign of Abijah is framed by the annalistic formula. Second Chronicles 13:1-2 offers (1) the year his reign began, (2) the length of his reign, (3) his mother's name, and (4) a theological evaluation (**war**). Second Chronicles 13:22–14:1 offers (1) further records of his reign, (2) his death and burial, and (3) his successor (Asa). The material between is the Chronicler's main interest, that is, his battle with Jeroboam (2 Chr 13:3-21). While the formulaic sections generally follow 1 Kings 15:1-2,6-8, the battle material is unique to Chronicles.

Some believe this is a striking example of the Chronicler's tendency to theologize his history and, in effect, create history for his own theological agenda. "It has long been accepted," Jones (425) writes, "that the Chronistic account cannot be regarded as historically reliable." His history is a reconstruction driven by theological rather than historical interests (Klein, "Abijah's," 210-217). He contrived it in order to interpret the relationship between north and south. The Chronicler turned Dtr's evil king Abijam into the good king Abijah (Jones, 420-434).

However, some believe the Chronicler's version is based on "authentic historical details" (JAPHET, 688; cf. SELMAN, 2:377-378). Several items support this assessment (Deboys, 48-62). Even though Dtr judges Abijah as one who walked in the ways of his father Rehoboam (1 Kgs 15:3), the Chronicler presses a more positive understanding of Abijah. His readers knew Dtr, so he cannot hide Abijah's true character. The short reign of Abijah does not fit the pattern of good kings in Chronicles. Something led the Chronicler to omit Dtr's evaluation and tell the story of this victory. Deboys (61) asks: "given the totally negative indictment of Abijah in Kings, how could [the Chronicler] have written this very different picture if he had no other information to go on?"

Deboys (59-62) argues that the Chronicler had a source available to him which reported Abijah's victory over Jeroboam. The annal also contained a summary of Abijah's speech. The Chronicler, then, reports this battle and recontexualizes the speech for his setting. The evidence for the annal is the specificity of the towns which Abijah captured and the analogy of other annals which preserve royal speeches.

Further, as Jones (431-432) notes, Dtr is also selective in his use of sources. He does not report every battle when it does not suit his purpose. For example, though Omri was the greatest king of the northern kingdom (known from noncanonical sources), Dtr gives only scant attention to his reign (1 Kgs 16:21-27). Dtr is not interested in telling the success stories of evil kings. He may have excluded Abijah's battle with Jeroboam for the same reason. The Chronicler includes it because Abijah's speech serves his theological interests.

But how do we account for the different evaluations of Abijah? The Chronicler does not provide a theological evaluation of Abijah unless the continual war between north and south constitutes a negative (JOHNSTONE, 2:50). But he says nothing explicit as he does for other kings, that is, the king was good or evil. Some conclude the Chronicler has a fully positive image of Abijah. But this is mistaken. Abijah's mother is credited with idolatrous worship which was probably present during Abijah's reign as well (cf. 2 Chr 15:16). Further, the people cry out to Yahweh, not the king (2 Chr 13:14). Abijah's spirituality is ambiguous. Indeed, this is the only king where the Chronicler does not have an explicit evaluation. The Chronicler leaves the door open for Dtr's evaluation while at the same time recognizing that during the reign of Abijah God did deliver Judah from Jeroboam. After all, even the evil king Rehoboam can humble himself on one occasion so that Jerusalem is spared. So, also, God delivered Abijah on one occasion even though his reign did not essentially glorify God.

1. The Formulaic Introduction (13:1-2)

The introduction is based on 1 Kings 15:1-2 with three exceptions. First, Dtr names the king "Abijam" ("Yam [a Canaanite deity] is his father"), but Chronicles has **Abijah** ("Yahweh is his father"). While theological motivation may have played a part in the use of "Abijah" rather than Abijam (Jones, 422-423), he was probably known by both names (DILLARD, 101). Dtr may have used Abijam, according to JAPHET (684), in order to avoid confusion with Jeroboam's son named Abijah (1 Kgs 14:1).

Second, the mother of Abijah in Chronicles is Michaiah (מִיכָיָהוּ, *mîkāyāhû*; NIV, **Maacah**), the **daughter of Uriel of Gibeah**. The mother of Abijam in Dtr is Maacah (מַעֲכָה), the daughter of

Abishalom. The difference in name is usually judged a scribal variation (LXX has Maacah [Μααχα]). If Abishalom is a variant spelling
for David's son Absalom, then it might be that Maacah is the granddaughter of Absalom but the daughter of Uriel (one of Absalom's
sons, JAPHET, 670-671).

Third, Chronicles omits Dtr's theological evaluation of Abijah
(1 Kgs 15:3-5) though the note that **there was war between Abijah
and Jeroboam** is a negative assessment.

2. The Battle with Jeroboam (13:3-21)

This material is unique to Chronicles, but probably based on
sources no longer available. The Chronicler uses this incident to
project his theological value — the northern kingdom should come
home to rest in the Davidic promise and divine temple presence.

This section divides into three parts: (1) Abijah's speech (2 Chr
13:3-12), (2) the report of the battle (2 Chr 13:13-19), and (3) the
results of the battle (2 Chr 13:20-21).

Abijah's Speech (13:3-12)

The speech has three parts: (1) narrative introduction (2 Chr
13:3-4a), (2) the Davidic covenant (2 Chr 13:4b-8a), and (3) cultic
faithfulness at the Solomonic temple (2 Chr 13:8b-12). Abijah
attempts to convince the northern army to reunite the country. His
appeal is rooted in two divine acts: God chose David, and he chose
Jerusalem. The north should accept God's election and renew their
covenant with David.

The actual speech (2 Chr 13:4b-12) flows from the past through
the present to the "imminent future" (JAPHET, 690). In the past, the
Lord gave the kingship to David, but Israel rebelled (2 Chr 13:4b-7).
Israel has an apostate priesthood and false gods while the Davidic king
still serves the Lord in Jerusalem (2 Chr 13:8-11). God will be with
David in this fight, so do not fight against God (2 Chr 13:12). Divine
action in the past, present, and future ground Abijah's confidence.

Narrative Introduction (13:3-4a)

Abijah advanced to **Mount Zemaraim in the hill country of**

Ephraim which is located in the original territory of Benjamin next to Ephraim proper (cf. Josh 18:22). Apparently, Jeroboam is on the defensive as Judah invades his territory.

The battle involved a huge number — too large for a single battle in Palestine. The numbers of 800,000 northern troops and 400,000 southern troops with 500,000 northern dead are excessive. For example, the 500,000 northern casualties exceed the total US dead in World War II (cf. DILLARD, 106). Some argue that "thousand" actually refers to a military unit (so it is 800 units versus 400 units), or that it refers to commanders (800 commanders versus 400 commanders). However, the numbers are probably "typological" (JAPHET, 689) or hyperbolic (THOMPSON, 262; SELMAN, 2:380). Judah was outnumbered 2 to 1 and won a decisive victory where more northerners were killed than the total number of Judah's army. The victory was a divine act.

The Davidic Covenant (13:4b-8a)

Abijah defiantly proclaims that God has chosen David's descendants to rule over Israel and that Jeroboam was a usurper. Abijah was probably engaging in the ancient art of "flyting" where hostiles trade insults in order to provoke the other (Eaton, 3-14). On the other hand, royal speeches before a battle are not unknown in the ancient world (Deboys, 54). Either scenario is easily imaginable.

Abijah's argument is twofold as he demands the attention of the northern army (**listen to me**; cf. 1 Chr 28:2; 2 Chr 15:2; 20:20; 28:11; 29:5). First, the divine promise (**kingship of Israel**) belongs **to David and his descendants forever by a covenant of salt** (2 Chr 13:5). The kingdom of David is the **kingdom of the LORD** (2 Chr 13:8a) because God gave it to him. It is a "covenant of salt." The exact social and religious background to this description is unknown, but it may reflect a similar idea among Arabs who acknowledge the sacredness of a bond that has been confirmed by eating salt together (DILLARD, 107). In parallel with Numbers 18:19, as JAPHET (691) points out, the covenant is "a divine grant (holy offerings//kingship) to a favoured beneficiary (Aaron//David) sealed by an eternal commitment." Thus, the "covenant of salt" is "a metaphor for a binding and immutable obligation." God has bound himself to David "by solemn, unbreakable covenant to enjoy an unparalleled privilege of access and intimacy." Davidic kingship has "sacral" status (JOHNSTONE, 2:53). To look elsewhere for a king is rebellion.

Jeroboam **rebelled against** the Davidic kingdom. **Some worthless scoundrels** (lit., "empty sons of Belial") took advantage of the **young and indecisive** (lit., "tender of heart") Rehoboam. Solomon was described as "young and tender" by David in 1 Chronicles 22:5 and 1 Chronicles 29:1. Who are these scoundrels? WILLIAMSON (252-253) believes it refers to Rehoboam's advisors and thus places the blame for the schism squarely on Rehoboam. However, the point is not to vitiate the northern sin but to emphasize it. Jeroboam rebelled and he (along with **all Israel**) now plans to **resist the kingdom of the LORD** in this battle (DILLARD, 108; SELMAN 2:380).

Temple Faithfulness (13:8b-12)

Abijah contrasts the unfaithfulness of Jeroboam with his own faithfulness. The northern army comes with their **golden calves that Jeroboam made to be your gods**. They have new gods and new **priests** for those gods. They drove the **priests of the LORD** from the north and appointed their own. Consequently, not only has the north rejected God's covenant with David, but they have also rejected God's covenant with the **sons of Aaron** and **the Levites** (cf. 1 Chr 15:2). They have cut themselves off from God's redemptive promises.

In contrast with the north, the south has remained steadfast. Abijah proclaims that **the LORD is our God, and we have not forsaken him**. His evidence is the ongoing rituals at the temple led by the sons of Aaron as the Levites **assist them**. The Lord is still worshiped at his temple in the city where he placed his name (twice daily **burnt offerings**, the **bread** of the **table**, and the lighting of the **lamps**).

The contrast is stated in 2 Chronicles 13:11: **We are observing the requirements of the LORD our God. But you have forsaken him.** Consequently, **God is with us** and if the north fights against Judah, they **fight against the LORD**. Cultic faithfulness at God's temple signals their allegiance to Yahweh and cultic unfaithfulness is rebellion.

While most of Abijah's speech has been descriptive, he now appeals to the army of Israel to desist their hostilities: **Men of Israel, do not fight against the LORD, the God of your fathers, for you will not succeed.**

Abijah's confidence, in the face of an army that outnumbers him two to one, is compelling. This confidence is the postexilic community's assurance. Despite their surroundings — a backwater province in the Persian Empire — God is with his people in his temple. God will prosper those who are faithful to him even when it seems hopeless. When God is your **leader** (lit., "at the head"), nothing is impossible and hope springs eternal.

The speech is a masterpiece of Chronicles's theology. It is grounded in God's election of David and Aaron. It calls for faithful response to God's covenantal grace. It exudes confidence in God's ultimate victory. This is the message of Chronicles itself. This speech is the canvas on which the rest of Chronicles's narrative about the relationship of Judah and Israel is written (2 Chr 14–28).

The Battle Report (13:13-19)

The battle report falls into three parts: (1) Jeroboam's pincer maneuver and Judah's response (2 Chr 13:13-15a), (2) Judah's victory (2 Chr 13:15b-18), and (3) annexation of additional territories (2 Chr 13:19).

Jeroboam's Maneuver and Judah's Response (13:13-15a)

Jeroboam had no intention of ceasing hostilities. Even while Abijah speaks, he is engaged in a classic pincer move against Judah. This apparently surprised Judah as they **turned and saw that they were being attacked at both front and rear**.

Judah's response is threefold. First, **they cried out to the LORD**. This is the only use of "cried out" (צעק, ṣāʿaq) in Chronicles. It is a lament term in the Psalms (Ps 34:17; 77:1; 88:1; 107:6,28). Solomon envisioned this circumstance in his temple prayer (2 Chr 6).

Second, the **priests blew their trumpets**. The significance of this sacral trumpeting is to announce the presence of the holy God who battles for his people. "The trumpets were," Kleinig (*Song*, 81) writes, "used to signal the presence of the heavenly King with his earthly armies as they marched into battle." The trumpets announced "the arrival of God on the field of battle" (JOHNSTONE, 2:56).

Third, the Judahite army **raised the battle cry**. They "cried out to the LORD," and the priests announced God's presence with their trumpets, and Judah confidently engages the battle.

337

The battle description has all the features of a typical "Holy War" scenario (DILLARD, 109; Jones, 426). It is prosecuted in the confidence of the Davidic covenant and God's temple presence. The people cry out to God, and he responds.

Victory (13:15b-18)

Chronicles attributes this victory to God's own hand: **God routed Jeroboam and all Israel** (2 Chr 13:15b), and **God delivered them into their hands** (2 Chr 13:16b). The narrative does not describe how this happened. Judah defeats an enemy twice its size. This was accomplished only by God's power. But the *modus operandi* is unknown.

The theological heart of the battle scene is 2 Chronicles 13:18. When Israel would not humble itself, seek God in the place where he put his name, and turn from their false gods (as per 2 Chr 7:14), God humbled them. Israel could have humbled itself just as Judah did under Rehoboam (2 Chr 12:6-7), or as Manasseh will (2 Chr 33:12,19,23), or even as future Israelites will (2 Chr 30:11). But they rejected God's gracious offer. The principle of 2 Chronicles 7:14-22 receives concrete expression in Israel's defeat and Judah's victory.

Israel had forsaken the Lord, but Judah **relied on the LORD, the God of their fathers**. This is the first time the verb שָׁעַן (*šā'an*, "relied") appears in Chronicles, a key term in this part of Chronicles (2 Chr 14:11; 16:7,8). In times of distress, when the people of God rely on the Lord, God will demonstrate his faithful love. The message for postexilic Judah is to humble itself, seek the face of the Lord, and turn from their evil ways. In response, God will prosper them just as he prospered Judah.

Annexation (13:19)

Abijah's victory was so complete that he annexed some Benjamite territory north of Jerusalem, including **Bethel** which was a cultic center for Jeroboam's apostate religion (1 Kgs 12:28-29). The capture of Bethel is a theological statement. Yahweh conquered the golden calves of Jeroboam. The annexation indicates that the war was a border dispute (JAPHET, 697). These border disputes continued through the history of the divided monarchy (cf. 2 Chr 16:6).

These cities are known from preexilic times. The list indicates that the Chronicler was using a historical source, perhaps even a royal victory annal or booty list (WILLIAMSON, 254-255; Deboys, 55-56).

The Results (13:20-21)

The Chronicler's final comment contrasts the battle's consequences for the respective kings. Jeroboam's loss of territory and power was never recovered during his reign, and just as the Lord delivered Judah, so he **struck** Jeroboam **down and he died**. The Chronicler uses the same word that he used in 2 Chronicles 13:15 ("routed"). God struck both Jeroboam's army and Jeroboam. God ultimately rejects the dynasty of Jeroboam (1 Kgs 14:7-11). Jeroboam, however, died the year after Abijah in 909 B.C.

Nevertheless, the Chronicler contrasts Jeroboam's demise (loss of territory and power, and death) with Abijah's **strength**, **wives**, and children. The Chronicler, as JOHNSTONE (2:58) notes, simply records the number "without comment either in approval or disapproval" though the notation "is probably meant to be adverse." Consequently, this is an implied negative evaluation that is consistent with his short reign. Nevertheless, while Jeroboam ultimately died as a result of this engagement, the king of Judah enjoyed a time of strength and family.

3. The Formulaic Conclusion (13:22–14:1a)

Chronicles follows 1 Kings 15:7-8 with two exceptions. First, Chronicles refers the reader to **the annotations of the prophet Iddo** where Dtr cites "the book of the annals of the kings of Judah." Iddo has been a source elsewhere (2 Chr 9:29; 12:15), but the term "annotations" (midrash, מִדְרָשׁ) is new. It probably refers to something like a commentary (DILLARD, 110). This work may have included a prophetic interpretation of Abijah's speech and battle.

Second, the Chronicler omits the repetitious 1 Kings 15:7b, "there was war between Abijam and Jeroboam," since it is already present in his introduction. The Chronicler adds that Asa's reign, the son of Abijah, was a time of **peace** (lit., "quiet"; cf. 1 Chr 22:9; 2 Chr 14:1,5,6; 20:30; 23:21). This contrast between Abijah ("war") and Asa ("peace") indicates the difference between their reigns. Abijah's wars were judgments, but Asa's peace was reward.

B. THE REIGN OF ASA (14:1b–16:14)

The Chronicler expands Dtr's account of Asa. As the chart below illustrates the Chronicler has added a battle with Cush, a covenant renewal, and two prophetic speeches (Knoppers, "Yahweh," 605). The Chronicler devotes 48 verses to Asa while Dtr only uses 16. As in the case of Rehoboam and Abijah, the Chronicler expands Dtr's narrative in order to emphasize significant theological themes for his postexilic readers.

Topic	1 Kings	2 Chronicles
Introduction	1 Kgs 15:9-11	2 Chr 13:23–14:1
Cultic Reforms	1 Kgs 15:12-15	2 Chr 14:2-8
Defeat of Zerah		2 Chr 14:9-15
Azariah's Oracle		2 Chr 15:1-7
Covenant Renewal		2 Chr 15:8-15
Further Reforms		2 Chr 15:16-18
War with Baasha	1 Kgs 15:16-17	2 Chr 15:19–16:1
Appeal to Ben-Hadad	1 Kgs 15:18-19	2 Chr 16:2-3
Israel Repelled	1 Kgs 15:20-21	2 Chr 16:4-5
Building Activity	1 Kgs 15:22	2 Chr 16:6
Hanani's Oracle		2 Chr 16:7-9
Asa's Rage		2 Chr 16:10
Diseased Feet	1 Kgs 15:23	2 Chr 16:12
Concluding Notices	1 Kgs 15:23-24	2 Chr 16:11-14

In expanding Dtr's account, the Chronicler has added chronological notations that exceed his narration of any other king.

1. 2 Chr 14:1 — **the country was at peace for ten years**
2. 2 Chr 15:10 — **They assembled . . . in . . . the fifteenth year of Asa's reign**
3. 2 Chr 15:19 — **no more war until the thirty-fifth year of Asa's reign.**
4. 2 Chr 16:1 — **in the thirty-sixth year of Asa's reign**
5. 2 Chr 16:12 — **in the thirty-ninth year of Asa's reign**
6. 2 Chr 16:13 — **in the forty-first year of his reign Asa died**

The Chronicler's periodization of Asa's reign permits him to narrate his story more specifically than Dtr. The Chronicler is interpreting the theological significance of Asa. In so doing, he does not necessarily contradict Dtr but selectively applies Dtr to his own post-exilic community (Steiner). Thus, Chronicles is a canonical interpretation of Dtr's Asa narrative. While 1 Kings 15 speaks generally, Chronicles specifies chronological periods. Thus, according to Dtr's introduction, Asa removed all the idols in his kingdom (1 Kgs 15:12-13), but Chronicles records that there were two such moments in Asa's reign — one early (2 Chr 14:2) and one after the battle with Zerah (2 Chr 15:13). Recognizing this periodization reconciles some "harmonization" problems between Dtr and Chronicles. For example, while Chronicles says that Asa removed all the high places (2 Chr 14:2), Dtr says not all were removed (1 Kgs 15:14). However, Chronicles distinguishes between the early reign of Asa and his later reign. In the early reign, all the high places were removed (2 Chr 14:2), but later in the reign not all were removed (2 Chr 15:17), which means that in the intervening 15 years many high places came back into use. Dtr speaks generally without attempting to differentiate stages in the progress of Asa's reign.

However, there are problems with Chronicles's chronology. Asa reigned 41 years (1 Kgs 15:10; 2 Chr 16:13), but a problem arises when 2 Chronicles 16:1 places the war with Baasha in the 36th year of Asa. This is impossible since Baasha was not alive during Asa's 36th year. After the death of Baasha, Elah became king of Israel in the 26th year of Asa (1 Kgs 16:8). This is a rather thorny problem, and several solutions have been offered (DILLARD, 123-125; "Asa," 212-217). One approach is theological. The periodization is theological rather than historical where he divides the reign into periods of blessing and punishment. The chronology, then, is simply a literary technique which accords well with ancient Near Eastern historiography (Cogan, 197-210; JAPHET, 703-705). But this literary device, as Dillard ("Asa," 214) comments, "swallows up the factuality of Scripture" and tends to "special pleading" as any problem could be solved by "theologizing." Another approach, popularized by Thiele (84-85; cf. WILLIAMSON, 255-258), argues that Chronicles's 35th and 36th years of Asa (2 Chr 15:19; 16:1) actually refer to a dating from the time of the schism (thus, the 15th and 16th years of Asa). Thiele supposes that Chronicles used an annalistic report that dated the war with Baasha from the schism and that this was attributed to the years of Asa's reign (perhaps a later scribe added the words "of Asa"). Perhaps the Chronicler intended his readers to date from the schism since they knew Dtr's dating. But this would be the only time the Chronicler dated from the schism, and there is no evidence of a textual history lacking the characterization of these years as belonging to Asa. Further, 2 Chronicles 15:10 contains the same expression, and clearly dates the reign of Asa. Another approach (McKenzie, *Chronicler's*, 101) is to suppose that a textual error has crept into the text so that it now reads 35/36 rather than 15/16. But there is no evidence to support this textual miscue. Steiner (229-231) proposes that Baasha in 1 Kings 15:16ff refers to the dynastic line of northern kings that harassed the south. Yet, as SELMAN (2:239) notes, "No solution, therefore, commends itself with any confidence."

The thematic thread which runs through the narrative is peace/rest. The verbs שָׁקַט (*šāqaṭ*, "quiet, rest, peace") and נוּחַ (*nûaḥ*, "rest") are used three times each in 2 Chronicles 14:5-7 and 2 Chronicles 14:1,7; 15:15 respectively. JOHNSTONE (2:59) follows this theme. Asa establishes peace through cultic reforms (2 Chr 14:1b-7), then defends peace against pagan invaders (2 Chr 14:8-15), then consolidates peace through covenant renewal (2 Chr 15:1-19), but, in the end, forfeits peace through lack of reliance on God (2 Chr 16:1-14).

Theologically, this thematic approach catches the heart of the narrative. Peace comes through cultic reform, covenant renewal, and seeking Yahweh. In fact, the language of "seeking" (דָּרַשׁ [*dāraš*] or בָּקַשׁ [*bāqaš*]) occurs more in the Asa narrative than in any other. Seven of Chronicles's forty-one uses of *dāraš* appear in 2 Chronicles 14–16 (cf. 2 Chr 14:4,7; 15:2,12,13; 16:12) and *bāqaš* occurs twice as well (2 Chr 15:4,15). Peace comes through seeking Yahweh, and one seeks Yahweh through cultic reforms and covenant renewal. The message for the Chronicler's postexilic community is clear: God will grant rest to those who seek him.

Structurally, the Asa narrative is divided into four sections: (1) introduction (2 Chr 14:1b-7), (2) war with Zerah the Cushite (2 Chr 14:8–15:19), (3) war with Baasha (2 Chr 16:1-10), and (4) conclusion (2 Chr 16:11-14).

1. Formulaic Introduction (14:1b-8)

This is the "establishment of peace" (2 Chr 14:1b-7; JOHNSTONE, 2:60). The theme is articulated in Chronicles's first line: **in his days**

the country was at peace for ten years. This is the Chronicler's own point since it does not appear in 1 Kings 15:8. Peace means the absence of war (2 Chr 14:5), but it also involves spiritual renewal as this introduction details Asa's cultic reforms and spiritual orientation. The reign of Asa, at least in its first ten years, was a time of spiritual renewal under a **good** king who did what was **right in the eyes of the LORD his God**.

Religious Reform (14:1b-5)

Asa's major reform was the removal of idolatry. According to Chronicles, **he removed the high places and incense altars in every town in Judah** along with **foreign altars**, **sacred stones**, and **Asherah poles**. In this early period of his reign, he stripped Judah of its idolatrous practices. Dtr, however, says that Asa did not remove all the high places (1 Kgs 15:14). It speaks generally about Asa's whole reign while Chronicles speaks specifically about the first ten years. The high places apparently returned later (2 Chr 15:17).

The precise identification of this idolatry is uncertain. The Asherah poles were probably representations of supposed female counterparts of Yahweh, the God of Israel. The use of incense stands, altars, and pillars may have involved foreign deities as well as Asherah worship (Day, "Asherah," 385-408).

Asa directs **Judah to seek the LORD** and **to obey his laws and commands**. Torah piety is the center of Asa's reform movement. The negative reformation (removing the idols) would have little effect if Judah did not turn its heart toward God. Turning away from evil is insufficient if there is not also a positive intent to seek God.

National Reform (14:6-8)

Asa was not idle during peace time. He built cities (cf. 2 Chr 11:10,11,23; 12:4) — whether they were fortresses or walled cities is a matter of dispute. Either is a sign of prosperity and independence.

In addition, Asa raised an army of 580,000 well-equipped men. This number contrasts with Zerah's million-man army (NIV, "vast army"; lit., "a thousand thousand") and 300 chariots. The numerical superiority is the same that Jeroboam had over Abijah (2 Chr 13:3) — a margin of 2 to 1. This hyperbole emphasizes the powerless position in which Asa found himself before an invading army (see comments at 2 Chr 13:3).

Theologically, God enabled this peace-time buildup because he gave them **rest**. **The land is still ours**, Asa proclaims, **because we have sought the LORD our God**. The peace of Judah has theological, not human, roots. The buildup is not the reason for peace, but peace is the occasion of the buildup. Defensive measures do not necessarily demonstrate a lack of faith on the part of God's people. God enables Asa to use prudence, wisdom, and stewardship to defend the nation.

2. War with Zerah the Cushite (14:9–15:19)

This war does not fit the theory of "immediate retribution." This is not divine punishment. In fact, Asa was a religious reformer. Consequently, this war was a divine test (Japhet, *Ideology*, 191-198). God, at the very least, permits Zerah's invasion in order to see if the hearts of his people truly depend on him (cf. 2 Chr 32:31). The function of testing must mitigate against any hard rule of "reward and punishment." God is still sovereign and may use all available means to test hearts (Hicks, *Trust*, 131-135). Therefore, "immediate retribution" must not overrule what even Chronicles recognizes as God's sovereign options. Immediate retribution, then, is not a mechanistic force in the cosmos, but a tool in the hands of a personal, sovereign God. The universe is not "governed by one consistent set of rules" to which God must bow. "Sometimes, YHWH would take the initiative and test pious kings" (Zvi, 223).

Most date the invasion in the eleventh year of Asa since he was at peace during his first ten years (2 Chr 13:23; WILLIAMSON, 256-259; DILLARD, 110). The invasion is dated ca. 899 B.C.

The War Described (14:9-15)

This section is "the defence of peace" (2 Chr 14:9-15; JOHNSTONE, 2:62). The blessing of peace is threatened by an invasion from the south. Asa defends this peace by relying on God rather than depending on a foreign alliance (cf. 2 Chr 16:1-10). Peace is given by God, and it is defended by trusting the giver.

Zerah Invades (14:9)

There is no extrabiblical information about **Zerah**, but apparently the Chronicler had sources available to him that are no longer extant (WILLIAMSON, 261-263). He is not the Egyptian Pharaoh Osorkon I since he was of Libyan origin and Zerah was a **Cushite** (Nubian — not Ethiopian — in the vicinity of modern Sudan; cf. Crocker, 27-31). Since Nubia was controlled by Egypt (ca. 899 B.C.), it is more likely that Osorkon sent a Nubian general named Zerah. Libyans are also included in this invasion force (cf. 2 Chr 16:8) which further supports an Egyptian incursion since Shishak's forces include Libyans and Nubians (2 Chr 12:3).

The invasion (Zerah reached **Mareshah** located west of Hebron just to the north of Lachish) was probably triggered by Asa's military buildup and his growing wealth (Kitchen, *Intermediate*, 309; cf. Crocker, 32-36). There is no reason to doubt its historicity given the known relationship between Egypt and Judah. Excavations at Beer-sheba show the city was destroyed during this period. Though written in the Chronicler's style, this does not undermine the historical nature of Zerah's invasion (any more than Chronicles's account of Shishak in 2 Chronicles 12 which is independently verified by Egyptian sources).

Asa Cries to the Lord (14:10-11)

Chronicles draws "the reader's attention to an impossible situation while at the same time preserving Asa as a model of calm and quiet confidence" (Steiner, 180). The two opposing armies meet for battle in the **Valley of Zephathah** which is otherwise unknown in the Hebrew Bible (Zephath is a Canaanite city in the region of Simeon in Judg 1:17).

Despite the desperate situation, Asa is confident. The term "cried" (קָרָא, *qārā'*; NIV, **called**) does not necessarily imply desperation (cf. 1 Chr 16:8). Twice Asa addresses the LORD as **our God**. His prayer moves from confession (**there is no one like you**) through petition (**help us**) to confidence (**do not let man prevail against you**).

Asa confesses that God alone is able **to help the powerless against the mighty**. The verbal root "help" (עָזַר, *'zr*; 95 times in Chronicles) is used twice in this verse. This expresses utter dependence on God. An alternative translation is "you do not take into account numbers or strength when you come to assist" (Steiner, 181). In either event, whether it is the powerless vs. the mighty or whether it is that numbers do not matter, God is confessed as the one who holds the victory in his hands.

Asa's confidence arises out of God. He relied (שָׁעַן, šāʿan; 2 Chr 13:18; 16:7-8) on God and came to this battle in his **name**. Invoking the name of God stresses the loyalty of his people and their confidence in his faithfulness. Judah exercised faith by coming to the battlefield. They petition God to defend his own honor. Will God let man prevail against him?

Victory for Judah (14:12-15)

As in the case of other battle scenes in Chronicles, there is no description of the military tactics that Judah used to rout the enemy. **The LORD struck down the Cushites** (cf. 2 Chr 13:15,20). While Asa's army **pursued them as far as Gerar**, it was God who defeated them. The Cushites **were crushed before the LORD**. The victory is theological, not human.

Gerar is located in the southwestern frontier of Judah. It was probably garrisoned by Egyptian troops. Judah took control of the area as they **plundered** surrounding **villages** (including the **camps of the herdsmen**). They returned to Jerusalem with **much booty**. The narrator emphasizes the quantity by repeating the Hebrew term רָבָה (rābāh, **large amount, much**).

While Asa's piety did not exclude the possibility of crisis, he bore witness to the victory of faith as he relied on God. War came to Asa during a time of peace and blessing. God tested the faith of Judah. Faith won the victory because faith relied on a faithful, sovereign God.

Covenant Renewal (15:1-18)

This section is "the consolidation of peace" (JOHNSTONE, 2:64). Israel renews their covenant with God. While the literary connection between the battle and the prophecy is evident, the chronology is problematic. While the battle followed the ten years of peace (899 B.C.), the festival is in the fifteenth year of Asa (1 Chr 15:10; 895 B.C.). The chronology presumes a period of time between the battle and the covenant festival. But exactly when the prophet spoke — at the return of the victorious army or just prior to the covenant festival — is unknown. Perhaps the prophet spoke to the returning army, and in response Asa pursued further reforms in his nation which culminated in a covenant festival in 895 B.C. If this is the case, then 899–895 B.C. were years of renewal and reform.

Second Chronicles 15:1-15 is unique to Chronicles, but 15:16-18 parallels 1 Kings 15:13-15. The unique material contains a prophetic word (2 Chr 15:1-8) and a covenant renewal festival (2 Chr 15:9-15). Second Chronicles 14–15 are a microcosm of God's hermeneutical method. God acts to redeem his people from the Cushite-led Egyptian army, and then he sends a prophet to interpret his actions. The prophet, as God's covenant messenger, explains the significance of the victory. The people, in grateful response, celebrate the victory and renew their covenant with God. God acts redemptively and interprets his actions.

The Chronicler's postexilic community have experienced God's redemptive work through release from Babylonian exile, and they have heard the voice of God's prophets (e.g., Zechariah, Haggai, Malachi). But will they dedicate themselves through covenant renewal?

The Prophetic Word (15:1-8)

Chronicles interprets God's redemptive act in 2 Chronicles 14 through a prophetic speech. Judah depends on the Lord, and God yearns for a reciprocal relationship with his people. Asa's response models how the postexilic community should respond to the prophetic voice.

The function of 2 Chronicles 15 is to drive home the summary points of 2 Chronicles 14:2-4. As Steiner (190-191) notes, 2 Chronicles 15 "draws out the message of chapter 14" and "underscores that Torah piety/seeking Yahweh must be an on-going pursuit."

The Prophetic Message (15:1-7). Chronicles explicitly notes the presence of the Spirit of God in four prophetic encounters (1 Chr 12:18; 2 Chr 15:1; 20:14; 24:20). These involve unknown prophets (**Azariah** is identified as the son of Oded the prophet in 2 Chr 15:8). Chronicles underscores the divine nature of the message from otherwise unknown prophets. Chronicles assumes the presence of the Spirit at work among God's messengers. The speech is a divine interpretation of God's redemptive work.

Second Chronicles 15:2 articulates the central theme of Chronicles (1 Chr 28:9; 2 Chr 7:14; cf. Deut 4:29; Jer 29:13-14; Isa 55:6). God seeks seekers, and **if you seek him, he will be found by you, but if you forsake him, he will forsake you**. This principle is prefaced with a succinct statement of the point: **The LORD is with you**

when you are with him. The presence of Yahweh is involved in "finding" Yahweh. When we seek him, he will be present. This draws out the contrast between "seeking" and "forsaking." Seeking entails the redemptive presence of God, but forsaking entails his absence (Mason, 125-127).

The description of Israel in 2 Chronicles 15:3-6 is problematic. Does this refer to the northern kingdom (JOHNSTONE, 2:65), a future moment in Judah's history, Judah's lapse into idolatry that Asa will reform, the period of the Judges, or a description of postexilic Judah? Most believe that the language reflects the period of the Judges when there was no monarchy (DILLARD, 120; SELMAN, 2:392). It also has affinities with both the northern kingdom and postexilic Judah. It is a prophetic lens through which to understand not only the past, but the present and future.

Just as in the times of the Judges when Israel was without God, priest, or law, so in the northern kingdom and in postexilic Judah — if they persist without God, priest, or law — God will act against his people. God is actively seeking his people, and if he must trouble them **with every kind of distress**, he will do what is necessary to turn his people's hearts to himself, even to the point of creating distress (Hicks, *Trust*, 126-131; cf. Isa 45:7). God is responsible for the distress that fills a land that has forsaken him. Nevertheless, there is hope. If **in their distress**, his people will turn to him and seek him, then he will be found (cf. Hos 5:15). God is active in the world toward that goal (cf. Acts 17:27).

Theologically, Israel lacked three key ingredients: (1) true God, (2) priests to teach, and (3) no law. Torah piety is significant for the Chronicler. Israel must seek God, hear the law, and heed their priests. Teaching was a priestly duty (cf. Lev 10:11; Deut 33:10; Jer 18:18). JAPHET (719) notes the similarities of this statement with Hosea 3:4. The absence of teachers and instruction leads to "a complete dearth of knowledge of the true God."

Azariah's sermon ends with an invitation. The past example of distress serves as a warning to Asa and his people (plural verbs). Azariah encourages strength (cf. 1 Chr 19:13; 22:13; 28:10,20; 25:8; 32:7) and perseverance (lit., "do not let your hands drop"). God is with them and he will be found (**rewarded**). Our strength and resolve are drawn from God's faithful presence. We continue to seek the Lord and engage in his work (cf. Gal 6:9-10), because God is active among his people and our work is not in vain (cf. 1 Cor 15:58; 2 Cor 4:1–5:10).

The Royal Response (15:8). Asa responds submissively. He **took courage** ("be strong" in v. 7). He takes up the challenge and begins a reform in **Judah and Benjamin** and in **the towns he had captured in the hills of Ephraim.** This indicates Chronicles's interest in the north's inclusion in the religious life of Judah. Asa pursues the theme of "all Israel" as much as possible. It also indicates that Asa had expanded his territory in the north. He captured territory in the hills of Ephraim (the southern region of the northern kingdom). Thus, the peace that reigned in Judah was a victorious one. This indicates that the Chronicler is aware that there were other battles with the north than the one in 2 Chronicles 16.

Asa's reforms were both positive and negative. He **removed the detestable idols** from the southern kingdom, and he repaired the temple complex, including the **altar** and the **portico of the LORD's temple.** Apparently, the temple had fallen into disrepair while at the same time idolatry flourished in parts of Judah and Benjamin. While Asa's reign was characterized by reform, the insidious nature of idolatry continually popped up and was, no doubt, encouraged by Asa's grandmother Maacah (cf. v. 16) who was herself an idolater. Asa even removes his grandmother from her position as queen mother.

The Covenant Festival (15:9-18)

The period of reform extended from immediately after the battle with Zerah in Asa's eleventh year to the climactic celebratory festival in his fifteenth year (899–895 B.C.). Chronicles both describes the festival and summarizes the reforms consistent with 2 Chronicles 15:8.

A Holy Assembly (15:9-15). Not only are **all Judah and Benjamin** present at this assembly, but also **people from Ephraim, Manasseh and Simeon** who lived within the confines of Asa's kingdom. It also included people **from Israel** who came to the festival because **they saw that the LORD his God was with** Asa. Thus, Chronicles emphasizes inclusiveness. All Israel is invited, and God seeks all Israel (cf. 2 Chr 34:6).

They celebrated the Feast of Weeks (Pentecost; Exod 23:16; 34:22; Lev 23:15-21), which is one of three pilgrim feasts of Israel (Passover and Feast of Tabernacles; cf. 2 Chr 8:13). The third month would have been May/June of 895 B.C. The feast is a "sacred assembly" (Num 28:26) that celebrates the harvest (Exod 34:22; Deut 16:10). In this context, it also celebrates reform, victory, and rededication.

The celebration portrays a new David and Solomon who leads Israel in festive worship (JOHNSTONE, 2:67). The number of animals implies a covenant meal (e.g., fellowship offerings). The Feast of Weeks included peace offerings (cf. Lev 23:19) which fits the section's "peace" motif. Covenant renewal involved a meal — just as it does for Christians at the Lord's table (1 Cor 10:14-22).

The center of the text is 2 Chronicles 15:12-14. The people **entered into a covenant to seek the LORD, the God of their fathers, with all their heart and soul**. This language is the essence of faithfulness — seeking the Lord with all your heart (cf. Deut 4:29; Ps 84:2). It is the greatest commandment (cf. Deut 6:5; 10:12; 11:13; 13:3; 30:6; Matt 22:37; Mark 12:30; Luke 10:27). They enjoined this oath with **shouting, trumpets and horns**. A noisy celebration overflowed with the joy of communion with God. Israel rejoiced at the temple and table of God for a week as they experienced God's peace.

As DILLARD (122) notes, "the execution of those who would 'not seek Yahweh, the God of Israel' (15:13) may seem harsh by modern standards, but it is in accord with Deut 17:2-7; 13:6-10." The covenant community must be united in its orientation toward the covenant of God. Such radical dedication prefigures the new heaven and new earth itself where all rebels are eternally rejected (Rev 21–22).

The concluding note (2 Chr 15:15) stresses divine faithfulness. Judah **sought God, and he was found by them**. Judah dedicated its whole heart to God through swearing a covenantal oath to him, and God blessed Judah with **rest**. God is faithful; he is with those who are with him. Worship arises out of covenantal relationship and the joy of communion. Worship is our response to the experience of God's gracious faithfulness.

Royal Reforms (15:16-18). After completing the covenant renewal narrative, Chronicles returns to 1 Kings 15:13-15 and closely follows its wording. Chronicles reads Dtr "as highlighting the extent of Asa's reform measures by drawing special attention to what must have been a painful action: he rid (עבר [*'br*]/סור [*swr*]) the land of idolatry and its accompanying practices" (1 Kgs 15:12), and **deposed his grandmother Maacah** (cf. 2 Chr 13:2) **from her position as queen mother.** "The effect," Steiner (207-208) writes, "is to portray this drastic action as one more manifestation of the on-going Torah piety required of God's people and exhibited in Asa's response to Azariah's preaching." Thus, seeking the Lord means covenant loyalty supersedes family loyalty.

The role of queen mother was quite significant. Unlike modern contexts where the queen mother has a ceremonial function, in the ancient Near East she was a "senior counselor to the king." Her role could even "circumscribe royal power to some extent and could represent the interests of people or court before the king, thereby providing a sort of buffer between king and people" (Andreasen, 191, 194). The removal of the queen mother was a political move that signaled idolatrous interests no longer had a voice in the royal court. The destruction of her **Asherah pole** would have sent a clear signal to idolaters within the nation. The Asherah was probably a female counterpart to Yahweh. Baal had a wife (Asherah) as well. It was usually represented by a wooden image or pole (Lipinski, 87-96; Day, "Asherah," 385-408). Her worship of Asherah had probably become part of the state cult and the reason why Asa's kingdom needed reform (Ackerman, 389-395).

Comparing 2 Chronicles 15:17 with 1 Kings 15:14, the Chronicler adds the words **from Israel** and omits the phrase **to the LORD** (NIV marks the words as supplied). Steiner (210-212; cf. WILLIAMSON, 272; SAILHAMER, 90) believes "from Israel" is the Chronicler's exegetical "clarification" of 1 Kings 15:14. The high places which Asa left standing were those in Israel (the northern kingdom). If so, there is no contradiction between 2 Chronicles 14:4 (where all the high places are removed from Judah) and 2 Chronicles 15:17 (where all the high places are not removed from Israel). Asa removed the high places that were accessible to him, but he could not remove all those in Israel (cf. DILLARD, 117-118). The text emphasizes Asa's Torah piety. His **heart was fully committed [to the Lord] all his life.**

But how does one square "all his life" with the stories in 2 Chronicles 16 where Asa fails to fully rely on God? Steiner (215-216) observes that the Chronicler is following his source once again and using a pattern that Dtr himself established. First Kings 15:14

characterizes Asa's life as dedicated to God throughout his whole life. Dtr characterizes kings this way even when they had major failings. First Kings 15:5 is an example. According to Dtr, David did "what was right in the eyes of the LORD and had not failed to keep any of the LORD's commands all the days of his life — except in the case of Uriah the Hittite." The Chronicler's history notes the exceptions in his life. Asa served the Lord all his life except in the war with Baasha and with regard to his foot disease. The Chronicler provides the exception that Dtr does not, consistent with Dtr's own method.

Theologically, even when the heart is fully dedicated to God, there are moments of weakness. Nevertheless, God accepts the heart even with the exceptions. The Chronicler emphasizes the dynamic relationship between God and his people: "if you seek the Lord, he will be found; and if you forsake him, he will forsake you." Asa illustrates both the first and the last. When Asa sought the Lord, he won a peace, but when he forsook the Lord, he lost the peace. The Chronicler, then, has reasons to include the full story of Asa that Dtr did not.

The dedication of **silver and gold** to the **temple** imitates David and Solomon (cf. 1 Chr 18:11; 22:3; 29:1-2; 2 Chr 5:1). This revives images of peace and blessing. The fully committed heart of Asa evidenced itself by gifts offered to God.

Conclusion (15:19)

While 2 Chronicles 15:19 seemingly parallels 1 Kings 15:16, their statements contrast.

2 Chr 15:19	1 Kgs 15:16
There was no more war until the thirty-fifth year of Asa's reign.	There was war between Asa and Baasha king of Israel throughout their reigns.

While the chronological problem was discussed in the introduction to 1 Chronicles 14, placing Chronicles and Dtr side-by-side highlights the significant difference. How can the Chronicler contradict his source so explicitly? Whereas Dtr believes there was war between Israel and Judah "throughout their reigns" (lit., "all their days"), the Chronicler believes that Asa lived in peace until his **thirty-fifth year**.

Steiner (221-223) suggests that the two texts do not have the same function though they are literary parallels. Second Chronicles 15:19 serves as the conclusion of 2 Chronicles 15:1-18 and thus describes the peace of Asa's reign in the light of his covenant renewal. However, 1 Kings 15:16 is an introduction to 1 Kings 15:17. Chronicles, as an exegete of Dtr, clarifies the structural relationship. Strictly, 2 Chronicles 15:19 is not parallel to 1 Kings 15:16 because it concludes the previous section rather than introducing the next one (as 1 Kgs 15:16 does). Chronicles understands that Asa had peace before his war with Baasha. The two texts do not have the same function and, therefore, are not parallel. Asa had a time of peace, but then he also had a time of war that filled the latter part of his reign. The Chronicler interprets Dtr's "all their days" as referring to the final years of Asa's reign. If the date is thirty-six years after the schism (894 B.C.) or a textual variant is the problem (15 instead of 35), then Asa would have experienced war with the northern kingdom during most of his reign (from 894–869 B.C.).

3. War with Baasha, King of Israel (16:1-10)

Asa is portrayed as a pious king who leads faithful Judah, but in a distressful situation with Baasha, Asa relies on the king of Aram. Consequently, Asa loses the blessing of rest. This section is the "forfeiture of peace" (2 Chr 16:1-10; JOHNSTONE, 2:70). Asa not only illustrates that God can be found when he is sought, but he also illustrates that God forsakes those who forsake him.

The War Described (16:1-6)

Though the Chronicler generally describes Asa's rule as one of peace, there was intermittent hostility between the north and south. Second Chronicles 15:8 states that Asa captured some of the hills of Ephraim. Thus, the Chronicler knows there have been some border disputes between Israel and Judah. Characterizing Asa's reign as peaceful is a broad generalization rather than a specific exclusion of any military action.

Second Chronicles 16:1-6 follows the account in 1 Kings 15:17-22 with a few significant alterations (e.g., 1 Kgs 15:17 does not date the incident).

The Threat of War (16:1)

If Thiele's dating (or a textual variant) is assumed (see introduction to 2 Chr 14), then the incursion by Baasha into Judah occurs in 894 B.C., just one year after the covenant renewal festival described in 2 Chronicles 15. Given the Chronicler's theological interpretation, this was another divine test, just as Zerah tested Asa during a time of peace and reform in 2 Chronicles 14. Baasha initiates hostility and Asa reacts. But will he react as he did with Zerah, or will he choose a different path? God tests the hearts of his kings (cf. 2 Chr 32:31).

Baasha **fortified** (lit., "built") **Ramah** in the territory of Benjamin (cf. Josh 18:25) only five miles north of Jerusalem. Apparently, Baasha reconquered his Ephraim territories and invaded Benjamin. Most probably, he intended to protect a key trade-route intersection at Ramah. This effectively controlled trade along east-west and north-south thoroughfares. Thus, the hostile intent was not only territorial but economic. He effectively blocked economic trade as well as any religious exchange between Israel and Judah. Thiele (84) suggests that the festival of 2 Chronicles 15 occasioned this action as it threatened Baasha's religious and political integrity.

Just as Asa had fortified cities in 2 Chronicles 14:6, so now Baasha builds a city on Asa's front porch. The theological function is to test Asa (Steiner, 231). The phrase **leaving and entering** (lit., "coming and going") was used to describe distress in 2 Chronicles 15:5. Will Judah seek God or someone else?

Asa's Reaction (16:2-3)

Unfortunately, the reliance on God is short-lived as Asa faces Baasha's hostile intent. While Asa rejects idolatry, he does not rely on God in this situation. Asa seeks a foreign alliance. He will trust **Ben-Hadad** rather than Yahweh (Knoppers, "Yahweh," 601-626). Instead of relying on God's covenant with David, Asa relies on his family's covenant with Ben-Hadad.

Chronicles shortens Dtr's account by omitting some incidentals (e.g., the fuller name of Ben-Hadad) and focuses the account on a "desperate king whose apparently implosive behavior betrays a complete reversal from the days when his heart" sought Yahweh and "supplied the temple treasury with consecrated" gifts (Steiner, 235). While he sought the Lord and gave to the temple during his reform, now he seeks out Ben-Hadad and offers the temple treasury as trib-ute. Asa hires a mercenary with temple money.

Aram (Syria) ruled territory to the northeast of Israel. The capital was Damascus. The hostility between Aram and Israel was perpetual (including the wars of David in 1 Chr 19), but there had apparently been a treaty between the kings of Aram and the Davidic dynasty. Asa appeals to this treaty as a plea for Ben-Hadad's assistance.

The War (16:4-6)

Asa's move is successful. **Ben-Hadad** prosecutes a war against the northern kingdom and captures Israelite territory. **Ijon** is one of the most northern cities in Israel, and **Dan** is an important religious cen-ter. Dtr includes "all Kinnereth" (a city located on the northwest coast of the Galilean Sea) and "Hazor" (archaeological evidence con-firms its destruction during this period). Instead of noting Hazor and Kinnereth, Chronicles substitutes **all the store cities of Naph-tali**. Such extensive domination would have included Hazor and Kinnereth. Aram now controlled international trade through the region. Chronicles substitutes **Abel Maim** for Dtr's "Abel Beth Maacah" which is probably updating a place name for his audience.

When Baasha retreats from **Ramah**, Asa fortifies **Geba** and **Mizpah** while destroying Ramah. The latter was located 2-3 miles northwest of Ramah, and the former about 2 miles due east of Ramah (DILLARD, 125-126). Asa secured his borders

Asa took initiative. He sought an alliance and secured his north-ern border. Asa succeeded. But his success was only apparent. Though Israel lost its store cities, Judah lost its temple treasury. Both are depleted and militarily disadvantaged.

Prophetic Opposition (16:7-10)

When Judah returns from fortifying two cities in Benjamin, God sends a prophet. The prophetic encounter in 2 Chronicles 15:1-7 is an encouraging call for reformation, but the message in 2 Chron-icles 16:7-9 is condemnation. Asa hears the prophetic word on two different occasions. He submits to one and rejects the other.

This section is unique to Chronicles. It provides a theological interpretation of Asa's seeming success against Baasha. What ap-peared a success was actually a failure. Asa failed the test of faith.

The Prophetic Message (16:7-9)

The **seer Hanani**, whose son is also a prophet (2 Chr 19:2; 20:34), is otherwise unknown in biblical history. He confronts Asa with his sin. Thus, he fulfills the role of Nathan with David or Isaiah with Hezekiah.

The prophetic speech has three points. First, if you had **relied** on Yahweh, God would have given not only Baasha but also the **king of Aram** into **your hand**. Asa limited his vision. If he had sought the Lord, God would have given him the whole land of Israel, including the regions of Syria. Instead of faith in Yahweh, he believed in Ben-Hadad. So, instead of ruling over the whole of the land, Asa only maintains his small kingdom in Judah. The postexilic community should learn that God can restore the kingdom in response to a people who seek him.

Second, the prophet reminds Asa of his previous faith and how God redeemed Judah from the hand of the Egyptians. If God delivered Judah from the overwhelming numbers of Zerah the Cushite, could he not deliver Judah from the border encroachment of Baasha? Whereas Asa relied on God in his battle with Zerah in 2 Chronicles 14:11 (cf. 2 Chr 13:18), here Asa relies on the king of Syria.

In support of this second point, the Chronicler articulates a vision of God that is significant for understanding the basic theme of Chronicles, that is, God seeks seekers. God delivers those who seek him because **the eyes of the LORD range throughout the earth to strengthen those whose hearts are fully committed to him**. The first part of the statement is taken from Zechariah 4:10b (perhaps a common expression in the postexilic era). God searches the earth. By his watchful presence, God is ready to help those who trust him. God is a seeker (1 Chr 28:9). He helps those who seek him. If Asa sought strength, he should have remembered that God strengthens those who seek him. If Asa had remained dedicated to God, then he would have found God and the strength to resist Baasha. Our confidence is that as we seek God, he will strengthen us for the task he has given us.

Third, the prophet announces Asa's punishment. His **foolish** act means that **from now on you will be at war**. Chronicles explains the continual war between Baasha and Asa that 1 Kings 15:16 assumes.

Chronicles exegeted Dtr so that the presence of continual war for a good king is explained by Asa's weakness.

The Royal Response (16:10)

Asa's response to the prophet is the opposite of his response to Azariah in 2 Chronicles 15:8. Instead of submitting, Asa is angered and rejects the prophetic message. He imprisons him (lit., "house of stocks") and begins a brutal oppression of **the people**. Asa's faithlessness likens him to Rehoboam who oppressed Israel. The nature of the oppression is uncertain. Is this religious persecution or economic? Whatever its meaning, Asa's anger against the prophet also turned against God's people. Asa's pride (the defeat of Baasha) blinded him.

The two responses of Asa to the prophetic word – one positive and one negative – are the choices available to the postexilic community (Mason, 54-55). How will they respond to the prophetic word? A submissive response brings blessing, but a prideful rejection brings trouble.

4. Formulaic Conclusion (16:11-14)

The Chronicler closely follows 1 Kings 15:23-24. However, he has some significant additions. Most significantly, the Chronicler interprets the meaning of Asa's foot disease. Chronicles exegetes Dtr.

Source Notation (16:11)

The source notation probably refers to nonextant materials. The book to which Chronicles refers is more extensive than Dtr since Chronicles's coverage of Asa is almost three times longer than Dtr. The Chronicler refers his readers to materials that were still extant in his own day for further details.

The Faithlessness of Asa (16:12)

While 1 Kings 15:23b mentions Asa's foot disease, Chronicles interprets it theologically. God punished Asa's faithlessness with this illness. Instead of seeking the Lord, he sought the assistance of his physicians. As soon as he encounters distress again, he still does not turn to the Lord. The last years of Asa's life must have been preoccupied with his own security, pride, and resourcefulness. This does not mean it is inappropriate to seek physicians, but it is only appropriate to seek them as we seek God. As long as God is primary, it is wise to use God's gift of medicine for healing. We must not separate the gift from its giver.

Death and Burial of Asa (16:13-14)

As JOHNSTONE (2:74-75) notes, the Chronicler "concludes his account of the reign of Asa with mostly his own data on the grandiose tomb and funeral arrangements Asa appointed for himself." It is a luxurious burial (**spices** and **perfumes**; cf. 2 Chr 9:1,9,24) that evokes images of David and Solomon.

What is the Chronicler's ultimate judgment of Asa? Does he die an evil king though for years he was a devout one? Dtr recognizes Asa as a good king. The Chronicler accepts that judgment as well, but the dynamic relationship between God and his people is more complicated than a broad generalization. The Chronicler recognizes the ups and downs of Asa's faith. Nevertheless, he retains the general characterization of Dtr (2 Chr 14:2) and provides Asa with an honorable burial. SELMAN (2:398) comments that "Asa's experience of the grace of God was merely dented rather than destroyed." Asa was committed to God all his life (2 Chr 15:17) though there were times of weakness and failure (similar to David).

C. THE REIGN OF JEHOSHAPHAT (17:1–21:1)

Dtr is more interested in Ahab than Jehoshaphat, but the Chronicler the reverse. Since Dtr details the deterioration of the north in anticipation of its exile, he emphasizes Ahab. The brief account of Jehoshaphat by Dtr sets the stage for the future degeneration of the south through Ahab's daughter. The Chronicler's intent, however, is quite different. He provides hope for the restored.

Topic	2 Chr	1 Kgs
The Reign of Nadab		15:25-32
The Reign of Baasha		15:33–16:7
The Reign of Elah		16:8-14
The Reign of Zimri		16:15-20
The Reign of Omri		16:21-28
The Reign of Ahab		16:29-34
Elijah Narratives		17:1–21:21
Ahab Conquers Aram (Syria)		20:1-43
Ahab and Naboth's Vineyard		21:1-29
Jehoshaphat Established as King	17:1-19	
War at Ramoth Gilead with Ahab	18:1-34	22:1-40
Prophet Confronts Jehoshaphat	19:1-3	
Jehoshaphat's Judicial Reforms	19:4-11	
Judah's War with Ammon	20:1-30	
The Reign of Jehoshaphat	20:30–21:1	22:41-51

Chronicles includes several stories about Jehoshaphat that are not found in 1 Kings. Chronicles and Dtr have different purposes. Dtr focuses on the causes of the exile, but Chronicles focuses on the hope of the restored. The reign of Jehoshaphat, in fact, receives more coverage than any other king of Judah in Chronicles (except Hezekiah). Jehoshaphat, therefore, is exemplary. His reign reflects the needs of the postexilic community. The Chronicler retains Dtr's ambivalent though fundamentally positive attitude toward Jehoshaphat (cf. 2 Chr 20:32-33; 1 Kgs 22:43-44), but he expands the positive aspects on the basis of sources available to him (WILLIAMSON, 278).

Knoppers ("Reform," 504) argues that Chronicles's Jehoshaphat narrative does not follow the more conventional methods of chronology (Asa) or climactic plot development (Rehoboam). Rather, it employs the narrative technique of parataxis where independent subnarratives are joined but not connected (chronologically or thematically). The Jehoshaphat narrative is four independent narratives joined only by the broad context of his reign. The four parts are: (1) Jehoshaphat's Religious Reforms (17:1-19), (2) War with Ramoth Gilead (18:1–19:3), (3) Jehoshaphat's Judicial Reforms (19:4-11), and (4) War with Ammon (20:1-30).

The effect is that Chronicles "juxtaposes" a good Jehoshaphat with a weak Jehoshaphat without reconciling the two. Jehoshaphat institutes godly reforms, but he also aligns himself with the north. The presentation of Jehoshaphat, then, is "multifaceted." While recognizing Jehoshaphat as a king like Asa, who sought the Lord, Chronicles also "proleptically" pronounces a verdict on alliances with the northern kingdom. Ultimately, Jehoshaphat's alliance is the downfall of the south. By the time Ahab's daughter (Athaliah) is on the throne, Knoppers ("Reform," 522-523) notes, the Davidic dynasty seems ended (2 Chr 22:10), priests no longer control the temple (2 Chr 23:18), temple resources are dedicated to Baal (2 Chr 23:18), and there are no more daily burnt offerings to Yahweh (2 Chr 24:14). Jehoshaphat, though he sought the Lord, planted the seeds of destruction as his successors (e.g., Jehoram and Ahaziah) aligned themselves with the north. Thus, Chronicles can extol Jehoshaphat's virtues while also anticipating the coming darkness his actions fostered.

In addition, Chronicles's Jehoshaphat narrative contains elements of Asa's narrative. DILLARD (129-130; "Jeshoshaphat," 17) argues that the Chronicler "has used the Asa narrative as a model for his account of Jehoshaphat." Both have two reforms and two battles. Second Chronicles 14–16 serves as a "type-scene" for Jehoshaphat so that they are purposeful analogies to heighten Chronicles's significant themes. Thus, Asa and Jehoshaphat are redemptive paradigms for the postexilic community. Jehoshaphat, unlike his role in Dtr as an addendum to Ahab, takes center stage in Chronicles's divided monarchy narrative (2 Chr 10–28). The postexilic community sees in his reign not only the reason for their own previous exile, but also the hope of restoration. When Jehoshaphat and Asa sought the Lord, they were blessed. When they relied on foreign alliances, they were forsaken. Chronicles narrates the relational character of God through the history of these two kings: God seeks those who seek him, and he forsakes those who forsake him.

The message for the postexilic community is obvious: seek Yahweh at his temple, rely on his faithfulness, and trust in the hope of his promises. Hope and peace belong to those who seek the Lord, but failure and unrest belong to those who forsake him.

1. Expanded Formulaic Introduction (17:1-19)

With the exception of the initial sentence (2 Chr 17:1a from 1 Kgs 15:24b), this material is unique to Chronicles. The introduction is expanded beyond its usual details (much like Asa) in order to commend Jehoshaphat's religious reforms which yield divine blessing.

Knoppers ("Reform," 505) suggests the following chiastic arrangement.

  a. Fortifications and Army (17:1-2)
  b. Commendation (17:3-4)
    c. Tribute and Respect (17:5)
      d. Reform (17:6)
      d′. Further Reforms (17:7-9)
    c′. International Tribute and Respect (17:10-11)
  b′. Increasing Greatness (17:12a)
  a′. Fortifications and Army (17:12b-19)

This structure stresses the center — Jehoshaphat's reforms. The surrounding material testifies to the blessings of his reign. Since Jehoshaphat sought the Lord, God blessed his reign with secure territory, a large army, and international respect.

Fortifications and Army (17:1-2)

Jehoshaphat **strengthened himself against** (or, "over") **Israel.** JAPHET (745) believes this refers to Jehoshaphat's consolidation of the regions mentioned in 2 Chronicles 17:2. The previous narrative hinted that there was internal unrest during the later years of Asa's reign (cf. 2 Chr 16:10b). However, given the continual war between Israel and Judah in the last years of Asa, the allusion to Asa's capture of cities in **Ephraim,** and the fact that Chronicles distinguishes between **Israel** and **Judah** in 2 Chronicles 17:4-5, the text probably refers to defensive measures against the northern kingdom. While eventually Jehoshaphat makes peace with Israel (Ahab; 1 Kgs 22:44), his reign begins defensively (DILLARD, 135). The Lord established (חָזַק, *ḥāzaq*) his kingdom (2 Chr 17:5; cf. 2 Chr 1:1).

Commendation (17:3-4)

The commendation of Jehoshaphat is similar to 2 Chronicles 20:32 (1 Kgs 22:43). The blessings of 2 Chronicles 17:1-2 are rooted in the fact that **the LORD was with Jehoshaphat**. Divine presence blessed his reign. Yet, not only is the Lord **with** him, but Jehoshaphat is supported by priests and Levites in 2 Chronicles 17:8-9 as well as a gathered army ("with" in 2 Chr 17:14-18).

"The reason for divine support," JOHNSTONE (2:78) writes, "is Jehoshaphat's exclusive loyalty to God." The contrast is strong: Jehoshaphat does not follow the **practices of Israel** (Baal worship), but rather he **sought the God of his father**. Chronicles uses the key word "seek" (*dāraš*) that was so important in 2 Chronicles 14–16. Like his father (2 Chr 14:4; 15:12), Jehoshaphat seeks Yahweh rather than the gods of the northern kingdom. The theological heart of Chronicles is that good kings seek Yahweh.

While the NIV reads **David** in 2 Chronicles 17:3 the reference is to Asa rather than David. Some Hebrew manuscripts and the LXX omit "David" (cf. NRSV). Probably an early scribe added "David" to the text in conformity with subsequent usage in 2 Chronicles 29:2 and 34:2 (DILLARD, 132). The reference to Asa underscores the "type-scene" nature of the Chronicler's presentation in 2 Chronicles 14–20. Further, the NIV inappropriately applies **in his early years** to Jehoshaphat when the line actually modifies his father (cf. NRSV). This mirrors the Chronicler's distinction between the early and latter Asa in 2 Chronicles 14–16.

Tribute and Respect (17:5)

Jehoshaphat did not exert his own strength to consolidate his kingdom. Rather, **the LORD established the kingdom under his control**. Kings do not rise and fall on their own but by God's sovereign decision.

All Judah recognizes the Lord's blessing, and they too bless Jehoshaphat with **gifts**. Consequently, Jehoshaphat, like David and Solomon (1 Chr 29:28; 2 Chr 1:12), possessed **great wealth and honor** (cf. 2 Chr 18:1). The glory of the Lord has reappeared in the material abundance of Jehoshaphat's reign (cf. 1 Chr 29:12). Hezekiah is the only other king whose wealth compared with David, Solomon, and Jehoshaphat (2 Chr 32:27).

Reform (17:6)

Jehoshaphat's devoted heart resulted in religious reform in

Judah. During the reign of Asa, probably during his later years, the **high places and the Asherah poles** returned to **Judah** (cf. 2 Chr 14:3,5; 15:17). Jehoshaphat removes this idolatry though it returns again before the end of his reign (Dillard, "Jehoshaphat," 18-19, n. 7; cf. 2 Chr 20:33).

The theological center, however, is Jehoshaphat's heart: it **was devoted to the ways of the LORD**. The verb "devoted" (גבה, *gābah*) is used negatively regarding Uzziah (2 Chr 26:16) and Hezekiah (2 Chr 32:25,26). It means to "make high" (an inflated heart). Literally, Jehoshaphat's heart was lifted up to the Lord. While wealth, honor, and power turned to pride in Uzziah and Hezekiah, Jehoshaphat's heart remained devoted.

"Heart language" (לב or לבב [*lēb/lēbab*] occur 64 times) in Chronicles is important. A devoted heart yields religious reform, and consequently, Jehoshaphat's kingdom enjoys peace, wealth, and international respect.

Further Reforms (17:7-9)

Jehoshaphat's reform was not simply negative, i.e., removal of idolatry. It was also positive, i.e., teaching Torah piety in **all the towns of Judah**. The king commissions five **officials**, nine **Levites**, and two **priests** to **teach in the towns of Judah**. The officials represented royal legitimization while the Levites and priests conducted the teaching ministry itself. An ideal king administered civil justice and was responsible for instructing the people in their religious duties (Deut 17:18-20; Whitelam, 17-37).

The teaching ministry of the Levites and priests is well-attested (Deut 33:10; Lev 10:11; Jer 18:18; Mal 2:7; Hag 2:11; Ezek 7:26; Neh 8:7; Hos 4:6). Religious reform is based on teaching and instruction.

Torah (**Book of the Law**) piety is the object of instruction. The Chronicler's allusion to Mosaic commandments throughout his narrative underscores the importance of the testimony of the written covenant (cf. 1 Chr 6:49; 15:15; 22:13; 2 Chr 8:13; 23:18; 25:4; 30:16; 33:8; 34:14; 35:6,12). It is an authoritative guide for the religious life of Israel. Just as the king followed the ways of the Lord, so must the people. The Chronicler appeals to an authoritative body of writings that served a canonical function (DILLARD, 134).

International Tribute and Respect (17:10-11)

The Davidic and Solomonic dimensions of Jehoshaphat's reign are evidenced through peace, international respect, and foreign tribute. There was no **war** because **the fear of the LORD fell on all the kingdoms of the lands surrounding Judah** (cf. 2 Chr 19:7; 20:29). This same fear subdued the nations during the time of David (1 Chr 14:17) and it pursued the enemies of Asa (2 Chr 14:14). Consequently, the reigns of Asa and Jehoshaphat are again tied together and linked with Davidic glory.

Tribute from the **Philistines** and **Arabs** (nomadic tribes in the Negev; cf. 2 Chr 21:16; 22:1; 26:7) resembles Solomonic glory though the extent of Jehoshaphat's influence is not as great.

Increasing Greatness (17:12a)

Jehoshaphat's realm grew larger (lit., "became upwardly great"). Chronicles uses an idiom that expresses increasing greatness (also describing Asa's foot condition; 2 Chr 16:12). While Asa declined in his later years because he did not seek the Lord, Jehoshaphat "grew great" because he did. "Grew great" rings with Davidic and Solomonic overtones (cf. 1 Chr 11:19; 29:25; 2 Chr 1:1; 9:22).

Fortifications and Army (17:12b-19)

The Chronicler returns to the theme of troops and fortification (2 Chr 17:1-2). He is more specific about these details (including names and numbers). Jehoshaphat is a well-entrenched monarch, blessed by God and secure in his borders.

Unexplained by the Chronicler, Amasiah **volunteered himself for the service of the LORD**. The only other use of this verb (הִתְנַדֵּב, *hithnadēb*, from *nādab*, "impel/make willing") refers to free-will offerings (1 Chr 29:6,9,14,17). As SELMAN (2:407) comments, "it shows that the sacrificial spirit of David's time was still evident," and the term "finds an echo in the New Testament" (Rom 12:1; 2 Tim 4:6; Heb 10:7).

The army totals 1.16 million men. The army is double the size of Asa's 580,000 (2 Chr 14:7) and is the largest army in Chronicles (besides David's census in 1 Chr 17). This may serve a hyperbolic function that increases Jehoshaphat's blessing above that of his father Asa and recalls David.

In 2 Chronicles 17 Jehoshaphat sought the Lord and reformed his kingdom. In response, God blesses him like David and Solomon (without reuniting all Israel). The message to the postexilic community is striking. Despite the failures of previous kings (Rehoboam and Asa's later years), God can renew the glory of David and Solomon through a people who seek him. God is not powerless. The hope of postexilic Judah is that God will make them great again as they seek the Lord through Torah piety.

2. War in Ramoth Gilead with Ahab (18:1–19:4a)

While Ahab and Jehoshaphat's war against Ramoth Gilead is essentially reproduced from Dtr, his introduction and conclusion contextualize this narrative for his readers. The chart below represents the differences (Knoppers, "Reform," 510).

Topic	2 Chr	1 Kgs
Riches and Glory	18:1a	
Marriage Alliance	18:1b	
Treaty	18:2-3	22:2-4
Prophecies	18:4-27	22:5-28
Joint Campaign	18:28-34	22:29-35
Ahab's Ignominious End		22:36-40
Prophetic Rebuke	19:1-3	
Residence in Jerusalem	19:4a	

The recontextualization appears in 2 Chronicles 18:1 and 2 Chronicles 19:1-4a. The relationship with Ahab is specified as a marriage alliance. Chronicles condemns Jehoshaphat's alliance because it was an act of covenant disloyalty.

The postexilic community must refuse foreign entanglements. If they seek the Lord, he will win battles for them and renew their blessings.

This story also illuminates the role of prophecy. Prophets speak for God and guide royal decision-making. Jehoshaphat (in contrast to Ahab) seeks out a Yahwehist prophet, but fails to heed him. In the aftermath of the battle, a Yahwehist prophet seeks out Jehoshaphat, but this time is heeded. Consequently, Jehoshaphat models how postexilic Judah might respond to their prophets. The people of God must hear and obey the voice of God's covenantal messengers.

The following structure accentuates the Chronicler's own introduction (2 Chr 18:1-2) and conclusion (2 Chr 19:1-4a) as it contextualizes his story.

   a. The Alliance Secured (18:1-2)
      b. False Prophets Testify (18:3-11)
         c. Micaiah's Prophecy (18:12-27)
      b′. True Prophet Confirmed (18:28-34)
   a′. Alliance Condemned (19:1-4a)

The centerpiece is the prophecy of Micaiah (2 Chr 18:12-27), which portrays Yahweh's role in the situation. The false prophets are proved liars by the actual series of events (2 Chr 18:3-11,28-34). True prophets are confirmed by the fulfillment of their prophecy. Consequently, the function of the Micaiah story in Chronicles is to condemn the alliance with the northern kingdom (Knoppers, "Reform," 512-513).

Jehoshaphat's alliance is a lapse in judgment. The prophetic condemnation recognizes that Jehoshaphat's heart was good (2 Chr 19:2-3). Even though Jehoshaphat was disloyal, his heart was nevertheless dedicated to God and God honored that heart. He did not die along with Ahab. Rather, because his heart sought the Lord, God delivered him.

Theologically, even good people can get so involved in bad alliances that they are blinded to their condition. For the Chronicler, even a "faithful king is *justus et peccator*" (righteous and sinner; Klein, "Reflections," 644). David became so involved in his adultery with Bathsheba that he became a murderer (2 Sam 12). Yet, when confronted by one of God's messengers, the heart that seeks God responds. David repented in the face of Nathan's rebuke, and Jehoshaphat renews his allegiance to Yahweh when he is confronted. God does not give up on Jehoshaphat (as he did Ahab) because he knows that he seeks him. As long as one truly seeks God, even when involved in evil alliances, God will be found. This is the story of Jehoshaphat and Ahab: one sought the Lord and the other did not. One was delivered and the other was not.

The Alliance Secured (18:1-2)

Chronicles portrays Jehoshaphat in 2 Chronicles 17 as a righteous king. Consequently, the events of 2 Chronicles 18 seem strange. The tension is introduced immediately by juxtaposing the first line of 2 Chronicles 18:1 (**Now Jehoshaphat had great wealth and honor**) with the second line (**he allied himself with Ahab by marriage**). The former repeats the warm approval of 2 Chronicles 17:5, but the latter anticipates the degeneration of Judah (2 Chr 21–22). Chronicles contextualizes the story of Ahab and Jehoshaphat by adding 2 Chronicles 18:1 to 1 Kings 22:2 so that the alliance is condemned (Knoppers, "Reform," 522-523).

Chronicles stresses the hospitality of Ahab (adding that **many sheep and cattle** were killed) and the temptation. In a sentence unique to Chronicles, Ahab **urged** (סוּת, *sûth*) **him to attack Ramoth Gilead**. "Urged" is the term Chronicles uses to describe how "Satan . . . incited David to take a census" (1 Chr 21:1). Ahab takes on the role of "Satan" in 2 Chronicles 18:2. Jehoshaphat is about to engage in a moral failure comparable to David's own. Just as David, Jehoshaphat fails a divine testing.

False Prophets Testify (18:3-11)

The prophetic motif dominates as Jehoshaphat and Ahab dicker over the kind of counsel they should seek. The prophetic voice often accompanied decisions for or against war. In biblical theology, often one prophet spoke the truth in contrast to many prophets who represented the popular consensus. To whom will the kings listen (cf. 2 Chr 20:20)?

Request for Prophetic Confirmation (18:3-5)

The marriage alliance probably entailed a mutual defense obligation. **I am as you are, and my people as your people; we will join you in the war**. However, consistent with 2 Chronicles 17, Jehoshaphat wants to **seek the counsel of the LORD**. The Judean king uses a key term — "seek" (דרשׁ, *dāraš*). As in 2 Chronicles 17, Jehoshaphat seeks Yahweh whereas Ahab begrudgingly agrees to inquire through his prophets (cf. 1 Chr 10:13-14). Though he has become entangled in an unholy alliance, Jehoshaphat wants to know the will of Yahweh. Jehoshaphat's heart is still dedicated to the Lord.

Ahab's 400 prophets answer the question. They encourage Ahab to go to battle since **God will give it into the king's hand**. These 400 will ultimately be arrayed against one prophet of Yahweh ("many" against the "one"). Ahab's prophets are probably prophets of Baal or, perhaps, prophets who have a dual commitment in this polytheistic and syncretistic setting (Baal, Yahweh, Asherah).

Request for Yahwehist Confirmation (18:6-11)

The prophets tell Ahab what he wants to hear, and Jehoshaphat detects the bias. Consequently, he asks: **Is there not a prophet of the LORD here whom we can inquire of?** Jehoshaphat uses the term "seek" (**inquire**; *dāraš*). He does not recognize Ahab's prophets as prophets of Yahweh. Jehoshaphat's desire to know the will of Yahweh reflects his heart. Even when Ahab reluctantly concedes that there is a prophet of Yahweh in Israel — **Micaiah son of Imlah** — and speaks badly of him, Jehoshaphat responds: **The king should not say that**. Though allied with Ahab, Jehoshaphat does not share Ahab's religious perspective.

Ahab does not expect any good news from Micaiah, but Jehoshaphat seeks the counsel of a Yahwehist prophet. As he is brought to the kings, the other prophets continue to prophesy. As the kings sit **on their thrones** at **the gate of Samaria**, the 400 prophets continually prophesied **before them**. Their public appearance on the **threshing floor** "reveals a greater concern for their public image than for discovering truth" (SELMAN, 2:410). Ahab may have been garnering public support for his venture.

Zedekiah son of Kenaanah symbolizes his message. JOHNSTONE (2:86) notes that though he claims to speak for Yahweh, he uses traditional Canaanite symbolism (bull). His name may even reflect his Canaanite heritage ("Kenaanah," Canaan). The 400 prophets no longer speak generally about "God" (or, gods) giving victory (2 Chr 18:5). Rather, given Jehoshaphat's desire for a word from Yahweh, they now proclaim **the LORD will give** the victory.

Even though they reflect some Canaanite values, Zedekiah's claim to speak for Yahweh may be true. According to Micaiah, they received a deceptive word from Yahweh.

Micaiah Prophesies (18:12-27)

The confrontation between true and false prophets is the heart of this narrative. The kings must decide whom they will heed. The entrance of Micaiah into the narrative plot underscores the prophetic conflict.

This section begins and ends with Micaiah's commitment to Yahweh's word (2 Chr 18:12-13,25-27). At the center is Ahab's sarcastic reception of the prophet (2 Chr 18:17). Sandwiched between these key points are Micaiah's prophetic message (2 Chr 18:14-16) and the revelation of Yahweh's intent (2 Chr 18:18-22). The prophetic confrontation unveils the heart of Ahab — he has no interest in serving Yahweh. Yet, the Chronicler is interested in Jehoshaphat. Where is his heart? That question is answered later in the narrative. Jehoshaphat must choose: Ahab or Yahweh?

Micaiah's Commitment to Yahweh's Word (18:12-13)

The prophets parrot royal interests as indicated by the **messenger** who summoned **Micaiah**. The prophets had conspired to speak "good" (**success**; 2 Chr 18:7,12,17) to the king as **one man**. SELMAN (2:410) notes the "long-established tradition going back at least to the eighteenth century BC kingdom of Mari that prophets should comply with royal policy." Micaiah, however, swears that he will speak whatever God tells him to speak.

Micaiah's Prophetic Message (18:14-16)

Given Micaiah's oath, his answer to Ahab's question in 2 Chronicles 18:14 is unexpected. The prophet encourages Ahab and Jehoshaphat to go to war. His plural imperatives are "go up" (**attack**) and "prosper" (**be victorious**) because **they will be given into your** (plural) **hand**. Significantly, Micaiah does not say "The LORD says . . ." (contrast 2 Chr 18:16). Micaiah tells Ahab what he wants to hear. Micaiah mocks the whole sham by which Ahab seeks the guidance of Yahweh through false prophets. That Ahab expects an unfavorable response from Micaiah indicates that his favorable response is satiric. Micaiah confirms this when he tells Ahab about his genuine vision.

Ahab recognizes Micaiah's satire. Perhaps it was the tone of his voice or his body language. Perhaps he knew it was not the word of Yahweh because it was not announced as such. Or, perhaps Ahab knew that Yahweh did not bless his venture. In any event, Ahab knew this was out of character for Micaiah. He forces Micaiah to **swear to the truth in the name of the LORD.**

The LORD said, "These people have no master. Let each one go home in peace." Micaiah predicts the death of Ahab. **Israel** will be **like sheep without a shepherd**. After the battle, Israel would go home in peace (שָׁלוֹם, *šālôm*). Perhaps the reference to peace is a hint to the kings that they should demobilize and send their armies home.

Micaiah's response offers some insight into the prophetic moment. He reports a vision — something he **saw**. But the vision did not stand alone. God interprets. Consequently, Micaiah's prophetic insight involved vision plus interpretation. A prophet reports his vision and interprets the vision.

Ahab's Response to Micaiah (18:17)

Ahab does not listen to the prophecy to hear the word of the Lord, but only to confirm his suspicions. True to his suspicions, Micaiah only prophesies **bad** ("evil, trouble") rather than **good** about Ahab. The long-standing antagonism between Ahab and the prophet of Yahweh reflects a sustained hostility between Ahab and Yahweh. Ahab's "itching ears" were not scratched by Micaiah.

Ahab rejects the prophecy. Micaiah unveils the future, and Ahab dismisses it. Ahab's sarcasm indicates he has no real interest in what Micaiah would say.

Micaiah's Revelation of the Counsel of Yahweh (18:18-22)

Micaiah is not finished. There is more to the vision. If Ahab wants to hear the truth (cf. 2 Chr 18:15), then he will hear the whole truth. The truth is that the word of his own prophets is also the word of Yahweh — **the LORD has put a lying spirit in the mouths of these prophets of yours**.

Micaiah describes a further vision (**I saw**). The prophet sees the throne room of God where **all the host of heaven** are gathered (cf. Isa 6:1-11). The angelic host are God's providential agents in the world. At this council, the Lord asks, **Who will entice Ahab king of Israel into attacking Ramoth Gilead and going to his death there?** God has his own "war council," and he intends to act against Ahab. He wants Ahab enticed into a fight where he will die. The time has come to remove this ungodly king. After some discussion, **a spirit came forward** and volunteered to entice Ahab by becoming **a lying spirit in the mouths of all his prophets**. The Lord not only sanctions the method, but he assures success. God authorizes a lie in order to accomplish his purposes. The action of the spirit is attributed to Yahweh himself in 2 Chronicles 18:22. The decision to entice Ahab through deception is sanctioned by God. Micaiah's prophetic declaration is that "the LORD has put a lying spirit in the mouth of these prophets of yours."

Yahweh's involvement generates some theological problems. Some argue that Yahweh has a "demonic" or "dark" side that accounts for this action. But this attributes a character flaw to Yahweh's nature which ultimately makes him undependable. Chronicles speaks too highly of the faithfulness of God to attribute this duplicity to Yahweh's "dark side." Others argue that the lying spirit is Satan. As such, God does not ordain the deception, but he permits it (as he permitted Job to suffer; cf. Mayhue, 135-163). But God seems more active than mere permission. The Lord authorizes the spirit to deceive and the Lord puts the spirit into the mouths of Ahab's prophets. The Lord is an active agent rather than a passive observer.

The lying spirit serves the purposes of God. He commissioned it, sent it, and put it into the mouths of the prophets. When Ahab hears his prophets confirm his plan, Ahab is determined to attack Ramoth Gilead. In this way, **the LORD has decreed disaster** for Ahab. The spirit, then, serves God and expresses divine intent. Just as the Spirit of God came upon other prophets in the Chronicler's narrative (1 Chr 12:18; 2 Chr 15:1), so this lying spirit came upon Ahab's prophets in order to seduce him.

Since Ahab has killed prophets of Yahweh, substituted Baal for Yahweh, and rules by his own selfish interests, the use of deception is appropriate. Ahab has forfeited his right to truth. He does not love the truth, but only himself. God deludes those who do not love the truth and permits them to sink further into the mire of their evil. God uses deception to accomplish his judgment. Paul writes that God sends some unbelievers "a powerful delusion so that they will believe the lie," and Paul's rationale is that God does this because they do not love the truth and they delight in wickedness (2 Thess 2:11-12). As Roberts (200) comments, divine deception — as present in several texts (e.g., Ezek 14:1-11; Ps 18:26-27; Isa 29:10) – is "poetic justice" for those who have hardened themselves against the will of God (cf. Chisholm, 11-28, who correlates "divine deceit" and "divine hardening.").

Nevertheless, Ahab still hears the truth. God always provides a way to discern the truth (cf. Deut 13:1-5). While the lying spirit testifies through Ahab's prophets, Micaiah proclaims the truth of God. Ahab is given the opportunity to choose between the lying spirit and the **word of the LORD**. Moreover, the whole process is unveiled for Ahab – he knows the divine intent in sending the lying spirit. Ahab's heart is not interested in a word from Yahweh. He calls for Micaiah only because Jehoshaphat insists. Ahab's interest is selfish. Therefore, God's actions toward him are "hardening" rather than "liberating."

Micaiah's Commitment to Yahweh's Word (18:23-27)

Zedekiah, Ahab's lead prophet, reacts aggressively to Micaiah's statement. The words and slap "contain an element of insolence and insult" (JAPHET, 765; cf. Job 16:10; Isa 50:6; Lam 3:30). Zedekiah believed he had received a word from Yahweh. He claims that the **spirit from the LORD** (or, Spirit of the Lord) was on him. Indeed, God had put a spirit into the mouth of Zedekiah, but Micaiah revealed that it was a lying spirit. Micaiah's response is sarcastic in tone. The day's events will prove who has spoken the word of the Lord. When Ahab is dead, Zedekiah will know the truth.

Ahab imprisons Micaiah (cf. 2 Chr 16:10) and restricts his diet to **bread and water**. The imprisonment was probably intended as a short-term measure, that is, **until I return safely** (lit., "in peace"). Afterwards, Ahab probably intended to execute him (like other prophets of Yahweh). To believe God is to believe his prophets, but to reject his prophets is to reject God (2 Chr 20:20).

Micaiah underscores the certainty of his prophecy. **Mark my words, all you people** is a declaration that "the whole world must witness his authenticity as a prophet" (JAPHET, 766). When Ahab does not return to his home in peace (**safely**), Micaiah's prophecy will be confirmed.

True Prophet Confirmed (18:28-34)

The narrative confirms Micaiah's prediction. But Chronicles is also interested in another question. What is the faith and heart of Jehoshaphat? The Chronicler subtracts most of the details about Ahab's death (cf. 1 Kgs 18:36-40) and adds some specifics about Jehoshaphat's fate (cf. 2 Chr 18:31b). These changes indicate the Chronicler's narrative interest. Jehoshaphat ultimately turns to the Lord, but Ahab continues in his unbelief.

Ahab's Plan (18:28-29)

Ahab persuaded Jehoshaphat to participate in the battle and serve as its main target. The primary tactic in ancient Near Eastern warfare was to kill the opposing king. Perhaps Jehoshaphat agrees to dress out in his royal regalia while Ahab disguises himself because Ahab was the target of the prophecy, not Jehoshaphat.

The theological function of Ahab's disguise, however, is to test the prophetic warning and avoid potential danger (WILLIAMSON, 276-277). Theologically, Ahab disguises himself in order to avoid God's judgment.

God Subverts Ahab's Plan (18:30-32)

The Arameans targeted Ahab since he troubled **Aram**. Jehoshaphat was an ally who had no independent interest in a fight with Aram. Yet, theologically, the motive is clear — Ahab is God's target (2 Chr 18:16).

The royal regalia deceived the Arameans, as Ahab had intended. But God was not deceived. Second Chronicles 18:31b is the Chronicler's addition to 1 Kings 22:32 (italicized below).

1 Kgs 22:32b-33	2 Chr 18:31b-32
So they turned to attack him, but when Jehoshaphat cried out, the chariot commanders saw that he was not the king of Israel and stopped pursuing him.	So they turned to attack him, but Jehoshaphat cried out, *and the* LORD *helped him. God drew them away from him,* for when the chariot commanders saw that he was not the king of Israel, they stopped pursuing him.

The addition makes the theological point. While Dtr makes no explicit mention of God's role or that Jehoshaphat was crying out to

God, Chronicles explains that Jehoshaphat called out to the Lord and God responded. Chronicles only uses the term **cried out** (זעק, *zā'aq*) in lament (1 Chr 5:20; 2 Chr 20:9; 32:20 – all unique to Chronicles). Yahweh, despite the fact that Jehoshaphat was allied with Ahab, delivered him (**the LORD helped him**; cf. the use of עזר (*'āzar*) in 1 Chr 5:20; 12:18; 2 Chr 14:11; 20:23; 25:8; 26:7; 32:8).

Jehoshaphat prayed and God answered. Thus, Chronicles's narrative emphasizes Jehoshaphat's fundamental orientation toward Yahweh despite his lapse. In his distress, Jehoshaphat turns to the Lord.

God drew Jehoshaphat's attackers **away from him**. Exactly how God did this is unspecified. God was at work in the battle to secure his ends, including the protection of Jehoshaphat. God enticed (סות, *sûth*) them, just as Ahab had urged (*sûth*) Jehoshaphat to join the battle in the first place (2 Chr 18:2). Consequently, Jehoshaphat was endangered by Ahab's enticement, but delivered by God's. God will protect those caught in the web of deceit and allied with evil if they will but seek him (cf. 1 Chr 28:9; 2 Chr 7:14; 15:2).

The Death of Ahab (18:33-34)

Ahab's deception could not escape God's sovereign purposes. A **random** arrow mortally wounded him. **All day long** the king of Israel watched the prophecy of Micaiah come true. At the end of the day it was clear who had spoken the truth.

Alliance Condemned (19:1-4a)

Second Chronicles 19:1-4 recontextualizes the prophetic confrontation in Samaria. Jehoshaphat is rebuked but restored. This models postexilic Judah's own rebuke and restoration. Moreover, God examines the heart rather than the technicalities of a person's life. God looks at the heart's direction rather than perfection.

Jehoshaphat in Jerusalem (19:1)

Unlike Ahab (2 Chr 18:26-27), Jehoshaphat **returned safely** (lit., "in peace") to his home (**palace**) as Micaiah promised some would (2 Chr 18:16). The Chronicler "considers Jehoshaphat one of the fortunate sheep" of Micaiah's oracle ("Knoppers, "Reform," 512).

Prophetic Encounter (19:2-3)

Jehu the seer (cf. 2 Chr 20:34) encounters the king in Jerusalem. His message is stern but gracious. The sternness derives from Jehoshaphat's covenantal disloyalty. Hate/love language was common in covenant formulations. Thus, "Jehoshaphat is being disloyal to his suzerain by 'helping the wicked' and being loyal to 'those who hate YHWH'. Fidelity to one precludes fidelity to the other" (Knoppers, "Reform," 513).

The Lord's **wrath** was demonstrated in the defeat of Jehoshaphat's army, but his grace is present in Jehoshaphat's return home in peace. God found some **good** in him. Apparently, this refers to the previous reformation in 2 Chronicles 17:3-6 where he destroyed the **Asherah poles** and **set** his **heart on seeking God**. Clearly, the Lord was gracious to Jehoshaphat in the light of his heart. Jehoshaphat's weakness did not entail his total destruction.

The theological principle embodied in this narrative interpretation (absent in 1 Kgs 22) is that God seeks the hearts of those who seek him. Even if we make alliances we should not make, nevertheless God is gracious toward those whose hearts seek him. This is analogous to "walking in the light" (1 John 1:6-10). As long as one walks in the light, that is, as long as one is oriented toward God's purposes and seeks the heart of God, God will graciously forgive.

The message for the postexilic community is obvious. Despite their checkered past and imperfect present, God is willing to receive all those who seek him, even those who had aligned themselves with idolatrous interests.

Jehoshaphat in Jerusalem (19:4a)

The phrase **Jehoshaphat lived in Jerusalem** corresponds with 2 Chronicles 19:1. "Jerusalem" serves as an inclusio that binds this section together. Despite his alliance with Israel, Jehoshaphat returned to dwell in Jerusalem. Jehoshaphat is where he is supposed to be — in Jerusalem rather than Samaria.

3. Judicial Reform (19:4b-11)

Second Chronicles 19:4b begins, like 2 Chronicles 19:1, with the verb "return" (שׁוּב, *šûb*, **went out again**). Jehoshaphat returned to his theological vocation. His goal is to turn Judah **back to the LORD, the God of their fathers**. Apparently, during his alliance with Ahab, Judah had spiritually degenerated.

This reform narrative is judicial. At the heart of judicial renewal is a theological vision (cf. 2 Chr 19:6-7). Judicial reform is one aspect of religious reform since the judges represent God. Judges must execute divine justice. Social justice is a biblical-theological concern throughout redemptive history (SELMAN, 2:416; Lev 19:15; Deut 16:19-20; 24:17; 27:19; 1 Sam 8:3; 2 Chr 9:8; Job 29:14; 31:13; Ps 72:1-2; 106:3; 112:5; Prov 28:5; 29:7; Isa 1:17; 10:2; 11:4; 28:17; 29:21; 32:1,16; 56:1; 68:1; Amos 2:7; 5:7,12,24; Micah 3:1; Mal 3:5).

Some believe this reflects postexilic reforms and, therefore, cannot refer to the time of Jehoshaphat. Further, Dtr does not mention this reform. However, the Chronicler may depend upon earlier sources for this material though the speeches are adapted to his theological ends (Whitelam, 185-189; cf. JAPHET, 771-774; DILLARD, 147-148). Dtr is generally uninterested in judicial reform and slights the reign of Jehoshaphat to concentrate on Ahab. Consequently, "there is no compelling reason to question the general accuracy of the account" (Wilson, "Judicial," 245). However, this judicial reform soon fell into disrepute (cf. Isa 1:23-26; 3:2,14; 7:3; Micah 3:1,9; 7:3).

Some believe this second reform is actually a doublet of the reform in 2 Chronicles 17 (Albright, "Judicial," 82). However, this reform is a renewal of the earlier one (Knoppers, "Reform," 514-515; cf. "Jehoshaphat's," 59-80). Just as Jehoshaphat returns to Jerusalem, he returns to his reformation agenda. The "early" Jehoshaphat returns, and he seeks God through reforming Judah's judicial institutions. Spiritual renewal involves social justice (cf. Ps 58). His relationship with Ahab was a momentary lapse.

JAPHET (771) divides this pericope into two sections: (1) Judah (19:5-7) and (2) Jerusalem (19:8-11). Each section follows the same literary pattern: (a) Appointment (19:5,8) and (b) Addresses (19:6-7,9-11).

Judges in Judah (19:4b-7)

Jehoshaphat's reform extends throughout the southern kingdom: **from Beersheba to the hill country of Ephraim** (cf. 2 Chr 17:2). Just as he had returned (*šûb*) to live in Jerusalem (2 Chr 19:1), Jehoshaphat intends to turn (*šûb*) Judah **back to the LORD** (2 Chr

19:4b). The narrative illustrates the principle of God's relationship with his people (2 Chr 7:14).

Appointment (19:4b-5)

Parallel with 2 Chronicles 19:8, Jehoshaphat **appointed judges** throughout Judah, particularly **in each of the fortified cities** (cf. 2 Chr 17:2). These judges exercised the juridical authority of the king. This is the imposition of monarchical authority when previously judicial matters may have been handled by local authorities. As Whitelam (192-197) argues, these judicial and administrative centers would have been the renewal of Davidic and Solomonic intentions as well as following the pattern of Rehoboam's administrative centers in 2 Chronicles 11. Jehoshaphat is not so much innovating as he is renewing and extending previous forms of monarchical justice (DILLARD, 148-149; Japhet, *Ideology*, 432; SELMAN, 2:417). The reform was a "practical attempt to reduce the jurisdiction of the local judicial authorities, which were under the influence of powerful families, and thereby eradicate corruption in the administration of justice throughout the realm" (Whitelam, 196). Local courts, therefore, were overseen by monarchical authorities to ensure justice in the land. Jehoshaphat extended "his own jurisdiction" and so restricted "the influence of the local courts" (Klein, "Jehoshaphat," 650). Theoretically, the king thereby protects the weak and innocent in his kingdom.

Address to the Judges (19:6-7)

Jehoshaphat's address articulates a theological vision of justice. As representatives of the king, judges must take seriously their role as instruments of divine justice. "Judicial authority in Israel was not the prerogative of autonomous power; rather it depended upon and expressed the rule of Yahweh and was to reflect his own attributes of righteousness, justice, and fairness" (DILLARD, 149).

The Hebrew root for "judge, justice" (שָׁפַט, *šāphaṭ*) is used 3 times in 2 Chronicles 19:6: **consider** (judge), **judging**, and **verdict**. The three qualities of "judging **carefully**" are characteristic of Hebrew descriptions of divine character. "The quality of divine judgment" is "just, impartial, and incorruptible" (JOHNSTONE, 2:93). This is the language of Deuteronomy 16:19: "Do not pervert justice or show partiality. Do not accept a bribe" (cf. Deut 10:17). Bribery was a particularly subversive crime since it favored the rich and oppressed the poor (cf. Exod 23:8; 1 Sam 12:3; Ps 15:5; Prov 17:23; Eccl 7:7; Isa 5:23; Micah 3:11).

This material serves several purposes. It portrays the social dimensions of religious reform. It supports the agenda of judicial reform in the postexilic community (cf. Ezra 7:25-26). It testifies to the nature of the kingdom as one which embodies social justice for all people. Christians, as instruments of the kingdom, are also instruments of divine justice in the world. They bear witness to the values of the kingdom.

Judges in Jerusalem (19:8-11)

While these officials are not specifically called "judges" in 2 Chronicles 19:8-11, they are given the task to **administer** (לְמִשְׁפַּט, *l⁰mišpaṭ*) **the law of the LORD and to settle** ("legal"; לָרִיב, *lārîb*) **disputes** (2 Chr 19:8). They function as judges in Jerusalem, but their main arena is religious, that is, they administer justice and settle disputes pertaining to Yahweh. The NIV's expression "law of the LORD" is not in the Hebrew text. The text simply reads "to the LORD."

Appointment (19:8)

Jehoshaphat sets up a judicial system in Jerusalem closely tied to the religious system at the temple. He appoints **Levites, priests and heads of Israelite families** to adjudicate concerning matters pertaining to the Lord. The use of the verb "judge" (**administer**, *l⁰mišpaṭ*) may indicate that this Jerusalem court was also a higher judicial authority (a supreme court; cf. 2 Chr 19:10). DILLARD (149) notes that such a court of higher appeal existed during the time of Moses (cf. Deut 1:8-18; Exod 18:17-26). The inclusion of Levites and priests is not surprising given their role as officials and judges in 1 Chronicles 23:4 (cf. 1 Chr 26:29). The integration of judicial and religious life reflected the theocratic nature of Israel though there is a delineation between the things that pertain to the Lord and the matters that concern the king (2 Chr 19:11).

Address to the Judges (19:9-11)

Jehoshaphat addresses his Jerusalem judges. His first admonition goes to the heart of the moral qualification of these judges. They **must serve faithfully and wholeheartedly in the fear of the LORD**. The Hebrew structure (using the prepositional prefix ב [bᵉ/be], "in") indicates three requirements: (1) *in* the fear of the Lord, (2) *in* faithfulness, and (3) *with* a whole heart. This is the only time in the Hebrew Bible where these three qualifications appear together. Judges must respect their role as divine representatives, act consistently with that role, and be wholly devoted to it.

Their role was not only to adjudicate various cases (including **bloodshed or other concerns of the law**), but also **to warn** (only time the word is used in Chronicles; "instruct") **them not to sin against the LORD**. They served as God's witnesses to his righteousness, in justice and in **wrath. Do this, and you will not sin**. When justice prevails in the land, God lives among them.

Jehoshaphat chose two servants to lead the justice system: **Amariah the chief priest will be over you in any matter concerning the LORD, and Zebadiah son of Ishmael, the leader of the tribe of Judah, will be over you in any matter concerning the king**. The judicial system, then, was divided between priestly (religious) and royal (civil) interests. This does not mean that the two interests are severed. Rather, they are appropriate divisions of labor. The reference to **Levites** as **officials** probably refers to "bureaucrats" who served both priestly and royal structures in Jerusalem (DILLARD, 150).

Jehoshaphat exhorts them to **act with courage** (lit., "be strong and do"; cf. the use of עשׂה ['āśāh, "do"] in 2 Chr 19:6,7,9,10). The just king expects just judges to act like the just God. They must exercise the strength and courage necessary for justice. God is **with those who do well**. "Good," JOHNSTONE (2:94) comments, "forms a fitting climax to the reform. It equally echoes sacramental theology: it is in the practice of the revealed goodness of God that the community realizes its own nature and destiny as good."

The call for justice is a never-ending plea on the lips of God's people. We pray for the fullness of the kingdom — with all its righteousness and justice — to come into the injustice so rampant in the fallen world. Spiritual renewal is never complete without social justice, and without social justice, the wrath of God may fall upon any nation.

4. War against Ammon (20:1-30)

As SELMAN (2:420) notes, 2 Chronicles 20 "contains one of the outstanding stories not only in [Chronicles] but in the whole Bible." It engages the reader so that one is led into a narrative world of faith, humility, prayer, lament, prophecy, and victory. The story assures the believing community of God's active work for the sake of his people. The language of this chapter is filled with prayer, prophecy, and praise. "It is as though God's work through Moses and David, in the psalms and the prophets, were all rolled together in this one incident" (SELMAN, 2:421).

This "war narrative" is not contextualized by either what precedes or follows. It is not linked to previous or subsequent events. However, DILLARD ("Jehoshaphat," 18) suggests that Chronicles's Jehoshaphat narrative is modeled after Asa (2 Chr 14–16). The war narrative of 2 Chronicles 20 is parallel to 2 Chronicles 14 and demonstrates royal piety and dependence upon God.

As with Asa, this war comes at a time of spiritual renewal in Judah. For Judah, JAPHET (783) notes, "armed conflict is a divine test, one more arena demanding concrete expression of religious integrity." The Chronicler's "main interest" lies in whether the nation passes the test. Consequently, instead of intricate battlefield details, the Chronicler provides a theological assessment of the war. War comes to Jehoshaphat, not as a punishment, but as a test (JOHNSTONE, 2:96).

The historicity of the war, however, has generated considerable debate; 2 Chronicles 20:1-30 is unique. Some believe the war is the Chronicler's own imaginative fiction. However, several have recently defended its historicity (DILLARD, 154-155; JAPHET, 783-784; WILLIAMSON, 291-293). The geographic details suggest authenticity, and the Chronicler is probably using an unknown source.

JAPHET (784) divides this pericope into four sections: (a) Background (2 Chr 20:1-4), (b) Assembly in Jerusalem (2 Chr 20:5-19), (c) War (2 Chr 20:20-28), and (d) Conclusion (2 Chr 20:29-30).

Background to the War (20:1-4)

After the spiritual and judicial reforms of 2 Chronicles 19, a transjordanian coalition invaded Judah. **Moabites**, **Ammonites**, and **Meunites** attacked Judah from the southeast (**from Edom**; MT reads

"Aram" [אֲרָם, *'rm*], but JAPHET [787] believes this is a textual corruption which should read "Edom" [אֱדֹם, *'dm*]). They probably crossed the Dead Sea at its lowest point (the ford opposite Masada) and then proceeded along the coast to **En Gedi**). From there they ascended into the wilderness area of Tekoa southeast of Bethlehem (cf. 2 Chr 20:20). There have been times in history when an army could have crossed the Dead Sea on dry land (as is true in 2001). Given possible low water tables, Judah's southwestern enemies seized an opportunity to attack her from the rear.

The actual enemies are confused in the textual history of 2 Chronicles 20:1-2. Where the NIV reads "Meunites" (LXX), the MT reads "Ammonites." The MT is redundant. Most follow the LXX. Their probable location was the southeastern region of the Dead Sea though some think they are nomadic Arabs operating south of Judah (cf. 1 Chr 4:41; 2 Chr 26:7; DILLARD, 155-156; JAPHET, 786). The association of the invading army with Mount Seir (2 Chr 20:10,22) confirms the southeastern hypothesis. Whatever the details, the invading army draws on the resources of Judah's southern and southeastern enemies.

What the NIV calls a **vast army** is literally a "great/large multitude" (הָמוֹן רָב, *hāmôn rāb*; 2 Chr 20:12,15). Abijah encountered a "vast army" in 2 Chronicles 13:8, and Asa prayed that the Lord would distinguish between the "powerless and the mighty" (רָב, *rāb*) as they encountered Zerah's "multitude" (הֶהָמוֹן, *hehāmôn*; 2 Chr 14:11). In 2 Chronicles 32:7 Hezekiah calms the fears of Israel when he reminds them that Assyria's "vast army" (*hehāmôn*) cannot defeat God's "greater power" (*rāb*). The battle is a contest between God and the nations.

Jehoshaphat determines to **inquire** and **seek help from the LORD**. Literally, 2 Chronicles 20:3a reads "Jehoshaphat was afraid, and he gave his face to seek the Lord." The Chronicler uses his favorite term — "to seek" (דרשׁ, *dāraš*). This is emphasized in 2 Chronicles 20:4 by twice using the other Hebrew term for "seek" (בקשׁ, *bāqaš*). Despite their fear and anxiety, instead of seeking an alliance, Jehoshaphat and Judah seek the Lord (cf. 1 Chr 28:9).

All Judah engages in a fast, and people **came from every town in Judah to seek** God. This is communal piety in a moment of crisis. Fasting is a spiritual discipline often exercised during times of mourning or fear (Esth 4:3; 9:31; Ps 69:10), particularly during war or calamity (Judg 20:26; 1 Sam 7:6; 31:13; 12:16-22).

Holy Assembly in Jerusalem (20:5-19)

All Judah comes to Jerusalem fasting and seeking the Lord. They gather as a holy assembly before the Lord at his temple. Judah models the appropriate response to approaching disaster: one seeks the Lord through prayer and worship at the place God has promised his presence. This holy assembly boldly approaches God on the basis of his promise in 2 Chronicles 6–7: God will hear the prayers of those who seek him.

Prayer (20:5-13)

Jehoshaphat's prayer (2 Chr 20:6-12), along with the prophetic response (2 Chr 20:15-17), is the narrative's theological heart. The prayer is bounded by the use of the Hebrew verb "to stand" (עמד, *'āmad*) and the presence of God (2 Chr 20:5,13). Judah stands before God to present their plea in the midst of their distress. It is a holy **assembly** (קָהָל, *qāhāl*; cf. 1 Chr 13:2-5; 15:3; 28:1,8; 29:1,10,20; 2 Chr 5:2-3; 6:3,12-13; 7:8) gathered to seek God.

Jehoshaphat Leads (20:5). Jehoshaphat is the representative of the people in their time of need. He speaks for the people in the place of God's presence: **at the temple of the LORD in the front of the new courtyard.**

Jehoshaphat Prays (20:6-12). Jehoshaphat's prayer is a lament. It contains the three major components of laments (cf. Ps 13): (1) praise (2 Chr 20:6-9), (2) complaint (2 Chr 20:10-11), and (3) petition (2 Chr 20:12). It is a national lament where Israel believes itself innocent but fearful of the situation. They recite God's past victories, complain about the present, and hope for the future (cf. Ps 44).

Jehoshaphat begins his lament with praise. It ascribes sovereignty to God (2 Chr 20:6) and recalls his past grace (2 Chr 20:7). The sovereignty of God means that **all the kingdoms of the nations** are under his control, **that no one can withstand** him, and that everything (**power and might**) is in his hands. In light of the great multitude coming against Judah, Jehoshaphat expresses confidence in God's sovereignty and historic graciousness. The descendants of Abraham, the **friend** of God, were given this land by God's divine judgment against **the inhabitants of this land before your people**. Jehoshaphat praises God's gracious intentions toward Israel. Judah, as a descendant of Abraham, inhabits the land by God's own power and grace.

The praise generates the lament question. Given God's intent to give the land to his people, why is the land invaded by **kingdoms of the nations**? If God is truly sovereign, why do the nations invade? The people ask legitimate questions in the light of God's sovereignty and gracious intent. If God is able and he is good, why is a pagan nation on the verge of subduing the land God gave to Abraham? The question is theodic.

Judah has just experienced spiritual renewal (2 Chr 19) and Jehoshaphat protests the innocence of his nation (2 Chr 20:8). Judah has built a **sanctuary for** the **Name** of God, and they rest in God's promises. Chronicles pictures the temple as the goal of the settlement of the land. Jehoshaphat appeals to Solomon's prayer at the dedication of the temple (2 Chr 6:14-42). Second Chronicles 20:9 is a summary of 2 Chronicles 6:28-30. Jehoshaphat's prayer rests on the promise of God at the dedication of the temple. God will **hear** and **save**.

The second part of the prayer is the complaint (2 Chr 20:10-11). The shift from praise to complaint is indicated by the Hebrew particle **but now** (וְעַתָּה, *wᵉʿattāh*; 2 Chr 20:10). Even though Judah sought renewal, God permits **Ammon, Moab and Mount Seir** to invade. They could not do so without God's permission because God rules over all the nations (2 Chr 20:6). Jehoshaphat expresses the complaint by blaming God for the present situation. If God had only let Israel destroy those nations when his people came out of Egypt, then this situation would not exist. When God forbade Israel from attacking these nations, Yahweh himself "created [the] present situation of distress" (Beentjes, "Tradition," 261).

These nations attack those who previously spared them. They seek to reverse the gift God gave his people. The use of the term **possession** reinforces the invasion's theological dimensions. This is its only use in Chronicles, but it occurs seven times in Deuteronomy (Deut 2:5,9,12,19; cf. Josh 12:6-7). Its significance is enhanced by the use of the verb form ("to inherit") in 2 Chronicles 20:7,11. Judah's relatives attempt to usurp divine boundaries of inheritance — Moab and Ammon descended from Abraham's nephew Lot (Gen 19:30-38) and Edom from Abraham through Esau (Gen 25:19-26). Will God permit these usurpers to tear away Israel's rightful inheritance?

The lament justifies God's judgment against the nations. This is a just war. In response to this unrighteous invasion, Jehoshaphat calls for divine justice (Good, 392-396). Kline (154-171) calls it an intrusion of God's eschatological judgment into history where God destroys the unrighteous as a prefigurement of his eschatological wrath (cf. Good, 390-391, 396 on Joel 4).

Second Chronicles 20:12 is Jehoshaphat's imprecatory (curse) petition. He calls upon God to **judge** the invading nations. The link between 2 Chronicles 19 and 20 is obvious. Jehoshaphat instituted judicial reform on the ground of God's righteousness, and now Jehoshaphat calls upon Yahweh to act justly. Indeed, the king uses his own name in his petition; *šāphaṭ* ("judge"). The one whose name means "Yahweh judges" calls upon Yahweh to judge.

Jehoshaphat confesses that he has no strength to face this multitude. They are too many and too powerful. Yet, Jehoshaphat confesses that all power and strength are in God's hands (2 Chr 20:6; כֹּחַ [kōaḥ] translated as **power** in 2 Chr 20:6 and 2 Chr 20:12). His petition expresses trust and humility.

The People Stand before the Lord (20:13). **All** Judah **stood** at the temple **before the LORD**. This narrative boundary (parallel with 20:5) underscores the solemn nature of the assembly. It is a communal lament.

This is the situation in which postexilic Judah found itself. They stood at the temple praying to God based upon his Davidic and Solomonic promises. They wondered whether God would hear. They wondered whether God still wanted them as his people. Just as Jehoshaphat appealed to the sovereignty and grace of God, so postexilic Judah stood at the temple making the same appeal.

The people of God seek the face of God in lament. They praise, complain, and petition. Though they wonder whether God will act on their behalf, in humility they seek his face. The confidence of God's people is the faithfulness of God. He will keep his promises, and the climactic testimony to that faithfulness is Jesus Christ. God answers all lament in Jesus Christ, but lament continues as we await the fullness of God's kingdom in the new heaven and new earth (Hicks, *Trust*, 183-212).

Prophetic Message (20:14-19)

As in the case of Solomon (2 Chr 6–7), God responds to Jehoshaphat's prayer. His response comes through a Spirit-prompted prophet.

The Prophet Jahaziel (20:14). Chronicles attributes the origin of a prophetic message to the movement of God's **Spirit** (cf. 1 Chr 12:18; 2 Chr 15:1; 24:29). This underscores the divine character of the message. While otherwise unknown, **Jahaziel** has quite a pedigree – a Levite whose ancestry is traced to the time of David (**Asaph**). Just as Jehoshaphat and the people stood before the Lord, so the prophet **stood in the assembly** to declare a word from God.

Jahaziel's prophecy represents a deliverance or "salvation oracle" (WILLIAMSON, 297-299). As DILLARD (157) notes, it closely follows the "prescribed speech from a priest before battle" (Deut 20:2-4). God hears and answers.

The Prophecy (20:15-17). The prophecy is bounded by the same instructions with similar rationales. Jehoshaphat, Judah, and Jerusalem are twice told, **Do not be afraid or discouraged** (2 Chr 20:15,17). The first rationale is **for the battle is not yours, but God's**. The second rationale is **the LORD will be with you**. The presence and power of God assure the battle's result. God gives the victory by his own strength. Consequently, if Judah will simply take up defensive positions at the **Pass of Ziz**, then God will fight for them.

Theologically, the salvation oracle of 2 Chronicles 20:17 recollects the language of the Exodus (JAPHET, 795; Beentjes, "Tradition," 264-266). The chart below parallels the almost identical Hebrew phrases in Exodus and Chronicles.

Exod 14:13-14	2 Chr 20:17
Do not be afraid	Do not be afraid
stand firm	take your positions
see the deliverance	see the deliverance
the Lord will bring you	the Lord will give you
the Lord will fight for you	you will not have to fight

Significantly, 2 Chronicles 20:16a and 20:17b bound the Exodus allusion with a kind of inclusio: **tomorrow** go down and **tomorrow** go out. This accentuates the Exodus reference. The prophet announces that God will deliver his people, just as he did in the Exodus. The God of the Exodus still reigns over the earth.

The God of the Exodus is the God of the Restoration as well. Just as God delivered his people from Egypt and from this invading army, so God delivered his people from Babylon and can yet deliver his people from Persia. The hope of Judah is Yahweh.

Response to Prophecy (20:18-19). Jehoshaphat receives the salvation oracle with worship. He and **all the people of Judah and Jerusalem fell down in worship before the LORD**. Worship is the proper response of God's people to what God has promised and what he does. Since we receive his promises by grace, we can only thank him.

While all Judah and Jerusalem were bowed on their faces, some of the Levitical musicians **stood up and praised the LORD, the God of Israel, with a very loud voice**. The celebration of praise and thankfulness is voiced in joyous, loud voices. The God of Israel is praised. The "God of Judah" is not biblical terminology. The Chronicler maintains the inclusiveness of his vision for the kingdom of God.

The War (20:20-28)

Though the most lengthy battle report in Chronicles, it is wholly the work of God. God wins the victory without Judah's army. Thus, the power of God removes any possibility for boasting. Judah can only glory in what God has done rather than boast about their role. The battle report, then, is paradigmatic of redemption itself. The redeemed cannot boast about their redemption except in boasting about what God has done. Paul voices this principle in Galatians 6:14, "May I never boast except in the cross of our Lord Jesus Christ."

The Worshiping Army (20:20-21)

Judah followed the instructions of the prophet and marched out to the **Desert of Tekoa** (about 15 miles southeast of Jerusalem). The army is a holy procession. Jehoshaphat offers a homiletic exhortation (2 Chr 20:20) and liturgical musicians lead the army into battle (2 Chr 20:21). In addition to instrumental accompaniment, the musicians included priestly trumpets (cf. 2 Chr 20:28) that announced God's presence on the battlefield. The Day of Yahweh is announced by a trumpet blast (DILLARD, 158; Exod 19:16,19; Isa 18:3; 27:13; Amos 2:2; Zeph 1:14-16; Zech 9:14). This is a liturgical army — the host of God worship as they go into battle.

Jehoshaphat's exhortation is brief — only seven words in Hebrew. These seven words are regarded by some as "the most concise summary" of Chronicles's message (Beentjes, "Tradition," 267). Throntveit (*Kings*, 118-119) argues it is the structural center of royal speeches in 2 Chronicles 13–30. However it not only addresses Jehoshaphat's army, but postexilic Judah. Jehoshaphat articulates the basic relational principle of the covenant: trust God and believe his prophets. When God's people trust him, they prosper.

The brief homily has a poetic structure. Despite the NIV's four lines, the Hebrew text only has three (cf. NRSV). It is given in an AAB synthetic parallelism where the A lines are synonymous (faith in God; faith in prophets) and the B line (successful) is the result or consequence of the A lines.

> Have faith in the LORD your God
> > have faith in his prophets
> > and you will be successful.

The promise of success is the same as David's promise to Solomon. As long as he sought the Lord, God would grant him success (1 Chr 22:11,13). When God is with his people, the enemy will not succeed (2 Chr 13:12). When Judah seeks God, they prosper (2 Chr 14:7). The language and circumstance of this text are reminiscent of Ahaz and Isaiah (Isa 7). There Ahaz did not believe Yahweh's prophet, and he did not succeed. Using Isaiah 7:9, Chronicles "has transformed the negative form" into a "positive summons." Chronicles has interpreted and applied a previous canonical text to Jehoshaphat's situation (JAPHET, 797).

In Chronicles the prophets are covenantal messengers who speak the promise and judgment of God. Heeding the prophets of Yahweh is heeding God. His language reflects Exodus 14:31 where the people "feared the LORD and put their trust in him and in Moses his servant." Just as Israel trusted God and his prophet in the Exodus, so now Jehoshaphat calls upon Judah to do the same (Beentjes, "Tradition," 267). The Redeemer God who delivered his people from Egyptian bondage is the same God who can deliver his people from this invasion.

Chronicles uses the Exodus as a paradigm for understanding the present experience of redemption. The Exodus provides the framework for thinking about God the Redeemer (cf. Ps 107). The power of the Exodus continues in the history of Israel.

In the same way, the power of the Redeemer God exhibited in the mighty act of God in Jesus Christ is not a mere past event. The power of the resurrection invades the daily lives of believers (Phil 3:11). The power of the resurrection, just as the power of the Exodus, is still at work among the people of God (Eph 1:15-22).

The Victory (20:22-25)

As the liturgical army begins to **sing** (lit., "shout" or "cry;" cf. 2 Chr 6:19) **and praise**, Yahweh defeats the enemy. JOHNSTONE (2:103) calls this a "realized sacramentalism: precisely at the moment of the acclamation of the Lord's arrival on the field of battle, the LORD himself intervenes."

The Lord initiated ambushes, and this generated a panic which resulted in the enemies' mutual annihilation. The tremendous amount of booty (**three days to collect it**; 2 Chr 20:25) indicates a large-scale panic as a defeated and fleeing army left much of its materiel on the battlefield. While various army groups (**Ammon, Moab**, and **Mount Seir**) destroyed each other, **the LORD set ambushes** that generated the self-destruction. Probably, the ambushes represent mistaken identity where the invaders, caught off guard, were routed by "mutual suspicion and self-destruction" (JAPHET, 798). The terrain of the Judean wilderness and the political intrigue of regional foes renders this scenario quite plausible.

Chronicles attributes the victory to Yahweh. The Judean army came to fight on a battlefield where they had already won. They collected the spoils. The defeat was complete, as is indicated by Chronicles's language: **defeated, destroy, annihilate, slaughtering, no one had escaped**.

The overtones of the Exodus are again unmistakable. When Jehoshaphat's army found **more than they could take away** (נצל, *nṣl*), Chronicles uses a term which describes the despoiling of the Egyptians (Exod 3:22; 12:36). God has reenacted the Exodus.

Holy Victory Assembly (20:26-28)

Judah gathered in a holy assembly in the **Valley of Beracah** (i.e., the Valley of Blessing). There Judah blessed (**praised**) **the LORD**.

They ascribed the victory to God. Worship is characterized by such an ascription so that God alone receives the credit, glory, and honor for his mighty works.

Just as "the beginning of national crisis finds Jehoshaphat and the people congregating and fasting at the temple, the end of the campaign finds Jehoshaphat and the people again at the temple in national celebration" (Knoppers, "Reform," 518). Whereas in a moment of lament, the people sought God at the temple through fasting, in victory they celebrate at the temple with musical praise and thanksgiving.

Judah rejoiced **over their enemies**. God judged the nations, just as Jehoshaphat requested (2 Chr 20:12). The people of God **rejoice** over God's righteous judgment. This triumphalism is matched in the New Testament where the saints rejoice over just judgments in avenging the blood of the saints (cf. Rev 19:1-8).

Interestingly, this "return" to Jerusalem (2 Chr 20:27) is quite different from Jehoshaphat's "return" in 2 Chronicles 19:1-4. The latter was a prophetic confrontation, but this is liturgical celebration. At the temple, where God himself rests (1 Chr 22:9; 28:2), Jehoshaphat celebrates the victory in which God gave Jehoshaphat rest (2 Chr 20:30).

Conclusion (20:29-30)

Yahweh demonstrated that he rules the nations (2 Chr 20:6). In consequence, **the fear of God came upon all the kingdoms** of the earth **when they heard how the LORD had fought against the enemies of Israel**. The language returns us to 2 Chronicles 17:10 which 2 Chronicles 20:29 repeats. Jehoshaphat has come full circle: spiritual renewal and reform brought peace, and peace is maintained by trusting God and his prophets.

5. Expanded Formulaic Conclusion (20:31–21:1)

Chronicles's expanded conclusion, partly based on Dtr, generates a few problems. The chart below represents the correlations and differences between 2 Chronicles and 1 Kings (Knoppers, "Reform, " 520).

Topic	2 Chr	1 Kgs
Introduction	20:31	22:41-42
Evaluation	20:32-33	22:43-44
Pact with Israel		22:45
Concluding Notice	20:34	22:46
Reforms		22:47
Regent in Edom		22:48
Pact with Ahaziah	20:35-36	
Shipbuilding Alliance	20:36	
Shipwreck	20:37	22:49
Pact with Ahaziah Refused		22:50
Death and Burial of Jehoshaphat	21:1	22:51

The Chronicler does not slavishly follow 1 Kings but expands and reorganizes it according to his own purposes. The major difference concerns Jehoshaphat's maritime adventure and his relationship with Ahaziah, king of Israel (2 Chr 20:35-37).

Standard Conclusion (20:31-34)

The Chronicler's conclusion contains fairly standard material. He supplies specific pieces of royal information (age, length of reign, supplemental sources (**Jehu**), and mother's name). Regarding the "Acts of Jehu," JAPHET (801) notes, the Chronicler probably used "some kind of a 'chronicle' from the monarchical period, which he conceived as having been written by successive generations of prophets." This larger source should be identified with "the book of the kings of Israel" (cf. 2 Chr 32:32), but it is not the canonical books of 1 & 2 Kings (since Jehu does not figure prominently in 1 Kings except at 1 Kings 16:1,7,12; DILLARD, 169). The prophet Jehu is known from his encounter with Jehoshaphat in 2 Chronicles 19:2, and his father was probably the **Hanani** imprisoned by Asa (2 Chr 16:7).

The evaluation of Jehoshaphat in 2 Chronicles 20:32-33 is almost verbatim from 1 Kings 22:43. Even though Jehoshaphat had his weaknesses (as did Asa), his life is characterized as one who **did what was right in the eyes of the LORD**. This characterization is possible because God looks to the heart rather than to the perfection of a person's life.

The Chronicler emphasizes the heart by the way in which he changes the wording of 1 Kings 22:44. While 1 Kings 22:43 reads "the people continued to offer sacrifices and burn incense there," 2 Chr 20:33 reads **the people still had not set their hearts on the God of their fathers**. For the Chronicler, the consistent idolatry of the people revealed their hearts. Even though Jehoshaphat was imperfect (e.g., unable to remove all the **high places**), his heart sought God.

As with Asa (2 Chr 14:5; 15:17), Jehoshaphat both removed but did not remove the high places (2 Chr 17:6; 20:33). Whatever may be the case with Asa's reign, the reappearance of the high places during the reign of Jehoshaphat is probably due to several factors, including his alliance with Ahab (which encouraged idolaters in Judah) and the fact that his people were not unanimous in seeking Yahweh. We may surmise that early in his reign Jehoshaphat removed all the high places, but they later returned (Dillard, "Jehoshaphat, 18-19, n. 7).

Appendix: Another Foreign Alliance (20:35-37)

While Jehoshaphat is a good king whose heart sought the Lord during his reign, he is no Solomon (whose maritime trade with Tarshish is mentioned in 2 Chr 9:21, NRSV). The Chronicler makes this clear by incorporating this short vignette about his failed maritime operations. It also provides yet another opportunity for the Chronicler to oppose foreign alliances (Knoppers, "Reform," 519-521).

While 2 Chronicles 20:35-37 appears to be based on 1 Kings 22:49-50, there are some differences. In Chronicles, **Jehoshaphat king of Judah made an alliance with Ahaziah king of Israel**, but in 1 Kings 22:50 Jehoshaphat refused to align himself with Ahaziah. Further, were the ships destroyed in port (as 2 Chr 20:37 may appear to say), or were they destroyed en route (as 1 Kgs 22:49 appears to say)?

While it is possible that the differences between Chronicles and Dtr are due to the Chronicler's use of a different textual tradition than MT, the two accounts can be harmonized by several scenarios (DILLARD, 160; SELMAN, 2:430). They may refer to two separate incidents. Or, they may refer to the same incident but from varying perspectives. For example, perhaps Ahaziah and Jehoshaphat contracted to build ships together, but Jehoshaphat wanted to control the actual shipping. In addition, Chronicles does not say that the ships were destroyed in port, but only that they were prevented from reaching Tarshish (NIV reads **to set sail to trade** when it could read, according to NRSV, "were not able to go to Tarshish").

The failure of Jehoshaphat's maritime operation is directly linked to his alliance with Ahaziah. Another prophet, like Jehu (2 Chr 19:2), condemns the alliance and prophesies that **the LORD will destroy what you have made**. Jehoshaphat's trust in the Lord, though genuine, was not perfect. The Lord "broke out"(פָּרַץ, *pāraṣ*) against Jehoshaphat (just as he had against David earlier, 1 Chr 13:11; 15:13). Jehoshaphat, like David, was spared, but his venture was halted.

Death and Burial of Jehoshaphat (21:1)

Jehoshaphat is a good king who receives an honorable burial. This contrasts with the burial his son will receive (2 Chr 21:19-20). Despite his weaknesses and failings, Jehoshaphat is one of the best kings of Judah (alongside of David, Solomon, and Hezekiah). The Chronicler's final conclusion concerning Jehoshaphat is that he "sought the LORD with all his heart" (2 Chr 22:9).

D. THE DARK DAYS OF JUDAH (21:2–23:21)

Second Chronicles 21:2-4 is unlike any other material in Chronicles's monarchical narrative. The sons of Jehoshaphat are listed in order to record their execution. While Jehoshaphat distributed wealth and cities to all his sons, he gave the throne to Jehoram. But when Jehoram was firmly established as king, he executed his brothers. Structurally, 2 Chronicles 21:2-4 introduces the monarchial crisis that will consume 2 Chronicles 21–23. Second Chronicles 21:5 begins Chronicles's more customary handling of a Davidic monarch. Thus, following the relatively good years of Davidic succession from Rehoboam to Jehoshaphat (2 Chr 10–20), the crisis years of Athaliah emerge in 2 Chronicles 21.

The introductory execution of Jehoshaphat's sons, the emphasis on the house of Ahab in 2 Chronicles 21–23, and the sustained crisis in the Davidic house (including three executions) bind these chapters together. These are the "dark days" of Judah. The successive reigns of Jehoram, Ahaziah, and Athaliah almost spell the end of the Davidic dynasty as Judah and Israel are practically one nation (family, religion, and national interests).

1. The Reign of Jehoram (21:2–22:1)

Separating 2 Chronicles 21:2-4 from 2 Chronicles 21:5-20 permits a chiastic understanding of the latter (DILLARD, 164).

(1) Chronology (21:5)
   (2) Wrongdoing (21:6-7)
      (3) Rebellion of Edom and Libnah (21:8-11)
         (4) Letter from Elijah (21:12-15)
      (3') Rebellion of Philistines and Arabs (21:16-17)
   (2') Punishment for Wrongdoing (21:18-19)
(1') Chronology (21:20)

This structure highlights Elijah's letter as the central theological point as a prophetic interpretation of the king's reign. Divine judgment comes because of the sinfulness of Jehoram's rule.

While Dtr summarized the evil reign of Jehoram in nine verses (2 Kgs 8:16-24), Chronicles expands it to twenty. Though some believe Chronicles's additions are midrashic and filled with creative imagination (Begg, "Constructing," 35-51), most believe they are based on historical sources no longer available (JAPHET, 806; DILLARD, 164; WILLIAMSON, 303). The following chart shows the relationship between Chronicles and Dtr.

Topic	2 Chr	2 Kgs
Jehoram Becomes King		2 Kgs 8:16
Jehoram Executes His Brothers	2 Chr 21:2-4	
Chronology	2 Chr 21:5	2 Kgs 8:17
Evaluation of Reign	2 Chr 21:6-7	2 Kgs 8:18-19
Edom and Libnah Revolt	2 Chr 21:8-10a	2 Kgs 8:20-22
Theological Evaluation	2 Chr 21:10b	
Letter from Elijah	2 Chr 21:12-15	
Philistia and Arabs Rebel	2 Chr 21:16-17	
Jehoram Becomes Ill	2 Chr 21:18-19	
Sources of Reign		2 Kgs 8:23
Death and Burial of Jehoram	2 Chr 21:20	2 Kgs 8:24

The Chronicler clarifies that Judah's calamities were a direct result of Jehoram's evil. He reverses the gains of Asa and Jehoshaphat. He loses control of Philistia, Arabia, and Edom. Jehoram subverts the religious reforms his fathers implemented. In one short reign (eight years), Jehoram destroys the accomplishments of his father's twenty-five and his grandfather's forty-one years (Begg, "Constructing," 43-47). Theologically, Jehoram is the degeneration of Judah.

Jehoram Establishes His Kingdom (21:2-4)

This section has no counterpart in any other history of a Davidic king. It introduces the threat against the Davidic dynasty that Jehoram's execution of his brothers embodies. This is the topic of 2 Chronicles 21–23 (WILLIAMSON, 304).

At first this transition seems relatively uneventful. Before his death Jehoshaphat, **king of Israel** (in reference to the southern kingdom in 2 Chr 12:1,6; 19:8; 21:2,4; 23:2; 24:5,16; 28:19,23,27; cf. Williamson, *Israel*, 102), distributed his wealth to his various sons, including the gift of particular cities where they functioned as administrators. Jehoram becomes king because he is **firstborn**. The explanatory note may have been necessary due to the horrendous memory of his reign (that is, to answer the question: "Why did Jehoshaphat make Jehoram king?"; cf. WILLIAMSON, 304).

After his father's death and **when Jehoram established himself firmly over his father's kingdom**, he executed **all his brothers**. His bloody deed also included **some of the princes of Israel**. The list of names (unlike other kings where the names of sons are not recorded) accentuates the horror of the deed.

The motivation for this fratricide is connected with the northern kingdom. Jehoram had married Athaliah, the daughter of Ahab. The northern kingdom (the Omride Dynasty) probably intended to annex Judah, or, at least, include it within its orbit. This bloodshed is "best interpreted against this background of dynastic rivalry and competition. What may have begun as a friendly alliance between Jehoshaphat and Ahab now threatens to annihilate the Davidides" (JAPHET, 807).

Instead of seeking God's own blessing where God establishes a throne in his kingdom (cf. 1 Chr 17:11; 2 Chr 1:1; 6:10; 7:18), Jehoram seeks his own way. He eliminates all his rivals. While the NIV may be correct (**over his father's kingdom**), it is also plausible to render the statement as "against" his father's kingdom. Thus, Jehoram establishes his own kingdom (rather than God's kingdom) by acting against his father's kingdom.

Jehoram Reigns (21:5-22:1)

Chronicles follows Dtr closely at points while adding new material. This section follows the more conventional style of monarchical reports with chronology, evaluation, and brief history.

Chronology (21:5)

According to Thiele (97), Jehoram became Jehoshaphat's co-regent in 853 B.C. and the sole ruler in 848 B.C. till his death in 841 B.C.

Wrongdoing (21:6-7)

This section follows 2 Kings 8:18-19 closely. Jehoram is the first king of Judah who is explicitly linked to the **ways of the kings of Israel**. While Jehoshaphat contracted an alliance with the northern kingdom, nevertheless he sought Yahweh with all his heart. But his son, Jehoram, who had **married a daughter of Ahab** (Athaliah), followed his father-in-law. This includes the introduction of Baal worship into the southern kingdom. The Chronicler assumes his readers know the evil of Ahab's reign.

Nevertheless, God does not **destroy the house of David** (1 Kgs 8:19 reads "house of Judah"). God's faithfulness comes to the forefront. Even though a son of David has aligned himself with the evil of the **house of Ahab**, God will keep his promise to David. "God's promise to David will determine future developments in defiance of human schemes" (JAPHET, 809). The Lord made a **covenant** with David — he will not destroy his dynasty (house).

Even in the face of such evil as Jehoram's fratricide, God remembers his covenant promise (cf. 1 Chr 17). The hope of the postexilic community is rooted in that same faithfulness.

Rebellion of Edom and Libnah (21:8-11)

In contrast to Jehoshaphat under whom **Edom** did not even have a king (cf. 1 Kgs 22:47), Jehoram cannot maintain his sovereignty over Edom (they appoint their **own king**). While it appears that

Jehoram successfully engaged Edom in battle (lit., "he rose up in the night and smote Edom"), he did not regain control. Judah would never again rule Edom the way it had during the time of David-Solomon and Asa-Jehoshaphat.

A consequence of Jehoram's unfaithfulness was the loss of southeastern (Edom) and western (**Libnah**, a city on the border of Judah and Philistia, perhaps even the residue of a Canaanite city-state [DILLARD, 166; JAPHET, 810-811]) territories. Chronicles provides the theological reason for this reversal: **because Jehoram had forsaken the LORD, the God of his fathers**. In fulfillment of his promise (1 Chr 28:9; 2 Chr 15:2), God forsakes Jehoram. Indeed, Libnah was one of the Levitical cities of Judah (Josh 15:42; 21:13; 1 Chr 6:57) that was lost to Canaanite interests; the Conquest is reversed as God has forsaken his Davidic king.

The rationale for this Godforsakenness is provided in 2 Chronicles 21:11. Though Asa and Jehoshaphat attempted to remove the high places from their realm, Jehoram **built high places on the hills of Judah** (the first to do so). Whereas Asa and Jehoshaphat attempted to turn the people to the Lord, Jehoram **caused the people of Jerusalem to prostitute** (זנה, *zānāh*, "to play the harlot") **themselves**. The shepherd of Judah (cf. 1 Chr 11:2; 17:6; 2 Chr 18:16) led his flock to destruction. The bride of God, Israel, became a prostitute. This language (*zānāh*) describes the exile of the transjordanian tribes (1 Chr 5:25). Jehoram **led Judah** into full-blown apostasy.

Letter from Elijah (21:12-15)

Elijah appears for the first time in Chronicles. A prophetic confrontation is expected in Chronicles (cf. 2 Chr 19:1-4), but Elijah is seemingly stepping outside his usual boundaries. He is Ahab's nemesis, not Judah's. But this is precisely the point. Elijah opposes the Baal worship of Ahab and once introduced into Judah, Elijah opposes it there as well.

The problem is that Elijah apparently died during the reign of Jehoshaphat (cf. 2 Kgs 2-3). THOMPSON (299; cf. SELMAN, 2:435-436) suggests that the letter was written during Jehoram's co-regency with Jehoshaphat (cf. 2 Kgs 1:17) when his tendencies were already well-known. Yet, this is problematic since the letter itself refers to the murder of his brothers (2 Chr 21:13). The chronology of 2 Kings

2-3 is not as clear as is sometimes thought. Elijah may have lived into the sole reign of Jehoram if the ministries of Elijah and Elisha overlapped to any significant degree (DILLARD, 167-168).

The Chronicler, based on some source no longer extant (probably a kind of prophetic handbook containing various speeches by prophets), believes the letter came from Elijah the arch antagonist of Ahab. The letter is composed in the Chronicler's typical language as he adapted Elijah's epistle to his own purposes. It is a kind of "redrafting rather than his composition" (SELMAN, 2:436).

The first half of the letter (2 Chr 21:12b-13) summarizes the evil of Jehoram's reign in language echoing the previous and subsequent verses (cf. 2 Chr 21:6 with 21:12; 21:11 with 21:13a; 21:4 with 21:13b; 21:17 with 21:14; and 21:18-19 with 21:15). It summarizes the narrative. Jehoram walked in the **ways of the kings of Israel**. He prostituted himself according the example of the **house of Ahab**. Further, he **murdered** his **own brothers** (which includes the value judgment **men who were better than you**). Elijah condemns Jehoram because he is like Ahab. Jehoram neither devoted himself to what was good (the ways of his fathers) nor avoided evil (the ways of Ahab).

Elijah pronounces judgment (2 Chr 21:14-15). The LORD will punish Jehoram — his **people, sons, wives**, and **everything** that belongs to him. Jehoram's full-scale apostasy will be matched by God's total forsakenness. God will **strike** a **heavy blow** against Jehoram and his realm. God prosecutes a kind of "negative exodus" as he curses Judah. God plagued Egypt (Exod 8:2; 12:13), and God will plague Judah (2 Chr 21:14,18). Just "as he had eliminated his brothers, so he is now to lose his sons" (JOHNSTONE, 2:112-113). Further, Jehoram himself will be struck (plagued in 2 Chr 21:18) with a mortal illness. When his people forsake him, God forsakes them. Chronicles's theology of retribution is fully unveiled.

Rebellion of Philistines and Arabs (21:16-17)

Unique to Chronicles, the nations who once brought tribute to Jehoshaphat now devastate Jehoram: **Philistines** and **Arabs** (2 Chr 17:11; cf. 2 Chr 26:6-7). The reference to the **Cushites** (or, Nubians) may denote a geographical reference (JAPHET, 814) or it may mean "at the direction of the Cushites" (JOHNSTONE, 2:113). The Cushites, under the influence of Egypt, may have encouraged raids against Judah in the light of the success of Edom and Libnah.

Chronicles attributes these raids to the Lord's arousal. Literally, the Lord stirred up the spirit of the Philistines and Arabs against Jehoram. This is the language of divine agency (cf. 1 Chr 5:26; 2 Chr 36:22). God works among the nations to accomplish his purposes, even to the point of arousing enemies against his people. The enemy that defeated Saul leaves only a single heir of David.

Jehoram lost everything his father left him. He lost secure territories on his south, southeastern, and southwestern borders. He lost his wealth as the invading Philistines and Arabs **carried off all the goods found in the king's palace**. He lost his family — **his sons** (with the exception of **Ahaziah, the youngest**). Jehoram suffered complete reversal.

The price of his sin is the near extinction of the house of David. Yet, God preserves a remnant — one son of Jehoram to whom God will show his faithfulness. Even in the midst of punishment, God remembers his promises. In the context of Chronicles's whole history, God's faithfulness is demonstrated in 2 Chronicles 36:22-23. In contrast to God's movement of the nations against Judah in 2 Chronicles 21, in 2 Chronicles 36:23 God stirs up Persia for the sake of Judah.

Punishment for Wrongdoing (21:18-19)

Jehoram himself suffered a painful and prolonged death. **The LORD afflicted Jehoram with an incurable disease of the bowels**. This plague (the reversal of blessing) lasted two years and caused **great pain**. His death was ignominious, and Chronicles lingers over its description as if to underscore the intensity of God's punishment.

There was no funeral fire for Jehoram (2 Chr 21:20). "The king who denied the righteous ways of his ancestors (v. 12) is himself denied the least sign of respect by his subjects: the funerary rites which all of his fathers had received" (JAPHET, 817). The Chronicler omits his usual ending of a king's life, that is, further sources, "direct succession" and "that he rested with his fathers." Thus, "in this matter-of-fact way, the author shows that he regarded Jerhoram's reign, as also those of his successors Ahaziah and Athaliah, as an aberration" (SELMAN, 2:437).

Chronology (21:20–22:1)

Though based on 1 Kings 8:24, the wording is changed and material is added. Jehoram **passed away** but **to no one's regret**.

Though **buried in the City of David**, he was not placed **in the tombs of the kings**. While Dtr simply reads that he was buried "with them" (his fathers) in the City of David, Chronicles clarifies that this means in the same city and not in the royal tombs.

The people of Jerusalem made Ahaziah, Jehoram's youngest and only remaining son, **king in his place**. The role of the inhabitants of Jerusalem is not unusual (cf. 2 Chr 23:1; 26:1; 33:24; 36:1), but in each case it followed "the violent death" of the preceding king. "The similar treatment of Ahaziah is another indication of [the Chronicler's] view that Jehoram's death should not be regarded as natural" (JAPHET, 818). The Chronicler alone clarifies that Ahaziah became king because he was the only son left (**Arabs killed all the older sons**).

2. The Reign of Ahaziah (22:2-9)

"The 'real subject' of Ahaziah's reign is the *house of Ahab*" (SELMAN, 2:437; 2 Chr 22:3,7,8). His reign was brief (one year) and dominated by his mother Athaliah, the daughter of Ahab. The kingdoms of Israel and Judah had become practically one.

The Chronicler follows the structure of Dtr in 2 Chronicles 22:2-6, but adds his own material in 2 Chronicles 22:7-9. The Chronicler omits a large amount of material (cf. 2 Kgs 9:1-26). He is only interested in the Davidic line except when the northern kingdom intersects with the southern kingdom.

As DILLARD (172-173) summarizes, substantial difficulties arise when Dtr and Chronicles are read together.

Topic	2 Chr	2 Kgs
Chronology	Murder of the house of Judah before Ahaziah's death (2 Chr 22:8-9)	Murder of the house of Judah after Ahaziah's death (2 Kgs 10:21-14)
Place of Death	Ahaziah is found in Samaria and killed in an unnamed place (2 Chr 22:9)	Ahaziah fled toward Ibleam and dies near Megiddo (2 Kgs 9:27)
Place of Burial	Appears to have been buried at the place of his death (2 Chr 22:9)	Ahaziah is buried in Jerusalem (2 Kgs 9:28)

Most find these accounts irreconcilable (MYERS, 2:126). WILLIAMSON (311-312) and JAPHET (823-824) believe the Chronicler has rewritten Dtr in order to express a theological judgment against Ahaziah.

However, the readers of Chronicles are familiar with 2 Kings. The Chronicler may have omitted some details (e.g., the exact place of burial) in order to emphasize a theological point. For example, the unspecified place of burial in Chronicles is a theological judgment — Ahaziah is unworthy to have his specific burial plot detailed. Chronicles does not contradict Dtr. Rather, the Chronicler left unsaid what was already known from Dtr in order to emphasize the ignominious nature of Ahaziah's life. Further, as DILLARD (173) suggests, the account of the murder of the house of Judah may have been "chronologically dislocated" in order for the Chronicler to end his account on the death of Ahaziah. In other words, the Chronicler does not intend his account as a chronology of events. THOMPSON (304) believes the Chronicler "was content to note the main facts and leave the chronological and geographical details for the reader to sort out in Kings."

Formulaic Introduction to Ahaziah's Reign (22:2-4)

According to MT, the age of Ahaziah is "forty-two" rather than **twenty-two** (NIV; 1 Kgs 8:26). However, "there seems no doubt that 'forty-two' is a textual error" due to the transmission (JAPHET, 820). Since Jehoram was forty years old at his death, his son could not have been forty-two (2 Chr 21:20).

Ominously, Chronicles notes that Ahaziah's mother, Athaliah, was the **granddaughter of Omri** (Ahab's father; cf. 2 Kgs 8:26). This stresses the domination of the Omride dynasty over Judah. In 2 Chronicles 22:3-4, Chronicles reproduces the statements of 2 Kings 8:27 but also adds some theological assessments.

2 Kgs 8:27	2 Chr 22:3-4
He walked in the ways of the house of Ahab	He walked in the ways of the house of Ahab
	for his mother encouraged him in doing wrong.
and did evil in the eyes of the LORD, as the house of Ahab had done	He did evil in the eyes of the LORD, as the house of Ahab had done
for he was related by marriage to Ahab's family	for after his father's death they became his advisers, to his undoing.

Ahaziah's evil is attributed to his connection with the house of Ahab. Consequently, just as the Omride dynasty fell under the judgment of God in 2 Kings 9, so Judah is judged. Just as Judah and Israel share a familial heritage, so they share God's wrath. The two nations suffer together. Ahaziah is headed for destruction (**undoing**) which was his father's fate (2 Chr 21:18).

The more significant question, however, is will the two dynasties fall together? The Omride dynasty is destroyed by Jehu. By juxtaposing the Omride and Davidic dynasties, Chronicles underscores the faithfulness of God. While Omri's royal line comes to an end, David's will, despite its seeming destruction, continue. This is an important point for the postexilic community.

War at Ramoth Gilead (22:5-6)

"While Jehoram of Judah is merely open to [Omride] influence," SELMAN (2:438) writes, "Ahaziah is fully co-operative." He follows the Omride counselors and aligns himself with **Joram son of Ahab king of Israel to war against Hazael king of Aram at Ramoth Gilead**. It appears that Ahaziah did not join Joram on the battlefield (he visits the wounded Joram in Jezreel), but he probably supplied troops and materiel.

However, the Chronicler is not interested in the war. His concern is the death of Ahaziah who visits his wounded uncle in Jezreel (near Mount Gilboa where Saul died in 1 Chr 10).

The Death of Ahaziah (22:7-9)

God judged the house of Ahab through the Aramean king and Jehu (1 Kgs 19:15-17; 2 Kgs 8:11-13). According to Chronicles, **God brought about Ahaziah's downfall** through his **visit to Joram**. This theological judgment is unique to Chronicles. God works to judge the evil of Ahab's house (including the king of Judah).

This judgment included the execution of **the princes of Judah and the sons of Ahaziah's relatives** (lit., "sons of the brothers of Ahaziah"). There is no chronological note as to when this happened — whether before or after Ahaziah died. The point is thematic, not chronological. God is cleaning house. The Chronicler assumes his readers' knowledge of 2 Kings.

Second Chronicles 22:9 parallels 2 Kings 9:27-28, but the accounts differ. It is difficult to reconcile them and perhaps unnecessary to do so. The Chronicler has 2 Kings before him. The

Chronicler's interest here is the death of Ahaziah, not the intrigue of the flight or where he died.

The death is theologically significant. The Chronicler does not specify the place of burial, but he does offer, unlike Dtr, the rationale for his burial. He is buried because he is a grandson of Jehoshaphat whom the people respect. While Jehoshaphat **sought the LORD with all his heart** (Jehoshaphat returned in peace; 2 Chr 19:1), Ahaziah dies in the northern kingdom as an act of divine judgment.

Unlike Jehoshaphat who had many sons to succeed him (cf. 2 Chr 21:1) and died in peace and prosperity, **the house of Ahaziah** had **no one** who was **powerful enough to retain the kingdom**. Judah, in the space of nine years, went from the wealth, territorial integrity, and peace of Jehoshaphat's reign to the near annihilation of the Davidic line. While spiritual renewal is a long process of faith formation, degeneration can happen swiftly.

Though this is analogous to the end of Saul (1 Chr 10:13-14; DILLARD, 175), it is best compared with the end of the Davidic line at the time of the exile (cf. Jer 22:29-30). This is the situation of the postexilic community. Will the Davidic line rise again? As SELMAN (2:442) comments, "the real problem is the conflict between the lack of an heir and God's eternal promise to David." Chronicles answers that the promise has not failed. Trust God and believe his prophets (2 Chr 20:20) — God will reign again through David.

3. The Reign of Athaliah (22:10–23:21)

Since the family connections are rather confusing, the following chart by JOHNSTONE (2:120) is helpful.

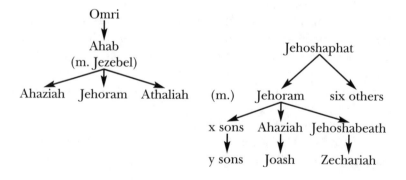

Jehoram killed his six brothers. The Philistine/Arab raid eliminated all the sons of Jehoram except Ahaziah (the daughter Jehoshabeath also survived). Upon the death of Ahaziah, Athaliah kills all the remaining males of David's house (except Joash whom Jehoiada hides). Thus, Joash is the sole surviving male heir of the Davidic house.

For six years it appeared that the house of David had come to an end and the promises of Yahweh had failed. But God preserved a remnant through his high priest Jehoiada. The promises of God cannot fail. Even though the house of Ahab came to an abrupt end (2 Kgs 10:1-17), the house of David remained under God's faithful protection.

The role of the queen mother is well-attested in the ancient Near East. She attained her full authority when her son came to the throne, but her authority was often dictated by the terms of the marriage contract. Further, if her son preceded her in death, she normally yielded her position to the mother of the successor (Spanier, 136-137). However, in this case, Athaliah seizes control by ridding herself of any potential rival (including her grandchildren).

The six-year reign of Athaliah receives little attention. There is no formulaic introduction or conclusion (e.g., age, line of descent, etc.). The narrative focuses on the preservation of the Davidic house (cf. 2 Chr 23:2-3). Though the events of 2 Chronicles 22:10–23:21 occur during the reign of Athaliah, the major topic is Joash and Jehoiada.

This section is divided into three parts: (a) the threat to Joash (22:10-12), (b) the enthronement of Joash (23:1-15), and (c) Judah's covenant renewal (23:16-21).

The Threat to Joash (22:10-12)

"Athaliah now attempts," SELMAN (2:442) writes, "what God had not been willing to do, that is, **destroy** finally" **the house of Judah**. Her northern family is extinct — the house of Ahab has been totally destroyed. She, to her knowledge, executed all the Davidic royal house (including her grandchildren). JOHNSTONE (2:121) suggests, based on a hint from 2 Chronicles 24:17, that "she has a power-base among certain of the nobility, who are intent on drawing Judah into the mainstream of traditional Canaanite culture." Consequently, alone and/or in concert with other leaders she is able to fully pursue the worship of her ancestral god (Baal).

DILLARD (179-180) suspects that Joash escaped notice because as a young child he had been put in the care of "wet nurses or foster mothers." As the executions proceeded, **Jehosheba** hid Joash among the other priestly children and temple devotees (like Samuel) that grew up in the shadow of the temple. As Ahaziah's sister, Jehosheba had access to the royal family, and as Jehoiada's wife she had access to the priestly environs. The story pits one woman (the wife of Jehoram) against another (the daughter of Jehoram).

The story line is similar to those of Moses (Exod 2:1-10) and Jesus (Matt 2). Despite the evil intentions of earthly powers, God's purposes cannot be thwarted.

Theologically, the postexilic community hopes in God's ability to preserve his people. They know he can raise up a nation from an infant. The postexilic community lives in the day of "small things" (Zech 4:10), but God uses "small things" to deliver his people. The preservation of Moses was a small thing, and so was the birth of Mary's son in Bethlehem. Both, however, became deliverers, and the kingdom of God now fills the whole earth.

The Enthronement of Joash (23:1-15)

Jehoiada initiates a coup d'etat against Queen Athaliah and installs Joash as the rightful king of Judah. However, as SELMAN (2:443) notes, the "underlying significance" of the coup is the restoration of Yahweh worship and covenant renewal. "Joash's succession therefore was really an attempt to retain Judah's distinctive *raison d'etre* in the face of the onslaught of Canaanite values." The renewal of the Davidic kingdom and Yahwehist worship are inseparably linked. One anticipates the other, just as in the postexilic community the renewal of temple worship anticipates the restoration of the Davidic monarchy.

Chronicles follows the sequence of 2 Kings 11:1-20, but there are significant additions and omissions. The Chronicler emphasizes the Levites while Dtr emphasizes the military leaders (DILLARD, 180-182). The two groups are intermingled in Chronicles as he first details the military leaders in 2 Chronicles 23:1 and then gives assignments to the Levites in 2 Chronicles 23:4.

Jehoiada's Preparations (23:1-7)

The Chronicler's interest in priests and Levites is clear as well as the theme of "all Israel" (cf. 2 Chr 23:2; **from all the towns**). Chronicles underscores the political (**heads of Israelite families**; cf. 1 Chr 29:6; 2 Chr 1:2; 5:2; 19:8; 35:10), military (**commanders**), and religious (**Levites**) support for Jehoiada. Chronicles specifies the names of the commanders. Though some believe the leaders of 2 Chronicles 23:1 are Levitical, Jehoiada would not have had to covenant with religious leaders. Without military support, Jehoiada could not have proceeded. Indeed, the assembled group of coup leaders constitute a "holy assembly" (קָהָל, *qāhāl*) which makes a **covenant with the king at the temple of God**. The sacred place, plus rightful heir, plus sacral assembly means a holy alliance.

Second Chronicles 23:2-3 is unique to Chronicles. Jehoiada articulates the theocratic and royalist agenda: **The king's son shall reign, as the LORD promised concerning the descendants of David.** Yahweh's covenant with David means that his sons should reign over Judah. It is a just coup based on divine promises. As DILLARD (181) comments, "this appeal is important in assessing the Chronicler's overall attitude to messianic/Davidic hopes during the post-exilic period: in [the Chronicler's] portrayal, the temple is not the seat of a satisfied theocratic status quo, but rather is the guardian and promoter of the Davidic succession." The temple and king are tied together in promise (David), history (Solomon), and hope (the future Messiah).

The coup was synchronized with the change of temple personnel (2 Chr 23:8). This would double the number of priests and Levites in the temple environs. Chronicles leaves the role of the military leaders unspecified, but they are apparently part of the scenario (2 Chr 23:8 includes "all Judah"). One third of the Levites would guard the **doors**, another third would be stationed at the **royal palace**, and another third **in the courtyards of the temple of the LORD**. Only the **priests and Levites** who were on duty were to **enter the temple of the LORD**. An inner circle of armed Levites protected the king.

Joash Crowned (23:8-11)

Jehoiada stationed his men and armed the **commanders** with **the spears and the large and small shields that had belonged to King**

David that were stored in the **temple**. Theologically, "it is certainly significant that king David's arms now serve . . . to secure the survival of the Davidic dynasty" (JAPHET, 833). These weapons may have been part of David's gifts to the temple (cf. 1 Chr 26:26; 2 Chr 5:1; 15:18).

Once everyone is in place, Jehoiada brings out **the king's son**. The public coronation in the temple courtyard involved four steps (as indicated by the successive "ands" in the Hebrew text): (1) Jehoiada crowns Joash, (2) Jehoiada presented him with the **covenant**, that is, "testimony," (3) the people proclaimed him king, and (4) they (the priests?) anointed Joash. The noun "crown" is a cognate of the verb "consecrate." "The crown," JOHNSTONE (2:128) notes, "is thus the symbol of exclusive dedication to the one to whose service he is set apart." The "testimony" (עֵדוּת, 'ēdûth) is probably a record of the duties and requirements of the king (1 Chr 29.19, cf. 1 Sam 10.25) though some have suggested a dedicatory inscription (SELMAN, 2:447). The public proclamation is recorded in 2 Chronicles 23:11: "**Long live the king!**"

The Death of Athaliah (23:12-15)

Athaliah contests the coronation. This moment will decide where the loyalty of the commanders, Levites, and people lie. But Athaliah stepped into an enthusiastic crowd which was determined to restore the Davidic throne. Athaliah was isolated, led out of the temple area, and executed at the royal gate.

Chronicles follows Dtr's account in 2 Kings 11:13-16, but with a few changes. Chronicles adds that the people rejoiced with the trumpeters, and **singers with musical instruments were leading the praises**. Levitical musicians led the people in praise to God for the successful restoration of the Davidic king. Literally, the singers "were causing to know" (וּמוֹדִיעִים [ûmôdî'îm]; cf. hifil of ידע [yāda'] in 1 Chr 16:8; 17:19) the praises (הַלֵּל, hallēl).

Jehoiada protects the sanctity of the temple by killing Athaliah outside its courts. In contrast with Athaliah's idolatry and bloodthirstiness, Jehoiada executes the judgment of God in a way that preserves the holiness of God's resting place. Nevertheless, Athaliah is rejected as queen because she was from the house of Ahab, a Baal worshiper and a murderer.

Covenant Renewal (23:16-21)

Chronicles elaborates on Dtr's account by adding temple details (2 Chr 23:18b-19 are unique), but otherwise follows 2 Kings 11:7-20. The additions signal the unity of king and temple. The restoration of the king (2 Chr 23:1-15) is followed by the renovation of the temple (2 Chr 23:16-21). The center of this unity is covenant renewal (cf. 2 Chr 23:16-21).

Reestablishing Yahweh Worship (23:16-17)

While Yahwehist worship was not extinct, it had been seriously damaged by competing interests (Baal worship), and the temple had fallen into disrepair (cf. 2 Chr 24:1-14). Jehoiada mediates the covenant renewal. He "cuts a covenant" (**made a covenant**) by sacrifice and renews the commitment of priest, king, and people to **be the LORD's people**. Jehoaiada represents the priesthood and Joash the royal interests. Together they celebrate a covenant renewal where God's faithfulness is invoked and their commitment is affirmed.

This commitment (**all the people**) resulted in the destruction of Baal worship in Jerusalem (similar to what happened when Jehu destroyed the house of Ahab; cf. 2 Kgs 9). The worship of Yahweh is exclusivistic. This is the first indication in Chronicles that Baal worship was so strong as to have a **temple**, but it is consistent with the kings walking in the ways of Ahab (cf. 2 Chr 22:4). Athaliah had confiscated dedicated articles from the temple of Yahweh to use in the temple of Baal (cf. 2 Chr 24:7).

As with Athaliah, the rival to the throne of David, so **Mattan the priest of Baal**, Jehoiada's rival, is killed (cf. Deut 13:5-10).

Reorganization of the Temple Cult (23:18-19)

Jehoiada restores the cultic integrity of the temple. He placed the temple rituals **in the hands of the priests, who were Levites**. The restoration of temple worship involved: (1) **burnt offerings** offered by priests according to the **Law of Moses** (1 Chr 24), (2) Levitical singers according to the Davidic regulations (1 Chr 25), and (3) Levitical **doorkeepers** who ensured **that no one who was in any way unclean might enter** (1 Chr 26). Chronicles highlights the sacrifices, music, and holiness of the temple parallel with 1 Chr 24-26.

Reenthronement of Davidic King (23:20-21)

The king has been anointed, his rival executed. Temple worship has a new beginning. Thus, Joash is led by a procession of **commanders, nobles, rulers**, and **all the people** from the temple into the royal palace to sit on the **royal throne**. The procession **through the Upper Gate** (only here in the Hebrew Bible) passes the Horse Gate where Athaliah was executed (JOHNSTONE, 2:136). The new king is enthroned and the old queen is dead.

The consequence is that **all the people of the land rejoiced** and **the city was quiet**. Rejoicing (cf. the same cognate in 2 Chr 23:18) is strongly cultic in flavor (cf. 1 Chr 16:10,31; 2 Chr 6:41; 7:10; 15:15). The joy of the people was a cultic celebration. The quietness of the city is God's blessing. The term "quiet" is part of the Davidic promise (1 Chr 22:9; 2 Chr 20:30). Israel rejoices in their worship, and God blesses his people with peace.

E. THE REIGN OF JOASH (24:1-27)

The "dark days" of Judah have passed and a new day has dawned under the guidance of the high priest Jehoiada. As long as Jehoiada lived, Joash remained faithful. After his death, Joash listened to other voices and abandoned what Jehoiada had accomplished. When Joash was left to himself, he lost his way.

The pericope divides into four sections. The first and last sections are Chronicles's normal formulaic introduction (2 Chr 24:1-3) and conclusion (2 Chr 24:25-27). The middle section, however, is the heart of the story which describes the good (2 Chr 24:4-16) and bad (2 Chr 24:17-24) years. The pivotal point is the death of Jehoiada (2 Chr 24:15-16).

Second Chronicles 24 parallels 2 Kings 12. Chronicles follows Dtr's formulaic introduction (2 Kgs 12:1-3) and conclusion (2 Kgs 12:19-21). Further, Chronicles follows 2 Kings's narrative of temple renovation (2 Kgs 12:4-16) and Hazael's invasion (2 Kgs 12:17-18). In addition to a few excisions (omits 2 Kgs 12:6-7 and 2 Kgs 12:19) and additions (adds 2 Chr 24:3-4,9-10,24), the major difference between Chronicles and Dtr is Jehoiada's death and Joash's subsequent apostasy (2 Chr 24:15-22). In Chronicles's story, the death of Jehoiada accounts for Joash's apostasy, and Joash's apostasy results in Hazael's invasion. The Chronicler did not invent this apostasy since Dtr presumes that, once he was no longer influenced by Jehoiada, Joash was not the faithful king he was previously (2 Kgs 12:3).

Thus, Chronicles interprets Hazael's invasion as a punishment for Joash's apostasy. This is absent from Dtr. The Chronicler reflects his characteristic interest in "immediate retribution" (DILLARD, 187). This literary pattern of good years followed by bad years is repeated by the Chronicler for the following two kings, Amaziah (2 Chr 25) and Uzziah (2 Chr 26). Thus, the periodization of the reigns into good and bad years, while not invented by the Chronicler, is used to make a significant theological point — God blesses those who seek him and forsakes those who reject him.

1. Formulaic Introduction (24:1-3)

The introduction includes the standard notations of when Joash began to reign (**seven**), how long he reigned (**forty years**), and the name of his mother (**Zibiah**).

The introduction contains a theological evaluation. **Joash did what was right in the eyes of the LORD all the years of Jehoiada the priest**. While Dtr reads "all the years Jehoiada the priest instructed him," Chronicles omits "instructed him." Chronicles emphasizes the guiding presence of Jehoiada's life. His death is the moment of transition in Joash's reign. As long as Joash was guided by the presence of a faithful leader, he followed that guidance. This underscores the importance of spiritual mentors.

Chronicles omits Dtr's troubling note that while spiritual renewal gripped Jerusalem, the people continued to sacrifice on the high places. Chronicles does not dispute this but applies it to Joash's apostate period (2 Chr 24:18).

2. The Good Years of Joash (24:4-16)

The good years of Joash involve efforts to restore the temple. The evil years will desecrate it. The temple is more central to the Chronicler's story than Dtr's because it figures into both the renewal and apostasy of the nation. Further, the Chronicler adds several details (Levites [2 Chr 24:5,6,11], Mosaic tax [2 Chr 24:6,9-10], and renovation [2 Chr 24:4,12]). Thus, the good years are temple years under the leadership of the high priest Jehoiada. Repairing the temple recalls the building of the temple in the days of David and Solomon as well as the initial construction of the tabernacle. The Chronicler, as in the Solomonic narrative, draws a parallel between the temple and the tabernacle (DILLARD, 187).

Renovation of the Temple (24:4-14)

While both Chronicles and Dtr report temple renovations during the reign of Joash, there are a few key differences (DILLARD, 188). Significantly, Chronicles describes this as a renovation (חדש, ḥdš; 2 Chr 24:4,12). For the Chronicler the renovation of the temple symbolizes and energizes renewal. The idea of "restoration" is deepened by the intent to rebuild **the temple of God according to its original design** (or, "proper condition," NRSV; 2 Chr 24:13). Presumably this alludes to the original pattern given by David in 1 Chronicles 28:11-12.

The renovation narrative divides into three sections: (1) Seeking Funds for the Renovation (2 Chr 24:4-7), (2) Funding Renovation through the Mosaic Tax (2 Chr 24:8-11), and (3) The Work of Renovation (2 Chr 24:12-14).

Seeking Funds for the Renovation (24:4-7)

Chronicles parallels Joash's intent to renovate the temple with David's intent to build one (lit., "had in my heart"; 1 Chr 22:7; 28:2; 2 Chr 24:4). JOHNSTONE (2:137) regards this as Joash's "impulsiveness" which is balanced by Jehoiada's prudence. Instead of using the royal treasury (as David did), Joash sent out the **priests and Levites** to **collect** money. It is unclear whether this was a voluntary contribution (**due** is not in the MT). Joash may have intended voluntary gifts (like David in 1 Chr 29). If this is the case, 2 Chronicles 24:5 is not parallel to 2 Kings 12:5 since Dtr involves the collection of owed taxes. Chronicles, however, mentions owed taxes in 2 Chronicles 24:6. Whatever may be the case, the Levites do not complete the task. The amount of time this involved (identified as the "twenty-third" year of Joash in 2 Kgs 12:7) is unstated.

The hesitancy of the **Levites** may derive from their own depleted funds. As 2 Chronicles 24:7 notes, temple resources (even the **sacred objects**) had been reallocated during the dark days (the sons of Athaliah) — holy funds for the unholy worship of Baal. This underscores the depravity that engulfed Judah (2 Chr 21–23). Apparently, the temple had no funds, and it was struggling to conduct its cultic activities. Perhaps Joash's interest in repairing the temple was not the highest priority for the priests and Levites.

Rather than using the royal treasuries, Joash seeks funds for repairing the temple from cultic taxation. Second Kings 12:4 describes this in a threefold manner: "money collected in census, the money received from personal vows and the money brought voluntarily to the temple." The first two are derived from Mosaic legislation — a census tax imposed for the upkeep of the tabernacle (Exod 30:12-16) and sacrificial monetary payments. The Chronicler collapses these three modes into one. JAPHET (844) suggests that the Chronicler is exegeting the older texts and applying them in his own context. This fits the Chronicler's own situation as he seeks to reinforce the support of the temple in the postexilic community.

In any event, the Mosaic regulations for supporting the tabernacle (**Tent of the Testimony**; Num 9:15; 17:7,8; 18:2) are applied to the temple. Joash applies the principles embedded in the Mosaic legislation. Chronicles's application means that the temple tax is the "ransom price of the entire community" because the temple is the "visible expression of the petition by the people for the sparing of their lives and of the acceptance by God of that petition." This entailed the "dedication of the whole of life to God." Thus, cultic taxation was an expression of Israel's "dependence" upon God's grace (JOHNSTONE, 2:138-139). All monetary gifts to divine interests testify that all that we have is by grace (cf. 2 Cor 8–9).

Funding Renovation through the Mosaic Tax (24:8-11)

Given the unexplained failure of the priests and Levites, Joash takes the initiative in collecting funds. Instead of a clerical itinerant collection, Joash commanded a **chest** be **made and placed outside, at the gate of the temple of the LORD**. He centralizes the collection of the **tax**. Joash intends Judah to obey the Mosaic regulation — it is a tax that is given **to the LORD** as **required of Israel in the desert**. The Chronicler applies Exodus 30:11-16 to the time of Joash and also to

411

his own postexilic community. Second Chronicles 24:9-10 emphasizes the Mosaic connection as well as the joyful response of the people which parallels the response of the people in 1 Chronicles 29:1-9
(as well as Exod 36:4-7). The people respond **gladly** to Joash's **proclamation**. The use of a chest for the collection of offerings is well-
known in ancient Near Eastern temples (DILLARD, 191).

There are several differences between 2 Kings 12:10-11 and
2 Chronicles 24:8-11. One is the location of the box. While Dtr
places the chest beside the altar, the Chronicler places it at the temple gate (probably where it was located in the Chronicler's own day).
He probably accommodated Dtr to his own time (THOMPSON, 315).
Another accommodation is the use of the term **money** (silver
coins?). While coinage was widespread in the postexilic era, it was
not during the time of Joash. The offerings would have been in the
form of precious metals, silver vessels, etc.

Interestingly, both royal and priestly personnel are involved in
the count and disbursement of the wealth. The king and priest are
linked together. Both Joash and Jehoiada are interested parties in
the renewal (2 Chr 24:12).

The Work of Renovation (24:12-14)

The king and Jehoiada handed over the funds to the foremen
who **hired** workers **to repair the temple**. Chronicles parallels the
building of the temple and the construction of the tabernacle. Both
conformed to a design or pattern (1 Chr 28:11-19; Exod 25:9,40),
and the repair work conforms to the **original design**. Further, just
as gifts were used to manufacture tabernacle utensils in Exodus 25
(cf. 31:1-10), they are used for the same purpose here (2 Chr 24:14).

As DILLARD (191) points out, there is no real tension between
2 Kings 12:14 and 2 Chronicles 24:14 though it seems problematic.
Chronicles comments on the surplus funds while Dtr comments on
the initial use of funds. Chronicles has collapsed all the monetary
collection into a single act while Dtr distinguishes between money
collected for the temple repairs from money collected for the priests
(2 Kgs 12:14-17).

Chronicles is interested in the overall point – the king and
his priest restored the temple cultus (both building and ritual). This
recalls Moses and David/Solomon. This is significant for the

Chronicler because it is the exact situation of his readers. They live in a time of a "restored" temple. It is important for them to remember earlier moments in their history (Moses, David, Joash) when worship was renewed. This calls the postexilic community to act, and it reassures them that just as God blessed the renovation of the temple during the days of Joash and Jehoiada, he will bless its renovation in their day.

Death of Jehoiada (24:15-16)

This is the transition from the good to the bad years of Joash's reign. It is unique to Chronicles. Jehoiada's long life (**a hundred and thirty**) surpasses Moses's one hundred and twenty years (Deut 34:7). The number of years is problematic since this is rare in the kingdom period and it would mean that Jehoiada married Jehoshabeath (daughter of Jehoram) when she was fifteen and he was eighty. But the marriage of older men and younger women was not uncommon (DILLARD, 196). Further, such a marriage served national interests as it linked the royal and priestly lines. In any event, 130 years is not impossible.

Jehoiada alone of nonroyal figures receives a royal burial in Chronicles (JOHNSTONE, 2:143), perhaps because he was a royal guardian and the protector of the Davidic line. The witness of his life is **the good he had done in Israel for God and his temple**. This description highlights the importance of the temple for the Chronicler. Jehoiada saved the Davidic line and assisted Joash in the renovation of the temple.

3. The Evil Years of Joash (24:17-24)

The transitional function of Jehoiada's death is indicated by the temporal notation in 2 Chronicles 24:17: **after the death of Jehoiada**. If the earlier reign of Joash reminded Chronicles's readers of David and Solomon, the latter reign evokes memories of Rehoboam (bad advice; 2 Chr 10:8-11) and Josah's apostate ancestors (Jehoram and Ahaziah; 2 Chr 21–23).

This section, with the exception of Hazael's invasion (2 Chr 24:23 with 2 Kgs 12:18), is unique to Chronicles. It explains Joash's assassination. His apostasy led to a violent death like his father

(2 Chr 22:9) and his grandmother (2 Chr 23:15). The Chronicler invokes his retribution theology to interpret Joash's demise.

The Evil (24:17-19)

Chronicles does not indicate how much time elapsed after Jehoiada's death before Joash headed into apostasy. Nevertheless, the shift is narratively abrupt. Whatever the rationale for Joash's apostasy, he listens to his **officials** (leaders) who embraced pluralism. The emergence of these leaders indicates that the royal house was probably divided during the "good" years, but they did not have the political power to press their concerns.

Interestingly, these leaders **paid homage** (וַיִּשְׁתַּחֲווּ, *wayyištaḥăwû*) **to the king**, which is the language used to describe the worship of Yahweh (cf. 1 Chr 16:29; 2 Chr 7:3,19,22; 20:18; 29:28-29; 32:12) and Amaziah's worship of Edomite gods (2 Chr 25:14; cf. 33:3). It may be used accomodatively of the king as long as it is remembered that he is a representative of Yahweh (cf. 1 Chr 29:20; cf. 21:21). The image here, as JOHNSTONE (2:144) suggests, is idolatrous in character — Joash receives worship and is led into pluralism.

With Joash's permission, the leaders of Judah reintroduced **Asherah poles and idols**. This is probably the reintroduction of Baal worship (which seems likely in the light of Athaliah) or perhaps simply a perverted Yahwehist worship. In either event, Chronicles characterizes their actions in the harshest terms possible: **They abandoned the temple of the LORD, the God of their fathers**. "Abandoned" (עֲזָב, *'āzab*) is one of the key theological words in Chronicles (28 times; cf. 1 Chr 28:9). It is used 5 times in this context (2 Chr 24:18,20[2],24,25). The leaders of Judah forsook the Lord, and in response God, as he promised he would (2 Chr 7:19-22), forsakes them.

Yahweh sent **prophets** to his **people** in order to **bring them back** (שׁוּב, *šûb*) **to him**. Even though his people had forsaken him and abandoned the temple, God yearned for his people. He sent covenantal messengers to turn them. His prophets **testified against** his people. Through his prophets, God pursues a redemptive agenda. He seeks to forgive (cf. 2 Chr 6:6:24,25,37,38; 7:14; 15:4; 30:9). This is a narrative version of Jehoshaphat's exhortation: "have faith in his prophets" (2 Chr 20:20).

Ultimately, God disciplines his people with exile because they would not turn to him (2 Chr 36:13). But despite this discipline, God is willing to receive his people back if they will but turn to him (cf. 2 Chr 7:14). The confidence of the postexilic community is that God is gracious and willing to forgive. The Chronicler calls his readers to hear the prophets in their own setting, just as we who live in the last days must hear the message of God's own Son (Heb 1:1-2).

Prophetic Warning (24:20-22)

While there were apparently many prophets, Chronicles highlights the priestly **Zechariah**. This prophet stands out because (1) he is the **son of Jehoiada** and (2) he is executed for his message. As JAPHET (849) notes, "Zechariah's intervention and his fate should be viewed in a political and historical context broader than the personal relationship between Joash and Jehoiada." He prophesied **before the people**. The conflict is between the priests (Zechariah) and the royal bureaucracy (Judean leaders). Zechariah's intervention was presumably regarded as treasonous.

The prophet questions the people under the inspiration of the **Spirit of God** (clothed with the Spirit; cf. 1 Chr 12:18). He brings the word of the Lord (**what God says**). His message is emphatic ("you" is pl): **Why do you disobey the LORD's commands? You will not prosper. Because you have forsaken the LORD, he has forsaken you**. Significantly, Zechariah uses the same word as Jehoshaphat ("successful" in 2 Chr 20:20). If they believe and heed the prophets, they will prosper, but if they do not, they will not. The people of God cannot prosper amidst Godforsakenness. God forsakes those who forsake him (1 Chr 28:9).

The leaders, **by the order of the king**, executed Zechariah by stoning (cf. Matt 23:35; Luke 11:50-51). Both the mode and place of death are important. "Zechariah, the son of the priest who had saved the throne for Joash, is murdered in the place where Joash was protected during the coup" (DILLARD, 192-193; 2 Chr 23:9-11,15-16). Even though Jehoiada preserved the holy place from bloodshed by removing Athaliah (2 Chr 23:13), Joash sanctions bloodshed in the holy place. Stoning is not an act of mob violence. It "was a judicial act undertaken by the whole community" (JOHNSTONE, 2:146; cf. 2 Chr 10:18). Joash's desertion of Yahweh is complete. Instead of purging evil from his presence, Joash purged God's goodness by stoning God's prophet (cf. Deut 17:5-7).

The theological comment of 2 Chronicles 24:22 is striking. Chronicles contrasts the **kindness** (חֶסֶד, *ḥesed*; steadfast love) of Jehoiada with Joash's apostasy. Despite Jehoiada's loving loyalty to Joash, the king would not show the same to Jehoiada's own son.

Zechariah's last words seem in tension with the last words of Jesus (cf. Luke 22:34) or Stephen (Acts 7:60; cf. DILLARD, 194). However, SELMAN (2:456) argues that this "prayer should not be compared unfavorably" because "Jesus actually quotes this incident in pronouncing judgment on his contemporaries" (cf. Matt 23:33-36; Luke 11:47-51). There are appropriate times to call upon God's justice (cf. Ps 58). Solomon's prayer envisioned just such a scenario where the innocent may seek justice in the temple courts (2 Chr 6:23). David called for divine justice without personal vengeance against Saul (1 Sam 24:15). Zechariah voices an appropriate cry for justice.

Punishment of Judah by Hazael (24:23-24)

The Chronicler returns to Dtr as he reports the campaign against **Aram**. While some believe the Chronicler has merely adapted Dtr's material at this point (JAPHET, 851-852), others believe he had access to an alternative description of the Aramaean invasion (WILLIAMSON, 325-326). Whatever the case, 2 Chronicles 24:24 is a theological assessment.

The invasion is disastrous. Just as the Philistines and Arabs executed judgment against Jehoram (cf. 2 Chr 21:16-17), so Aram executes judgment against Joash. The invasion is so successful that **all the leaders of the people** are killed (cf. 2 Chr 24:17) and Jerusalem itself is plundered. The smaller army defeats the larger one (contrast 2 Chr 13:3-18; 14:8-15; 20:27).

Judgment comes, of course, **because Judah had forsaken the LORD**. The spoils (including temple articles; cf. 2 Kgs 12:19) were taken to Damascus (just as the wealth of Solomon's temple was taken to Egypt; cf. 2 Chr 12:9). God rejected both Joash and Rehoboam because they had forsaken him (cf. 2 Chr 12:5; 24:24).

4. Formulaic Conclusion (24:25-27)

The formulaic conclusion includes the normal items, such as (1) death of the king, (2) burial of the king (though unusual since it is **not in the tomb of the kings**), (3) historical sources, and (4) his successor (**Amaziah**). The Chronicler follows the bare outlines of 2 Kgs 12:20-22 but adapts it to the unique material his narrative contains. While Dtr only refers to a conspiracy, the Chronicler explains that its roots are found in the opposition to the death of Jehoiada's **son**. The Chronicler identifies the conspirators as the sons of **Ammonite** and **Moabite** women as if to call attention to God's "foreign" judgment of his own king. They bear witness to the "constant readiness of destructive powers to invade Israel from the world of nations, if Israel in any way falls short of the destiny envisaged for her" (JOHNSTONE, 2:148).

Joash dies violently, just like his father and grandmother. God judges Joash's reign. The prophetic interpretation was preserved in **the annotations on the book of the kings** to which the Chronicler refers his readers. The word "annotations" (מִדְרַשׁ) is sometimes translated "commentary" or transliterated "midrash." While some have seized "on this particular title as a significant clue to unraveling the complex question of the nature of the Chronicler's sources," it is "doubtful" that this is what the Chronicler intends (WILLIAMSON, 326). More likely, in addition to Dtr, the Chronicler had a prophetic book available to him that contained the oracles against Joash.

The reign of Joash underscores the value of spiritual mentors. But mentoring only lasts so long. At some point, Joash must adopt his own faith. Instead of following his godly mentor, he listened to others. This epitomizes the fallen heart. While Joash did what was right in the eyes of Yahweh, he only did so under the tutelage of Jehoiada. Ultimately Joash did not have a heart for God. When unrestrained, that heart killed God's prophet (cf. Matt 21:33-46; Acts 7:51-53).

F. THE REIGN OF AMAZIAH (25:1–26:2)

Following PRATT (379), this table portrays the relationship between Chronicles and Dtr. The Chronicler's additions reshape Dtr's narrative to make a different point. While Dtr is primarily interested in the war with Israel, the Chronicler is interested in the journey from good to evil.

Topic	2 Chr 25–26	2 Kgs 13–14
Events in the North		13:1–14:1
Introduction to Amaziah's Reign	25:1-4	14:2-6
War with Edom	25:5-13	14:7
Theological Evaluation	25:14-16	
War with Israel	25:17-24	14:8-14
Kings of Israel		14:15-16
Conclusion to Amaziah's Reign	25:25–26:2	14:17-22

Chronicles basically ignores the events in the northern kingdom but expands the details of Amaziah's war with Edom. Most importantly, Chronicles adds a theological section which details Amaziah's idolatry and Yahweh's displeasure.

The theological assessment is the literary center of story. The Chronicler structures his narrative in a concentric fashion (adapted from Graham, "Aspects," 81-84).

    1. Introduction to Amaziah's Reign (2 Chr 25:1-4)
      2. War with Edom (2 Chr 25:5-13)
        3. Amaziah's Idolatry (2 Chr 25:14-16)
      2'. War with Israel (2 Chr 25:17-24)
    1'. Conclusion of Amaziah's Reign (2 Chr 25:25–26:2)

The literary and theological structure focuses on the central part of the story — Amaziah's idolatry. Chronicles divides the reign of Amaziah into two periods: (1) preidolatry and (2) postidolatry. The former is blessed (victory over Edom), but the latter is cursed (defeated by Israel).

The Chronicler's unique material (2 Chr 25:5-16) has generated doubt about its historicity. Since periodization and immediate retribution is so characteristic of his hermeneutical method, many suppose his account is more theology than history (Graham, "Aspects," 89, n. 26). Further, while Chronicles portrays Amaziah as moving from Yahweh-seeker to an idolater, Dtr assesses his reign as a relatively good king (cf. 2 Kgs 14:3-4).

However, Dtr's assessment of Amaziah is not all good. The king of Israel, speaking for the narrator, accuses Amaziah of pride (2 Kgs 14:10). Israel's victory over Amaziah is an implied judgment in Dtr.

The Chronicler illuminates this implication. But does the Chronicler fabricate a scenario in order to press his own theological agenda? JAPHET (859; cf. WILLIAMSON, 327-329) believes that sources lie behind the Chronicler's account. The details of the Ephraimite band, the organization of the army, and the Edomite war are not fabrications, but derived from historical sources. DILLARD (197) suggests that the "fact that the prophet is unnamed" tends to confirm "the genuineness of the narrative" because if the Chronicler "were composing of whole cloth, one would expect that the prophet be given a name or associated in some way with some other known prophetic figure."

Amaziah is the second of three kings (Jehoash and Uzziah) who started out good, but ended up bad. The theological point is perseverance and consistency. SELMAN (2:458-459) reminds us that the repetitious character of some of these stories (another good king gone bad) may seem tiresome. But the stories remind us that God is patient. They warn us about our own temptations. No one "is immune from pride and complacency," and perseverance is a necessary virtue.

1. Formulaic Introduction (25:1-4)

The introduction contains the standard elements: (1) the age Amaziah began to rule (**twenty-five**); (2) the length of his reign (**twenty-nine**); (3) his mother's name (**Jehoaddin**); and (4) a theological evaluation (**he did what was right in the eyes of the LORD, but not wholeheartedly**). Even though Amaziah reigned twenty-nine years (796–767 B.C.), much of this (perhaps twenty-four) was as co-regent with his son (Thiele, 113-116; DILLARD, 198).

The theological evaluation is unique. He is the only king who is assessed as doing what was right but not with a "whole heart." Since this changes the wording in 2 Kings 14:3 ("he did what was right in the sight of the LORD, but not as his father David had done"), Amaziah's lack of a "whole heart" is significant. "Wholeheartedness" was expected (cf. 1 Chr 28:9; 29:19; 2 Chr 15:17; 19:9). It explains his subsequent actions. Externally, he did what was right, but his heart was neither loyal nor committed. His "rightness" derived from external motives rather than from those of a "whole heart."

The standard introduction is extended in order to narrate the fate of those who assassinated Jehoash. No rationale is offered for their execution (which may have been justice, revenge, or simply consolidation of power). The account is taken from Dtr, including the citation of Deuteronomy 24:16. Amaziah executes the **officials who had murdered his father**, but he spares their children in accordance with Mosaic **Law**. In Chronicles, the citation "illuminates and interprets the outcome of Amaziah's reign" since "Amaziah was assassinated at the end of [the Chronicler's] narrative 'for his own sin'" (Graham, "Aspects," 86). Ironically, the text cited to praise Amaziah is also used to condemn him.

2. War against Edom (25:5-13)

While the war against Edom receives only brief mention in Dtr (2 Kgs 14:7), it becomes the first half of the Chronicler's narrative. Though Amaziah displays some virtues (e.g., he listens to the prophet), the narrative is rather negative. He becomes embroiled in a war in which he should never have engaged and enlists mercenaries he should never have hired. His "rightness" is colored by a disloyal heart (2 Chr 25:2), which is unveiled when he worships Edomite gods (2 Chr 25:14-16).

Preparations for War (25:5-10)

Amaziah prepares for battle by (1) appointing his **commanders**, (2) mustering his army (300,000 men over **twenty years old**), and (3) hiring 100,000 warriors **from Israel**. As DILLARD (199) points out, the number of Judeans is smaller than Asa (580,000) and Jehoshaphat (1.16 million), and this may "explain why Amaziah hired the additional troops." In any case, the numbers are probably typological (cf. 2 Chr 14:8-9).

JOHNSTONE (2:153) posits Exodus 30:11-16 as the background to this mustering. According to Exodus 30:13, every male mustered into the army had to pay a half-shekel "redemption" which would be dedicated to the sanctuary. Three hundred thousand men would produce 150,000 shekels, or "50 talents of silver." Thus, Amaziah took what belonged to the temple and used it to hire mercenaries at double the rate. "No wonder the unnamed 'man of God' is outraged" (2 Chr 25:7).

As Graham ("Aspects," 87) points out, "while 300,000 Judean troops should have been sufficient to subdue Edom (10,000 Edomites eventually fell in battle and 10,000 more were captured and executed), the fearful Amaziah hired additional troops from Israel." Amaziah does not exemplify the trust of Asa (2 Chr 14) or Jehoshaphat (2 Chr 20). The irony is that Israel became a more destructive enemy than Edom, and they plunder Judah twice in the narrative (2 Chr 25:13,24). Amaziah's righteousness is superficial.

An unnamed **man of God** (cf. 1 Chr 23:14; 2 Chr 8:14; 11:2) confronts Amaziah. The prophet assumes a typical role in Chronicles. God is with Judah, not Israel. This "enshrines" the "central affirmations of Jerusalemite 'Immanuel' theology" (JOHNSTONE, 2:154; cf. 1 Chr 11:9). There is one God, and he has one kingdom, king, and sanctuary. While Yahweh will receive any who come to his temple, Chronicles does not endorse the northern kingdom. **The LORD is not with Israel**. The question is whether Amaziah will trust in Yahweh who has **power to help** (cf. 1 Chr 12:18) **or to overthrow**. He can either go **courageously** (cf. קזח, ḥāzaq in 1 Chr 19:13; 22:13; 28:10,20; 2 Chr 15:7) into battle as one who trusts God, or he can attack with the Ephraimites. God helps those who trust him but overthrows those who do not.

Amaziah is double-minded. He has already paid his mercenaries. Why should he not go ahead and use them? Amaziah not only lacks trust but also misplaces his trust. He does not know Yahweh since, as the prophet says, **the LORD can give you much more than that**. The call to trust the Lord instead of mercenaries is a "colossal challenge to normal scales of human values: better to sever connections made even at high cost, if these relationships are illicit" (JOHNSTONE, 2:154).

The mercenaries are angry. Even though they retained their wages, they lost potential booty in Edom. Consequently, they plunder Judah as they return home (2 Chr 25:13). The booty they should have received in battle, they took from Judahites from Samaria to Beth Horon. "The irony," Graham ("Aspects," 87) writes, "lies in Amaziah's concern for losing a hundred talents of silver, while the entire success of the Edomite campaign hung in the balance, and in the fact that he never anticipated the angry reaction of the Israelite troops, who had been deprived of their plunder."

The Battle (25:11-13)

Amaziah gained some resolve from the prophet's words. He "took courage" (NRSV; *ḥāzaq* in 2 Chr 25:8) and defeated the Edomites. The identification of the battle site ("Sela" [a transliteration of the Hebrew] in NRSV; **a cliff** in NIV) is disputed (DILLARD, 200; Hart, 91-95), but the battle must have raged in the region of Edom southeast of Judah. No motive for the war is given.

The mass execution of 10,000 Edomites seems horrendous by modern standards, but the practice was widespread in the ancient Near East. Further, the execution may have a theological purpose. JOHNSTONE (2:156) argues that this is a narrative display of the Davidic right "to exercise dominion over Edom." It is an extension of divine justice among the nations. As with the Canaanites, divine eschatological justice at times intrudes into history to execute justice and demonstrate the election of his people.

3. Theological Evaluation (25:14-16)

Amaziah's victory did not engender faith, but apostasy. In contrast to David who destroyed his enemy's idols (1 Chr 14:12), Amaziah brings them to Jerusalem. Conquering kings would take idols as plunder and erect them in their own land (DILLARD, 201; cf. 2 Chr 36:7). This indicated that the gods had abandoned their people and supported the conquering nation. Amaziah – whose heart was not "whole" – brings the Edomite gods to Jerusalem and becomes a pluralist. Since the Edomite **gods** aided his victory, he worships them alongside Yahweh. Amaziah's pride (cf. 2 Chr 25:19) finds refuge in Edomite deities rather than full submission to Yahweh.

In response, Yahweh was angry (cf. 1 Chr 13:10) and sent an unnamed **prophet** to question him: **Why do you consult this people's gods, which could not save their own people from your hand?** The logic of the question is impeccable from a monotheistic standpoint, but in the context of the pluralistic ancient Near East it fell on deaf ears. Amaziah does not recognize Yahweh as the only God. The question uses one of Chronicles's key terms – "seek" (**consult**; cf. *dāraš* in 1 Chr 28:9; 2 Chr 7:14). Why do you seek Edomite gods instead of Yahweh?

The king, however, is committed to pluralism, and he does not recognize the prophet as **an adviser to the king**. Amaziah, the royal representative of Yahweh, does not recognize the **prophet** whom Yahweh **sent**. While prophets may not have been titled officials in the royal court, they do represent Yahweh. Instead of answering the prophet's question, Amaziah asks his own: **Why be struck down?** Ironically, Amaziah's question predicts his own fate for rejecting Yahweh.

The prophet pronounces judgment: **I know that God has determined to destroy you**. This destruction was averted in Rehoboam's day because the nation humbled itself (cf. 2 Chr 12:7,12), but Amaziah refused to humble himself.

The Hebrew term הִשְׁחִית (*hišḥît*, "destroy," from שׁחת) links the narratives of Jehoash, Amaziah, and Uzziah. All three are given over to destruction (2 Chr 24:23; 25:16; 26:16) because of their pride (Prov 16:18). In addition, all three kings were warned and refused to listen to Yahweh's godly representatives (2 Chr 24:19; 25:16; 26:18-19). The typical pattern is: (1) pride, (2) warning, (3) refusal to listen, and (4) destruction.

The message for the postexilic community is clear (2 Chr 20:20). Listen to God's prophets, humble yourself before the Lord, and he will raise you up. But if your pride neglects or rejects God's prophets, he will destroy you.

4. War against Israel (25:17-24)

Chronicles follows Dtr rather closely (2 Kgs 14:8-14) but recontextualizes it. Dtr does not mention the worship of the Edomite gods. Rather, Dtr attributes the loss to Amaziah's pride (2 Kgs 14:10), as does the Chronicler (cf. 2 Chr 25:19). The war with Israel is divine punishment (2 Chr 25:20) whereas it is primarily foolhardiness in Dtr. The two ideas are not mutually exclusive though they serve different functions.

Preparations for War (25:17-20)

Chronicles often refers to the counsel that kings took with their officials (cf. 1 Chr 13:1; 2 Chr 10:6; 22:4). Amaziah consults with **his advisers** even as he refuses to heed Yahweh's prophet. This cabinet meeting results in a battle plan against Israel. Amaziah invites **Jehoash**, the **king of Israel**, to a battle. The phrase **meet me face to face** is a euphemism for war (cf. 2 Chr 25:21).

Jehoash is not anxious for battle though he is certain of its outcome. He tries to convince Amaziah "to desist from a planned course of action, out of a realistic appraisal of his own strength" with a fable. The fable portrays the thistle as a "naïve country-bumpkin, who does not realize how small he really is" (Solomon, 129). Amaziah's optimism is generated not only by his recent victory over Edom (2 Chr 25:19), but also by Israel's recent losses (cf. 2 Kgs 12:18–13:5). But Amaziah was only a **thistle** and did not realize it.

But who is the **cedar** and who is the **wild beast**? PRATT suggests that the cedar is Edom (PRATT, 388). The thistle had the gall to align itself with a cedar. This alliance is Amaziah's covenant with the Edomite gods. Though this generates pride, Jehoash counsels that a wild beast may trample the thistle. In other words, basking in the pride of an Edomite victory, Judah may find itself defeated by a larger foe. Israel is the wild animal (anticipating a succession of wild animals in the coming history — Assyria and Babylon; cf. Solomon, 130). Unless Judah wants to be crushed like a thistle, it should **stay at home**. Otherwise, there will be **trouble** (lit., "evil").

Amaziah did **not listen**. He failed to heed another warning due to divine determination. Second Chronicles 25:20 is the most theological verse in the narrative. Amaziah intended to attack Israel because God intended to **hand them over** in punishment. This is a divine act. Chronicles explicitly attributes this battle to God's own work — literally, "it was from God" (the same word appears in 1 Chr 5:22). God hardened the prideful heart of Amaziah in order to punish him (Prov 21:1; cf. Rom 9:15-18).

The Battle (25:21-22)

In the light of Amaziah's arrogance, **Jehoash** takes the initiative and engages Judah at **Beth Shemesh** (a Levitical city on the northwest frontier of Judah near a major "access route to Jerusalem;" JOHNSTONE, 2:160). When Yahweh was with Judah, they defeated Israel (2 Chr 13:15) or other enemies (2 Chr 14:12; 20:22), but when Yahweh is against Judah, they are defeated by their enemies (2 Chr 6:24). Israel is the instrument of God's anger.

Aftermath (25:23-24)

Typologically prefiguring the exile to come, Amaziah is **captured** (only use in Chronicles) and **Jehoash** takes **hostages** (only use in Chronicles, probably royal family and aristocracy) **to Samaria**. Other kings will experience mini-exiles (Ahaz in 2 Chr 28; Manasseh in 2 Chr 33). Further prefigurement is seen in the destruction of part of Jerusalem's wall (about 200 yards from the northern gate to the western wall). This thwarts the military advantage of the city and depletes their confidence. Judah will not so readily seek battle if the wall of their capital city has a huge breach. It was not repaired until the reign of Uzziah (2 Chr 26:9). The irony is that the very gods that Amaziah brought into Jerusalem to worship are the reason Jerusalem is plundered. The gods of Edom could not protect Edom, and they could not protect Jerusalem. Yahweh alone reigns.

5. Formulaic Conclusion (25:25–26:2)

The conclusion of Amaziah's reign includes the standard elements: (1) sources (**the book of the kings of Judah and Israel**); (2) burial; and (3) his successor (**Uzziah**).

While the Chronicler is dependent upon 2 Kings 14:17-22, he provides an interesting theological twist in 2 Chronicles 25:27. The conspirators who assassinated Amaziah had been planning his death **from the time that Amaziah turned away from the LORD**. Apparently, there was a religious reform party in Judah who resented Amaziah's introduction of Edomite gods. Perhaps this group also gave Uzziah his reformist mentality. The conspirators were not alone because **all the people of Judah took Uzziah** and **made him king**. Divine blessing accompanied this appointment as Uzziah **rebuilt Elath and restored it to Judah**, but only **after Amaziah rested with his fathers**.

The ironies continue to pile up in this narrative (Graham, "Aspects," 89). A king is expected to flee to his home for protection (Jerusalem), not to **Lachish**. Further, a king is expected to ride on a horse into his royal city as a victor rather than as a rejected king. The king who became king because his father was assassinated died by the hand of conspirators. The one who executed his father's assassins was himself executed by assassins for his own sin.

Amaziah was a king who did right but not with a whole heart. He is a negative model in the Chronicler's history. When the whole heart does not seek God, double-mindedness will eventually express itself in ungodly attitudes or actions.

G. THE REIGN OF UZZIAH (26:3-23)

Uzziah is the third successive king (Joash, Amaziah) whose reign is characterized by righteousness early but by evil in his last years. The pattern of Uzziah's narrative is introduction (2 Chr 26:3-5), good years (2 Chr 26:6-15), evil years (2 Chr 26:16-21), and conclusion (2 Chr 26:22-23).

Despite his lengthy fifty-two year reign, 2 Kings is brief (2 Kgs 14:21-22; 15:1-7). While 2 Kings only gives nine verses to Uzziah (2 Kgs 14:21-22; 15:1-7), Chronicles gives twenty-three (2 Chr 26:1-23). Chronicles divides Uzziah's reign into two parts: a time of blessing parallel to 2 Kings 14:22 (rebuilt Elath) and a time of curse parallel to 2 Kings 15:5 (struck with leprosy). The Chronicler builds his narrative around this dual theme of blessing and curse along with Dtr's introduction (2 Kgs 15:1-4) and conclusion (2 Kgs 15:6-7; cf. WILLIAMSON, 332-333). The Chronicler renders Dtr's account more "theologically coherent" in terms of the rationale for the good king's leprosy (JAPHET, 876). Second Chronicles 26:5-20a is unique to Chronicles, probably based on an additional source (WILLIAMSON, 333; DILLARD, 206; JAPHET, 877).

Theologically, ALLEN (345) suggests that this "royal trilogy" presses the point that faithful perseverance is necessary (cf. Heb 3:14). Joash, Amaziah, and Uzziah are narrative illustrations which encourage believers to persevere. The postexilic community returned to the land full of faith only to lose heart as the promises of God were not realized according to their expectations. Contemporary believers also falter on the same ground. Chronicles, like Hebrews 3–4, calls for perseverance.

1. Formulaic Introduction (26:3-5)

The introduction contains the usual information: (1) length of reign (**fifty-two years**), (2) age when he began to reign (**sixteen**), (3) his mother's name (**Jecoliah**), and (4) theological evaluation (**he did what was right in the eyes of the LORD**) in relation to his predecessor (**just as his father Amaziah had done**). Chronicles reprints 2 Kings 15:2-3.

The theological evaluation receives a different twist in Chronicles which adds 2 Chr 26:5 but omits 2 Kings 15:4. The Chronicler explains Uzziah's righteousness and omits Uzziah's failure to remove all the high places. Chronicles minimizes his failures during the early part of his reign. Indeed, Uzziah's righteousness is contingent on his mentor. Uzziah **sought** (1 Chr 28:9) **God during the days of Zechariah, who instructed him in the fear of God.** Just as his grandfather Joash (2 Chr 24:2), Uzziah was a faithful king while he was under the influence of a godly mentor.

Zechariah is unknown in other biblical sources. WILLIAMSON (334; JAPHET, 878) believes the name was found in the Chronicler's source. Though possibly a prophet, the Chronicler usually identifies prophets. Zechariah is probably Uzziah's teacher in the royal court. Literally, he "caused" Uzziah "to understand the fear of God." Thus, Uzziah was educated in the fear of the Lord.

Chronicles's additional material (2 Chr 26:5) emphasizes the critical word "seek" (דָּרַשׁ, *dāraš*) as the key to **success**. The term is used twice and is directly correlated with Uzziah's blessing (cf. 2 Chr 14:7; 31:21). God blesses those who seek him, and he forsakes those who forsake him (cf. 1 Chr 28:9).

2. Uzziah's Accomplishments (26:6-15)

His accomplishments are the content of the success which God gave Uzziah. God's blessings are narrated in three categories: (1) territorial expansion (26:6-8), (2) economic development (26:9-10), and (3) military buildup (26:11-15).

Territorial Expansion (26:6-8)

Uzziah extended his territorial borders in the west-southwest (**Philistines**), southeast (**Arabs** and **Meunites**) and east (**Ammonites**). This expansion created a regional stir as even Egypt recognizes **his fame**.

Chronicles emphasizes his victory over the Philistines by noting the three cities he conquered, two of which were major centers

(**Gath** and **Ashdod**). **Jabneh** is probably Jabneel (Josh 15:11). Given the western and southwestern interests of these battles, Uzziah was probably seeking to control trade along the international coastal highway. This control fueled his economic growth (2 Chr 26:9-10) and military buildup (2 Chr 26:11-15).

The implied contrast between Saul who did not seek the Lord (2 Chr 10:13-14) and Uzziah who did (2 Chr 26:5-6) is clear. God defeats the enemies of those who seek him. Thus, **God helped** Uzziah **against the Philistines** but defeated Saul.

While the identification of the **Arabs who lived in Gur Baal** is uncertain, it has been identified with Gari (east of Beersheba) named in the Amarna letters (WILLIAMSON, 335). "Arab" is a general name for nomadic tribes in the regions south and southeast of Judah. Meunites (cf. 2 Chr 20:1) are generally associated with Edom (southeast of Judah). Ammonites are the traditional enemy of Israel east of the Jordan River. God restored territorial integrity to Judah because Uzziah sought the Lord.

This restoration has a theological function (JOHNSTONE, 2:164-165). God reasserts, through his vicegerent, his Lordship over the nations. His fame, while not Solomonic in proportions, is analogous to that era. On a limited scale, Uzziah enjoys Solomonic success (צלח, ṣālaḥ; 1 Chr 29:23), fame (2 Chr 9:1) and territory (**border of Egypt**; 2 Chr 9:26). As long as Uzziah sought God, he prospered (cf. 1 Chr 22:11,13; 28:9).

Economics (26:9-10)

Uzziah's prosperity is evidenced in his building and agricultural projects. Building projects repair the damage done by Jehoash of Israel (2 Chr 25:23). "The fact that Jeroboam of Israel does not interfere with these works may imply that Judah had regained its independence" (JAPHET, 881).

Economic growth came both through trade (controlling the intercoastal highway) and agricultural development (Rainey, "Wine," 57-62; Graham, "Vinedressers," 55-58). Uzziah must have had a particular love for agriculture (**he loved the soil**). Many **towers** (watchtowers) and **cisterns** were needed in the wilderness to graze **livestock** (e.g., near Bethlehem). The **fields and vineyards** would be located in the hills. This was the most **fertile** soil in Judah and the constant target of Philistine aggression. The defeat of the Philistines enables agricultural development and economic growth in the Shephelah (the **foothills** between the coast and the mountainous terrain of Jerusalem and Hebron).

"There is," THOMPSON (329) writes, "widespread archaeological support for building activity in Uzziah's day." This includes a seal with Uzziah's name discovered in a cistern at Tell Beit Mirsim as well as many towers and cisterns that date from this period (WILLIAMSON, 336-337).

Military (26:11-15)

Uzziah protected his economic growth through a military buildup. His army was **well-trained**; well-managed by **Jeiel the secretary and Maaseiah the officer under the direction of Hananiah**; well-led with **2,600 family leaders** (reflecting a tribal organization); well-equipped with **shields, spears, helmets, coats of armor, bows, slingstones**, and **machines designed by skillful men** (not catapults, but defensive protection for archers and stone-throwers; cf. DILLARD, 209-210); and well-populated with **307,500 men** ("the size of the conscript army seems reasonable enough," JAPHET, 882).

There is also extrabiblical literary evidence of Uzziah's prodigious army. Uzziah was part of a coalition in 742 B.C. that resisted the encroaching imperial interests of the Assyrian king Tiglath-pileser III. He is mentioned in the Assyrian texts as "Azriyau of Yaudi" (Azariah of Judah, the name of Uzziah in 2 Kgs; cf. Thiele, 139-162). Uzziah's army, in coalition with others, prevented Assyrian incursions during his reign.

Second Chronicles 26:15b is a transition point in the narrative. It summarizes Uzziah's **fame** (see v. 8) which is due to divine help (עֲזַר, 'āzar; cf. 2 Chr 26:7). But it also anticipates his fall in 2 Chr 26:16-21. Uzziah's fame **spread** across the region **until he became powerful**. The term "powerful" links 2 Chr 26:7-8 with 2 Chr 26:15. The Lord made him powerful (חָזַק, ḥāzaq; cf. 2 Chr 1:1), but Uzziah becomes prideful (2 Chr 26:16). The statement "he became powerful" may refer to Uzziah's self-assertion (as in the case of Rehoboam in 2 Chr 12:13 and Jehoram in 2 Chr 21:4). The noun form (חָזְקָה, ḥezqāh) of the verb is used in 2 Chr 26:16 — "Uzziah became powerful." Divine blessing becomes the occasion for stumbling.

3. Uzziah's Sin (26:16-21)

While Dtr notes the leprosy (2 Kgs 15:5; "the LORD afflicted the king with leprosy"), the Chronicler explains the reason. JAPHET believes that the original source of this story is a "priestly homily on Uzziah's leprosy predating [the Chronicler] but reworked and integrated by him" (JAPHET, 877). Thus, the Chronicler does not invent an explanation but incorporates material from a source other than Dtr. The explanation permits the Chronicler to apply the principle of blessing/curse (cf. 1 Chr 28:9).

Prosperity was the occasion of Uzziah's fall. Faithfulness in the midst of prosperity demands integrity. Uzziah failed the test of prosperity. Three successive verbs are connected by the Hebrew conjunction *waw* ("and"): his heart *was great*, he *was unfaithful*, and he *entered* the temple. The root of Uzziah's sin is **pride**. Literally, "his heart was high (great) to his own destruction." This contrasts with Jehoshaphat whose "heart was high (great) in the ways of the Lord" (2 Chr 17:6; cf. 2 Chr 32:25-26). A "high heart" is the opposite of God's call for humility (cf. 2 Chr 7:14).

This pride led to unfaithfulness (מעל, *mā'al*; cf. 1 Chr 5:25; 9:1; 10:13; 2 Chr 26:16,18; 28:19; 29:6; 30:7; 36:14). Chronicles specifies the unfaithfulness as the king's entrance into the Holy Place **to burn incense on the altar of incense**. The king blatantly violated a Mosaic prescription (cf. Exod 30:1-10; Num 16:40; 18:1-7). Critical scholars dismiss this explanation as a late anachronism since some believe the priestly prescriptions did not arise till late in the history of Israel. However one dates the priestly material in the Pentateuch, it is consistent with ancient Near Eastern rituals that the priests have a special role in the burning of incense (cf. DILLARD, p. 210). While the Chronicler provides no specific occasion for this royal intrusion into the priestly ministry, he links it to Uzziah's pride. There are no mitigating circumstances. JOHNSTONE (2:167-168) suggests that "there must have been a strong desire on the part of the monarchy to reassert the right of the king to act as High Priest for his people; perhaps this is one of the attractions of the old Canaanite religion — that the king could officiate directly in the cult."

Despite his long-term loyalty, Uzziah presumes on the holiness of God by entering the Holy Place. While the Chronicler emphasizes the grace of God, he insists as well on his transcendent holiness. One does not enter God's presence with pride. Only the **priests, the descendants of Aaron, have been consecrated to burn incense**. They are sanctified ministers. Whoever else enters **will not be honored by the LORD God**.

Azariah, the high priest, and **eighty other courageous priests of the LORD followed** Uzziah into the temple where they "stood against him" (**confronted**). They are described as "sons of valor" (**courageous**; cf. 1 Chr 5:18; 11:22; 26:7-9,30,32; 2 Chr 28:6), which has military overtones. They were prepared to evict the king from the **sanctuary**. They asserted the priestly right as a matter of God's honor. Uzziah was enraged by the audacity of such priestly insolence (the verb for "rage" is used twice). Asa was also outraged when he imprisoned the prophet who opposed him (2 Chr 16:10). The word also describes the excessive plundering by Israel's army (2 Chr 25:10). Instead of humility and self-abasement (cf. 2 Chr 7:14), Uzziah rejects the priestly instruction. Such rage and confrontation may indicate that this was the culmination of a whole series of incidents.

Uzziah is struck with **leprosy** after he is confronted. That God's "judgment" falls "only after explicit rejection of a warning from God" is a familiar one in Chronicles (WILLIAMSON, 338). The king is warned: **leave the sanctuary**. Uzziah's heart refuses to submit. This is no mere cultic violation, but a rejection of God's explicit will after the truth has been clarified. Uzziah is condemned for his pride, not for an inadvertent (ignorant or mistaken) violation. He is judged by his heart, not by the mere violation of cultic rules. His pride and rage reveal a heart that no longer seeks the Lord (contrast Jotham in 2 Chr 27:6).

Before the priests can evict Uzziah, **the LORD had afflicted him** with leprosy. Apparently, the leprosy began as a slow growth (though it appeared suddenly). The priests scattered quickly since they did not wish to become unclean through contact with a leper, and Uzziah hurriedly left the temple (hoping to arrest its spread?). The significance of the moment is captured by recalling the same biblical language that describes Miriam's leprosy in Numbers 12:10 (SELMAN, 2:471): "Aaron turned toward her and saw that she had leprosy" (cf. **Azariah . . . looked at him, they saw that he had leprosy on his forehead**).

JOHNSTONE (2:169) calls attention to the theological significance of the forehead. The high priest wears a turban with a gold pendant over the forehead which reads "Holy to the Lord" (Exod 28:36-38). In contrast to the holiness that should pervade the Holy Place and in punishment of Uzziah's prideful assertion of priestly rights, the leprosy begins on his forehead. Where the high priest's pendant proclaims "Holy to the Lord," Uzziah's forehead says "Unclean before the Lord."

The Hebrew term does not exactly correspond with the disease we know as leprosy (DILLARD, 211; Hulse, 87-105; also NIV fn). It is much broader and includes all kinds of infectious skin diseases — all of which would exclude one from Israel's camp (cf. Lev 13:36; Num 5:1-4; 12:15; 2 Kgs 7:3).

Due to cleanliness laws, Uzziah **lived in a separate house** till he died, and he was **excluded** (lit., "cut off") **from the temple of the LORD**. God reverses Uzziah's intent. While Uzziah intended to represent Judah in the temple cult, now he can no longer enter the temple. Nothing could be worse since the temple is the place of forgiveness, grace, and divine presence.

Given Uzziah's leprosy, his son, **Jotham**, begins a co-regency (750 B.C.; cf. Thiele, 106-107). Uzziah lived his last ten years in isolation from his kingdom, family, and God.

4. Formulaic Conclusion (26:22-23)

The Chronicler returns to 2 Kings 15:6-7 for the conclusion, but he substitutes the source that Dtr cites ("the book of the annals of the kings of Judah") with his own source, **the prophet Isaiah son of Amoz**. This is the first citation of a writing prophet in Chronicles, but it does not refer to the canonical book. "Since *Isaiah's* call came in the year of Uzziah's death (Is. 6:1)," SELMAN (2:472) writes, "Isaiah probably collected earlier material" (cf. 2 Chr 32:32). Perhaps this material was incorporated into a larger history to which the Chronicler had access (DILLARD, 211).

Uzziah is not buried with the other kings. This is an extension of his last ten years. The Chronicler explains what Dtr does not: he was buried separately because he was a leper.

In human terms, Uzziah was a great king. He reigned a long time, raised a large army, reconquered territory, and rebuilt the

Judean economy. In his early years he sought the Lord and listened to the instruction of Zechariah. The status, wealth, power, and strength of Judah during his reign were immense (almost Solomonic). However, in just a few years, as Isaiah knew (Isa 6:11-12), the cities of Judah would lie ruined and uninhabited. As long as Uzziah sought the Lord, he was blessed. But when he forsook God, God forsook him (cf. 1 Chr 28:9).

Uzziah's defiance is the beginning of the end for Judah as the critical term "unfaithful" rears its ugly head in the Chronicler's narrative. Earlier it described the exile (1 Chr 5:25; 9:1) and the destruction of the house of Saul (1 Chr 10:13-14). Now it becomes common in the Chronicler's narrative (cf. 2 Chr 33:19; 36:14). The Babylonian exile of Judah lies on the horizon.

H. THE REIGN OF JOTHAM (27:1-9)

The previous three kings (Joash, Amaziah, Uzziah) were a mixed bag. Early in their reigns, as they listened to their godly counselors, they were good kings. Towards the end of their reigns they forsook the Lord. They failed to persevere. Jotham breaks the cycle.

Jotham's reign anticipates the next two kings. SELMAN (2:472) calls these three kings "alternating" kings. Righteous Jotham is followed by the unmitigated evil of Ahaz. But Ahaz is followed by Hezekiah who is compared with David and Solomon. Chronicles's description of Jotham, Ahaz, and Hezekiah breaks with the mixed reviews of the previous three kings (Joash, Amaziah, Uzziah). Jotham, Ahaz, and Hezekiah receive a "single consistent judgment" (DILLARD, 214; cf. WILLIAMSON, 341).

The Chronicler's Jotham narrative is no mere extension of Uzziah's reign. This may be true for Dtr, but the Chronicler's narrative transitions the story from a mixture of good and evil (Uzziah) to unmixed good (Jotham) to unmixed evil (Ahaz). Though brief, the narrative has an important structural function. Jotham demonstrates how blessing can follow punishment. Every generation has the hope of renewal. The postexilic community needs the hope of blessing following punishment, and they need the warning that evil can follow righteousness.

This "three-generation sequence of a faithful man followed by a wicked son and a faithful grandson corresponds exactly to the situation described in Ezekiel 18:1-20, on which [the Chronicler's] pattern is probably based" (SELMAN, 2:473). Each person is responsible for their own wickedness and righteousness, and each community is responsible for its orientation to seek or forsake God.

Chronicles follows the basic structure of Dtr. The introduction and conclusion are essentially that of 2 Kings 15:32-38. However, the major difference is the addition of 2 Chronicles 27:3b-6.

1. Formulaic Introduction (27:1-2)

The introduction contains the normal information: (1) age of king when he began to rule (**twenty-five**), (2) length of reign (**sixteen years**), (3) name of his mother (**Jerusha**), and (4) theological evaluation (**he did what was right**).

The chronology is problematic. While Chronicles assigns sixteen years to Jotham's reign, 2 Kings 15:30 says that Hoshea became king of Israel in the "twentieth year of Jotham son of Uzziah." The problem is complex, but Thiele (106-107, 199-200) suggests that Jotham's reign fell into three parts. First, he reigned ten years as co-regent with his father Uzziah (750–740 B.C.). Second, he reigned six years as sole ruler (740–735 B.C.). Third, he reigned four years with his son Ahaz as co-regent (735–732 B.C.). Thus, Dtr's "twentieth" year includes Ahaz's co-regencies while Chronicles's "sixteen" refers only to his sole rule (he led the nation while his father was diseased; cf. 2 Chr 26:11 and 1 Chr 5:17 where the military buildup is attributed to Uzziah in one text and Jotham in another). However, 2 Kings 17:1 says that Hoshea became king of Israel in the "twelfth" year of Ahaz (rather than the fourth as depicted in the text above). Thiele (199) attributes this to an editorial or scribal misunderstanding, but other solutions have been suggested (Stigers, 81-90; see comments on 2 Chr 29).

The evaluation is emphasized. Jotham **did what was right in the eyes of the LORD, just as his father Uzziah had done**. This is a wholly positive assessment of Jotham. In fact, in order to clarify that he only followed his father in righteousness, Chronicles adds that **unlike** Uzziah **he did not enter the temple** (lit., "palace") **of the LORD** (cf. 2 Chr 26:15-21). The language is exactly the same: Uzziah went into the palace (2 Chr 26:16), but Jotham did not (2 Chr 27:2).

Given the same language, this does not mean Jotham did not worship at the temple, but that he did not go where he was not entitled.
The Chronicler's addition is actually a substitution — he supplies a
positive where Dtr has a negative. Where Dtr reads that Jotham did
not remove the high places (2 Kgs 15:35), Chronicles compliments
the king in that he did not commit sacrilege as his father did.
Chronicles often omits references to the high places (DILLARD, 215;
cf. 2 Chr 25:2 with 2 Kgs 14:4; 2 Chr 26:4 with 2 Kgs 15:4).

Nevertheless, Chronicles does not ignore the fact that the people
continued their corrupt practices. Corruption (שָׁחַת, *šāḥath*) involves the idea of "destruction," that is, these practices ate away at
Judah's heart like a cancer. It would come to full fruition during the
reign of Ahaz (cf. 2 Chr 28). Consequently, while Jotham exhibited
personal righteousness, his people destroyed themselves through
idolatry. Ahaz would bring the nation to the brink of exile.

2. The Accomplishments of Jotham (27:3-6)

Unlike the previous three kings (Joash, Amaziah, Uzziah), Chronicles's description of Jotham's reign is unmixed. Unique to Chronicles
(except for 2 Chr 27:3a), it solidifies the righteous ways of Jotham.
God blessed the good king Jotham.

Building Projects (27:3-4)

Second Kings 15:35b notes the first building project (**the Upper
Gate of the temple of the LORD**), but the other details are unique to
Chronicles. He improved the City of David (**the hill of Ophel**), built
additional **towns** in the mountains (where his father had vineyards;
cf. 2 Chr 26:10), and **towers** in the forested regions. The description recalls similar projects of his father (cf. 2 Chr 26:9-10 with 2 Chr
27:3-4).

Military Victory (27:5)

Jotham's blessings continue in the mode of his father's (cf. 2 Chr
26:6-8). While Uzziah expanded his territory in the south (Philistia
and Edom), Jotham maintains control over the transjordanian
region. Just as Uzziah received tribute from the Ammonites (2 Chr

26:8), so Jotham squelched (**conquered**, וַיֶּחֱזַק [*wayyeḥĕzaq*] – one of the Chronicler's favorite words for the strength of a king; 2 Chr 1:1; 12:13; 13:21; 17:1) an **Ammonite** rebellion and exacted an annual tribute. "The tribute was substantial, something over three tons of *silver* and approximately *ten thousand* donkey loads of *barley*" (SELMAN, 2:475). While some believe the Chronicler added this Ammonite victory to enhance his status, JAPHET (892) notes "there is still no reason to doubt the facts themselves."

General Assessment (27:6)

Jotham became **powerful** through these blessings. The same Hebrew word lies behind "powerful" and "conquered" (2 Chr 27:5), and also described Uzziah (cf. 2 Chr 26:8,15).

The reason for Jotham's strength is theological. While the NIV reads **he walked steadfastly before the LORD his God**, the text more literally reads "he ordered his ways" (NRSV). Chronicles sometimes uses the phrase "ordered heart(s)" (cf. 1 Chr 29:18; 2 Chr 12:14; 19:3; 20:33; 30:19). To "order a way" and "to order a heart" are essentially synonymous. One can order their hearts in one direction or another – to good (1 Chr 29:18; 2 Chr 19:3; 30:19) or evil (2 Chr 12:14; 20:33). The Psalms use this phrase to refer to a "steadfast heart" (cf. 57:7; 78:8,37; 108:1; 112:7) and that God strengthens hearts (10:17). Ezra, for example, had a heart set on the study of the Law (Ezra 7:10).

Theologically, this contrasts Uzziah and Jotham. While Uzziah turned his strength into pride and arrogantly presumed to enter the Holy Place, Jotham did not enter the Holy Place but set his heart on the ways of God. This is the critical difference between Uzziah and Jotham. Uzziah "made his heart great" (2 Chr 26:16), but Jotham "ordered his heart" toward the Lord (2 Chr 27:6).

This is the difference between good and evil, that is, how the heart orients life toward obedience or disobedience. God does not total up the amount of obedience and disobedience (e.g., Jotham did not get rid of the corrupt practices of his people as a perfect king would). Rather, he looks at the heart. Jotham was blessed because his heart was set on God, but Uzziah was cursed because his heart was arrogant.

The question for the postexilic community is, where is your heart? Whom or what does it seek? Jesus called believers to seek first the kingdom of God (Matt 6:33), and he warned that whatever they treasure, that is where their heart is (Matt 6:21). In the context of prosperity and materialism, what do we treasure? Uzziah's prosperity turned to pride, but Jotham's prosperity served his faith. The difference is a matter of the heart.

3. Formulaic Conclusion (27:7-9)

The conclusion contains the normal information, plus a repeat of some of the information in the introduction (2 Chr 28:1): (1) sources **(in the book of the kings of Israel and Judah)**, (2) death and burial of Jotham, and (3) his successor **(Ahaz)**. A theological evaluation is implied by his burial **in the city of David** with **his fathers**.

Interestingly, the Chronicler substitutes 2 Kings 15:36's "what he did" with **all his wars and the other things he did**. This fits his narrative description of Uzziah and Jotham: wars and projects. Both indicate divine blessing, and the plural "wars" means the Chronicler knows more than he is telling.

I. THE REIGN OF AHAZ (28:1-27)

In contrast to his father, Ahaz represents extreme degeneration in Judah. The narrative moves from three ambiguous kings (mixture of good/bad in Joash, Amaziah, and Uzziah) to unmixed righteousness in Jotham to unmitigated evil in Ahaz. Unlike Dtr where Manasseh is the worst king of Judah (2 Kgs 21), Chronicles portrays Ahaz as the worst. (Manasseh repents in Chronicles, and the sins of Ahaz are more numerous.) The following chart places the two kings side by side (adapted from Smelik, 172; the asterisk indicates what is not in 2 Kings).

King Ahaz (2 Chr 28)	King Manasseh (2 Chr 33)
not doing what is right in the eyes of the Lord	doing evil
walking in the ways of the kings of Israel	
*making idols for Baal	[making an image/idols]
*burning incense at Valley of Ben Hinnom	
child sacrifice	child-sacrifice
doing abominations	doing abominations

sacrificing in the high places	
sacrificing on the hills and under every green tree	
asking for help from Assyria	
*promoting debauchery in Judah	seducing people
plundering the temple	
*unfaithfulness	*unfaithfulness
*not repenting	[repents]
*sacrificing to the gods of Damascus	[worshiping the heavenly host]
*destroying the vessels in the temple	
*closing the temple	
*making illicit altars in Jerusalem	[making altars for the Baals and the heavenly hosts]
*making high places	building high places
*provoking to anger	provoking to anger
*defiling the temple	
	sin
	making Asherahs
	illicit divination

The Chronicler's additions emphasize Ahaz's sins. Ahaz embraced idolatry, and he undermined the temple cultus. He trusted foreign kings and gods. Unlike Manasseh, he refused to repent, and upon his death he received an ignoble burial. Ahaz epitomizes the evil which ultimately results in exile.

The function of 2 Chronicles 28 is to manifest the degeneration of Judah and prepare for the exile (cf. 2 Chr 28:19,22; 36:14). SELMAN (2:477) notes that the repeated use of "prisoners" or "to take captive" (from the root שׁבה, šābah) betrays exilic overtones. The Hebrew root is used 9 times in 2 Chronicles 28 (5,8,11,13-15,17) while only used 11 times elsewhere in Chronicles (cf. 2 Chr 6:36-38 for six of those). Judah experienced a "mini-exile" in the aftermath of their war with Israel (DILLARD, 219) as well as the plundering of the temple (cf. 2 Chr 28:21). After Ahaz, Hezekiah (2 Chr 29–32) "points to obedience and cultic fidelity as the condition of restoration" (DILLARD, 220).

The contrast between Ahaz and Hezekiah is strong. Chronicles expands Dtr's account of Hezekiah and lauds his accomplishments (even somewhat diminishing Josiah's). Hezekiah receives more attention in Chronicles than any other king besides David and Solomon. Structurally and rhetorically, Ahaz is a new Saul and Hezekiah is a new David. While Ahaz is unfaithful (like Saul), Hezekiah is faithful (like David). Hezekiah reverses everything Ahaz did. Thus, 2 Chronicles 29 begins a third major section in the Divided Kingdom (2 Chr 10–36). It is a new beginning for both Judah and the northern Israelites who remain in the land. Williamson (*Israel*, 114) argues that under Hezekiah north and south were reunited. Hezekiah begins a "new era in Israel's history" (Smelik, 182).

Further, 2 Chronicles 13 and 2 Chronicles 28 stand in contrast to each other as two opposing bookends to this section (2 Chr 13–28). While Abijah pleaded with rebellious Israel to renew covenant with them (2 Chr 13), in 2 Chronicles 28 rebellious Israel comes to the aide of their southern brothers (2 Chr 28:9-15). Abijah's speech in 2 Chronicles 13 and the speeches by Israelite leaders in 2 Chronicles 28 serve the end of reuniting north and south (Williamson, *Israel*, 114-118). In addition, just as the north stood condemned because of their idolatry in the days of Abijah, Judah also stood under God's anger because of their idolatry in the days of Ahaz. Both north and south were unfaithful (Smelik, 179-180).

Chronicles's introduction (2 Chr 28:1-4) and conclusion (2 Chr 28:26-27) essentially follow 2 Kings 16:1-4,19-20. However, 2 Chronicles 28:5-25 is new material even though the topics and structure echo Dtr (SELMAN, 2:476): Judah's war with Aram and Israel (2 Kgs 16:5-6; 2 Chr 28:5-15), appeal to the Assyrian King (2 Kgs 16:7-9; 2 Chr 28:16-21), and Ahaz's apostasy (2 Kgs 16:10-18; 2 Chr 28:22-25). The Chronicler's additions are indicative of his theological agenda (e.g., inclusion of the north in Yahwehist worship and the temple in Jerusalem). The result is that Dtr and Chronicles exhibit different, though not mutually exclusive, interests in Ahaz's reign (Smelik, 143-145). The political (Aram, Israel, and Judah) and religious intrigues (alliance with Assyria) of Ahaz's reign also appear in Isaiah 7.

The structure of 2 Chronicles 28 is chiastic (JAPHET, 896). Between the introduction and conclusion are two statements concerning the sins of Ahaz (28:2-4,22-25). Between the two sections devoted to Ahaz's sin is the long narrative that details his punishment (2 Chr 28:5-21). The central section parallels two invasions — one from the Israel/Aram alliance (2 Chr 28:5-15), and the other from the Philistines and Ammonites (2 Chr 28:16-21). Thus, the Chronicler's narrative introduces the king, describes the king's sins, punishes the king, describes his sins again, and concludes with the king's death and burial. This is a narrative about "crime and punishment."

1. Formulaic Introduction (28:1)

The introduction includes the normal points (except the name of his mother): (1) age when he began to reign (**twenty**), (2) how long he ruled (**sixteen years**), and (3) a theological evaluation (**he did not do what was right in the eyes of the LORD**).

Ahaz is the wicked son of a righteous man (Jotham) who was followed by a righteous son (Hezekiah). Ezekiel 18 describes this scenario. Will a righteous son bear the sin of his wicked father? Will a righteous father save his wicked son? Ezekiel's answer is that each will bear their own responsibility. Chronicles is Ezekiel's theology in narrative form (DILLARD, 220).

A difficulty arises, however, in the chronology of Ahaz and Hezekiah. If Hezekiah is twenty-five when he begins to reign (2 Chr 29:1), but his father dies at thirty-six, this means that Hezekiah was born when Ahaz was eleven. This is possible, but highly unusual. (See 2 Chr 29:1-2.)

2. The Sin of Ahaz (28:2-4)

The basic characteristic of Ahaz's apostasy is that **he walked in the ways of the kings of Israel** (cf. 2 Chr 21:6, 13; 22:3-4). Clarifying Dtr's cryptic reference, Chronicles specifies Baal worship. The "dark days" of Judah return under Ahaz's leadership (cf. 2 Chr 21–23).

His idolatry is heightened by the idolatrous worship of Canaanite gods through **sacrifices in the Valley of Ben Hinnom** (cf. 2 Chr 33:6) as well as sacrificing **his sons in the fire**. These are the **detestable** things for which **the LORD had driven** out the Canaanites (cf. Deut 7:22-26). Judah, as Israel before her, follows the Canaanites. This anticipates the exile just as the Canaanites were driven from the land. Child sacrifice was common in Canaanite religion, and Chronicles emphasizes Ahaz's sin with the plural **sons** (whereas 2 Kgs 16:3 only reads "son").

Further, while some kings removed the **high places**, Ahaz worships at these sanctuaries. Their pervasive presence in Judah is indicated by the phrase **on the hilltops and under every spreading tree**.

3. Divine Punishment for Sin (28:5-21)

This is the middle part of the chiasm. It is bounded on either side by the sins of Ahaz (2 Chr 28:2-4,22-25). Thus, the apostasy provides the rationale for Judah's defeat and captivity. Just as there are two descriptions of apostasy, so there are two invasions. The first is the invasion by the Aram-Israel alliance (2 Chr 28:5-15) and the second is the invasion by Philistines and Edomites (2 Chr 28:16-21). Judah is invaded from the north and the south.

The punishment of Judah involves the loss of territory, people (death and captivity), and economic resources (the wealth of the nation despoiled or liquidated as tribute). The resultant Judah is small, poor, and defenseless. The sin of Ahaz destroyed the near Solomonic glory of his grandfather's kingdom (cf. 2 Chr 26).

However, this national condition parallels the state of the postexilic community as a small, poor, and defenseless Persian province in Judah. The postexilic community can identify with Judah's situation. They can also identify with Hezekiah's "restoration" and renewal in 2 Chronicles 29–31. While despair may overwhelm the postexilic community, Chronicles offers hope through renewal.

Judah Defeated by Israel [and Aram] (28:5-15)

Dtr and Chronicles portray the Aram-Israel attack differently (cf. Hos 5:8–7:16). While it is a combined siege that does not ultimately sack Jerusalem in Dtr (and Isa 7), in Chronicles it appears as two separate attacks which included the subjugation of Jerusalem. While Dtr emphasizes the preservation of a remnant, Chronicles emphasizes the total defeat of Judah. The Chronicler separates Aram and Israel (though he does not deny that they were aligned) because he wants to stress the relational dimension between Israel and Judah. The Chronicler does not say that Jerusalem was sacked, and Dtr says that Ahaz paid tribute from the temple treasuries (2 Kgs 16:8). Consequently, the discordance between Dtr and Chronicles is not as great is as sometimes portrayed (SELMAN, 2:479-480).

Aram and Israel intended to persuade Judah to join their alliance against Assyria, but Judah refused and sought an alliance with Assyria. In response, Aram and Israel attacked Judah in the hopes of installing their own king on the throne which would effectively end the Davidic dynasty (cf. Isa 7:6).

There are similarities between this narrative and the parable of the Good Samaritan (Luke 10:25-37). The following chart highlights them (adapted from Spencer, 320-321).

Topic	2 Chr 28:5-15	Luke 10:25-37
Victims	Judeans and Jerusalem citizens	Implicitly a Jew from Jerusalem
Injuries	Nakedness	Stripping of Clothes
	Beating (LXX: πληγήν, plēgēn)	Beating (πληγάς, plēgas)
	Spoils	Robbing
Attackers	Aramean and Israelite warriors	Undesignated robbers
Leaders	Prophet (Oded)	Priest
	Ephramite Rulers	Levite
Place of Healing	Jericho	Jericho
Healing Ministry	Anointing (with oil)	Pouring oil and wine
	Transport on a Donkey	Transport on a Donkey
	Clothing the naked	Clothing implied
Ministers of Healing	Northern Israelites	Samaritan
Theology	Love for Brothers (3 times)	Love for Neighbor (3 times)

Both story lines involve Judeans (Jews) who were stripped, beaten, and robbed. Both involve northern Israelites (Samaritans) who anointed, clothed, and transported the injured to Jericho. Both are obedient to Leviticus 19:17-18 where Israel is told to love their neighbors and brothers (Spencer, 333-337). They differ, however, concerning the role of the leaders. While the leaders in Jesus' parable ignore the injured man, the leaders of Israel persuade the attackers to help the injured. The leaders of Israel manifest a love for their brothers that the priest and Levite did not. Given the similarities and the indicting example, Jesus probably recounted the parable of the Good Samaritan as a hermeneutical application of the themes embraced by 2 Chronicles 28:5-15. "Essentially," Spencer (347) writes, in line with Chronicles, "Jesus, and Luke represent an unbroken chain of prophets calling for loving unity among the people of God, unfettered by social discrimination."

The significance for the postexilic community is threefold. First, the mercy of the northern Israelites which embraced "brotherhood" with the south is a model for how postexilic Judah should treat northern Israelites who seek God. As THOMPSON (338) comments, the Chronicler "did not regard the *people* of the Northern Kingdom as an affront to God but only treated their counterfeit monarchy (a rival to the house of David) and their counterfeit shrines at Dan and Bethel (rivals to the temple of Solomon) as illicit." Second, the only political leaders involved in the actual movement of the narrative are the Ephramite rulers. Indeed, Ahaz is called **king of Israel** (2 Chr 28:19) as if there were no king in the north. Nevertheless, kingless Israel may serve God if they seek him. Faithfulness does not depend on a king. Consequently, the kingless postexilic community can follow the example of these Israelites. Third, the northern Israelites listened to God's prophet (cf. 2 Chr 20:20). The Chronicler encourages his readers to listen to God's messengers (Zvi, 239-246).

Second Chronicles 28:5-15 is divided into four parts of almost equal length (JAPHET, 897): (1) the attack, (2) Oded's speech, (3) Ephraimite rulers' speech, and (4) healing. The first and last balance each other — the attack is followed by healing. The middle two balance each other — persuasive speeches.

The Attack (28:5-8)

While the Chronicler gives brief attention to Aram and focuses his narrative on Israel, both receive the same theological evaluation. The invasions are the consequence of Ahaz's apostasy. **Therefore the LORD his God handed him over to the king of Aram . . . He was also given into the hands of the king of Israel**. The theological evaluation also appears in verse 6: **because Judah had forsaken the LORD, the God of their fathers**. The key term is "forsake" ("apostasy"; cf. 1 Chr 28:9). God forsakes whoever forsakes him.

Both nations took **prisoners** to their home capitals — Aram to **Damascus** and Israel to **Samaria**. Judah experiences a mini-exile. Further, Judah experienced some significant deaths among their leaders — **Maaseiah the king's son, Azirkam the officer in charge of the palace, and Elkanah, second to the king**. Judah's leadership was devastated.

The numbers, as DILLARD (222) comments, "are higher than historically probable," especially the death of 120,000 in a single day.

As Zvi (234-235) comments, "neither [the Chronicler] nor the community could have failed to grasp the huge discrepancy between these numbers and their common experience." Consequently, unless one understands "thousands" as units (SELMAN, 2:479), the numbers are probably hyperbolic to indicate the devastating depopulization of Judah by Aram and Israel (DILLARD, 222).

The Prophet Oded (28:9-11)

The northern kingdom had a **prophet of the LORD** among them. There were Yahwehist strains still extant in the north, even on the eve of their exile into Assyria (722 B.C.). **Oded** the **prophet** confronts the returning **army** in **Samaria**. The capital of the northern kingdom rings with meaning for postexilic readers as they experience Samaria's hostility in their own day.

The structure of Oded's speech is partially obscured by the NIV (JAPHET, 902). The first word of the speech (untranslated by NIV and NRSV) is "behold."

Accusation	Response
[Behold] because the LORD, the God of your fathers, was angry with Judah, he gave them into your hand. But you have slaughtered them in a rage that reaches to heaven (28:9)	And now (וְעַתָּה, wᵉʿattāh) you intend to make the men and women of Judah and Jerusalem your slaves (28:10a)
But aren't you also guilty of sins against the LORD your God? (28:10b)	Now (וְעַתָּה, wᵉʿattāh) listen to me! Send back your fellow countrymen you have taken as prisoners, for the LORD's fierce anger rests on you. (28:11)

"Behold" sets up the contrast between what God has done and what Israel has done. God gave Israel victory over Judah, but Israel abused Judah. They **slaughtered them in a rage**, that is, excessively. **Heaven** noticed their enormous rage (cf. 2 Chr 16:10; 26:19). Israel should have been restrained by their guilt before God and their cry for mercy against Assyria. Only the merciful receive mercy (Matt 5:7; Jas 2:13). War without mercy is criminal (ACKROYD, 176; cf. Zech 1:15; Isa 10:15; 40:2; Hos 1:4; Hab 2:2-20).

Israel's guiltiness, vengeance, greed, and bloodthirstiness emboldened them to enslave their relatives and violate the Torah (cf. Lev 25:42-46). They "subdued slaves" (לִכְבֹּשׁ לַעֲבָדִים, likbōš *la'ăbādîm*). Nehemiah 5:5 uses the same words to describe the situation of some families in the postexilic community. The Chronicler rebukes those in his own community who enslave the sons and daughters of relatives for economic profit. They must return their **fellow countrymen** (lit., "brothers") or else the Lord will turn his anger on Israel.

Oded "castigated them for their war crimes, and tried to awaken in them feelings of regret by stressing the natural friendship that existed between Judah and Ephraim" (Luria, 259). They did not defeat their relatives by their own strength. This prophetic message assumes "that the northerners are an organic part of the people of Israel" (JAPHET, 903).

Leaders of Ephraim (28:12-13)

Some of the leaders (lit., "heads") **in Ephraim** heeded the words of the prophet and opposed the enslavement of Judah. These four leaders apparently do not represent King Pekah, but they have sufficient influence to persuade Israel to relent. The absence of the king serves the interests of the Chronicler toward reunification under Hezekiah (the northern kingdom went into exile during the reign of Ahaz; cf. 2 Chr 30:6). The specificity of the names betokens the historical nature of this account (DILLARD, 222).

The leaders reinforce the prophetic message: to enslave Judah is to bring more guilt upon Israel. God is already angry with Israel, and this would further exacerbate the situation. The leaders are Yahwehists (their names contain God's name, *Yah*) and are concerned about Israel's relation to their God.

The two speeches indicate the Chronicler believed that both north and south "were still children of Israel and should worship the God of Israel" (Zvi, 237). The Chronicler did not view northern Israelites as outsiders, but as relatives to be reclaimed and reincorporated into the religious and political life of Jerusalem (Braun, "Reconsideration," 59-62). The two speeches demonstrate a continuity with the south. Zvi (237) summarizes the points well:

> The report of these actions conveys a clear meaning: (1) the people of the north were Yahwehistic; (2) they had prophets like the southerners; (3) their prophets had the same characteristics as the southerners, that is, they were warning speakers, preachers;

and (4) the same divine rules, such as warning before punishment, the possibility of repentance, and accountability before God, all applied to the northerners as well as to the southerners.

Postexilic Judah, therefore, must be inclusive and seek out northern believers. The north is not finally and irrevocably rejected. Grace and forgiveness are as open to them as they are to southern believers. Israel and Judah, both north and south, must heed God's prophets, seek his face, and humble themselves before the Lord (cf. 1 Chr 28:9; 2 Chr 7:14).

The Healing (28:14-15)

Israel obeys the word of the prophet and its leaders. They collect all their booty (in men and spoils) and present it **in the presence of the officials and all the assembly** (הַקָּהָל, *haqqāhāl*), a holy convocation (cf. 1 Chr 13:2). This is significant because there are times, according to the Chronicler, "when the north, through its acknowledgement of theological principles, can act as 'Israel'" (JOHNSTONE, 2:184).

A committee (**men designated by name**) returned all the spoils to Judah. They **clothed all who were naked, provided them clothes and sandals, food and drink, and healing balm**. They carried the **weak** on **donkeys**. They returned the Judahites to their **countrymen** ("brothers") **at Jericho**. The oasis of Jericho is an appropriate symbol as the returning exiles find refreshment at the place where Israel first entered the land of promise. Jericho was also the traditional border between Ephraim and Benjamin (cf. Josh 16:1; 18:12,21).

The northerners "are described as complying with YHWH's will not because they came to the Temple to worship, but because they freed the captive, fed the hungry, watered the thirsty, and clothed the naked" (Zvi, 243; cf. Isa 58:7; Ezek 18:5-9). This imitates the God of Israel (Deut 29:4; Ps 146:7-8) as they obey the word of the prophet (Mason, 93-95). The Chronicler invites them to participate in the temple cult (Hezekiah in 2 Chr 30), but the fundamental value is the imitation of God. They treated their neighbors in the way God would treat them. Israel manifests the heart of God. It is also the ethic of Jesus (cf. Matt 25:31-46) where mercy, justice, and faithfulness are the supreme values (cf. Matt 12:7; 23:23).

Judah Defeated by Edomites and Philistines (28:16-21)

While the first invasion was from the north, the second comes from the south. The Philistines and Edomites regain territories they lost under Uzziah (2 Chr 26:6-7). Ahaz attempts to prevent this by appealing to the king of Assyria, but to no avail. God has determined to reduce Judah to almost nothing and this sets the stage for restoration and renewal during the reign of Hezekiah.

Seeks Assyria's Help (28:16)

While Dtr places Ahaz's application for help in the context of the Aram-Israel invasion, Chronicles emphasizes the Philistine-Edomite context. This is not problematic since the confluence of invasions was probably connected. Edom, for example, opposed Assyria, and they may have been part of the concerted attack on Judah because they refused to join an alliance against Assyria (cf. 2 Kgs 16:6). Isaiah 7 condemns Ahaz's reliance on Assyria.

Edomites and Philistines Defeat Judah (28:17-18)

Edom is located to the southeast of Judah and Philistia to the southwest. Thus, the southern border changes drastically as a result of Judah's defeat. Edom **carried away prisoners**, and **the Philistines** probably reoccupied cities they had lost to Uzziah as well as raiding the **foothills** (*Shephelah*) and **Negev** (southern wilderness area; e.g., Beersheba and Arad). They even occupied some towns in the foothills, including important agricultural centers such as **Beth Shemesh, Aijalon and Gederoth**. This left Judah with only the mountain regions around Jerusalem and Hebron. The size and economic stability of Judah was significantly reduced.

Theological Evaluation (28:19)

If only Ahaz had humbled himself (like Manasseh; cf. 2 Chr 33:19,23), God would have reversed the effects of his defeats. However, when Ahaz would not humble himself, **the LORD humbled Judah because of Ahaz**. The reason for this humbling is twofold: (1) Ahaz **promoted wickedness in Judah** and (2) he **had been most unfaithful to the LORD**. Ahaz is the most unfaithful of all kings (cf. 1 Chr 5:25; 9:1) – he is **most unfaithful** (וּמָעוֹל מַעַל, *ûmā'ôl ma'al*) or "unfaithfully unfaithful."

Seeks Assyria's Help (28:20-21)

The alliance with Assyria never materializes, and Assyria subjugates Judah. According to Assyrian documents, Ahaz paid tribute to Tiglath-pileser (*ANET*, 282). Ahaz liquidated the temple and royal assets in order to hire the Assyrian king, but it turned out that the payment was a tribute rather than a partnership. The one "helper" to which Ahaz appeals gives him **trouble instead of help**. Literally the text reads "he distressed him instead of establishing him." Ahaz leaned on Assyria to "establish" him when in the history of Judah it was the Lord who "established" kings (2 Chr 1:1; 17:1; 27:6) and strengthened hearts (2 Chr 16:9). Ahaz looked for help in the wrong place.

Assyria overran Philistia during the campaign of 734 B.C. He left an Assyrian detachment in Philistia to prevent Egyptian intrusion. Tiglath-pileser returned in 732 B.C. and further subjugated the whole region, extracting tribute from Israel and capturing Damascus (DILLARD, 223).

4. The Sin of Ahaz (28:22-25)

Even in his distress (like Manasseh's in 2 Chr 33:12), Ahaz did not humble himself. Ahaz is the worst king of Judah because he did not repent. Manasseh repented, but Ahaz hardens himself in his evil and becomes **even more unfaithful to the LORD**. For the third time in this narrative, Ahaz is described as unfaithful (cf. 2 Chr 28:19[2],22). This explains his Godforsakenness (cf. 1 Chr 28:9; 2 Chr 7:11-22).

This further description of the sins of Ahaz parallels the previous description (2 Chr 28:2-4). Ahaz expands his idolatry. He includes the **gods of Damascus**. Ahaz gives the glory of Aram's victory to their gods rather than recognizing it as the will of Yahweh. He gives the glory of Yahweh to other gods (cf. Isa 42:8,11). Ahaz is a theological opportunist — he will turn to whatever god he thinks might help. Because he did not seek **help** from Yahweh, his idolatry becomes the moment of his "stumbling" (**downfall**; cf. 2 Chr 25:8).

While 2 Chronicles 28:2-4,22-23 focused on Ahaz's idolatry, 2 Chronicles 28:24-25 focuses on his attitude toward the temple and Yahweh worship. "Ahaz," DILLARD (219) notes, "shut the doors of the temple, put out the lamps and stopped the offerings of incense and sacrifices (2 Chr 29:7), and neglected the shewbread (2 Chr 29:18)." Further, he **set up altars at every street corner in Jerusalem** and **built high places to burn sacrifices to other gods**.

The very thing the leaders of Israel feared (2 Chr 28:9-13), Ahaz discounted. By turning to other gods, Ahaz **provoked the LORD, the God of his fathers, to anger**. The kingdom that had rejected David in 1 Chronicles 13 showed mercy to David out of respect for Yahweh. But the kingdom of David itself rejected Yahweh. The Davidic kingdom is no guarantee of divine favor — if the Davidic king forsakes God, God will forsake him (1 Chr 28:9).

The postexilic community is aware that the same thing could happen again. The Chronicler teaches his community that the kingdom of David must seek Yahweh and it must include their northern relatives who also seek him. Likewise, the church also must seek God while not excluding others who seek him. We must practice faithfulness with mercy. We must overcome the schisms of the past by seeking the God of Jesus and embrace all who faithfully embrace him.

5. Formulaic Conclusion (28:26-27)

The conclusion contains the standard elements: (1) source materials (**the book of the kings of Judah and Israel**), (2) burial, and (3) his successor (**Hezekiah**). However, Ahaz **was not placed in the tombs of the kings of Israel**. This unfaithful king died without honor (cf. 2 Chr 21:20; 24:25; 26:23; 33:20).

III. THE REUNITED KINGDOM (29:1-36:23)

The northern kingdom is in exile. Only the southern kingdom remains. Even though the north has experienced the judgment of God, the Davidic kingdom with its temple offers hope. Hezekiah, therefore, speaks in a conciliatory manner. His speech invites the north to participate in the worship of Yahweh at the Jerusalem temple (2 Chr 30:6b-9). Just as Abijah's speech (2 Chr 13:4b-12) set the tone of 2 Chronicles 13-28, so Hezekiah's sets the tone of 2 Chronicles 29-36.

Hezekiah's speech to a judged nation addresses the Chronicler's postexilic community. All Israel (north and south) are invited to the temple to worship Yahweh. Whether it is the judged northern kingdom in Assyrian exile or the judged southern kingdom in Babylonian exile, the restored community in postexilic Jerusalem invites all Israel to return to Yahweh at the temple.

Second Chronicles 29–36 portrays a reunited kingdom. While "disunity" and tension marked the relationship between north and south in 2 Chronicles 10–28, in 2 Chronicles 29–36 unity reappears (Throntveit, *Kings*, 120; cf. PRATT, 416). This is not a reunion of Davidic and Solomonic proportions, but a cultic (temple) unity. The kingdom is reunited theologically. This is the reunion that the Chronicler seeks for his postexilic community as they await the restoration of a Davidic king.

However, despite two good kings (Hezekiah and Josiah), Judah's evil is punished by a general exile. Despite the reform attempts, Jerusalem follows Samaria into exile. Thus, what happened to Israel in 722 B.C. eventually happens to Judah in 586 B.C.

The Chronicler narrates the story of Judah's fall with both explanation and hope. He explains the sin that generates the exile, but he also provides hope. Hezekiah offers reconciliation to the remnant of Israel, Manasseh is exiled but then restored, and Josiah reaches out to the north as well. Exiled people are not hopeless. Just as Hezekiah (good) followed Ahaz (an evil king which involved an exile) and Josiah followed Manasseh (an evil king which included an exile), the postexilic community expects a Davidic king to follow their exile (Konkel, 233). The Chronicler reminds the returnees that God seeks them.

A. THE REIGN OF HEZEKIAH (29:1–32:33)

King Hezekiah receives more attention in Chronicles than any other Judean king. Behind David and Solomon, Hezekiah is the most important king. Jehoshaphat (2 Chr 17–20) ranks fourth (in terms of space).

Scholars have debated whether Chronicles portrays Hezekiah as a new David or a new Solomon, or both (Throntveit, "*Kings*, 121-125; "Hezekiah," 302-311). There are parallels between Hezekiah and both David and Solomon. For example, Hezekiah does what is right as his father David did (2 Chr 29:2). He restores Davidic personnel

(2 Chr 29:11-14; 31:2,11-20) and music to the temple (2 Chr 29:25-
26). The Chronicler also compares the celebration of the Passover
to the time of Solomon (2 Chr 30:26), and it lasted two weeks (2 Chr
30:23) just like Solomon's temple dedication (2 Chr 7:8-9). Chronicles also emphasizes Hezekiah's wealth (2 Chr 32:27-29) and his
respect among the nations (2 Chr 32:23). Thus, Hezekiah embodies
the values and significance of both David and Solomon (DILLARD,
228-229). The United Kingdom under David and Solomon is renewed in the Reunited Kingdom of Hezekiah. Hezekiah was not
greater than David and Solomon but God renewed his covenant
with David and Solomon in the reign of Hezekiah. This testifies to
God's faithfulness and grounds the hope of renewal for the postexilic community.

Seventy percent of Chronicles is not present in Dtr. For example,
what Dtr describes in six verses (2 Kgs 18:1-6), Chronicles expands
to eighty-two (2 Chr 29:1–31:21).

Topic	2 Chr	2 Kgs
The Fall of the Northern Kingdom		17:1-41
Formulaic Introduction	29:1-2	18:1-3
Restoration of the Temple	29:3-36	
Renewal of the Passover	30:1-27	
Removal of Idolatry	31:1	18:4
Temple Personnel	31:2-19	
Evaluation of Hezekiah's Reign	31:20-21	18:5-6
Judah and Assyria	32:1-21	18:13–19:27
The Success of Hezekiah	32:22-23	18:7-8
The Fall of the Northern Kingdom		18:9-12
Hezekiah's Illness	32:24-26	20:1-11
Hezekiah's Wealth and Achievements	32:27-30	
Hezekiah and the Babylonians	32:31	20:12-19
Formulaic Conclusion	32:32-33	20:20-21

While Dtr briefly notices Hezekiah's reforms, Chronicles dwells on
them. Dtr is primarily interested in Hezekiah as a model of trust in
the face of the Assyrian threat (Knoppers, "None," 411-431). Chronicles is interested in Hezekiah as a reformer who renews the worship
of Yahweh. Consequently, the expanded section concerns the re-
opening, purification, and dedication of the temple (2 Chr 29); the
celebration of the Passover (2 Chr 30); and the appointment of

temple personnel (2 Chr 31). In addition, the Chronicler shortens Dtr's material concerning the Assyrian invasion, Hezekiah's illness, and the visit of the Babylonian envoys. The Chronicler supplies what Dtr does not discuss, but the Chronicler truncates what he assumes his readers already know. He concentrates on what is most significant to his readers.

The expanded sections have been the subject of considerable debate. Some believe this material is theological propaganda. Significantly, none of the major topics of 2 Chronicles 29–32 are noticed in Dtr: (a) the purification and restoration of the temple (2 Chr 29:3-36); (b) the observance of the Passover (2 Chr 30:1–31:1); (c) the appointment of temple personnel (2 Chr 31:2-19); and (d) the description of Hezekiah's economic and military activities (2 Chr 32:27-30).

Current scholarship is reevaluating this doubt. For example, Vaughn (224-225) has demonstrated that there is solid extrabiblical (including archaeological and epigraphical) corroboration for the description of Hezekiah's reign in 2 Chronicles 32:27-30. JAPHET (914-915, 935, 960-961) argues that the Chronicler depends upon other sources or historical memory (oral tradition) for his unique material.

The Passover is increasingly seen as a historic moment. While earlier scholars rejected this Passover as the Chronicler's creation (duplicating Josiah in 2 Chr 35), many argue that it is based upon a source, perhaps even available to Dtr though unused due to his own particular interests (cf. Rosenbaum, 23-43; McKenzie, *Chronicler's*, 173; DILLARD, 240-241). At the very least, JAPHET (935) argues, "the story is based on some authentic tradition concerning a celebration of Passover in Jerusalem during the reign of Hezekiah."

As for Hezekiah's reforms in 2 Chronicles 29, most believe it is an imaginative telling of the Chronicler's theology and reject its historicity, especially Ahaz's closing of the temple (JAPHET, 918; Handy, "Hezekiah's,"111-115). "Few," however, would locate the reform "exclusively in the imagination" of the Chronicler (Moriarty, 401), and many give it historical credence (MYERS, 2:169; Todd, 288-293; Rowley, "Hezekiah's," 395-431; Rosenbaum, 23-43). While the closing of the temple is unknown in Dtr, it seems unlikely that the Chronicler would invent it. The closing of the temple was a significant event in the historical memory of Judah which, in turn, remembers the reformation of Hezekiah. Its absence from Dtr says more about Dtr's purposes (more interested in Josiah than Hezekiah) than it does about historicity. The Chronicler emphasizes this point due to the importance he attaches to the temple.

The Hezekiah narrative may be divided into four main parts: (1) Formulaic Introduction (2 Chr 29:1-2), (2) Religious Reform (2 Chr 29:3-31:21), (3) Hezekiah's Trials (2 Chr 31:1-31), and (4) Formulaic Conclusion (2 Chr 31:32-33). While the introduction and conclusion are fairly standard, the middle sections are related to Dtr in different ways. Hezekiah's reforms expand Dtr's brief treatment, but Hezekiah's trials condense Dtr's fuller discussion.

1. Formulaic Introduction (29:1-2)

The introduction to Hezekiah's reign is derived from 2 Kings 18:2-3 and contains the standard data: (1) age when he began to rule (**twenty-five**), (2) length of reign (**twenty-nine years**), (3) mother's name (**Abijah**), and (4) a theological evaluation (**he did what was right in the eyes of the LORD**).

Hezekiah is like **his father David**. Hezekiah returns the nation to the days of David and Solomon. The promises of God are renewed in Hezekiah's time. While this phrase is derived from 2 Kings 18:3, the Chronicler's retention is more than simply reproduction. It stakes out a theological perspective that is illuminated by Hezekiah's Davidic restoration project.

The text, however, poses the "single greatest problem in the chronology of the kings" (Thiele, 39). First, if Hezekiah is twenty-five when he begins to reign (2 Chr 29:1), but his father dies at thirty-six (2 Chr 28:1), this means that Hezekiah was born when Ahaz was eleven. This is possible, but unusual. Second, when compared with 2 Kings 18:10,13, a further problem emerges. Second Kings 18:10 states that Samaria was captured by the Assyrians in the sixth year of Hezekiah (722 B.C.), but 2 Kings 18:13 states that Sennacherib besieged Jerusalem during the fourteenth year of Hezekiah (701 B.C.). The dates, based on Assyrian documents, create an internal tension in Dtr's account: if 722 B.C. is Hezekiah's sixth year, then 701 B.C. cannot be his fourteenth.

While this chronological quandry has generated many solutions (Konkel, 9-43 surveys them), Thiele (174-5) dates the twenty-nine year reign of Hezekiah as 715 to 686 B.C. However, Thiele believes that an error crept into the final redaction of 2 Kings which creates the chronological impasse. It is possible that Hezekiah was a co-regent with his father early in his life (ca. 727/726 B.C.) and that he did not begin his sole reign until 715 B.C. (Horn, 40-52; Konkel, 43; Stigers, 81-90). Or, 2 Kings 18:13 may refer to Sennacherib's invasion of 714 B.C. and thus date Hezekiah's accession to the throne from 726 B.C. (PAYNE, 4:533-542 and "Relationship," 40-52; Goldberg, 360-390). Whatever the case, the dates for Hezekiah's reign are uncertain and problematic. This commentary assumes Thiele's dating for the reign of Hezekiah (715–686 B.C.) preceded by a co-regency with his father.

2. Religious Reform (29:3–31:21)

While Hezekiah reigned twenty-nine years, the Chronicler devotes three of his four chapters to the religious reforms which occurred in his first seven months (715 B.C.). The Chronicler's interest is theological. The reforms of Hezekiah provide a model for the postexilic community.

Restoring the Temple (29:3-36)

As SELMAN (2:485) points out, not only does Hezekiah follow David and Solomon, but Chronicles also sets him in explicit contrast with Jeroboam I of Israel (2 Chr 13:8-12) who rejected the temple and Ahaz (2 Chr 28:22-24) who defiled it. Hezekiah invites the northern Israelites to join Judah at the temple (cf. 2 Chr 13:8-12), and he reopens what Ahaz closed.

Hezekiah's proactive restoration provides a model for the postexilic community who restored the temple. Even though the prophets Haggai and Zechariah pushed Judah to complete the temple, there were times during the postexilic period when the temple sank into disrepair and virtual disuse. The Chronicler's emphasis probably reflects a similar situation in his own community.

The principle of restoration is also important in Christian theology, and it proceeds according to a pattern. For Christians, this pattern is theological and christological in character. It is not a blueprint of specific details (e.g., sacrificial rituals performed by Levitical prescription) but a call to image God through imitating the life and ministry of Jesus Christ. The church is the community of God founded on the ministry, death, and resurrection of Jesus. Just as Israel sought God in the temple, Christians seek God through Jesus Christ.

Chronicles describes Hezekiah's restoration of the temple in three movements: (1) Purification (29:3-19), (2) Dedication (29:20-30), and (3) Celebration (29:31-36).

Purification of the Temple (29:3-19)

Ahaz defiled the temple before he closed it. It had also fallen into disrepair. Consequently, the first task is to reopen, purify, and repair the temple. Hezekiah gathers the priests and the Levites to prepare the temple for divine worship.

JAPHET (915) sees three divisions: (1) Hezekiah's Address (29:3-11), (2) Levitical Consecration (29:12-17), and (3) Levitical Report to Hezekiah (29:18-19).

Hezekiah Addresses the Levites (29:3-11). In the **first month** of his reign, Hezekiah reversed his father's religious orientation. He **opened** what Ahaz closed (2 Chr 28:24) — **the doors of the temple**. However, its usefulness depends on the purification of its servants and sanctuary. Consequently, Hezekiah gathers the **priests and the Levites** in front of the sanctuary (**east side**).

Second Chronicles 29:5 and 11 frame the speech with second-person invocations (JAPHET, 917): **Listen to me, Levites** (2 Chr 29:5) and **My sons, do not be negligent** (2 Chr 29:11). Hezekiah calls upon the Levites to **consecrate** themselves and the temple in order to fulfill their responsibilities as temple servants. The body of the speech falls into three parts as indicated by "formulaic markers:" (1) "because" (כִּי, *kî*; 2 Chr 29:6, untranslated by the NIV), (2) "and behold" (וְהִנֵּה, *wᵊhinnēh*; 1 Chr 29:9, untranslated by the NIV), and (3) **now** (עַתָּה, *'attāh*; 1 Chr 29:10). The body of the speech moves from the explanation for the need for consecration (2 Chr 29:6-8) to an explanation for Judah's **captivity** (2 Chr 29:9) to Hezekiah's intention to renew Judah's **covenant with the LORD** (2 Chr 29:10).

Frame: Invocation (29:5)
  Body: Explains the Need for Consecration (29:6-8)
  Body: Explains the Current Situation of Judah (29:9)
  Body: Explains Hezekiah's Intention (29:10)
Frame: Invocation (29:11)

Interestingly, Hezekiah only addresses the Levites (2 Chr 29:5) even though the priests and the Levites were assembled (1 Chr 29:4). While some think this is the result of careless redaction (Welch, *Work*, 103-107), Chronicles uses Levites to include both priests and nonpriests (JAPHET, 917; THOMPSON, 343; JOHNSTONE, 2:190). The speech assumes priestly functions (**to burn incense**; 2 Chr 29:11; cf. 2 Chr 26:18). Further, priests participated in the purification of the sanctuary (2 Chr 29:16). Thus, Hezekiah addresses all the temple servants – the Levitical clan (cf. "Levitical priests" in 2 Chr 30:27).

The Levites must assume the function which God intended for them: **to stand before him and serve him, to minister before him and to burn incense** (2 Chr 29:11). The former phrase may describe nonpriestly personnel such as musicians (cf. 1 Chr 6:32 where the NIV translates "stand" as "performed") or those who assist the priests (cf. 2 Chr 8:14). This phrase is a general description of the Levitical order (cf. Num 16:9; Deut 10:8; 18:5; cf. 1 Chr 15:2; 16:4). The latter phrase, however, is appropriate only for priests who alone may burn incense (cf. 2 Chr 26:18). Hezekiah calls the Levites back to their original function – they are ministers of worship at the holy temple. Consequently, they must consecrate (קָדַשׁ, *qādaš*; 3 times in 2 Chr 29:5) themselves and the temple.

Purification ("to make holy") involves cleanliness rituals, including appropriate washings ("immersions"; cf. Lev 8:6; 14:8-9; 15:5-11,13,16,18,21-22,27; 17:15; 22:6). The temple and its servants had become polluted (**defilement**; הַנִּדָּה [*hanniddāh*] is only used here in Chronicles, but numerous times in Lev 15 and Num 19). The pollution and closing of the temple was analogous to its destruction.

Hezekiah explains the need for reconsecration (2 Chr 29:6-8). The Levites should consecrate themselves because (*kî*) **our fathers were unfaithful**. The Chronicler uses one of his key terms to describe the faithlessness of Ahaz. Unfaithfulness (מַעַל, *ma'al*) generates the exile of both Israel (1 Chr 5:25) and Judah (1 Chr 9:1) as well as the death of Saul (1 Chr 10:13). It is the reason for Judah's present captivity (2 Chr 29:9) which refers to the Edomite invasion under Ahaz (2 Chr 28:17).

Chronicles describes Ahaz's unfaithfulness: (1) **they did evil in the eyes of the LORD**, (2) they **forsook** the Lord, (3) they **turned** away from **the LORD's dwelling place**, and (4) "they gave their backs" to the Lord. This is the only place where these four descriptors are given together. This heightens the sin of Ahaz and accentuates the exilic punishment due to Judah. The southern kingdom deserved exile — they forsook the Lord (cf. 1 Chr 28:9; 2 Chr 7:14-22; 15:2).

Chronicles describes what Ahaz did to the temple (2 Chr 29:7). He not only **shut the doors** and **put out the lamps**, he did not permit any sacrifices to Yahweh. The sacrifices, even the daily **burnt offerings**, ceased. The worship of Yahweh was snuffed out.

Just as Judah forsook Yahweh, so he forsakes them. God responded to Judah's pollution with **anger** (cf. 2 Chr 28:25). The result is that **Judah and Jerusalem** had become an **object of dread and horror and scorn**. Jeremiah 29:18 similarly describes the exilic condition of Judah. Ahaz's unfaithfulness is punishable by exile ("captivity") — which was partially accomplished in his own reign (cf. 2 Chr 28:17). Thus, the Chronicler draws a parallel between the situation of Hezekiah and the situation of his own readers who have returned from exile and now seek God in a new temple (PRATT, 423).

Judah is on the verge of full exile like its northern neighbor. Only Hezekiah's reforms prevent the full implementation of God's anger. His commitment to renew Judah's **covenant with the LORD** will **turn away** the divine anger. Literally, the Hebrew reads "with my heart to cut a covenant with Yahweh" (2 Chr 29:10). Chronicles uses "heart" language to underscore the depth of Hezekiah's intention. His reforms arise out of his heart and express his heart-orientation toward Yahweh.

The Chronicler's postexilic community must renew their covenant with God, turn from unfaithfulness, and seek God at his temple. Hezekiah's confidence is the confidence of the postexilic community: God is faithful, and he will find those who seek him.

Levites Consecrate Themselves (29:12-17). "The Levites do not answer the king in words," JAPHET (920) comments, "but in deeds."

Parallel with 1 Chronicles 15:4-10, representatives are chosen from the Levitical clans to carry out the work of purification. Two representatives are chosen from the three major clans of Levi: (1) Kohath, (2) Merari, and (3) Gershon. Two representatives are chosen from the three major musical divisions: (1) **Asaph**, (2) **Heman**, and (3) **Jeduthun**. In addition, two representatives are chosen from "the great Kohathite family of Elizaphan" (DILLARD, 235). Thus, the total number of leaders is fourteen, perhaps symbolic of the task ($7\times2 =$ 14). The list not only symbolizes the completeness of the purification task (JAPHET, 921), but also the full involvement of the whole Levitical clan (PRATT, 425). These representatives **assembled their brothers** (2 Chr 29:15).

The Levitical clans purified (sanctified) themselves through ritual washings and then **they went in to purify the temple**. Chronicles only uses the term "purify" (טִהַר, *tihar*) to describe the reforms of Hezekiah (2 Chr 29:15-16,18; 30:18) and Josiah (2 Chr 34:3,5,8). This was done **as the king had ordered, following the word of the LORD** which contrasts with Ahaz's conduct (2 Chr 29:15). The heart that seeks God will keep his word, but those who do not follow Yahweh's word (cf. 1 Chr 15:15) and rebelliously pursue their own way demonstrate an unfaithful heart (cf. 1 Chr 10:13).

The purification of the temple was accomplished in two stages (JAPHET, 922). First, the temple was cleansed (*tihar*). This involved the removal of all unclean items (whatever negated the holiness of the sanctuary). The **priests went into the sanctuary** and carried out whatever was **unclean**, and then the **Levites took it** to the **Kidron Valley**. The distinction is important since only the priests may go inside the temple's inner parts (לִפְנִימָה, *liphnîmāh*; lit., "within"). The Levites took the unclean items to the valley where "pagan cult objects were also burned" (DILLARD, 235) during the reigns of Asa (2 Chr 15:16) and Josiah (2 Chr 35:14).

Second, the temple was consecrated (קָדַשׁ, *qādaš*). This was the positive procedure of hallowing the utensils of the temple as well as its holy space.

The cleansing of the temple took sixteen days which indicates the depth of its depravity and the sad state of its condition (the sanctification of the temple after Antiochus Epiphanes' desecration took only eight days; cf. 2 Macc 2:12; JAPHET, 923). Unfortunately, this was too late to observe the Passover on its official day (the fourteenth day of the first month). The Passover was rescheduled for the fourteenth day of the second month in 2 Chronicles 30 (cf. Num 9:1-11).

Levites Report to Hezekiah (29:18-19). Hezekiah told the Levites to do something, they did it, and now they report that they have done it. The report focuses on the temple **utensils** and **table articles**. The reason Chronicles emphasizes the "temple vessels" is the continuity they symbolize between pre- and postexilic Jerusalem (Ackroyd, "Temple," 166-181). While the building would be destroyed, the Solomonic utensils survived the exile (cf. 2 Chr 4:19-22; 36:18; Ezra 1:7-11; Dan 5:2-3,23; 2 Kgs 25:14-15). Thus, the postexilic community takes a particular interest in the history of the utensils because they are a link to Solomon's temple (DILLARD, 235).

The two stages of purification are represented in this report. First, they **purified** (*tihar*) **the entire temple of the LORD**, including the **altar** and table. Second, they **prepared and consecrated** (*qādaš*) **all the articles that King Ahaz removed in his unfaithfulness**. They dedicated and sanctified all the articles necessary for the worship of Yahweh at his temple. The temple is ready for rededication.

The body of Hezekiah's speech began with Ahaz's unfaithfulness and the report of the Levites ends with Ahaz's unfaithfulness. Hezekiah's reforms contrast with Ahaz's apostasy. Hezekiah's faithfulness seeks mercy just as Ahaz's apostasy engendered wrath. The postexilic community must make their choice: will they follow Hezekiah or Ahaz?

Dedication of the Temple (29:20-30)

The postexilic community recognizes in Hezekiah's rededication festival the same kind of event in which they themselves have participated. Just as the temple was shut down during Ahaz's reign, so it was destroyed during the Bablyonian exile. Just as Hezekiah rededicated the temple and restored its theological meaning for Judah, so the postexilic community rebuilt and rededicated the temple in its own time. Hezekiah models faithfulness, and God's response to Hezekiah's reforms anticipates God's own faithfulness to postexilic Judah.

Just as Hezekiah had gathered the priests and Levites, he **gathered** the **city officials** (the leaders of the people) to go up to the

temple of the LORD. Thus, Hezekiah, the priests, the Levites, and the officials gather for the rededication of the temple. This gathering of Judah is called an **assembly** (2 Chr 29:23), a holy convocation (קָהָל, *qāhāl*; cf. 1 Chr 13:4). The leaders of God's people (king and officials) bring sacrifices to the priests who slaughter them on **the altar of the LORD.**

Preparation of the Sacrifices (29:20-24). The temple must be dedicated, like the tabernacle (Exod 40; Heb 9) and the Solomonic temple (2 Chr 5–7), with blood rituals. **Blood** is **sprinkled** on the **altar** as a dedicatory and atoning ritual. As sprinkling of the blood inaugurated the Mosaic covenant (Exod 24), Hezekiah renews the covenant by analogous dedicatory rites.

Two kinds of sacrifices are offered by the **priests** in the dedication of the temple. First, **burnt offerings** are offered (cf. 2 Chr 29.24,27). This would include the **bulls, rams,** and **lambs.** This is a dedicatory offering — the whole animal is burned up to God. This symbolizes the dedication of the worshiper.

Second, a **sin offering** is offered with **goats.** The sin offering is an atonement offering that removes the sin of the people from the sight of God. The **king and the assembly** placed their sin on the goats by the laying of the hands. Their sin was removed from the people and transferred to the goats.

Significantly, the burnt offering and the sin offering were **for all Israel.** Atonement is for all Israel, and not just for Jerusalem or Judah but also for northern Israel. Milgrom (159-161) suggests that the offerings were made three times each — once for the royal house, once for the sanctuary, and once for the people. Thus, a total of 84 animals were sacrificed ($3 \times [7+7+7+7]$). This number symbolically represents "all Israel" since 84 is 7×12, or the complete number (7) times the number of the tribes of Israel (12).

Theologically, the postexilic temple is not only for the Babylonian exiles, but also for the Assyrian exiles. The temple is the place where all God's people can find the throne of grace, just as in Jesus Christ all nations find grace (Heb 4:14-16). The cross is the blood ritual for Christians, and there the new covenant was dedicated and the people of God are sanctified (Heb 9:11-28).

Preparation for Worship (29:25-26). Second Chronicles 29:25-26 describes the preparation of the liturgical musicians for divine worship. The text presumes the details of 1 Chronicles 15–16, 25. The **Levites** served God musically through **cymbals, harps and lyres** while the **priests** served God with **trumpets**. The trumpets announce the presence of God, the cymbals call attention to the sacrifice, and the lyres and harps accompany the singers during the actual sacrificial ritual (1 Chr 16). While the trumpets were commanded by Moses (Num 8:9-10), the other instruments were **prescribed by David** (thus, they are called **David's instruments**) **and Gad the king's seer and Nathan the prophet**. This is the same as **commanded by the LORD through his prophets**. The text affirms that David's innovation was sanctioned by a prophetic word. The commandment of David was a commandment from Yahweh through the prophets (the same Hebrew term, מִצְוָה [*miṣwāh*], describes both David and Yahweh). The instruments, then, were divinely authorized. Indeed, according to Chronicles, David is one of the prophets (DILLARD, 236). Thus, unlike Ahaz or Uzziah, Hezekiah acted properly according to the word of the Lord.

Chronicles balances the ritual sacrifices with musical liturgy. The musical proclamation ("prophesying" in 1 Chr 25:1-7) of the sacrifice is theologically significant. The sacrifice and music form a symbiotic relationship. When Israel worships, it worships through sacrifice and song. Indeed, the musical instruments themselves become part of the temple utensils or vessels. The instruments were stored in the temple (1 Chr 16:42) because they belonged to the Lord (2 Chr 30:21). The instruments belong among the "vessels of service" (1 Chr 9:28; 23:26; 28:13; 2 Chr 24:14) handled by the Levites in distinction from the "holy vessels" handled by priests (1 Chr 9:29; 22:19; 2 Chr 5:5; cf. Kleinig, *Song*, 78). The instruments, therefore, were a significant part of the sacrificial ritual itself as the temple served its purpose of grace, atonement, and fellowship.

This emphasis may indicate that the postexilic community devalued the musical ministry. Chronicles gives this ministry an exalted status: divinely authorized, part of the temple ritual, and the function of the Levites who stand before the Lord (cf. 1 Chr 16:4). Music is no addendum to divine liturgy. It is an integral part of the worship of God's people.

Israel Worships (29:27-30). The animals are now burned though they were slaughtered earlier. The slaughter and blood ritual (sprinkling), along with the reinstitution of the Levitical choir and band, were part of the preparation for the main event, that is, the lighting of the altar (cf. 2 Chr 5–6).

As the sacrifices burn, Israel worships. The musical ritual remembered, thanked, and praised God (cf. 1 Chr 16:4) as the smoke of the **burnt offering** rose up to God. The incense, smoke, and song are the offering of God's people as they enter his royal palace (cf. 1 Chr 29:1). The **whole assembly** (*qāhāl*) **bowed in worship**. The singing and playing continued until the animals were fully consumed. The people bowed in worship as the Levitical musicians performed and the priests conducted their ritual.

Once the sacrifices were burned up, Hezekiah and **everyone present with him knelt down and worshiped**. In this serious moment of temple dedication, Hezekiah orders **the Levites to praise the LORD** with song. Even though the burnt offering is complete, the musical praise of God continues as the Levites **sang with gladness** (cf. 1 Chr 15:16,25; 2 Chr 23:18; 30:21). The Levites provided a musical homily for the whole assembly.

Celebration of the Temple (29:31-36)

The dedication of the temple is complete. The temple is open and ready for divine service. Consequently, Hezekiah invites everyone to bring sacrifices to the temple to celebrate the renewed covenant and the gracious presence of God.

Hezekiah Invites Worship at the Temple (29:31a). Hezekiah's invitation is directed toward Jerusalem and Judah since this is the context of 2 Chronicles 29. Now that the official (priestly) sacrifices are completed (both burnt offerings and sin offerings), the populace is invited to bring their own sacrifices. Their participation in the festivities that day sanctified them, that is, they "filled the hand" in a kind of priestly ritual (**dedicated**). In some sense, all God's people are priests (cf. 1 Chr 29:5 for the same expression).

Specifically, Hezekiah invites them **to bring sacrifices and thank offerings to the temple of the LORD**. Thank offerings are a form of peace (*shalom*) offerings (Lev 7). The worshiper sacrifices the animal, the fat is burned up to God, part of the animal is given to the priest to eat, and the rest of the animal is eaten by the worshipers. The meal symbolizes the peace between God, the community, and the worshiper. The meal thanks God for his gracious presence.

Christians have such a meal. They break bread and drink wine at the table of the Lord. They drink the cup of thanksgiving and give thanks for the peace that God has established through Jesus Christ (1 Cor 10:16).

Israel Brings Its Sacrifices (29:31b-35a). The people respond with **sacrifices and thank offerings** as well as additional **burnt offerings** (**seventy bulls, a hundred rams**, and **two hundred male lambs**). Their sacrifices included **six hundred bulls and three thousand sheep and goats**. These animals were peace or thank offerings. The worshipers ate with God in celebration of the restored temple (cf. Deut 27:6-7).

Significantly, Chronicles uses "heart" language again (**hearts were willing**). Unlike some presentations of the Chronicler's liturgical theology, Graham ("Setting," 124-141) recognizes that the most significant point about worship ritual for the Chronicler is the orientation of the heart. The heart that seeks God is accepted by him.

The response overwhelmed the priests. There was not a sufficient number of **consecrated** priests to meet the demand. As a result, the **Levites helped them**. In other words, given the circumstances, the Levites assumed priestly functions since they had **been more conscientious in consecrating themselves than the priests had been**. Though the Chronicler is a stickler for ritual perfection, this situation permitted Levitical transgression of priestly prerogatives.

This is not necessarily a negative view of the priesthood. The point is the joy and spontaneity of that day. The religious officials were unprepared for the enormity of Jerusalem's response. the Chronicler does not intend a denigration of the priesthood but only a recognition that in specific ad hoc situations nonpriests may serve in priestly functions for the larger goal of fellowship between God and his people. The ad hoc character of the permission is underscored by the phrases **until the task was finished** and **until other priests had been consecrated** (JAPHET, 930-931). The Levites did what was normally assigned to the priests. Their intrusion into the priestly sphere, however, was accepted by God due to the special circumstances (lit., 2 Chr 29:34 reads: "only the priests were too few").

Yet, according to Leviticus 1:5-6, the worshipers themselves were permitted to skin their own animals. The Chronicler does not explain why, in this circumstance, it is expected that only the priests could do so. Perhaps, as PRATT (430) suggests, "the widespread apostasy of the generation before Hezekiah made it necessary to take extra precautions against syncretism among the laity." In any event, the Levites serve in an extraordinary way due to special circumstances.

The Temple Restored (29:35b-36). **The temple of the LORD was** established (כּוּן, *kûn*) and **the people rejoiced at what God had** established (*kûn*) **for his people.** JOHNSTONE (2:199) comments that "as the worship of God was undertaken, so, sacramentally, God undertook for the people." This reflects, as so often in Chronicles (1 Chr 28:9; 2 Chr 7:14), God's relational character. The people responded to God's anger with faithful seeking, and God responded to their seeking with his gracious presence. Consequently, as in 2 Chr 7:10, the people rejoice over what God has done for them.

Significantly, Israel does not see this day as something it has done for itself. Rather, it revels in the joyous knowledge that God has established himself once again in their presence. The joy arises out of what God has done rather than out of what Israel has done.

The restoration (and transformation) of grace is not a human act. It is a divine work. Though we exert effort, turn our hearts to God, and seek his face, it is God who works in us and through us to do his will and effectively establish his transforming presence in our midst. God works in us to accomplish his purposes and transform our lives into the image of his Son (cf. Phil 2:11-12).

Renewing the Passover (30:1–31:1)

The Passover account in Hezekiah generates three major problems (SELMAN, 2:493-535; WILLIAMSON, 360-365). First, what is the relationship between the Passover and the Feast of Unleavened Bread? Second, what is the relationship between the Passovers in 2 Chronicles 30 (Hezekiah) and 2 Chronicles 35 (Josiah)? Third, is Chronicles's account historical?

Scholars have generally discounted Hezekiah's Passover as theological propaganda. However, this is changing. DILLARD (240) argues that "it would be quite surprising for [the Chronicler] in his idealization of Hezekiah to create *de novo* details of the observance of the Passover in which the praxis was not strictly orthodox." Would the Chronicler create a "heterodox fantasy" with such huge "irregularities"

(DILLARD, 240; cf. Moriarty, 406)? Why would he create a Passover account that differs from his Josianic account (Eves, 124)? But why would Dtr not include Hezekiah's Passover (as he did Josiah's) if, in fact, it did occur? Following Rosenbaum (35-36), Eves ("Role," 123) suggests that Dtr omitted Hezekiah's Passover in order to emphasize Josiah. While Chronicles is more interested in Hezekiah, Dtr is more interested in Josiah — both record what is important for their purposes.

The second problem is more complex. There are similarities and differences between 2 Chronicles 30 and 35 which demonstrate that the Chronicler did not replicate his Josianic account (Eves, 315-320). Eves (318-319) argues that Hezekiah's Passover reflects the priestly tradition found in Exodus 12–13 and Numbers 9 while Josiah's Passover reflects the tradition found in Deuteronomy 16:1-8. The Chronicler intentionally patterns the two accounts after two different traditions. These are two different understandings of the Passover in the Chronicler's postexilic community. The Chronicler promoted "legitimate diversity in Passover praxis. These accounts, therefore, functioned as parallel, non-harmonized texts that expressed the spectrum of legitimate Passover interpretation" (Eves, 320). The Chronicler, then, reconciles a community that is divided over Passover practices by noting the diverse practices of their ancestors.

Eves' historical reconstruction is possible as the Torah does reflect two Passover practices (Exod 12 and Deut 16). However, these practices envision changing circumstances — from homes to a central location (e.g., the temple). Eves overplays the differences between the two Passover accounts. The differences reflect more situational or occasional elements. Some see the differences as so minor that it is argued that Hezekiah's Passover is an anachronistic reduplication of Josiah's (COGGINS, 270). If anything, the two Passover accounts confirm that Israel legitimately adapted the Passover traditions to their circumstances in order to faithfully worship Yahweh. Further, Chronicles may emphasize certain aspects of Hezekiah's Passover in order to pattern it after Solomon's dedication of the temple and thus ensure Hezekiah's status as a "Second Solomon" (Eves, 128-132).

The third problem is the relationship between the Passover and the Feast of Unleavened Bread (DILLARD, 241-243). Scholars have generally believed that the Feast of Unleavened Bread (a pilgrimage feast to a central sanctuary) was originally separate from the Passover meal (originally based in families or homes). The two festivals appear together in Leviticus 23. McConville (*Law*, 99-123) argues that the two have always been joined in biblical legislation and that varying practices reflect differing situations in the history of Israel.

Despite these problems, the heart of the Chronicles account of Hezekiah's Passover is theological. The celebration of the Passover remembers the Exodus, emulates the arrival of the ark into Jerusalem in 1 Chronicles 13, 15–16, and the dedication of the temple by Solomon (2 Chr 7), and celebrates the reunion of north and south at the temple. Chronicles employs the language of 2 Chronicles 7:14 to highlight this significant moment of national repentance and fellowship (WILLIAMSON, 368). Just as God promised Solomon in response to his prayer (2 Chr 7:14), if Israel will "humble" (2 Chr 30:11), "pray" (2 Chr 30:18), "seek" (2 Chr 30:19), and "turn" (2 Chr 30:9), God will "hear" (2 Chr 30:20) and "heal" (2 Chr 30:20).

Hezekiah's Passover becomes a national moment (north and south) for celebrating God's grace through his temple presence in the land which God gave them. It is a national moment when the hearts of God's people were turned to him and God responded with grace. Chronicles encourages the postexilic celebration of the Passover for the same reason. Hezekiah models the Passover for postexilic Judah: postcaptivity north and south are reconciled in a newly dedicated temple.

JAPHET (936) divides Hezekiah's Passover into two sections: (1) Preparations (2 Chr 30:1-12) and (2) Celebration (2 Chr 30:13–31:1).

Preparations for the Passover (30:1-12)

The preparations for the Passover include: (1) the declaration of intention (2 Chr 30:1-5), (2) the invitation to the northern tribes (2 Chr 30:6-9), and (3) the response of the people (2 Chr 30:10-12).

Second Chronicles 30 parallels the ark narrative in 1 Chronicles 13, 15–16 (Graham, "Setting," 131-132). Just as David consulted with his leaders and the whole assembly agreed (1 Chr 13:1-4), so did Hezekiah (2 Chr 30:2-4). In both cases it seemed right in the eyes of the assembly (1 Chr 13:4; 2 Chr 30:4). Everyone, including priests and Levites, are invited to join the holy convocation (1 Chr 13:2,5;

2 Chr 30:1). In both cases the king intended to reform past mistakes (David would consult the ark whereas Saul did not, 1 Chr 13:3; Hezekiah reformed the kingdom). Both convocations were joyous and accompanied with musical celebration (1 Chr 13:8; 2 Chr 30:21-23,26). Both involved the sanctification of priests and Levites as well as accompanying sacrifices (1 Chr 15:12-15,26; 2 Chr 29:4-15; 30:15-17,22,24), even though David's first abortive attempt to move the ark lacked both (cf. 1 Chr 13:1-14). Hezekiah imitated the David of 1 Chronicles 15 rather than the unholy assembly of 1 Chronicles 13. "Therefore," Graham ("Setting," 132) notes, "it appears that Hezekiah showed proper respect for God and so avoided David's disaster with Uzzah."

Graham ("Setting," 132-133) also notes connections with Solomon. Second Chronicles 30:26 compares this celebration with Solomon. This Passover follows a rededication of the temple (2 Chr 29) that echoed Solomon's own dedication (2 Chr 5–7). Both experienced tremendous joy (2 Chr 5:13; 7:6,10; 30:21-23,26) and offered huge sacrifices (2 Chr 5:6-7; 7:1,4-5; 30:15-16,22,24). Hezekiah's invitation (2 Chr 30:6-9) and prayer (2 Chr 30:18b-19) reflect Solomonic language from his own prayer (2 Chr 6) and God's response (2 Chr 7:14). Solomon's plea that foreigners be permitted to seek God at the temple (2 Chr 6:32-33) is fulfilled in Hezekiah's Passover when aliens are part of the celebration (2 Chr 30:25).

Theologically, Hezekiah's Passover had both Davidic and Solomonic meaning as all Israel celebrated God's grace. Worship is a time of unity, thankful remembrance and seeking God's face. "In short," Graham ("Setting," 141) writes, "it is a time for the reorientation of the human heart — to remember what God has done in the past and to infuse the present with hope for a future life of well-being and communion with God."

Intention to Celebrate the Passover (30:1-5). Hezekiah intends a national celebration that includes **all Israel and Judah**. The Chronicler cites **letters to Ephraim and Manasseh** (2 Chr 30:1). Further, in the resumptive repetition of 2 Chronicles 30:5, the Chronicler's proclamation goes **throughout Israel, from Beersheba to Dan** (from south to north). Hezekiah models inclusiveness. Postexilic Judah must also welcome their northern relatives to the Jerusalem temple.

The Law specifies that the Passover is celebrated on the fourteenth day of the first month, but the nation decided to celebrate it in **the second month**. Why does Hezekiah delay the Passover? Most believe the Chronicler assumes the "Second Passover" law of Numbers 9:2-14 as the explanation for the delay (DILLARD, 243-244; SELMAN, 2:496; Fishbane, 154-159). This law permits those who are unclean at the time of the first month to celebrate the Passover in the second month once they are clean. Hezekiah's temple and nation were unclean on the fourteenth day of the first month and thus could not celebrate the Passover. Hezekiah, therefore, extends the individual legislation of Numbers 9 to a national level. The whole nation will celebrate the Passover in the second month rather than the first.

Chronicles is "apologetic" (defensive) about the date and recognizes that it is irregular (JAPHET, 939). The rationale provided in 2 Chronicles 30:3 is twofold. First, **not enough priests had consecrated themselves** for the celebration. During the dedication rites the Levites had to assist the priests in the sacrificial ritual because there were too few of them (2 Chr 29:34). A Passover would include many more animals. Second, the people were not yet **assembled in Jerusalem**. The temple cleansing had taken the first half of the first month to complete, and once it was complete, there was not enough time for a pilgrimage festival in Jerusalem.

The Chronicler's rationale for the irregularity does not invoke Numbers 9 (it may lie in the background as a principle, but he does not cite the Torah as he does in other instances), and his rationale includes more than Numbers 9 explicitly permits. JAPHET (939-940) correctly notes that Numbers 9:6-13 involves individuals who are unclean because they came in contact with the dead or who missed the Passover because they were far away from home. Neither are the case in 2 Chronicles 30. Further, Numbers 9 permits a *second* Passover, but it does not authorize a wholesale abrogation of the first. For the Chronicler, it was not the uncleanness of the people or the fact they lived far away that permitted the cancellation of the first Passover date, but the insufficient number of consecrated priests and the inability to gather the people in Jerusalem so quickly. These exigencies permitted a new Passover date so that it could be celebrated in that calendar year. PRATT (433) comments:

"[Hezekiah] was no pedantic legalist, insisting on precise and wooden application of the Law. Hezekiah's situation was unusual and this extraordinary situation required the application of precedents in Mosaic Law in creative ways. The fact that Hezekiah postponed only one month demonstrates the king's desire to adhere to Mosaic standards, but his unique situation required ingenious application."

The gracious renewal of fellowship with God is more important than the particulars of the Passover date. Mercy takes precedence over sacrifice; or grace takes precedence over ritual (cf. Hos 6:6; Matt 9:13; 12:7). The law of Numbers 9 is itself a reflection of God's merciful intention rather than his unyielding demand for ritualistic perfection. Thus, contrary to some construals, the Chronicler is no extreme ritualist or perfectionistic legalist (WILLIAMSON, 330-331; Graham, "Setting," 135-140).

Hezekiah anticipated a large celebration after the rededication of the temple (2 Chr 30:5). He sought renewal among his people in a way that echoed the Golden Age of David and Solomon. He expected **large numbers**.

Hezekiah's Invitation to Northern Israel (30:6-9). While it appears that the letter is primarily addressed to the northern tribes, Chronicles's preface sends it **throughout Israel and Judah**. This reflects the "leveling down" of Israel and Judah during Ahaz's reign so that effectively both were in exile as defeated peoples (WILLIAMSON, 366). Not only Israel, but Judah must repent. The proclamation goes out from Beersheba to Dan (2 Chr 30:5). Nevertheless, the letter is directed at the northern tribes (**people** [lit., "children"] **of Israel**) since Hezekiah had already made a similar appeal to Jerusalem and Judah in 2 Chronicles 29:5-9 through the priests and Levites.

Building on PRATT (434) and JAPHET (942), the structure of the letter is:

i. Opening (30:6b): **Return to the LORD**
  ii. Negative Imperatives (30:7-8a):
     Do not be like your fathers and brothers, who were unfaithful
     Do not be stiff-necked, as your fathers were
  ii'. Positive Exhortations (30:8b-d).
     Submit to the LORD

Come to the sanctuary
Serve the LORD
i'. Closing (30:9): **If you return to the LORD.**

The letter articulates the "guiding principle" in the opening and closing (PRATT, 434). The use of the verb "return" (שׁוּב, *šûb*) forms an inclusio and occurs 6 times. God will return to them and return (**come back**) their exiled relatives to their land if they will return (**turn**) to him. This expresses the fundamental theological principle of Chronicles (1 Chr 28:9; 2 Chr 7:14-22; 15:2). God finds those who seek him, and whoever returns to him, God will return to them. Further, the call to return is grounded in the character of God. Israel is called to serve the Lord because (כִּי, *kî*; untranslated by the NIV) **if you return**, God will return you to your land. The ground of this principle is that **the LORD your God is gracious and compassionate** (the only time these two words occur together in Chronicles; cf. Exod 34:6; Ps 86:15; 103:8; 111:4; 145:8). God is faithful and **he will not turn his face from you if you return to him**. Thus, this principle expresses the relational and gracious heart of God.

The language assumes an exilic condition for the northern kingdom. The letter is addressed to the remnant **who are left** in the land (cf. 2 Chr 36:20). They have **escaped** the successive incursions of the Assyrian **kings** in the last twenty years.

The negative imperatives remind the north of their past. Their ancestors were **unfaithful** (applied to Judah in 2 Chr 9:1) and **stiffnecked** (applied to a Judean king in 2 Chr 36:13). As a result, God **made them an object of horror** (cf. 2 Chr 29:8), and God turned his anger on them (cf. 2 Chr 29:8). The letter does not stand arrogantly over Israel, but rather Judah stands alongside of Israel. They both have been made a horror and both suffered God's anger. They both have been unfaithful (cf. 2 Chr 29:6). One fallen relative reaches out to another. The letter invites Israel to join Judah in their return to God.

The positive imperatives (**submit, come**, and **serve**) build on each other. "Submit" is literally "give the hand" (cf. 1 Chr 29:24) which is a pledge of loyalty. Secondly, Israel is invited to come to the **sanctuary** which God has given to his people **forever**. Coming to the sanctuary embraces God's faithfulness. The Davidic covenant (cf. 2 Chr 6:41-2) is forever and found in the temple of Yahweh. Thirdly, they should **serve the LORD**. In this context, "serve" has a liturgical meaning. Hezekiah invites Israel to offer their loyalty to the Lord, come to his temple and worship him. This constitutes "returning" to God.

The theological message for the postexilic community is at least twofold. First, they are in the same situation as the northern kingdom. They are a remnant who survived the Bablyonian exile. The principle speaks to them: **if you return to the LORD**, then God will return to you. The postexilic community should embrace the hope rooted in God's faithfulness and his gracious intent. Second, the postexilic community should offer a similar letter to their northern neighbors. The principle applies as much to the north in 400 B.C. as it did in 715 B.C. God yearns for the reunion of his people in his holy presence. The Babylonian remnant must accept the Assyrian remnant.

Of course, this theological principle, rooted in the character of God, is also true today. God is faithful, and he will always receive those who seek him. The faithfulness of God means that Christians accept each other (Rom 15:5-7).

Israel's Response to the Letter (30:10-12). Hezekiah's letter parallels Abijah's speech in 2 Chronicles 13:4-12. Abijah's invitation was soundly rejected, but Hezekiah's invitation is partially accepted. Those who reject Hezekiah's invitation continue to identify with Jeroboam. But those who accept must be accepted as God accepts them.

The opposition to the **couriers** was sufficiently strong that even though the letter was intended for Beersheba to Dan, the couriers did not reach Dan (located in Naphtali). They only went as far as **Zebulun**. This may indicate that the vast majority of the north rejected Hezekiah's plea with scorn and ridicule (though DILLARD [244] thinks other regions may have been too depopulated by the Assyrians to provide much enthusiasm for Hezekiah's invitation). Literally, "they played against them and mocked them" (cf. Jer 20:7; Ps 59:9). In other words, "they laughed them to scorn" (NRSV). Such a reaction indicates the vast distance that separated Israel and Judah. Even God's own people can eventually so harden themselves that they laugh at the prospect of worshiping God at his own temple.

Nevertheless, some northerners (**Asher, Manasseh and Zebulun**) accepted Hezekiah's invitation. In contrast to most of the north, these pilgrims **humbled themselves** (כָּנַע, *kāna'*) — a characteristic term for submission (cf. 2 Chr 7:14). Some even immigrated to Judah (2 Chr 31:6). There is archaeological support for an influx of Israelites into the south. Though many returned to their northern homes, some remained in Jerusalem. Excavations have revealed that Jerusalem was expanded during Hezekiah's reign, perhaps to accommodate northern immigrants and western refugees from Philistine and Assyrian threats (Broshi, 21-26; cf. Graham, "Setting," 137, n. 37).

In contrast to the majority report in the north, the south fully embraced Hezekiah's project. Judah shared a **unity of mind** (lit., "one heart"). They were united in their support of **the king and his officials** as they too intended to follow **the word of the LORD** (though this Passover had some irregularities).

God receives the credit for unity in Judah. Literally, the "hand of God was on Judah to give them one heart." The "hand of God" is involved in "all true revivals" (THOMPSON, 353). God creates unity among his people. Consequently, Paul prays that God give the Jews and Gentiles in the Roman church unity (Rom 15:5-6). The difference between those who scorn Hezekiah's invitation and those who accept it is a matter of the heart (cf. 2 Chr 30:19). Among hearts that seek him, God works unity, but among those who seek their own interests, God works wrath.

Celebration of the Passover (30:13–31:1)

Hezekiah leads the people in a Passover celebration unlike any since the reign of Solomon (2 Chr 30:26). The description of the Passover may be divided into five parts: (a) Introduction: Assembly (2 Chr 30:13-14), (b) The Sacrifices (2 Chr 30:15-20), (c) the Feast (2 Chr 30:21-22), (d) the Extended Feast (2 Chr 30:23-27), and (e) Conclusion: Going Home (2 Chr 31:1).

Introduction: The Assembling (30:13-14). God blessed Hezekiah with a **large crowd** (עַם־רָב, *'am-rāb*) **of people** (2 Chr 30:13; cf. 2 Chr 30:5) to celebrate the Passover and the subsequent **Feast of Unleavened Bread in the second month**. Chronicles portrays the Passover and Feast as joint celebrations where the Feast follows on the heels of the Passover. On the Feast, see Exodus 23:14-17 and Deuteronomy 16:16-17 (cf. 2 Chr 8:13). "As elsewhere in both the OT and NT," DILLARD (245) comments, "the two festivals were so closely associated that the entire celebration could be denominated by either designation."

As this large crowd entered Jerusalem, they took up the banner of reform. While the temple had been cleansed, the country and the city of Jerusalem had not. Consequently, as these pilgrims entered Jerusalem, **they removed the altars in Jerusalem and cleared away the incense altars**. Their religious zeal for Yahweh motivated a thorough cleansing of the city just as the temple had been cleansed. Eventually, the land itself is cleansed (cf. 2 Chr 31:1). Reform begins at the temple, moves through the city, and then throughout the land. They demonstrated their intention to serve only Yahweh as the pagan altars were burned in the **Kidron Valley** (where the unclean items of the temple were burned; cf. 2 Chr 29:16). The people gathered as a holy **assembly** (קָהָל, *qāhāl*; used 9 times in 2 Chr 30:2,13,17,23-25; cf. 1 Chr 13:1-4).

The Sacrifices (30:15-20). The religious zeal of the populace not only removed pagan altars, but they also came to the temple and **slaughtered the Passover lamb**. The laity (rather than the priests and Levites) killed their own animals (as in the original Passover in Exod 12). In fact, there is a contrast between the laity and the **priests and the Levites** in verse 15: the laity were fully consecrated to kill their lambs while the clergy were scrambling to fully prepare themselves through consecration by means of **burnt offerings**. The shame which the clergy experience is due to the zeal of the laity, and their state of unpreparedness for such a large number.

However, the priests and the Levites finally **took up their regular positions as prescribed in the Law of Moses**. Once the family had killed the lamb, priests **sprinkled** the **blood** on the altar. The Passover is a regular "sacrifice" (cf. Exod 34:25; 2 Chr 35:11) where the blood of the animal is sprinkled (as in Lev 1:5,11; 3:2,8,13). JAPHET (950) believes the Passover took on the characteristics of a peace offering. The Passover sacrifices also recall the blood ritual of the original Passover (cf. Exod 12:7,22-23) and serve an atoning function (Exod 12:13; cf. SELMAN, 2:499).

However, a problem arises. While the temple and clergy have been sanctified, **many in the crowd had not consecrated themselves**. Consequently, they could not kill their own animals. Due to their uncleanness, **the Levites had to kill the Passover lambs** for them.

Unclean people cannot kill consecrated lambs. The Chronicler demonstrates a concern for cultic ritual by noting the substitution of the Levites for the worshipers. The Chronicler does not simply dismiss ritual but follows it as closely as possible (e.g., 2 Chr 30:16).

But may unclean people eat the Passover? The text indicates that they did. Unclean people, especially **many** unclean **who came from Ephraim, Manasseh, Issachar and Zebulun**, ate what was clean. This is a clear violation of the Law of Moses and its cultic rituals. Chronicles states that they **ate the Passover contrary to what was written**. This is the opposite of what Chronicles has stressed, that is, Hezekiah celebrated the Passover according to what was written (2 Chr 30:5,12; cf. 1 Chr 16:40; 2 Chr 23:18; 31:3). Hezekiah had a clear understanding of temple and sacrificial ritual as he encouraged Levites who performed well (2 Chr 30:22). But in this case Hezekiah permitted unclean northerners to eat contrary to what was written.

Some have invoked Numbers 9 as a specific authorization for unclean people to eat the Passover. But Numbers 9 does not address this situation. Eves ("Role," 213) argues that "the original intent of the Numbers passage is to allow those who are unclean at the time of the Passover feast to be ceremonially clean by the Second Passover and able to keep it. However, the working assumption of the passage is that at the time of the Second Passover they will be cultically clean. To a considerable degree, however, this is not the case in regard to Hezekiah's Passover. Incredibly, another ingenious alteration (if not rejection) of the Numbers legislation is that Hezekiah knowingly allows *unclean* people to eat the Passover (2 Chr 30:17,18)."

The issue in Numbers 9 is not whether or not unclean people may eat the Passover. The unclean are prohibited from eating. The presumption of Numbers 9 is that those who eat a "second Passover" will be clean when they eat it. Numbers 9 does not authorize unclean people to eat the Passover. This situation in Chronicles violates Numbers 9 and explicitly violates Leviticus 7:19-21 regarding sacrificial meals (which includes the Passover).

Why was not this cultic violation punished with death, as in the case of Uzzah in 1 Chronicles 13 or even Nadab and Abihu in Leviticus 10? Why is not this cultic violation punished as Uzziah's was (2 Chr 26)? Hezekiah's prayer answers the question and reveals the essence of the Chronicler's theology of worship (Graham, "Setting," 136-140). Uzzah was part of an unholy convocation, and he dared to touch the presence of God (cf. 1 Chr 13). Nadab and Abihu arrogantly contradicted the command of God by taking the fire from a place other than God prescribed (cf. Lev 10). The principle which Hezekiah articulates here — and consistent with the whole of Chronicles — is that the heart makes the difference and not ritualistic technicalities.

The prayer appeals to the gracious promise of God in 2 Chronicles 6–7 (cf. 2 Chr 7:14). God accepts those who seek him, and Hezekiah adds **even if he is not clean according to the rules of the sanctuary**. The critical point is the orientation of the person — the one **who sets his heart on seeking God**. This phrase combines two extremely important words in Chronicles: "heart" and "seeking." Hezekiah prays for the forgiveness (lit., "to provide atonement") of those who violated the divine ritual out of a heart that sought God. The guiding principles of forgiveness are: (1) the goodness of God (1 Chr 28:9; 29:14-17) and (2) the orientation of the heart. God forgives those who seek him even when they violate his cultic rules. This is the principle of mercy over sacrifice (Hos 6:6; Matt 9:13; 12:7).

God accepted unclean worshipers because their hearts sought him. The text explicitly records, as if to emphasize the legitimacy of Hezekiah's request, that **the LORD heard Hezekiah and healed the people** (cf. 2 Chr 7:14). Significantly, the Chronicler commends Hezekiah's actions: "in everything . . . he sought his God and worked wholeheartedly" (2 Chr 31:21).

WILLIAMSON (370) notes that 2 Chronicles 30:18-20 clarifies that 2 Chronicles 7:14 is not to be interpreted cultically, but according to the heart. The ritual is not the most important thing. Even the Sabbath with all its strict regulations and penalties was secondary to human needs and suffering (Hicks, "Sabbath," 79-92). The Sabbath was made for humanity, not humanity for the Sabbath (cf. Mark 2:23–3:6). Ritual is made for humanity, not humanity for ritual. Rituals serve the ends for which God has designed them, but they must never be used to repress the heart that seeks God.

The Feast (30:21-22). The people ate their meals with **great rejoicing** as the **Levites and priests sang** with instrumental accompaniment **to the LORD every day**. The scene is celebratory: the people eat while the clergy sing the praises of God and proclaim his acceptance of his people (1 Chr 16:4). God rejoices over his people as they rejoice over his gracious presence.

The Levites (inclusive of the priests) performed their service to the Lord well and they also participated in the festival as **they ate their assigned portion and offered fellowship offerings**.

The fellowship (*shalom*) offerings involved communion (peace) between God, the priests, and the worshiper. God ate the fat (it was burned up to him), the priests ate the right thigh and breasts, and the worshiper ate the rest (cf. Lev 7). To eat the Passover, or to eat the fellowship offerings as part of the **Feast of Unleavened Bread**, was to eat with God (cf. Deut 27:6-7). The Feast is a communal event: God and his people at peace with each other.

Christianity celebrates its own thanksgiving meal in the Lord's Supper. There we give thanks and experience the communion of God with his people (1 Cor 10:16). We sit at the Lord's table and feast on our Passover Lamb as the Lord himself sits at table with us. The joy of the fellowship offerings of ancient Israel should surround the table of the Lord Jesus in his church.

The Extended Feast (30:23-27). The enthusiasm of the joyous celebration in 2 Chronicles 30:21-22 overflows into the extension of the celebration for an additional week (cf. Solomon's two-week affair in 2 Chr 7:8-10). There is no precedent in the Law of Moses for such an extension, but the king and his **officials** provide the animals for another week of festive meals. The number of animals (**a thousand bulls and seven thousand sheep and goats . . . a thousand bulls and ten thousand sheep and goats**) is necessary to feed the large assembly.

The ranks of consecrated priests also continue to grow. Priests, perhaps those arriving from the countryside, are still undergoing ritual cleansing. Consecration is not abrogated even though it is dealt with mercifully.

The roll call of participants in 2 Chronicles 30:25 highlights several important items. Four groups are identified: (1) **entire assembly of Judah**, (2) **priests and Levites**, (3) **all who had assembled from Israel**, and (4) **aliens who had come from Israel and those who lived in Judah**. The list's inclusiveness is apparent. Everyone who lives in Judah and Israel (laity and clergy alike) was free to come to the festival — including aliens in the land. Theologically, "alien" connects with David's prayer in 1 Chronicles 29:15. Israel is itself an alien in the earth, but nonetheless blessed by God. So, also, Israel as an alien must receive the aliens in her midst (cf. Exod 12:48-49 on aliens eating the Passover). The participation of the aliens fulfills part of the mission of Israel to serve the nations.

The joy and blessing of this festival recalls the Golden Age of the United Monarchy. There are two indications of this in 2 Chronicles 30:26-27. First, Chronicles explicitly connects the joy of this moment with Solomon (2 Chr 30:26). The joy is rooted in its inclusiveness. At least for this brief moment, Israel and Judah are united. Second, the prayers of the **priests and the Levites** are **heard** by God from **his holy dwelling place**. This is the language of Solomon's prayer in 2 Chronicles 6. The blessing that closed the festivities, as DILLARD (245) supposes, was probably Numbers 6:22-27. Since blessing is a priestly duty, it is probably best to render "Levitical priests" rather than priests and Levites (MT has no "and;" cf. WILLIAMSON, 371-372). The theological point, however, is that God is with his people once again.

The point for the postexilic community is that God's blessings will come upon them as well. Even in their uncleanness, they must seek the Lord in his temple. But will they imitate their ancestors and seek the Lord?

The theological question is a perennial one. Jesus asked whether he would find faith on earth when he returned again (Luke 18:8). The writer of Hebrews wonders whether his audience will continue to seek God faithfully even as he offers example after example of faithful seeking (Hebrews 11:6). Who seeks the Lord? This is the rallying cry for the people of God. Let everyone who seeks the Lord submit, come, and worship him (cf. 2 Chr 30:8).

Conclusion: Going Home (31:1). The zeal that enthused the pilgrims to cleanse the city of Jerusalem (2 Chr 30:14) enthused them to cleanse the land. The **Israelites** who attended the feast purified **towns of Judah** as well as **Ephraim and Manasseh** from pagan idols. They destroyed **sacred stones** and **Asherah poles** as well as **the high places and the altars**. This iconoclasm reached into the north as well as the south. Worship zeal empowered bold action.

Most scholars believe this was part of Hezekiah's recentralization project (parallel with 2 Kgs 18:4). He systematically removed altars (whether to pagan gods or to Yahweh) from local sanctuaries and centralized the worship of Yahweh in the Jerusalem temple. This was particularly necessary in light of the recent idolatry of Ahaz as well as the history of the northern kingdom. Archaeological evidence supports this picture. Dismantled altars in Arad and Beersheba, dating from the time of Hezekiah, have been found. Thus, "there is no reason to doubt that a dismantling of altars throughout the kingdom of Judah took place during Hezekiah's reign" (Rainey, "Hezekiah's," 334). Hezekiah's recentralization project restored Solomonic worship.

Restoring the Temple Personnel (31:2-21)

Second Chronicles 29–30 covers only two months of Hezekiah's reign. They were filled with religious reform and renewal. He restored the temple and the Passover. His attention now turns to the support of the temple personnel and their permanence. This takes five months. Consequently 2 Chronicles 29–31 detail incidents within the first seven months of his twenty-nine year reign. Chronicles devotes only a single chapter to the rest of his reign. Almost as much attention is given to the support of temple personnel as to the Assyrian invasion (2 Chronicles 32:1-23). The Chronicler is focused on the temple because this is what is significant for his readers.

DILLARD (251) notes that this chapter may seem remote to contemporary readers, but for the Chronicler's readers "this section would have been full of the utmost practical relevance for godly living." Postexilic readers needed to hear how tithing brings God's blessing and how they are responsible for the support of the temple cultus. For the Chronicler "it was a lesson from history that needed to be heard in his own day, for it remained the pathway to success and blessing" (2 Chr 31:21).

Permanent Appointment of Priests and Levites (31:2-4)

Given the temple restoration (2 Chr 29) and religious renewal (2 Chr 30), Hezekiah appoints the **priests and Levites to divisions** for the temple's regular functioning. Hezekiah emulates David (1 Chr 23–26; esp. 1 Chr 23:18-19) and Solomon (2 Chr 8:14) as he reinstitutes the temple cultus. While David and Solomon were founders, Hezekiah is a restorer.

The function of the priests and Levites is described in general terms. The priests, of course, **offer burnt offerings and fellowship offerings**, while the Levites assisted them in their priestly ministry (2 Chr 8:14; cf. 1 Chr 23:13). The Levites functioned as general ministers (**to minister**; cf. 1 Chr 6:32; 15:2; 16:4,37) at the temple and they composed the Levitical choir and band. The Levitical singers remember, give thanks, and praise God (cf. 1 Chr 16:4). Thus, both the priests and Levites are ministers of the temple, but they serve different functions. The former lead the sacrificial ritual while the latter perform the musical one. It is better to translate "within the gates" (cf. NRSV) rather than **at the gates** (NIV) since clerical functions were performed in the temple courts and the gatekeepers served at the gates (DILLARD, 248).

Significantly, the priests and Levites minister within the gates of **the LORD's dwelling** or, more literally, the Lord's camp (cf. 1 Chr 9:19). This contrasts the "camp of the Assyrian king" (2 Chr 32:21) and "the Lord's camp." The Jerusalem temple is the place where God is permanently camped, and no earthly power can assail it. The Lord of Hosts is encamped in Jerusalem "in a state of perpetual mobilization" (JOHNSTONE, 2:207). This expression also "belongs to the period of the Tent" (cf. Num 2:17) and "illustrates faithfulness to Mosaic principles" (SELMAN, 2:503).

Once the ritual is established, the next task is its support. Hezekiah assumes the responsibility of providing the daily sacrifices (**morning and evening burnt offerings**) as well as the regular festivals (including **Sabbaths, New Moons and appointed feasts**). These are daily, weekly, monthly, and annual moments of worship. The law prescribes the festivals but does not obligate the king to supply the animals (cf. Lev 23; Num 28–29). Thus, Hezekiah is generous, much like David (cf. 1 Chr 29:1-10) and Solomon (2 Chr 9:10-11). Hezekiah models generosity for the people.

However, at some point it became the king's responsibility to provide the regular sacrificial offerings (Ezek 45:17,22; 46:2; cf. the king's "portion" in 2 Chr 31:3). It was the practice of Persian kings (cf. Ezra 6:9-10). The postexilic community, however, was without a king, and so Nehemiah prescribed a temple tax to ensure a proper subsidy for regular temple offerings (Neh 10:32-39; 12:44).

While Hezekiah will provide the regular sacrificial animals (his "portion"), he **ordered the people** to financially support **the priests**

and Levites so they could devote themselves (lit., "be strong") **to the Law of the LORD.** The laity must support the clergy so they can give their full attention to their ministry in the temple and the study of the Law. The reference to the Law instead of the expected "temple" may indicate the growing interest in the study of the Law in the postexilic period (WILLIAMSON, 374; cf. Ezra 7:10; Mal 2:6-7). **The portion** (מְנָת, *m*ᵉ*nāth*; also 2 Chr 31:3 though untranslated) **due** to the clergy assumes the clerical share of the harvest (including tithes, first fruits, etc.; cf. Lev 6:14–7:36; Num 18:8-32; Deut 14:27-29; 18:1-18; 26:1-15) which were probably suspended during the reign of Ahaz (PRATT, 442).

This section models the maintenance of the temple and the sustenance of its ministers. The king has his portion and the people have theirs. This was a continual problem in the postexilic community (cf. Neh 13:10; Mal 3:8-10) due to hardships and faithlessness. The Chronicler rebukes this lethargy and exhorts his readers to fulfill their responsibilities.

Immediate Provisions for the Temple Cultus (31:5-8)

The people respond to Hezekiah's proclamation (**order**; lit., "the word"). Two groups are pictured. First, **the Israelites generously gave** (lit., "multiplied") from their harvests. They gave a tenth **of everything**. This probably refers to the Israelites who returned to the northern territories. A second group, however, is **the men of Israel and Judah who lived in the towns of Judah**. This refers to Israelite immigrants and native Judahites. They also brought a tenth of their possessions (including **herds and flocks**) as well as tithes from things that had been dedicated as holy (Num 18:19). "Between Israel and Judah, everything possible was contributed, as a sign of prosperity and blessing" (JAPHET, 965). These gifts are called "offerings" ("contributions") in 2 Chronicles 31:10. They are gifts to the Lord from the blessings the Lord gave his people.

The people keep their "portion" and the law of the Lord. Their dedication to the temple resulted in **heaps** (lit., "heaps of heaps" or "heaping heaps") of gifts. Their giving continued from the **third** to the **seventh month** which parallels the two harvest seasons (DILLARD, 250; May/June grain harvest at Pentecost and September/October fruit and vine harvests at the Feast of Tabernacles). The scenario, then, entailed a Passover celebration in the second month followed by tithing and first-fruit gifts from the ensuing two harvests. The Passover was followed by the festive celebrations of Pentecost and the Feast of Tabernacles. Thus, the seasonal festivals bracketed the celebration of the restoration of the temple. Second Chronicles 31 is a continuation of the celebration begun in 2 Chronicles 29–30.

When Hezekiah **saw the heaps**, he blessed (**praised**) the LORD (cf. 1 Chr 29:10,20). To bless the Lord is to ascribe to him what is due him, but to bless the people is to place upon them what belongs to the Lord. In gratitude (like David in 1 Chr 29:10 and Solomon in 2 Chr 6:3), the people give God credit for his generosity (cf. 2 Chr 31:10) and at the same time ask God to bless his people even more richly than he has in the past. Worship entails both blessing God and his people; it includes praise and intercession (cf. 2 Chr 30:27).

Permanent Provisions for the Temple Cultus (31:9-19)

The huge response by the people created a problem — **Hezekiah asked the priests and Levites about the heaps**. Where will such an abundance be stored, and how can this ensure the permanence of the clerical ministry? Second Chronicles 31:9-10 raises the problem and 2 Chronicles 31:11-19 provides the solution.

The Problem (31:9-10). The heaps create a problem because after the immediate needs of the clerical ministry were met, a **great amount is left over**. God had so **blessed his people** that there was too much and no place to store it. The purpose of the provisions is clear from Azariah's statement that the clerics **had enough to eat**. The ministry is supported by gifts.

Azariah is not listed in the succession of high priests in 1 Chronicles 6:3-15 and, more than likely, he is not the priest who rebuked Uzziah (2 Chr 26:17) forty years earlier. However, 1 Chronicles 6 is not exhaustive. DILLARD (250) suggests that he is the grandson of that Azariah which seems probable in the light of the widespread practice of papponymy (a son named after the grandfather; DILLARD, 251; WILLIAMSON, 375).

The Solution (31:11-19). Hezekiah solves the problem by (1) preparing **storerooms** attached to the temple and (2) appointing Levites to supervise the provisions. Thus, the Levites were given the responsibility of collecting (cf. Neh 10:37), managing, and distributing the tithes. Specifically, **Conaniah**, assisted by **his brother Shimei**, along with ten other **supervisors** were charged with the collection and storage of provisions. **Kore**, assisted by six others, was responsible for distributing them **in the towns of the priests**.

The distribution, however, was not only for those living in the cities, but also for those serving at the temple (2 Chr 31:16-18). While the NIV reads **three years old**, the text should read "thirty." In Hebrew, the difference between "three" (שָׁלוֹשׁ, *šālôš*) and "thirty" (שְׁלֹשִׁים, *š^elōšîm*) is minor, and 1 Chronicles 23:3 gives "thirty" as the age of enrollment. Most scholars emend the text to read "thirty" supposing that there was a problem in its transmission (DILLARD, 251). At thirty, men could begin serving in the temple (Jesus' age in Luke 3:23).

Twenty is also a significant age for enrollment (2 Chr 31:17). Thirty may refer to priests and twenty to Levites, but age requirements apparently varied according to circumstances. For example, Levites may be thirty (1 Chr 23:3), twenty-five (Num 8:24), or twenty (2 Chr 31:17). Presumably, the age requirement may have changed due to circumstances such as the number of priests and Levites available to perform the necessary tasks.

Summary of Hezekiah's Reform (31:20-21)

This paragraph parallels 2 Kings 18:5-7. "There are also striking points of contact with [2 Chr] 7:11, which was seen to have been deliberately shaped by [the Chronicler] into a conclusion of the dedication of the temple under Solomon" (WILLIAMSON, 377). This paragraph concludes 2 Chronicles 29:3–31:19. It summarizes Hezekiah's faithfulness in reforming the temple and nation.

The positive theological evaluation of Hezekiah echoes 2 Chronicles 29:2. In contrast with his father Ahaz, Hezekiah did **what was good and right and faithful before the LORD his God**. This summary, however, is directly related to his temple service (just as Solomon's faithfulness is temple-focused). This is specified in 2 Chronicles 31:21 — **in everything that he undertook in the service of God's temple and in obedience to the law and the commands**.

This is particularly interesting in light of the fact that several irregularities were present in 2 Chronicles 29–30. Levites participated in sacrificial rituals designed only for priests. The Passover was kept in the wrong month. Hezekiah permitted unclean people to eat the Passover. He extended the Feast of Unleavened Bread for an additional week. Nevertheless, his actions are regarded as **faithful** because **he sought his God and worked wholeheartedly**. Hezekiah's faithfulness is characterized by his orientation (seeking) and dedication (whole heart).

Consequently, **he prospered**. Solomon prospered (1 Chr 22:13 and 2 Chr 7:11). It describes the blessing of God upon Asa (2 Chr 14:7), Jehoshaphat (2 Chr 20:20), and Joash (2 Chr 26:5). Those who forsake the Lord do not prosper (2 Chr 24:20), but those who seek the Lord do.

3. Hezekiah's Trials (32:1-31)

While Dtr devoted a few verses to Hezekiah's reform (2 Kgs 18:1-8), Chronicles gave it three chapters (2 Chr 29–31). However, while Chronicles only devotes a single chapter to other topics (2 Chr 32), Dtr focuses his history on those incidents (2 Kgs 18:9–20:21). Their interests are different. Chronicles emphasizes religious reform and temple celebrations, but Dtr emphasizes political intrigue. Chronicles answers questions about temple worship, but Dtr answers questions about whom the king trusts. Their histories are different though not mutually exclusive.

Chronicles summarizes the other events of Hezekiah's reign. Chronicles follows but shortens the accounts of 2 Kings while adding some unique sections of his own (PRATT, 448, 456). Chronicles exalts Hezekiah (like David and Solomon) while not passing over his failures.

Topic	2 Chr	2 Kgs	Isa
Sennacherib Invades	32:1	18:13	36:1
Hezekiah's Preparations	32:2-8		
Hezekiah's Submission		18:14-16	
Sennacherib's Propaganda	32:9-19	18:17-35	36:2-22
Reactions to Threats	32:20	18:36–19:34	37:1-35
Divine Intervention	32:21	19:35-37	37:36-38
Hezekiah's Exaltation	32:22-23		
Hezekiah Becomes Sick	32:24a	20:1	38:1
Hezekiah Prays	32:24b	20:2-8	38:2-6,21,22

The Prayer of Hezekiah		38:9-20	
God Answers Hezekiah	32:24c	20:9-11	38:7-8
Hezekiah's Pride, Repentance, Blessing	32:25-26		
Hezekiah's Prosperity	32:27-30		
Hezekiah Receives the Babylonians	32:31	20:12-19	39:1-8

Chronicles contexualizes the three major episodes, (1) the Assyrian siege of Jerusalem, (2) Hezekiah's illness, and (3) the Babylonian envoys, differently. The events are contextualized by the previous reform. The question is whether Hezekiah will continue his trust in the Lord throughout his reign or will vacillate as other kings who started out well but nevertheless ended badly (e.g., 2 Chr 25–27). These three events test Hezekiah's faith. The third episode is called a testing (2 Chr 32:31), and this illuminates the whole context.

Some key themes in this chapter are pride, trust, and humility. When Jerusalem is threatened, whom will Hezekiah trust? Pride is the issue. Through trials (whether war, illness, or prosperity), God probes the hearts of his people. Despite Hezekiah's wholehearted devotion to God in his reform (2 Chr 31:21), God tests Hezekiah to know what is in his heart (2 Chr 32:31).

This "testing" motif fills the story line of Scripture. Abraham is tested (Gen 22:1). Israel is tested (Deut 8:1-5). Job is tested (Job 23:1-12). Jesus is tested (Matt 4:1-11). Paul is tested (1 Thess 2:4). Believers are tested (Judg 2:22; 3:4; Ps 17:3; 66:10; Isa 48:10; Zech 13:9; 2 Cor 8:8; Jas 1:12). The whole world is tested (Rev 3:10). Believers pray for testing (Ps 26:2; 139:23). As God seeks hearts, he tests them (cf. 1 Chr 29:17). In 2 Chronicles 32 God tests Hezekiah.

Hezekiah and the Assyrians (32:1-23)

Chronicles's account of the Assyrian invasion is brief when compared with 2 Kings 18:13–19:27. While the Chronicler adds a section on preparations for the invasion and a conclusion, he omits almost all the political details (e.g., the rebellion in 2 Kgs 18:7-8; the tax in 2 Kgs 18:14-16, etc.). His interest is theological rather than political. He provides enough of the story to make his point without duplicating Dtr's details. It is "theological commentary" (JAPHET, 977).

The invasion by the Assyrian King Sennacherib has occasioned discussion due to difficulties in 2 Kings. Some have postulated two invasions while others have dismissed the biblical accounts as contradictory (Millard, "Sennacherib's," 61-77; Shea, 401-418; Rowley, "Hezekiah's," 395-431; Konkel, 45-115). These difficulties primarily concern 2 Kings (Fewell, 79-90). Chronicles interprets the invasion by Sennacherib in 701 B.C. which is confirmed by extrabiblical evidence (Na'aman, "Sennacherib's," 61-86).

Theologically, the key question is whether God can deliver Jerusalem from such a massive invading power. The term הִצִּיל (*hiṣṣîl,* "save, deliver," from נצל, *nṣl*) occurs 9 times in 2 Chronicles 32:12-17 (and only 3 times elsewhere in Chronicles). The issue is confidence and assurance. Is Hezekiah confident that God can deliver? SELMAN (2:508) notes that this demonstrates that Yahweh "really rules in Israel," and "aims to stimulate faith in Israel's God rather than admiration for Israel's king." The Lord reigns — Hezekiah is only his servant. Confidence and assurance arise out of God's ability to deliver his people. It is not vested in human kings. God is the one who saves and justifies (cf. Rom 8:31-39).

The Invasion (32:1)

While based on 2 Kings 18:13 (cf. Isa 36:1), the Chronicler recontextualizes the announcement of the invasion. First, he reminds the reader of Hezekiah's previous reforms (lit., "after these things [temple rededication and Passover] and these trustworthy [אמת, *'ĕmeth*] deeds"). But the appearance of an invading force seems problematic in the light of Hezekiah's faithfulness. DILLARD (256) believes there is an implicit retribution. But the Chronicler links this narrative with the previous one about Hezekiah's faithfulness. This is "a divine test" (JAPHET, 980). The situation is similar to that of Asa in 2 Chronicles 14 where his reformed nation was challenged by an invader from the south. Hezekiah, after his reforms, is challenged by an invader from the north.

Second, the Chronicler states Sennacherib's intention to capture Judah's **fortified cities** whereas in Dtr it is an accomplished fact. The Chronicler is relatively unconcerned about those cities as he concentrates on the fate of Jerusalem and its temple. The Chronicler does not deny that Sennacherib captured them, but the statement of intention provides a better context for the discussion of Jerusalem which follows (absent from Dtr).

Sennacherib captured forty-six Judean cities. The Assyrian annal also declares that Sennacherib trapped Hezekiah in Jerusalem like a caged bird, took 200,150 captives and obtained 30 talents of gold and 800 talents of silver (*ANET*, 288). However, he does not say he captured Jerusalem. Unlike Sennacherib's (and others) descriptions of victories, he does not replace the king, devastate the capital city, or despoil it. For example, while Sennacherib describes in detail his defeat of the kings of Ashkelon and Ekron, his description of Hezekiah is more like his son's description of his siege of Tyre in 671 B.C. which he did not capture. Sennacherib captured many cities in Judah; he did not capture Jerusalem. The Assyrian records are consistent with the Chronicles picture (Millard, "Sennacherib's," 68-70).

The Preparations (32:2-8)

This section is unique. As the siege of Jerusalem loomed ahead, Hezekiah prepared his city and his people. Isaiah also confirms this preparation (Isa 22:8-11) even though it is not mentioned in Dtr.

Theologically, what is the function of these preparations? Does the Chronicler commend them or does the narrative implicitly question them (cf. Isa 22:11)? The Chronicler is never theologically neutral. A positive assessment of these preparations would see building projects as a sign of blessing (DILLARD, 257) and the words of Hezekiah in 2 Chronicles 32:7-8 as indicative of his intent (JAPHET, 981-982). Most follow this positive interpretation (THOMPSON, 361; SELMAN, 2:509-511; JOHNSTONE, 2:212-214; WILLIAMSON, 380). However, a negative assessment is based on the example of Jehoshaphat who first sought the Lord and only after a prophetic word began preparations for battle (cf. 2 Chr 20:3-20). Asa built up his armies after he sought the Lord (2 Chr 14:4). The context of 2 Chronicles 32 indicates that these preparations are viewed negatively since pride and failure are the setting of the other two episodes in 2 Chronicles 32. The Chronicler "had little interest in idealizing Hezekiah" (PRATT, 450). Hezekiah's failures are tempered by his implicit trust in God as the text always resolves the failures quickly. Consequently, these preparations are probably a prideful reaction to an Assyrian invasion (thus, consistent with 2 Kgs 18:13-18 where Hezekiah attempts to "buy off" Sennacherib and 2 Kgs 20:6 where the deliverance of the city is still in question due to Hezekiah's pride). Instead of seeking God first, Hezekiah made preparations first. Trusting in God was almost an afterthought (cf. Isa 22:8-11). Ultimately, Hezekiah placed his trust in God, but he followed the wrong order: "get prepared, then trust in God." The Chronicler's order is "trust in God, and then get prepared."

Hezekiah's preparations fall into three categories. First, he secures his water supply and denies the Assyrians access to the spring of Gihon (2 Chr 32:3-4). Second, he repairs the walls, **towers**, and **supporting terraces** in the city of Jerusalem (2 Chr 32:5a). Archaeological evidence confirms the expansion of Jerusalem (tripling its size) and perhaps the identification of the wall mentioned here (Avigad, 129-134; Broshi, 21-26). Third, he equipped his military with new weapons and appointed **military officers over the people** (2 Chr 32:5b-6). These are all practical matters which seem natural as preparations for a siege.

Despite the lack of trust, Hezekiah ultimately assembles the people and speaks "to their hearts" (**encouraged them with these words**). In this speech (2 Chr 32:7-8) Hezekiah resembles Jehoshaphat in 2 Chronicles 20:15-17. Here the theological message shines. Ultimately, the preparations will not defeat the Assyrian king, but God himself will. Hezekiah ultimately places his trust in God though the trial also revealed flaws in his character (e.g., 2 Kgs 18:20-25). Consequently, Chronicles's abbreviated account offers the heart of Hezekiah in 2 Chronicles 32:7-8 (unparalleled in Dtr) which seeks God (2 Chr 32:19-21) in response to Assyrian threats (2 Chr 32:9-19). Chronicles does not assume that Hezekiah never flinched or wavered. Chronicles implicitly says what Dtr records. Ultimately, Hezekiah trusted God and sought his deliverance.

The language of 2 Chronicles 32:7-8 is familiar (cf. 2 Chr 20:15-17). **Be strong and courageous** (cf. Deut 31:6-7; 31:23; Josh 1:6-7,9) appears in 1 Chronicles 22:13 and 28:20. **Do not be afraid or discouraged** (cf. Deut 1:21; 31:8; Josh 8:1; 10:25) appears in 1 Chronicles 22:13 and 28:20 as well as in Jehoshaphat's speech (2 Chr 20:15,17). This language links Hezekiah with David and Solomon as well as Moses and Joshua.

There is reason for alarm because Sennacherib brings a **vast army**. Twice before Judah had faced "vast armies" (2 Chr 13:8; 20:12), and in both cases God delivered his people. History teaches that God delivers those who seek him. Thus, **confidence** is gained by memory and reflection on the faithfulness of God (lit., "the people leaned on the words of Hezekiah"). God is willing and able. His **power** is **greater** than the Assyrian king's, and the Lord's arm is stronger (cf. Jer 17:5 on **arm of flesh**). Literally, despite the vastness of his army, the vastness of the Lord is greater. God is committed to **help** and to **fight our battles** (2 Chr 18:31). "'Our battles' are sacramentally his battles" (JOHNSTONE, 2:214). God helps those who ask him (cf. 2 Chr 14:11; 18:31; on "help" in Chronicles, see 1 Chr 12:18).

Sennacherib Threatens Jerusalem (32:9-19)

Sennacherib sends **officers** to Jerusalem to intimidate **Hezekiah** and his **people**. This was not uncommon in the ancient world (cf. 2 Kgs 20:2-12). While the official **siege** of **Jerusalem** had not yet begun (or perhaps Sennacherib is conducting two sieges at once — one at **Lachish** and one at Jerusalem), advance forces are probably already forming around Jerusalem. The message is "designed both to instill fear and to arouse discontent with Hezekiah" (DILLARD, 258). They even spoke in **Hebrew** so the populace could understand them (2 Chr 32:18).

Chronicles mentions the siege of Lachish in southeast Judah. This siege was so significant that Sennacherib told its story in a relief on one of his palace walls (Ussishkin). Even more interesting is the absence of such a relief concerning the conquest of Jerusalem. This silence indicates Sennacherib's embarrassment regarding Jerusalem, that is, he was unable to complete what he began (Millard, "Sennacherib's," 72). He never captured Jerusalem as he did Lachish.

Chronicles's rendition of Sennacherib's speech is "a masterly combination of several speeches" (2 Kgs 18:10-25,27-35; 19:9-13) which reduces the "variety of arguments" in 2 Kings "to a single theme" (SELMAN, 2:511). Sennacherib attacks Hezekiah's claim that Yahweh will deliver Jerusalem. As an abbreviation of 2 Kings 18–19, 2 Chronicles 32:9-19 focuses the point: Sennacherib of Assyria versus Yahweh of Jerusalem.

While 2 Kings 18–19 emphasizes the term "trust" or "rely" (בטח, *bāṭaḥ*; 9 times in 2 Kgs 18:5,19,20-22,24,30; 19:10), the term only occurs in two texts in Chronicles: 1 Chronicles 5:20 and 2 Chronicles

32:10. The former text recounts the victory of the transjordanian tribes over the Hagrites. God answered their prayer because "they trusted in him." Sennacherib raises this question for Judah: can they trust God? Chronicles's whole history answers that question affirmatively (2 Chr 32:7-8). Nevertheless, it is a persistent question for the people of God. Is God trustworthy? The story of God answers that Yahweh is faithful. Israel must trust Yahweh (cf. 2 Chr 32:15 with 2 Chr 20:20).

Sennacherib's argument is twofold. First, he questions Hezekiah's loyalty to Yahweh (2 Chr 32:12). Hezekiah is deceptive and misleads his people (2 Chr 32:11,15). He subverted the worship of Yahweh by tearing down the **high places and altars** to him throughout the nation. The king surmises that is why he is able to ravage the cities of Judah. There are no altars to Yahweh in them. Therefore, those cities are destroyed. In the ancient Near East "the common assumption was that gods were pleased to have many altars" (PRATT, 453). Sennacherib appeals to some potential discontent among the people for the lack of Yahwehist altars. However, God chose the site of his single altar in Jerusalem.

Second, he questions Yahweh's power (2 Chr 32:13-14). Sennacherib has conquered the **gods** of other **nations**. Twice the Assyrian king refers to the "gods of the nations" (2 Chr 32:17). Ironically, Yahweh, as ruler of all the nations (2 Chr 20:6), empowers Sennacherib to conquer those gods (cf. 2 Chr 15:6; Isa 10:5-19). Yahweh conquered the "gods of the nations" through Sennacherib. Now Sennacherib ignorantly challenges the very God who enabled his victories. He misinterpreted his own experience.

Sennacherib's mistake is that his messengers **spoke about the God of Jerusalem as they did about the gods of the other peoples of the world**. They did not recognize the sovereignty of Yahweh over all the nations nor distinguish between **the work of men's hands** (idols) and Yahweh. Instead, they taunted (insulted; cf. 1 Chr 20:7) Yahweh.

Hezekiah Prays and God Answers (32:20-21)

King Hezekiah and the prophet Isaiah (2 Chr 32:20,32; 36:22) respond to these threats with trust (cf. 2 Chr 32:24; 33:13). They **cried out in prayer to heaven** (lit., "prayed and cried out to heaven").

489

While 2 Kings 19:1-34 describes the prayer, Isaiah's role, and the divine response in great detail, Chronicles summarizes the episode in a simple, but theologically pregnant, phrase. The verb "pray" (הִתְפַּלֵּל, *hithpallēl*) appears 8 times in Solomon's temple prayer (2 Chr 6). It also appears in God's assurance to Solomon that "if my people . . . pray and seek my face . . . then I will hear from heaven and will forgive their sin and will heal their land" (2 Chr 7:14). Ten of the fifteen occurrences of this verb are found in 2 Chronicles 6–7 along with seventeen of Chronicles's thirty-five uses of "heaven" (2 Chr 6:13-14,18,21,23,25-27,30,33,35,39; 7:1,14). Second Chronicles 32:20 recalls Solomon's prayer and remembers the promises of God. Thus, Hezekiah and Isaiah depend on the faithfulness of God. The verb "cried out" appears 4 times in Chronicles. In every case the people of God are distressed (1 Chr 5:20; 2 Chr 18:31; 20:9; 32:20). When his people cry out, God hears and delivers.

When Assyrian annals are compared with each other, Sennacherib's report of his attack on Jerusalem indicates that he did not capture and despoil the city. His own report says that he did not receive tribute from Hezekiah until after he had arrived back in Nineveh (*ANET*, 288). Assyrian annals report victories and their extent, including whether the city was captured. Thus, Assyrian documents confirm that something extraordinary happened at Jerusalem because they do not report the obeisance and humiliation that is characteristic of surrendering cities. Whatever the exact *modus operandi*, Sennacherib broke off his siege and returned home (Millard, "Sennacherib's," 70-72, 76-77).

Chronicles interprets the withdrawal of Sennacherib as a divine act, even more directly than the extended version of 2 Kings 19:35-37. **The LORD sent an angel** (cf. 1 Chr 21:12-30). While the **camp** may allude to Lachish (WILLIAMSON, 385), the Chronicler presupposes a knowledge of 2 Kings and his abbreviation does not intend to contravene the events of 2 Kings 18–19. The time between Sennacherib's multiple threats ("letters" in 2 Chr 32:17) and this deliverance is unstated. This may have provided sufficient opportunity for Sennacherib to complete his siege of Lachish and besiege Jerusalem. The Chronicler's account is truncated (e.g., 185,000 dead Assyrians in 2 Kgs 19:35). The summary is a generalization (**annihilated all the fighting men and the leaders and officers in the camp**).

Chronicles emphasizes the divine answer to prayer. Not only does Sennacherib's army withdraw, but Sennacherib himself is punished. God delivered Jerusalem and judged Sennacherib. The Assyrian king was assassinated by his own sons (*ANET*, 288-289). However, Sennacherib was not killed till 681 B.C. (after Hezekiah died). The Chronicler telescopes the events of withdrawal and assassination without necessarily implying that one immediately followed the other. The two-part answer to Hezekiah's prayer is separated by twenty years. "To look for answers to prayer only in the short term," SELMAN (2:513) writes, "is often to miss what God is doing." Ironically, the very god Sennacherib sought for his own protection was the very god in whose house he was killed. The taunt that Sennacherib placed at the feet of Yahweh came back to haunt him as his own god could not protect him from his own sons.

Conclusion (32:22-23)

Unique to Chronicles, this section summarizes the theological meaning of Sennacherib's withdrawal. Divine deliverance engenders gratitude among the people (**offerings**) and respect among the nations. In fact, the term "offerings" is sometimes used in Chronicles in reference to "tribute" (cf. 1 Chr 18:2,6; 2 Chr 17:11; 26:8) or "gifts" to the king (cf. 2 Chr 17:5). Judah brought **gifts** ("precious things," NRSV) to Hezekiah as a form of gratitude to replenish the wealth of the kingdom. Ironically, now **all the nations** respect Hezekiah (lit., "he is carried [exalted] in the eyes of all the nations"). The nations whom Sennacherib defeated honor Hezekiah. This parallels David and Solomon (1 Chr 14:17; 2 Chr 9:23-24). The nations recognize that the Lord reigns (cf. 1 Chr 16:24,31) as the people of God are delivered (cf. 1 Chr 16:35).

The NIV follows the MT (**took care of them** or guided them; וַיְנַהֲלֵם, *way°nahălēm*), but the NRSV follows the Vulgate and LXX ("he gave them rest;" κατέπαυσεν [*katepausen*] = נוּחַ [*nwḥ*]). The words were probably confused in textual transmission. "Rest" is better because this connects Hezekiah with David and Solomon (as well as Asa and Jehoshaphat) and reflects the "rest" theology of Chronicles (cf. 1 Chr 22:9,18; 23:25; 2 Chr 14:6-7; 15:15; 20:20). As God rests in his temple, so his people rest in the land he has given them.

Ultimately, Hezekiah and his people pass the trial. While their initial reaction was less than flattering, ultimately they cried out to God and trusted in his faithfulness. The trial revealed a heart of faith.

Hezekiah and His Illness (32:24-26)

Chronicles summarizes 2 Kings 20:1-11 (cf. Isa 38:1-22). The incidental way in which Chronicles refers to the **miraculous sign** assumes a knowledge of Dtr.

Second Chronicles 32:24 is another example of trial, human prayer, and divine response (like 2 Chr 32:1-23). Hezekiah's illness should be understood as a trial or discipline (cf. Isa 38:15-19). Though the Chronicler does not say explicitly, he assumes the Lord is responsible for this illness as a testing of Hezekiah's heart (cf. Isa 38:15, "he himself has done this"). The recognition of Hezekiah's **proud** heart in 2 Chronicles 32:35 confirms this. Faced with this trial, Hezekiah prayed (cf. 2 Chr 32:20) and God answered (deliverance; cf. 2 Chr 32:21). SELMAN (2:514) notes that "healing " miracles are rare in the Hebrew Bible and often associated with prophets (cf. Exod 15:22-26; Num 21:7-9; 1 Kgs 17:17-24; 2 Kgs 4:8-41). The term "miraculous" reflects the "wonders" of God's work in Egypt (its only other use in Chronicles is 1 Chronicles 16:12; cf. Exod 4:21; 7:1,9; 11:9-10; Deut 4:34; 6:22; 7:14; 26:8; 34:11; Ps 78:43). However, the prayer for healing is common in Psalms (cf. 6:2; 30:2; 41:4; 103:3; 107:20). Prayers for healing are legitimate, but God is sovereign — he may or may not heal according to his purposes.

Dating the illness is problematic, but it was prior to or synchronous with Sennacherib's siege of Jerusalem (**in those days** identifies the general time frame, and 2 Kgs 20:6 assumes the city is already endangered). The Chronicler's account is topical. He narrates three separate trials — Sennacherib, illness, and the Babylonian envoys (2 Chr 32:31). However, they are linked by the same general time period. The exact chronological relationship between them, however, is disputed (JAPHET, 992-994; WILLIAMSON, 385-387).

The illness and subsequent visit by the Babylonian envoys were probably prior to Sennacherib's siege. Some believe the Babylonian visit was political in character. Perhaps they intended to enlist Hezekiah in a rebellious plot after the accession of Sennacherib in 705 B.C. (DILLARD, 259). The illness and the report of a miraculous sign would have been the occasion of their visit, and Sennacherib's invasion would have been a response to these political intrigues.

The exact relation between verses 24 and 25 is problematic. Verse 24 is a summary of 2 Kings 20:1-12 and verses 25-26 may be the Chronicler's theological commentary on Hezekiah's illness and its linkage with Sennacherib's invasion. If so, then verse 25 does not refer to a further incident but is an interpretation of the illness itself. The Chronicler contextualizes the illness in this manner: (1) Hezekiah is prideful (perhaps his preparations for the invasion are part of this), (2) God responds with wrath (e.g., the illness in the context of a potential threat from Sennacherib), (3) Hezekiah repents (prays), and (4) God removes the wrath (e.g., healing as well as ultimate deliverance from Sennacherib). The term **wrath**, however, may have a longer view in mind, that is, the exile. It should not be limited to Hezekiah's illness, but as part of a complex set of circumstances that tended toward exile. Nevertheless, due to Hezekiah's humility, the fullest expression of divine wrath was delayed for over a century (cf. 2 Chr 36). Jerusalem and the temple were not destroyed during Hezekiah's reign.

Whatever the exact provenance of 2 Chronicles 32:25-26, the theological point is clear. Pride brings wrath, but humble prayer brings deliverance. Hezekiah's **heart was proud** (lit., "his heart was high"). Uzziah is so described in 2 Chronicles 26:16. However, Hezekiah's response to God's wrath was quite different from Uzziah's. Hezekiah **repented** (lit., "humbled"; cf. the use of כָּנַע [kāna'] in 2 Chronicles 7:14; 30:11; 32:26; 33:12,19,23; 34:27; 36:12).

The model for the postexilic community is obvious. If they will humble themselves, seek God, and pray, God will hear and deliver. This is the faithfulness of God and consequently the confidence of all believers.

Hezekiah and the Babylonians (32:27-31)

Second Chronicles 32:27-29 is unique to Chronicles and not in chronological order. From the building programs and prosperity, it appears that this describes Hezekiah's kingdom prior to the devastation of Sennacherib's invasion. This prosperity created pride in Hezekiah (cf. Uzziah, 2 Chr 26:16). It is a time of blessing (2 Chr 32:29-30) as God established (**succeeded**; צָלַח, ṣālaḥ) Hezekiah as he did other faithful kings (2 Chr 20:20; 26:5), including David and Solomon (1 Chr 29:23). The word links this text with 2 Chronicles

31:21 ("prospered") and confirms that the **great riches and honor** (2 Chr 32:29; cf. 1 Chr 29:12,28; 2 Chr 1:12 for descriptions of David and Solomon; also 2 Chr 17:5; 18:1) describe Hezekiah's reign between his reform and Sennacherib's invasion (715–701 B.C.).

Since this material is unique to Chronicles, some have doubted its historical basis. However, Vaughn (112) concludes that cities in the Judean hill country (the Shephelah) "experienced four times more settlement and development of resources during the reign of Hezekiah than during the reign of Josiah." "The archaeological data," Vaughn (113) continues, "point to a reign with much economic buildup and great civil and administrative power." Vaughn believes Dtr omitted this emphasis on Hezekiah's prosperity in order to exalt Josiah. The data supports the prosperity of Hezekiah even though Dtr does not mention it.

Another piece of supporting data is the existence of jars with royal seals discovered in Lachish, Jerusalem, Gibeon, Beth Shemesh, Jericho, Arad, and over fifty other sites. Vaughn (202) demonstrates that these royal vessels had an economic function as they served as a "commodity which was traded or deployed to government employees throughout Hezekiah's kingdom." The existence of these jars testifies to Hezekiah's wealth in wine and oil. Vaughn (228) concludes that the Chronicler used reliable historical data which was derived "from a historical source or a historical remembrance of facts not recorded in Kings."

The building projects are signs of wealth and glory ("honor"): (1) **treasuries** for his **silver and gold, precious stones, spices, shields and all kinds of valuables**; (2) **buildings to store the harvest of grain, new wine and oil**; (3) **stalls for various kinds of cattle, and pens for the flocks**; and (4) **villages** (cities).

A fifth building project was a monumental task. Parallel to 2 Kings 20:20, Chronicles records that Hezekiah **channeled the water** from the **Gihon spring** down **the west side of the City of David**. Dtr describes it as a "tunnel" which is now known as the Siloam Tunnel (discovered in 1837; cf. Shanks, "Jerusalem's," 20-38, 64). While some dispute this identification (Rogerson, 138-149), most date the tunnel to the time of Hezekiah (Hendel, 233-237; Cahill, 184-185; Norin, 37-48). The tunnel contained an inscription which described the channel as an **outlet** (מוֹצָא, *môṣā'*), the term used in 2 Chronicles 32:30. Modern visitors to Jerusalem can walk through the tunnel and wonder at its achievement.

The Babylonians visit Hezekiah after his illness and God's **miraculous** healing (same word in 2 Chr 32:24,31). We may surmise that not only do the Babylonians come to curry political favor in an alliance against Assyria (the **envoys were sent by the rulers of Babylon**), but also, as Chronicles indicates, **to ask him about the miraculous sign**. Their interests may be scientific or astrological (JAPHET, 996).

The Chronicler's interest is the divine function of this visit. Even when Babylonian envoys visit a Judean king at the behest of their own rulers, God has a purpose. God uses this moment to **test** (נסה, *nsh*; only time this verb is used in Chronicles, but see its use in Gen 22:1; Exod 16:4; 20:20; Deut 4:34; 8:2,16; 13:3; Judg 2:22; 3:1,4; Ps 26:2). The specific purpose of the test is **to know everything that was in his heart** (cf. Deut 8:2). God seeks hearts (1 Chr 28:9), probes hearts (cf. 1 Chr 29:17), and judges according to the heart (2 Chr 6:30; 30:18-20). Apparently, Hezekiah failed the test due to his pride (at least according to 2 Kgs 20:12-19). Nevertheless, the Chronicler assumes that Hezekiah — despite his consistent problem with pride — did not permit his failure to turn his heart away from God.

The moment of testing unveils the heart so that even God may say to his faithful ones, "Now I know that you fear God" (Gen 22:12). It is unnecessary to think about this metaphysically (the relationship between probing and omniscience). Since this is a narrative, we read it from a narrative perspective, that is, from within the story. This is how we live our own stories. We do not stand outside of it to think metaphysically, but we live within it as moments of self-discovery. In the narrative of Chronicles, though God reigns over the nations, all things come from him, and he is at work in everything, God too discovers with narrative eyes the hearts of his people. What God knows outside of this narrative construct is not the Chronicler's concern. He writes his narrative as we live ours — from the inside.

Second Chronicles 32 provided a series of "testing moments" (trials) for Hezekiah. God probes and tests. God seeks hearts and is found by humble hearts. God probes our hearts and yearns for a response of faith, trust, and humility. As we respond to his seeking,

God responds with gracious deliverance. But the question is not whether God will seek or respond graciously. God is always seeking and always willing to respond. The question is whether when God finally delivers his people in the coming of the Son of Man, will he find faith on the earth (cf. Luke 18:8)?

4. Formulaic Conclusion (32:32-33)

Parallel with 2 Kings 20:20-21, the conclusion contains the standard information: (1) sources (**written in the vision of the prophet Isaiah son of Amoz in the book of the kings of Judah and Israel**), (2) burial, and (3) successor (**Manasseh**).

However, there are unique features to Chronicles's conclusion. For example, while 2 Kings refers to "the book of the annals of the kings of Judah," Chronicles specifies Isaiah. "The inclusion of this source in a larger collection, 'the book of the kings of Judah and Israel,' indicates that this is not the canonical book of Isaiah" (DILLARD, 260).

Hezekiah is **honored** due to his wholehearted orientation toward Yahweh. The people recognize his piety, and the Chronicler underscores it by his conclusion. The Chronicler calls attention to the **acts of devotion** ("mercy, covenant loyalty," חֶסֶד, *ḥesed*) that he did not have opportunity to report but are available in his source. Just as Yahweh is *ḥesed* (mercy; 1 Chr 16:34,41; 2 Chr 5:13; 6:14,42; 7:6; 20:21), so was Hezekiah. Even in his conclusion, the Chronicler reminds us that Hezekiah was a new David and Solomon as *ḥesed* reigned in the lives of God's people (cf. 2 Chr 35:26).

JOHNSTONE (2:221) summarizes: "Despite these shortcomings Hezekiah's reign is on the whole a success (marked by 'deeds of loyalty', v. 32), warranting (v. 33) the recognition of burial in the 'ascent' (not otherwise noted in the Hebrew Bible) to the royal tombs."

B. THE REIGN OF MANASSEH AND AMON (33:1-25)

The reigns of Manasseh and Amon are grouped together because they are evil kings. Despite Manasseh's repentance, it did not materially transform the religious interests of the people who had been weaned on his evil. Amon epitomizes the socialization of the nation as he remained evil even though his father had repented. Moreover, Manasseh and Amon are united in their disregard for Yahweh but sandwiched between the major reforms of Hezekiah (2 Chr 29–32) and Josiah (2 Chr 34–35).

The differences between Dtr and Chronicles are so transparent that this chapter is exemplary for thinking through the different purposes of Dtr and Chronicles. The following table illustrates the differences and similarities.

Topic	2 Chr 33 2	Kgs 21
The Sins of Manasseh	33:1-9	21:1-9
The Lord Spoke to Manasseh	33:10	21:10
The Condemnation of Manasseh		21:11-16
The Exile and Restoration of Manasseh	33:11-13	
The Reformation of Manasseh	33:14-17	
The Conclusion of Manasseh's Reign	33:18-20	21:17-18
The Reign of Amon	33:21-25	21:19-26

Dtr condemns Manasseh and Chronicles rehabilitates him. Manasseh is responsible for the exile in Dtr, but is a model of restoration in Chronicles. The two historians are using Manasseh to serve different ends. Dtr uses his reign to justify the exile, but the Chronicler uses it to encourage his postexilic community.

Amon is an addendum to Manasseh so that the historical succession of kings in Judah is complete. However, the Chronicler's use of the term "humble" (*kāna'*) in both accounts links them — both positive (2 Chr 33:12,19) and negative (2 Chr 33:23). The contrast between father and son encourages the postexilic community to find blessing through humility but expect punishment through pride.

The contrast between humility and pride is a significant biblical theme (cf. Prov 11:2; 29:23; Isa 2:11; Jas 1:9-10). The parable of the Pharisee and the tax collector in Luke 18:9-14 illustrates the difference. God himself displayed humility in the incarnation where the one who existed in the form of God did not exploit his status but humbled himself for the sake of others (Phil 2:1-11, NRSV). God seeks humble hearts and forsakes prideful ones.

1. The Reign of Manasseh (33:1-20)

Perhaps no other story in Chronicles has generated more negative historical criticism. Skepticism reigned until recent years. Earlier scholars doubted that Manasseh was ever taken captive because, in part, Assyrian records do not document it. Others have doubted that Manasseh would have been taken to Babylon rather than Nineveh. Still others doubt that Manasseh would have ever repented of his evil. The result is that the story of Manasseh is a testing ground for the historical reliability of Chronicles. Was Manasseh exiled in Babylon and later restored?

Scholarly skepticism is not only based on the lack of historical confirmation in extrabiblical sources, but also on the theological tendencies of the Chronicler (North, 383-386). Some believe the Chronicler has fabricated an incident in order to account for Manasseh's long reign. The Chronicler's concept of immediate retribution must entail that Manasseh repented and was blessed with fifty-five years. Consequently, the Chronicler invents Manasseh's repentance in order to explain his lengthy reign (ACKROYD, 198; COGGINS, 286-289). In addition, others believe the Chronicler has deliberately created a typological situation where Manasseh's exile and restoration prefigure his own community's fate (the exile and restoration of Judah; cf. WILLIAMSON, 389; Van Keulen, 212-222). Manasseh's repentance provides a model for his postexilic community and grounds their hope in divine grace.

Despite past skepticism, the "historical data" of the story is increasingly accepted (JAPHET, 1001-1004; Bulbach). First, many believe the Chronicler did not invent or fabricate this account but that he derives it from another source (Schniedewind, 450-461). The Chronicler does not invent new historical data, and most scholars recognize that he had sources which at least date to the time of Rehoboam (cf. 2 Chr 12). The Chronicler's methodology reflects a careful, though theological, use of his sources (cf. 2 Chr 33:18-19).

Second, the relationship between Manasseh and Assyria is hindered by the scarcity of Assyrian sources, but some general perspectives are clear (Gane, 21-32). Manasseh is mentioned in the Assyrian records as a loyal vassal who provides labor, military assistance, and supplies for Assyrian interests and military campaigns.

Third, there is a scenario in Assyrian history which might account for this exile as well as its location in Babylon. Tatum (504-511) places Manasseh's exile in the context of internal Assyrian civil strife. Shamash-shum-ukin, king of Babylon (652-648 B.C.) and brother of the Assyrian king Ashurbanipal, rebelled and enlisted support from several nations, including some Phoenicians and Arab tribes near Judah. Ashurbanipal defeated his brother in 648 B.C. and marched against his allies. If Manasseh joined the rebellion, Ashurbanipal would have marched against him. There is archaeological evidence that Arad was destroyed during this period. Consequently, it is probable that Ashurbanipal defeated Manasseh as part of his brother's attempted coup d'etat. Ashurbanipal would have taken Manasseh to Babylon (the site of the rebellion and his imperial location for a few years). Chronicles's placement of Manasseh in Babylon correlates with the only time Assyrian monarchs were located there.

Fourth, there is evidence of leniency on the part of Ashurbanipal toward some of his rebellious vassals. Since Ashurbanipal was interested in having a buffer between himself and Egypt, he permitted vassal states to remain in his western regions. The Assyrian records document one such occasion. The Rassam Cylinder records Ashurbanipal's mercy to Necho, a king in Egypt, after he rebelled against Assyria. The kings were brought to Ashurbanipal in Nineveh. While others were executed, Necho was spared and reinstalled in Egypt "with a more favorable treaty than before" (Gane, 25; cf. *ANET*, 294). This scenario is exactly the one Chronicles records concerning Manasseh. The historical plausibility of the Chronicler's account is confirmed by Ashurbanipal's treatment of Necho. As a vassal buffer state, "not only would the Assyrians have tolerated Manasseh's administrative tightening, it is perfectly conceivable that they would have encouraged it" (Tatum, 344).

If this historical context is the most plausible setting for 2 Chronicles 33:10-13, then this event falls in the last years of Manasseh. According to Thiele (176-178), the total reign of Manasseh was 696-642 B.C. If Manasseh's rebellion, exile, and restoration was in the context of Ashurbanipal's defeat of his brother in 648 B.C., this means that Manasseh's repentance was in his old age and his reformation was short.

The Chronicler's theological interests need not mean that he fabricated stories. While some believe the lengthy reign may need explanation, the Chronicler does not think so. He does not bring chronology into his account, and the length of reign has no function in the narrative. "The fact that no such connection is made between Manasseh's repentance and the long rule," Tatum (228) writes, "argues strongly against any connection of the two in [the Chronicler's'] mind."

The typological function cannot be denied. It is present in other stories (Ahaz and Hezekiah). The exile and restoration of Manasseh typifies the exile and restoration of Judah. However, the question remains whether history provided the occasion for typology or whether theology created history. Given the Chronicler's general method, extant archaeological evidence, and a possible Assyrian context for this exile in Babylon, it appears the burden of proof falls on those who would deny the historicity of Manasseh's exile, repentance, and restoration. I conclude that the Chronicler had a reliable source which detailed this story. He incorporated the story into his narrative and interpreted it typologically.

But if Manasseh repented, why did not Dtr mention it? Many believe Dtr's silence indicates that the Chronicler's account is theologically motivated. However, Dtr is also theologically motivated. He does not tell all he knows (cf. his allusions to sources for further details). Dtr pegged Manasseh as the epitome of the exile, not restoration. Written during the exile, Dtr focuses on the reason for the exile, not the typology of restoration (DILLARD, 265-266). Further, the Chronicler focused on the individual while Dtr is concerned about the nation. Thus, the Chronicler is concerned about the immediate setting of Manasseh's life while Dtr "takes a long-term view" of the nation (SELMAN, 2:517).

PRATT (463) suggests that the Manasseh story is told in chiastic fashion. He suggests the following schematization:

  a. Introduction: Manesseh is king (33:1)
    b. Manasseh's transgressions (33:2-9)
      c. Punishment and Restoration (33:10-13)
    b'. Religious Restoration (33:14-17)
  a'. Conclusion: death and burial (33:18-20)

McMillion (7) notes that this "concentric structure," where the "elements of the story radiate outward from" the center, focuses on Manasseh's repentance. The structure not only highlights the center, but emphasizes the reversal of Judah's religious life (McMillion, 9-11). The carved image (סֶמֶל, *semel*) which was set up in 2 Chronicles 33:7 is torn down in 2 Chronicles 33:15. The altars (מִזְבְּחוֹת, *mizb°hôth*) which Manasseh built on the temple hill in 2 Chronicles 33:4-5 are torn down in 2 Chronicles 33:15. The foreign gods which he introduced to Judah in 2 Chronicles 33:4-5 are removed in 2 Chronicles 33:15. While "Manasseh led Judah and the people of Jerusalem astray" in 2 Chronicles 33:9, Manasseh "told Judah to serve the LORD" in 2 Chronicles 33:16.

In this context of "reversal," the central point is Manasseh's repentance and deliverance. Second Chronicles 33:12-13 contains the language of 2 Chronicles 6-7. Manasseh typifies God's response to his exiled people. When the people of God are captive in a foreign land, if they will humble themselves, seek him, and pray, God will listen and restore (cf. 2 Chr 7:14). This is the hope of the Chronicler's postexilic readers. If God will receive Manasseh back from exile, then postexilic Judah may also hope in God's gracious faithfulness. If God will forgive Manasseh, then God will renew his grace with anyone, including postexilic Judah and even a Jeffrey Dahmer (who was immersed into Christ during the last year of his life).

Formulaic Introduction (33:1-2)

The introduction to Manasseh's reign follows the standard formula: (1) his age when he began to reign (**twelve**, begun as a co-regent with his father in 696 B.C.), (2) how long he ruled (**fifty-five years**; the longest of any king in Israel's history), and (3) a theological evaluation (**he did evil in the eyes of the LORD**).

The Chronicler follows Dtr closely except he omits a standard introductory feature, i.e., the name of Manasseh's mother, Hephzibah. WILLIAMSON (390) argues that the mother is omitted due to her idolatrous background just as he omitted the name of Asa's mother in 2 Chronicles 14:1 (cf. 2 Chr 15:16). However, the names of the mothers are absent for the rest of the Chronicler's narrative. This may reflect a change in historiographic method (JAPHET, 1004; DILLARD, 267) or absence in his source (McKenzie, *Chronicler's*, 174-176).

The theological evaluation is the most significant element of his introduction since this is what he immediately elaborates (2 Chr

33:3-9). Theologically, Manasseh's evil is compared with the evil of the Canaanites (**nations**) whom God drove out of Palestine. Their evil reached a boiling point and became so great that God punished it (cf. Gen 15:16; Deut 9:4-5). To describe Judah as **following the detestable practices of the nations the LORD had driven out** was as severe a critique as one could offer. It prepares us for the coming exile since just as God removed the Canaanites, so he will remove his people.

Manasseh's Sin (33:3-9)

Following 2 Kings closely, Chronicles details the sins of Manasseh. Significantly, the subjects of the verbs are singular: **he rebuilt, he also erected, he bowed down**, etc. The text focuses on the sins of Manasseh as God's personal representative. This emphasis is heightened by the quotation of God's speech to David and Solomon in 2 Chronicles 33:7-8. The king is responsible to lead the people in God's ways, but this king fails on a personal level and renews idolatry in the land after his father had forbidden it. According to McMillion (6), "a major focus of [2 Chr 33:1-20] is on the lone figure of Manasseh as responsible for both good and evil."

The sins of Manasseh are many. As JAPHET (1004) notes, this list is no "random conglomeration." It is framed by theological evaluations in 2 Chronicles 33:2 and 33:9. The list is punctuated with two words from Yahweh (2 Chr 33:4 and 2 Chr 33:7-8). The first set of sins concerns his idolatry (2 Chr 33:3-4), and the second set (2 Chr 33:5-8) concerns his deviant practices in the worship of other gods.

Manasseh's idolatry was wide-ranging. He decentralized the worship of Yahweh by rebuilding the **high places**. He reintroduced Baal worship in Judah (cf. 2 Kgs 21:3). He also introduces a "new cult" into the life of Judah, an "astrological" or occultist religion that worshiped the **starry hosts** (JOHNSTONE, 2:223). Manasseh went beyond Ahaz in his pluralism (cf. 2 Chr 28). Manasseh created a pantheon in the **temple of the LORD** as **he built altars** there.

Theologically, this is repugnant to God's intent for his temple. God placed his **Name** in the temple. Idolatry exchanges the God of all the nations for the gods of the nations. Idolatry, especially the worship of starry hosts, deifies "the creation at the cost of the creator" and honors "the sign rather than the reality" (JOHNSTONE, 2:223). Manasseh not only reverses the actions of **his father Hezekiah** but turns the religion of Israel on its head. Instead of obedience in response to God's gracious placing of his Name among his people, Manasseh seeks other gods and puts them in Yahweh's temple.

The second list of sins specifies several deviant practices. The two lists are linked by repeating Manasseh's erection of altars in the temple, specifically in **both courts** (inner and outer) **of the temple**, and by specifying the starry hosts as objects of worship. Manasseh's new religious commitments, however, entailed practices that were specifically forbidden (cf. Lev 19:26; 20:17; Deut 18:10-14). **He sacrificed his sons in the fire**, practiced the occult (including **sorcery, divination and witchcraft**), and sought guidance from **mediums and spiritists**. The latter practice is one of the reasons for Saul's removal (cf. 2 Chr 10:13-14). If Saul was unfaithful, Manasseh is even more so. Indeed, these are the practices of the **nations** whom God dispossessed (Deut 18:14). Finally, Manasseh placed a **carved image** of Yahweh in the temple. Given the religious consciousness of the ancient Near East, Israel may have been embarrassed by the fact that their God had no "image." The northern kingdom provided images of Yahweh at Dan and Bethel. Now Manasseh carves one.

Theologically, Manasseh has reversed the days of David and Solomon. The temple in which Yahweh dwelt has been defiled by other gods and an idolatrous image. Manasseh **put** an image where God put his Name (2 Chr 33:7). The contrast could not be greater.

Chronicles charges Manasseh with responsibility for this apostasy. While 2 Kings 21:9 reads "but the people [lit., "they"] did not listen," Chronicles omits this note and places the burden on Manasseh. He **led Judah and the people of Jerusalem astray, so that they did more evil than the nations the LORD had destroyed before the Israelites**. Verses 2 and 9 balance each other, and the narrative stresses Manasseh's own personal responsibility. This does not excuse the people, but it focuses the decline on Manasseh's leadership. This is the only time in Chronicles where the verb "led . . . astray" is used (lit., "caused to err," from תעה, * tā'āh*).

Leadership is a critical factor in the spiritual health of a community. It is relatively easy to lead a people into idolatry, but more difficult to lead them out. Manasseh will try after his repentance, but his leadership will be ineffective as the people continued to worship at the high places even though it was "only to the LORD their God" (2 Chr 33:17).

Manasseh's Punishment and Restoration (33:10-13)

This is the core of the pericope and the theological heart of Chronicles. The exile, repentance, and restoration of Manasseh is the story of Judah. God's gracious acceptance of penitent Manasseh is God's gracious acceptance of penitent postexilic Judah.

Though the core of the concentric structure of 2 Chronicles 33:1-20, these verses (2 Chr 33:10-13) have their own concentric structure (PRATT, 463).

(1) Manasseh Ignores God (33:10)
    (2) Manasseh Taken Captive from Jerusalem (33:11)
        (3) Manasseh Prays for Deliverance (33:12)
    (2') Manasseh Brought Back to Jerusalem (33:13a)
(1') Manasseh Acknowledges God (33:13b)

God warns his people through his prophets (cf. 2 Chr 33:18). Though the prophets are not mentioned by the Chronicler, they are specified in 2 Kings 21:10 along with a prophetic message (2 Kgs 21:10-15). Some believe that the absence of prophets in the Chronicler's account means that God spoke directly to Manasseh. However, this is unnecessary since it may reflect stylistic abbreviation rather than theological interests. Further, Chronicles also records that **the LORD spoke to Manasseh and his people, but they paid no attention**. The message was not only for Manasseh, but for Judah. This assumes a prophetic role so common in Chronicles (JAPHET, 1008-1009; cf. 2 Chr 12:5; 15:8; 18:6; 21:12; 25:15-16; 28:9).

Manasseh probably joined a Babylonian coup d'etat against the Assyrian king Ashurbanipal. The coup failed and the participants were punished, including western states that supported the Babylonian pretender. The method by which Manasseh was transported is well known from reliefs that picture captives led by a chain anchored in their **nose** and **shackles** on their feet (*ANEP*, no. 447). Consistent with that scenario, Manasseh was taken to **Babylon** from where the Assyrian king ruled in the aftermath of the failed coup. Babylon suits the interests of Chronicles since it offers a historical reference point from which to think typologically about the future exile of Judah in Babylon.

But this forced appearance in Babylon was no mere human decision to humiliate Manasseh. **The LORD brought against them the**

army of Assyria. This is divine retribution for Manasseh's evil. It encompassed the whole nation (**against them**; which assumes a military campaign), but the narrative focuses on Manasseh who was exiled in Babylon. Ironically, the God who captured cities for his people (cf. the verb לכד [lākad] in 1 Chr 15:11; 18:4; 2 Chr 13:19; 15:8) now empowers an enemy to capture the king (cf. 2 Chr 12:4; 28:18; 32:11).

The language of 2 Chronicles 33:12-13 abounds with Solomon's language in 2 Chronicles 6-7. Both envision a moment of distress (צרר [ṣārar]; 2 Chr 6:28; 33:12) and people who seek ("entreat" here but synonymous with "seeking") the **favor** of God ("before you" in 2 Chr 6:24; 2 Chr 33:12). Both envision humility (2 Chr 7:14; 33:13) and prayer (2 Chr 6:19,20,21,24,26,32,34,38; 7:14; 33:13). In both, God listened (2 Chr 6:19-21,23,25,27,30,33,35,39; 7:12,14; 33:13). In both, the prayers are characterized as pleas (2 Chr 6:19,29,35,39; 2 Chr 33:13), and God "returns" them to their privileged status (2 Chr 6:25; 33:13; cf. 2 Chr 6:37-38). When God's people turn to him, he returns to them (cf. 2 Chr 7:14). Manasseh, as the text emphatically notes with the pronoun "he" (הוא, hû', omitted in NIV), **knew that the LORD** *he* **is God**. Thus, as in the prayer of Solomon, God makes himself known by his graciousness (2 Chr 6:33; 2 Chr 33:13).

Manasseh's repentance and prayer is a specific instantiation of Solomon's temple prayer. God is faithful; he keeps his promises. If his people will seek him — wherever they are (Babylon or postexilic Judah) — God will graciously find them. God restored Manasseh to his throne.

The story of Manasseh underscores the grace of God like no other text in Scripture. The evil perpetrated by God's anointed leader is unimaginable. Its depth and extent rivals Ahaz. But, the grace of God abounds more than sin. "Where sin increased, grace increased all the more" (Rom 5:20). When one seeks God, the grace of God knows no bounds. Whether it is a thief on a cross (Luke 23:39-43), or the "worst" of sinners (1 Tim 1:16), God forgives those who humble themselves and seek him.

Manasseh's Reformation (33:14-17)

Upon his return to Jerusalem, Manasseh initiates a national renewal in building projects, fortifications, and religious reformation.

Archaeological findings confirm a national buildup in the second half of the seventh century B.C. (650–600). Bulbach and Tatum survey the evidence and conclude that the latter part of Manasseh's reign witnessed a significant rise in prosperity and building activity.

The projects described in 2 Chronicles 33:14 are military in nature, but would a recent rebel be permitted to pursue such fortifications? While some believe this creates a tension, Tatum (504-510) points out that this is exactly what Ashurbanipal did with Necho of Egypt. In order to consolidate his support, he reinstalled Necho while executing other kings. Necho provided a buffer between Assyria and other potential enemies in Egypt. Tatum suggests the same is true for Manasseh. Ashurbanipal could have encouraged this buildup as a buffer between him and a rising power in Egypt.

The religious reformation reverses Manasseh's sins in 2 Chronicles 33:3-9. He removes the **foreign gods** and **the image from the temple of the LORD**. He removes the **altars** he placed on the **temple hill**. Further, he **restored the altar of the LORD**. In essence, Manasseh rededicates the temple and reinstitutes the worship of Yahweh. The renewal is celebrated with **fellowship offerings and thank offerings**. Israel eats with its God and celebrates his deliverance. The times of David, Solomon, and Hezekiah have returned (1 Chr 16:2; 29:9; 2 Chr 7:7; 29:35).

Manasseh led in the renewal just as he had led the apostasy. He **told Judah to serve the LORD** (cf. 1 Chr 28:9). However, the popularity of the high places and the previous decentralization of Yahweh worship meant that the people **continued to sacrifice at the high places**. Manasseh was successful in removing idolatry from the land, but he could not fully recentralize the worship of Yahweh. It is difficult to undo the harm one has done with their own life. Nevertheless, God is merciful, compassionate, and gracious.

Formulaic Conclusion (33:18-20)

Chronicles's conclusion to the Manasseh pericope contains the standard items: (1) sources (**records of the seers**), (2) death and burial, and (3) his successor (**Amon**). These elements are based on 2 Kings 21:17-18 with a few changes (e.g., while Chronicles reads **in his palace**, Dtr reads "in his palace garden").

The most significant change is the source Chronicles cites (2 Chr 33:18-19). While 2 Chronicles 33:18 is generally regarded as a citation of 2 Kings, 33:19 appeals to a different source. Schniedewind (456, 460-461) argues that verse 18 appeals to a non-Dtr source and that verse 19 is his homiletic application. This is partly indicated by the use of resumptive repetition — the repetition of **his prayer** in 2 Chronicles 33:18-19. Thus, "[the Chronicler's] composition begins with received historical traditions. In these cases, [the Chronicler] is not simply an inventor of history; rather he is a creative theological interpreter."

Therefore, the Chronicler's homiletic intent is summarized in 2 Chronicles 33:18-19. Schniedewind (457-458) argues that אֱלֹהִים (*'ĕlōhîm*, **God** or gods) refers to Manasseh's idolatries. In response, God sent his prophets, but Manasseh would not listen. However, his humble prayer to Yahweh was received compassionately despite **all his sins and unfaithfulness** (cf. 1 Chr 5:25; 9:1; 10:13; 2 Chr 12:2). Despite his unfaithfulness which generated an exile, God restored him through his humble, prayerful seeking (2 Chr 7:14).

The message of Chronicles is the amazing grace of God. This grace was demonstrated over and over again in the history of Israel, and it reached its fullest expression in the love of God at the cross of Jesus. There God demonstrated his love and offered his grace, even to we who were still his enemies. The grace of God is greater than human sin, even the sin of Manasseh.

2. The Reign of Amon (33:21-25)

Chronicles devotes little attention to Amon. The brevity of his reign contributes to this. However, the Chronicler makes a theological point. This is evident in the use of the term "humble" (כָּנַע, *kāna'*). Manasseh humbled himself and God restored him to his throne, but Amon did not humble himself so he was assassinated. He applies his theology of retribution — those who seek God are found, but those who forsake him are forsaken. Chronicles follows the text of 2 Kings 21:19-26 with few changes and omissions.

Formulaic Introduction (33:21-22a)

The introduction contains the standard elements except the name of the queen mother is omitted: (1) age when he began to reign (**twenty-two**), (2) how long he reigned (**two years**), and (3) theological evaluation (**he did evil in the eyes of the LORD**).

Divine Judgment against Amon (33:22b-24)

Chronicles elaborates the theological evaluation and interprets his death as divine punishment. While 2 Kings 21:20 refers to Amon as one who did evil "as his father Manasseh had done," the Chronicler clarifies this. He repeats Dtr's phrase but explains that **Amon worshiped and offered sacrifices to all the idols Manasseh had made**. The Chronicler specifies the manner in which Amon followed his father. However, the Chronicler also specifies the manner in which he differed. Though Manasseh humbled himself, Amon did not. Therefore, he was punished. While the Chronicler does not offer an explicit theological comment on Amon's death, his theological hermeneutic is assumed.

The rationale for Amon's assassination is unknown. Malamat ("Historical," 26-29) believes it was the result of political intrigue where pro-Egyptian **officials** murdered him because he was pro-Assyrian. Others suggest that it was motivated by religious convictions where proreform officials (late Manasseh) sought to reverse Amon's religious policies (Nielsen, 103-106). **The people of the land** killed the conspirators, and this may indicate a lack of popular support for the conspirator's reform movement (and thus a rejection of Manasseh's reforms; cf. JOHNSTONE, 2:231). The people of the land wanted to retain their local sanctuaries.

At bottom, however, the motives are unknown (JAPHET, 1014). Whatever the case, whether political, religious, or both, the Chronicler does not comment on the motives. His interest is punitive: Amon suffered the fate of those who do not seek God.

Formulaic Conclusion (33:25)

The conclusion contains some standard elements, such as (1) death and (2) successor (**Josiah**), but lacks any reference to his burial or sources used. The omission of these details probably serves the Chronicler's interest in abbreviation. Amon's narrative is kept as short as possible (JAPHET, 1014).

C. THE REIGN OF JOSIAH (34:1–36:1)

Chronicles's account of Josiah follows the structure of Dtr closely. However, there are significant differences as Chronicles adds,
omits, elaborates, and abbreviates.

Topic	2 Chr	2 Kgs
Introduction to Josiah's Reign	34:1-2	22:1-2
Josiah's Eighth-Year Reform	34:3-7	
Temple Repairs	34:8-14	22:3-7
Discovery of the Book	34:15-21	22:8-13
Consultation with Huldah	34:22-28	22:14-20
Josiah Charges the People	34:29-31	23:1-3
Josiah's Eighteenth-Year Reform	35:1-3	23:4-20
Josiah Keeps the Passover	35:1-19	23:21-23
God's Anger toward Judah		23:24-27
The Death of Josiah	35:20–36:1	23:28-30

The Chronicler has an early reform in Josiah's eighth year, but Dtr
does not. The eighteenth-year reform is abbreviated by the Chronicler
but is the central focus of Dtr. The Chronicler, however, expands the
account of the Passover to which Dtr only gives passing attention. The
Chronicler omits Dtr's comment on the anger of the Lord and expands the account of Josiah's death. Why does the Chronicler so radically change Dtr's account?

JAPHET (1019-1020) succinctly summarizes the theological problems inherent in Dtr's account for the Chronicler. The reform of the
temple in 2 Kings 23 indicates that Judah was saturated in idolatry
for the first seventeen years of Josiah's reform. If Amon died so
quickly for his sin, why does Josiah reign so long in the midst of his
nation's idolatry? The Chronicler responds by positing a reform
prior to the temple renovation and justifying Josiah's reign by his
own personal piety.

However, as DILLARD (277) points out, in both 2 Kings and
2 Chronicles the discovery of the book of the law is the central
point. Everything leads up to the discovery of the book in 2 Chronicles, but everything flows from the discovery of the book in 2 Kings.
The discovery of the book incites major reform in Dtr. The reform
is progressively extended from the temple, through the city,
throughout Judah, and into the north. Chronicles sees incremental

reform that leads to the discovery of the book, and the discovery explodes into covenant renewal.

The two accounts are not as "contradictory" as they might first appear. Glatt-Gilead (21-25) argues that the first Josianic reforms (2 Chr 34:3-7) were royal initiatives without any hint of "communal participation." Josiah, it appears, was conducting his own "private crusade." However, after the discovery of the book of the law, the reform movement took on a communal dimension. Further, the temple repairs in Dtr assume some kind of reform prior to the discovery of the book (WILLIAMSON, 397-398). Dtr focuses on the public and communal dimensions of reform. Chronicles is interested in the king's own personal piety as the source of reform movements in Judah.

In short, both writers shape their narrative in order to emphasize their central points. Harmonization, while possible, is unnecessary since neither gives us the whole story and each tells the story in view of their own specific purposes. "Each author," Washburn (78) writes, "was more interested in building up to his own particular high point than he was in giving us a chronology of Josiah's reign." Neither are exhaustive nor necessarily contradictory (SELMAN, 2:527).

Chronicles divides Josiah's reign into chronological periods: (1) in the eighth year Josiah began to seek God (2 Chr 34:3a); (2) in the twelfth year he began to purge Judah and Jerusalem of high places, Asherah poles, carved idols and cast images (2 Chr 34:3b); and (3) in the eighteenth year he began to purify the land and the temple (2 Chr 34:8). While some think the chronological notes are examples of ahistorical framing (Cogan, 203-205), Cross and Freedman (56-58) believe the years correspond with significant events in the history of the Assyrian empire. The decreasing power of Assyria may have encouraged Josiah's reform, but such a specific correlation is unlikely. Nevertheless, there is no reason to seriously doubt the chronological structure since it serves no theological purpose.

Glatt-Gilead recognizes "nine sub-units" in 2 Chronicles 34–35 in a concentric structure. Huldah's prophetic word is the center from which the rest of the narrative ripples to the discovery and implementation of the book of the Law. The ripples further move to the purification of the land, and then to cultic purification. The chart below underscores the thematic character of the Chronicles account (Glatt-Gilead, 21-22):

1. Formulaic Introduction (34:1-2)
   2. Cultic Purification of Judah and Jerusalem (34:3-5)
      3. Cultic Purification of the North (34:6-7)
         4. Discovery of the Book (34:8-18)
            5. Prophecy of Huldah (34:19-28)
         4'. Implementation of the Book (34:29-32)
      3'. Cultic Purification of the North (34:33)
   2'. Celebration of the Passover (35:1-19)
1'. Extended Formulaic Conclusion (35:20–36:1)

This structure highlights the significance of Huldah and the direction she gives to Josiah's reformation. This thematic reorganization of Dtr keeps Huldah and the book at the center just as it is in Dtr but recognizes that Josiah's piety preceded the discovery of the book. Huldah's prophecy provides the "turning point" in the narrative because now Josiah "is at pains to insure the people's obedience" (Glatt-Gilead, 23).

Theologically, this structure stresses the authority of both the prophetic word and written Scripture. The book lays a claim on Josiah, and the word of a prophetess confirms the authority of Scripture. Thus, king and people stand under Scripture as it unveils God's intent for his people. The reformation begins in Josiah's seeking God but finds its communal dimension when Scripture is applied to the people. Inner personal piety is incomplete without communal renewal under the authority of Scripture.

1. Formulaic Introduction (34:1-2)

The introduction contains the standard elements: (1) his age when he began to reign (**eight**), (2) how many years he reigned (**thirty-one**), and (3) theological evaluation (**he did what was right in the eyes of the LORD**). What is lacking, as with Manasseh and Amon, is the name of the Josiah's mother (present in 2 Kgs 22:1).

The theological evaluation is extended to compare Josiah with **David** (cf. 2 Chr 28:1; 29:2) in his **not turning aside to the right or to the left**. While only used here in Chronicles, it appears several times in Dtr (Deut 5:32; 17:11,20; 28:14; Josh 1:7; 23:6; cf. Prov 4:27). It refers to the rejection of idolatry (cf. Deut 28:14). Josiah is like David (2 Chr 34:3) and followed David (2 Chr 35:4,15).

2. Cultic Purification of Judah and Jerusalem (34:3-5)

This material is unique and creates a tension with the record in 2 Kings since the reformation there seems to begin only after the discovery of the book of the law. However, temple repairs indicate that some kind of reform was already in progress when the book was discovered. Nevertheless, it is difficult to see how Josiah could purge **high places, Asherah poles, carved idols and cast images** from **Judah and Jerusalem** (2 Chr 34:3) and there yet remain idolatrous elements in the temple (2 Kgs 23:4). Further, the burning of the **bones** of idolatrous **priests** precedes the discovery of the book in Chronicles (2 Chr 34:5), but follows the discovery of the book in Dtr (2 Kgs 23:16,20). Washburn (62) concludes that topical arrangement dominates the two authors rather than strict chronology. Indeed, given Chronicles's chronological notes, Dtr is more topically driven than Chronicles.

When Josiah was sixteen years old, **he began to seek the God of his father David**. The king orients his heart toward Yahweh. The Chronicler utilizes one of his key terms — "seek" (דרשׁ, *dāraš*; cf. 1 Chr 28:9; 2 Chr 7:14). When Josiah was twenty years old, **he began to purge Judah and Jerusalem** of its high places (alternative worship sites for Yahweh) and idolatry (including **Baals**). He destroyed the idolatrous **altars** in his realm. Washburn (65) argues that 2 Chronicles 34:4 parallels 2 Kings 22:20 so that Josiah's work was twofold: (1) destruction of the altars and (2) execution of idolatrous priests. THOMPSON (373) suggests that the early ministries of Zephaniah and Jeremiah had some influence on the young king.

Significantly, Chronicles specifically states **he began** to reform. Chronicles recognizes this reformation's personal dimension (a royal initiative, perhaps unsupported by the people) and the fact that it was in its initial stages (the reformation was only beginning). Thus the singular ("he") and the verb ("began") are indicators which distinguish Chronicles's account from Dtr's. The initiatives Josiah began here may not have been fully implemented until after the discovery of the book of the law.

3. Cultic Purification of the North (34:6-7)

The demise of Assyrian power may have enabled Josiah to extend control over the northern territories (**Manasseh, Ephraim,** and **as far as Naphtali**; cf. DILLARD, 278-279). As Josiah's control increased, he also pursued cultic reform in the north (**throughout Israel**; lit., "in all the land of Israel — from **Simeon** in the south to **Naphtali** in the north"). The kingdom is culticly reunited (emphasized in 2 Chr 34:6,7,9,21,33; 35:17-18; cf. 2 Kgs 23:15-17,19-20). Theologically, all Israel returns to the worship of Yahweh (Ogden, 26-34).

The inclusion of the phrase **he went back to Jerusalem** indicates that the Chronicler is consciously following the narrative of 2 Kings 23 (cf. 2 Kgs 23:20). However, its repositioning before the discovery of the book indicates the topical character of the two narratives. The Chronicler recontextualizes Dtr's overtly topical treatment with some chronological sensitivity (PRATT, 473). In any event, the Chronicler is not attempting to deceive readers who already know 2 Kings. Rather, he is recontextualizing the story to demonstrate the piety of Josiah.

4. Discovery of the Book in the Temple (34:8-18)

When Josiah was twenty-six years old (**eighteenth year**), he decided to **repair the temple of the LORD**. This is as part of the purification of the **land and temple**. Unfortunately, as SELMAN (2:530) notes, some translations place this in the past tense (NRSV: "when he had purged the land and the temple"), but the Hebrew is an infinitive — **to purify** (NIV). The reformation is ongoing which now turns to repairing the temple. Josiah intended to restore the temple in order **to purify the land and the temple** (PRATT, 478). Chronicles focuses on this **eighteenth year** because this is the year of the discovery of the book, the prophetic word from Huldah, and the Passover covenant renewal (cf. 2 Chr 35:19).

This pericope depends on 2 Kings 22:3-10 but with some significant additions. For example, Chronicles includes northerners (**Manasseh, Ephraim and the entire remnant of Israel** as well as **all the people of Judah and Benjamin and the inhabitants of Jerusalem**). Chronicles emphasizes the "all Israel" character of this temple renovation. Tithes were collected from both north and south, which assumes the ongoing operation of the temple or even reform (cf. 2 Kgs 22:4). Theologically, the inclusion of the north encourages the postexilic community to include the north in their temple life.

Another significant addition to 2 Kings 22 is 2 Chronicles 34:12b-

14. Chronicles not only adds details about the **Levites** (including musicians — those who "understood the utensils of song"; cf. 1 Chr 16, 25), but also specifies that the book which was found is **the Book of the Law of the LORD that had been given through Moses** and that it was found *in* **the temple of the LORD** (2 Chr 34:15). Scholars generally believe that the **Book of the Law** is Deuteronomy (JAPHET, 1030, and DILLARD, 280-281; perhaps the whole Pentateuch). Josiah's reign began with an allusion to a favorite phrase in Deuteronomy (cf. 2 Chr 34:2). Further, that it was found **in** the temple has fostered speculation that a copy of the Law was "deposited in the cornerstone of the temple when it was built" and discovered during the repair work (Washburn, 75, n. 56). Others, however, believe that Deuteronomy was authored during this time period and both Dtr and the Chronicler are seeking to ascribe antiquity to something that was actually relatively new. But such a late date for Deuteronomy is suspect (cf. DILLARD, 280).

Washburn (75, n. 56) conjectures that "virtually all copies of the Law of Moses were lost or destroyed during the reigns of Manasseh and Amon." This explains the "great excitement" that surrounds its discovery.

The list of workers and the type of jobs they performed (2 Chr 24:9-12) indicate the extent of the renovation. The temple must have been in significant disrepair through neglect or abuse. Previous kings (except for the last years of Manasseh) had allowed the temple **to fall into ruin** (a point unique to Chronicles; 2 Chr 34:11). Given Chronicles's chronology, the temple had not seen faithful activity for almost sixty-five years (from the death of Hezekiah to the eighteenth year of Josiah, 686 to 621 B.C.).

Hilkiah (cf. Elayi, 54-56), the high priest, found the **Book of the Law** and gave it to **Shaphan**. Shaphan informs the king that **Hilkiah the priest has given me a book**. He reads it aloud ("read" is lit. "call out") in the presence of the king.

5. Prophecy of Huldah (34:19-28)

This is the literary and theological center of Chronicles's Josiah narrative. Josiah hears **the words of the Law**, seeks the will of the Lord, hears the words of a prophetess, and responds with a renewed determination to reform the religion of all Israel. The central motif is the normative function of the Book of the Law in the religious reformation and the confirmation that book receives from Huldah the prophetess. Josiah seeks the Lord through Scripture and prophetess. Thus, Josiah submits to divine authority. The narrative, therefore, offers a model of submissive faith — the people of God hear the word of the Lord and obey. Josiah humbled (כָּנַע, *kāna'*; 2 Chr 34:27; cf. 2 Chr 7:14) himself before God. The narrative proceeds in two stages: (1) Josiah determines to seek God's will (2 Chr 34:19-22) and (2) Huldah speaks God's will (2 Chr 34:23-28).

Josiah Seeks God's Will (34:19-21)

In response to hearing the Law, Josiah **tore his robes** in remorse and contrition (cf. 2 Chr 34:27; 1 Kgs 21:27; Isa 36:22; 37:1). Josiah wants to know what the will of the Lord is. Consequently, he commands five men to **inquire of the LORD**. The five are (1) **Hilkiah** the high priest, (2) **Ahikam son of Shaphan**, (3) **Abdon**, (4) **Shaphan**, and (5) **Asaiah the king's attendant**. The Shaphan family has a significant future (Ahikam is the father of Gedaliah, governor of Judah; cf. 2 Kgs 25:22), and Shaphan is one of the leaders of the temple renovation (2 Chr 34:8). This is Judah's spiritual and political leadership.

Josiah charges his officials and the high priest. They are to **inquire** ("seek;" *dāraš* as in 1 Chr 28:9; 2 Chr 7:14) **of the LORD**. However, only here in Chronicles (elsewhere only in Jer 21:2) is "seek" combined with the Hebrew word "on behalf of" (בְּעַד, *ba'ad*). Josiah seeks intercession (JOHNSTONE, 2:240). The term *ba'ad* denotes "the other role of the prophet: praying on behalf of his people" (JAPHET, 1032; cf. 1 Sam 12:19; 1 Kgs 19:4). Josiah does not merely seek guidance, he seeks prayer to avert the curses (**the LORD's anger**) Deuteronomy promised.

This intercession is for Josiah (**me**) and **for the remnant in Israel and Judah**. Josiah needs intercession as the one who represents the kingdom of God in his person and office. The prayer for the remnant of the nation assumes a "remnant theology" of the reunited nation of Israel and Judah. "From the time of Hezekiah," PRATT (484) writes, "the remnant of the North and South had been reunited under the leadership of David's sons." Josiah seeks intercession for the remnant.

Josiah articulates the need for this intercession: **because our fathers have not kept the word of the LORD; they have not acted in accordance with all that is written in this book**. The book bears the authority of God. The word of the Lord is given in the book. Since the nation has failed to obey the word, the LORD's anger (cf. 2 Chr 12:7; 28:9; 34:25; 36:16) is **great**.

Josiah's words are words for the postexilic community. The anger of the Lord was poured out on Judah because their fathers had sinned. Now that they have been restored to their land and rebuilt the temple, they must pay heed to the words of the book. They are the remnant of Judah, and they must follow the model of Josiah — hear the words, seek the mercy of God, and follow the book's prescriptions.

Huldah Reveals God's Will (34:22-28)

Huldah receives the longest introduction in Chronicles. She is identified as the wife of **Shallum** who was the **keeper of the wardrobe** (only place where this task is mentioned). This function and his pedigree indicate that he is a Levite (JOHNSTONE, 2:241) since he probably kept the priestly garments (cf. Lev 8:7-9). The location of the **Second District** is unknown but probably refers to the "expansion to the western hill of the city" where refugees from the north, including Levites, were settled (JOHNSTONE, 2:241; cf. 2 Chr 32:9 and JAPHET, 1035).

Huldah is called a **prophetess** (only one of four in the OT; Exod 15:20; Judg 4:4; Neh 6:14; cf. Luke 2:36; Acts 2:17-18; 21:9; 1 Cor 11:5; Rev 2:20). Even though many male prophets were available (including Jeremiah and Zephaniah), these men seek out Huldah. Priest (367) suggests that as the wife of a "Temple functionary" and probably a "cult prophetess" (a prophet connected with the liturgy of the temple), it was reasonable to ask her about the authenticity of the book and its significance. A woman delivers God's word to the king of Judah.

Her message is twofold as indicated by the structural repetition of **tell** Josiah **this is what the LORD says**. The first message is God's announcement that he is **going to bring disaster on this place and its people** (2 Chr 34:24-25). The second is a personal one for Josiah that his **eyes will not see all the disaster I am going to bring on this place** (2 Chr 34:26-28).

The first announces Judah's eventual punishment. Huldah defines the nature of the disaster ("evil," רָעָה, *rā'āh*; cf. 2 Chr 18:22; 2 Chr 25:19; 2 Chr 34:24,28). The divine punishment is **all the curses written in the book**, the lists in Deuteronomy 27–28 (perhaps also Lev 26). These curses include exile and deportation. Huldah also provides the rationale for this disaster — **because they have forsaken me** and pursued idolatrous practices. "Forsake" (עזב, *'āzab*; cf. 1 Chr 28:9; 2 Chr 7:14-23; 2 Chr 12:1,5; 15:2) is the Chronicler's term for apostasy, which is most visibly expressed in idolatry.

Most scholars believe that since Huldah's prophecy does not reflect any awareness of Josiah's earlier reforms, it assumes that no reformation was underway or, at least, that Dtr's narrative is historically superior to Chronicles's. However, Weinfeld (cited by Glatt-Gilead, 19) argues that Huldah's prophecy is not simply about recent events in Josiah's reign, but is about the cumulative effects of Judah's idolatry, particularly the reigns of Manasseh and Amon. Further, "it is conceivable that Huldah's silence regarding Josiah's record stems not from a *complete* lack of reform activity by Josiah before his eighteenth year, but from the limited nature of that activity" (Glatt-Gilead, 19). Consequently, Huldah's words are not necessarily inconsistent with the Chronicler's narrative (at least the Chronicler did not think so).

While Josiah sought out Huldah for intercession, instead she announces God's judgment. The disaster is coming. God has already decided the fate of Judah. Consequently, there is no intercession (cf. Jer 15:1). The **anger** of the Lord will accomplish its goal, just as it did against the Canaanites whose cup was full (cf. 2 Chr 33:2,9). God will create this disaster as he punishes his people (cf. Isa 45:7).

However, the second message from the Lord is merciful. God answers Josiah's seeking. Just as disaster comes upon Judah because it has forsaken God, so mercy comes to Josiah because he has **humbled** (2 times in 2 Chr 34:27) himself **before God**. This is the language of 2 Chronicles 7:14-23: humility, forsakenness, seeking, and mercy. Josiah responded to God in humility because his **heart was responsive** (lit., "soft"). God hardens hard hearts (cf. 2 Chr 25), but he mercifully embraces soft ones.

The difficult part of Huldah's word is her assurance that Josiah will be buried in **peace** (2 Chr 34:28). Given that Josiah is mortally wounded in battle (2 Chr 35:20-24), how can this be characterized as peaceful? Priest (366-368) suggests that Dtr's literary tradition reflects different redactions, but this does not explain how a final redactor could retain both Huldah's prophecy and Josiah's violent death. DILLARD (282) suggests the Chronicler "understood the first half of Huldah's prophecy (going to his grave in peace) as defined by the second half (not seeing the destruction of Jerusalem)." In other words, Josiah will be buried in peace because he will not experience the Babylonian destruction (disaster). He will thus have peace because he did not experience the evil (disaster) God intends for Jerusalem and the temple (PRATT, 487). Others believe Huldah's prophecy is conditioned on Josiah's continual seeking. When Josiah refused to hear the word of God, he forfeited his peaceful death (2 Chr 35:22).

The two messages illustrate God's relational approach to humanity. In the first message, God forsakes his people because they forsake him, but in the second God finds Josiah because he seeks him. National disaster is not averted because the nation does not seek him, but Josiah himself will not experience this evil because he humbled himself (2 Chr 7:14).

The postexilic community, settled again in the land of promise, should view Huldah's message as one of warning, but also grace. God has reversed the disaster (curse) and restored his people. God is seeking them, but the question is whether the postexilic community will seek God.

6. Implementation of the Book in the South (34:29-32)

Josiah responds humbly to Huldah's prophecy. He submits to the prophetic warning. He extends his personal humility to a communal level. He **called together all the elders of Judah and Jerusalem**. The elders are mentioned elsewhere in Chronicles (1 Chr 11:3; 15:25; 21:16; 2 Chr 5:2,4; 10:6,13) as an esteemed group of leaders, probably representative of the people of the land in their local villages. Thus, in a way reminiscent of Moses, Josiah and the elders **went up to the temple of the LORD** (that is, to the dwelling place of God; cf. Exod 24:9-11). Just as the covenant began in Exodus 24, so it is renewed by the representatives of the people.

Josiah and the elders are joined by **the men of Judah, the peo-**

ple of Jerusalem, the priests and the Levites (where 2 Kgs 23:2 reads "prophets") — indeed, **all the people from the least to the greatest**. The text stresses the inclusiveness of the assembly though only **Judah and Jerusalem** are mentioned. The assembly heard **all the words of the Book of the Covenant**. Josiah retraces his steps in order to include the people in the reforming movement.

SELMAN (2:534) calls attention to the word **covenant**. The term occurs four times in 2 Chronicles 34:30-32. Scripture is the **Book of the Covenant**, the **covenant is written** in the **book**, the people pledged themselves in **accordance with the covenant of God**, and Josiah **renewed the covenant**. Covenant embodies the relationship between God and his people. It contains the history of God's gracious work, but it also contains God's expectations. Josiah leads his people in a national covenant renewal. The king and the people stood in God's holy temple and rededicated themselves to a covenantal relationship **in the presence of the LORD**. Literally, Josiah "cut a covenant" with Yahweh (2 Chr 34:31), which entailed some sacrificial rituals as in Exodus 24 (cf. 2 Chr 6:11; 23:3,16; 29:10).

The pledge to keep the covenant involves (1) an inward orientation (**with all his heart and soul**) and (2) outward obedience. This is similar to David's charge to Solomon (1 Chr 22:19; 28:9) and Solomon's prayer to God (2 Chr 6:38; cf. 2 Chr 15:12), but, more significantly, it reflects the language of Deuteronomy (cf. Deut 4:29; 6:5; 10:12; 11:13,18; 13:3; 26:16; 30:6,10).

7. Cultic Purification of the North (34:33)

Second Chronicles 34:32-33 is unique to Chronicles. Verse 32 stresses the involvement of all the southern clans (**everyone in Jerusalem and Benjamin**) and verse 33 stresses the involvement of the north (**all who were present in Israel**). Consequently, paralleling 2 Chronicles 34:6-7, the reunited kingdom finds unity in their faithfulness to Yahweh. He completes the reform initiated earlier as "all Israel" renews their covenant with God.

Josiah's leadership is essential. His personal piety launched the reform and his zeal pursued it at the national level. However, while Josiah's heart was dedicated to God, his people did not always follow suit. After his death they returned to their idolatrous practices

(as long as he lived, they did not fail to follow the LORD). Idolatry was deeply embedded into the psyche of Israel and Judah. Even a national renewal could not eradicate its vestiges that would later give birth to the national disaster decreed for Judah. Chronicles, therefore, anticipates the next stage in Judah's history and prepares the reader for the disaster Huldah announced.

8. Celebration of the Passover (35:1-19)

Chronicles expands Dtr's Passover account. While Dtr summarizes it in 2 Kings 23:21-23, Chronicles explores its theological significance. Second Chronicles 35:1b-17 is unique. This is the second Passover Chronicles describes (cf. 2 Chr 30), but the first in 1–2 Kings. Few seriously doubt the historicity of this event though many believe the details belong more to the Chronicler's time than to Josiah's (JAPHET, 1041). But such a judgment depends on one's assessment of the history of Israel's religion. If the organization of 1 Chronicles 23–26 is early and/or Davidic, then the details of 2 Chronicles 35 are appropriate for Josiah's reign.

In addition to the parallel between 2 Chronicles and 2 Kings, the apocryphal book 1 Esdras begins with 2 Chronicles 35–36. While the relationship between 2 Chronicles, Ezra–Nehemiah, and 1 Esdras is disputed (DILLARD, 286-287), 2 Chronicles 35 is clearly 1 Esdras' source. Yet, as an ancient copy of 2 Chronicles 35–36, 1 Esdras may shed some light on the text of 2 Chronicles 35–36 (cf. Talshir, "Deaths," 213-236).

Josiah is the leader of this Passover. He is the subject of every third person singular verb in 2 Chronicles 35:1-19. The pericope is bounded by three key words: Josiah, celebrated ("did"), the Passover (2 Chr 35:1,19). Josiah keeps the Passover according to the Law as seen by the constant references to the Levites and priests, as well as the written standards of worship (cf. 2 Chr 35:4,6,12). This Passover is an exemplar of ritual faithfulness that arises out of Josiah's heart to seek God. No other Passover was like it in the history of the monarchy (2 Chr 35:18).

Following JAPHET (1040), Chronicles's account is divided into four sections: (a) Heading (2 Chr 35:1), (b) Preparations (2 Chr 35:2-9), (c) Celebration (2 Chr 35:10-17), and (d) Summary (2 Chr 35:18-19).

Heading (35:1)

The heading contains the inclusio with which the Chronicler will end his pericope (2 Chr 35:19). He rephrases 2 Kings 23:21,23 to fit his own literary pattern. In Dtr Isaiah commands the people to keep the Passover, but the Chronicler emphasizes Josiah (**Josiah celebrated the Passover**) though the text literally reads "they slaughtered . . ." so that the people are included. In addition, the heading firmly plants this celebration in the Law. It was celebrated **in Jerusalem** on the lawful day (**fourteenth day of the first month**; cf. 2 Chr 30:2,15; Exod 12:6; Num 28:16).

Preparations (35:2-9)

This section is a "flashback" which describes the preparations made before the slaughter of the animals. The preparations are twofold: (1) clerical (2 Chr 35:2-6) and (2) royal (2 Chr 35:7-9). The clerics (Levites and priests) prepared themselves for the sacrificial rituals, and the king (and his officials) provided sacrificial animals.

Clerical Preparations (35:2-6)

The clerical preparations are twofold: **priests** (2 Chr 35:2) and **Levites** (2 Chr 23:3-6). The emphasis on the Levites probably reflects the special needs of the Chronicler's audience where the function of the Levites was neglected or abused. Josiah **appointed the priests to their duties and encouraged them in the service of the LORD's temple**. Appointment (lit., "causing to stand") and encouragement (lit., "strengthening") demonstrated Josiah's leadership. The priests attend to their duties (cf. 2 Chr 7:6; 13:11; 23:6) and service (1 Chr 23:28; 23:32; 29:35) at the behest of the king.

The Levites, however, receive more attention than the priests. They are identified as those who teach **all Israel** and who are holy **to the LORD** (2 Chr 35:3). They are "teachers and monitors of Israel's practice of holiness" (JOHNSTONE, 2:246). While teaching is associated with priests (1 Chr 15:3), the Levites also have a teaching role (cf. 2 Chr 17:7-8).

In accordance with their teaching function and holy status, Josiah gives them two instructions (2 Chr 35:3): (1) **put the sacred** (holy) **ark in the temple** (only the holy may handle the holy) and

521

(2) **serve the LORD your God and his people Israel**. The former command is perplexing since Chronicles has never indicated that the ark had ever been removed from the temple. JOHNSTONE (2:247) believes this is an example of "timeless contemporaneity" where the moment of Solomon's movement of the ark into the temple is relived. Thus, it is a literary construct which highlights this liturgical moment. However, it is possible that Manasseh or Amon had removed the ark for some reason and the Levites had begun the practice of carrying it through the city rather than locating it in God's holy place (PRATT, 491-492). Whatever the case, the placement of the ark in the temple reminds the readers of Solomon's dedication of the temple in 2 Chronicles 5–7. **Solomon**, after all, built the temple as a resting place for the ark (cf. 2 Chr 6:41-42; 1 Chr 28:2).

The second command is general but receives specification in the following verses. The service of the Levites is threefold: (1) **prepare yourselves by families**; (2) **stand in the holy place**; and (3) **slaughter the Passover lambs, consecrate yourselves and prepare [the lambs] for your fellow countrymen**. The first refers to the arrangement of the Levites into **divisions** by **David** (1 Chr 24) and Solomon (2 Chr 8:14).

The second instruction places the Levites in the holy place to insure that all the families of Israel are served. The Levites function as the liaison between divine holiness and the fellowship of the people with God. They serve **the lay people** and facilitate their enjoyment of the presence of God.

The final instruction concerns the actual Passover sacrifice itself. In contrast to Deuteronomy 16:5-6 (cf. Exod 12:3-6,21) where the laity sacrifice their own Passovers and in contrast to Hezekiah's Passover where the Levites sacrificed only for those who were unclean (2 Chr 30:15-17), Josiah appoints the Levites as the slayers of the Passover lambs. They will sanctify and prepare the lambs for use by the worshipers ("countrymen" or "brothers"). Interestingly, even though not in exact obedience with Deuteronomy and Exodus, the Chronicler regards Josiah's instructions as **doing what the LORD commanded through Moses**. Perhaps the Levites were given this task because Josiah wanted to insure cleanliness or due to the numbers of people (DILLARD, 290).

Royal Preparations (35:7-9)

As in the case of Hezekiah (2 Chr 29:31-36; 30:24; 31:3), the king and his royal **officials** take responsibility for providing the animals for the national festival. **Sheep and goats** are prescribed by the law (Exod 12:3-5; Deut 16:2), but **cattle** (bulls) are not. However, the bulls were probably part of the week-long Feast of Unleavened Bread which followed the Passover (Num 28:16-25).

The number of animals detailed are realistic (DILLARD, 290). More than 41,000 animals would feed a huge crowd in Jerusalem for a week (cf. 2 Chr 29:21). The week-long festival involved celebratory meals featuring sacrificed animals.

Celebration (35:10-17)

Unlike his description of Hezekiah's Passover (2 Chr 30), the Chronicler details the specifics of Passover observance. His purpose is not only to legitimate Josiah's Passover and testify to its faithful adherence to Mosaic law, but also to model a Passover for his own community.

As JAPHET (1051) points out, the celebration is framed by notes concerning the preparation of the service (2 Chr 35:10,16). This separates the liturgical ritual (2 Chr 35:10-15) from the eating of the meal (2 Chr 35:16-17). The ritual involved two parts: (1) the sacrificial ritual (2 Chr 35:10-13) and (2) the Levitical and priestly personnel (2 Chr 35:14-15).

The sacrificial ritual consists of a series of actions: (1) slaughter of the **lambs**, (2) sprinkling of the **blood** which symbolizes atonement, (3) skinning of **the animals** in preparation for eating, (4) cooking the animal, and (5) serving the **people**. In addition, the clergy also **set aside burnt offerings** for later use. This was done **as is written in the Book of Moses** which probably refers to "the regulations concerning peace or fellowship offerings, of which Passover was a type" (PRATT, 493; cf. Lev 3:6-16; 7).

However, the cooking method is problematic. The words **roasted** and **boiled** in 2 Chronicles 35:13 are the same Hebrew term. The account seems to harmonize Exodus 12:8-9 (prohibited boiling and specified roasting with fire) and Deuteronomy 16:7 (prescribed boiling; NIV reads "roast" where the Hebrew reads "boil"). Literally, Chronicles reads that the animals were "boiled with fire" (2 Chr

35:13). Eves (119) believes this is a conflation of competing Passover cooking methods. There is no concern for the cooking method for the Passover animals whatsoever in the Hezekiah narrative. The difference between Exodus and Deuteronomy may reflect different historical circumstances (Exodus in Egypt, but Deuteronomy at the sanctuary; cf. JOHNSTONE, 2:253). Or, "boil" may be understood as a general term meaning "cook." Thus, "cook with fire" is equivalent to "roasting" (JAPHET, 1053; THOMPSON, 383).

After preparing animals for the people, the clergy also prepared some for themselves and continued **sacrificing the burnt offerings and the fat portions** (part of the fellowship offerings) **until nightfall**. In addition, the **musicians** proclaimed the grace of God as **prescribed by David** (1 Chr 16, 25; on the link between musicians and seers [prophets], cf. 1 Chr 25:1-6) and the **gatekeepers** protected God's holiness (cf. 1 Chr 26).

Second Chronicles 35:16-17 describes the actual eating of the Passover. **The Israelites who were present celebrated** (lit., "did") **the Passover at that time and observed the Feast of Unleavened Bread for seven days**. The week-long feast was enjoyed by the "sons (children) of Israel" which identifies Judah and Jerusalem with Israel. Judah is Israel.

Summary (35:18-19)

The Chronicler picks up the story in 2 Kings 23:22-23 with his summary. However, he changes the wording so that Dtr's "judges" is specified as **the prophet Samuel**. He elaborates the significance of this Passover as inclusive of **the priests, the Levites and all Judah and Israel who were there with the people of Jerusalem**. In comparison with 2 Chronicles 30:26,"the number of offerings and celebrants at Josiah's Passover exceeded that of Hezekiah" (DILLARD, 291). Josiah's Passover receives the highest ranking in the history of the monarchy.

The inclusion of all Judah and Israel serves the Chronicler's purpose. Passover is for all Israel — north and south. Postexilic Judah should follow the models of Hezekiah and Josiah as they include northerners in their celebration. The triumphal atmosphere of Josiah can, by the blessing of God, be repeated in postexilic Judah.

9. Extended Formulaic Conclusion (35:20–36:1)

Chronicles expands the conclusion found in 2 Kings 23:28-30. It contains the standard elements: (1) sources (**Laments** and **the book of the kings of Israel and Judah**), (2) the death and burial of Josiah, and (3) Josiah's successor (**Jehoahaz**).

Chronicles also narrates the death of Josiah in 609 B.C. Apparently, the Chronicler thought that Josiah's death needed more explanation than was provided by Dtr. Chronicles differs from Dtr in some particulars. For example, the Chronicler adds **Carchemish** as the place where Neco intended to fight (Dtr only refers to the Euphrates though Babylonian sources verify Carchemish), that Josiah intended to **meet him in battle** (Dtr only says he intended to "meet" Neco), that Neco delivers a message from God to Josiah (absent from Dtr), that Josiah **disguised himself** for the battle (absent from Dtr), and that Josiah died in Jerusalem (Dtr says he was brought to Jerusalem already dead).

While earlier scholars even doubted there was a battle between Neco and Josiah (Welch, "Death," 255-260), the publication of Babylonian sources has squelched this doubt (DILLARD, 288; Malamat, "Josiah's Bid," 274-278). It is now generally recognized that conditions for a battle were ripe. The Babylonians had forced Assyria to relocate its capital at Carchemish in 610 B.C., and Egypt already had a presence there (Malamat, "Josiah's Bid," 274). Josiah had grown in power as Assyria declined. His anti-Assyrian stance put him at odds with Neco who marched to aid Assyria against ascendant Babylon. Josiah's intentions were hostile (2 Kgs 23:29's "meet" is ambiguous and does not necessarily contradict Chronicles). Josiah died as a result of the battle.

JAPHET (1041) argues that the Chronicler takes the formulaic Dtr account and builds it into a story "with a series of protagonists, changing scenes, two monologues, and a plot developing through a dramatic turn of events to a tragic conclusion." The primary elements of 2 Kings 23:29-30 are present in 2 Chronicles 35:20,24a and 36:1. However, the question is whether the Chronicler fabricated the additional details or depended upon other sources. While JAPHET (1042-1044), Talshir ("Deaths," 215-236), and Begg ("Death of Josiah," 1-8) believe this is a theological story generated by the

Chronicler, WILLIAMSON (408-410; "Death of Josiah," 242-248; "Reply," 9-15) and DILLARD (288-289) believe it is based on authentic sources close to the events (perhaps a different version of 2 Kgs). The lack of the Chronicler's characteristic vocabulary (e.g., humble, seek, forsake, heart, unfaithful) indicates that he is not inventing this plot but depends on another source (perhaps Jeremiah's laments [2 Chr 35:25]).

The rest of Scripture is silent about the death of Josiah (Frost, 369-382), even Jeremiah (Rowton, 128-130). The only theological interpretation of the death of Josiah in Scripture is Chronicles. Apparently, the death of such a good king was difficult to explain. It probably created a theodic problem in the Chronicler's own community. Thus, the Chronicler's expansion of Dtr is directly related to offering a theological interpretation that is consistent with the themes of his own work.

Chronicles understands Josiah's death as a divine response to his disobedience: **he would not listen to what Neco had said at God's command**. The theological intent is clear. Josiah, in this last moment, stands with the kings of Judah who did not listen to God (2 Chr 25:16,20). In fact, there are evident parallels between Ahab and Josiah. Just as Ahab disguised himself, so does Josiah (cf. 2 Chr 18:29; 35:22). Just as archers shot Ahab, so they wounded Josiah (2 Chr 18:33; 35:23). Just as Ahab requested removal from the battlefield, so does Josiah (2 Chr 18:33; 35:23). Further, just as Jeroboam would not listen to Abijah's declaration that the Lord was with Judah, so Josiah would not listen to Neco's announcement that God was with him (2 Chr 13:4,12; 35:21). The threat to **destroy** Josiah is the same word used in warning rebellious kings (2 Chr 24:23; 25:16). Thus, Josiah follows the evil of previous kings. The Chronicler's interpretation of the death of Josiah, then, belongs to his theology of retribution (DILLARD, 292). Despite his many faithful years (632–609 B.C.), Josiah fails to heed God's word in what would turn out to be the last episode of his life. Josiah dies because he sins. JOHNSTONE (2:255-257) calls this a "negative Passover." The destroyer who destroyed Egypt (cf. 1 Chr 21:12) now destroys Josiah.

The most difficult aspect of this interpretation is that Neco, a pagan Pharaoh, becomes the conduit of divine revelation. In 2 Chronicles 35:21 Neco declares that he has no **quarrel** with Josiah.

Then he reports that **God has told me to hurry; so stop opposing God, who is with me, or he will destroy you**. The irony is explosive. God uses Israel's long-standing enemy (Egypt) to deliver Josiah, but Josiah will not listen. However, is it conceivable that a Jewish king would receive a word of God from an Egyptian Pharaoh? Should not Josiah have been skeptical? It may be that the Chronicler "assumed his audience knew other information that authenticated the divine origin of Neco's message" (PRATT, 497). This is confirmed by 1 Esdras 1:26-27 where Jeremiah verifies the words of Neco. Whatever the method, kings in Chronicles are not without a certain word from God, and the role of a prophet like Jeremiah is not inconceivable in the situation. In any event, "his language is no more shocking than that of other non-Israelites" (SELMAN, 2:542; Gen 20:3-7; Matt 27:19).

Why would God have been displeased with Josiah's move? Chronicles has articulated a conservative stance regarding Israel's involvement in international politics. Begg ("Death of Josiah," 3-4) notes that the Chronicler often links a reforming king with an international incident in order, I think, to test their faith (cf. Asa in 2 Chr 14, Jehoshaphat in 2 Chr 20, Hezekiah in 2 Chr 32). JOHNSTONE (2:256) argues that the reestablishment of the ark in the temple (2 Chr 35:3) entails pacification just as in the days of Solomon. Consequently, the desire for international interventionism is inappropriate for the king whose theological base is the temple. Josiah displays a lack of trust in God's presence at the temple and seeks a wider influence than God has given him (analogous to 1 Chr 21).

One further difficulty appears in the text. While 2 Kings 23:30 states that "Josiah's servants brought his [dead] body" to Jerusalem (NIV leaves the Hebrew word "dead" [מֵת, *mēth*] untranslated; cf. NRSV: "carried him dead"), 2 Chronicles 25:24 states that Josiah died in Jerusalem. But this is not a significant problem because the Hebrew term in 2 Kings 23:30 is a participle and may be rendered "dying" (Washburn, 60-61, n. 6). He was carried to Jerusalem mortally wounded ("dying") and died there. Though 2 Kings 23:29 states that Neco killed Josiah at Meggido, this is a telescoped point.

The end of Josiah's reign is ignominious. The Chronicler is forced to comment due to the nature of his death. However, Josiah was a faithful king who walked in the ways of his father David (2 Chr 34:2). But even a faithful king suffers for disobedience, though this does not change the Chronicler's basic perspective. Even though he died in an unfaithful act, Josiah is ranked alongside David.

Theologically, our lives are scattered with acts of unfaithfulness. We are not perfect royal priests anymore than Josiah or David. But God is faithful and gracious as he looks in our hearts and judges us by our intent to seek him. The story of Josiah is a story of faithfulness but it is tainted by his last act of unfaithfulness. This does not, however, overshadow, undermine, or reverse Chronicles's theological evaluation in 2 Chronicles 34:2. Josiah is taken home, buried with his fathers, and lamented by male and female singers (unlike other kings; cf. Jer 22:18; 34:5). God is gracious, even in an unfaithful act that leads to death. Consequently, even suicide, as a last unfaithful act, does not mean that God has forsaken someone. God judges the heart and life rather than one's last act.

D. THE REIGN OF THE LAST KINGS OF JUDAH (36:2-23)

After the extended narration of Hezekiah (2 Chr 29–32) and Josiah (2 Chr 34–35), the Chronicler's story comes to a quick close. Chronicles briefly rehearses the reigns of the last four kings of Judah. Structurally, they form one account as they emphasize the exilic horizon of Judah's future. The Chronicler "has created a single, uniform 'exilic' generation," and this is the fiftieth generation (49 from Abraham to Josiah) from the creation of the world in the Chronicler's account. The fiftieth generation goes into exile. The restoration, then, is a Jubilee — the return from exile is a liberating proclamation (JOHNSTONE, 2:260-261).

Chronicles radically condenses the account in Dtr (2 Kgs 23:30–25:30) and adds a brief note from Ezra 1:2-3 (2 Chr 36:22-23). Discussions about what version of Dtr was available to the Chronicler are interesting (McKenzie, *Chronicler's*, 206) but ultimately unnecessary (DILLARD, 297). PRATT (499) provides this comparison (with some modifications):

Topic	2 Chr	2 Kgs
The Reign of Jehoahaz		
Summary of Reign	36:2	23:30b-31a
Maternal Notice		23:31b
Theological Evaluation		23:32
Trouble and Exile	36:3-4	23:23-24
The Reign of Jehoiakim		
Tribute to Egypt		23:35
Summary of Reign	36:5a	23:36a
Maternal Notice		23:36b
Theological Evaluation	36:5b	23:37
Trouble and Exile	36:6-7	24:1-4
Other Sources	36:8a-c	24:5
Death		24:6a
Successor	36:8d	24:6b
Babylonian Dominance		24:7
Reign of Jehoiachin		
Summary of Reign	36:9a	24:8a
Maternal Notice		24:8b
Theological Evaluation	36:9b	24:9
Trouble and Exile	36:10a-b	24:10-16
Successor	36:10c	24:17
Reign of Zedekiah		
Summary of Reign	36:11	24:18a
Maternal Notice		24:18b
Theological Evaluation	36:12-14	24:19-20
Trouble and Exile	36:15-21	25:1-26
Jehoiachin Released		25:27-30

The Chronicler's purpose is indicated by how he handles
2 Kings. He abridges the reigns of the first three kings as well as
every "trouble and exile" section, but expands the theological evaluation of Zedekiah. His treatment of the first three kings amounts to
the combination of formulaic introductions and conclusions. He
adds a text from Ezra 1:2-3 to Dtr and subtracts the note about
Jehoiachin's release. Consequently, Zedekiah (who receives more
attention than all the other three kings combined) and Ezra hold the
key to interpreting the ending of Chronicles.

Chronicles prepares us for this ending by repetitively noting the
exile of each of the successive kings. The unity of these kings is their

respective exiles and the alternating lengths of service: three months, followed by eleven years, followed by three months and ending with eleven years. Interestingly, in each case where Dtr records the death of the king, Chronicles omits it (cf. 2 Kgs 23:34; 24:6). JAPHET (1064) surmises that the Chronicler has no interest in events outside the land of Israel and thus does not record the death of these kings in exile. The Chronicler stresses exile — exile is Judah's punishment. Each time Babylon exiles a king, it despoils the temple (2 Chr 36:8,10,14). Thus, the temple and the Davidic dynasty are linked (WILLIAMSON, 412).

Zedekiah, however, holds the key to the final act of divine punishment. Chronicles justifies the exile in the light of his reign. Yahweh's repeated attempts to delay the exile are frustrated by the unfaithfulness of his people. Josiah illustrated how God might delay the disaster if Judah would humble itself, but the final kings of Judah did not follow Josiah. Finally, the cup of God's wrath was poured out on Judah during the reign of Zedekiah.

However, this wrath was not forever. God initiated the return of his people from Babylon to Judah. He moved the heart of Cyrus to proclaim a release. This redemptive act revealed the passing of divine wrath. They will not only return, but they will rebuild the temple.

This merciful divine initiative is the ending of Chronicles. The first readers, living in the postexilic situation, would see this as hopeful and gracious. God wants his people back. He moved the Persian king. He initiated redemption. He wants his temple rebuilt. God seeks his people. Structurally, the Chronicler ends his narrative where it began (1 Chr 10): exile (the unfaithfulness of Saul) and hope (Davidic dynasty). Just as the previous exile ended in God's glory through the reign of David and Solomon, so the postexilic community has the hope of future glory as well (WILLIAMSON, 412).

Christians, of course, understand this move from wrath to redemption through the cross of Christ. In the cross the wrath of God is displayed and propitiated (Rom 3:25-26). The justice of God is demonstrated, but also the love of God is proclaimed. In Christ the wrath of God has passed away and God reconciles the world to himself. God seeks seekers, and the work of Christ has enabled God to be both just and justifier (Hicks, "What," 53-63). While Chronicles's first readers looked back to Cyrus' decree as an act of redemptive love in the passing of wrath, Christians look back to the cross for God's climactic act of redemption. There the God who is light propitiated himself because he loved us (1 John 1:16–2:2; 4:10-16).

For chronological purposes, the material below assumes Thiele's (182-191) dating for both the Judean kings and the Bablyonian incursions into Judah.

King of Judah	Dates	International Intervention
Josiah	640–609	Egypt Defeats Josiah, 609
Jehoahaz	609	Egypt Deposes Jehoahaz, 609
Jehoiakim	609–598	Egypt Enthrones Jehoiakim, 609
		Egypt Defeated at Carchemish, 605
		Babylon Besieges Jerusalem, 605
Jehoiachin	598–597	Babylon Besieges Jerusalem, 597
Zedekiah	597–586	Babylon Destroys Jerusalem, 586

The above conclusions involve a complicated assessment of 2 Chronicles, 2 Kings, Jeremiah, Ezekiel, Daniel, and the Babylonian records. Some dates are questionable, but the differences are relatively minor (Tadmor, 226-230; Malamat, "Last Kings," 135-156; Malamat, "Twilight," 123-145). Stern (26-54) surveys the wealth of evidence available for this period of history.

1. The Reign of Jehoahaz (36:2-4)

The Chronicler's summary of the reign of Jehoahaz contains the standard elements of his formulaic introductions and conclusions with a few missing items (e.g., maternal origin): (1) age when he began to reign (**twenty-three**), (2) length of reign (**three months**), (3) exile (**carried him off to Egypt**), and (4) successor (**Eliakim**, renamed **Jehoiakim**). Interestingly, the theological evaluation in 2 Kings 23:32 is omitted (cf. Jer 22:11-17). But the tenor of the narrative is negative: he is **dethroned** by the **king of Egypt** and assessed a heavy tribute. Further, he is exiled in Egypt (the land of Israel's earlier captivity).

Why did the king of Egypt dethrone **Jehoahaz** and install his older brother Eliakim whom he renamed Jehoiakim? Malamat ("Twilight," 126-127) believes that the anti-Assyrian party in Judah elevated Jehoahaz over Eliakim despite the latter's firstborn status and **Neco** wanted a king who was conciliatory to Egyptian interests (and thus pro-Assyrian and anti-Babylonian). With the defeat of Josiah, Judah serves Egypt as a vassal state.

2. The Reign of Jehoiakim (36:5-8)

The Chronicler's summary of the reign of Jehoiakim contains the standard elements of his formulaic introductions and conclusions with a few missing items (e.g., maternal origin): (1) age when he began to reign (**twenty-five**), (2) length of reign (**eleven years**), (3) theological evaluation (**he did evil in the eyes of the LORD**), (4) exile (**bound him with bronze shackles to take him to Babylon**), (5) sources (**book of the kings of Israel and Judah**), and (6) successor (his son **Jehoiachin**).

Jehoiakim is pro-Egyptian, and when Neco is defeated at Carchemish in 605 B.C. (Jer 46:2), Judah submits to **Nebuchadnezzar**. Jerusalem suffered a siege in 605 B.C. (cf. Dan 1:1-2). Indeed, Judah suffered a series of humiliations before the Babylonians from 605–600 (Malamat, "Twilight," 129-132). It was most likely during one of these incidents that Jehoiakim was bound with bronze shackles in order to take him to Babylon. Whether he was actually deported or not is unstated, but the historical setting does not exclude the possibility (Mercer, 179-192; Green, 108-109). MCCONVILLE (266) believes this was a symbolic gesture and Jehoiakim was never actually deported. In any event, the Chronicler does not report Jehoiakim's death in 598 B.C. Instead he retains the "exilic" atmosphere.

Babylon's first siege of Jerusalem involved a despoliation of the temple. The reversal is startling — the articles that belong to the **temple of the LORD** were put into Nebuchadnezzar's **temple** in Babylon (reversing Amaziah; cf. 2 Chr 25:14).

In contrast with Josiah (2 Chr 35:26), Jehoiakim's obituary refers to the **detestable things** (abomination) **he did**. This word is only used regarding Ahaz (2 Chr 28:3), Manasseh (2 Chr 33:2; cf. 2 Chr 34:33), Jehoiakim (2 Chr 36:8), and Zedekiah (2 Chr 36:14). It encompasses their idolatry, defiling of the temple, and probably child sacrifice. The days of Ahaz and Manasseh returned with

Jehoiakim. Jeremiah, said much about this evil king (cf. Jer 22:18; 25:1; 26:21; 35:1,9; 36:29-32; 45:1).

3. The Reign of Jehoiachin (36:9-10)

The Chronicler's summary of the reign of **Jehoiachin** contains the standard elements of his formulaic introductions and conclusions with a few missing items (e.g., maternal origin): (1) age when he began to reign (**eighteen**; MT reads "eight," but this is certainly a scribal error; cf. 2 Kgs 24:8; DILLARD, 296), (2) length of reign (**three months**), (3) theological evaluation (**he did evil in the eyes of the LORD**; cf. Jer 22:24-28),and (4) exile (**brought him to Babylon**).

Nebuchadnezzar conducted a campaign against Judah in 598–597 B.C. He captured the city in March, 597 B.C. The *Babylonian Chronicles* confirm the data in 2 Chronicles 36:10: the king is enslaved, Babylon receives tribute, and Nebuchadnezzar appoints his own king (DILLARD, 300). Jehoiachin is taken to Babylon, but ultimately released in 561 by Amel-Marduk (cf. 2 Kgs 25:27; Jer 52:31; Tadmor, 230). Administrative records document his presence in Babylon (*ANET*, 308). Jehoiachin eventually died in Babylon.

As JAPHET (1067) notes, "the drastic abbreviation of Jehoiachin's story results in a new perspective on the destruction." The Chronicler does not concentrate on Jehoiachin, but Zedekiah. He plays down the humiliation of this forced exile in order to heighten the final destruction. Begg ("Babylon," 147, 151-152) suggests that the Chronicler's interest is not focused on Babylon as much as the Persian period. The Chronicler ends his work with Babylon (punishment) in the background and Persia (hope) in the foreground. Hope replaces wrath.

4. The Reign of Zedekiah (36:11-21)

Nebuchadnezzar appointed Zedekiah, the uncle of Jehoiachin and brother of Jehoiakim, "king over Judah and Jerusalem" (2 Chr 36:10). Zedekiah, then, is the third son of Josiah to reign in Jerusalem. However, the Hebrew reads "brother" rather than "uncle." Yet, the term is best understood in the general sense of "relative" which could include an uncle (2 Kgs 24:17; Jer 37:1; SELMAN, 2:547;

DILLARD, 296), or it is a scribal error where the original text read "his father's brother" (JAPHET, 1068).

The Chronicler follows Dtr (cf. Jer 52), but also adds considerable material to the story of Zedekiah. He pours all the Babylonian horror into the end of Zedekiah's reign in order to heighten the finality of the punishment and the intensity of God's wrath. The chart below represents what is unique and parallel in the Chronicles account.

Topic	2 Chr	2 Kgs	Jer
Formulaic Introduction	36:11-12	24:18-19	52:1-2
Zedekiah Rebels	36:13a	24:20b	52:3b
Theological Evaluation	36:13b-16a		
The Wrath of God	36:16b	24:20a	52:3a
God Acts against Zedekiah	36:17		
The Fall of Jerusalem		25:1-7	52:4-11
The Exile of Judah	36:18-20	25:8-21	52:12-30
Theological Interpretation	36:21		

Chronicles condenses the material about the fall and exile of Judah into a few verses, but adds material not found in 2 Kings or Jeremiah (e.g., the temple in 2 Chr 36:18). The Chronicler also adds a theological interpretation to the events. He explains the obstinacy of Judah (2 Chr 36:13b-16a), identifies the Babylonian invasion as a divine act (2 Chr 36:17), and offers a rationale for seventy years of exile (2 Chr 36:21).

Formulaic Introduction (36:11-12)

The introduction includes the standard elements minus maternal origins: (1) age when he began to reign (**twenty-one**), (2) length of reign (**eleven years**), and (3) theological evaluation (**he did evil in the eyes of the LORD**). The theological evaluation is expanded in comparison with the previous three kings as well as adding to 2 Kings 24:9. Zedekiah **did not humble himself before Jeremiah the prophet, who spoke the word of the LORD**. The failure to listen to God's prophet (2 Chr 25:20) and to humble himself is characteristic of evil kings in Chronicles (2 Chr 33:23). Significantly, the Chronicler uses one of his key theological terms: "humble" (כנע, kāna'; cf. 2 Chr 7:14; 12:7,12; 33:12,19; 34:27). Jeremiah plays a key role as God's prophetic voice in Judah (cf. Jer 21; 24:8; 27:1,3,12; 28:1; 32:1-5; 34:21; 38:14-24; 39:1-6; 49:34).

Theological Evaluation (36:13-16)

The evaluation assesses the king (2 Chr 36:13), leaders (2 Chr 36:14), Yahweh (2 Chr 36:15), and the response of Judah (2 Chr 36:16). The king rebelled against Nebuchadnezzar and Yahweh, the leaders embraced the **detestable practices of the nations,** God sent prophets among them to warn them, and Judah's final response was to mock **God's messengers.** Chronicles portrays a dynamic relationship between God and his people that degenerates into a final display of God's **wrath.** God seeks his people, but they reject him. He demonstrates his patience through messengers, but ultimately the king, **leaders of the priests,** and **people** forsake him. God, faithful to his relational principle (1 Chr 28:9; 2 Chr 15:2), forsakes those who forsake him.

Since the punishment had already been announced during the reign of Josiah (cf. 2 Chr 34:24), why does God send messengers? What is the function of Jeremiah if God has already determined to destroy Jerusalem and the temple (even from the time of Manasseh, according to 2 Kgs 23:26; 24:3). The language of Jeremiah abounds in this section (cf. Jer 26:5; 29:19). His function may be similar to Huldah in 2 Chronicles 34. She announces the judgment, but she announces a delay due to the humility of Josiah. The constant messengers, then, are God's continual pleading and yearning for reconciliation with his people. He would delay the disaster to come though he would not back off his determination to punish Judah for her sins. God sends messengers because he has **pity on his people and on his dwelling place.**

Judah's cup of evil becomes full as its king **became stiff-necked and hardened his heart and would not turn to the LORD.** Literally, the text reads that "he hardened (stiffened) his neck and strengthened his heart against returning to the LORD." A stiff-necked people evokes images of Israel's own history (Exod 32:9; 33:3,5; 34:9; Deut 9:6,13; 10:16; 31:27; Neh 9:16-17,29). Jeremiah characterizes Judah in this manner (Jer 7:26; 17:23; 19:15). It also appears in Hezekiah's appeal to the north (2 Chr 30:8). The king thus hardened his neck and strengthened his resolve (heart). He refused to repent ("turn"; שׁוּב [*šûb*] in 2 Chr 6:23-26,37-38; 7:14,19; 15:4; 30:6). The word "return" is a favorite word in Jeremiah (cf. Jer 3:7-22; 4:1). The wording, in the context of Chronicles, implies that if Zedekiah had turned back to God, he would have been received graciously (especially in the light of comparing 2 Chr 24:19 with 36:16). But he would not (cf. Matt 23:37).

The leaders of the priests and the people did not return either. They **became more and more unfaithful** (מָעַל [*ma'al*] repeated twice as in 2 Chr 28:19). Only the days of Ahaz compare with this description (2 Chr 28:3,19). Evil took root and fully blossomed. Just as the Canaanites experienced the wrath of God for their abominations, so Judah will experience God's wrath. Even the priests, entrusted with the holiness of the temple, defiled the place which God had consecrated. This is the only place in Chronicles where priests actively defile the temple. The Lord's wrath was **aroused against his people and there was no remedy**.

The insolence of the people is pictured in their response to the divine messengers. They **mocked**, **despised**, and **scoffed at his prophets**. This is the only time in the Hebrew Bible where all these verbs occur in the same sentence. The emphatic character is hard to miss. God does not forsake his people because of a few mistakes or some lack of legal understanding or because they ignorantly crossed a line in the sand. Rather, God forsakes his people because they have forsaken him and rebelliously rejected his repeated warnings. The exile of Judah was not a malicious act on the part of a legalistic God. Rather God punished an abuse of his gracious disposition. Unfaithfulness (1 Chr 2:7; 9:1; 10:13-14), understood as rebellious arrogance, is the criteria of God's judgment.

Divine Wrath (36:17-21)

God sends wrath upon his people, city, and temple. The God who pitied his people and sent messengers to them again and again is now the God who has no pity. The term "pity" (חָמַל, *ḥāmal*) appears in 2 Chronicles 36:15 and 36:17 (translated **spared**). The time for pity is past.

Description of the Fall of Jerusalem (36:17-19)

It is uncertain who the subject of the verb **killed** is — it may be either Nebuchadnezzar or God himself. Whatever the case, the action is initiated and empowered by God. Chronicles understands the Babylonian devastation of Jerusalem as an expression of divine wrath. God destroyed his own temple. **God handed** everyone **over to Nebuchadnezzar**.

The description of the devastation is paralleled in 2 Kings and Jeremiah with the exception of 2 Chronicles 26:18. Once again, the temple is front and center for the Chronicler. The temple's vessels are exiled and its environs burned. The completeness of the destruction is emphasized by the repeated use of **all** (לֹכ, *kol*; 5 times in 2 Chr 26:17-18).

Description of the Exile (36:20-21)

While Nebuchadnezzar put many to the **sword**, Chronicles stresses that a **remnant** remained. The remnant goes into exile, but it is this remnant that also returned and founded the community for whom the Chronicler writes. Just as there was a remnant of Israel in the time of Josiah (2 Chr 34:9), so there is a remnant that returns during the **kingdom of Persia**.

Seventy years is the prescribed length of the exile. This number, derived from Jeremiah (Jer 29:11-12; 29:10; cf. Dan 9:2), has generated considerable discussion (cf. Winkle). Some believe the number is symbolic, that is, an unspecified period of distress analogous to a single life-span (THOMPSON, 391). There is evidence that 70 years was a representative number for desolation (e.g., Essarhaddon "states that Marduk ordained the desolation of Babylon to last seventy years"; De Vries, "Sabbath," 98). Others, however, believe it is an exact or round number. PRATT (508) suggests the seventy years extends from the time of the first deportation (605 B.C.) till the decree of Cyrus (539 B.C.) or the year Judah first returned (538 B.C.) which is roughly seventy years but not exactly. Others (Whitley, 60-72) suggest the exile began in the final destruction of Jerusalem (586 B.C.) and ended in the rebuilding of the temple (516 B.C.). However, the exile actually ended with the return to the land not with the building of the temple. There is evidence that the seventy years has been variously interpreted by several biblical writers (Applegate, 91-110). Consequently, different biblical writers may have interpreted the number differently for different purposes (e.g., Zechariah probably dates it from 586–516 B.C. [cf. Zech 1:12-17], but Daniel perhaps from 605–536 [Dan 9:2]).

But how does the Chronicler understand the number? PRATT

(508) believes that the ending of Chronicles provides the clue. It is dated from Cyrus' edict in 539 B.C. (perhaps the return of the remnant in 538). This means seventy is essentially a round number since the first possible deportation is 605 B.C. However, the Chronicler's interests are primarily theological and not chronological. While Jeremiah is the one who prophesied the seventy years, only the Chronicler interprets it theologically.

The Chronicler roots his interpretation in Leviticus 26:34-35. This is one of the curses. If evil pervades the land (Lev 26:43) and Israel is exiled, "then the land will enjoy its Sabbath years all the time it lies desolate and you are in the country of your enemies . . . the land will have the rest it did not have during the Sabbaths you lived in it" (Lev 26:34-35).

The land was to rest every seven years (Lev 25:1-7). In that sabbath year Israel was to grow no crops but depend upon God's provisions. After seven sabbatical years, Israel was to proclaim a Jubilee (Lev 25:8-13) in the fiftieth year. Apparently, according to Chronicles, Israel did not follow this law. Consequently, the seventy years of the exile are the seventy years of rest which the land should have received since the time of the monarchy. $70 \times 7 = 490$ years which is roughly the beginning of Saul's reign (ca. 1040 B.C.). While De Vries ("Sabbath," 101) thinks the number is symbolic, the Chronicler may have intended an actual counting back to the period of the Judges. Perhaps, just as with the Passover (cf. 2 Chr 35:18 where Samuel is a reference point), Israel had not celebrated the sabbath year since the days of Samuel. If the Edict of Cyrus and the return to the land in 539/538 B.C. is the end of the seventy years, then 490 years would be roughly the early reign of Saul (WILLIAMSON, 418).

DILLARD (301-302) suggests that Leviticus 26:40-45 looms in the background. The text promises restoration and grace. Though Judah had "paid for their sin," God "had not forgotten his covenant." Does God still favor his people? Does he still love them? The Chronicler (from the genealogies beginning with Adam to the end of his work) "is answering that question with a ringing affirmation. He is saying in effect, 'God has loved us from the foundation of the world; we are a prepared people brought to a prepared land. It is a new day.'"

5. The Restoration (36:22-23)

The Chronicler concludes by citing Ezra 1:1-2. While some believe this indicates that the same author wrote Chronicles and Ezra (Haran, 18-20), the Chronicler cites Ezra in order to link his book with the history he already knows (Ezra and Nehemiah). The Chronicler wants his readers to continue the story in Ezra. But, more importantly, it is not simply an incidental link to another historical work. Rather, it is a significant theological conclusion to the whole of Chronicles. Without it Chronicles is incomplete (contra WILLIAMSON, 419). The conclusion assures the remnant of Judah that Yahweh is still **with** them.

Applegate (98-99) contrasts the "no remedy" (מַרְפֵּא לְאֵין עַד, *'ad lᵊ'ên marpē'*; 2 Chr 36:16; cf. Jer 21:7) with the Edict of Cyrus. In Jeremiah the term refers to the restoration (or, the remedy; cf. Jer 33:6). The divine remedy for the exile is the decree of Cyrus. God reverses his exile and enables a restoration. God remedies the remediless situation.

Theologically, God enables his people to **go up** (עלה, *'ālah*). He is with them, and by his grace, they will go up. This is the last word in Chronicles. It describes the exodus of God's people from Egypt into the land of promise (cf. Exod 3:8,17; 13:18; 33:1,3). Moses pleads with Pharoah to let God's people "go up" to worship (Exod 10:25; untranslated in the NIV). Moses "goes up" on Mount Sinai (Exod 19:20; cf. 24:1,9,12). It is also the word used to describe going up to worship at the temple (Ps 24:3). In the Diaspora, it took on the meaning of "pilgrimage to Jerusalem, immigration to Israel" (JOHNSTONE, 2:275). The final words of Chronicles, then, bespeak the restoration of God's people. The people of God are invited to "go up" to worship — to return to Judah, rebuild the temple, and experience the gracious fellowship of God.

The restoration arises out of divine initiative. As far as Chronicles narrates, the people did not pray the restoration into being. They did not humble themselves, repent, or return to God. Rather, God, in his sovereign election, decided to bring his people back. When God **moved the heart of Cyrus**, it was an expression of grace. God took the initiative to redeem his people. He enabled Cyrus (gave him **all the kingdoms of the earth**) and commissioned him (**he has appointed me to build a temple for him**).

This divine initiative is important. The postexilic community wonders whether God will take them back or not, whether God will renew his grace among them. The answer is staring them in the face. God expressed his intention to renew his fellowship with his people by returning them to their land and rebuilding the temple. The fact that they are in the land is testimony to God's electing grace (cf. Mal 1:1-5).

Despite the many difficult circumstances which create doubt about God's love, Yahweh has already testified to his love in Jesus Christ (Rom 8:31-39). Whatever the problems or trials, God has assured us of his love. The fact that God sent his Son as a propitiation for our sins reveals the certainty of his love. Just as Chronicles looked back to the Edict of Cyrus and the subsequent rebuilding of the temple as a demonstration of God's love, so Christians look back to the cross as the climactic demonstration of that same love. Therefore, just as the postexilic community rested in the confidence of God's grace, so Christians rest through the love of God in Jesus Christ.

Date Due

Code 4386-04, CLS-4, Broadman Supplies, Nashville, Tenn., Printed in U.S.A.